UNDERSTANDING SECURITIES LAW

THIRD EDITION

By

Marc I. Steinberg

Radford Professor of Law
School of Law
Southern Methodist University

LEXIS Publishing™

LEXIS®-NEXIS® • MARTINDALE-HUBBELL®
MATTHEW BENDER® • MICHIE™ • SHEPARD'S®

Library of Congress Cataloging-in-Publication Data
Steinberg, Marc I.
Understanding securities law/by Marc I. Steinberg.--3rd ed.
p. cm. --(Understanding series)
Includes bibliographical references and index.
ISBN 0-8205-4865-0 (pbk.)
1. Securities--United States. I. Title. II. Understanding series (New York, N.Y.)
KF1440 .S74 2001
346.73'092--dc21

This publication is designed to provide accurate and authoritative information in regard to the subject matter covered. It is sold with the understanding that the publisher is not engaged in rendering legal, accounting, or other professional services. If legal advice or other expert assistance is required, the services of a competent professional should be sought.

Editorial Offices
2 Park Avenue, New York, NY 10016-5675 (212) 448-2000
201 Mission St., San Francisco, CA 94105-1831 (415) 908-3200
701 East Water Street, Charlottesville, VA 22902-7587 (804) 972-7600
www.lexis.com

ACKNOWLEDGMENTS

First Edition

I wish to thank a number of individuals for their help regarding this project. In particular, my thanks to Professors Alan Bromberg, Dennis Honabach, and Mark Sargent for their comments. I thank Ralph Ferrara, Robin Goldman, Sam Gruenbaum, Will Kaulbach, Joe Kempler and Richard Starr, all of whom were my coauthors for certain publications, portions of which appear herein. My thanks also to Callaghan & Co., publishers of my treatise on Securities Practice: Federal and State Enforcement (1985) (updated annually) (coauthored with Ralph Ferrara), and to Law Journal Seminars-Press, publisher of my treatise on Securities Regulation: Liabilities and Remedies (1984) (updated annually) for granting their permission for me to use excerpts from the respective treatises. I also thank several law reviews in which I authored articles for granting their permission to use certain portions thereof herein, including the Cornell Law review (67 Cornell L. Rev. 557 (1982), 66 Cornell L. Rev. 27 (1980)) and Fred B. Rothman & Co., the Emory Law Journal (30 Emory L.J. 169 (1981)), the Journal of Corporation Law (11 J. Corp. L. 1 (1985)), the Loyola of Los Angeles Law Review (13 Loyola Univ. (L.A.) L. Rev. 247 (1980) (coauthored with Samuel Gruenbaum), the University of Maryland Law Review (46 Md. L. Rev. 923 (1987)) (coauthored with Robin Goldman), the University of Pennsylvania Law Review (129 U. Pa. L. Rev. 263 (1980)) (coauthored with Ralph Ferrara) and Fred B. Rothman & Co., and the Vanderbilt Law Review (40 Vand. L. Rev. 489 (1987)) (coauthored with Will Kaulbach).

From the University of Maryland Law School, I thank Bob Krusen for his research assistance, Anne Rollins for her comments, and LuAnn Marshall, Gwen Davis, and Eileen Gretes for their expert secretarial help. This book was written while I was a member of two faculties, the faculties of the University of Maryland Law School and the Southern Methodist University School of Law. I thank both institutions and their respective deans, Mike Kelly at Maryland and Paul Rogers at SMU, for their support of this project.

I wish to dedicate this book to my friends at The University of Maryland School of Law. I've been fortunate to teach during the past six years at this superb institution with wonderful colleagues and students. As I enthusiastically join the SMU Law faculty on a more permanent basis, I will miss my friends at the Maryland Law School.

June 1989

Second Edition

The Second Edition to this reference text comes during my seventh year at SMU. It has been a fine seven years and I thank the university and my colleagues.

This project was funded by summer research grants (including the William Hawley Atwell Fund) from SMU Law School. I thank Dean Paul Rogers and the Atwell Fund for their support.

I owe many thanks to several individuals for helping this project become reality. I certainly thank the contribution of all those mentioned in the acknowledgments to the First Edition as well as the publishers who granted permission for me to use excerpts from my other books and articles.

For the Second Edition, I thank my secretary, Ms. Kathleen Vaughan, for her significant assistance. I also thank Professor Alan Bromberg, Mr. Ralph Janvey, Mr. Daryl Lansdale, Mr. Bruce Mendelsohn, Mr. Chris Olive and Mr. Buddy Reece as well as my research assistants, Mr. Cory Farley, Ms. Julie Herzog, and Mr. Cliff Murray, for their meaningful input. My thanks as well to The International Lawyer granting permission for me to use excerpts from my article that appeared in 29 Int'l Law 43 (1995). I again thank Law Journal Seminars-Press for granting permission for me to use excerpts from my treatise, Securities Regulation: Liabilities and Remedies (1995).

I dedicate this Second Edition to my good friend and colleague Professor Alan R. Bromberg. Professor Bromberg truly is the preeminent scholar in the United States in the areas of the law relating to securities fraud and partnership law. He also is a wonderful and generous individual. His help and guidance through my years at the University of Maryland and here at SMU have meant so very much to me. I thank you Alan.

August 1995

Third Edition

Fifteen years have elapsed since the publication of the First Edition of Understanding Securities Law. As this reference text undergoes modification due to securities law developments and the author's prerogative, I thank the contribution of all those mentioned in the acknowledgments to the First and Second Editions as well as the publishers who have granted permission for me to use excerpts from my other books and articles.

This project was funded by summer research grants from the SMU School cf Law. I thank Dean John Attanasio and the Law School for their generous support.

For the Third Edition, I thank my secretary, Ms. Judy Parsley, for her significant assistance. I also thank my research assistants Mr. Jeff Brown, Mr. Noah Hansford, Mr. Barrett Howell, and Mr. Jason Myers for their meaningful input.

I dedicate this Third Edition to my parents Gerald and Phyllis Steinberg in honor of their fifty-ninth wedding anniversary. I am a lucky man to have two wonderful and loving parents. Mom and Dad, thanks so very much for your love, support, and guidance.

September 2000

SUMMARY TABLE OF CONTENTS

TABLE OF CONTENTS

Chapter 4
THE REGISTRATION PROCESS

Chapter 5
RESALES AND REORGANIZATIONS

Chapter 6
DUE DILIGENCE AND SECURITIES ACT LIABILITY

Chapter 8
ALTERNATIVE REMEDIES

Chapter 14
SEC ENFORCEMENT

Chapter 1

INTRODUCTION

§ 1.01 Purpose of Text

The purpose of this reference text is to provide a general understanding of the key issues that a student will face in the basic securities regulation course. As a consequence, the text's scope principally focuses on the Securities Act of 1933 (hereinafter called the "Securities Act" or "1933 Act") and the Securities Exchange Act of 1934 (hereinafter called the "Exchange Act" or "1934 Act"). In this respect, the text addresses pertinent Congressional amendments to these Acts as well as Securities and Exchange Commission regulatory developments. State securities statutes (also known as "blue sky" laws) also are covered. For students wishing a broader subject matter treatment or more intense coverage of a particular issue (such as tender offers or SEC enforcement), the sources cited in § 1.03 should be consulted.

Securities regulation is a difficult course. At the same time, it is intellectually challenging and generates provocative policy issues. It thus has the potential of being one of the more interesting yet demanding courses in the law school curriculum. This text hopefully will stimulate student interest and help make the course's subject matter more understandable.

§ 1.02 Overview

Enacted in the aftermath of "The Great Crash," the Securities Act of 1933 (hereinafter the "Securities Act" or "1933 Act") and the Securities Exchange Act of 1934 (hereinafter the "Exchange Act" or "1934 Act") have become the principal governors of federal securities law regulation. Basically, the 1933 Act deals with the initial offer and sale of securities while the 1934 Act primarily concerns trading and regulation in the secondary markets. Both Acts also prohibit manipulative and deceptive practices. Undoubtedly, the central focus of the federal securities laws is that of disclosure, thereby providing shareholders and the marketplace with sufficient information to make relevant decisions and to be apprised of significant developments. Congress thus sought to promote investor protection and the maintenance of fair and orderly markets. Generally, in enacting these Acts, Congress declined to adopt a merit approach. Rather, irrespective of the value or fairness of a transaction or other corporate action, the investor may decide for him or herself *after* receiving disclosure of pertinent information.

It bears mentioning that the Exchange Act addresses a number of other matters, including oversight of brokers, dealers, and the stock exchanges, as well as proxy and tender offer regulation. In addition, the Exchange Act, as amended by the 1975 Amendments, directs the Securities and Exchange Commission to facilitate the establishment of a national market system.

In addition to the 1933 and 1934 Acts (and amendments thereto), Congress has enacted other securities legislation: the Public Utility Holding Company Act of 1935, the Trust Indenture Act of 1939, the Investment Company Act of 1940, the Investment Advisers Act of 1940, and the Securities Investor Protection Act of 1970. Also, the individual states have passed their own securities statutes, called "Blue Sky" laws.[1] A number of these statutes, depending on the particular state, provide for significant investor protection and substantive regulation.

The Securities and Exchange Commission (hereinafter called the "SEC" or the "Commission") is the agency that administers and enforces the federal securities laws. Not surprisingly, the Commission during the years has had both its ardent supporters and outspoken critics.[2] Nonetheless, as described in the New York Times, "the agency created in 1934 to enforce [the securities] laws, the Securities and Exchange Commission, is still widely regarded as the nation's finest independent regulatory agency."[3]

Turning to state securities regulation, the first such statute was enacted in Kansas nearly a century ago. Today, all the states have enacted some form of "blue sky" law designed to apply to securities activities within their individual borders. In general, these statutes seek to regulate such activities by one or more of the following routes: "(1) to prohibit fraud in the offer and sale of securities; (2) to require and regulate licensing of investment advisors, broker-dealers, and their agents; (3) to require the registration of securities, and (4) to determine that the securities meet certain standards which are often referred to as 'merit' or 'fair, just, and equitable' standards."[4]

§ 1.03 Selected References

There are a number of useful books and treatises on securities regulation. These works include:

---

[1] This term came into being due to the original purpose of the "blue sky" laws which was to prevent "speculative schemes which have no more basis than so many feet of blue sky." *Hall v. Geiger-Jones Co.*, 242 U.S. 539, 550 (1917).

[2] See R. Karmel, *Regulation by Prosecution — The Securities and Exchange Commission Versus Corporate America* (1982); H. Kripke, *The SEC and Corporate Disclosure: Regulation in Search of a Purpose* (1979); J. Seligman, *The Transformation of Wall Street — A History of the Securities and Exchange Commission and Modern Corporate Finance* (1982); M. Steinberg, *Corporate Internal Affairs — A Corporate and Securities Law Perspective* (1983). Compare Macey, *Administrative Agency Obsolescence and Interest Group Formation: A Case Study of the SEC at Sixty,* 15 Cardozo L. Rev. 909 (1994), with Ratner, *The SEC at Sixty: A Reply to Professor Macey,* 16 Cardozo L. Rev. 1765 (1995). See also, Hicks, *Securities Regulation: Challenges in the Decades Ahead,* 68 Ind. L.J. 791 (1993).

[3] Miller, *S.E.C.: Watchdog 1929 Lacked,* New York Times, Oct. 31, 1979, at D.1. See also, D. Vise & A. Coll, *Eagle on the Street* (1991); *The SEC at 60,* Nat'l L.J., July 18, 1994, at Section C (articles contained therein).

[4] Walker & Hadaway, *Merit Standards Revisited,* 7 J. Corp. L. 651, 653 (1982). See generally Macey & Miller, *Origin of the Blue Sky Laws,* 70 Tex. L. Rev. 347 (1991); J. Long, *Blue Sky Law* (1999); L. Loss, *Commentary on the Uniform Securities Act* (1976).

Bader, W. Reece, *Securities Arbitration.*

Bainbridge, Stephen M., *Securities Law: Insider Trading.*

Bialkin, Kenneth & Grant, William, *Securities Underwriting.*

Bloomenthal, Harold S., *Going Public and the Public Corporation.*

Bloomenthal, Harold S., *Securities and Federal Corporate Law.*

Bloomenthal, Harold S. & Wolff, Samuel, *International Capital Markets and Securities Regulation.*

BNA Securities Regulation & Law Report (weekly service).

Borden, Arthur M., *Going Private.*

Branson, Douglas H., *Corporate Governance.*

Bromberg, Alan R. & Lowenfels, Lewis D., *Securities Fraud and Commodities Fraud.*

Brown, J. Robert Jr., *The Regulation of Corporate Disclosure.*

Cane, Marilyn Blumberg & Shub, Patricia A., *Securities Arbitration: Law and Procedure.*

CCH Blue Sky Law Reporter (weekly service).

CCH Federal Securities Law Reporter (weekly service).

Cohn, Stuart R., *Securities Counseling for New and Developing Companies.*

Federal Securities Act of 1933 (A.A. Sommer Jr., ed.).

Federal Securities Exchange Act of 1934 (A.A. Sommer Jr., ed.).

Ferrara, Ralph C., Rivkin, David W., & Crespi, Gregory S., *Stockbroker Supervision.*

Ferrara, Ralph C., Nagy, Donna M. & Thomas, Herbert C., *Insider Trading and the Wall.*

FitzGibbon, Scott & Glazer, Donald W., *Legal Opinions.*

Fleischer, Arthur, *Tender Offers: Defense, Responses and Planning.*

Fletcher, C. Edward, *Arbitrating Securities Disputes.*

Frankel, Tamar, *The Regulation of Money Managers.*

Frankel, Tamar, *Securitization.*

Friedman, Howard M., *Securities Regulation in Cyberspace.*

Garner, Brian A., *Securities Disclosure in Plain English.*

Hazen, Thomas Lee, *The Law of Securities Regulation.*

Hicks, J. William, *Civil Liabilities: Enforcement and Litigation Under the 1933 Act.*

Hicks, J. William, *Exempted Transactions Under the Securities Act of 1933.*

Insights (monthly periodical).

Jacobs, Arnold, *Litigation and Practice Under Rule 10b-5.*

Janvey, Ralph S., *Regulation of the Securities and Commodities Markets*.

Johnson, Charles J., Jr., *Corporate Finance and the Securities Laws*.

Johnson, Philip McBride & Hazen, Thomas Lee, *Commodities Regulation*.

Karmel, Roberta S., *Regulation by Prosecution — The Securities and Exchange Commission Versus Corporate America*.

Kaufman, Michael J., *Securities Litigation: Damages*.

Kripke, Homer, *The SEC and Corporate Disclosure: Regulation in Search of a Purpose*.

Langevoort, Donald C., *Insider Trading: Regulation, Enforcement and Prevention*.

Lee, Ruben, *What Is an Exchange? The Automation, Management, and Regulation of Financial Markets*.

Legislative History — Securities Law Committee, Federal Bar Association, *Federal Securities Laws: Legislative History 1933-1982*.

LEXIS-NEXIS (computer service).

Lipton, David A., *Broker-Dealer Regulation*.

Lipton, Martin & Steinberger, Erica, *Takeovers and Freezeouts*.

Long, Joseph C., *Blue Sky Law*.

Lorne, Simon M., *Acquisitions and Mergers: Negotiated and Contested Transactions*.

Loss, Louis, *Fundamentals of Securities Regulation*.

Loss, Louis & Seligman, Joel, *Securities Regulation*.

Malloy, Michael P., *The Corporate Law of Banks*.

Phillips, Susan M. & Zecher, J. Richard, *The SEC and the Public Interest*.

Poser, Norman S., *Broker-Dealer Law and Regulation: Private Rights of Action*.

Poser, Norman S., *International Securities Regulation*.

Review of Securities & Commodities Regulation (M. Finkelstein ed.) (bi-monthly periodical).

Romeo, Peter J. & Dye, Alan L., *Section 16 of the Securities Exchange Act of 1934: Treatise and Reporting Guide*.

Russo, Thomas A., *Regulation of the Commodities Futures and Options Markets*.

Sargent, Mark A., *D & O Liability Handbook*.

Sargent, Mark A. & Honabach, Dennis R., *Proxy Rules Handbook*.

Securities Law Techniques (A.A. Sommer ed.).

Securities Regulation Law Journal (M. Steinberg editor-in-chief) (quarterly periodical).

Securities Underwriting: A Practitioner's Guide (K. Bialkin & W. Grant eds.).

Seligman, Joel, *The SEC and the Future of Finance.*

Seligman, Joel, *The Transformation of Wall Street — A History of the Securities and Exchange Commission and Modern Corporate Finance.*

Shapiro, Susan, *Wayward Capitalists.*

Soderquist, Larry, *Understanding the Securities Laws.*

Steinberg, Marc I., *Corporate Internal Affairs: A Corporate and Securities Law Perspective.*

Steinberg, Marc I., *Corporate and Securities Malpractice.*

Steinberg, Marc I., *International Securities Law: A Comparative Analysis.*

Steinberg, Marc I., *Securities Regulation: Liabilities and Remedies.*

Steinberg, Marc I. & Ferrara, Ralph C., *Securities Practice: Federal and State Enforcement.*

Thomas, Randall S. & Dixon, Catherine T., *Aranow & Einhorn on Proxy Contests for Corporate Control.*

Vise, David A. & Coll, Steve, *Eagle on the Street.*

Wallstreetlawyer.com (monthly periodical).

Wang, William K.S. & Steinberg, Marc I., *Insider Trading.*

Waters, Michael D., *Proxy Regulation.*

Westlaw (computer service).

West's CD-ROM Federal Securities Law Library.

Wolfson, Nicholas, *The Modern Corporation: Free Markets vs. Regulation.*

Chapter 2

DEFINITION OF A "SECURITY"

§ 2.01 Introduction

Failure on counsel's part to recognize that a "security" is present can be disastrous. As will be seen in the following chapters, absent an exemption, no offer or sale of a security generally can take place unless a registration statement is in effect. Because the requirements for meeting any particular exemption may be complex, failure on counsel's part to perceive that his or her client's "deal" involves a security often means that the securities are being sold in violation of the securities laws. Under such circumstances, the Securities and Exchange Commission (SEC), state securities commissioner(s), and private parties may bring suit. Even criminal liability, depending on the circumstances, may be imposed. Hence, many deals have been scuttled, parties held liable, and lawyers sued for failure on counsel's part to recognize that a "security" was present.

The definition of "security" in the Securities Act of 1933 and the Securities Exchange Act of 1934[1] ("the Acts") covers a broad range of transactions. Although the term includes familiar instruments such as stock, notes, bonds, and "in general, any instrument commonly known as a 'security,'" the statutory definition also encompasses a wide variety of novel and unique instruments. Such instruments have included, for example, interests in "pyramid" sales schemes, chinchillas, whiskey warehouse receipts, and beavers. Ordinarily, these rather novel types of instruments come within the securities laws because they are held to be "investment contracts."

The term "security" is defined in Section 2(1) of the Securities Act of 1933 and Section 3(a)(10) of the Securities Exchange Act of 1934. Although the language of these statutes somewhat differs, they have been construed in an identical manner. Fairly broad at first glance, the instruments set forth in the statutory definitions are only the starting point. This is due to the phrase "unless the context otherwise requires," which precedes each of the provisions. This phrase, as will be seen, focuses on the economic reality of the transaction, and hence, is very significant.

§ 2.02 Overview of Key United States Supreme Court Decisions

The Supreme Court has construed the definition of a "security" several times in an attempt to clarify the statutory definitions contained in the securities acts.[2] In its decisions, the Court has rejected a literal

---

[1] Securities Act of 1933 § 2(1), 15 U.S.C. § 77b(1); Securities Exchange Act of 1934 § 3(a)(10), 15 U.S.C. § 78c(a)(10).

[2] See *Reves v. Ernst & Young*, 494 U.S. 56 (1990); *Gould v. Ruefenacht*, 471 U.S. 681 (1985);

interpretation of the statutes, adopting instead a more flexible view that looks to the economic reality of the particular plan or scheme addressed.

In the first such case, *SEC v. C.M. Joiner Leasing Corp.*,[3] the Court recognized that, although the statutory definition makes specific reference to a number of "standardized" investment devices, "the reach of the [Securities] Act does not stop with the obvious and commonplace."[4] Therefore, as the Court suggested, other "[n]ovel, uncommon, or irregular devices" may fall within one of the definition's more descriptive categories, such as "investment contract," if the facts so warrant.[5]

In *SEC v. W.J. Howey Co.*[6] the Supreme Court subsequently explained that the term "investment contract" had been employed in previously enacted state "blue sky" laws and had come to signify "a contract or scheme for 'the placing of capital or laying out of money in a way intended to secure income or profit from its employment.' "[7] The transaction in *Howey* involved the offering of small parcels of land in a citrus grove in Florida, coupled with a service contract for cultivating and marketing the produce. The prospective purchasers were informed that the venture was not economically feasible without arranging for a service contract. In holding that the instrument offered was an "investment contract" and, hence, a security, the *Howey* Court emphasized that "investment contract" embodies a "flexible rather than a static principle" and that the term had been broadly construed by state courts as a means of protecting the investing public. "Form was disregarded for substance and emphasis was placed upon economic reality."[8] Reasoning that Congress was aware of prior judicial interpretation of "investment contract" when it employed the term in defining "security" and noting that a broad construction was consistent with the federal securities laws' remedial intent, the *Howey* Court devised a standard to

---

Marine Bank v. Weaver, 455 U.S. 551 (1982); *International Bhd. of Teamsters v. Daniel*, 439 U.S. 551 (1979); *United Hous. Found., Inc. v. Forman*, 421 U.S. 837 (1975); *Tcherepnin v. Knight*, 389 U.S. 332 (1967); *SEC v. United Benefit Life Ins. Co.*, 387 U.S. 202 (1967); *SEC v. Variable Annuity Life Ins. Co. of Am.*, 359 U.S. 65 (1959); *SEC v. W.J. Howey Co.*, 328 U.S. 293 (1946); *SEC v. C.M. Joiner Leasing Corp.*, 320 U.S. 344 (1943). Cases not discussed in the following discussion include *SEC v. Variable Annuity Life Insurance Co. of America*, 359 U.S. 65 (1959) (holding variable annuity contracts to be securities); *SEC v. United Benefit Life Insurance Co.*, 387 U.S. 202 (1967) (holding that a "flexible fund annuity contract" was a security).

[3] 320 U.S. 344 (1943) (holding that the sale of assignments of oil leasehold subdivisions constituted a sale of securities).

[4] *Id.* at 351.

[5] *Id.* The Court looked to such factors as "what character the instrument is given in commerce by the terms of the offer, the plan of distribution and the economic inducements held out to the prospect." *Id.* at 352-53.

[6] 328 U.S. 293 (1946) (holding that the sale of units in a citrus grove development together with service contracts for cultivating and marketing the produce constituted a sale of securities).

[7] *Id.* at 298 (quoting *State v. Gopher Tire & Rubber Co.*, 146 Minn. 52, 56, 177 N.W. 937, 938 (1920)).

[8] 328 U.S. at 298.

comport with this background.[9] Under what has become known as the "*Howey* test," an investment contract is a transaction or scheme that involves "an investment of money in a common enterprise with profits to come solely from the efforts of others."[10] This test has been elaborated upon by both the Supreme Court and lower federal courts. These decisions are discussed later in this chapter.

In *Tcherepnin v. Knight*,[11] the Court reiterated that "remedial legislation should be construed broadly to effectuate its purposes" and that "[e]ven a casual reading of [Section] 3(a)(10) of the 1934 Act reveals that Congress did not intend to adopt a narrow or restrictive concept of security in defining that term."[12] Therefore, in its early post-*Howey* decisions construing the Acts, the Court adopted a flexible, expansive interpretation of the three-part *Howey* test. The lower courts, expanding on the *Howey* test, followed suit.[13] By the mid-1970s, however, the Supreme Court retreated from this remedial approach.

The decision that signaled the Court's retreat was *United Housing Foundation, Inc. v. Forman*.[14] In *Forman* the Court held that shares of stock in a cooperative housing project purchased by individuals who were residents of the apartment complex were not securities. The Court assessed the economic realities of the transaction: the shares purchased did not confer the attendant rights that ordinarily accompany stock, were not transferable to a non-tenant, could not be pledged or encumbered, carried no voting rights in relation to the shares owned, and had to be offered back to the cooperative housing corporation at their initial selling price. In determining whether such shares of stock constituted securities, the Court rejected a literal approach and refused to require that the transaction, evidenced by the sale of "stock," be considered a security transaction merely because the statutory definition of a security contains the words "any stock." Instead, the Court stressed that "*economic reality*," not form, should control: "Because securities transactions are economic in character Congress intended the application of these statutes to turn on the economic realities underlying a transaction, and not on the name appended thereto."[15]

---

[9] *Id.* at 299 (defining the term "investment contract" to encompass "a flexible rather than a static principle, one that is capable of adaptation to meet the countless and variable schemes devised by those who seek the use of the money of others on the promise of profits").

[10] *Id.* at 301.

[11] 389 U.S. 332 (1967).

[12] *Id.* at 336-39 (also stating that "form should be disregarded for substance and the emphasis should be on economic reality").

[13] See, e.g., *SEC v. Koscot Interplanetary, Inc.*, 497 F.2d 473 (5th Cir. 1974) (holding that a franchise-like "pyramid" promotion scheme involved securities even though the investors exerted some effort, provided that the promoters' efforts were the undeniably significant ones); *SEC v. Glenn W. Turner Enters., Inc.*, 474 F.2d 476, 482 (9th Cir. 1973) (looking to "whether the efforts made by those other than the investor are the undeniably significant ones, those essential managerial efforts which affect the failure or success of the enterprise"); *infra* notes 38-43 and accompanying text.

[14] 421 U.S. 837 (1975).

[15] *Id.* at 849.

After finding that the shares of stock in *Forman* lacked the attributes of ordinary stock, the Court also declined to view the instruments as investment contracts. The Court reasoned that the securities laws are inapplicable when the purchaser is "motivated by a desire to use or consume the item purchased," rather than by the anticipation of receiving a return on his or her investment.[16] In *Forman*, the purchasers of stock sought adequate and affordable housing to live. Accordingly, they were not investors and did not purchase a "security."

Similarly, in *International Brotherhood of Teamsters v. Daniel*,[17] the Supreme Court applied the "economic reality" concept to constrict, rather than to broaden, the definition of "investment contract." Specifically, the Court held that a noncontributory, compulsory pension plan is not an investment contract and, hence, not a security. In a noncontributory, compulsory pension plan, the employer contributes the necessary payments, not the employee who ultimately benefits from the plan. The Court applied the three-pronged *Howey* test for an investment contract. Concentrating on the economic reality of the plan, the Court observed that "an employee is selling his labor primarily to obtain a livelihood, not making an investment" and, therefore, concluded that the *Howey* test's "investment of money" element was not satisfied.[18] Moreover, the employer's contributions to the fund were not the equivalent of an "investment" by the employee because no fixed relationship existed between the employer's contributions and the employee's potential benefits. The Court also found that the pension fund's assets did not depend on profits yielded by the efforts of others. To the contrary, the vast majority of the income generated derived from the employer's contributions and thus was independent from the efforts of the fund's managers. In addition, actual receipt of benefits from the fund depended on whether employees met certain individual eligibility requirements, not on the financial success of the fund itself.[19]

The *Daniel* Court further supported its holding by concluding that the enactment of ERISA, which expressly regulates pension plans,[20] eliminated the need for coverage under the securities laws:

> The existence of this comprehensive legislation governing the use and terms of employee pension plans severely undercuts all arguments for extending the Securities Acts to noncontributory, compulsory pension plans. Congress believed that it was filling a regulatory void when it enacted ERISA, a belief which the SEC actively encouraged. Not only is the extension of the Securities Acts . . . not supported by the language and history of those Acts, but in light of ERISA it serves no general purpose. . . . Whatever benefits employees might derive from the effect

---

[16] *Id*. at 852-53.

[17] 439 U.S. 551 (1979).

[18] *Id*. at 560–61.

[19] *Id*. at 561–62.

[20] See Employee Retirement Income Security Act of 1974 (ERISA), 29 U.S.C. §§ 1001-1461.

of the Securities Acts are now provided in more definite form through ERISA.[21]

Thus, in both *Forman* and *Daniel* the Supreme Court employed the language, if not quite the spirit, of the *Howey* "economic reality" test to exclude transactions that otherwise might fall within the definition of "investment contract." This trend was further evidenced by the Court's decision in *Marine Bank v. Weaver*.[22] At the outset of its analysis, the *Marine Bank* Court paraphrased the prefatory language to Section 3(a)(10) of the Exchange Act, stating that the terms included in the Act's definitional section are not to be considered securities if "the context otherwise requires." The Court then asserted that "Congress, in enacting the securities laws, did not intend to provide a broad federal remedy for all fraud."[23] It concluded that neither a conventional certificate of deposit nor an agreement given as consideration for pledging the certificate of deposit to guarantee a bank loan constituted a security under the federal securities laws.

In addressing the certificate of deposit issue, the *Marine Bank* Court elevated the presence of other comprehensive regulation, a factor of inferential importance in *Daniel*, to paramount significance. The Court commenced its analysis by distinguishing the withdrawable capital shares in *Tcherepnin v. Knight* on the ground that the *Tcherepnin* purchasers received dividends based on the savings and loan associations' profits, rather than at a fixed rate of interest, and also received voting rights. The *Marine Bank* Court observed that the withdrawable capital shares in *Tcherepnin* "were much more like ordinary shares of stock and 'the ordinary concept of a security,' . . . than a certificate of deposit."[24] Then, looking to the context of the transaction, the Court turned to the differences it perceived between a certificate of deposit and other long-term debt obligations. The Court focused not so much on the particular attributes of these instruments, but rather on the existence of comprehensive federal regulation governing the banking industry. Moreover, unlike the holder of a long-term debt obligation who assumes the risk of the borrower's insolvency, the purchaser of a certificate of deposit is almost assured of repayment due to the availability of depositor insurance. Accordingly, the Court concluded that "[i]t is unnecessary to subject issuers of bank certificates of deposit to liability under the antifraud provisions of the federal securities laws since the

---

[21] 439 U.S. at 569–70 (citations omitted). On the other hand, voluntary contributory pension plans may be securities. See *Uselton v. Commercial Lovelace Motor Freight, Inc.*, 940 F.2d 564 (10th Cir. 1991); Securities Act Release Nos. 6188 (1980), 6281 (1981). But see *Matassarin v. Lynch*, 174 F.3d 549 (5th Cir. 1999) (interest in a mandatory employer-funded employee option plan held not a security); *Conrad v. Colgate-Palmolive Co.*, 686 F.2d 1230 (7th Cir. 1982) (contributory voluntary pension plans are not securities). See generally Bromberg, *The Employee Investor & ESOPS and Other Employee Benefit Plans as Securities*, 19 Sec. Reg. L.J. 325 (1992).

[22] 455 U.S. 551 (1982).

[23] *Id*. at 556.

[24] *Id*. at 557.

holders of bank certificates of deposit are abundantly protected under the federal banking laws."[25]

Likewise, the Court observed that the profit-sharing agreement present in *Marine Bank* was not the type of transaction that "comes to mind when the term 'security' is used" and concluded that the agreement differed in several respects from other unusual arrangements found to involve securities. Specifically, the Court noted that the agreement was a private transaction, negotiated one-on-one, with no prospectus distributed to potential investors; that the agreement was unique (as evidenced by the provisions allowing the Weavers to use the barn and pasture), lacked "equivalent value" to other investors, and was not designed to be traded publicly; and that the Weavers' "veto" power over future loans gave them a measure of control over the business. Therefore, although the Court did not apply the *Howey* test expressly, it held that the agreement was not a security despite the profit-sharing provision.[26]

Indeed, the *Marine Bank* Court may have impliedly modified the *Howey* test. Under this possible modification, an instrument may not be deemed an investment contract, irrespective of the *Howey* three-part test being met, if (1) the transaction involves a novel or unique instrument, (2) that is not capable of mass distribution or public trading, (3) when no offering document has been distributed, and (4) the transaction is negotiated privately and involves few individuals.

On the other hand, in *Landreth Timber Co. v. Landreth*[27] and *Gould v. Ruefenacht*,[28] the Supreme Court held that common stock having the attributes normally associated with this instrument is a security. In so holding, the Court rejected the approach embodied by the sale of business doctrine. That doctrine stood for the proposition that the incidental transfer of stock to manifest the sale of a closely-held business is not a security with respect to those who are entrepreneurs rather than passive investors.[29] In refusing to adopt the doctrine, the Supreme Court indicated that scrutiny of a transaction's economic substance is necessary only when the instruments involved are "unusual . . . not easily characterized as 'securities.'"[30] Hence, the Court distinguished *Forman* by reasoning that the stock involved in the cases at bar bore all the characteristics traditionally associated with common stock, which the Court described as follows: "(i) the right to receive dividends contingent upon an apportionment of profits; (ii) negotiability; (iii) the ability to be pledged or hypothecated; (iv) the conferring of voting rights in proportion to the number of shares owned; and (v) the capacity to appreciate in value."[31]

---

[25] *Id.* at 558–59.

[26] *Id.* at 559–60.

[27] 471 U.S. 681 (1985).

[28] 471 U.S. 701 (1985).

[29] See, e.g., *Christy v. Cambron*, 710 F.2d 669 (10th Cir. 1983); *King v. Winkler*, 673 F.2d 342 (11th Cir. 1982); *Canfield v. Rapp & Son, Inc.*, 654 F.2d 459 (7th Cir. 1981).

[30] *Landreth*, 471 U.S. at 690.

[31] *Id.* at 686. See *Gould*, 471 U.S. at 704–06.

Looking to the "plain meaning" of the statutory definition of a "security," the Supreme Court held that traditional stock necessarily falls within the Acts' coverage. Reconciling this approach with the economic reality test, the Supreme Court in a subsequent case reasoned: "*Landreth Timber* does not signify a lack of concern with economic reality; rather it signals a recognition that stock is, as a practical matter, always an investment if it has the economic characteristics traditionally associated with stock."[32]

In *Reves v. Ernst & Young*,[33] the Court rejected the *Landreth Timber* rationale in the note context. Unlike "stock," which by its nature (if it has the attributes typically associated with such an instrument) is within the class of instruments Congress intended to regulate under the securities laws, the same cannot be said of "notes," which are used in a variety of settings, some of which are commercial and others of which involve investments. Hence, since "notes" are not necessarily securities, the Court, after searching for a proper standard to be applied, opted for the "family resemblance" test.[34] As elaborated upon later,[35] this test encompasses the "motivations" of a reasonable buyer and seller to engage in the transaction, the plan of distribution, the reasonable expectations of the investing public, and the presence of a risk reducing factor.[36] Applying the family resemblance test, the Court held that the notes at issue were securities.[37]

§ 2.03   Key Issues for "Investment Contract" Analysis

The discussion that follows addresses three key issues (i.e., "solely from the efforts of others," "expectation of profits," and the "common enterprise" requirement) that arise in determining whether an ownership interest satisfies the *Howey* investment contract test. They are analyzed at this point for ease of organization and understanding. Emphasis is made that these three issues surface when analyzing whether any interest in an enterprise (such as an interest in a general partnership, limited liability company, or joint venture) meets the *Howey* investment contract test, and, hence, is a security under federal law.

---

[32] *Reves v. Ernst & Young*, 494 U.S. 56, 62 (1990). Subsequent cases continue to address the issue concerning the security law status of instruments called stock. See, e.g., *Seger v. Federal Intermediate Credit Bank of Omaha*, 850 F.2d 468 (8th Cir. 1988) (applying *Forman* criteria, lender's Class B "stock" did not have characteristics normally associated with such an instrument and, hence, was not a security); *One-O-One Enterprises, Inc, v. Caruso*, 848 F.2d 1283 (D.C. Cir. 1988) (option to purchase stock deemed a security relying on *Landreth)*; *McVay v. Western Plains Service Corporation*, 823 F.2d 1395 (10th Cir. 1987) (interpreting *Forman*, loan participation certificates held not to be "stock" within scope of the securities laws because such certificates "lack[ed] any of the basic attributes of true stock"); *B. Rosenberg & Sons, Inc. v. St. James Sugar Coop., Inc.*, 447 F. Supp. 1 (E.D. La. 1976), *aff'd*, 565 F.2d 1213 (5th Cir. 1977) (applying *Forman*, common stock in sugar coop held not a security).

[33] 494 U.S. 56 (1990).

[34] *Id.* at 64–67.

[35] See *infra* notes 81–105 and accompanying text.

[36] 494 U.S. at 66–67.

[37] *Id.* at 67–73.

[A] "Solely from the Efforts of Others"

The Supreme Court in *Howey* stated that one of the requirements for an instrument to be an investment contract is that the investor must expect to derive "profits *solely* from the efforts of the promoter or a third party."[38] One of the issues often present in determining whether limited partnership interests and similar investments are securities under the *Howey* test is how strictly the term *solely* from the efforts of others should be construed. A number of federal appellate court decisions have discussed the issue.

One such case is the Fifth Circuit's decision in *SEC v. Koscot Interplanetary, Inc.*[39] The *Koscot* court adopted a test first enunciated by the Ninth Circuit in *SEC v. Glenn W. Turner Enterprises, Inc.*[40] In *Turner* the court announced that the critical inquiry is "whether the efforts made by those other than the investor are the undeniably significant ones, those essential managerial efforts which affect the failure or success of the enterprise."[41] This *Koscot/Turner* test rejects a literal interpretation of "solely" and has been widely followed.[42] Nonetheless, a number of other courts have expressed this standard in more narrow terms, inquiring "whether the investor has meaningfully participated in the management of the [venture] in which it has invested such that it has more than minimal control over the investment's performance."[43] The Supreme Court, although not expressly adopting a more flexible formulation of this aspect of the *Howey* test, appears to have acquiesced in such a formulation. For example, in *United Housing Foundation, Inc. v. Forman*, the Court opined that "profits [must] be derived from the entrepreneurial or managerial efforts of others."[44]

[B] "Expectation of Profits"

The Supreme Court has identified two forms of "profit" that meet the *Howey* investment contract test: (1) "capital appreciation resulting from the development of the initial investment," and (2) "a participation in earnings resulting from the use of investors' funds."[45] In so holding, the Court rejected the plaintiffs' argument in *Forman* that their tax deductions were

---

[38] 328 U.S. at 298 (emphasis added).

[39] 497 F.2d 473 (5th Cir. 1974).

[40] 474 F.2d 476 (9th Cir. 1973).

[41] *Id.* at 482.

[42] See, e.g., *Goodman v. Epstein*, 582 F.2d 388 (7th Cir. 1978).

[43] *Steinhardt Group, Inc. v. Citicorp*, 126 F.3d 144, 152 (3d Cir. 1997).

[44] 421 U.S. 837, 852, n.16 (1975). For more recent cases applying the "efforts of others" standard, see, e.g., *Webster v. Omnitriton Int'l, Inc.*, 79 F.3d 776 (9th Cir. 1996) (fact that investors exerted some efforts does not preclude securities law coverage); *Steinhardt Group, Inc. v. Citicorp*, 126 F.3d 144 (3d Cir. 1997) (holding that due to limited partner's retention of "pervasive control over its investment in the limited partnership," no investment contract present); *SEC v. Life Partners, Inc.*, 102 F.3d 587 (D.C. Cir. 1996) (holding that interests in viatical settlements are not investment contracts because purchaser's profit depended on when the insured died rather than on a third party's managerial efforts).

[45] 421 U.S. at 852.

a form of profit. Nonetheless, lower courts have held that an investor's desire for favorable tax consequences may not prevent the instrument from being a security so long as there was also an expectation of profit in real terms.[46]

Another key point is that the securities laws generally do not apply where the purchaser is principally motivated by a desire to use or consume the interest acquired. For example, because the plaintiffs in *Forman* were motivated mainly by the desire to obtain affordable and decent housing, rather than seeking a return on the acquisition, the securities laws were not applicable.[47] As a more recent example, in *Rice v. Branigar Organization, Inc.*[48] Justice Powell, sitting by designation on the Eleventh Circuit, opined that purchases of beach front lots and equity memberships in an adjacent country club were not securities. The court asserted that the purchasers acquired the beach front lots and country club memberships "primarily to use them, not to derive profits from the entrepreneurial efforts of the developers." Moreover, "[t]he overall emphasis in the promotional material was clearly placed on enjoying the beauty . . . and the amenities of the club and community." Hence, the court held: "where those who purchase something [have] the primary desire to use or consume it, the security laws do not apply."[49]

[C] The "Common Enterprise" Requirement

As the Supreme Court pointed out in *Howey*, an essential ingredient for the finding of an investment contract is that there be a "common enterprise." Generally, there are two types of common enterprise: horizontal commonality and vertical commonality. All courts have held that horizontal commonality is sufficient to meet this aspect of the *Howey* test. Generally, horizontal commonality looks to the relationships that exist between an individual investor and the pool of other investors. Under this standard, a pooling of the interests of the investors is essential to finding the existence of an investment contract. Hence, "no horizontal common enterprise can exist unless there . . . exists between [the investors] themselves some relationship which ties the fortunes of each investor to the success of the overall venture."[50]

---

[46] See, e.g., *Goodman v. Epstein*, 582 F.2d 388 (7th Cir. 1978).

[47] See 421 U.S. at 853–54.

[48] 922 F.2d 788 (11th Cir. 1991).

[49] *Id.* at 790–91. For a more recent decision on this point, see *Teague v. Bakker*, [1998 Transfer Binder] Fed. Sec. L. Rep. (CCH) ¶ 90,182 (4th Cir. 1998) (holding that jury was properly instructed for *Howey* investment contract test to inquire whether the purchasers acquiring lodging in a vacation park were primarily attracted by the prospective financial return or by enjoyment of the lodging).

Note, however, if an instrument has the usual characteristics of traditional stock, the securities laws will apply. This is so even if the purchaser intends to be an active entrepreneur who seeks to "use or consume" the business acquired. See *Gould v. Ruefenacht*, 471 U.S. 701 (1985); *Landreth Timber Co. v. Landreth*, 471 U.S. 681 (1985). These cases are discussed earlier in this chapter, *supra* notes 27–32 and accompanying text.

[50] *Curran v. Merrill Lynch, Pierce, Fenner & Smith, Inc.*, 622 F.2d 216, 224 (6th Cir. 1980), *aff'd on other grounds*, 456 U.S. 353 (1982).

The lower courts widely disagree, however, on whether "vertical commonality" satisfies the *Howey* common enterprise element. A number of courts hold that only horizontal commonality (and not vertical commonality) satisfies the common enterprise requirement.[51] On the other hand, other courts deem "vertical commonality" to be sufficient. As explained by one court, there are two types of vertical commonality:

> There is a split in the courts that have applied the "vertical commonality" approach regarding precisely what is necessary to satisfy this standard. The courts applying the more restrictive definition state that "vertical commonality" exists where "the fortunes of the investor are interwoven with and dependent upon the efforts and success of those seeking the investment or third parties." . . . Thus, [one view] appears to require . . . that there be a "direct relation between the success or failure of the promoter and that of his investors."

> A broader definition of "vertical commonality" seems to have been articulated by [some courts holding] that "the requisite commonality is evidenced by the fact that the fortunes of [the investor(s)] are inextricably tied to the efficacy of the [promoter's efforts]". . . . Thus, . . . the broader definition merely requires a link between the fortunes of the investors and the efforts of the promoters.[52]

§ 2.04 Application of the *Howey* Test to Specific Ventures

[A] Limited Partnerships

The judicial analysis of whether partnership interests fall within the definition of a security has proceeded along the lines of whether a partnership interest is an "investment contract."

Since state law governing the operation of limited partnerships traditionally prohibited limited partners from performing significant managerial functions, courts usually held that these interests met the *Howey* requirement that profits be derived essentially from the efforts of others. Analysis often focused upon both the terms of the partnership agreement and on the actual extent of managerial participation by the limited partners.[53]

It should be emphasized, however, that a court still must make an independent examination of whether the limited partnership interest meets

---

[51] See, e.g., *Salcer v. Merrill Lynch, Pierce, Fenner & Smith, Inc.*, 682 F.2d 459 (3d Cir. 1982); *Milnarik v. M.S. Commodities, Inc.*, 457 F.2d 274 (7th Cir. 1972).

[52] *Mechigian v. Art Capital Corp.*, 612 F. Supp. 1421, 1427 (S.D.N.Y. 1985) (citations omitted). For further discussion, see Chang, *Meaning, Reference and Reification of a Security*, 19 U.C. Davis L. Rev. 403 (1986); Gordon, *Common Enterprise and Multiple Investors: A Contractual Theory for Defining Investment Contracts and Notes*, 1988 Colum. Bus. L. Rev. 635 (1988); Monaghan, *An Uncommon State of Confusion: The Common Enterprise Element of Investment Contract Analysis*, 63 Fordham L. Rev. 2135 (1995); Comment, *Defining an "Investment Contract": The Commonality Requirement of the Howey Test*, 43 Wash. & Lee L. Rev. 1057 (1986).

[53] See, e.g., *L&B Hospital Ventures, Inc. v. Healthcare Int'l, Inc.*, 894 F.2d 150 (5th Cir. 1990); *Mayer v. Oil Field Systems Corp.*, 721 F.2d 59 (2d Cir. 1983).

[C] Limited Liability Companies

An issue not yet resolved is whether interests in a limited liability company (LLC) are securities. An LLC is a relatively recent creature of statute, effective in nearly all of the states. As a flexible form of non-corporate business organization, an LLC allows a planner to choose pass-through taxation without classification as an S corporation. Beginning in 1988, the Internal Revenue Service (IRS) began classifying LLCs as partnerships for tax purposes, thus legitimizing the LLC's pass-through tax structure. Thus, the LLC avoids double taxation and corporate formalities and allows a pass-through of income and loss to its members for tax purposes. Further, LLC investors (referred to as "members") may take an unrestricted role in management without sacrificing limited liability. The LLC also need not have any member subject to unlimited liability as is required in limited partnerships.[65]

The *Howey* investment contract test applies to determining whether LLC interests are securities. It may be argued that LLC interests are not investment contracts since most of the state statutes vest management power in the LLC members. This power arguably signifies that LLC members are not relying essentially on the efforts of others. Under this approach, LLC interests are similar to interests in a general partnership and, therefore, ordinarily are not investment contracts. Nonetheless, depending on the provisions contained in the LLC operating documents and the surrounding circumstances (such as the expertise required to operate the business), application of the *Williamson* factors may result in the LLC interests satisfying the *Howey* test.[66]

Moreover, even though LLC interests are not labeled stock, such interests are issued by an entity called a "Company." Since the typical issuance of an equity interest by a commercial enterprise calling itself a company or corporation is stock, the argument may be made that LLC interests should be analyzed pursuant to the *Forman-Landreth Timber* "ordinary attributes of stock" standard. Applying this standard, an investor's interest in a limited liability company may have characteristics similar to those associated with stock. Analysis as to whether LLC interests are securities also may be made by applying the "family resemblance" test enunciated in *Reves v. Ernst & Young*.[67]

---

[65] See generally M. Sargent, *Limited Liability Company Handbook* (1996).

[66] See *Keith v. Black Diamond Advisors, Inc.*, 48 F. Supp. 2d 329 (S.D.N.Y. 1999); Goforth, *Why Limited Liability Company Membership Interests Should Not Be Treated as Securities and Possible Steps to Encourage This Result*, 45 Hastings L.J. 1223 (1994); McGinty, *Are Interests in Limited Liability Companies Securities?*, 25 Sec. Reg. L.J. 121 (1997); Ribstein, *Form and Substance in the Definition of a "Security": The Case of Limited Liability Companies*, 51 Wash. & Lee L. Rev. 807 (1994); Sargent, *Are Limited Liability Company Interests Securities?*, 19 Pepperdine L. Rev. 1069 (1992); Wells, *Limited Liability Company Interests as Securities: An Analysis of Federal and State Actions Against Limited Liability Companies Under the Securities Laws*, 73 Den. U.L. Rev. 425 (1996).

[67] See Steinberg & Conway, *The Limited Liability Company as a Security*, 19 Pepperdine L. Rev. 1105 (1992). But see sources cited *supra* note 66. The *Forman-Landreth Timber* "ordinary attributes of stock" standard is discussed *supra* notes 27–32 and accompanying text. The *Reves* "family resemblance" test is addressed *infra* notes 80–105 and accompanying text.

[D] Property Interests Combined with Service Contracts

The factual setting presented to the Supreme Court in *Howey* has been repeated numerous times in a variety of contexts. Courts repeatedly have looked beyond a strict statutory construction and have examined the economic reality of the transaction to determine whether a property interest combined with some form of service contract constitutes a security (termed the "aggregation" approach). The *Howey* analysis applied by the courts in these cases usually can be broken down into three issues: First, are the investors dependent on other investors and/or the promoter for a return on their investment ("common enterprise")? Second, is the interest bought in order to obtain a financial return or for other reasons ("expectation of profits")? Third, do the investors participate in the venture to such a degree that they are not dependent "solely on the efforts of others" for their profits?[68]

The applicability of the securities laws in this context may arise where there is the offer and sale of condominium units, or other units in a real estate development, coupled with an arrangement for the promoter or its designee to perform certain rental services for the purchaser. Such agreements may be held to involve the offer and sale of an investment contract or a participation in a profit sharing arrangement within the meaning of the securities acts. On this subject, the SEC has expressed the following view:

> [T]he offering of condominium units in conjunction with any one of the following will cause the offering to be viewed as an offering of securities in the form of investment contracts:
>
> 1. The condominiums, with any rental arrangement or other similar service, are offered and sold with emphasis on the economic benefits to the purchaser to be derived from the managerial efforts of the promoter, or a third party designated or arranged for by the promoter, from rental of the units.
>
> 2. The offering of participation in a rental pool arrangement; [or]
>
> 3. The offering of a rental or similar arrangement whereby the purchaser must hold his unit available for rental for any part of the year, must use an exclusive rental agent or is otherwise materially restricted in his occupancy or rental of his unit.
>
> In all of the above situations, investor protection requires the application of the federal securities laws.[69]

Note that a security may exist in additional situations other than the three classified above in the SEC release. For example, in *Hocking v. Dubois*, the Ninth Circuit expansively applied the *Howey* test to a condominium *resale* coupled with a rental agreement between the purchaser and a rental agent recommended by but not affiliated with the real estate broker.[70] The decision has raised concerns among real estate brokers that their

---

[68] See, e.g., *Westchester Corp. v. Peat Marwick Mitchell & Co.*, 626 F.2d 1212 (5th Cir. 1980); *Continental Marketing Corp. v. SEC*, 387 F.2d 466 (10th Cir. 1967).

[69] Securities Act Release No. 5347 (1973).

[70] 885 F.2d 1449 (9th Cir. 1989) (en banc).

recommendation of a leasing agent (even if not affiliated with such broker) in connection with the sale as well as resale of a vacation-type condominium may trigger application of the securities laws.[71]

[E] Franchises

Conventional franchising agreements (which also may take such forms as dealerships, distributorships, or leasing arrangements) generally have been held not to constitute "investment contracts." The rationale is that pursuant to these arrangements, the franchisee exerts meaningful efforts.[72] Nonetheless, it is important to emphasize that the label "franchise" is not determinative. Where the franchisee has not been granted realistic authority to exercise significant managerial rights and responsibilities with respect to the enterprise, an investment contract may be held to exist.[73] Moreover, where a franchise agreement is really a pyramid scheme, in which profits are sought from the sale of other "franchises" through the main efforts of the promoter and/or third parties (rather than from the sale of products), an investment contract normally will be recognized.[74]

§ 2.05 The Risk Capital Test

The *Howey* test is the prevalent standard for ascertaining the existence of an investment contract under both federal and state law. Nonetheless, the risk capital test remains an important state law alternative to the *Howey* standard. Although not generally adopted by the federal courts, the risk capital test has been embraced by a number of states by statute or case law. Importantly, application of the risk capital test may lead to a finding of a "security" under the applicable state law where the *Howey* test would hold that no security interest is present.

The risk capital test was first recognized by the California Supreme Court in *Silver Hills Country Club v. Sobieski*,[75] in an opinion written by Justice Traynor. There, the California Commission of Corporations successfully argued that the offer and sale of memberships in a country club to be operated for profit were securities under California law. The proceeds from such memberships were to be used for club improvements, and members and their immediate families were entitled to use club facilities. Even though the benefits to be received were non-pecuniary, the court, applying the risk capital test, held that the membership interests were securities. Justice Traynor stated:

---

[71] See Rumsey, *Resort Condominiums and the Federal Securities Laws*, 18 Colo. Lawyer 229 (1989); Comment, *Hocking v. Dubois: Applying the Securities Laws to Condominium Resales*, 58 Fordham L. Rev. 1121 (1990).

[72] See, e.g., *Meyer v. Dans un Jardin*, 816 F.2d 533 (10th Cir. 1987).

[73] See, e.g., *SEC v. Aqua-Sonic Products Corp.*, 687 F.2d 577 (2d Cir. 1982); Securities Act Release No. 5211 (1971).

[74] See *Piambino v. Bailey*, 610 F.2d 1306 (5th Cir. 1980); Johnson & Campbell, *Securities Law and the Franchise Agreement*, 1980 Utah L. Rev. 311 (1980).

[75] 55 Cal. 2d 811, 361 P.2d 906, 13 Cal. Rptr. 186 (1961).

We have here nothing like the ordinary sale of a right to use existing facilities. Petitioners are soliciting the risk capital with which to develop a business for profit. The purchaser's risk is not lessened merely because the interest he purchases is labelled a membership. Only because he risks his capital along with other purchasers can there be any chance that the benefits of club membership will materialize.[76]

The risk capital test has been adopted by a number of state courts and legislatures.[77] The Oklahoma statute, for example, has a far-reaching risk capital test, defined as an "investment of money or money's worth including goods furnished and/or services performed in the risk capital of a venture with the expectation of some benefit to the investor where the investor has no direct control over the investment or policy decisions of the venture."[78]

It is important to note that generally under the risk capital test (1) there is no horizontal common enterprise required, (2) (similar to the *Howey* line of cases) non-pecuniary benefits are sufficient, and (3) the *Howey* "solely from the efforts of others" standard is relaxed.

Irrespective of whether the risk capital or the *Howey* test is employed, it may be argued that some courts have not adequately focused on the prospective investor's position at the time that the transaction occurs. Instead, such courts too often may concern themselves with the investor's anticipated position after the deal is struck. Yet, because the critical issues arise during the offer, negotiation, and purchase stages, it is at these stages that courts should assess whether the interests at stake warrant application of the securities laws.[79]

§ 2.06 Debt Securities

A substantial portion of case law has addressed whether certain debt instruments are securities under federal and state law. One threshold issue is that the definitions pertaining to debt securities in Section 2(1) of the Securities Act and Section 3(a)(10) of the Exchange Act are not precisely the same. Further, the Securities Act definition, although exempting notes of less than nine months maturity from the registration requirement, specifically includes "evidence(s) of indebtedness." The Exchange Act definition of security (§ 3(a)(10)), on the other hand, specifically excludes notes of less than nine months maturity. Nonetheless, the coverage of the two Acts, as the Supreme Court has held, "may be considered the same."[80]

---

[76] 361 P.2d at 908.

[77] See, e.g., *State, Commissioner of Securities v. Hawaii Market Center, Inc.*, 52 Haw. 642, 485 P.2d 105 (1971); Ga. Code Ann. § 97-102(a)(16); Okla. Stat. tit. 71, § 2(20)(P); Coffey, *The Economic Realities of a "Security": Is There a More Meaningful Formula?*, 18 Case W. Res. L. Rev. 367 (1967).

[78] Okla. Stat. tit. 71, § 2(20)(P).

[79] On this point, see Carney & Fraser, *Defining a "Security: Georgia's Struggle with the Risk Capital Test*, 30 Emory L.J. 73 (1981).

[80] *Reves v. Ernst & Young*, 494 U.S. 56, 61 n.1 (1990).

[A] Notes

Prior to the Supreme Court's decision in *Reves v. Ernst & Young*,[81] the lower federal courts were sharply divided on the applicable criteria to be employed in determining the security law status of "notes." The tests utilized included the "family resemblance" approach,[82] the "commercial/ investment" standard,[83] the "risk capital" test,[84] and the *Howey* criteria.[85] Given the divergent approaches, the Supreme Court's decision in *Reves*, although far from being a model of clarity, helps to resolve ambiguities in this area.

The instruments in *Reves* were demand notes, such notes being uncollateralized and uninsured, paying a variable rate of interest adjusted monthly to be higher than that paid by local financial institutions but not being linked to the earnings of the business. In determining the proper standard to adopt, the Court declined to adhere to the *Howey* test in the "note" context. The *Reves* Court reasoned: "To hold that a 'note' is not a 'security' unless it meets a test designed for an entirely different variety of instrument 'would make the Acts' enumeration of many types of instruments superfluous,' and would be inconsistent with Congress' intent to regulate the entire body of instruments sold as investments."[86] On the other hand, the Court rejected the *Landreth Timber* formula in the note context. Unlike "stock," which by its nature (if it has the attributes typically associated with such an instrument) is within the class of instruments Congress intended to regulate under the securities laws, the same cannot be said of "notes," which are used in a variety of settings, some of which are commercial and others of which involve investments. Hence, since "notes" are not necessarily securities, the Court, after searching for a proper standard to be applied, opted for the "family resemblance" test.[87]

---

[81] 494 U.S. 56 (1990).

[82] See, e.g., *Exchange National Bank of Chicago v. Touche Ross & Co.*, 544 F.2d 1126 (2d Cir. 1976).

[83] See, e.g., *Baurer v. Planning Group, Inc.*, 669 F.2d 770 (D.C. 1981). As set forth in this text's first edition:

Several courts have adopted the commercial/investment test where the focus is on the underlying character of the transaction. Applying the "unless the context otherwise requires" language of Sections 2(1) and 3(a)(10) as well as the economic reality concept, courts adhering to this view hold that a note is not a security where it arises from a commercial transaction even when its terms are literally within the Acts' coverage. In making this determination, the courts have focused on such factors as the use of the funds (to fund current expenses rather than long-term projects), whether the note is collateralized (and, hence, less "risky"), the number of purchasers (limited to few or marketed to many), the level of sophistication of the purchasers (is the purchaser a bank or an uninitiated investor), and whether the note has a short maturity.

M. Steinberg, *Understanding Securities Law* 25–26 (1989).

[84] See, e.g., *Great Western Bank & Trust v. Kotz*, 532 F.2d 1252 (9th Cir. 1976) (looking at such factors as the length of the note's maturity, whether the note is collateralized, the relative size of the debt in relation to the size of the borrower's business, and the use of the proceeds).

[85] See *supra* notes 6-10, 38–52 and accompanying text.

[86] 494 U.S. at 62–63.

[87] *Id.* at 65.

Under the family resemblance test, a "note" exceeding nine months duration is presumed to be a security.[88] The presumption may be rebutted by a showing that the note bears a strong resemblance (by looking to the four-factor "family resemblance" test) to an instrument that has been excluded from the reach of the securities laws or that application of the "family resemblance" test evidences that the note ought to be excluded. As stated by the Supreme Court:

> We conclude that in determining whether an instrument denominated a "note" is a "security," courts are to apply the version of the "family resemblance" test that we have articulated here: a note is presumed to be a "security," and that presumption may be rebutted only by a showing that the note bears a strong resemblance (in terms of the four factors we have identified) to one of the enumerated categories of instruments. If an instrument is not sufficiently similar to an item on the list, the decision whether another category should be added is to be made by examining the same factors.[89]

Prior application of this test reveals that the following notes are *not* securities:

1. The note delivered in consumer financing;

2. The note secured by a mortgage on a home;

3. The short-term note secured by a lien on a small business or some of its assets;

4. The note evidencing a "character" loan to a bank customer;

5. Short-term notes secured by an assignment of accounts receivable;

6. A note formalizing an open-account debt incurred in the ordinary course of business; and

7. Notes evidencing loans by commercial banks for current operations.[90]

Hence, the "family resemblance" test consists of the following four factors:

(1) *The motivations that would prompt a reasonable buyer and seller to enter into the transaction.* "If the seller's purpose is to raise money for the general use of a business enterprise or to finance substantial investments and the buyer is interested primarily in the profit the note is expected to generate, the instrument is likely a 'security.'" On the other hand, if the note is exchanged to promote some commercial or consumer purpose, it is less likely to be a security.[91]

(2) *The plan of distribution of the instrument.* If there exists "common trading for speculation or investment," the note more likely will be viewed

---

[88] For notes having a duration of nine months or less, the Court declined to address whether this presumption applied. *Id.* at 65, n.3.

[89] *Id.* at 65.

[90] *Id.*, citing, *Chemical Bank v. Arthur Andersen & Co.*, 726 F.2d 930 (2d Cir. 1984); *Exchange National Bank v. Touche Ross & Co.*, 544 F.2d 1126 (2d Cir. 1976).

[91] 494 U.S. at 67.

as a security. To establish such common trading, it must be shown that the notes were "offered and sold to a broad segment of the public." The notes need not be traded on an exchange.[92]

(3) *The investing public's reasonable expectations.* Where, for example, notes are advertised and otherwise marketed as an "investment" and no countervailing factors would lead a reasonable person to doubt this characterization, a security may be recognized. Accordingly, "[t]he Court will consider instruments to be 'securities' on the basis of such public expectations, even where an economic analysis of the particular transaction might suggest that the instruments are not 'securities' as used in that transaction."[93]

(4) *The existence of a risk reducing factor.* For example, securities law application may well be deemed unnecessary when another regulatory framework significantly reduces the risk.[94]

Applying the "family resemblance" test to the case at bar, the Supreme Court in *Reves* held that the notes came within the purview of the securities laws. The notes were sold in an effort to raise capital for general business operations and were purchased by investors in order to earn a profit, the plan of distribution was widespread, the public's reasonable expectations were that the notes were securities as they were advertised as investments, and there was no risk-reducing factor, such as the presence of other comprehensive regulation, that minimized the risk of loss. Moreover, the "demand" nature of the notes did not take them outside the reach of the federal securities laws as this feature did not significantly lessen the investment's risk (as phrased by the Court, "demand only eliminates risk when and if payment is made"). Accordingly, the Court held that such promissory notes are securities.[95]

In light of the Supreme Court's decision in *Reves* and lower court application post-*Reves*, the following points are set forth:

(1) *Rejection of the Howey Test.* The Court's rejection of the *Howey* test in the "note" context seemingly is significant. With the exception of "stock," some lower courts had advocated that the *Howey* test be applied, irrespective of the nature of the instrument. The Supreme Court's rejection of this interpretation may signal that *Howey*'s relevance is confined to investment contract analysis.

Indeed, if any applicable standard may have widespread application in the definition of "security" setting, it is the "family resemblance" test. Referring to this test, the *Reves* Court stated that the factors comprising that test are the ones that the Court has looked to "in deciding whether a transaction involves a 'security.' "[96]

---

[92] *Id.* at 67–68.

[93] *Id.* at 66.

[94] *Id.* at 67.

[95] *Id.* at 67–73.

[96] *Id.* at 66.

(2) *Definition of "Profit."* The Court's definition of "profit" in *Reves* is important. Under *Howey*, profits generally have been limited to capital appreciation or participation in the earnings of the business. If this definition were to be applied in the "note" context, many such instruments (such as the one present in *Reves*) would not have the requisite "profit" attributes to be defined as an investment coming within the purview of the securities laws. For example, the "demand" notes in *Reves* paid a fixed rate of interest, not being keyed to profits. Importantly, the Court held that the *Howey* definition of "profit" did not apply in this context and may well be confined to solely investment contract analysis.

Thus, in the "note" setting, profit means an investment having a valuable return "which undoubtedly includes interest."[97] As a result, it may be asserted that in order for a note to have a "valuable" return, it must pay interest to the holder above the generally prevailing rate offered by instruments that are deemed "safe." Such "safe" instruments would include notes that are adequately insured and other instruments where the rate of default (both from a prospective and historical view) is practically nil. Generally, an investor purchases a note not having these more secure characteristics for the purpose of receiving a return that may be deemed "substantial," and hence, "valuable." At the same time, when an investor seeks a more valuable return, the risk of loss is magnified.[98]

(3) *Application of Four-Prong Test.* In adopting the four-prong "family resemblance" test, the Supreme Court declined to state whether all factors must be met or whether the standard calls for balancing the various factors. The Court's language in *Reves* is somewhat ambiguous. After *Reves*, several lower court decisions have suggested that a note may be a security even though all four factors have not been met.[99]

(4) *Plan of Distribution.* After *Reves*, it was uncertain whether the inquiry as to plan of distribution focused on whether the notes *in fact* were distributed to a broad segment of the public or whether this prong would be satisfied if the notes were *capable* of being so distributed. Although the *Reves* Court did not refer to the "capability" of mass distribution, the cases relied on by the Court support this proposition.[100] Nonetheless, post-*Reves*,

---

[97] *Id.* at 68, n.4.

[98] Nonetheless, some courts have construed the "profit" prong narrowly. See, e.g., *Guidry v. Bank of LaPlace*, 740 F. Supp. 1208, 1213 (E.D. La. 1990) (applying family resemblance test, court stated that "profit generation was impossible due to the fixed interest rate"). But see *Stoiber v. SEC,* 161 F.3d 745 (D.C. Cir. 1998) (applying *Reves,* court held that notes were securities, reasoning in part that purchasers of notes were motivated to earn a profit from loan interest); *National Bank of Yugoslavia v. Drexel Burham Lambert, Inc.*, 768 F. Supp. 1010, 1015 (S.D.N.Y. 1991) (stating that "a fixed interest rate is a feature of many notes undoubtedly covered by the federal securities laws").

[99] See Kerr & Eisenhauer, *Reves Revisited*, 19 Pepperdine L. Rev. 1123, 1157 (1992) (stating that "[m]ost courts seem to have adopted a balancing approach") (citing cases *id.* at 1157, n.296).

[100] See 494 U.S. at 66, 68, *relying on, Landreth Timber*, 471 U.S. at 687, 693 (1985) (stock of closely held corporation not traded on any exchange held to be a "security"); *Tcherepnin v. Knight*, 389 U.S. 332, 337 (1967) (nonnegotiable but transferable "withdrawable capital shares" in savings and loan association held to be a "security"); *Howey*, 328 U.S. 293, 295 (1946) (units of citrus grove and maintenance contract held to be "securities" although not traded on an exchange).

lower court decisions generally have looked to the distribution that occurred *in fact* rather than to the capability of distribution.[101]

(5) *Risk-Reducing Factors.* After *Reves*, a number of lower court decisions have relied on the fact that the notes at issue were collateralized as a basis for excluding such notes from securities law coverage.[102] Hence, along with the presence of another regulatory framework that significantly reduces the risk of loss,[103] lower courts view collateralization of notes as a key risk-reducing factor.

(6) *Notes Not Exceeding Nine Months.* The Supreme Court's holding articulates that a "note" is presumed to be a "security" unless the note bears a strong resemblance (by looking to the four-factor "family resemblance" test) to an instrument that has been excluded from the securities laws' reach or unless application of the "family resemblance" test indicates that the note ought to be excluded. The Court, however, declined to address whether this presumption applies to securities with a maturity not exceeding nine months. Chief Justice Rehnquist, writing for a four member dissent, would exclude notes of nine months or less duration from the scope of the securities laws as a matter of law.[104] While a literal interpretation of the nine-month exemption contained in Section 3(a)(10) of the Exchange Act would exclude such instruments from that Act's reach all together, the exclusion in Section 3(a)(3) of the Securities Act would exclude such instruments from the registration provisions. The antifraud provisions of the 1933 Act would still apply to such instruments. Irrespective of the difference in this statutory language, the Court has consistently held, and reaffirmed in *Reves*, that the coverage of the two Acts is the same. Moreover, each definition is prefaced by the term "unless the context otherwise requires." Employing this language, courts have applied an approach rooted in economic reality to determine whether a particular instrument is a security.

There can be little question that, from a general perspective, the shorter time period one's money is in another's hands, the less the risk of loss. It also can be stated with confidence, however, that such a time period is far from a guarantee of repayment. Other factors are equally, if not more, important, such as the solvency of the seller of the note, the intended use of the proceeds, general market conditions, and the rate of interest required to be paid to service the debt. Indeed, financings extended in leveraged buyouts evidence that fairly short-term debt can often be at risk of default.

---

[101] See, e.g., *Pollack v. Laidlaw Holdings, Inc.*, 27 F.3d 808 (2d Cir. 1994); *Banco Espanol de Credito v. Security Pacific National Bank*, 973 F.2d 51 (2d Cir. 1992).

[102] See, e.g., *Resolution Trust Corporation v. Stone*, 998 F.2d 1534 (10th Cir. 1993).

[103] See *Reves*, 494 U.S. at 67; *Trust Company of Louisiana v. N.N.P., Inc.*, 104 F.3d 1478 (5th Cir. 1997) (applying "family resemblance" test and holding notes at issue were securities, court pointed to lack of other regulatory framework to protect the investors).

[104] 494 U.S. at 77–81 (Rehnquist, C.J., dissenting in part).

Hence, a note's duration, although relevant, should not be determinative for securities law coverage.[105]

[B] Certificates of Deposit

The definitive case in this area is *Marine Bank v. Weaver*[106] where the Court focused on the existence of depositor insurance and the pervasive federal regulation over banking. Accordingly, the Court held that a certificate of deposit (CD) purchased from a federally regulated bank is not a security. Given the widespread impact of the Federal Deposit Insurance Company and other federal insurance, the *Marine Bank* holding would in practical terms seem to have very wide impact. Note, however, that application of the federal securities laws to a CD issued by a state chartered non-federally insured bank or a foreign bank may not be foreclosed by *Marine Bank.*

A number of post-*Marine Bank* decisions help highlight the questions involved. For example, in *Wolf v. Banco Nacional de Mexico,*[107] the Ninth Circuit was faced with the issue of whether *Marine Bank's* analysis applies to CDs issued by a foreign bank. More precisely, the issue presented in *Wolf* was whether a certificate of deposit in Mexican pesos in a Mexican bank was a security under U.S. law. The district court, relying on *Marine Bank's* emphasis on the protection given to depositors by the federal banking laws, held that, since the Mexican deposits were outside the U.S. banking regulatory system, *Marine Bank* did not control. Reversing, the Ninth Circuit held that the Mexican CD was not a security in that the issuing bank was sufficiently regulated and repayment in full was virtually guaranteed. The court stated: "When a [domestic or foreign] bank is sufficiently well regulated that there is virtually no risk that insolvency will prevent it from repaying the holder of one of its certificates of deposit in full, the certificate is not a security for purposes of the federal securities laws."[108]

In *Tafflin v. Levitt,*[109] the Fourth Circuit applied *Marine Bank* to state regulation. There, the Fourth Circuit held that Maryland's regulatory and

---

[105] For articles addressing *Reves* and its ramifications, see, e.g., Brown & Breckinridge, *Notes Qualifying as Securities in the Wake of Reves: Recent Developments,* 31 Rev. Sec. & Comm. Reg. 1 (1998); Gordon, *Interplanetary Intelligence About Promissory Notes as Securities,* 69 Texas L. Rev. 383 (1990); Kerr & Eisenhauer, *Reves Revisited,* 19 Pepperdine L. Rev. 1123 (1992); Quinn, *After Reves v. Ernst & Young, When Are Certificates of Deposit "Notes" Subject to Rule 10b-5 of the Securities Exchange Act?"* 46 Bus. Law. 173 (1990); Schneider & Cohen, *Reves v. Ernst & Young: A Note-Worthy Departure in Defining "Security,"* 23 Rev. Sec. & Comm. Reg. 191 (1990); Steinberg, *Notes as Securities: Reves and Its Implications,* 51 Ohio St. L.J. 675 (1990); Warren, *The Treatment of Reves "Notes" and Other Securities Under State Blue Sky Laws,* 47 Bus. Law. 321 (1991); Comment, *Bank Loans as Securities: A Legal and Financial Economic Analysis of the Treatment of Marketable Bank Assets Under the Securities Act,* 40 UCLA L. Rev. 799 (1993).

[106] 455 U.S. 551 (1982). See *supra* notes 22–26 and accompanying text.

[107] 739 F.2d 1458 (9th Cir. 1984). See *West v. Multibanco Comermex,* 807 F.2d 820 (9th Cir. 1987).

[108] 739 F.2d at 1463.

[109] 865 F.2d 595 (4th Cir. 1989).

insurance system with respect to state-chartered savings and loans compelled the conclusion that the certificates of deposit were not securities.

Not all courts agree with the foregoing cases. For example, the Tenth Circuit in *Holloway v. Peat, Marwick, Mitchell & Co.,*[110] rejected *Marine Bank's* functional regulation approach to state regulation. In holding passbook savings accounts and thrift certificates (issued by a financial institution subject to state oversight) to be securities, the court asserted that "under the supremacy clause [of the U.S. Constitution] our focus must be on federal regulation; *state regulatory schemes cannot displace the [Securities] Acts.*"[111]

---

[110] 900 F.2d 1485 (10th Cir. 1990).

[111] *Id.* at 1488 (emphasis added). See also *Olson v. E.F. Hutton & Co.,* [1991-1992 Transfer Binder] Fed. Sec. L. Rep. (CCH) ¶ 96,554 (8th Cir. 1992); *Sanderson v. Roethenmund,* 682 F. Supp. 205 (S.D.N.Y. 1988).

In addition to the sources cited previously in this chapter, for further coverage on definition of "security," see generally Arnold, *The Definition of a Security Under the Federal Securities Laws Revisited,* 34 Clev. St. L. Rev. 249 (1986); Bradford, *Expanding the Investment Company Act: The SEC's Manipulation of the Definition of Security,* 60 Ohio St. L.J. 995 (1999); Branson & Okamoto, *The Supreme Court's Literalism and the Definition of "Security" in the State Courts,* 50 Wash. & Lee L. Rev. 1043 (1993); Chiappinelli, *Reinventing a Security: Arguments for a Public Interest Definition,* 49 Wash. & Lee L. Rev. 957 (1992); Corgill, *Securities as Investments at Risk,* 67 Tulane L. Rev. 861 (1993); Gabaldon, *A Sense of a Security: An Empirical Study,* 25 J. Corp. L. 307 (2000); Lowenfels & Bromberg, *What Is a Security Under the Federal Securities Laws?,* 56 Albany L. Rev. 473 (1993); McGinty, *What Is a Security?,* 1993 Wisc. L. Rev. 1033 (1993); Rosin, *Historical Perspectives on the Definition of a Security,* 28 S. Tex. L. Rev. 575 (1987); Steinberg & Kaulbach, *The Supreme Court and the Definition of "Security": The "Context" Clause, "Investment Contract" Analysis, and Their Ramifications,* 40 Vand. L. Rev. 489 (1987).

Chapter 3

ISSUER EXEMPTIONS FROM REGISTRATION

§ 3.01   Securities Exempt from Registration

The general rule is that, absent an exemption, all offers or sales of securities must be registered pursuant to Section 5 of the Securities Act of 1933 ("Securities Act" or "1933 Act"). Note, importantly, that the securities law antifraud provisions apply irrespective of whether an exemption from registration exists. There are two general types of registration exemptions: transactional exemptions and securities exempt from registration. The latter covers specific securities or categories of securities that are never required to be registered under Section 5, largely due to the intrinsic character or nature of the issuer itself. These exempt securities include, for example, certain short-term promissory notes or bills of exchange; securities issued or guaranteed by municipalities, state or federal governments; and securities issued by nonprofit, religious, educational or charitable organizations.[1]

Moreover, some securities, although exempt from the 1933 Act's registration requirements, come under the supervision of another federal or state governmental authority. For example, with respect to securities issued by national banks, the Comptroller of the Currency has developed a regulatory framework somewhat similar, yet many feel not as rigorous, as that developed by the Securities and Exchange Commission ("SEC"). On the other hand, the securities of bank holding companies are not exempt from registration under the federal securities laws.[2]

Significantly, it is the transactional exemptions from registration that play the important role in this context. As a consequence, the chapter will focus on these exemptions.

§ 3.02   Why Perfect a Transactional Exemption?

As stated above, unless an exemption from registration is available, all offers or sales must be registered pursuant to Section 5 of the Securities Act. Given this consequence, one may ask "why perfect a transactional exemption from registration rather than registering the offer or sale under Section 5 of the 1933 Act?" There are several reasons why a transactional exemption often is the preferred route. Keep in mind that the following discussion somewhat simplifies the pertinent requirements.

---

[1] See Securities Act Section 3(a)(2)-3(a)(8), 15 U.S.C. § 77c(a)(2)-(a)(8), for a listing of the securities exempt from registration.

[2] See generally L. Loss & J. Seligman, *Securities Regulation* 1142-1210 (3d ed. 1989).

Generally, in order to register an offer or sale under Section 5 and have what is called a "public offering" or "to go public,"[3] a registration statement must be filed with the Securities and Exchange Commission. In addition, the statutory prospectus, which is part of the registration statement, must be provided to the purchaser at the time that the security is delivered or at the time the confirmation of the sale is received, whichever occurs earlier. The registration statement (of which the prospectus is a part) is no ordinary document. The disclosures required are detailed and complex, the document's length is massive, and the costs of preparing the registration statement, including accountant, attorney, investment banker and printer fees, easily can run into the tens if not hundreds of thousands of dollars.

The costs and nature of the registration statement are due largely to Section 11 of the 1933 Act which, in practical effect, imposes a "due diligence" requirement upon certain parties, including the issuer's directors and certain executive officers, the underwriters, and the experts, including the accountants (with respect to those portions of the registration statement that an accountant has "expertised"). Attorneys, unless they act as experts,[4] are not subject to Section 11 liability. Counsel, nonetheless, is integrally involved in the registration process. He or she frequently is delegated by the issuer, underwriter, or other parties potentially liable under Section 11 to perform the requisite "due diligence" on their behalf. Other fundamental aspects of counsel's role in this process involve the drafting of the language contained in the registration statement, advising whether certain disclosures should or must be made, and acting as informal mediator between the various parties involved.

The concept of "due diligence," its significance, and the steps that must be taken to fulfill this mandate are addressed in Chapter 6. In theory, "due diligence" is a defense that may be asserted by the subject party rather than an affirmative obligation. It is certainly true that if the statements made in the registration statement are true or if no lawsuit is ultimately brought, no liability will be incurred for failure to exercise due diligence. If an action is instituted and a material misstatement or omission is shown, however, liability often may be avoided under Section 11 only by proving the performance of due diligence. In the realities of corporate practice, therefore, due diligence is a necessity rather than a discretionary function.

Hence, the "due diligence" requirement is given "teeth" by the liability consequences. In general, if there is a material misrepresentation or nondisclosure in the nonexpertised portion of the registration statement, parties subject to Section 11 liability, except experts and the issuer (which is strictly liable), can avoid such liability only by showing that they had

---

[3] The terms "public offering" and "going public" are often not synonymous. In short, the initial public offering ("IPO") made by an enterprise constitutes "going public." On the other hand, a successful corporation that has gone public decades ago may make public offerings of its securities on a periodic basis.

[4] Counsel acts as an expert, for example, if he or she proffers an opinion contained or referred to in the registration statement. An accountant, by certifying financial statements contained in the registration statement, is the party who frequently is sued as an expert under Section 11.

conducted a reasonable investigation and, after such investigation, had no reason to believe and did not believe that the registration statement contained any materially false or misleading statement.

With respect to expertised portions of the registration statement, nonexperts are not required to investigate. They need show only that they had no reason to believe and did not believe that the expertised portions of the registration statement contained any materially false or misleading statements. Moreover, experts are potentially liable under Section 11 only for those portions of the registration statement which they "expertised." They can avoid Section 11 liability by showing that, with respect to the expertised portions of the registration statement, they had conducted a reasonable investigation and, after such investigation, had no reason to believe and did not believe that such expertised portions of the registration statement contained any materially false or misleading statements.

While the issuer is the only party that has no "due diligence" defense under Section 11 and is subject to strict liability, it may well be insolvent. The result is that aggrieved plaintiffs seek redress against the "deep pockets," frequently the underwriters and the accountants. Because of the severe financial ramifications that can amount to several million dollars, parties potentially subject to Section 11 liability seek to ensure that abundant due diligence is performed and extensive disclosure made, including the potentially negative consequences and risks of the venture.

Hence, the costs of having a "registered" offering under the Securities Act frequently will be substantial. For a start-up venture or a business in severe financial difficulty, the costs of a public offering normally will prove prohibitive. Moreover, it is next to impossible to consummate successfully a registered offering unless receptive investment bankers can be retained to underwrite the offering and the financial markets are favorable. These conditions are exacerbated in cases where enterprises with little or no previous earnings history seek to "go public." As some of the "high-tech" and "research" companies have shown, however, these problems are not insurmountable.

Even if a financially successful registered offering can be made, it may be advisable for the client nonetheless to perfect a transactional exemption. By refraining from "going public," the enterprise essentially is keeping its financial affairs and related matters private among its various participants. By "going public," however, the enterprise, pursuant to the disclosure requirements of the securities laws, will be hanging its dirty linen out for public viewing.[5] The enterprise, pursuant to certain provisions of the Securities Exchange Act, such as Section 13(a) or Section 15(d), will be required to file annual, quarterly, and other periodic reports with the SEC as well as to provide periodic reports to its shareholders and the pertinent self regulatory organizations. Moreover, other sections of the Exchange Act,

---

[5] Cf. *Schlick v. Penn-Dixie Cement Corp.*, 507 F.2d 374, 384 (2d Cir. 1974); Kilman, *Giant Cargill Resists Pressure to Go Public as It Pursues Growth*, Wall St. J., Jan. 9, 1997, at A1 (stating that "Cargill is the nation's largest closely held company, generating annual revenues approaching $60 billion, and it perhaps best demonstrates the benefits of being private").

such as Section 13(b)'s recordkeeping and internal accounting control provisions, will become applicable. Hence, the enterprise, by having a registered offering, will be faced not only with public scrutiny but saddled with high accounting and legal fees as well as the persistent threat of litigation due to the consequences of public disclosure.

For the above reasons as well as others (such as, by taking the corporation public, the insiders may potentially risk loss of control through a hostile takeover), it may well be advisable and indeed necessary to procure a transactional exemption from registration. It should not be surprising that, given the above, the vast majority of offerings are made under a transactional exemption rather than by a registered offering pursuant to Section 5 of the Securities Act. In many instances, therefore, counsel will seek the viability of a transactional exemption before advising that a registered offering go forward. Hence, an examination of the offering process begins with the transactional exemptions.

§ 3.03   Transactional Exemptions — Introductory Points

Prior to turning to a discussion of the transactional exemptions from 1933 Act registration, certain introductory points should be made:

First, the following material in this chapter addresses exemptions from Securities Act registration that are transactionally based. Hence, for each separate *transaction*, an exemption from registration must be perfected.

Second, the relevant parties for the purposes of this chapter who are seeking to come within the transactional exemptions are primary issuers of securities. For example, a corporation issuing authorized but unissued stock or a limited partnership issuing interests to its participants would each be viewed as a primary issuer while a shareholder who seeks to transfer his or her shares to another would not be so viewed.

Third, accordingly, individuals reselling their stock must register any offer or sale unless they likewise perfect an exemption. The exemption that normally would be invoked in this context is Section 4(1) of the Securities Act which exempts from the registration requirements of Section 5 offers or sales made by any person "other than an issuer, underwriter, or dealer." The subject of resales is addressed in Chapter 5.

Fourth, the party seeking the exemption has the burden of proving that it has perfected the exemption by establishing that it has satisfied the necessary conditions for invoking the exemption. Failure to carry this burden signifies that no transactional exemption has been perfected, resulting in liability under the Securities Act for failure to register the offer or sale in question.

Such failure to register gives rise to SEC and perhaps criminal liability for violation of Section 5 and to private recovery under Section 12(a)(1) of the 1933 Act. Generally, Section 12(a)(1) grants to the purchaser the right to rescind the transaction in an action brought against the seller for violation of Section 5. In effect, the provision imposes strict liability upon the seller for failure to comply with Section 5's registration requirements. Generally, the state securities laws have similar provisions.

Fifth, consistent with the federal securities laws in general, the interstate commerce requirement must be met in order for federal jurisdiction to be invoked in the transactional exemption context. This requirement normally is shown without difficulty. Use of the mail or any means or instrumentality of interstate commerce is sufficient. An intrastate telephone call, for example, satisfies the federal jurisdictional requirement.

Sixth, even if a transactional exemption has been perfected, thereby obviating the need to register the offering, the antifraud provisions of the securities acts nonetheless fully apply. The antifraud provisions most frequently invoked are Section 17(a) of the Securities Act, Section 10(b) of the Exchange Act, and Rule 10b-5 promulgated by the SEC pursuant to its Section 10(b) rulemaking authority.

Seventh, as a final important point, federal law is not the only source of regulation in this setting. The state "blue sky" laws also frequently apply and present additional dilemmas for the corporate practitioner and his or her client. With certain exceptions, to perfect an exemption, in addition to satisfying the requirements of federal law, the securities regulations of *each* state where *any* offer or sale is made also must be satisfied. To the credit of the SEC and the states, significant progress has been made in coordinating the federal and state transactional exemption scheme, thereby alleviating much of the burden in complying with this multi-faceted regulatory framework. Moreover, as discussed later in this chapter, federal legislation enacted in 1996 preempts state regulation of certain exempt offerings.

§ 3.04 The Burden of Proof File, SEC No-Action Letters and Rescission Offers

[A] Burden of Proof File

Questions frequently arise, particularly in the litigation setting, regarding an issuer's compliance with an exemption from registration. As the law stands, the issuer (as the party seeking to perfect an exemption) has the burden to prove that it has satisfied the requirements for invoking an applicable exemption from registration. To satisfy this criteria, the attorney or the issuer (with the assistance of counsel) should maintain a "burden of proof" file. Such a file, if properly maintained, goes a long way toward showing that the issuer conducted the offering in compliance with the conditions for invoking the exemption.[6]

The importance of properly maintaining a burden of proof file is illustrated by the Sixth Circuit's decision in *Mark v. FSC Securities Corporation*.[7] Holding that the defendants had failed to perfect the Rule 506 exemption, the court alluded to the inadequate procedures utilized:

---

[6] See L. Wertheimer, *Securities and Partnership Law for MLPs and Other Investment Limited Partnerships* § 7.01 (1988).

[7] 870 F.2d 331 (6th Cir. 1989).

[T]he documents [introduced at trial] offered no evidence from which a jury could conclude [that] the issuer reasonably believed each purchaser was suitable so as to warrant a Rule 506 exemption. Instead, all that was proved was the sale of twenty-eight limited partnerships, and the circumstances under which those sales were *intended* to have been made. The mere fact that the limited partnership interests were sold cannot support a conclusion that they were sold in compliance with the conditions contemplated by the Rule 506 exemption. The blank subscription document and offeree questionnaire simply do not amount to probative evidence, when it is the answers and information received *from* purchasers that determines whether the conditions of the Rule 506 exemption have been met. Because there was no evidence from which a jury could conclude that the issuer had the requisite belief, nor from which a jury could determine the reasonableness of any such belief, [the issuer] FSC has failed to sustain its burden of proving an exemption under Rule 506 of Regulation D.[8]

[B] SEC No-Action Letters

Although not specifically related to transactional exemptions from registration, this is a good point to mention the SEC "no-action" letter process. Under this process, counsel advises the SEC staff (not the Commission itself) in writing of his or her client's contemplated conduct. Such contemplated conduct may involve, for example, questions related to a Regulation D offering, resales of stock, or proxy statements. The staff generally responds by either issuing a no-action letter or by refusing to issue such a letter. At times, the staff's response communicates solely an enforcement posture — namely, whether the staff would recommend to the Commission that an enforcement action be initiated if the contemplated conduct were undertaken in the manner set forth in the written request. In other staff responses, in addition to the enforcement position taken, the staff may articulate interpretations of applicable SEC rules and regulations as they pertain to the proposed conduct. In either situation, the staff's views are not those of the Commission and are not binding in any manner. Notwithstanding the informal status of SEC no-action letters, they unquestionably have great significance and are relied upon by market participants and their attorneys.[9]

Not surprisingly, the SEC staff's refusal to approve a no-action request normally results in the affected parties not engaging in the contemplated conduct. Even if the staff issues a no-action letter, however, that does not ensure that the client's conduct will not be challenged. Private parties are not bound by an SEC no-action letter and may sue irrespective of the issuance of such a letter. Moreover, although very unlikely to happen, the

---

[8] *Id.* at 337 (emphasis in original).

[9] See Nagy, *Judicial Reliance on Regulatory Interpretations in SEC No-Action Letters: Current Problems and a Proposed Framework*, 83 Cornell L. Rev. 921, 924 (1998).

SEC retains its discretion to institute an enforcement action even though its staff has issued a no-action letter covering the very same conduct.[10]

[C]　Rescission Offers

An ever present fear for securities counsel and his or her client is that a securities law violation has occurred that is material to the transaction. For example, in a Rule 505 offering, suppose that either before or after the transaction "closes" counsel discovers that there are 36 non-accredited purchasers rather than the allotted maximum of 35 or that there was general solicitation in connection with the offering. Is there any curative action that the issuer may take? Insofar as purchasers are concerned, the issuer may make a "rescission offer" that fully informs the purchasers of all material facts and provides such purchasers with the right to rescind.

Needless to say, counsel who is responsible for the transaction will be in an uncomfortable position. If counsel does nothing, permitting the "deal" to go forward and the issuer to use the funds, he or she may be liable under the securities laws. Alternatively, if the mistake happens to be counsel's doing, he or she may be liable to the client for malpractice. Moreover, even if a rescission offer may cut off a purchaser's right to sue (although it may not), the SEC and state authorities retain their prerogative to bring an enforcement action.

Rescission offers may occur in the private or public offering context. If a rescission offer is made in the private offering setting, an exemption from registration must be perfected. Otherwise, compliance with the Securities Act registration requirements may be necessary.[11]

§ 3.05　　The Section 4(2) Private Offering Exemption

Section 4(2) of the Securities Act exempts from the registration requirements "transactions by an issuer not involving any public offering." There is no monetary limit to the amount of funds that can be raised under this exemption. The provision's legislative history expresses Congress' intent to exempt those transactions from registration "where there is no practical need for [such] application . . . [or] where the public benefits are too remote."[12] As subsequently construed, courts have looked to a number of factors in determining the availability of the Section 4(2) private offering exemption.

A good starting point in ascertaining the requirements of the Section 4(2) private offering exemption is the Supreme Court's decision in *Securities and*

---

[10] See *New York City Employees' Retirement System v. SEC,* 45 F.3d 7 (2d Cir. 1995); *In re Morgan Stanley & Co.,* Securities Exchange Act Release No. 28990 (1991). See generally R. Haft, *Analysis of Key No-Action Letters* (1999-2000); Lemke, *The SEC No-Action Letter Process,* 42 Bus. Law. 1019 (1987); Nagy, note 9 *supra.*

[11] See Bromberg, *Curing Securities Violations: Rescission Offers and Other Techniques,* 1 J. Corp. L. 1 (1975); Rowe, *Rescission Offers Under Federal and State Securities Law,* 12 J. Corp. Law 383 (1987).

[12] H.R. Rep. No. 85, 73d Cong., 1st Sess. 5 (1933).

Exchange Commission v. Ralston Purina Co. [13] In that case, the company made asserted private offerings to scores of "key" employees, many of whom held non-managerial positions. The Supreme Court, observing that the burden of proving the perfection of an exemption from registration is upon the party relying upon the availability of such an exemption, held that the company had not satisfied this burden. The availability of the Section 4(2) private offering exemption, according to the Court, should turn upon "whether the particular class of persons affected needs the protection of the [Securities] Act." [14] Accordingly, the private offering exemption, among other things, requires that all persons to whom offers are made are to be provided with or are to have access to the type of information that would be contained in a registration statement. [15]

The lower federal courts subsequent to *Ralston Purina* have had numerous occasions to construe the Section 4(2) exemption. [16] Although the principles emerging from these cases are not crystal clear, the following points can be made:

First, as construed by some courts, the Section 4(2) exemption turns on whether *all offers* (rather than actual purchases) are made in accordance with the exemption. A single noncomplying offer may invalidate the entire offering. For example, the Fifth Circuit has stated: "[W]e have held that the defendant must establish that each and every offeree either had the same information that would have been available in a registration statement or had access to such information." [17]

Second, although the courts and the SEC have not placed a finite number on how many offers can be permissibly made under the Section 4(2) exemption, it is clear that certain limits, depending on the circumstances, apply. [18]

Third, related to the above point, is that, pursuant to the Section 4(2) exemption, the issuer cannot engage in general solicitation or advertising. The precise limits of what conduct constitutes general solicitation so as to make unavailable the Section 4(2) exemption (as well as the Rule 505 and Rule 506 exemptions of Regulation D) are unclear. For example, a seminar held for an offering where twenty-five existing clients of adequate sophistication attend should be permitted while a seminar for a particular offering open to all clients of a major broker-dealer (e.g., Merrill Lynch) should be deemed general solicitation. [19]

---

[13] 346 U.S. 119 (1953).

[14] *Id.* at 124.

[15] *Id.* at 124-27.

[16] See, e.g., *SEC v. Murphy*, 626 F.2d 633 (9th Cir. 1980); *Seenson v. Engelstad*, 626 F.2d 421 (5th Cir. 1980); *Lawler v. Gilliam*, 569 F.2d 1283 (4th Cir. 1978).

[17] *Swensen v. Engelstad*, 626 F.2d 421, 425-26 (5th Cir. 1980). See *Mark v. FSC Securities Corp.*, 870 F.2d 331, 334 (6th Cir. 1989).

[18] See *Ralson Purina*, 346 U.S. at 125.

[19] The SEC has issued no-action letters in this context. See § 3.04[B] *supra*. See also, Cohn, *Securities Markets for Small Issuers: The Barrier of Federal Solicitation and Advertising Prohibitions*, 38 U. Fla. L. Rev. 1 (1986).

Fourth, an issuer should take certain precautions against resales, such as obtaining written commitments by purchasers that they are acquiring for investment purposes (called an investment letter), placing appropriate legends on the certificates, and issuing stop transfer instructions. These procedures help the issuer to perfect the Section 4(2) exemption in the event that purchasers subsequently resell their stock. It may well be, however, that the absence of these steps does not nullify an otherwise valid Section 4(2) exemption if no distribution in fact takes place.[20]

Fifth, all offerees must be financially sophisticated or be advised by someone who has the requisite acumen (called an offeree representative). Under case law, individual wealth does not make one sophisticated for Section 4(2) private placement purposes.[21]

Sixth, irrespective of whether an offeree (or offeree representative) has financial acumen, "[s]ophistication is not a substitute for access to the [type of] information that a registration statement would disclose."[22] In short, if offerees have not received the type of information that registration would elicit, they cannot bring any alleged "sophistication" to bear in deciding whether or not to invest.[23] Hence, all offerees must be provided with the type of information (not necessarily identical) that would be contained in a registration statement or have access to such information.

Ascertaining which offerees have "access" to registration-type information may be problematic. Relevant factors include promoter or high level executive status in the enterprise, family ties, a privileged relationship based upon prior business dealings between the parties, and economic bargaining power that enables an offeree effectively to obtain the registration-type information.[24]

As a final comment, some courts have looked to two additional factors in determining whether the Section 4(2) exemption has been perfected: the number of units offered and the size of the offering.[25] These factors, however, often are irrelevant. For example, the offer and sale by an issuer of one million corporate debentures for $500 million to five sophisticated institutional investors (such as insurance companies), having effective access to registration-type information, normally should be within the Section 4(2) private offering exemption.

---

[20] See *Livens v. William D. Witter, Inc.,* 374 F. Supp. 1104, 1110 (D. Mass. 1974); Schneider, *The Statutory Law of Private Placements,* 14 Rev. Sec. Reg. 870, 881 (1981).

[21] See *Doran v. Petroleum Management Corp.,* 545 F.2d 893, 903 (5th Cir. 1977). For a more relaxed standard, see *Acme Propane, Inc. v. Tenexco, Inc.,* 844 F.2d 1317, 1321 (7th Cir. 1988).

[22] *Doran,* 545 F.2d at 902. See *United States v. Custer Channel Wing Corp.,* 376 F.2d 675, 678 (4th Cir. 1967).

[23] See *Hill York Corp. v. American International Franchises, Inc.,* 448 F.2d 680, 690 (5th Cir. 1971).

[24] See *Doran v. Petroleum Management Corp.,* 545 F.2d 893, 903 (5th Cir. 1977); Schneider, *supra* note 20, at 877.

[25] See, e.g., *SEC v. Continental Tobacco Co.,* 463 F.2d 137, 158 (5th Cir. 1978).

§ 3.06 Rule 506 of Regulation D

As seen from the preceding discussion, perfecting a Section 4(2) exemption is no easy matter. In addition, the alleged vagueness of judicial decisions, setting forth relevant Section 4(2) criteria, resulted in the securities bar clamoring for an SEC "safe harbor" rule. In 1974, the Commission responded by adopting Rule 146. As stated by the SEC in a subsequent release:

> Section 4(2) of the Securities Act of 1933 provides that offers and sales of securities by an issuer not involving any public offering are exempt from the registration provisions of the Act. Rule 146 provides objective standards for determining when the exemption is available. The main conditions of the rule require that (1) there be no general advertising or soliciting in connection with the offering; (2) offers be made only to persons the issuer reasonably believes have the requisite knowledge and experience in financial and business matters or who can bear the economic risk; (3) sales be made only to persons as described above except that persons meeting the economic risk test must also have an offeree representative capable of providing the requisite knowledge and experience; (4) offerees have access to or be provided information comparable to that elicited through registration; (5) there be no more than 35 purchasers in the offering; and (6) reasonable care be taken to ensure that the securities are not resold in violation of the Act's registration provisions.[26]

Rule 146 was severely criticized by the securities bar. Indeed, the rule was viewed as more restrictive than the case law construing the Section 4(2) statutory exemption.[27] Responding to this criticism and in an effort to facilitate capital formation, the SEC promulgated Regulation D in 1982. Rule 506, one of the rules promulgated by the Commission pursuant to Regulation D, is a "safe harbor" to the Section 4(2) exemption and supersedes Rule 146. Compliance with Rule 506 thus may be viewed as an alternative method to perfect the Section 4(2) private offering exemption. Moreover, federal legislation enacted in 1996 preempts state regulation of Rule 506 offerings (but does not preempt Section 4(2) offerings).

Generally, Rule 506 is available to any issuer. There is no limit to the aggregate price of the securities offered. Although Rule 506 does not limit the number of offerees, no advertising or general solicitation is permitted under the rule. Hence, depending on the circumstances, offers to a large number of offerees may be viewed as general solicitation, resulting in loss of the exemption.[28] The number of nonaccredited purchasers is limited to thirty-five plus an unlimited number of accredited investors. If any of the purchasers are not accredited, then specified disclosure must be made to such nonaccredited purchasers (see chart in § 3.10). As addressed later, a substantial compliance standard applies to Rule 506 offerings (see § 3.07).

---

[26] Securities Act Release No. 5913 (1978).

[27] See, e.g., *Woolf v. S.D. Cohen & Co.*, 515 F.2d 591, 612 n.14 (5th Cir. 1975), *vacated and remanded on other grounds*, 426 U.S. 944 (1976).

[28] See *supra* note 19 and accompanying text.

Unlike prior Rule 146, there is no requirement under Rule 506 that the issuer determine that the purchaser can bear the economic risk of the investment. Suitability determinations, however, must be made for nonaccredited purchasers. Except for accredited investors, the issuer prior to sale must "reasonably believe" that each purchaser either alone or with his or her "purchaser" representative has such knowledge and experience in financial and business matters that he or she is capable of evaluating the merits and risks of the prospective investment. (See the Appendix for this chapter). Moreover, the issuer must take certain actions to guard against resales (e.g., obtaining purchaser investment letters) in order to help ensure that a "distribution" does not occur.[29] In addition, the issuer is required to provide written disclosure to all nonaccredited purchasers regarding limitations on resale.[30] And, as discussed in § 3.15, principles of "integration of offerings" generally apply to Regulation D offerings.

An important concept under Rule 506 (as well as under Rule 505) is that of an "accredited investor." Under Regulation D, accredited investors irrebuttably are deemed to have access to registration-type information and to possess investment sophistication. Under Rule 501, accredited investors include not only certain institutional investors but also "fat cat" individual investors. These persons include those whose net worth at the time of the purchase exceeds $1 million (including the value of one's residence) and those who had an individual income exceeding $200,000 in each of the two most recent years (or $300,000 joint income with one's spouse) and who reasonably anticipate such an income for the current year.[31] Significantly, in a Rule 505 or 506 offering involving accredited investors, there is no mandated delivery of information to such accredited investors as Regulation D presumes that these investors can fend for themselves.

It is noteworthy that Rule 506 expands the Section 4(2) private offering exemption in at least two ways. First, unlike Section 4(2), which applies to both offers and sales, Rule 506 focuses on purchaser (rather than offeree) qualification. Hence, for example, Rule 506, unlike Section 4(2), requires that only purchasers meet the sophistication standards. Second, institutions and wealthy individuals irrebuttably are deemed under Regulation D to be sophisticated and to have access to the type of information that a registration statement would provide. Case law under Section 4(2), particularly with respect to wealthy individual investors, disagrees with the SEC's position.[32]

Significantly, federal legislation enacted in 1996 preempts state regulation of offerings coming within Rule 506 (see § 18(b)(4)(D) of the Securities Act). States nonetheless may set forth notice filing requirements and collect

---

[29] See Securities Act Release Nos. 6389 (1982), 6758 (1988); *supra* note 20 and accompanying text. See generally J.W. Hicks, *Limited Offering Exemptions: Regulation D* (1999).

[30] See Rule 502(d) of Regulation D.

[31] See SEC Releases note 29 *supra*.

[32] See M. Steinberg, *Corporate Internal Affairs A Corporate and Securities Law Perspective* 44-49 (1983). But see Kripke, *Has the SEC Taken All the Dead Wood Out of Its Disclosure System?*, 38 Bus. Law. 833 (1983).

fees with respect to such offerings. States also retain their authority to bring enforcement actions for fraudulent conduct in connection with such offerings. However, with respect to the requisite parameters of the Rule 506 exemption, the states no longer have any role.[33]

Irrespective of the Rule 506 exemption, Section 4(2) still is the key exemption in certain contexts. For example, under Rule 506, disclosure of specified information must be provided to all purchasers who are not accredited. On the other hand, Section 4(2) allows an offeree's access to the applicable information to substitute for the providing of such information. In view of the costs generated in supplying such information, particularly in offerings of relatively small financial amounts, Section 4(2) may provide an attractive alternative. However, with respect to offerings made pursuant to the Section 4(2) *statutory* exemption (unlike the Rule 506 exemption), the states may continue to impose their own requirements.[34]

§ 3.07 Rules 507 and 508 — Substantial Compliance Standard and Filing of Form D

After the SEC's adoption of Regulation D, additional criticism was heard. Two major points were: (1) the unduly technical requirement that the Form D be filed with the Commission as a condition of a Regulation D exemption; and (2) the need for a "substantial compliance" standard so that minor and inadvertent errors would not result in loss of a Regulation D exemption. After consideration, the SEC responded to these assertions by adopting a "substantial compliance" standard in Rule 508 and by eliminating the Rule 507 disqualification provisions. Hence, in deleting the Form D filing requirement as a condition to the pertinent Regulation D exemption, the Commission stated:

> The proposals to eliminate the Form D filing requirement as a condition to every Regulation D exemption and the Rule 507 disqualification provisions were favorably received by the public commenters. These revisions have been adopted without change. The Rule 503 requirement to file a Form D within 15 days of the first sale of securities remains, but will no longer be a condition to the establishment of any exemption under Regulation D. Rule 507 will serve as a disqualification to the use of Regulation D for future transactions by any issuer, if it, or a predecessor or affiliate, has been enjoined by a court for violating the filing obligation established by Rule 503. The Commission has the authority to waive a disqualification upon a showing of good cause.[35]

---

[33] See Bagnell and Cannon, *The National Securities Markets Improvement Act of 1996: Summary and Discussion*, 25 Sec. Reg. L.J. 3 (1997).

[34] See generally J.W. Hicks, *Limited Offering Exemptions: Regulation D* (1999); Donahue, *New Exemptions from Registration Requirements of the Securities Act of 1933: Regulation D*, 10 Sec. Reg. L.J. 235 (1982); Warren, *A Review of Regulation D: The Present Exemption Regimen for Limited Offerings Under the Securities Act of 1933*, 33 Am. U.L. Rev. 355 (1984); Sargent, *The New Regulation D: Deregulation, Federalism and the Dynamics of Regulatory Reform*, 68 Wash. U. L.Q. 225 (1990); Note, *Regulation D: Coherent Exemptions for Small Business Under the Securities Act of 1933*, 24 Wm. & Mary L. Rev. 121 (1982).

[35] Securities Act Release No. 6825 (1989).

In other words, the timely filing of the Form D with the SEC is not a condition for perfecting a Regulation D exemption. The issuer nonetheless is required to file a Form D and, if such issuer is enjoined for failing to file the Form D, the failure to do so acts as a disqualification for such issuer to use a Regulation D exemption in the future. In its discretion, the SEC may waive any such disqualification upon a showing of good cause.

As discussed above, the SEC promulgated a "substantial compliance" standard for offerings pursuant to the Rule 504-506 exemptions. As set forth by the Commission, the "substantial compliance" standard contained in Rule 508 may be explained as follows:

> Rule 508 provides that an exemption from the registration requirements will be available for an offer or sale to a particular individual or entity, despite failure to comply with a requirement of Regulation D, if the requirement is not designed to protect specifically the complaining person; the failure to comply is insignificant to the offering as a whole; and there has been a good faith and reasonable attempt to comply with all requirements of the regulation. Rule 508 specifies that the provisions of Regulation D relating to general solicitation, the dollar limits of Rules 504 and 505 and the limits on non-accredited investors in Rules 505 and 506 are deemed significant to every offering and therefore not subject to the Rule 508 defense. Further, the rule specifies that any failure to comply with a provision of Regulation D is actionable by the Commission under the Securities Act.[36]

§ 3.08 The Meaning of "General Solicitation"

In order to satisfy several of the exemptions from Securities Act registration, there must not be any advertising or general solicitation. This ban on general solicitation is a necessary condition to such exemptions as those provided by Section 4(2), Rule 505, Rule 506, and Section 4(6).[37] Note, however, that Rule 508 (substantial compliance) provides no defense for violation of the general solicitation prohibition in Regulation D offerings.[38] Unfortunately, the meaning of general solicitation at times remains elusive. To gain a general understanding of what type of conduct violates the ban on general solicitation, such as under Rule 502(c) of Regulation D, a number of no-action letters issued by the SEC's Division of Corporate Finance are helpful.

According to the Commission, analysis of Rule 502(c)[39] focuses on two separate inquiries:

> First, is the communication in question a general solicitation or general advertisement? Second, if it is, is it being used by the issuer or by someone

---

[36] *Id.* See Sargent, *The New Regulation D: Deregulation, Federalism, and the Dynamics of Regulatory Reform*, 68 Wash. U. L.Q. 225 (1990).

[37] For the circumstances where general solicitation is permitted in Rule 504 offerings, *see* § 3.09[B][1] *supra.*

[38] See § 3.07 *supra.*

[39] Securities Act Release No. 6455 (1983).

on the issuer's behalf to offer or sell the securities? If either question can be answered in the negative, then the issuer will not be in violation of Rule 502(c).

The former inquiry is generally regarded as the more difficult. In general, to avoid general solicitation in Regulation D offerings, the no-action letters issued by the SEC staff frequently require a preexisting relationship between the issuer (or its agents) and the prospective investors which is of some substance and duration or which allows the issuer to evaluate the prospective investor's financial standing and sophistication. Note that the number of prospective investors solicited is not controlling. However, it is apparent that certain conduct, such as the use of the media to offer securities, is prohibited by the general solicitation ban of Rule 502(c).[40]

The first no-action letter addressing general solicitation under Rule 502(c) was *Woodtrails-Seattle, Ltd.*,[41] wherein the SEC staff found that the mailing of written offers to 330 prospective investors who had previously invested with the issuer over the last three years did not constitute general solicitation. The staff reasoned that the general solicitation ban had not been violated because of the *pre-existing relationships* between the general partner and the prospective investors, as evidenced by the general partner's determination that the proposed investment was suitable for each of the prospective investors.[42]

In the staff's view, a key basis underlying the pre-existing relationship requirement is to aid the issuer in assessing investor suitability, namely, that a potential investor is capable of evaluating the merits and risks of a proposed investment prior to it being offered.[43] Nonetheless, even if a potential investor possesses some degree of financial sophistication and/or wealth, if no preexisting relationship exists between the potential investor and the issuer, the issuer may not solicit such prospective investor without violating the general solicitation ban.[44]

Subsequent no-action letters issued by the SEC staff stress the *substance* of the relationship between the issuer and the solicitees and the importance of a "*cooling-off*" period between the beginning of a substantive relationship and the point in time at which that investor may be solicited to invest in a particular offering. In *E.F. Hutton & Co.*,[45] and *Bateman Eichler, Hill Richards, Inc.*,[46] the staff addressed the use of "questionnaire" materials

---

[40] *Id.*

[41] See *Woodtrails-Seattle, Ltd.*, 1982 SEC No-Act. LEXIS 2662 (Aug. 9, 1982).

[42] See *id.* at *1-2.

[43] See *Mineral Lands Research & Marketing Corp.*, 1985 SEC No-Act. LEXIS 2811 (Dec. 4, 1985).

[44] See *In the Matter of Kenman Corp. and Kenman Sec*, 1985 SEC LEXIS 1717, n. 6 (April 19, 1985). See also, Interpretive Release on Regulation D, Securities Act Release No. 33-6455, 17 C.F.R. Pt. 231, 1983 SEC LEXIS 2288 (March 3, 1983), Q. 60, ("The mere fact that a solicitation is directed only to accredited investors will not mean that the solicitation is in compliance with Rule 502(c). [Rule 502(c)] relates to the nature of the offering not the nature of the offerees.").

[45] See *E.F. Hutton & Co.*, 1985 SEC No-Act. LEXIS 2917 (Dec. 3, 1985).

[46] See *Bateman Eichler, Hill Richards, Inc.*, 1985 SEC No-Act. LEXIS 2918 (Dec. 3, 1985).

by broker-dealers to pre-qualify potential investors for future private offerings. These letters were generic questionnaires that were to provide relevant information for each potential client, including the respondent's personal financial circumstances and investment sophistication. Bateman Eichler also proposed to have an account executive follow up on the questionnaire's responses for the purpose of procuring additional financial information about the respondents.[47]

In addressing the use of questionnaires to establish a substantive pre-existing relationship, the SEC staff stated in *E.F. Hutton* that "substantive relationships may be established with persons who provide satisfactory responses to questionnaires that provide [the broker-dealer] with sufficient information to evaluate the prospective offerees' sophistication and financial circumstances."[48] However, the staff believed that the responses to both the E.F. Hutton and Bateman Eichler questionnaires in fact were inadequate to determine the level of sophistication and financial circumstances of the prospective offerees.[49]

In light of the staff's position in *Woodtrails-Seattle, E.F. Hutton,* and *Bateman Eichler,* one may conclude that a "substantive" pre-existing relationship may be established by showing that the issuer was sufficiently aware of the potential investor's financial circumstances and sophistication because: (1) the potential investor had previously invested with the issuer and the offeree's relationship with the issuer had existed for some duration; or (2) the potential investor had been effectively pre-screened. It is important to note the distinction between the two situations, the former involves a relationship with a *previous* investor, while the latter involves a recently established relationship with a *new* customer. That is, a previous investor would be one who the issuer would know was suited to invest in the proposed offering because the investor had similarly invested with the issuer in the past. This is distinct from a new customer whose financial background and sophistication is known by the issuer because of the prescreening process, thus enabling the issuer to determine that the proposed offering is a suitable investment for the new customer.

Of equal importance to the SEC staff in determining whether certain contact with *new* customers constitutes general solicitation is whether "sufficient time" elapsed between the pre-qualification of the new customer and the participation by the issuer or its agents in the particular offering under consideration.[50] This "cooling-off" period has been underscored in a

---

[47] See *id.* at *4-5.

[48] *E.F. Hutton, supra* note 45, at *1-2.

[49] Unfortunately, the SEC did not specifically explain why the E.F. Hutton and Bateman Eichler questionnaires were inadequate. See *E.F. Hutton, supra* note 45, at *2; *Bateman Eichler, supra* note 46, at *2. Furthermore, the SEC did not address the fact that Bateman Eichler account executives would follow up to receive additional information from the prospective offerees. See *id.* However, in reference to the E.F. Hutton Letter, a former Associate Director of the Division of Corporation Finance suggested "a form designed to establish sophistication for purposes of Rule 506 would generally be sufficient . . ." McCoy & Aalbregtse, *Partnership Disclosure and Regulation D Developments,* Thirteenth Ann. Sec. Reg. Institute, U. Cal. S.D., Dec. 1985, at 6.

[50] See *E.F. Hutton, supra* note 45, at *1-2; *Bateman Eichler, supra* note 46, at *1-2.

number of no-action letters issued by the staff as the key in determining that the relationship between the issuer and the customer is, in fact, "pre-existing." The no-action letter issued in *H.B. Shaine & Co.*[51] illustrates the interplay between the "substantive" and "cooling-off" period requirements of the general solicitation ban set forth by the Commission, and provides an example of how broker-dealers can avoid violating the ban on general solicitation while still soliciting new investors for private offerings.

In *H.B. Shaine*, the broker-dealer intended to send pre-qualifying questionnaires to both established Shaine clients and individuals with whom Shaine had no previous relationship in order to determine which potential customers were accredited within the meaning of Regulation D or sophisticated within the meaning of Section 4(2) of the Securities Act (if the investor is accredited under Regulation D, it is presumed that such investor is sophisticated for purposes of Rule 506).[52] The H.B. Shaine questionnaire also sought other information to inform the broker-dealer about the respondent's ability to evaluate the risks and merits of potential offerings, including the respondent's own opinion about his or her ability to do so.[53] In response, the Commission stated:

> We understand that the proposed questionnaire is generic in nature and that sufficient time will have elapsed between the respondent's completion of the questionnaire and the completion or inception of any particular offering. The Division is of the view that the procedure outlined in your letter would establish a preexisting substantive relationship with a respondent provided that the respondent furnishes complete responses to the questionnaire. We take no position as to whether the information obtained from the questionnaire is sufficient to form a reasonable basis for believing an individual to be accredited or sophisticated.[54]

This same analysis was extended to Internet solicitations in the IPONET no-action letter.[55] In general, the IPONET letter illustrates the standards set forth by the SEC staff regarding the proscription of general solicitation in private offerings. IPONET proposed the posting of private offerings in a password-protected page.[56] In order to receive a password to view the posted offerings, W.J. Gallagher & Co., through the IPONET web-site, would "solicit individuals who meet the 'accredited investor' or sophisticated investor standards of Regulation D," as determined by a questionnaire to be completed on-line and verified by W.J. Gallagher & Co.[57] Once the investor receives his or her password, the "IPONET site will only allow an Accredited Investor access to those private offerings which are posted subsequent in time to the Accredited Investor qualification with IPONET."[58]

---

[51] See *H.B. Shaine & Co., Inc.*, 1987 SEC No-Act. LEXIS 2004 (May 1, 1987).

[52] See *id*. at *4.

[53] See *id*.

[54] *Id*. at *1.

[55] See *IPONET*, 1996 SEC No-Act. LEXIS 642 (July 26, 1996).

[56] See *id*. at *2.

[57] *Id*. at *7.

[58] *Id*. at *9.

First, because IPONET involves the use of an Internet web-site, it is clear that the number of potential investors that view the IPONET web-site plays no part in the determination of whether the ban on general solicitation has been violated. Second, in order to receive a password, the potential investor must be sophisticated or accredited under Regulation D. This ensures that the Commission's underlying objective of the substantive pre-existing relationship standard is met, i.e., the issuer is aware of the potential investor's financial circumstances and level of sophistication. Further, because the issuer must have adequate information to make that determination, the relationship between the potential investor and the issuer is considered to be "substantive." Finally, because the potential investor is not able to view any offerings that were initiated or under consideration at the time the potential investor was under pre-qualification review, the requisite "cooling-off" period is met and the relationship is considered "pre-existing" according to the Commission.

The second inquiry in the two-step analysis of what conduct falls within the scope of Rule 502(c), is whether the general solicitation is being used by the issuer or by someone on the issuer's behalf to offer or sell securities. This second inquiry can be broken into two elements: (1) by the issuer or by someone on the issuer's behalf; and (2) to offer or sell securities. Cases in which the use of general solicitation is "by the issuer" are often straightforward. In general, if a communication is in an issuer's name or the management solicits a potential investor, it is clearly "by the issuer." However, what is meant by the language "nor any person acting on its behalf" of Rule 502(c) is more difficult to determine. The Commission apparently deems third party communications to be *not* on the issuer's behalf if the issuer has not influenced the content of the communication in any way and the communication bears no direct connection to a current or pending offer by the issuer.[59]

Focusing on the issue of whether a particular communication constitutes an offer to sell securities, the Commission's analysis is similar to that used by the Commission to determine what types of communication, other than a prospectus, can be made during a public offering.[60] Hence, communications related to a particular offering that occur after that offering has closed and have no "immediate or direct bearing on contemporaneous or subsequent offers or sales of securities" are clearly not part of an offer or sale.[61]

---

[59] See *Richard Daniels*, 1984 SEC No-Act. LEXIS 2874 (Dec. 19, 1984) (SEC finding that proposed newsletter setting forth public information concerning all limited partnerships in Arizona, making no mention of any issuer or offerings, and prepared completely independent of contact with any issuers not in violation of the ban on general solicitation); *Tax Investment Information Corp.*, 1983 SEC No-Act. LEXIS 1737 (Feb. 7, 1983) (finding lack of facts concerning any issuer's connection with proposed newsletter analyzing Regulation D offerings in Louisiana to preclude SEC staff's judgment that proposed activity not general solicitation). See generally Martin & Parsons, *The Preexisting Relationship Doctrine Under Regulation D: A Rule Without Reason?*, 45 Wash. & Lee L. Rev. 1031, 1038-39 (1988).

[60] See R. Haft, *supra*, note 10, at § 3.05; L. Loss & J. Seligman, *Securities Regulation*, 1437-45 (3d ed. 1995). See generally Daugherty, *Rethinking the Ban on General Solicitation*, 38 Emory L.J. 67, 115-23 (1989).

[61] *Alma Securities Corp.*, 1982 SEC No-Act. LEXIS 2647, *2 (Aug. 2, 1982).

However, communications that occur before or during a particular offering requires an analysis of the circumstances surrounding the communication to determine if an offer or sale of a security has occurred. For example, the "questionnaire" no-action letters discussed above did not constitute offers to sell securities because the questionnaires did not mention any specific offerings under consideration that were currently being offered. [62] However, in *Gerald F. Gerstenfeld*, [63] the SEC staff found that an institutional advertisement relating to a syndicator that sold securities in private placements and invited potential investors to contact the syndicator for additional information to be general solicitation because "the primary purpose of the advertisement is to sell securities and to condition the market for future sales if the syndicator expects in the near future to offer and sell securities." [64] Hence, the analysis employed by the Commission in *Gerstenfeld* is the same used by the Commission to address "gun-jumping" in the pre-filing period of registration. [65]

§ 3.09   The Limited Offering Exemptions

The statutory limited offering exemptions are contained in Sections 3(b) and 4(6) of the Securities Act. These exemptions reflect Congressional concern that small enterprises should not be unduly burdened in raising capital. Note, moreover, that Congress' enactment of Section 28 of the Securities Act in 1996 gives the SEC broad exemptive authority to create additional exemptions from registration.

[A]   The Section 4(6) Exemption

Generally, Section 4(6) exempts from registration under the 1933 Act offers and sales by any issuer solely to one or more "accredited investors" if the total offering price does not exceed the amount permitted under Section 3(b) of the Act (currently $5 million). No advertising or public solicitation is permitted in connection with a Section 4(6) offering, and the issuer must file a notice of such sales made pursuant to the exemption with the SEC. [66]

[B]   The Section 3(b) Exemptions

Generally, Section 3(b) contains an exemption for small offerings, empowering the Commission to exempt from registration any offering of securities where the aggregate amount of such offering does not exceed $5,000,000.

---

[62] In *Bateman Eichler*, it was proposed that the account executives would not send any offering materials for at least 45 days following the "questionnaire" mailing. See *Bateman Eichler, supra* note 46, at *5.

[63] *Gerald F. Gerstenfeld*, 1985 SEC No-Act. LEXIS 2790 (Dec. 3, 1985).

[64] *Id.* at *2. Thus, in contrast to *Bateman Eichler*, the fact that investors could receive additional information concerning current or pending offers as soon as it was requested from the syndicator represented an "offer for securities" according to the SEC.

[65] See § 4.02[A] *infra*.

[66] See Securities Act Release No. 6256 (1980).

The most significant rules that the SEC has promulgated pursuant to this authority are Regulation A and Rules 504, 505, and 701. Section 28 of the Securities Act, enacted in 1996, enables the Commission to increase the monetary amount otherwise available under these exemptions.

[1] Rule 504

The SEC adopted Rule 504 to facilitate the capital raising needs for the small start-up company. The exemption is not available for investment companies and reporting entities under the Exchange Act (i.e. those registrants which must file periodic reports with the SEC). In a Rule 504 offering, the issuer need not determine whether the purchaser is sophisticated; nor does the issuer need to provide a purchaser representative for the unsophisticated. There are no specified federal disclosure requirements in a Rule 504 offering and there is no express limit on the number of offerees and purchasers. Offerings made pursuant to the Rule 504 exemption (in aggregation with all other securities sold in reliance on any exemption under Section 3(b) or in violation of Section 5) during any twelve-month period have a ceiling of $1 million. [67]

In fact, the Rule 504 offering exemption permits the issuer to conduct, in essence, a "mini-public" offering where general solicitation is permitted and purchasers in such offerings acquire freely transferable securities. In order for general solicitation to be permitted and the securities acquired to be freely transferable, one of two conditions must be met:

- the transactions are registered under a state law requiring public filing and delivery of a disclosure document before sale. For sales to occur in a state without this sort of provision, the transactions must be registered in another state with such a provision and the disclosure document filed in that state must be delivered to all purchasers before sale in both states; or

- the securities are issued under a state law exemption that permits general solicitation and general advertising so long as sales are made only to "accredited investors" as that term is defined in Regulation D. [68]

Where neither of these conditions is satisfied, Rule 504 prohibits advertising and general solicitation and deems the securities acquired restricted. These restrictions were necessary, according to the SEC, to curb abuse of the Rule 504 exemption in the markets for "microcap" enterprises. [69]

---

[67] See Securities Act Release Nos. 6389 (1982), 6758 (1988).

[68] Securities Act Release No. 7644 (1999).

[69] *Id.* Offerings involving securities of microcap enterprises often are associated with low prices per share, limited public information, thin capitalization, and little, if any, analyst coverage. In the 1999 Release, the SEC stated:

Recent market innovations and technological changes, most notably, the Internet, have created the possibility of nationwide Rule 504 offerings for securities of non-reporting companies that were once thought to be sold locally.

In some cases, Rule 504 has been used in fraudulent schemes to make prearranged "sales" of securities under the rule to nominees in states that do not have registration or prospectus

Thus, except for the conditions set forth above, Rule 504 may be viewed as a blanket federal exemption from registration for offerings not exceeding $1 million. The SEC believes that the remedial provisions of the federal securities laws, in conjunction with state regulation, are sufficient protection in these smaller offerings.

[2] Rule 505

Rule 505 provides any issuer that is not an investment company with an exemption from registration under Section 3(b) of the Securities Act for sales of securities to (what the issuer reasonably believes are) not more than thirty-five nonaccredited purchasers and to an unlimited number of accredited investors. In aggregation with other offerings made pursuant to exemptions available under Section 3(b) (or sold in violation of Section 5), an issuer pursuant to Rule 505 may raise up to $5 million during any twelve-month period. In a Rule 505 offering, general solicitation or advertising is prohibited and restrictions on resale apply.[70] As in Rule 506 offerings, issuers under the Rule 505 exemption must provide written disclosure to all nonaccredited purchasers regarding limitations on resale (see Rule 502(d)). And, as set forth in § 3.07, a substantial compliance standard applies to offerings made pursuant to the Rule 505 exemption.

The availability of the Rule 505 exemption is conditioned upon the disclosure of specified information to nonaccredited purchasers. Unlike Rule 506, however, the issuer need not make a determination that the purchaser is sophisticated. If unsophisticated, there is no requirement that the investor have a purchaser representative.[71] Finally, the Rule 505 exemption is unavailable to issuers that have engaged in certain misconduct ("bad boy" disqualifiers). For example, an issuer subject to an SEC injunction within the previous five years may not avail itself of the Rule 505 exemption.[72]

[3] Rule 701

In 1988, the SEC adopted Rule 701 pursuant to Section 3(b) of the 1933 Act. In 1999, the Commission increased the monetary amount that may

---

delivery requirements. As a part of this arrangement, these securities are then placed with broker-dealers who use cold-calling techniques to sell the securities at ever-increasing prices to unknowing investors. When their inventory of shares is exhausted, these firms permit the artificial market demand created to collapse, and investors lose much, if not all, of their investment. This scheme is sometimes colloquially referred to as a "pump and dump."

See generally Cohn, *The Impact of Securities Laws on Emerging Companies: Would the Wright Brothers Have Gotten Off the Ground?*, 3 J. Sm. & Emer. Bus. Law 315 (1999); Hass, *Small Issue Public Offerings Conducted over the Internet: Are They "Suitable" for the Retail Investor?*, 72 S. Calif. L. Rev. 67 (1998).

[70] See Securities Act Release No. 6389 (1982).

[71] For further discussion on this point, see Friedman, *On Being Rich, Accredited, and Undiversified: The Lacunae in Contemporary Securities Regulation*, 47 Okla. L. Rev. 291 (1994); Warren, *A Review of Regulation D: The Present Exemption Regimen for Limited Offerings Under the Securities Act of 1933*, 33 Am. U.L. Rev. 355 (1984). See also, Bradford, *Transaction Exemptions in the Securities Act of 1933: An Economic Analysis*, 45 Emory L.J. 591 (1996).

[72] For a complete listing of the disqualifiers, see Rule 262 of Regulation A, 17 C.F.R. § 230.262.

be raised under Rule 701 by invoking its exemptive authority under Section 28 of the Securities Act. Generally, Rule 701 provides an exemption from registration for offers and sales of securities for certain compensation benefit plans adopted for the participation of employees, officers, directors, consultants, and advisers of an eligible company. Rule 701's availability is limited due to the fact that companies eligible to use the exemption must not be subject to the periodic reporting requirements of the Exchange Act. As a preliminary note to the rule makes clear, Rule 701 is designed to facilitate the issuance of securities for compensation. As a consequence, the rule does not exempt offers and sales that are intended to raise capital.[73]

So long as the offering is made solely to eligible purchasers, Rule 701 permits such offerings to be public in nature, thereby permitting general solicitation. In a Rule 701 offering, unless more than $5 million of securities are to be sold, there are no specific disclosure requirements.[74]

Where sales exceed the $5 million threshold, the required disclosure consists of:

- a copy of the compensatory benefit plan or contract;

- a copy of the summary plan description required by the Employee Retirement Income Security Act of 1974 ("ERISA") or, if the plan is not subject to ERISA, a summary of the plan's material terms;

- risk factors associated with investment in the securities under the plan or agreement; and

- the financial statements required in an offering statement on Form 1-A under Regulation A.

Limitations on resales, however, do apply. The monetary amount of securities that can be offered and sold pursuant to Rule 701 during any twelve-month period is the greatest of the following: (1) $1 million, (2) 15 percent of the company's total assets, or (3) 15% of the outstanding securities of the class of securities issued.[75]

Importantly, because of the exemption's compensatory (rather than capital raising) purpose, offerings made pursuant to Rule 701 are not aggregated with offerings made pursuant to the other Section 3(b) exemptions. Nor are the monetary ceilings for other offerings made pursuant to the other Section 3(b) exemptions affected by Rule 701 offers and sales. Moreover, "integration of offering" problems are minimized because Rule 701 "specifically state[s] that all offers and sales pursuant to its rubric are deemed to be a part of a single, discrete offering; consequently, Rule 701 transactions need not be integrated into any other offering made by the issuer or vice versa."[76]

---

[73] See Securities Act Release No. 6768 (1988). See generally Robbins, *Securities Offerings to Employees, Consultants, and Advisers Under Rule 701*, 31 Rev. Sec. & Comm. Reg. 51 (1998).

[74] See Securities Act Release No. 7645 (1998).

[75] *Id.*

[76] *Id.* For restrictions on resales regarding securities issued in Rule 701 offerings, see Chapter 5.

[4] Regulation A

In 1992, the SEC amended Regulation A in an effort to enhance capital formation by small business.[77] Although Regulation A is an exemption from registration for non-reporting companies, it in fact permits generalized interstate public offerings of up to $5 million during any 12-month period, including up to $1.5 million in non-issuer resales. The Regulation imposes no limit on the number of offerees or purchasers and authorizes the use of broker-dealers to advertise and distribute the securities. Purchasers of securities acquired in a Regulation A offering generally may resell such securities without being subject to restrictions on resale imposed by SEC rules such as 147 and 505-506. In addition, like Rule 508 in Regulation D, Regulation A contains a "substantial compliance" standard.

An offering pursuant to Regulation A may very much resemble a "mini-public" offering. Indeed, the filing with the SEC of an "offering statement" (like a registration statement in a registered offering) is required. There, however, are some important differences, including:

- Because Regulation A offerings are exempt from registration, there is no Section 11 liability (for materially false or misleading statements contained in the registration statement) and no requirement for the issuer to file with the SEC periodic reports under the Exchange Act.

- The Regulation A exemption is not available for any issuer if it or its affiliated persons, executive officers, or other like persons have been subject to certain discipline during the previous five years, including a criminal conviction relating to the sale of securities and the imposition of an SEC injunction (see Rule 262 —"bad boy" disqualifications).

- Prior to conducting a Regulation A offering, a prospective issuer may "test the waters" for potential investor interest by means of oral and written communications.

- The information required to be contained in a Regulation A offering statement generally is not as extensive as that mandated in a registration statement. For example, a registration statement must contain audited financial statements.

- Unlike the Rule 505, 506, and 701 exemptions, purchasers in a Regulation A offering are not subject to limitations on resale.

A relatively frequent use of the Regulation A offering exemption is by privately-held (nonreporting) issuers for employee stock option and purchase plans. Note that this remains true in many circumstances even after the SEC's adoption of Rule 701 for the following reason: while stock purchased under the Rule 701 exemption is subject to limitations on resale, securities acquired pursuant to the Regulation A exemption are not restricted. As discussed in Chapter 5, limitations on resale may pose intolerable burdens upon those who wish to freely resell their stock into the market.

---

[77] Securities Act Release No. 6949 (1992). See generally Bradford, *Regulation A and the Integration Doctrine: The New Safe Harbor,* 55 Ohio St. L.J. 255 (1994).

The state securities regulators have expressed grave reservations regarding the SEC's Regulation A amendments, particularly the "test the waters" provision. For example, one prominent state regulator opined that the SEC was "embarking on an attempt to facilitate the sale of the riskiest securities in the market to the least sophisticated of buyers" and predicted that the states would reject the SEC's amendments. Without such state cooperation, it is clear that any simplification of the federal requirements is illusory. Hence, because an issuer must perfect exemptions from both state and federal registration, the SEC small business initiatives will only become significant if a sufficient number of states adopt coordinated exemptive regulations. [78]

Nonetheless, a number of states have adopted modified versions of "testing the waters." Although generally not as broad as the SEC's Regulation A, these state versions provide some flexibility for assessing potential investor interest prior to incurring the major expenses associated with a public offering. [79]

§ 3.10 Comparative Chart

Given the complexity of the various requirements for perfecting the issuer transactional exemptions from registration discussed in §§ 3.05-3.09, the following chart may prove helpful. Remember, however, that the chart may simplify certain of the requirements. Reference should be made to the pertinent SEC rules, releases, and the preceding discussion in this chapter.

---

[78] See 24 Sec. Reg. & L. Rep. (BNA) 1139, 1297 (1992). See generally, Campbell, *Blue Sky Laws and the Recent Congressional Preemption Failure*, 22 J. Corp. L. 175 (1997); Sonsini, *Regulation A*, 16 Rev. Sec. Reg. 781 (1983); Steinberg, *The Emergence of State Securities Laws: Partly Sunny Skies for Investors*, 62 U. Cincinnati L. Rev. 395 (1993).

[79] See Ariz. Rev. Stat. Ann. § 44-1845; 70 Pa. Cons. Stat. Ann. §§ 1-203, 1-205; NASAA Proposed Statement of Policy on Solicitation of Interest (Test the Waters), NASAA (CCH) ¶ 4141 (1993).

Chart of Selected Securities Act Exemptions

Item	Rule 504	Rule 505	Rule 506	Rule 701	Reg. A	§4(2)	§4(6)
Aggregate Offering Price Limitation	$1,000,000 (12 mos.)	$5,000,000 (12 mos.)	Unlimited	Depending on certain factors, at least $1,000,000 (12 mos.)	$5,000,000 (12 mos.)	Unlimited	$5,000,000
Number of investors	Unlimited	35 plus an unlimited number of accredited investors	35 plus an unlimited number of accredited investors	Unlimited but must be an eligible purchaser	Unlimited	Uncertain but evidently a finite number of offerees depending on the circumstances	An unlimited number of accredited investors only
Investor Qualification	None required	No sophistication requirements	Purchaser must be sophisticated (alone or with representative); accredited investors presumed to be qualified	Purchaser must be employee, officer, director, consultant or advisor of an eligible company who has acquired the securities as compensation	None required	Exact requirements uncertain; offeree must receive or have access to the type of information that registration would disclose; also, sophistication standards apply – offeree must be financially sophisticated (alone or with representative)	Accredited investors only
Commissions	Permitted	Permitted	Permitted	Permitted	Permitted	Permitted	Permitted
Limitations on Manner of Offering	General solicitation and advertising permitted if state registered or sold only to accredited purchasers	No general solicitation or advertising permitted	No general solicitation or advertising permitted	General solicitation and advertising permitted	General solicitation and advertising permitted	No general solicitation or advertising permitted	No general solicitation or advertising permitted
Limitations on Resale	Not restricted if state registered or sold only to accredited purchasers	Restricted	Restricted	Restricted	Not Restricted	Restricted	Restricted
Issuer Qualifications	Among others, no reporting or investment companies	No investment companies or issuers disqualified under Regulation A	None	No reporting companies	Among others, no reporting or investment companies; "bad boy" disqualifiers apply	None	None
Filing with SEC	Form D required but not as a condition of exemption	Form D required but not as a condition of exemption	Form D required but not as a condition of exemption	No notice of sales required	Filings required	No notice of sales required	Form 4(6) required
Information Requirements	No information specified	In either a Rule 505 or 506 offering, see SEC Rule 502(b) for information requirements	In either a Rule 505 or 506 offering, see SEC Rule 502(b) for information requirements	No information specified except if greater than $5 million sold	Information specified in Regulation A	Investors receive or have access to the type of information that registration would disclose	No information specified

§ 3.11 Rule 1001 — The "California" Exemption

Showing its administrative flexibility, the SEC adopted Rule 1001 to provide a federal exemption from registration in order to coordinate with a California exemption from state registration for small business issuers. Rule 1001 exempts from registration "offers and sales up to $5,000,000 that are exempt from state qualification under paragraph (n) of Section 25102 of the California Corporations Code."[80] The Rule 1001 exemption was promulgated by the SEC under Section 3(b) of the Securities Act to enhance capital raising by small businesses, while maintaining adequate investor protection. A closer look at the requirements of Rule 1001 reveals that this

---

[80] Securities Act Release No. 7285, [1996 Transfer Binder] Fed. Sec. L. Rep. (CCH) ¶ 85,803, at 88,807 (SEC 1996).

exemption is broader than the exemptions provided by Rules 505 and 506 of Regulation D.

California Section 25102(n) limits the exemption to issuers that are California corporations or other business entities that are formed under California law, including partnerships and trusts.[81] In addition, a non-California corporation may use the exemption if more than 50 percent of its outstanding voting securities are held by California residents and at least 50 percent of its property, payroll, and sales, as determined for state tax purposes, can be attributed to California.[82] The California exemption is not available to investment companies subject to the Investment Company Act of 1940.[83]

To perfect the exemption, an eligible issuer must be able to show that "sales of securities are made only to qualified purchasers or other persons the issuer reasonably believes, after reasonable inquiry, to be qualified purchasers."[84] Section 25102(n) sets forth its own definitions of qualified purchasers, which are similar, but not the same as, accredited purchasers under Regulation D. Examples of qualified purchasers include:

- any person purchasing more than $150,000 of securities in the offering; or

- a natural person whose net worth exceeds $500,000, or a natural person whose net worth exceeds $250,000 if such purchaser's annual income exceeds $100,000 — in either case the transaction must involve:

    (a) only one-class voting stock (or preferred stock establishing the same voting rights);

    (b) an amount limited to no more than 10 percent of the purchaser's net worth; and

    (c) a purchaser able to protect his or her own interests (alone or with the guidance of a professional advisor).[85]

The solicitation permitted under California Section 25102(n) is less restrictive than that of Rules 505 and 506 of Regulation D (which prohibit general solicitation). An eligible issuer under Rule 1001 is permitted to "test the waters" by distributing to qualified and non-qualified purchasers a written general announcement that contains certain specified information.[86] The SEC has previously accepted this general announcement

---

[81] See Cal. Corp. Code § 25102(n)(1).

[82] See Cal. Corp. Code § 25102(n)(1), 2115.

[83] See Cal. Corp. Code § 25102(n)(1).

[84] Cal. Corp. Code § 25102(n)(2).

[85] Securities Act Release, *supra* note 80, at 88,007-88,008.

[86] For example, such specified information includes:

  (i)   The name of the issuer of the securities,

  (ii) The full title of the security to be raised, [and]

  (iii) The anticipated suitability standards for prospective purchasers.

Cal. Corp. Code § 25102(n)(5)(A). The issuer also has the option of providing additional information, such as the nature of the issuer's business, its geographic location, and/or the probable price range of the security being offered. See Cal. Corp. Code § 25102(n)(5)(B).

process in connection with a "mini-public" offering pursuant to a Regulation A exemption, discussed earlier in this chapter. However, telephone solicitation is specifically prohibited until it can be determined that the prospective purchaser is deemed qualified.[87] As a general rule, all offers, oral and written, are limited to qualified purchasers.[88]

The California exemption sets forth further requirements. For example, issuers are required to "provide certain purchasers who are natural persons a disclosure document as specified in [SEC] Rule 502 of Regulation D five days prior to any sale or commitment to purchase."[89] In addition, securities issued pursuant to the exemption are "restricted."[90] This resale restriction and the $5,000,000 offering limitation are the only two federal requirements that are imposed independent of California Section 25102(n).

The SEC has stated that any state enacting a transaction exemption similar to California's is eligible to receive the same exemption.[91] To date, the SEC has not formally received any request from a state other than California.[92]

§ 3.12   NASAA — Model Accredited Investor Exemption

In an effort to stimulate capital formation for small companies and promote greater uniformity in state securities regulations, the North American Securities Administrators Association (NASAA)[93] approved the Model Accredited Investor Exemption. In those states in which the Accredited Investor Exemption is adopted, issuers may avoid state registration requirements if securities are sold only to persons "who are or the issuer reasonably believes are accredited investors."[94] The model exemption incorporates by reference the SEC definition of accredited purchaser set forth in Rule 501 of Regulation D. The model exemption is regarded as a simpler version of the "California Exemption" and the SEC's corresponding Rule 1001. Importantly, however, the SEC has not promulgated a federal exemption from registration that coordinates with NASAA's model exemption. Thus, issuers that rely on the model exemption to avoid state registration requirements must also register the offering under the federal securities laws or perfect a federal exemption.

In order to sell securities pursuant to NASAA's model exemption, the issuer must reasonably believe that the purchaser is accredited as defined in SEC Rule 501(a). For example, an issuer offering securities under the

---

[87] See Cal. Corp. Code § 25102(n)(6).

[88] See Securities Act Release No. 7285, *supra* note 80, at 88,008.

[89] *Id.*

[90] 17 C.F.R. § 230.1001(c).

[91] See Securities Act Release No. 7285, *supra* note 80, at 88,009.

[92] See *id.* See also, Bradford, *The SEC's New Regulation CE Exemption: Federal-State Coordination Run Rampant*, 52 U. Miami L. Rev. 429 (1998); § 3.12 *infra*.

[93] NASAA is a voluntary organization comprised of securities regulatory authorities of the fifty states, the Commonwealth of Puerto Rico, Guam, Mexico, and the provinces of Canada.

[94] Model Accredited Investor Exemption § A.

model exemption may sell such securities to any person that has a net worth (or the issuer reasonably believes has a net worth) at the time of purchase of $1 million or greater. In contrast, the California exemption requires sales to be made only to "qualified purchasers," which are distinguished from accredited investors under Regulation D. By utilizing the accredited investor definition promulgated by the SEC, the model exemption enhances federal-state uniformity in this respect.

The model exemption is limited to issuers that are not in the development stage and have "no specific business plan or purpose" to effectuate a merger or acquisition.[95] In addition, subject to certain exceptions, the model exemption disqualifies an issuer from using the exemption if the issuer or any of its affiliated persons (such as an officer, director, or general partner) have been subject to certain disciplinary action ("bad boy" disqualifiers).[96] Similar to SEC Rules 505 and 506, restrictions on resale apply.[97]

Importantly, the model exemption allows the issuer to use a general advertisement to "test the waters" if such advertisement contains specified information mandated by the model exemption.[98] Note that an issuer is not required to use a general advertisement.[99] Similar to the California exemption, the permitted use of a general advertisement under the model exemption is a departure from the general solicitation ban imposed by Rules 505 and 506 of Regulation D. An issuer is not disqualified from using the

---

[95] Model Accredited Investor Exemption § B.

[96] Model Accredited Investor Exemption § D(1)(a)-(d). Hence, a "bad boy" disqualifier exists if such person is subject to, or has been in the last five years subject to, a state, federal or judicial order, judgment, or decree, or "has been convicted of any criminal offense in connection with the offer, purchase, or sale of security, or involving fraud or deceit." However, the model exemption lifts the disqualification of the issuer in any of the aforementioned situations if: (1) the subjected party is licensed or registered in the state in which the disqualifying order, judgment or decree was entered; (2) the court or regulatory agency issuing the order, judgment or decree waives the disqualification before any offer is made; or (3) the issuer demonstrates that, in the exercise of reasonable care, that it did not know of the existing disqualification. See Model Accredited Exemption § D(2)(a)-(c).

[97] Model Accredited Investor Exemption § C.

[98] See Model Accredited Investor Exemption § E(2)(a)-(f). Information required in the general advertisement includes:
  (a) the name, address and telephone number of the issuer of the securities;
  (b) the name, a brief description and price (if known) of any security to be issued;
  (c) a brief description of the business of the issuer in 25 words or less;
  (d) the type, number and aggregate amount of securities being offered;
  (e) the name, address and telephone number of the person to contact for additional information; and
  (f) a statement that:
    (i) sales will only be made to accredited investors;
    (ii) no money or other consideration is being solicited or will be accepted by way of this general announcement; and
    (iii) the securities have not been registered with or approved by any state securities agency or the U.S. Securities and Exchange Commission and are being offered and sold pursuant to an exemption from registration.

[99] See Model Accredited Investor Exemption § E(1).

model exemption should a non-accredited investor receive the general advertisement.[100]

In addition to the use of a general advertisement, an issuer under the model exemption has the option to provide additional information to offerees. Such additional information is to be provided pursuant to one of two delivery requirements. First, the model exemption allows the additional information to be delivered via "an electronic database that is restricted to persons who have been prequalified as accredited investors."[101] This approach appears consistent with the SEC staff's IPONET no-action letter,[102] wherein the staff agreed that prequalifying an investor as accredited and allowing a "cooling off" period between the potential investor's prequalification and the point in time in which that investor is offered a particular security creates a "substantive preexisting relationship" and therefore does not violate the ban on general solicitation imposed by Rules 505 and 506 of Regulation D, as well as Sections 4(2) and 4(6) of the Securities Act. Second, the issuer may deliver additional information if the issuer reasonably believes that the recipient of the additional information is an accredited investor.[103]

Finally, telephone solicitation is permitted if the issuer reasonably believes that the solicited investor is accredited prior to placing the call.[104] This provision grants to issuers considerable leeway to solicit investors under the model exemption. Furthermore, this appears to be a departure from the SEC's view that there must be a substantive pre-existing relationship established to avoid violation of the ban on general solicitation in the private offering context. Today, several states have adopted the model exemption.[105]

§ 3.13 Intrastate Offerings

Section 3(a)(11) of the Securities Act provides an exemption from registration with respect to "[a]ny security which is a part of an issue offered and sold only to persons resident within a single State or Territory, where the issuer of such security is a person resident and doing business, or, if a corporation, incorporated by and doing business within, such State or Territory." The rationale underlying the intrastate offering exemption is based on "the probability that investors in local enterprise will have adequate familiarity with [such enterprises] and an acknowledgment that [local] issuers will be relatively small and thus less able to bear the burden of federal registration,"[106] thereby leaving the respective states as the

---

[100] See Model Accredited Investor Exemption § H.

[101] Model Accredited Investor Exemption § F(1).

[102] See § 3.08 *supra*.

[103] See Model Accredited Investor Exemption § F(2).

[104] See Model Accredited Investor Exemption § G.

[105] See Securities Act Release No. 7664 (1999) (stating that sixteen states have adopted the model exemption and other states may do so in the relatively near future); § 3.08 *supra*.

[106] Deaktor, *Integration of Securities Offerings,* 31 U. Fla. L. Rev. 465, 481 (1979).

principal regulators in such offerings. In 1974, the SEC, in order to establish more definitive standards regarding the intrastate exemption, promulgated Rule 147 to serve as a safe harbor.[107] If the conditions of the rule have not been met, the party still may assert the availability of the Section 3(a)(11) statutory exemption. Unlike the exemption provided by Rule 147 and unlike those exemptions provided by Rules 504-506 of Regulation D as well as Section 4(2) of the Securities Act, which are available only to the issuer, the Section 3(a)(11) exemption also may be used under certain circumstances by shareholders seeking to resell their stock.

[A]   The Section 3(a)(11) Exemption

The Section 3(a)(11) exemption, as well as the Section 3(a)(9) and Section 3(a)(10) exemptions (addressed in § 3.14 of this chapter), are categorized in the Securities Act as exempt securities rather than transactional exemptions from registration. In practical effect, however, these exemptions come into play only where there is a transaction that meets the criteria of the applicable exemption. For example, the Section 3(a)(11) exemption, concerning securities that are offered and sold pursuant to an intrastate offering, is invoked only where there is an offering (e.g., a transaction) which meets the exemptive requirements of the statute.

Generally, the principal issues that come into play concerning the Section 3(a)(11) exemption deal with the concepts of "resident," "doing business within the state," and restrictions on resale. For purposes of the statutory intrastate exemption, offers only can be made to persons "resident" in a single state or territory. An offer to a single nonresident evidently voids the exemption, thereby giving rise to liability if no other exemption is perfected. Moreover, the SEC historically has defined "residence" to be similar to that of "domicile" which looks to the state of mind of the offeree. This subjective standard has been criticized for its uncertainty.[108]

Second, under the Section 3(a)(11) exemption, the issuer must be a person resident and "doing business" within the state in which the offering takes place. From the statutory definition, it is clear that the issuer must be incorporated in that state. Generally, the term "doing business" has been interpreted to mean that a "substantial," though not necessarily "exclusive," portion of the issuer's business must be conducted in that state. How much business is sufficiently substantial to validate use of the exemption seems unclear.[109]

With respect to restrictions on resale, a purchaser of securities offered under either the Section 3(a)(11) or Rule 147 exemption may resell without restriction to another bona fide resident. For an offer or sale by a purchaser

---

[107] See Securities Act Release No. 5450 (1974). See generally Morrissey, *Think Globally, Act Locally: It's Time to Reform the Intrastate Exemption*, 20 Sec. Reg. L.J. 59 (1992).

[108] See Securities Act Release Nos. 4434 (1961), 5450 (1974); Thomforde, *Exemptions from SEC Registration for Small Businesses*, 47 Tenn. L. Rev. 1, 28-29 (1979).

[109] See, e.g., *Chapman v. Dunn*, 414 F.2d 153 (6th Cir. 1969); Thomforde, *supra* note 108, at 29.

to a nonresident to be permitted, however, the issue of the securities offered must have "come to rest." While the SEC is said to have taken the position that a one-year holding period normally is necessary under Section 3(a)(11) before there is a resale to a nonresident,[110] courts may adopt a shorter resale period. In this regard, one court held that a seven-month holding period, although not within the Rule 147 safe harbor, nonetheless was of sufficient duration for Section 3(a)(11) purposes:

> The Court is of the opinion that the seven month period from the time of initial sale to the time of resale [to an out-of-state resident] is sufficient for the offering to come to rest. Plaintiffs argue that Rule 147 requires nine months before a resale can be made. The Court concludes that Rule 147 provides only a safe harbor [to the Section 3(a)(11) exemption]; compliance with [Rule 147's] provisions ensures that the SEC will take no action. But it does not follow that, as plaintiffs argue, that non-compliance necessarily means that the statute and its policies have been violated . . . Accordingly, defendants have complied with Section 3(a)(11) . . . .[111]

[B] The Rule 147 Exemption

In an effort to minimize the uncertainty surrounding the scope of the Section 3(a)(11) intrastate exemption, the SEC promulgated Rule 147 as a safe harbor. In the release adopting Rule 147, the Commission stated:

> Section 3(a)(11) was intended to allow issuers with localized operations to sell securities as part of a plan of local financing. Congress apparently believed that a company whose operations are restricted to one area should be able to raise money from investors in the immediate vicinity without having to register the securities with a federal agency. In theory, the investors would be protected both by their proximity to the issuer and by state regulation. Rule 147 reflects this Congressional intent and is limited in its application to transactions where state regulation will be most effective. The Commission has consistently taken the position that the exemption applies only to local financing provided by local investors for local companies. To satisfy the exemption, the entire issue must be offered and sold exclusively to residents of the state in which the issuer is resident and doing business. An offer or sale of part of the issue to a single non-resident will destroy the exemption for the entire issue.[112]

Rule 147 sets forth more objective criteria in defining the parameters of the intrastate exemption. Similar to Section 3(a)(11), Rule 147 has no monetary ceiling on the amount of funds that can be raised or on the number of offerees or purchasers. Offers and sales can only be made to

---

[110] See *In re Brooklyn Manhattan Transit Corp.*, 1 S.E.C. 147 (1935); Thomforde, *supra* note 108, at 29-30.

[111] *Busch v. Carpenter*, [1984-1985 Transfer Binder] Fed. Sec. L. Rep. (CCH) ¶ 91,810 (D. Utah 1984).

[112] Securities Act Release No. 5450 (1974).

residents of the state where the offering occurs. A single offering to a non-resident invalidates the exemption. Rule 147 defines "residence" to mean principal residence at the point in time that the offer and sale occur, thereby rejecting the subjective concept of "domicile."

With respect to the issuer's qualifications to use Rule 147, the enterprise must be incorporated or organized in the offering state and must be "doing business" within that state. The rule enumerates four specific criteria for defining the term "doing business within a state": (1) the enterprise must have its principal office within that state; (2) the enterprise must derive at least eighty percent of its gross revenues "from the operation of a business . . . or from the rendering of services within such state"; (3) the enterprise must have at least eighty percent of its assets situated within the state; and (4) the enterprise must use at least eighty percent of the funds raised by the offering for operations within the state.[113]

To come within Rule 147's safe harbor, while resales to residents can immediately be transacted, a period of nine months from the date of the last sale by the issuer must transpire before resales to non-residents are permitted. Issuers must take certain precautions to guard against illicit resales. These measures include disclosing in writing the resale limitations to all offerees, placing legends on the certificates describing the resale limitations, issuing stop transfer instructions to the transfer agent, and receiving a written representation from each purchaser declaring bona fide residence in the state of the offering.[114]

[C] ALI Federal Securities Code

It has been asserted that the Section 3(a)(11) and Rule 147 intrastate exemptions are unduly restrictive. If so, criticism should be directed toward Congress and not the Commission, which is bound by Section 3(a)(11)'s scope when adopting a safe harbor rule pursuant to that statute. The approach taken by the American Law Institute's (ALI) Federal Securities Code may be more appropriate. The ALI Code labels such offerings "local offerings" and does not confine them to a single state (§ 514). Section 514 of the ALI Code focuses solely on purchasers of securities rather than offerees. State lines under Section 514 no longer are necessarily controlling as the SEC is given authority, after evaluating economic characteristics and population, to define contiguous areas encompassing a number of states or a state and a contiguous foreign country. Moreover, Section 514 permits up to five percent of the securities in such an offering to be sold to no more than five percent of all purchasers who neither work nor reside in the localized area.

Prior to consultation with and determination by the SEC to support the ALI Code, Section 514 permitted up to twenty percent of the securities in a "local offering" to be sold to no more than five percent of "non-local" purchasers. In view of the provision's objective of facilitating local financing

---

[113] *Id*. See Thomforde, *supra* note 108, at 31-32.
[114] See Rule 147(f), 17 C.F.R. § 230.147(f).

for local business, the SEC believed that the percent of securities sold "non-locally" should be decreased. The change to five percent was subsequently made.

In 1980 the SEC announced its support for congressional enactment of the ALI Code, provided that revisions it sought and obtained from the ALI Reporter and his group of advisers were not significantly amended during the legislative process.[115] The ALI Code, however, has not been introduced in either the U.S. House of Representatives or the Senate and its prospects for enactment are dim.

§ 3.14   The Section 3(a)(9) and 3(a)(10) Exemptions

Section 3(a)(9) of the Securities Act exempts from the registration requirements certain bona fide recapitalizations, namely, "[a]ny security exchanged by the issuer with its existing security holders exclusively where no commission or other remuneration is paid or given directly or indirectly for soliciting such exchange." Section 3(a)(10) generally exempts from registration securities that are issued in exchange for bona fide legal claims, securities, or property interests when a court or other specified tribunal, after conducting an adversary proceeding on the transaction's fairness, grants such approval. Traditionally, the Section 3(a)(10) exemption has been invoked in three situations: (1) settlement of private lawsuits; (2) reorganization of insolvent business organizations outside of bankruptcy litigation; and (3) reorganization of solvent business organizations.[116]

While both the Section 3(a)(9) and 3(a)(10) exemptions reflect Congress' concern for the financially troubled enterprise that seeks internal readjustment without having to comply with the 1933 Act's costs of registration, an issuer may have a number of motives for utilizing these exemptions. Indeed, the financial status of an issuer does not affect the availability of these exemptions. For example, in practice the Section 3(a)(10) exemption "has been availed of almost exclusively by financially sound issuers involved in reorganization or other exchanges for a variety of legitimate ongoing business purposes."[117]

§ 3.15   Integration of Offerings

Under the concept of integration of offerings, what apparently may seem to be separate offerings instead are construed as one integrated offering. Because of the fairly distinct requirements for each exemption, otherwise

---

[115] See Securities Act Release No. 6242 (1980). See also, Morrissey, note 107 *supra*.

[116] See generally J.W. Hicks, *Exempted Transactions Under the Securities Act of 1933*, ¶ 3.02 (rev. ed. 1999); Glanzer, Schiffman & Packman, *Settlement of Securities Litigation Through the Issuance of Securities Without Registration: The Use of Section 3(a)(10) in SEC Enforcement Proceedings*, 50 Fordham L. Rev. 533 (1981); Mann, *The Section 3(a)(10) Exemption: Recent Interpretations*, 22 U.C.L.A. L. Rev. 1247 (1975).

[117] Ash, *Reorganizations and Other Exchanges Under Section 3(a)(10) of the Securities Act of 1933*, 75 Nw. U. L. Rev. 1, 10 (1980). See Hicks, *Recapitalization Under Section 3(a)(9) of the Securities Act of 1933*, 61 Va. L. Rev. 1057, 1060-61 (1975).

exempt offerings are unlikely to qualify for an exemption once they are integrated, thereby resulting in a violation of the Securities Act's registration requirements. Moreover, if a purported exempt offering is integrated with a registered offering, the exemption will be destroyed, again resulting in liability.

Rule 152 is an exception to the above general principle, providing that the Section 4(2) exemption is still available "although subsequently . . . the issuer decides to make a public offering and/or files a registration statement." The purpose of the rule is to permit "those who have contemplated or begun to undertake a private offering to register securities without incurring any risk of liability as a consequence of having first contemplated or begun to undertake a private offering."[118]

In determining whether offers and/or sales should be integrated, the SEC has set forth a five factor analysis:

(1)   Whether the offerings are part of a single plan of financing;

(2)   Whether the offerings involve issuance of the same class of securities;

(3)   Whether the offerings have been made at or about the same time;

(4)   Whether the same type of consideration is received; and

(5)   Whether the offerings are made for the same general purposes.[119]

The SEC and the courts continue to apply this analysis.[120]

In order to provide greater certainty for issuers, the SEC, pursuant to its rulemaking authority, has adopted integration "safe harbor" rules. For example, Rule 502(a) of Regulation D in part provides:

Offers and sales that are made more than six months before the start of a Regulation D offering or are made more than six months after completion of a Regulation D offering will not be considered part of that Regulation D offering, so long as during those six month periods there are no offers or sales of securities by or for the issuer that are of the same or a similar class as those offered or sold under Regulation D . . . .[121]

Rule 147(b)(2), as another example, has a similar "safe harbor" from integration with respect to the intrastate offering exemption.

Remember that Rules 147(b)(2) and 502(a) are "safe harbor" provisions. If the issuer engages in offers or sales during the six-month period prior

---

[118] Securities Act Release No. 305 (1935). See *In re JAI*, Inc., [1990 Transfer Binder] Fed. Sec. L. Rep. (CCH) ¶ 79,505 (SEC No-Action Letter 1990) (applying Rule 152, SEC staff states that the making of a registered offering after an otherwise exempt private offering under Section 4(2) would not nullify the Section 4(2) exemption); Johnson & Patterson, *The Reincarnation of Rule 152: False Hope on the Integration Front*, 46 Wash. & Lee L. Rev. 539 (1989); Securities Act Release No. 4761 (1965).

[119] Securities Act Release No. 4552 (1962).

[120] See, e.g., *SEC v. Murphy*, 626 F.2d 633 (9th Cir. 1980).

[121] See also discussion of integration of offerings with respect to Rule 701 in § 3.09[B][3] *supra*.

to commencement or after completion of the purportedly exempt offerings, the five factor analysis outlined above will be applied to determine whether the apparently separate offerings should be integrated.[122]

As a final point, the principle of *integration* of offerings must be distinguished from that of *aggregation* of offering price used for purposes of the Section 3(b) exemptions. The following example provided by the SEC serves aptly to distinguish the two concepts:

> The Commission is aware that in computing the aggregate offering price [for offerings made pursuant to the Section 3(b) exemptions] issuers frequently misunderstand the interaction of the concepts of aggregation and integration as applicable under Rules 504(b)(2)(i) and 505(b)(2)(i). Aggregation is the principle by which an issuer determines the dollar worth of exempt sales available directly under Section 3(b) of the Securities Act. Integration is a principle under which an issuer determines overall characteristics of its offering. The following examples illustrate the application of these concepts. An issuer that has conducted an offering under Rule 505 in May [1994] must aggregate the proceeds from that offering with the proceeds of a Rule 505 offering conducted in December [1994]. [On the other hand,] if the May offering had been under Rule 506 [which is a "safe harbor" to the § 4(2) exemption], it would not need to be aggregated with the December offering. In either case, the May offering should be exempt from principles of integration by virtue of the safe harbor provision in Rule 502(a). If a Rule 506 offering had been conducted in July [1994], the integration safe harbor would not be available as to a subsequent Rule 505 offering in December. Although the proceeds from the July [Rule] 506 offering would not be added to the December [Rule] 505 aggregate offering price under aggregation principles, they would have to be included if the two offerings [were] integrated. Assuming the two offerings were integrated, then the issuer would have to evaluate all characteristics of the combined transactions, e.g., number of investors, aggregate offering price, etc., when determining the availability of an exemption.[123]

§ 3.16   State "Blue Sky" Law Exemptions

With certain exceptions and subject to the preemptive provisions of the National Securities Markets Improvement Act of 1996, unless an exemption from state registration is perfected, any offer or sale within a particular state must be registered. The result is that perfecting a federal exemption from registration frequently is only half the battle. Exemptions often must be found on the state level in any state where the security is offered or sold.

---

[122] See generally, Bradford, *Regulation A and the Integration Doctrine: The New Safe Harbor*, 55 Ohio St. L.J. 255 (1994); Deaktor, *Integration of Offerings*, 31 U. Fla. L. Rev. 465 (1979); Morrissey, *Integration of Securities Offerings — The ABA's "Indiscrete" Proposal*, 26 Ariz. L. Rev. 41 (1984); Shapiro & Sachs, *Integration Under the Securities Act: Once an Exemption, Not Always . . .* , 31 Md. L. Rev. 3 (1971); Wallace, *Integration of Securities Offerings: Obstacles to Capital Formation Remain for Small Businesses*, 45 Wash. & Lee L. Rev. 883 (1988).

[123] Securities Act Release No. 6389 (1982). For further discussion, see §§ 3.05-3.10 *supra*.

Until recently, there was little uniformity between the federal and state exemption framework. The promulgation of the Uniform Limited Offering Exemption (ULOE) by the North American Securities Administrators Association (NASAA) and its subsequent adoption (in whole or substantial part) by several states eased this uniformity problem. With qualifications, the Uniform Limited Offering Exemption exempts offerings sold in compliance with Rules 501-503 and 505 of SEC Regulation D.[124] In certain respects, however, the NASAA Exemption is more protective of investor interests than Regulation D. For example, investor sophistication or suitability standards may apply in Rule 505 offerings (unlike the SEC's 505).

After the adoption of Regulation D and ULOE, additional criticisms were voiced. Two of the more significant points concerned the unnecessarily technical requirement that the Form D be filed with the applicable agency as a condition of the exemption and the desirability for the adoption of a "substantial compliance" standard so that minor and inadvertent mistakes would not cause the exemption to be lost. The Commission's release proposing the foregoing changes was viewed by a number of state administrators as overly broad. For example, the Maryland Securities Division registered its strong opposition to the SEC proposals. In addition to viewing the Form D filing requirement as critical to its investigatory efforts, Maryland perceived that the availability to issuers and related parties of a "good faith and reasonable defense" would be unduly burdensome to its overall enforcement program.[125]

Due to the input by NASAA and the individual states, the Regulation D and ULOE changes were more modest than otherwise would have occurred. Pursuant to SEC Rule 507, the timely filing of the Form D is no longer a condition for perfecting a Regulation D exemption. The issuer nonetheless is required to file a Form D, and if such issuer is enjoined for failing to file the Form D, the failure to do so acts as a disqualification for such issuer to use a Regulation D exemption in the future. In its discretion, the SEC may waive any such disqualification upon a showing of good cause.

A substantial compliance standard was added to both Regulation D and ULOE. The standard's reach, however, is far less encompassing than proponents had advocated. As stated by the Commission in the 1989 adopting release:

> Rule 508 [of Regulation D] provides that an exemption from the registration requirements will be available for an offer or sale to a particular individual or entity, despite failure to comply with a requirement of Regulation D, if the requirement is not designed to protect

---

[124] Securities Act Release No. 6389 (1982). Rule 504, discussed in § 3.09[B][1] *supra*, leaves solely to the individual states the authority to prescribe disclosure of specified information and certain other requirements with respect to offerings made within the parameters of that exemption. State regulation of offerings under Rule 506 generally is preempted by the 1996 federal legislation.

[125] Letter from Ellyn L. Brown, Esq., Maryland Securities Commissioner to the SEC (May 12, 1988).

specifically the complaining person; the failure to comply is insignificant to the offering as a whole; and there has been a good faith and reasonable attempt to comply with all requirements of the regulation. Rule 508 specifies that the provisions of Regulation D relating to general solicitation, the dollar limits of Rules 504 and 505 and the limits on non-accredited investors in Rules 505 and 506 are deemed significant to every offering and therefore not subject to the Rule 508 defense.[126]

Nonetheless, both Rule 508 and the ULOE counterpart provide that such "inadvertent" failures to comply are subject to enforcement actions by the SEC and the respective states.[127]

Critics assert that, as adopted, the substantial compliance defense leaves unsettled far too many questions and subjects issuers and their associates to a continuing saga of astronomical liability exposure. When merely technical rather than fraud violations are at issue, one may contend that public policy should call for greater flexibility in the enforcement regimen, particularly given our country's need to foster capital-raising activities. Moreover, the failure to include matters relating to general solicitation within the substantial compliance defense without clearly delineating what constitutes such conduct plays havoc upon all those associated with the raising of capital in the private markets.[128]

The above points, although meritorious, did not sway a number of the state administrators who viewed their primary mission as safeguarding the interests of unsophisticated investors in their respective jurisdictions. Faced with this situation, the SEC elected to coordinate the Regulation D changes with NASAA, presumably due to the Commission's perception that the states' acquiescence was necessary to make the exemption process function in an efficient manner.[129]

The attitude of certain states in favor of strong investor protection provisions is intriguing when compared to the "race to the bottom" approach[130] taken by some of these very same states under the applicable corporation laws. Perhaps one response is that the state securities laws are

---

[126] Securities Act Release No. 6825 (1989).

[127] Rule 508(b) of Regulation D; Uniform Limited Offering Exemption, 33 NASAA Rep. (CCH) ¶ 6201, at 6104 (1989).

[128] See Cohn, *Securities Markets for Small Issuers: The Barriers of Federal Solicitation and Advertising Prohibitions*, 38 U. Fla. L. Rev. 1 (1986); Daugherty, *Rethinking the Ban on General Solicitation*, 38 Emory L.J. 69 (1989); Martin & Parsons, *The Preexisting Relationship Doctrine Under Regulation D: A Rule Without Reason?*, 45 Wash. & Lee L. Rev. 1031 (1988); Sargent, *The New Regulation D: Deregulation, Federalism and the Dynamics of Regulatory Reform*, 68 Wash. U. L.Q. 225 (1990).

[129] See generally Maynard, *The Uniform Limited Offering Exemption: How "Uniform" is "Uniform?" — An Evaluation and Critique of the ULOE*, 36 Emory L.J. 357 (1987); Rossi, *The Uniform Limited Offering Exemption*, 16 Rev. Sec. Reg. 875 (1983); Sargent, *State Limited and Private Offering Exemptions: The Maryland Experience in a National Perspective*, 13 U. Balt. L. Rev. 496 (1984); Sargent, *Blue Sky Law: The SCOR Solution*, 18 Sec. Reg. L.J. 93 (1990); sources cited in note 128 *supra*.

[130] See, e.g., Cary, *Federalism and Corporate Law: Reflection upon Delaware*, 83 Yale L.J. 663 (1974).

designed in part to protect the individual investor against so-called speculative shady promoters while enabling corporation laws favoring management
hopefully will induce publicly-held companies to incorporate within the
respective states, thereby bringing in a welcome source of revenues in the
form of franchise fees.

This supposed state-SEC accommodation did not entirely persuade the
U.S. Congress. In an effort to reduce overlapping regulation and simplify
the regulatory framework, Congress enacted the National Securities Markets Improvement Act of 1996. This reallocation of regulatory authority,
including the preemption of state regulation of certain exempt offerings,
and in particular Rule 506 offerings, represents a major change in the
federal-state relationship in the securities law setting.[131] In addition to
preempting Rule 506 offerings, the 1996 federal legislation defines the following as "covered" securities, thereby providing the SEC with exclusive
authority over the registration of such securities:

(1) securities issued by investment companies registered with the Commission under the Investment Company Act of 1940 (Investment Company Act); (2) securities offered or sold to "qualified purchasers," as that
term will be defined by Commission rule; (3) all securities that are listed
or authorized for listing on the New York Stock Exchange (NYSE), the
American Stock Exchange (AMEX), or quoted on the Nasdaq National
Market System (NMS), or listed or authorized for listing on any other
national securities exchange that the Commission finds has listing
standards that are "substantially similar" to these exchanges or Nasdaq,
including securities of an issuer that rank senior to listed securities, and
(4) securities issued in connection with certain specified transactions that
are exempt under the Securities Act.[132]

§ 3.17 Extraterritorial Application — Regulation S

Although not an exemption from Securities Act registration, adherence
to the provisions of Regulation S signifies that the registration mandates
of Section 5 are not applicable. Regulation S represents an attempt by the
SEC to clarify the extraterritorial application of the 1933 Act's registration

---

[131] See Bagnell & Cannon, *The National Securities Markets Improvement Act of 1996: Summary and Discussion*, 25 Sec. Reg. L.J. 3 (1997).

[132] *Id.* at 5-6. See Campbell, *The Impact of NSMIA on Small Issuers*, 53 Bus. Law. 575
(1998); Friedman, *The Impact of NSMIA on State Regulation of Broker-Dealers and Investment
Advisers*, 53 Bus. Law. 511 (1998); Miller & O'Brien, *The National Securities Markets
Improvement Act of 1996*, 30 Rev. Sec. & Comm. Reg. 23 (1997); Sargent, *The National
Securities Improvement Act — One Year Later*, 53 Bus. Law. 507 (1998); Sargent, *Blue Sky
Mysteries of the National Securities Markets Improvement Act*, 25 Sec. Reg. L.J. 91 (1997).

Pursuant to the 1996 legislation, the SEC has authority to preempt state regulation with
respect to offerings made to "qualified purchasers" who, due to their wealth and sophistication,
are deemed not to need state registration. See § 18(b)(3) of the Securities Act. By invocation
of this authority, the SEC could define the term "qualified purchaser" in such a manner so
as to preempt state regulation of Rule 505 and Regulation A offerings. The Commission has
not done so, and it appears unlikely that it will. See Campbell, *Blue Sky Laws and the Recent
Congressional Preemption Failure*, 22 J. Corp. L. 175 (1997).

requirements.[133] This effort seeks to ease undue regulatory burdens on issuers and those seeking to resell, thereby fostering a more efficient international securities market.[134]

In Regulation S, the SEC embraced a territorial approach to the extraterritorial application of registration under the Securities Act. This approach is based on the notion that the registration requirements of the Securities Act are intended to protect the U.S. capital markets and all investors in such markets, whether U.S. residents or foreign nationals. Regulation S represents a change in emphasis, from attempting to protect U.S. persons irrespective of where they are located, to protecting the integrity of the U.S. capital markets. For registration purposes, the Commission decided to rely upon the laws in the jurisdictions in which the transactions occur rather than the U.S. Securities Act. The Commission stated: "The territorial approach recognizes the primacy of the laws in which a market is located. As investors choose their markets, they choose the laws and regulations applicable in such markets." Adherence to this approach is premised on the principles of comity and the expectations of participants in the global markets. The territorial approach thus forms the basis of the Regulation S regulatory framework.[135]

It bears emphasis that Regulation S is directed at Securities Act registration. The extraterritorial application of the U.S. securities laws have a broader reach with respect to the antifraud provisions, such as Section 10(b) of the Exchange Act.[136]

Regulation S comprises four rules: Rule 901, 902, 903, and 904. Rule 901 contains a general statement that reflects the SEC's new territorial approach. Rule 901(a) states that only offers and sales of securities inside the United States are subject to Section 5. This statement reflects a shift from previous SEC policy (namely, that Section 5 was to protect all U.S. citizens no matter where such persons lived or invested) to a basically geographical approach under Regulation S.[137]

The primary inquiry under the new regulatory scheme, as stated in Rule 901, is whether the offer and sale of securities occurs "outside the United States." If the offer and sale are outside the United States within the

---

[133] See Securities Act Release No. 6863 (1990). The adoption of Regulation S superseded Securities Act Release No. 4708 (1964) and the interpretive and no-action letters relating thereto.

[134] See Wolff, *Offshore Distributions Under the Securities Act of 1933: An Analysis of Regulation S*, 23 L. & Pol'y Int'l Bus. 101 (1991-1992).

[135] See Securities Act Release No. 6863 (1990); Thalacker, *Reproposed Regulation S*, 683 PLI/Corp. 799 (1990).

[136] For case law, see, e.g., *Consolidated Gold Fields PLC v. Minorco, S.A.*, 871 F.2d 252 (2d Cir. 1989); *Zoelsch v. Arthur Andersen & Co.*, 824 F.2d 27 (D.C. Cir. 1987); *Bersch v. Drexel Firestone, Inc.*, 519 F.2d 974 (2d Cir. 1975). As the Second Circuit stated in *Consolidated Gold Fields*, "the antifraud provisions of American securities laws have broader extraterritorial reach than American filing requirements." 871 F.2d at 262. Note, moreover, that the state blue sky laws remain applicable. *Id.* For further discussion, see § 7.13 *infra*.

[137] See Securities Act Release No. 6863 (1990), *superseding*, Securities Act Release No. 4708 (1964); note 133 *supra*.

meaning of Rule 901, the registration provisions of Section 5 are not applicable; if the offer or sale occurs within the United States, the registration provisions (absent the perfection of an exemption) are applicable. However, determining whether an offer and sale have occurred outside the United States is not necessarily an easy matter to resolve.

The SEC provides that whether an offer and sale are made outside the United States is to be determined on an ad hoc basis. To clarify when an offer and sale will be considered outside the United States, Regulation S provides two nonexclusive safe harbor provisions in Rules 903 and 904. If the offer and sale satisfy the conditions of either of the safe harbor provisions, such transaction will be deemed to have occurred outside the United States and outside the reach of Section 5. Hence, perfecting a safe harbor provides assurance that the registration provisions of the Securities Act will not apply.

Regulation S comprises two safe harbor provisions: (1) an issuer safe harbor (Rule 903) and (2) a safe harbor for resales (Rule 904). All offers and sales, whether made in reliance on the issuer or the resale safe harbor, must satisfy two general conditions. In addition, the issuer must satisfy specific conditions that are set out in each safe harbor provision.[138]

[A]   General Conditions

The general conditions applicable to all offers and sales, whether based on the issuer or resale safe harbor, are that: (1) the offer or sale is made in an "offshore transaction;"[139] and (2) there are no "direct selling efforts"[140] in the United States in connection with the distribution or resale of the securities.[141] To engage in an "offshore transaction" there can be no offer or sale to a person in the United States[142] and either of two additional requirements must be satisfied.[143] The first of the alternative requirements is that the buyer is outside the United States, or the seller reasonably believes that the buyer is outside of the United States, at the time the buy order is originated.[144] If an employee of an entity formed under the laws of the United States places the buy order while abroad, the requirement

---

[138] See Securities Act Release No. 6863 (1990).

[139] Rule 902(i).

[140] Rule 902(b).

[141] Rule 903(a), (b). See McLaughlin, *"Directed Selling Efforts" Under Regulation S and the U.S. Securities Analyst*, 24 Rev. Sec. & Comm. Reg. 117 (1991). These two conditions are herein referred to as "general conditions."

[142] Reversing the approach in Securities Act Release No. 4708, Regulation S defines "U.S. Person" as "any natural person resident in the United States," rather than a U.S. citizen regardless of location. Rule 902(o)(1)(i). Therefore, selling to a U.S. citizen living abroad will not automatically prevent the transaction from being considered an offshore transaction. However, Rule 902(i) makes clear that offers and sales specifically targeted at identifiable groups of U.S. citizens abroad, such as members of the armed forces, will not be offshore transactions. Rule 902(i)(2). The phrase "offshore transaction" is defined in Rule 902(i). *Id.*

[143] Rule 902(i)(1)(ii)(A).

[144] *Id.*

that the buyer be outside the United States is satisfied.[145] The second alternative means of satisfying the "offshore transaction" requirement is to execute the transaction on a designated offshore securities market.[146] However, if the seller or its agent knows that the transaction has been pre-arranged with a buyer in the United States, the second alternative will not be satisfied.[147]

The second general condition that must be satisfied in order for an offer and sale to be considered "outside the United States" is that there be no "direct selling efforts" in the United States. For purposes of the issuer safe harbor, neither the issuer, distributors, nor their respective affiliates may engage in direct selling efforts in the United States. Failure to adhere to this condition will result in loss of the safe harbor for all participants in the offering.[148]

"Directed selling efforts" are defined as any activity that could reasonably be expected to have the effect of conditioning the market in the United States for any of the securities being offered in reliance on Regulation S.[149] Specifically, placing advertisements with television or radio stations reaching the United States or in publications with a general circulation[150] in the United States, mailing printed material to U.S. investors, or conducting promotional seminars in the United States are considered "direct selling efforts."[151] Rule 902(b), however, excludes certain types of advertising from the definition of "direct selling efforts." These exceptions include advertisements that are required under either U.S. or foreign law and "tombstone" advertisements[152] that are placed in publications that have less than twenty percent of their total circulation in the United States. Additionally, sellers are permitted to visit and inspect real estate and other facilities located in the United States without engaging in "direct selling efforts."[153]

[B] Issuer Safe Harbor — Rule 903

The "issuer" safe harbor is applicable not only to the actual issuer but also to the issuer's distributors, their respective affiliates, and persons acting on behalf of the foregoing.[154] The safe harbor may be utilized by both

---

[145] Securities Act Release No. 6863 (1990). This holds true when the buyer is an investment company or its investment advisor. *Id.*

[146] Rule 902(a) specifically identifies the markets that the SEC considers to be "designated offshore securities markets." See Rule 902(a).

[147] Rule 902(i)(1)(B)(2).

[148] Rule 903(b).

[149] Rule 902(b).

[150] A definition of publications with a general circulation in the United States is provided in Rule 902(c)(2).

[151] Rule 902(b).

[152] In order to qualify as a "tombstone" ad that will not be considered conditioning the U.S. market for a foreign offering, the ad must meet the specific requirements set forth in Rule 902(b)(iii).

[153] Rule 902(b).

[154] Rule 903. Therefore, references to the term "issuer" hereinafter will refer to the issuer, its distributors, any respective affiliates, or any person acting on behalf of the issuer, distributors, or affiliates.

U.S. and foreign issuers offering securities outside the United States. Similar to the previous SEC policy, the conditions that must be satisfied to meet the issuer safe harbor differ depending on the type of securities being offered. For purposes of Regulation S, the SEC separates securities into three categories: Category I, Category II and Category III. The categorization of securities is based on the likelihood that the securities will flow back to the United States. As the probability that the securities will flow back to the United States increases, the procedural requirements necessary to avoid registration become more difficult. Under the Regulation S regulatory scheme, Category I securities are subject to the least regulatory restraints and Category III securities are subject to the most.[155]

Category I securities are securities of "foreign issuers"[156] for which there is no "substantial U.S. market interest,"[157] securities offered and sold in "overseas directed offerings,"[158] securities that are backed by the full faith and credit of a "foreign government,"[159] and securities sold pursuant to certain employee benefit plans.[160] Because the SEC concluded that these

---

[155] See SEC Release No. 6863, (1990). See Cogan & Kimbrough, *Regulation S Safe Harbors for Offshore Offers, Sales and Resales*, 4 Insights No. 8, at 3 (1990).

[156] The definition of "foreign issuer" is contained in Rule 902(f). Basically, a foreign issuer may be a foreign government, a national of any foreign government, or a corporation or other entity formed under the laws of a foreign country.

[157] Whether a "substantial U.S. market interest" exists depends on the type of security being offered. Generally, if the foreign issuer is offering equity securities, a substantial U.S. market interest is deemed to exist at the commencement of the offering if: (1) the securities exchanges and inter-dealer quotation systems in the United States in the aggregate constitute the single largest market for such securities; or (2) twenty percent or more of the trading of the class of securities took place on a securities exchange or inter-dealer quotation system located in the United States and less than fifty-five percent of such trading took place in a foreign securities market. Rule 902(n).

A substantial U.S. market interest in a foreign issuer's debt securities is deemed to exist upon commencement of the offering if: (1) 300 or more U.S. persons are the aggregate record holders of the issuer's debt securities, its non-participating preferred stock and its asset-backed securities; (2) U.S. persons hold $1 billion or more of the outstanding indebtedness of the foreign issuer; or (3) U.S. persons hold twenty percent or more of the outstanding debt securities of the foreign issuer. Rule 902(n)(2).

Definitions for U.S. market interest in warrants, non-participating preferred stock, and asset-backed securities are provided in Rule 903. The other members in the issuer's chain of distribution, such as the underwriter and its affiliates, may rely on the written representation of the issuer that it has a reasonable belief that there is no substantial U.S. market interest in its securities. See SEC Release No. 6863 (1990).

[158] Two types of offerings can qualify as "overseas directed offerings." See Rule 902(j). One is an offering of a foreign issuer's securities directed to residents of a single country other than the United States. The other is an offering of non-participating preferred stock, nonconvertible debt securities, and asset-backed securities of a domestic (U.S.) issuer directed to a single foreign country. Under this latter type of offering, the principal and interest of the securities must be denominated in non-U.S. currency. *Id.* When any participant in the issuer's syndicate knows or is reckless in not knowing that a substantial portion of the offering will be sold or resold outside that country, the offering will not qualify as an overseas directed offering. See Rule 904(c).

[159] "Foreign government" is defined as "the government of any foreign country . . . provided that such person would qualify to register securities under the Securities Act on Schedule B." Rule 902(e).

[160] Rule 903(c). An offering made to employees of either a domestic or foreign issuer

securities were the least likely to flow back to the United States, it put only minimal procedural requirements upon them.[161] Accordingly, to satisfy the issuer safe harbor, an issuer of Category I securities need only satisfy the general conditions described above: (1) an "offshore transaction;" and (2) no "direct selling efforts" in the United States. Under the Category I issuer safe harbor, sales to U.S. investors overseas are permissible.[162] Nonetheless, participants should be cognizant of preliminary note 2 to Regulation S, which excludes from the regulation's protection any plan or scheme to evade the registration provisions of the Securities Act.[163] In sum, prior to the promulgation of Regulation S, the applicability of the federal securities laws to offerings falling under Category I was unclear. Today, Regulation S clarifies the reach of the Securities Act's registration requirements in this context and sets forth relatively minimal regulatory burdens with respect to such offerings.

Offerings falling within the second issuer safe harbor, Category II, are those by foreign and U.S. companies that are subject to the Exchange Act's reporting requirements as well as offerings of debt securities by non-reporting foreign issuers.[164] To qualify for the Category II issuer safe harbor, the issuer must satisfy not only the general conditions but must also comply with certain selling restrictions.[165]

There are two types of selling restrictions applicable to offerings of securities falling within Category II: (1) "transactional restrictions" and (2) "offering restrictions." The transactional restrictions prohibit offers and sales of such securities in the United States or to a "U.S. person"[166] during a restricted period lasting forty days.[167] Additionally, a distributor selling the securities prior to the end of the restricted period to certain securities professionals (such as dealers) is required to send a "confirmation or other notice"[168] to such professionals advising them that they are subject to the

---

pursuant to a qualified employee benefit plan may be made under Category I as long as certain conditions are met. The specific conditions set forth in Rule 903(c) are similar to those contained in no-action letters relating to Release 4708. See SEC Release No. 6863.

[161] Securities Act Release No. 6863 (1990).

[162] See Rule 903.

[163] See Preliminary Note 2 to Regulation S.

[164] Rule 903(2). This category also includes foreign issuers offering nonparticipating preferred stock and asset-backed securities. *Id.*

[165] The SEC placed these selling restrictions on Category II securities offerings due to the Commission's belief that Category II securities are more likely to flow back to the United States than are the securities included in Category I. See SEC Release No. 6863 (1990).

[166] Rule 903(c)(2). A "U.S. person" as defined in Rule 902(o) focuses not on U.S. citizenship, but on U.S. residency. SEC Release No. 6863 (1990). Therefore, U.S. investors, distributors and the like residing overseas may engage in their respective activities without the issuer losing the Regulation S safe harbor protection. *Id.*

[167] Rule 903(c)(2)(iv). The forty day restricted period begins to run on the later of the date of the offering's closing or the date the first offer of securities is made to persons other than distributors. See Rule 902(m).

[168] "Confirmation or other notice," as used in Rule 903(c)(2)(iv), allows various types of notice to fulfill the distributors' notice requirement. See SEC Release No. 6863 (1990). This confirmation includes notice given over the telephone or computer generated notice given on a screen, provided the seller keeps written records that notice was provided. *Id.*

same restrictions on offers and sales that are applicable to the distributor.[169]

In addition, the issuer and its entire distribution syndicate must adhere
to certain "offering restrictions" (which basically are procedures) to meet
the Category II and Category III issuer safe harbors.[170] These offering
restrictions are procedures that impact the entire offering process and that
seek to ensure compliance with the conditions imposed.[171] Generally, as
currently formulated, the procedures require that all distributors[172] agree
in writing that all offers and sales during the applicable restricted period
be made only in accordance with a Regulation S safe harbor or pursuant
to registration under the Securities Act or an exemption therefrom.[173] Furthermore, the issuer, distributors, and their respective affiliates must
include statements in all offering materials that the securities have not
been registered under the Securities Act and may not be offered or sold
in the United States or to U.S. persons unless the securities are registered
or an exemption from registration is perfected.[174]

The final safe harbor category, Category III, applies to all securities not
within Categories I or II. This category includes offerings of non-reporting
U.S. issuers and equity securities of non-reporting foreign issuers when
there is a substantial U.S. market interest in such securities. The SEC
imposes the most rigorous restrictions on offerings falling within this
category due to the Commission's position that these securities have the
highest probability of flowing back to the United States.[175]

As is the case in the first two categories of securities, the general
conditions that the offer and sale be made in an "offshore transaction" and
that there be no "direct selling efforts" in the United States or to a U.S.
person are applicable to Category III securities. Moreover, the offering restrictions applicable to Category II offerings discussed above also are
applicable to offerings under Category III. However, the transactional
restrictions applicable to Category III offerings are more demanding than
those required under Category II.[176]

The transactional restrictions applicable to Category III offerings are
similar to the restrictions existing (under SEC Securities Act Release No.
4708) prior to the promulgation of Regulation S. Due to the Commission's

---

[169] Rule 903(c)(2)(iv).

[170] Securities Act Release No.6863 (1990).

[171] *Id.*

[172] "Distributor" is defined as "any underwriter, dealer, or other person who participates,
pursuant to a contractual arrangement, in the distribution of the securities . . . ." Rule 902(c).

[173] Rule 902(h)(1).

[174] Rule 902(h)(2). The statements of the restrictions must be made on the cover or inside
cover page of any prospectus or offering circular, in the underwriting section of any prospectus
or offering circular, and in all advertisements of the offering. Rule 902(h)(2)(i)(ii) & (iii).

[175] Securities Act Release No. 6863 (1990). See Bai, *U.S. Registration Requirements for
Multi-National Offerings*, (pts. 1 & 2), 25 Rev. Sec. & Comm. Reg. 131, 144 (1992), 25 Rev.
Sec. & Comm. Reg. 151, 157 (1992).

[176] Securities Act Release No. 6863 (1990).

belief that debt offerings of Category III securities are less likely to flow back to the United States, the SEC imposes less stringent transactional restrictions upon them than it does upon equity securities.[177]

Debt securities offered pursuant to Category III are subject to a forty day restricted period.[178] During this period the securities may not be sold to U.S. persons or for the account (or benefit) of U.S. persons.[179] The debt securities must be represented by a temporary global security that is not exchangeable for definitive securities until the forty day restricted period has expired. When the global security is exchanged for the definitive security, certification must be effected that a non-U.S. person owns the security or that a U.S. person purchased securities in a transaction that was exempt from the registration requirements of the Securities Act.[180] If a distributor or other person receiving a selling concession sells prior to the expiration of the forty day restricted period, it must send a "confirmation or other notice" to the purchaser stating that the purchaser is subject to the same restrictions on offers and sales that apply to the distributor.[181]

The transactional restrictions applicable to equity offerings under the third issuer safe harbor — Category III — are even more demanding than the restrictions applicable to debt securities in the same category. Rule 903(c)(3)(iii) prohibits equity securities offered under Category III from being sold to a U.S. person or for the account (or benefit) of a U.S. person for a period of one year.[182] Furthermore, the purchaser of the security must certify that it is not a U.S. person and is not acquiring the securities for the account (or benefit) of any U.S. person.[183] In addition, the purchaser must agree to resell only if it adheres to one of three conditions, namely, that such resale is made in accordance with Regulation S, pursuant to a registration statement, or under an exemption from registration.[184] If a U.S. issuer is utilizing the Category III safe harbor, it must place a legend on the securities offered stating that all transfers are prohibited except as set forth above.[185] Finally, the issuer is required, either by contract or pursuant to a provision in its bylaws, articles or charter, to refuse to register any transfer not in accordance with the foregoing.[186]

[C] Resale Safe Harbor

The resale safe harbor generally is available only to security holders who are not issuers, affiliates of an issuer, distributors, or affiliates of a

---

[177] Id.

[178] Rule 903(c)(3)(ii)(A).

[179] See Rule 902(m).

[180] Rule 903(c)(3)(i)(B).

[181] Rule 903(c)(iv). Nondistributors are not required to provide such notice. See Securities Act Release No. 6863 (1990).

[182] Rule 903(c)(3)(iii)(A).

[183] Rule 903(c)(3)(iii)(B)(1).

[184] Rule 903(c)(3)(iii)(B)(1).

[185] Rule 903(c)(3)(ii)(B)(3).

[186] Rule 903(c)(3)(iii)(B)(4).

distributor. Nonetheless, under certain circumstances, officers and directors of an issuer and securities professionals may use the resale safe harbor.[187] By satisfying all conditions of the resale safe harbor, the registration requirements of the Securities Act can be avoided.[188] In general, other than securities professionals[189] and officers and directors of an issuer, persons may sell in reliance on the resale safe harbor simply by satisfying the general conditions applicable to Regulation S transactions — (1) a resale in an offshore transaction, and (2) without direct selling efforts in the United States.[190]

An officer or director may rely on the resale safe harbor if, in addition to meeting the general requirements, the officer or director is an affiliate solely by virtue of his or her position and there is paid no special selling compensation in the resale transaction.[191] With respect to securities professionals, they may not knowingly offer or sell securities to U.S. persons during the applicable restricted period.[192] If the securities professional is selling to another securities professional, a trade confirmation or other notice must be sent to such purchaser reciting the applicable restrictions.[193]

[D] The 1998 Regulation S Amendments

In 1998, the SEC adopted amendments to Regulation S. The amendments reflect the Commission's concern with certain abusive and problematic practices in connection with offers, sales, and resales of securities made in offshore transactions purportedly pursuant to Regulation S.[194] The 1998 Regulation S amendments accordingly focus on market participants who

---

[187] Without this exception, officers and directors would be considered affiliates and therefore would be unable to utilize the resale safe harbor.

[188] See Rule 904.

[189] Persons who are considered securities professionals include: "dealers and persons receiving a selling concession, fee or other remuneration in respect of the securities offered or sold, which may include subunderwriters." Securities Act Release No. 6863 (1990).

[190] Rule 904(a), (b).

[191] Rule 904(c)(2).

[192] Rule 904(c)(1).

[193] Rule 904(c)(1)(ii). The applicable restrictions are that the securities may be offered and sold during the restricted period only in accordance with the provisions of Regulation S, if the securities are registered, or pursuant to an available exemption from the registration requirement. *Id.* For discussion on Rule 144A, see § 5.07 *infra*. See generally Berger, *Offshore Distributions of Securities: The Impact of Regulation S*, 3 Transn'l Law. 578 (1990); Bloomenthal, *Distributions Outside the U.S. — Regulation S*, 10 Sec. & Fed. Corp. L. Rep. 161 (1988); Bradley, *Regulation S: Tempest in a Safe Harbor*, 25 Rev. Sec. & Comm. Reg. 185 (1992); Karmel, *SEC Regulation of Multijurisdictional Offerings*, 16 Brook. J. Int'l L. 3 (1990); Longstreth, *Global Securities Markets and the SEC*, 10 U. Pa. J. Int'l Bus. L. 183 (1988); Steinberg & Lansdale, *Regulation S and Rule 144A: Creating A Workable Fiction in an Expanding Global Securities Market*, 29 Int'l Law. 43 (1995); Thalacker, note 135 *supra*; Wolff, note 134 *supra*.

[194] See Securities Act Release No. 7505, [1997-1998 Transfer Binder] Fed. Sec. L. Rep. (CCH) ¶ 86,006 (SEC 1998). See Barron, *The SEC Acts to Slam the Door on Regulation S Abuses*, 26 Sec. Reg. L.J. 211 (1998); Lewis, *Offers Under Regulation S: How Safe is the Harbor?*, 30 Rev. Sec. & Comm. Reg. 205 (1997).

purport to conduct legitimate offshore Regulation S placements but actually place the securities offshore in an effort to evade registration requirements.[195] The amendments seek to impede abusive practices in connection with placements of equity securities by U.S. issuers,[196] while "promot[ing] capital formation and efficient, competitive markets."[197] Hence, the amendments "should prevent further abuses . . . but also allow continuous reliance on Regulation S in legitimate offshore offerings."[198]

Thus, the 1998 Regulation S amendments:

1.   Classify the equity securities of all U.S. issuers (both reporting and nonreporting companies) placed offshore under Regulation S as "restricted securities" within the meaning of Rule 144;[199]

2.   Align the Regulation S restricted period for these equity securities issued by all U.S. enterprises with the Rule 144 holding periods by lengthening from 40 days to one year the period during which persons relying on the Regulation S safe harbor may not sell these securities to U.S. persons, unless pursuant to registration or an exemption therefrom (termed the "distribution compliance period");[200]

3.   Impose certification, legending, stop transfer, and other requirements for sales of equity securities by all U.S. (reporting and nonreporting) issuers;[201]

4.   Require purchasers of these equity securities sold by U.S. issuers to agree not to engage in hedging transactions with regard to such securities unless such transactions are in compliance with the Securities Act;[202]

5.   Unless certain conditions are satisfied, prohibit the use of promissory notes as payment for these equity securities;[203] and

---

[195] Securities Act Release No. 7505, [1997-1998 Transfer Binder] Fed. Sec. L. Rep. (CCH) ¶ 86,006 (SEC 1998). See the SEC's release proposing amendments to Regulation S, Securities Act Release No. 7392, [1997 Transfer Binder] Fed. Sec. L. Rep. (CCH) ¶ 85,909 (SEC 1997).

[196] See Securities Act Release No. 7505, [1997-1998 Transfer Binder] Fed. Sec. L. Rep. (CCH) ¶ 86,006 (SEC 1998). Note that the Commission declined to address potentially abusive practices in Regulation S equity offerings of foreign issuers.

[197] Securities Act Release No. 7392, [1997 Transfer Binder] Fed. Sec. L. Rep. (CCH) ¶ 85,909, at 89,292 (SEC 1997).

[198] See SEC Release No. 7505, *supra* note 194, at 80,157. These abuses occurred especially with respect to "the securities of thinly capitalized or microcap companies. These types of securities are particularly vulnerable to fraud and manipulation because little information about them is available to investors." *Id.*

[199] See Rules 903, 905 of Regulation S, 17 C.F.R. §§ 230.903, 230.905.

[200] *Id.* See Rule 144(a)(3), 17 C.F.R. § 230.144(a)(3) (defining "restricted securities to include equity securities of all domestic issuers acquired in a transaction or chain of transactions subject to the conditions of . . . Regulation S"). See also, notes 193-194 *supra.*

[201] Rule 903(b)(3)(iii)(B) of Regulation S, 17 C.F.R. § 230.903(b)(3)(iii)(B). See SEC Release No. 7505, *supra* note 196, at 80,162.

[202] *Id.*

[203] SEC Release No. 7505, *supra* note 196, at 80,164.

the *Howey* investment contract test. Whether or not a partnership interest is "limited" for state law purposes is significant but not determinative. This is illustrated by *Gordon v. Terry*.[54] In that case, a limited partnership was formed for the purposes of buying and selling undeveloped land. The limited partners had explicit voting power on whether or not specific pieces of land should be sold and at what time. The Eleventh Circuit held that these interests did not pass the *Howey* test and, hence, were not securities. Similarly, in a more recent decision, the Third Circuit in *Steinhardt Group, Inc. v. Citicorp*,[55] concluded that "the limited partner retained pervasive control over its investment in the limited partnership such that it cannot be deemed a passive investor under *Howey* and its progeny."[56]

This issue has become more prevalent due to the fact that nearly all states have enacted the Revised Uniform Limited Partnership Act (RULPA). This Act provides limited partners with a "safe harbor" to exercise considerable authority, yet retain their status as limited partners. For example, under Section 303(b) of RULPA a limited partner, while still retaining his/her limited partner status, may engage in such actions as "consulting with and advising a general partner" regarding the partnership business, serving as an officer or director of a corporation which is a general partner of the limited partnership, and voting on a number of important subjects, such as "a change in the nature of the business" and "the admission or removal of a general partner." Moreover, if the limited partnership agreement so provides, the limited partner may enjoy a right of approval over *any* matter related to the partnership's business.[57]

In sum, interests in a limited partnership generally are securities because limited partners ordinarily rely on the general partners to exercise the essential efforts. However, in those situations where limited partners have the capability to exert meaningful efforts, the *Howey* investment contract test may not be met.

[B] General Partnerships

Since general partnerships do not possess the same restrictions on participation in management as limited partnership interests, they normally fail to satisfy the *Howey* "solely from the efforts of others" standard. Several courts in the 1960s and 1970s applied *Howey* in a fairly literal manner and held that general partnership interests were not securities.[58]

---

[54] 684 F.2d 736 (11th Cir. 1982).

[55] 126 F.3d 144 (3d Cir. 1997).

[56] *Id.* at 145. See *Gordon v. Terry*, 684 F.2d 736 (11th Cir. 1982).

[57] See *Steinhardt Group, Inc. v. Citicorp*, 126 F.3d 144, 155 (3d Cir. 1997) (concluding that limited partner's adherence to safe harbor provided by Delaware Revised Uniform Limited Partnership Act "not controlling" for investment contract analysis); Everhard, *The Limited Partnership Interest: Is It a Security? Changing Times*, 17 Del. J. Corp. L. 441 (1992) (asserting that in those situations where "the powers retained by the limited partners are so pervasive that they are in a position to adequately protect themselves, . . . the protections of the federal securities laws are neither appropriate nor necessary").

[58] See, e.g., *Sandusky Land Ltd. v. Uniplan Group, Inc.*, 400 F. Supp. 440 (N.D. Ohio 1975).

In *Williamson v. Tucker*,[59] the Fifth Circuit may have "rescued" general partnership interests from being declared outside the scope of the securities laws as a matter of law. That case involved a series of joint ventures each of which owned an undivided interest in certain real estate. The participants in each joint venture retained substantial control over the prospect pursuant to the joint venture agreements that they signed. The Fifth Circuit stated that, in spite of the form which the investment took, if the investor was in fact unable to exercise meaningful management powers because of his or her dependence on the promoter or a third party, then the general partnership or joint venture interest could be designated a security under federal law. The court went on to delineate three sets of circumstances where this could happen: First, an interest could be a security if the agreement between the parties leaves so little power in the hands of the investor that power is distributed as it would be in a limited partnership. Second, a security also could be present if the investor is so inexperienced and unknowledgeable in business affairs as to be incapable of intelligently exercising his or her partnership powers. Finally, the *Williamson* court stated that a security could be present if the investor is so dependent on some unique "entrepreneurial or managerial" ability of the promoter or manager that he or she cannot in all practicality replace the manager or otherwise exercise meaningful partnership powers.[60]

The *Williamson* decision thus is an expansion of the circumstances under which general partnership or joint venture interests may be found to be securities. A number of cases in other circuits have examined general partnership interests under the analysis set forth in *Williamson*.[61] On the other hand, some courts have rejected its application as being too expansive.[62] One such view posits that each general partner as a matter of law enjoys the right of ultimate control over the venture, hence signifying that each such general power may exert meaningful managerial efforts and thus negating securities law coverage.[63] Another approach, broader than the preceding standard but narrower than *Williamson*, solely focuses on the terms of the general partnership agreement. Applying this approach, regardless of a particular general partner's lack of financial sophistication or lack of control actually exercised, the general partnership agreement's inclusion of "real power" in the general partners signifies that the securities laws do not apply.[64]

---

[59] 645 F.2d 404 (5th Cir. 1981).

[60] *Id.* at 417–25.

[61] See, e.g., *Koch v. Hankins*, 928 F.2d 1471 (9th Cir. 1991).

[62] See, e.g., *Goodwin v. Elkins & Co.*, 730 F.2d 99 (2d Cir. 1984).

[63] *Id.* at 103–05 (Garth, J., opinion announcing judgment of the court).

[64] See, e.g., *Banghart v. Hollywood General Partnership*, 902 F.2d 805, 808 (10th Cir. 1990) ("[R]egardless of the control actually exercised if a partnership agreement retains real power in the general partners, then an investment in the general partnership is not a security. Thus, our determination of whether a general partnership interest can be characterized as a security turns on the partnership agreement."). See generally Note, *General Partnership Interests as Securities Under the Federal Securities Law: Substance over Form*, 54 Fordham L. Rev. 303 (1985).

6.   Clarify that offshore resales under Rule 901 or Rule 904 of equity securities of U.S. issuers, classified as "restricted securities" as defined in Rule 144, will not affect the restricted status of those securities or otherwise cleanse the securities of their restricted status.[204]

[E]   Facilitating Global Trading

By promulgating Regulation S the SEC has acknowledged the existence of a global economy and the important role of international securities transactions. While not a panacea, Regulation S establishes a uniform U.S. framework with respect to international securities offerings. Moreover, Regulation S decreases some of the ambiguity that existed under the prior regulatory regimen. Regulation S, aside from creating a more flexible approach with fewer regulatory burdens, has been used in conjunction with Rule 144A to increase investment in foreign issuers and to expand international securities trading in general (see § 5.07 *infra*).

---

[204] M. Steinberg, *International Securities Law — A Contemporary and Comparative Analysis* 194-198 (1999). See Rule 905 of Regulation S, 17 C.F.R. § 230.905.

APPENDIX 3

LIMITED OFFERING MATERIALS

INVESTOR:

_____

Name

PRIVATE PLACEMENT QUESTIONNAIRE
(ALL INFORMATION IS AND SHALL REMAIN CONFIDENTIAL)

The information contained herein is being furnished in order to enable you to determine whether a sale of a Limited Partnership interest (the "Partnership Interest") in _____, a Texas limited partnership (the "Partnership") may be made to the undersigned (the "Investor") without registration of the Partnership Interest under the Securities Act of 1933, as amended, or any applicable state securities law. This Questionnaire is not an offer to purchase or acceptance of an offer to sell a Partnership Interest, but is, in fact, a response to a solicitation of information to provide you a basis for determining the appropriateness of any sale to the undersigned prospective Investor.

1. FOR INDIVIDUAL INVESTORS:
    Name:_____Telephone:_____
    Home Address (street, city, state and zip): _____

    _____

    How long a resident of state of residence:_____
    Date of Birth:_____ U.S. Citizen: Yes _____ No_____
    College: _____ Degree: _____ Year_____
    Graduate School:_____ Degree: _____ Year_____
    Social Security Number:_____
    Business (Name):_____
    Address:_____

    _____

    Telephone:_____
    Nature of Business:_____
    Your Position and Duties:_____

    Communications should be sent to (check one):
    _____ Residence address _____ Business address
    Any other prior occupations, positions or duties during
    past five years:_____

    _____

    _____

2. FOR INVESTORS THAT ARE CORPORATIONS, PARTNERSHIPS, TRUSTS OR OTHER ENTITIES:

Name:_____

Address of principal office:_____

Telephone: _____

Date and state of incorporation or organization:_____

_____

Taxpayer Identification Number:_____

Nature of Business:_____

Individual Authorized to Execute this Questionnaire:

_____

Name and Title

Name of record and beneficial owners of entity:

_____

FOR ALL INVESTORS:

3. Relationship to the Partnership or the General Partner:

_____

_____

4. The undersigned is an officer or director of a publicly-held company:

                Yes _____   No _____

If yes, specify._____

5. The undersigned beneficially owns 10% or more of the voting securities of a publicly-held company:

                Yes _____   No _____

If yes, specify._____

6. I _____ have_____ have not personally invested in investments sold by means of private placements within the past 5 years.

7. I consider myself to be an experienced and sophisticated investor. Yes _____ No _____

If so, on what basis?_____

_____

8. I, the undersigned individual or person authorized to execute this Questionnaire, consider myself to have such knowledge of the Partnership and its business and such experience in financial and business matters to enable me to evaluate the merits and risks of an investment in the Partnership, should I be given an opportunity to so invest.

                Yes _____   No _____

9. Listed below are the categories of accredited investors, as defined by Regulation D, promulgated under the Securities Act of 1933, as amended. Please check the appropriate space provided below if the Investor falls within one or more of these categories.

The undersigned meets one or more of the following "accredited" categories as indicated in the space provided below (check all appropriate categories).

_____ A.   A natural person whose net worth or joint net worth with spouse exceeds $1,000,000. Net worth includes homes, furnishings and automobiles.

_____ B.   A natural person whose income, exclusive of spouse's income, exceeded $200,000 in each of the last two years and who reasonably expects an income in excess of $200,000 in the current year, or whose income, together with spouse's income, exceeded $300,000 in each of the last two years and who reasonably expects such combined income to exceed $300,000 in the current year.

_____ C.   A bank, insurance company, registered investment company, employee benefit plan if the investment decision is made by a bank, insurance company or registered investment adviser; or an employee benefit plan with more than $5 million of assets.

_____ D.   A private business development company as defined in Section 202(a)(22) of the Investment Advisers Act of 1940.

_____ E.   A tax exempt organization (IRC Section 501(c)(3) exemption), corporation, Massachusetts or similar business trust, or partnership, not formed for the specific purpose of acquiring the Interests offered, with assets in excess of $5 million.

_____ F.   An entity in which all the equity owners are accredited investors under A through E above.

If the Investor does not qualify in an accredited category above, please indicate this in the space provided below.

_____G.   The Investor does not qualify in any accredited category as indicated above.

The undersigned intends to have an attorney, accountant, investment advisor or other consultant act as its Purchaser Representative in connection with this investment.
Yes _____ No _____
If yes, please furnish the information indicated below:
Name:_____ Telephone:_____
Firm:_____
Address:_____
If the undersigned utilizes a Purchaser Representative, the Representative will be required to complete a questionnaire to be supplied by the Partnership.
If the undersigned is an individual, was your personal income from all sources for the previous calendar year more than (initial highest number applicable):
_____ $150,000 _____ $200,000 _____ $250,000

If the undersigned is an individual, is your net worth (exclusive of home, furnishings and personal automobiles) in excess of (initial highest number applicable):

_____ $150,000 _____ $250,000 _____ $500,000
_____ $750,000 _____ $1,000,000 _____ $2,000,000

If the undersigned is an entity which checked Item F of Paragraph 9 hereof in reliance upon the accredited investor categories set forth in items A and B of Paragraph 9, please state the name, address, total personal income from all sources for the previous calendar year, and the net worth (exclusive of home, furnishings, and personal automobiles) for each equity owner of said entity.

_____

_____

_____

_____

_____

If the undersigned does not qualify in any accredited category as indicated in Paragraph 9 hereof, items A through F, please provide answers to the following questions: (Accredited investors may omit answers to this paragraph 14.)

(a)   State total assets of the undersigned, including cash, stocks and bonds, automobiles, real estate, and any other assets: $_____

(b)   State total liabilities of the undersigned, including real estate indebtedness, accounts payable, taxes payable, and any other liabilities: $_____

(c)   State annual income of the undersigned, including salary, securities income, rental income, and any other income: $_____

(d)   State annual expenses of the undersigned, excluding ordinary living expenses, including real estate payments, rent, property taxes, and other expenses: $_____

(e)   Do you expect the amount of assets, liabilities, income, and expenses of the undersigned, as stated above, to be subject to significant change in the future?

Yes _____   No _____

If yes, explain.

_____

_____

(f)   Does the undersigned own stocks which have been purchased on a margin basis?

Yes _____   No _____

If yes, explain.

_____

_____

(g)   Has the undersigned ever filed for bankruptcy?

Yes _____   No _____

(h)   Are there any outstanding judgments against the
        undersigned?

Yes _____   No _____

If the answer to either of (g) or (h) above is yes,
explain fully on a separate sheet of paper.

(i)   Bank Reference:_____

        Address of Bank:_____

        _____

        Bank Telephone:_____

        Person to Contact:_____

The information contained herein is complete and accurate and the
Investor will notify you promptly of any change in any of such information.
Specifically, the Investor hereby certifies that the information contained
above concerning the residency of the Investor is true and correct. The
Investor realizes and understands that, but for the truth of the information
contained herein, the Investor would not receive consideration by the
General Partner pertaining to this investment.

If this Questionnaire is completed on behalf of a corporation, partnership,
trust or estate, I, the person executing on behalf of the Investor, represent
that I have the authority to execute and deliver this Questionnaire on behalf
of such corporation, partnership, trust or estate.

DATED: _____, 2000.

IF INDIVIDUAL INVESTOR:

_____

(Signature)

_____

(Printed Name)

IF CORPORATION, PARTNERSHIP,
TRUST,
ESTATE OR REPRESENTATIVE:

_____

Name of Investor

By:_____

Name:_____

Title:_____

SUBSCRIPTION AGREEMENT

The undersigned hereby subscribes for a Limited Partner Interest in _____, a Texas limited partnership (the "Partnership") in the amount set forth below.

1. Subscription. Subject to the terms and conditions hereof, the undersigned hereby irrevocably subscribes for a Limited Partnership interest (the "Partnership Interest") in the Partnership for a total purchase price of $_____. The undersigned hereby tenders with this Subscription Agreement a check payable to the order of _____ or wire transfer, in the amount of $_____.

2. Closing. The undersigned understands the General Partner intends to make an initial closing of the Partnership Interests on _____, 2000, and thereafter will open the partnership on a quarterly basis for additional capital contributions from existing or new Limited Partners. If you do not accept this subscription, this Subscription Agreement, together with the funds and other documents delivered to the Partnership, shall be promptly returned to the undersigned with interest, if any.

3. Determination of Compliance. The undersigned agrees that this subscription is subject to the following terms and conditions:

(a) You shall have the right, in your sole discretion, to accept or reject all or part of this subscription and to determine whether the Subscription Agreement has been properly completed and whether all suitability requirements have been satisfied. If you find this subscription to be defective, deficient or noncomplying, the subscription price will be promptly returned without interest or deduction.

(b) This subscription is not transferable or assignable.

4. Receipt of Information. The undersigned hereby acknowledges receipt of the _____ Private Placement Memorandum, and a copy of the Limited Partnership Agreement which governs the rights of Limited Partners and the operation of the Partnership, and the undersigned acknowledges that he has had reasonable time and opportunity to examine those documents. The undersigned further acknowledges that the Partnership is a suitable investment only for sophisticated investors; that the Partnership Interests are being offered and sold under an exemption from registration under the Securities Act of 1933, as amended, and appropriate state securities laws; and that the offering has not been submitted to or reviewed by the Securities and Exchange Commission, the State Securities Board of Texas, the securities regulation agency of any other state or any other governmental agency.

5. Representation of Purchaser. The undersigned hereby makes the following representations, declarations, and warranties to you, with the intent that the same be relied upon in determining the suitability of the undersigned to invest in the Partnership:

(a) Individual Investor: I am of legal age and a resident of the State of _____; or (aa) Partnership, Trust or other Entity: The investor has been organized in compliance with applicable law of the State of _____, is presently in existence, and has the power to invest in the Partnership.

(b) The undersigned understands that an investment in the Partnership is an illiquid investment, which means that:

(i) The undersigned must bear the economic risk of investment in the Partnership for an indefinite period of time, since the Partnership Interests have not been registered under the Securities Act of 1933 nor any state securities laws and cannot be sold unless the Partnership Interests are either subsequently registered under said Act and applicable state laws (which is neither contemplated by nor required of the Partnership) or an exemption from such registration is available; and

(ii) There is no established market for the Partnership Interests and that it is not anticipated that any public market for the Partnership Interests will develop in the near future.

(c) The undersigned represents that this investment is being made for the account of the undersigned; the undersigned has not offered or sold any portion of the Partnership Interest for which the undersigned hereby subscribes to any other person and has no present intention of dividing such Partnership Interest with others or reselling or otherwise disposing of any portion of such Partnership Interest, either currently or after the passage of a fixed or determinable period of time, or upon the occurrence or nonoccurrence of any predetermined event or circumstance.

(d) The undersigned represents that none of the following has been represented, guaranteed, or warranted to the undersigned by any broker, the Partnership, their agents or employees, or any other person, expressly or by implication:

(i) The length of time that the undersigned will be required to remain as the owner of the Partnership Interest;

(ii) The profit to be realized, if any, as a result of investment in the Partnership; or

(iii) The past performance or experience on the part of the Partnership, or any partner or affiliate, their partners, salesmen, associates, agents, or employees or of any other person, will in any way indicate the predicted results of the ownership of the Partnership Interest.

(e) The undersigned has adequate means of providing for current needs and possible personal contingencies and has no need for liquidity in the investment in the Partnership. The undersigned is either (i) an "accredited investor" (as indicated in the Private Placement Questionnaire), or (ii) has a personal net worth in excess of three (3) times the amount to be invested in the Partnership and could afford to sustain a loss of the entire investment in the Partnership in the event such loss should occur.

(f) The undersigned has made an independent examination of the investment and has depended on the advice of counsel and accountants to the undersigned and agrees that you have no responsibility with respect to such matters and such advice.

(g) The undersigned understands that the Partnership is newly formed and has no operating history; the undersigned has carefully reviewed and relied solely upon the Private Placement Memorandum and independent investigations made by the undersigned or by representative(s) of the undersigned, if any, in making the decision to purchase the Partnership Interest hereby subscribed for, and the undersigned has a full understanding and appreciation of the risks involved.

(h) The undersigned understands that any offering literature used in connection with this offering has not been prefiled with the Attorney General or Securities Commission of any state and has not been reviewed by the Attorney General or Securities Commission of any state.

(i) The undersigned understands that any and all documents, records and books pertaining to this investment have been made available for inspection by the undersigned, his attorney and/or accountant, and that the books and records of the Partnership will be available, upon reasonable notice, for inspection by investors during reasonable hours at the principal place of business of the Partnership. The undersigned represents that he has had an opportunity to ask questions of and receive answers from the General Partner, or a person or persons acting on its behalf, concerning the terms and conditions of this investment.

6. Indemnification of the Partnership and the General Partner. The undersigned understands the meaning and legal consequences of the representations and warranties contained herein, and hereby agrees to indemnify and hold harmless the Partnership, the General Partner, and their agents and employees from and against any and all loss, damage or liability due to or arising out of a breach of any representation or warranty of the undersigned contained in this Subscription Agreement. Notwithstanding any of the representations, warranties, acknowledgments or agreements made herein, the undersigned does not in any manner waive any rights granted to the undersigned under United States Federal or state securities laws.

7. Power of Attorney. In order to induce the General Partner to accept the subscription of the undersigned, and in consideration of the General Partner's agreement to serve as General Partner of the Partnership, the undersigned hereby irrevocably constitutes and appoints the General Partner, with full power of substitution, his true and lawful attorney for him and in his name, place and stead for his use and benefit, to execute:

    (a)   the Partnership Agreement in the form provided to the undersigned or as the same may be thereafter amended;

    (b)   all amendments to the Certificate of Limited Partnership and Partnership Agreement regarding a change in name of the Partnership, its address, or that of the General Partner or any Partner, or the admission or withdrawal of a Partner;

    (c)   all amendments adopted in accordance with Section 11.04 of the Partnership Agreement;

(d) all certificates and other instruments necessary to qualify or continue the Partnership in the states where the Partnership may be doing business;

(e) all conveyances or other instruments or documents necessary, appropriate or convenient to effect the dissolution and termination of the Partnership.

The undersigned hereby agrees to be bound by any representations made by the General Partner or its substitutes acting pursuant to this Power of Attorney, and the undersigned hereby waives any and all defenses which may be available to him to contest, negate or disaffirm its actions or the actions of his substitutes under this Power of Attorney. The powers herein granted are granted for the sole and exclusive benefit of the undersigned and not on behalf of any other person, in whole or in part. This Power of Attorney is hereby declared to be irrevocable and a power coupled with an interest which will survive the death, disability, dissolution, bankruptcy or insolvency of the undersigned.

8. Subscription Not Revocable. The undersigned hereby acknowledges and agrees that the undersigned is not entitled to cancel, terminate or revoke this Subscription Agreement or any agreements of the undersigned hereunder and that this Subscription Agreement shall survive the dissolution, death or disability of the undersigned.

9. Representative Capacity. If an investment in the Partnership is being made by a corporation, partnership, trust or estate, I, the person signing on behalf of the undersigned entity, represent that I have all right and authority, in my capacity as an officer, general partner, trustee, executor or other representative of such corporation, partnership, trust or estate, as the case may be, to make such decision to invest in the Partnership and to execute and deliver this Subscription Agreement on behalf of such corporation, partnership, trust or estate as the case may be, enforceable in accordance with its terms. I also represent that any such corporation, partnership or trust was not formed for the purpose of buying the Partnership Interest hereby subscribed.

10. Restrictions on Transferability. The undersigned understands and agrees that the purchase and resale, pledge, hypothecation or other transfer of the Partnership Interest is restricted by certain provisions of the Limited Partnership Agreement of _____ and that the Partnership Interest shall not be sold, pledged, hypothecated or otherwise transferred unless the Partnership Interest is registered under the Securities Act of 1933, as amended, and applicable state securities laws or an exemption from such registration is available.

11. Number and Gender. In this Agreement the masculine gender includes the other two genders and the singular includes the plural, where appropriate to the context.

IN WITNESS WHEREOF, the undersigned has executed this Subscription Agreement on the date set forth below.

Date of Execution: _____

IF INDIVIDUAL INVESTOR:

_____

(Signature)

_____

(Printed Name)

IF CORPORATION, PARTNERSHIP,
TRUST,
ESTATE OR REPRESENTATIVE:

_____

Name of Investor

By:_____

Name:_____

Title:_____

APPROVED THIS____DAY
OF_____, 2000.

By:_____

General Partner

PURCHASER REPRESENTATIVE QUESTIONNAIRE

The information contained herein is being furnished for consideration by the General Partners in determining whether the sale of Limited Partnership interests in _____, a Texas Limited Partnership (the "Partnership") may be made to:

_____

(Printed or typed name of potential Limited Partners)

The undersigned understands that (i) the General Partners will rely upon the information contained herein for purposes of such determination, (ii) the Limited Partnership interests will not be registered under the Securities Act and may not be registered under the securities laws of the Limited Partner's state of residence in reliance upon exemptions from the registration provisions thereof and (iii) this Questionnaire is not an offer of the Limited Partnership interests or any other securities to the undersigned or to the above-named prospective Limited Partner.

The undersigned is acting as Purchaser Representative for the above-named Limited Partner(s) and is furnishing the following representations and information:

1. The undersigned is not an affiliate of the Partnership (as defined hereafter), except as set forth below. (Write "No Exceptions" or set forth exceptions and give details.)

_____

_____

_____

_____

The only permitted exceptions are those stated below: A Purchaser Representative may not be an affiliate of the Partnership (director, officer, or other employee of the Partnership or of the General Partners or beneficial owner of 10% or more of any class of equity interest in the Partnership or of the General Partners), except where the purchaser is:

(a) related to the purchaser representative by blood, marriage or adoption, no more remotely than as a first cousin;

(b) any trust or estate in which the purchaser representative and any persons related to him or her, as specified in subparagraph (a) or (c), collectively have more than 50% of the beneficial interest (excluding contingent interests) or of which the purchaser representative serves as trustee, executor or in any similar capacity; or

(c) any corporation or other organization in which the purchaser representative and any persons related to him or her, as specified in subparagraph (a) or (b), collectively are the beneficial owners of more than 50% of the equity securities (excluding directors' qualifying shares) or equity interests.

2.   The undersigned believes that he/she has sufficient knowledge and experience in financial and business matters to be capable of evaluating, alone or together with other Purchaser Representatives of the purchaser, or together with the purchaser, the relative merits and risks of an investment in the Partnership. Such opinion is based upon the following information; if the undersigned has relied upon, in part, the expertise of additional Purchaser Representatives or others, their names and addresses are indicated below. (Please describe personal investment experience, business experience, profession and education.)

_____

_____

_____

_____

_____

3.   There is no material relationship or agreement between the undersigned or any of his/her affiliates and the Partnership or its affiliates which now exists or is mutually understood to be contemplated or which has existed at any time during the previous two years, nor has the undersigned or any of his/her affiliates received any compensation from the Partnership or its affiliates as a result of any such relationship, except as set forth below. If you and your firm are participating in the solicitation of purchasers in connection with this private placement or any prior offerings by the General Partners or their affiliates, please (a) so state, (b) separately indicate the total compensation to be received and (c) make sure that the purchaser reads, answers and signs the statements at the end of this Purchaser Representative Questionnaire. (Write "No Exceptions" or set forth exceptions and give details.)

_____

_____

The foregoing information is complete, correct and may be relied upon by the General Partners and the Partnership. The undersigned agrees to promptly advise of any changes in the foregoing information which may occur prior to the termination of the offering.

Signed this _____ day of _____ 2000, at _____ (City and State)

_____	_____
Firm Name	Signature
_____	_____
Street Address	Type or Print Name

_____   _____
City, State and Zip Code   (Area Code) Telephone Number

IMPORTANT NOTE TO PURCHASER:

If the answer to question 3 above is anything other than "No Exceptions," it means that your Purchaser Representative may at some future date have, presently has, or within the past two years had, a material relationship with the Partnership or its affiliates and will receive or has received compensation therefor. Accordingly, you should understand that such person may have a conflict of interest between such Purchaser Representative's impartial representation of you as a purchaser representative and such Purchaser Representative's past, present, or future relationship with the Partnership or its affiliates. After consideration of the effects such a conflict of interest may have upon such Person's acting as your Purchaser Representative and, if such Person is to so act, you should acknowledge that you have been advised in writing by the Purchaser Representative, prior to completion of the Subscription Agreement, of such potential conflict of interest and that you desire such person to act as your Purchaser Representative.

I have been advised in writing by my Purchaser Representative, prior to my completion of the Subscription Agreement, of the potential conflict of interest described in question 3 above.

Yes _____   No _____

I desire the above named person to act as my Purchaser Representative.

Yes _____   No _____

Signed this _____ day of _____ 2000, at _____ (City and State)

IF INDIVIDUAL INVESTOR:

_____

(Signature)

_____

Printed Name)

IF CORPORATION, PARTNERSHIP, TRUST, ESTATE OR REPRESENTATIVE:

_____

Name of Investor

By:_____

Name:_____

Title:_____

Chapter 4

THE REGISTRATION PROCESS

§ 4.01   Overview of the Registration Process

To protect investors and the integrity of the securities markets, the Securities Act of 1933 has two basic objectives: (1) to provide investors with adequate and accurate material information concerning securities offered for sale and (2) to prohibit fraudulent practices in the offer or sale of securities. The registration framework of the Act seeks to meet these goals by imposing certain obligations and limitations upon persons engaged in the offer or sale of securities. For the Securities Act's registration framework to apply, the interstate commerce requirement must be met. This normally is satisfied without difficulty.

Pursuant to Section 5, a public offering of securities requires that a registration statement be filed with the Securities and Exchange Commission (SEC). As a general matter, before the registration statement is filed, there can be no offers to sell or offers to buy the securities in question. After the filing of the registration statement, oral offers and written offers by means of a Section 10 prospectus are permissible. Until the registration statement becomes effective, however, there can be no sale of the securities. Moreover, the registration requirements of the applicable state securities laws must be met.

Under federal law, the main purpose of registration is to provide adequate and accurate disclosure of material information concerning the issuer (as well as affiliates and certain other parties) and the securities the issuer (which, for example, may be a corporation or a limited partnership) proposes to offer. The disclosure of this information, in the form of a Section 10 prospectus, enables investors to evaluate the securities offered and thus make informed investment decisions.

The registration of a securities offering with the SEC does not mean that the offering is considered to be a good risk. The Commission does not have the authority to prevent an offering from going to market because it considers the investment to be of a speculative nature. Rather, the main role of the federal securities laws in this setting is to require the accurate disclosure of material information.

On the other hand, a number of states apply "merit" regulation to certain securities offerings. Under this standard, the pertinent state securities administrator can prevent an offering from going forward because it is not "fair, just and equitable." Under merit regulation, therefore, adequate disclosure is not the only criterion. The substantive fairness of the offering also may be scrutinized.

It also should be pointed out that neither the SEC nor the states verify the truthfulness of the disclosures made in the registration statement. That a registration statement becomes effective in no way vouches for the veracity of the information contained therein. In this regard, both federal and state law prohibit materially false and misleading statements, with civil and criminal remedies available to redress such violations. For example, as discussed in Chapter 6, Section 11 of the 1933 Act imposes civil monetary liability against certain persons who fail to establish "due diligence" (except the issuer which is strictly liable) for any misstatement or omission of a material fact contained in a registration statement; Section 12(a)(1) provides that a purchaser may rescind, or alternatively, recover damages against any person who offers or sells a security in violation of Section 5; Section 12(a)(2) likewise grants the purchaser the right to rescind or to recover damages against any person who sells a security by means of a prospectus or oral communication that includes a materially false or misleading statement if such seller fails to show the exercise of reasonable care; Section 17(a), as addressed in Chapter 8, provides a remedy to the SEC for redressing any fraudulent or deceptive conduct committed in the offer or sale of securities; and Section 24 of the Securities Act provides for criminal penalties for the willful violation of any provision of the Securities Act or any rule or regulation promulgated by the SEC thereunder. Moreover, as discussed in Chapter 7, suit under certain circumstances may be brought under Section 10(b) of the Securities Exchange Act for any materially false or misleading statement contained in a registration statement.

Section 5 of the Securities Act may be viewed as the central provision of the federal registration framework. Subject to certain exceptions, the provision prohibits any person from using the mails or any means of interstate commerce to offer a subject security for sale unless a registration statement has been filed with the SEC and, with respect to any written communication, unless such communication meets the requirements of Section 10.[1] Section 5 also has the effect of prohibiting any sales of the subject securities unless a registration statement is effective and a statutory (Section 10(a)) prospectus has been sent or given to the investor. The terms "offer to sell" and "sale" are defined broadly in Section 2(a)(3).[2] The term "prospectus" is defined expansively in Section 2(a)(10). The information required to be contained in a registration statement is specified in Section 7; and Section 10 details the contents of the prospectus (remember that the statutory prospectus is part of the registration statement).

---

[1] There are a number of exceptions to this general principle. See Section 2(a)(10) of the Securities Act. For example, one exception occurs in the post-effective period where the "communication" is accompanied or preceded by the sending or giving of a statutory Section 10(a) prospectus to the investor. In that case, the separate "communication" need not meet the requirements of Section 10.

[2] The terms "sale" and "sell" are defined in Section 2(a)(3) to include "every contract of sale or disposition of a security for value." The term "offer" includes "every attempt or offer to dispose of, or solicitation of an offer to buy, a security or interest in a security, for value." See *Rubin v. United States*, 449 U.S. 424 (1981) (a pledge of stock as collateral for a loan is an "offer or sale" of a security under § 17(a) of the Securities Act).

Pursuant to the requirements of Section 5(b)(1), a prospectus must meet the requirements of Section 10. Because the term "prospectus" is defined broadly in Section 2(a)(10),[3] a person engaged in the offering process should be wary. As defined in Section 2(a)(10), a prospectus generally includes any written communication that is used to sell securities in a public offering. Such written communications include confirmations, letters, brochures, circulars, notices, and advertisements that offer securities for sale. Hence, in general, *with certain exceptions*, any written communication to potential investors offering the subject securities for sale in a public offering will constitute a prospectus, irrespective of whether such communication occurs before or after the effective date of the registration statement.

Generally, a Section 10 prospectus describes the issuer, affiliated persons, and the securities to be offered. The prospectus, among other things, may be viewed as being both a selling and a disclosure document. As a selling document, it is used by underwriters and dealers for the purpose of helping to persuade investors to purchase the securities. A more commonly-held view, however, is that the prospectus, as a disclosure document, serves to protect the various parties from liability. From this perspective, information placed in the prospectus traditionally has been conservative, focusing on historically-based information and clearly warning prospective investors of any risks involved. The SEC's promulgation of Rule 175 and Item 303 of Regulation S-K (& Regulation S-B) signal a new era for facilitating the disclosure of forward-looking statements and other "soft" (rather than historical) information (see §§ 4.07, 10.01-10.02, 10.05 *infra*). Enactment of the Private Securities Litigation Reform Act of 1995 also encourages issuers to engage in disclosure of "forward-looking" or "soft" information. (See §§ 4.07, 7.06[D], 10.05[D] *infra*).

§ 4.02 Framework of Section 5

When speaking of making a public offering, the concept of *"in registra-tion"* is sometimes heard. Generally, the term refers to the entire registra-tion period, commencing at least from the time that the issuer reaches an understanding with the managing underwriter prior to the filing of the registration statement to the time that the prospectus delivery require-ments terminate in the post-effective period.

From a structural perspective having legal ramifications, Section 5 covers three basic time periods for making offers and sales of securities during a registered offering: (1) the pre-filing period, (2) the waiting period, and (3) the post-effective period. The following discussion will address each of these time periods.

---

[3] Note that the Supreme Court has construed the term "prospectus" narrowly for purposes of Section 12(a)(2) of the Securities Act. See *Gustafson v. Alloyd Company*, 513 U.S. 561 (1995), *discussed in*, § 6.09 *infra*.

[A] The Pre-Filing Period

[1] Overview

The *pre-filing* period is the time period before a registration statement has been filed with the SEC. During this time period, among other prohibitions, Section 5(c) prohibits the use of the mails or any means or interstate commerce to offer to sell or offer to buy the securities offered.[4]

Certain activities, however, are not deemed to be an offer to sell or an offer to buy. For example, Section 2(3) exempts negotiations and agreements between the issuer and any underwriter or among underwriters who are or will be in privity of contract with the issuer. Rule 135 permits an issuer to make an announcement of a proposed public offering, provided that only the information specified in the rule is released. Moreover, pursuant to Rules 137-139, dealers may publish certain information about specified issuers in the pre-filing period (as well as in the waiting and post-effective periods).

As a general proposition, however, during the pre-filing period, the concept of "offering" for sale is given a broad interpretation. Publication of information about the issuer or its securities, prior to the filing of a registration statement, may be considered to constitute an "offer to sell." Although the publication is not an express offer, it may be viewed as conditioning the public market or stimulating interest in the securities to be registered (more colorfully referred to as "gun-jumping"). Hence, during the pre-filing period, the issuer and other participants must be cautious regarding the publication of information.

[2] Conditioning the Market ("Gun-Jumping")

A major concern in the pre-filing period is that statements made by the issuer and others will be construed as "conditioning the market" ("gun-jumping"), and, hence, constitute an "offer to sell" in violation of Section 5(c). The SEC has issued a number of releases on this issue. In this regard, the Commission has asserted that "the publication of information and statements, and publicity efforts, made in advance of a proposed financing which have the effect of conditioning the public mind or arousing public interest in the issuer or in its securities constitutes an offer in violation of the Act." Nonetheless, the SEC takes the position that, particularly if a current practice, the flow of *factual* information by publicly-held companies to shareholders and the marketplace should be encouraged. Hence, according to the Commission, publicly-held issuers should:

(1) Continue to advertise products and services.

(2) Continue to send out customary quarterly, annual, and other periodic reports to stockholders.

---

[4] For example, Section 5(a) prohibits the use of the mails or any instrument or means of interstate commerce to sell or to deliver securities for purposes of sale before the effective date of the registration statement.

(3) Continue to publish proxy statements and send out dividend notices.

(4) Continue to make announcements to the press with respect to factual business and financial developments; i.e., receipt of a contract, the settlement of a strike, the opening of a plant, or similar event of interest to the community in which the business operates.

(5) Answer unsolicited telephone inquiries from stockholders, financial analysts, the press and others concerning factual information.

(6) Observe an "open door" policy in responding to unsolicited inquiries concerning factual matters from securities analysts, financial analysts, security holders, and participants in the communications field who have a legitimate interest in the corporation's affairs.

(7) Continue to hold stockholder meetings as scheduled and to answer shareholders' inquiries at stockholder meetings relating to factual matters.[5]

On the other hand, newly implemented practices or increased activity of existing practices (e.g., increasing the company's advertising in the mass media) should be avoided when the issuer's securities are "in registration." Moreover, during this time, the issuer and its personnel should not provide opinions concerning values. As a key point, the SEC's position provides comfort to only publicly-held enterprises. Issuers having their initial public offerings (IPOs) are not extended such comfort.

With respect to gun-jumping, an interesting issue is the effect of such SEC rules as Rule 175 that allow forward-looking information. For example, as discussed in § 4.07[C], Rule 175 permits an issuer under certain conditions to make forward-looking statements in registration statements, annual reports, and certain other documents filed with the SEC. Although the Commission has advised issuers to avoid making such forecasts or projections when its securities are in registration,[6] this position was taken prior to the SEC's adoption of Rule 175. As a result, Rule 175 by its terms permits an issuer to make predictive statements in its annual report even though it contemplates filing a registration statement in the near future, such as within the next two weeks. Given the SEC's concerns with "gun-jumping," however, an issuer may not find sufficient comfort in Rule 175 in this context, particularly if the issuer has not made forward-looking statements in its SEC-filed documents on a regular basis.[7]

---

[5] SEC Securities Act Release No. 5180. Accord, Securities Act Release No. 7856 (2000).

[6] See sources cited note 5 *supra*. See also, SEC Securities Act Release Nos. 3844 (1957), 4697 (1964).

[7] See generally *SEC v. Thomas D. Kienlen Corporation*, 755 F. Supp. 936 (D. Ore. 1991); Chiappinelli, *Gun-Jumping: The Problem of Extraneous Offers of Securities*, 50 U. Pitt. L. Rev. 457 (1989).

[3] Effect of Rule 135

Under Rule 135, a notice given by an issuer in the pre-filing period that complies with the provisions of the rule is not deemed an "offer to sell," and hence may be released without violating Section 5(c). Generally, a Rule 135 notice, in addition to containing only certain specified information, states that the issuer intends to make a public offering of securities and that such offering will be made only by means of a prospectus. Note that the rule prohibits the underwriters from being named in the notice and that judicial authority has interpreted the rule to prohibit valuations from being contained in the notice.[8] The purpose of these prohibitions "is designed to prevent an issuer from arousing investor interest before a registration statement covering the securities proposed to be offered has been filed; investors are intended to have an opportunity to evaluate the disclosures there contained."[9]

The Second Circuit in its seminal decision in *Chris-Craft Industries, Inc. v. Bangor Punta Corporation*[10] construed Rule 135 as setting forth an exclusive list. Issuer notices that go beyond Rule 135 and which are not otherwise required by another SEC regulation constitute "an offer to sell," thereby violating Section 5(c). The Second Circuit in *Chris-Craft* reasoned:

> When it is announced that securities will be sold at some date in the future and, in addition, an attractive description of these securities and of the issuer is furnished, it seems clear that such an announcement provides much the same kind of information as that contained in a prospectus. Doubtless the line drawn between an announcement containing sufficient information to constitute an offer and one which does not must be to some extent arbitrary. A checklist of features that may be included in an announcement which does not also constitute an offer to sell serves to guide the financial community and the courts far better than any judicially formulated "rule of reason" as to what is or is not an offer. Rule 135 provides just such a checklist, and if the Rule is not construed as setting forth an exclusive list, then much of its value as a guide is lost.[11]

On the other hand, in certain situations, such as a tender offeror making a securities exchange offer and thereby becoming subject to the SEC's tender offer rules, an issuer may be required to disclose information that goes beyond the specified Rule 135 list. In such situations, it appears that Section 5 is not violated in the pre-filing period where disclosure of the pertinent information is required by a specific SEC rule and the issuer's purpose in making the disclosure is not to "condition the market" for the securities "in registration."[12]

---

[8] See *Chris-Craft Industries, Inc. v. Bangor Punta Corporation*, 426 F.2d 569 (2d Cir. 1970) (en banc).

[9] Letter from the SEC to Judge Lasker, dated January 6, 1978, quoted in, *Sheinberg v. Fluor Corp.*, 514 F. Supp. 133, 139-40 (S.D.N.Y. 1981). The court in *Sheinberg* adopted this position.

[10] 426 F.2d 569 (2d Cir. 1970) (en banc).

[11] *Id.* at 574 (citation omitted).

[12] See *Sheinberg v. Flour Corp.*, 514 F. Supp. 133 (S.D.N.Y. 1981); note 9 *supra*.

[4] Transactions Between Market Professionals

In addition to Rule 135, certain other actions are exempt from constituting an offer to sell or an offer to buy, and, hence, are permitted in the pre-filing period. For example, negotiations and agreements between the underwriter and the issuer or among underwriters who are (or will be) in privity with the issuer are allowed in the pre-filing period.[13]

Importantly, unless otherwise exempted, the prohibitions of Section 5 apply to transactions and discussions between market professionals. In this regard, an "offer to buy" in the pre-filing period by a dealer not in privity with the issuer to an underwriter who is in privity with the issuer constitutes a violation of Section 5(c). Likewise, an "offer to sell" in the pre-filing period by an underwriter in privity with the issuer to a dealer who is not violates Section 5(c). The prohibitions of Section 5 in the waiting and post-effective periods also apply to transactions and discussions between market professionals, unless otherwise exempted.[14]

Turning to another point, an individual investor who contacts his/her broker-dealer in the pre-filing period to buy a few shares of a company's stock to be issued in the public offering normally does not violate Section 5. That is because the individual, unless he/she is deemed to be engaged in a "distribution," has the Section 4(1) exemption that exempts from the Section 5 registration requirements "transactions by any person other than an issuer, underwriter, or dealer." (See Chapter 5). On the other hand, the broker-dealer's offer to sell to the investor in the pre-filing period shares of such company to be issued in the public offering would violate Section 5(c). Unlike the investor, the broker-dealer neither has the Section 4(1) exemption nor can it invoke any other exemption in this context.

[5] Rules 137, 138, and 139

Rules 137, 138, and 139 permit broker-dealers to engage in specified "safe harbor" activities in the pre-filing period without violating Section 5. Rules 137-139 apply as well to the waiting and post-effective periods. For a broker-dealer to invoke these rules, the issuer must be an Exchange Act reporting entity having its securities registered on Form S-2 or S-3 (or F-2 or F-3, which are for foreign issuers), discussed in § 4.06[A].[15]

Generally, Rules 137-139 establish standards for ascertaining the circumstances under which broker-dealers, without violating Section 5, may publish information concerning an S-2 or S-3 issuer which proposes to conduct a registered public offering.

Rule 137 is directed at broker-dealers who are not participating in the public offering — in other words, those dealers who are not in privity of contract either with the issuer or with any underwriter of the offering (i.e.,

---

[13] See Section 2(a)(3) of the Securities Act. Moreover, communications under Rule 135 relating to business combination transactions must be filed with the SEC as required by Rule 425.

[14] See, e.g., *Byrnes v. Faulkner, Dawkins & Sullivan*, 550 F.2d 1303 (2d Cir. 1977).

[15] All references will hereafter be made only to U.S. issuers who register their Securities Act offerings on such Forms as S-1, S-2, or S-3.

such dealers are not purchasing the securities offered from the issuer or from any of the underwriters). Generally, Rule 137 allows a nonparticipating dealer in its regular course of business to publish and distribute information, recommendations, and opinions concerning securities of an Exchange Act reporting company that has filed or intends to file a 1933 Act registration statement.

Turning to Rule 138, that rule "permits a broker-dealer participating in an offering of non-convertible senior securities registered on Form [S-2 or S-3] to publish opinions or recommendations concerning the issuer's common stock, and vice versa."[16]

Rule 139 is directed at those broker-dealers who publish research reports containing information, recommendations, or opinions and who are or will be "participants" in the issuer's public offering. In its amendment of the rule, the SEC elected to distinguish between S-2 and S-3 companies (discussed in § 4.06[A]). Although both S-2 and S-3 issuers are subject to the periodic reporting obligations of the Exchange Act, the S-3 issuers, being larger than their S-2 counterparts, have a wider market following, thereby ensuring adequate dissemination of information regarding such issuers. Consequently, broker-dealers research reports under the Rule 139 safe harbor are less regulated for S-3 issuers than for S-2 issuers.

Generally, for S-2 issuers, Rule 139 requires that information, opinions, or recommendations regarding such issuers be contained in a publication that is published at regular intervals in the normal course of business. The publication must consist of a comprehensive list of securities or include similar information concerning a substantial number of enterprises in the issuer's "sub-industry." Any opinion or recommendation contained in the publication may not be given greater space or prominence than that given to other securities (or companies) and may not be more favorable than the last previous opinion or recommendation published by the broker-dealer prior to its participation in the offering.

With respect to S-3 issuers, Rule 139 extends its safe harbor to require only that broker-dealer research reports that include information, recommendations, or opinions regarding such issuers be distributed with reasonable regularity in the normal course of business. In distinguishing between S-2 and S-3 issuers, the Commission reasoned:

> Amending Rule 139 will enhance the efficiency of the markets by allowing a greater number of research reports to provide a continuous flow of essential corporate information into the marketplace. The amended Rule is structured to differentiate between companies eligible to use Form S-3 (and Form F-3) and other registrants. This structure facilitates the functioning of the integrated disclosure system by increasing the flow of information most broadly as to S/F-3 companies, those companies whose marketplace following is relied upon to replace reiteration of all company-oriented information in the prospectus. Moreover, the marketplace following provides the basis for allowing more research as

---

[16] SEC Securities Act Release No. 5101 (1970).

to S-3/F-3 companies to come within a Section 5 safe harbor because it lessens the opportunity to condition the market for such companies' securities.[17]

A question may be raised whether, in adopting amendments to Rule 139, the SEC has gone too far to accommodate large (i.e., S-3) issuers and participating dealers at the expense of the investing public. Arguably, the rule permits participating dealers to more easily condition the market for S-3 issuers. For example, a participating dealer may publish with reasonable regularity and in the normal course of business research reports highly recommending the purchase of the securities of an S-3 issuer whose registration statement for a prospective public offering will be filed with the SEC in the near future. On the other hand, it may be asserted that, even if this conduct is permitted by Rule 139 and hence is not a violation of Section 5, the antifraud provisions (such as Section 10(b) of the Exchange Act) still apply.

The Commission's amendments to Rule 139 with respect to S-3 issuers may raise certain inconsistencies with some of the other rules. For example, under Rule 135, as discussed in § 4.02[A][3], issuers are quite limited in what they can say in a notice released in the pre-filing period; for example, the underwriters for the offering cannot be named. Yet, under Rule 139, dealers wishing to participate in the offering (although they cannot engage in "offers to buy" in the pre-filing period) can make in the pre-filing period highly favorable recommendations for the purchase of the S-3 company's securities without violating Section 5. A question certainly can be asked whether this distinction makes sense. The inconsistency in the Commission's administrative framework with respect to the registration process may well be due to its hodge-podge adoption and amendment of various rules rather than making a concerted effort to scrutinize the entire process.

[B] The Waiting Period

[1] Overview

After the registration statement is filed with the Commission, the *waiting period* commences. In this time period, subsections (a) and (b) of Section 5 are applicable. Section 5(b)(1) prohibits the use of the mails or any means of interstate commerce to transmit any prospectus, unless such prospectus meets the requirements of Section 10. Since Section 2(a)(10) defines a prospectus to include any written offer, there is no bar against verbal offers during the waiting period. However, the contents and form of written offers are limited by Section 2(a)(10) and Section 10 (as well as SEC rules).

During the waiting period (as well as the post-effective period), no written offers may be made except by means of a Section 10 prospectus. Pursuant to Section 5(a), the securities may not be sold nor may offers to buy be accepted unless the registration statement has become effective. The

---

[17] SEC Securities Act Release No. 6550 (1984). See Securities Act Release No. 7132 (1995) (clarifying availability of Rules 138 and 139).

"tombstone ad" and the Rule 134 "identifying statement," both of which are not deemed to be prospectuses under Section 2(a)(10), may be published during the waiting period (as well as during the post-effective period). During the waiting period, issuers and underwriters customarily conduct "roadshows" to prospective institutional investors, securities professionals, and others as a means to present the issuer and the securities offered in a favorable light. These devices are used to ascertain what parties are interested in the securities and the extent of such interest.

During the waiting period, no written sales literature, namely, so-called "free writing," is allowed. Hence, during this period, written offering materials may not be used, other than a Section 10 prospectus, a tombstone ad, or an identifying statement. Normally, through the use of oral communications and Section 10 prospectuses, underwriters and dealers solicit indications of interest from prospective purchasers during the waiting period. In this regard, through a number of no-action letters, the SEC staff has allowed the use of electronic media by issuers and underwriters to conduct roadshows for audiences consisting of sophisticated investors and securities professionals. The SEC staff has acquiesced in the view that such electronic roadshows are not prospectuses within the meaning of Section 2(a)(10) of the Securities Act.[18]

[2] SEC's Power of Acceleration

Under Section 8(a) of the Securities Act, a registration statement becomes effective the twentieth day after it is filed with the SEC. Significantly, the filing of any amendment commences the twenty day waiting period anew. Moreover, an issuer typically files its registration statement with a legend (referred to as the "delaying amendment" pursuant to Rule 473) voluntarily waiving this twenty-day period in favor of waiting until the SEC elects to clear the registration statement.

Pursuant to Section 8(a), the Commission has the power of acceleration, meaning, for example, that it can determine to have the registration statement become effective immediately after the last amendment is filed. In practice, this power of acceleration along with the issuer's waiver of the twenty-day period referred to above gives the Commission a good deal of leverage. Imagine if an issuer, after filing its last amendment, would have to wait twenty days before being able to have the registered securities sold. In many situations, given the volatile nature of the financial markets, the offering, twenty days later, no longer may find a receptive audience. The end result is that the Commission staff may be able to "persuade" the issuer and affiliated parties to disclose more information than they otherwise would prefer.

The SEC has reduced its leverage somewhat in this context by adopting Rule 430A. Under Rule 430A, issuers engaging in offerings of securities for cash no longer are required to file a pre-effective "pricing" amendment (i.e.,

---

[18] See, e.g., *In re Charles Schwab & Co.*, 1999 WL 1038050 (Nov. 12, 1999); *In re Private Financial Network*, [1997 Transfer Binder] Fed. Sec. L. Reg. (SEC) ¶ 77,332 (March 12, 1997).

information relating to price and the underwriting syndicate). Today, specified changes can be made with respect to such matters as price and volume information after the registration statement's effective date, provided that such changes do not materially alter the disclosure contained in the registration statement. In the Release adopting Rule 430A, the SEC pointed out that the rule does not alter an issuer's disclosure obligations. According to the Commission, Rule 430A is intended to "minimize the risk of disruption of a registrant's marketing schedule caused by the need to file a pricing amendment and wait until the registration statement is declared effective."[19]

Moreover, as a condition to granting acceleration, the SEC may require the respective parties to undertake certain actions. For example, in order that market professionals can adequately advise their customers, particularly in an initial public offering, the Commission under Rule 460 "will not accelerate the effective date of a registration statement unless the preliminary prospectus . . . is distributed to underwriters and dealers who it is reasonably anticipated will be invited to participate in the distribution of the security to be offered or sold."[20] Also, in determining whether to accelerate a registration statement's effective date, the Commission will consider, particularly for a nonreporting company under the Exchange Act, whether reasonable steps have been taken to furnish preliminary Rule 430 prospectuses to prospective purchasers.[21] As a final example, under Item 512(h) and 702 of Regulation S-K, the issuer, in order to request acceleration of the effective date of the registration statement, must disclose, inter alia, any arrangement to indemnify any director, officer or controlling person of the issuer against liabilities arising under the Securities Act. A subject issuer, pursuant to Item 510, also must disclose that such indemnification with respect to a director, officer, or controlling person of the issuer, "in the opinion of the Securities and Exchange Commission . . . is against public policy as expressed in the [Securities] Act and is, therefore, unenforceable."

[C] The Post-Effective Period

[1] Overview

After the registration statement becomes effective, the *post-effective* period commences. Sales of the subject securities now may be made. Written offers continue to be regulated by Section 5(b) as in the waiting period. Under Section 2(a)(10), "free writing" is permitted in the post-effective period. Hence, without violating Section 5, subject parties during this period may distribute any written material (such as glossy brochures) so long as

---

[19] SEC Securities Act Release No. 6714 (1987). See Securities Act Release No. 6964 (1992).

[20] SEC Securities Act Release No. 4968 (1969).

[21] *Id.*

the literature is accompanied or preceded by a statutory Section 10(a) prospectus or its equivalent.[22]

The contents of the statutory prospectus are specified in Section 10(a). Unlike the preliminary prospectus, which is used in the waiting period (see Rule 430), the statutory prospectus is used only after the registration statement becomes effective. This is because the preliminary prospectus has certain incomplete information.

During the post-effective period, Section 5 has the effect of requiring that a Section 10(a) statutory prospectus be sent or given to purchasers of securities. Note, however, that a Section 10(b) summary prospectus (see Rule 431) may continue to be used by certain issuers in the post-effective period for solicitation purposes only. This is due to the fact that a summary prospectus meets the requirements of Section 10, and, hence, is permitted under Section 5(b)(1). If there is "free writing" (including a confirmation of sale), however, a statutory Section 10(a) prospectus or its equivalent[23] must be transmitted. Otherwise, such "free writing" constitutes a separate prospectus under Section 2(a)(10), thereby resulting in a violation of Section 5(b)(1). Moreover, if the securities are mailed to the customer for purposes of sale, Section 5(b)(2) requires that such securities must be accompanied or preceded by a Section 10(a) prospectus.

The use of electronic media in this context raises significant liability concerns. For example, the SEC in 1995 adopted the "envelope" theory, positing that an issuer's sales literature containing a hyperlink to its statutory prospectus enables the final prospectus to be viewed directly as if it were packaged in the same envelope as the sales literature. Therefore, the final [statutory] prospectus would be considered to have accompanied the sales literature. Consequently, the placing of sales literature in a discussion forum on a web site would satisfy [Securities Act] delivery obligations provided that a hyperlink that provides direct access to the final [statutory] prospectus is included.[24]

---

[22] See Securities Act Release No. 7168 (1995) (adopting Rule 434). As set forth by the SEC in the adopting release:

Rule 434 permits participants in eligible offerings to convey prospectus information in more than one document and allows such documents to be delivered to investors at separate intervals and in varying manners. Rule 434 does not require that a final, integrated prospectus be delivered to investors. In the aggregate, however, all required information will still be disclosed to investors prior to or at the same time as a confirmation is sent . . . .

[23] See Securities Act Release No. 7168 (1995) (excerpt of Release quoted in note 22 *supra*). In that Release, the Commission also stated:

[I]n eligible offerings . . . persons may comply with their prospectus delivery obligations by delivering a preliminary prospectus, a term sheet, if necessary, and a confirmation. The term sheet is required to include all information material to investors with respect to the offering that is not disclosed in the delivered preliminary prospectus or the confirmation.

. . .

Rule 434 requires that the preliminary prospectus and the term sheet, taken together, not materially differ from the disclosure included in the effective registration statement . . . .

See generally Barker, *SEC Registration of Public Offerings Under the Securities Act of 1933*, 52 Bus. Law. 65 (1996).

[24] SEC Securities Act Release No. 7233 (1995). See Securities Act Release No. 7288 (1996).

More recently, opining on whether such sales literature would be deemed part of the prospectus, thus raising Section 11 and 12(a)(2) liability exposure, the SEC commented that "if an issuer includes a hyperlink *within* a Section 10 prospectus, the hyperlinked information would become a part of that prospectus" but that a "hyperlink from an external document to a Section 10 prospectus . . . would not result in the non-prospectus document being deemed part of the prospectus."[25]

[2] Dealer Prospectus Delivery Requirements

In the post-effective period, dealers are subject to the prospectus delivery requirements, noncompliance with which results in a violation of Section 5(b). In order to help ensure that there is adequate information disseminated to the investing public, Section 4(3), as modified by SEC Rule 174 pursuant to the Commission's rulemaking authority under that statute, generally requires that either a participating or nonparticipating dealer must provide a Section 10(a) statutory prospectus for sale purposes in the following circumstances:

(1) Under the language of Section 4(3), if the issuer has not previously sold its securities pursuant to an earlier effective registration statement, a dealer must provide a statutory prospectus up to ninety days after the effectiveness of the registration statement or after the securities have been bona fide offered to the public, whichever is later.

Pursuant to rule, the SEC has modified the foregoing requirement (see Rule 174). In effect, the Commission reduced the prospectus delivery requirement for dealers, other than participating dealers selling any unsold allotment, to twenty-five days after the effectiveness of the registration statement or twenty-five days after the securities were bona fide offered to the public, whichever is later. Rule 174 applies to issuers who were not previously reporting companies and whose securities are now exchange-listed or traded in the National Association of Securities Dealers' Automated Quotation System (NASDAQ). On the other hand, for offerings by previously non-reporting issuers whose stock is not traded on an exchange or the NASDAQ, the prospectus delivery requirement of ninety days is retained.[26]

(2) If the issuer has previously sold its securities pursuant to an earlier effective registration statement, Section 4(3) provides that a dealer must provide a prospectus up to forty days after the public offering has commenced. Rule 174, in effect, nullifies this aspect of Section 4(3), however, by providing that a dealer generally is not subject to the prospectus delivery requirements if the issuer is a reporting company under the Exchange Act.

(3) Irrespective of the time period expired, either under Section 4(3) or Rule 174, a participating dealer selling part of its unsold allotment must adhere to the prospectus delivery requirements.

---

[25] SEC Securities Act Release Act No. 7856 (2000) (emphasis added).

[26] See SEC Securities Act Release 6763 (1988).

[3] The Section 4(4) Exemption

A word also needs to be said about Section 4(4). That provision exempts from the prospectus delivery requirements unsolicited brokers' transactions (as opposed to a "distribution") executed on an exchange or in the over-the-counter market. Note here that the intermediary must be effecting the transaction for "the account of others" (see § 3(4) of the Exchange Act) and not for its own account. If the manner, amount, and other characteristics of the sale(s) are deemed to constitute a "distribution," however, the Section 4(4) exemption is unavailable (as it applies only to "transactions"). Moreover, the transaction must be at the customer's behest and must take place on an exchange or in the over-the-counter market.

[4] Loophole?

An argument can be made that there is a loophole in the prospectus delivery framework. For example, a participating dealer may telephone a customer in either the waiting or post-effective period to inquire whether the investor is interested in purchasing securities pursuant to the registered offering. After the customer expresses his or her desire to buy the stock, the dealer in the post-effective period mails the customer a confirmation of sale accompanied by a statutory Section 10(a) prospectus. The statutory prospectus thus is the first written communication that the investor receives. The dealer's conduct is permitted provided that the issuer is a reporting company under the Exchange Act. If the issuer is not a reporting company, however, SEC Exchange Act Rule 15c2-8(b) deems it a violation of such rule (not Section 5 of the Securities Act) for a broker or dealer to fail to "deliver a copy of the preliminary prospectus to any person who is expected to receive a confirmation of sale at least 48 hours prior to the mailing of such confirmation."

As a result, insofar as Exchange Act reporting companies are concerned, it may be asserted that in practice the prospectus delivery requirements often may be an "empty gesture." Moreover, in part because the remedies provided for violation of Rule 15c2-8(b) are uncertain, it may be the case that investors who purchase stock in initial public offerings are all too often doing so without receiving the preliminary prospectus.

[D] Chart of Time Periods

The following chart hopefully will help clarify the conduct permitted as well as prohibited during the pre-filing, waiting, and post-effective periods.

Time Period

Pre-Filing	Waiting	Post-Effective
Offers to sell as well as offers to buy are prohibited — see §§ 2(a)(3), 5(c).	Oral offers and written offers by means of a § 10 prospectus are permitted — see §§ 2(a)(10), 5(b)(1), 10(b), Rules 430, 431.	Sales may be made only if a statutory § 10(a) prospectus or its equivalent has been sent or given to the investor — see §§ 2(a)(10), 5(b), 10(a), Rules 430A, 434.
Sales are prohibited — see §§ 2(a)(3), 5(a). Negotiations and agreements between the issuer and any underwriter or among underwriters who are or will be in privity with the issuer are permitted — see § 2(a)(3).	Securities may be sold and offers to buy may be accepted only in the post-effective period — see §§ 2(a)(3), 5(a).	§ 10 summary prospectus permitted to be used by certain issuers for solicitation purposes only — see §§ 5(b)(1), 10(b), Rule 431.
		Preliminary § 10 prospectus not permitted during post-effective period — see Rule 430. "Free-writing" permitted only in the post-effective period and only if such material accompanied or preceded by a statutory § 10(a) prospectus or its equivalent — see §§ 2(a)(10), 5(b)(1), 10(a), Rules 430A, 434. Both the "tombstone ad" and the "identifying statement" may be used — see § 2(a)(10), Rule 134.
Issuer may make an announcement of a proposed public offering in compliance with Rule 135.	Both the "tombstone ad" and the "identifying statement" may be used — see § 2(a)(10), Rule 134.	
Pursuant to Rules 137-139, a broker or dealer may publish certain information about specified issuers. This is also the case in the waiting and post-effective periods. With respect to all three time periods, the interstate commerce requirement must be met in order for § 5 to apply.		Prospectus delivery requirements for dealers are subject to § 4(3) and Rule 174.

Pre-Filing	Waiting	Post-Effective
		Unsolicited brokers' transactions without prospectus delivery requirements permitted if such transactions (as opposed to a "distribution") executed on an exchange or in the over-the-counter market — see § 4(4).

§ 4.03   The "Misleading" Prospectus

In *SEC v. Manor Nursing Centers, Inc.*,[27] the Second Circuit considered whether material misrepresentations or nondisclosures contained in a statutory prospectus signified that, in addition to incurring antifraud liability, the prospectus failed to meet the requirements of Section 10(a) of the 1933 Act and, hence, violated Section 5(b)(2) of that Act. In that case, the violations were premised on the defendants' failure to amend or supplement the prospectus to reflect changes which occurred in the post-effective period that made the previous information furnished materially false and misleading. The Second Circuit held that Section 5(b)(2) had been violated, stating:

> We hold that implicit in the statutory provision that the prospectus contain certain information is the requirement that such information be true and correct. A prospectus does not meet the requirements of § 10(a), therefore, if information required to be disclosed is materially false and misleading. Appellants violated § 5(b)(2) by delivering Manor securities for sale accompanied by a prospectus which did not meet the requirements of § 10(a) in that the prospectus contained materially false and misleading statements with respect to information required by § 10(a) to be disclosed.[28]

The Manor Nursing analysis is subject to criticism because it imposes essentially strict liability, thereby nullifying the due diligence and reasonable care defenses contained in Sections 11 and 12(a)(2) of the Securities Act (see Chapter 6). For this reason, a number of courts have limited its holding to apply only where the prospectus or a like document is egregiously incomplete or permeated with misrepresentations.[29] Other courts, in analogous situations, have completely rejected *Manor Nursing's* rationale.[30]

---

[27] 458 F.2d 1082 (2d Cir. 1972).

[28] *Id.* at 1098.

[29] See, e.g., *Byrnes v. Faulkner Dawkins & Sullivan*, 413 F. Supp. 453 (S.D.N.Y. 1976), *aff'd on other grounds*, 550 F.2d 1303 (2d Cir. 1977).

[30] See, e.g., *SEC v. Blazon Corp.*, 609 F.2d 960 (9th Cir. 1979).

One such case is *SEC v. Southwest Coal & Energy Company*.[31] There, the SEC relied by analogy on *Manor Nursing*, arguing that the issuer had never properly qualified for a Regulation B exemption since its Schedule D offering sheets were materially false and misleading. Such materially defective offering sheets, the SEC asserted, did not meet Regulation B's initial filing requirements, thereby violating Section 5(a) and 5(c). The Fifth Circuit rejected this contention, reasoning that such an interpretation would impose strict liability and vitiate the defenses available under other provisions of the securities laws (e.g., Sections 11, 12(a)(2), and 17(a) of the Securities Act and Section 10(b) of the Exchange Act). The court stated:

> That an offering sheet which formally complies with the disclosure requirements of Schedule D is misleading in some respect, should not automatically render void *ab initio* a Regulation B exemption obtained on the basis of that offering. Rather, representations and material nondisclosures may be adequately dealt with under the pertinent antifraud provisions expressly designed for that purpose, instead of under § 5(a), (c) which is more appropriately focused upon failures to adhere to the prescribed formal mechanisms or procedures.[32]

The view expressed above, on balance, is correct. To hold that a Section 5 violation occurs whenever a security is sold pursuant to a materially false or misleading statement in the prospectus or like document, such as an offering circular, would negate the defenses otherwise available. Such a result is one that Congress could not have intended.

On the other hand, if the thrust of *Manor Nursing* is confined to issuers of registered offerings, then the decision may be viewed as compatible with Section 11. Hence, because Section 11 holds issuers strictly liable for making material misrepresentations or nondisclosures in a registration statement, the *Manor Nursing* rationale is consistent with the framework of Section 11, provided that it is limited only to issuers.[33]

§ 4.04 A Brief Look at the Process of a Public Offering

The advantages and disadvantages of going public are addressed in § 4.05. In addition, the process of the initial public offering and the ramifications thereof are described in excerpts from articles contained in the textbook.[34]

---

[31] 624 F.2d 1312 (5th Cir. 1980).

[32] *Id.* at 1319 (citations omitted).

[33] In this regard, the Commission has certain enforcement powers if the registration statement is materially false or misleading. The most significant such power is the "stop order" pursuant to Section 8(d) of the Securities Act. See McLucas, *Stop Order Proceedings Under the Securities Act of 1933: A Current Assessment*, 40 Bus. Law. 515 (1980). See generally A. Bromberg & L. Lowenfels, *Securities Fraud and Commodities Fraud* § 6.11 (2000); M. Steinberg, *Securities Regulation: Liabilities and Remedies* § 5.02 (2000).

[34] See M. Steinberg, *Securities Regulation* 266–82 (3d ed. 1998), containing excerpts from, Schneider, Manko & Kant, *Going Public: Practice, Procedure, and Consequences*, 27 Vill. L. Rev. 1 (1981); Schneider & Shargel, *"Now That You Are Publicly Owned. . ."*, 36 Bus. Law. 1631 (1981).

In brief, and put simplistically, the process of a public offering may be analogized to the sale of commercial goods. In a public offering, the distribution chain normally is as follows: Issuer — Underwriters — Participating Dealers — Investors/Purchasers (who may be individuals or institutions). Generally speaking, the larger in dollar size and the greater the geographical area where the selling activity takes place, the larger the number of underwriters and dealers who will comprise the distribution chain to effectuate the offering. Note the similarity to the sale of commercial goods: Manufacturer — Wholesalers — Retailers — Consumers. As with the sale of commercial goods where wholesalers may sell directly to the public, underwriters also may bypass the "dealer-link" and sell the securities directly to investors. This may occur, for example, when an underwriter (such as Merrill Lynch) has a national retail brokerage capacity with which to market the securities directly to investors.

Underwriting agreements for the most part are on a "firm commitment" basis. This means that the underwriters agree to purchase the securities from the issuer (at a discount) with the intent to resell them to participating dealers and/or investors. Although the underwriters incur the risk of "being stuck" with the securities if there is insufficient buyer interest, this risk is minimized due to the fact that, during the "waiting" period (when offers can be made), purchaser interest can be estimated with a fair degree of accuracy. And, importantly, the underwriters' obligations normally are subject to several conditions, including various "outs" to not close should certain adverse developments arise prior to the closing date. Hence, because the underwriters are not obligated until the "eve" of the offering's effective date when the underwriting agreement is finalized to, inter alia, determine the desired number of shares to be offered and fix the offering price per share, they have a strong indication of the market's likely response to the offering.[35]

Another type of underwriting agreement is on a "best efforts" basis. In this situation, the underwriters act as agents for the issuer. Rather than purchasing the securities outright from the issuer and incurring the risk of insufficient investor interest in such securities or the specter of a "bear" market, the underwriters, acting as agent for the issuer, locate buyers utilizing their "best efforts." These types of offerings may be used for start-up or financially troubled enterprises where there is a substantial degree of uncertainty regarding the offering's, as well as the company's, ultimate success. Because investors may wish some degree of comfort when they part with their money in these types of offerings, such offerings frequently may be made on "a part or none" or "an all or nothing" basis. This means that, unless the requisite number of shares as stated in the registration statement are sold to bona fide purchasers and the proceeds

---

[35] See C. Johnson, *Corporate Finance and the Securities Laws*, 97-101 (2d ed. 1997); Schneider, Manko & Kant, *Going Public: Practice, Procedure and Consequences*, 27 Vill. L. Rev. 1, 24 (1981).

are received by a specified date, all funds will be returned to the prospective investors.[36]

In either a "firm commitment" or "best efforts" underwriting arrangement, the obligations of the underwriters normally are subject to various contractual conditions. Pursuant to such an arrangement, for example, underwriters may have the right not to close the "deal" if specified adverse developments arise before the closing date (such as the presence of adverse market conditions) or if the issuer fails to comply with its many representations and warranties. Moreover, the underwriters condition their obligations by bargaining for the receipt of certain legal opinions and/or representations from counsel for the issuer.[37]

A word should be said about the underwriting syndicate and dealer group. The syndicate is headed by the main underwriter or main underwriters (there, for example, may be three main underwriters in a fairly large offering). These underwriters generally are the ones to negotiate with the issuer and are delegated by the other underwriters in the syndicate to perform the due diligence functions. To effectuate the desired distribution, the main underwriter(s) will locate and bring in other underwriters which desire to take part in the offering. Generally, these "lower-tier" underwriters in the offering will purchase a significantly smaller number of shares from the issuer than the main underwriter(s). Although all underwriters are jointly and severally liable for material misstatements in the registration statement, Section 11(e) mitigates this potentially harsh effect somewhat by limiting an underwriter's damages to the dollar amount of the securities offered by such underwriter to the public. Moreover, Section 11(g) expressly permits a party to recover contribution.

Members of the dealer group ("participating" dealers), as discussed in § 4.02, are not in privity with the issuer. These are broker-dealers who for one reason or another (such as inability or a conscious desire not to commit the necessary funds) are not members of the underwriting syndicate but who nonetheless deem it in their financial interests to become a "participant" in the offering. Hence, they purchase from underwriters an allocated number of shares offered and resell them to their customers, their profit being the difference between the purchase price from the underwriters and the price of resale to their customers. Although dealers are not subject to Section 11 liability, they may incur liability under other provisions for making material misstatements (or omissions), for violating the prospectus delivery requirements, and for material misrepresentations (or nondisclosures) contained in the prospectus.

---

[36] See Rule 10b-9, 17 C.F.R. § 240.10b-9; Securities Exchange Act Release No. 11532 (1975). See generally Frelich & Janvey, *Understanding "Best Efforts" Offerings*, 17 Sec. Reg. L.J. 151 (1989).

[37] See Schneider, Manko & Kant, *Going Public: Practice, Procedure and Consequences*, 27 Vill. L. Rev. 1, 24 (1981). See generally L. Loss & J. Seligman, *Securities Regulation* 315-595 (3d ed. 1989); Such opinions, representations, or statements from counsel raise serious liability concerns. See Glossary *infra* defining the term "Comfort Opinion." See generally S. FitzGibbon & D. Glaser, *Legal Opinions* (1992); A. Jacobs, *Opinion Letters in Securities Matters* (rev. ed. 1990); M. Steinberg, *Corporate and Securities Malpractice* (1992); Rice & Steinberg, *Legal Opinions in Securities Transactions*, 16 J. Corp. L. 375 (1991).

§ 4.05 "Going Public" — Pros and Cons

Briefly, the *advantages* of an enterprise going public and having its initial public offering (IPO) include:

1. The funds obtained from the offering may be used for capital formation purposes as well as for retiring existing indebtedness.

2. The insiders may sell a substantial portion of their stock and thereby become (if they aren't already) millionaires.

3. A public offering, by improving the company's financial position, will enable it to have access to capital on more favorable terms.

4. The funds desired from the offering may enable the company to expand by acquiring other businesses.

5. By offering stock remuneration packages tied to a public market, the enterprise will be in a better position to hire and retain quality personnel.

6. By having a public market for its stock, the company may become better known, thereby possibly resulting in improved profits.

On the other hand, perceived *disadvantages* of going public include:

1. The costs of an IPO, particularly when compared to other methods of procuring funds, are high.

2. Due to shareholder concern for the short-term, management may discount long-term strategies in order to put emphasis on the company's stock prices.

3. Management, through its sale of stock, may lose control of the enterprise and become subject to a hostile takeover.

4. By going public, the enterprise becomes a reporting company under the Securities Exchange Act. Such a consequence may be viewed as having several disadvantages to insiders including:

    a. The company now must file periodic and annual reports, comply with the internal accounting controls and recordkeeping mandates of the Foreign Corrupt Practices Act (even if all of the company's operations are domestic), be subject to the federal proxy provisions, as well as a number of other requirements.

    b. The expenses of complying with Exchange Act requirements will be substantial.

    c. Insiders lose much of their privacy as their salaries, perquisites, and transactions with the issuer must be disclosed pursuant to SEC rules.

    d. Due to such mandated disclosure, there is a greater risk of shareholder litigation.

    e. Insiders are subject to the short-swing six-month trading provisions of Section 16 of the Exchange Act, thereby resulting in loss of liquidity and potential liability.

Given the above, the decision to go public may not be an easy one. Moreover, the registration process, including the planning, preparation, structuring, and timing of a public offering, is a major undertaking for all parties concerned. [38]

§ 4.06   The Integrated Disclosure Framework

The SEC's integrated disclosure system was adopted to ameliorate the expenses and duplication that were prevalent as a result of two different reporting mandates under the 1933 Act and the 1934 Act. In seeking to make disclosure as uniform as practicable under the two Acts, the SEC promulgated Regulation S-K and Regulation S-X (accounting rules), which act as the key sources for ascertaining the disclosures required to be made. For enterprises generally with annual revenues and a public float of less than $25 million, Regulation S-B rather than Regulation S-K applies (see discussion later in this section).

This is not to imply, however, that the disclosures contained in the various documents filed with the Commission are identical. For example, with respect to the annual report on Form 10-K and the annual report to shareholders, the SEC took the following position:

> The Commission has determined to require only portions of the Form 10-K and the annual report to security holders to have equivalent disclosure because these documents are not necessarily used in an identical manner. Disclosure requirements in annual reports evolved in the context of shareholders making voting decisions. The Form 10-K has traditionally confirmed information previously delivered to investors and other users making economic decisions about the company and, as a result, has been more detailed. [39]

Hence, under the Commission's integrated disclosure framework, registrant reporting has been simplified in three ways: "(1) disclosure requirements are made uniform under the Securities Act and the Exchange Act; (2) Exchange Act periodic reporting is used to satisfy much of the disclosure necessary in Securities Act registration statements; and (3) the use of informal shareholder communications is encouraged, but not required, to satisfy formal statutory requirements under both Acts." [40]

This emphasis on Exchange Act periodic disclosure under the integrated disclosure system induced the SEC to require that a majority of the registrant's directors sign the annual Form 10-K. Such a signature requirement was necessary, according to the Commission, in order to encourage directors "to devote the needed attention in reviewing the Form 10-K and

---

[38] See sources cited notes 34-37 *supra*.

[39] SEC Securities Act Release No. 6231 (1980).

[40] SEC Securities Act Release No. 6331 (1981).

Note that under the Electronic Data Gathering, Analysis, and Retrieval System (EDGAR), subject registrants must submit to the SEC virtually all documents (such as filings) electronically. See generally Westerberg, *EDGAR*, 26 Rev. Sec. & Comm. Reg. 173 (1993).

to seek the involvement of other professionals to the degree necessary to give themselves sufficient comfort."[41]

The integrated disclosure process, although calling for meaningful non-duplicative information, has evoked important liability concerns. These liability issues, related to the concept of "due diligence," are addressed in Chapter 6.

[A] Registration Forms

To implement the integrated disclosure system, the Commission adopted three registration forms, Forms S-1, S-2, and S-3. These Forms serve as the basic framework for registered offerings under the Securities Act. Incorporation by reference from 1934 Act reports is permitted only as to Forms S-2 and S-3:

> The registration statement for the first category is Form S-1. It requires complete disclosure to be set forth in the prospectus and permits no incorporation by reference. [Stated generally,] Form S-1 is to be used by registrants in the Exchange Act reporting system for less than three years and also may be used by any registrants who choose to do so or for whom no other form is available. [Subsequently, the SEC adopted Securities Act registration forms for small business issuers which may be used in lieu of the Form S-1 and which contain less rigorous disclosure requirements.]
>
> The second category of registration statement is Form S-2 which combines reliance on incorporating Exchange Act reports by reference with delivery to investors of streamlined information. Registrants in the Exchange Act reporting system for three years may use this Form, which allows them to choose to either: (1) Deliver a copy of their annual report to security holders along with the prospectus describing the offering or (2) present registrant-oriented information comparable to that of the annual report in the prospectus along with the description of the offering. In either case, the more complete information in the Form 10-K is incorporated by reference into the prospectus.
>
> Form S-3, in reliance on the efficient market theory, allows maximum use of incorporation by reference of Exchange Act reports and requires the least disclosure to be presented in the prospectus and delivered to investors. Generally, the Form S-3 prospectus [which can be used in primary offerings of common stock by issuers which have been in the Exchange Act reporting system for twelve months and which prior to such offering have $75 million of voting stock outstanding held by non-affiliates ("public float")] will present the same transaction-specific information as will be presented in a Form S-1 or S-2 prospectus. Information concerning the registrant will be incorporated by reference from Exchange Act reports. The

---

[41] SEC Securities Act Release No. 6231 (1980). See Brown, *Deregulation and the Annual Report to Shareholders*, 15 Sec. Reg. L.J. 423 (1988).

prospectus will not be required to present any information concerning the registrant unless there has been a material change in the registrant's affairs which has not been reported in an Exchange Act filing or the Exchange Act reports incorporated by reference do not reflect certain restated financial statements or other financial information.[42]

The rationale largely underlying incorporation by reference of Exchange Act reports into 1933 registration statements is that information regularly furnished to the securities markets through 1934 Act periodic reports is digested by the marketplace and reflected in the price of the issuer's securities, thereby eliminating the need to reiterate such information in the public offering context. Hence, this theory postulates that the securities markets, by analyzing the available information and accurately valuing the information in the price set for a security, are efficient. The efficient market theory has received Supreme Court approbation with respect to the issue of "reliance" in Section 10(b) litigation,[43] discussed in Chapter 7.

For mergers and certain other reorganizations, the Form S-4 registration statement may be used. This Form is discussed in Chapter 5.

In 1992, as part of its Small Business Initiatives, the SEC adopted Regulation S-B to facilitate the access of small business issuers to the public securities markets. Generally, a small business issuer has annual revenues of less than $25 million and a public float (the aggregate market value of such issuer's voting stock held by non-affiliates) of less than $25 million. Only U.S. or Canadian issuers are eligible and investment companies, irrespective of their domicile, are excluded. Moreover, in order to be eligible, if a purported small business issuer is a majority-owned subsidiary of another corporation, its parent also must satisfy the above definition of small business issuer.[44]

Regulation S-B serves as the central depository that references disclosure requirements for 1933 and 1934 Act filings for small business issuers in the integrated disclosure system. Thus, Regulation S-B provides for simplified disclosure and parallels Regulation S-K. The two Securities Act registration forms in the S-B framework are Form SB-1 and Form SB-2. As adopted, Form SB-1 is designed for those small business issuers that seek to transition from non-reporting to reporting status ("transitional" issuers). Based on a simplified and less rigorous model of disclosure, Form SB-1 may be used by transitional small business issuers to register securities offerings of up to $10 million during any twelve-month period.[45] Turning to Form SB-2, which has been called by the SEC as "the designated Securities Act registration form for small business issuers," no dollar limits exist for offerings on Form SB-2 and it "may be used for both initial and repeat offerings, and for both primary and secondary offerings."[46] Although

---

[42] SEC Securities Act Release No. 6383 (1982). See Securities Act Release No. 6964 (1992).

[43] See *Basic, Inc. v. Levinson*, 485 U.S. 224 (1988).

[44] See Securities Act Release No. 6949 (1992).

[45] See Securities Act Release No. 6996 (1993).

[46] Securities Act Release No. 6949 (1992).

seemingly expansive, the Form SB-2 in practice is not nearly so because it can be employed only by those entities meeting the definition of small business issuer.

[B] Shelf Registration

One of the Commission's significant actions with respect to the integrated disclosure framework was its adoption of Rule 415, the "shelf" registration rule. Generally, Rule 415 concerns the Securities Act registration of securities to be offered or sold on a delayed or continuous basis in the future. Significantly, the rule allows Form S-3 issuers to file primary-at-the-market offerings of equity securities which they plan to offer within two years of the effective date of the registration statement.[47] As will be addressed in Chapter 6, Rule 415 raises significant liability questions.

§ 4.07 The Mandatory Disclosure System

This Section addresses five timely issues in the securities regulation field: (1) the debate surrounding the securities acts' mandatory disclosure system, (2) the SEC's "plain English" disclosure requirements, (3) issuer disclosure of forward-looking information, (4) issuer disclosure obligations with respect to the "MD&A" — management discussion and analysis, and (5) issuer disclosure of qualitative, in addition to quantitative, information.

[A] The Disclosure Debate

The propriety of Congress' enactment of a mandatory securities law disclosure system has generated much debate over the last three decades. As discussed throughout this chapter, issuers must disclose certain material and other specified information when publicly offering securities pursuant to the Securities Act's registration framework. Moreover, once an issuer engages in a public offering, it is required under the Exchange Act to provide the SEC and its shareholders with annual and other periodic reports. Whether such a mandatory disclosure system is appropriate and the type of information that should be subject to compelled disclosure have been subject to debate.

Critics of the mandatory disclosure system argue that the system produces considerable costs yet few benefits.[48] The quality of disclosure, according to critics, yields little useful information. Professor Kripke, for example, opined:

---

[47] SEC Securities Act Release No. 6499 (1983). See Banoff, *Regulatory Subsidies, Efficient Markets, and Shelf Registration: An Analysis of Rule 415*, 70 Va. L. Rev. 135 (1984); Maynard, *Blue Sky Regulation of Rule 415 Shelf-Registered Primary Offerings: The Need for a Limited Form of Federal Preemption*, 22 Ariz. St. L.J. 89 (1990).

[48] See, e.g., H. Manne, *Insider Trading and the Stock Market* (1966); Benston, *The Value of the SEC's Accounting Disclosure Requirements*, 44 Acct. Rev. 515 (1969); Stigler, *Public Regulation of the Securities Markets*, 37 J. Bus. 117 (1964).

> [T]he Commission's disclosure system cannot be given high marks either for performance or on a cost/benefit basis. . . . The system was founded not on disclosure of "all material facts," but on disclosure of events in the past which the Commission could objectively verify. This historical perspective was assumed for the inefficient purpose of preventing blatant securities fraud and for the less apparent purpose of protecting the Commission from criticism for issues that turn sour. In recent years, while the Commission has shown commendable willingness to try to modernize the system, development and economic theory have outrun adaptation of the system.[49]

Proponents of a mandatory disclosure system assert that, in the absence of such a system: (1) some registrants would engage in fraudulent disclosure practices, (2) insider perquisites and salaries as well as underwriter costs would be excessive, (3) current state laws and self-regulatory oversight by themselves would be inadequate for enforcement purposes, (4) the threat of civil and criminal actions would not induce the appropriate level of disclosure, and (5) investors would lose confidence in the integrity of the securities markets.[50]

A point that should be raised is the role that disclosure under the federal securities laws has on normative corporate conduct. As this author has stated:

> Although the rationale underlying disclosure is not based primarily on influencing corporate internal affairs but rather on providing shareholders and the marketplace with sufficient information to make intelligent decisions and to be apprised of significant developments, there is little question that disclosure has a substantial impact on the normative conduct of corporations. In this regard, the Commission's disclosure policies . . . have not only had an effect of deterring unlawful or questionable conduct but have played a positive role in influencing the establishment of improved standards of conduct.[51]

---

[49] Kripke, *Fifty Years of Securities Regulation in Search of a Purpose*, 21 San Diego L. Rev. 257 (1984).

[50] See Seligman, *The Historical Need for a Mandatory Corporate Disclosure System*, 9 J. Corp. L. 1, 9 (1979). See generally Coffee, *Market Failure and the Economic Case for a Mandatory Disclosure System*, 70 Va. L. Rev. 717 (1984); Easterbrook & Fischel, *Mandatory Disclosure and the Protection of Investors*, 70 Va. L. Rev. 669 (1984); Fanto, *The Absence of Cross-Cultural Communications: SEC Mandatory Disclosure and Foreign Corporate Governance*, 17 Nw. J. Int'l L. & Bus. 119 (1996); Fox, *Retaining Mandatory Securities Disclosure: Why Issuer Choice Is Not Investor Empowerment*, 85 Va. L. Rev. 1335 (1997); Palmiter, *Toward Disclosure Choice in Securities Offerings*, 1991 Colum. Bus. L. Rev. 1 (1999); Romano, *Empowering Investors: A Market Approach to Securities Regulation*, 107 Yale L.J. 2359 (1998).

[51] M. Steinberg, *Corporate Internal Affairs: A Corporate and Securities Law Perspective* 29 (1983). See R. Stevenson, *Corporations and Information — Secrecy, Access and Disclosure* 81-82 (1980) ("Today the disclosure requirements of the securities laws are used, in a variety of ways, for the explicit purpose of influencing a wide range of corporate primary behavior. . . ."); Weiss, *Disclosure and Corporate Accountability*, 34 Bus. Law. 575 (1979) ("[O]ne of the central themes of the system by which large corporations are governed [is] that corporate decisionmaking be regulated through mandatory disclosure requirements rather than direct government intervention.").

[B] Plain English Disclosure Requirements

In 1998, the SEC adopted the plain English disclosure rules primarily to address concerns that disclosure documents were too complicated to be effectively used by many individual investors. The principal focus of these rules is clarity of prospectus disclosure. Because prospectuses are drafted in significant part to avoid liability that may ensue from a public offering, language used in prospectuses traditionally has been often highly technical and legalistic. This complexity, in turn, impairs the ability of investors to make knowledgeable judgments regarding the merits of the securities being offered. Under the plain English disclosure rules, the Commission requires issuers to write the cover pages, summary, and risk factors sections of prospectuses in plain English. Further, the SEC has provided specific guidance on how to make the entire prospectus clear, concise, and under-standable.[52]

The plain English rule (Rule 421) sets forth requirements with respect to the front and back cover pages, the summary, and the risk factors sections of the prospectus. These requirements include:

- Short sentences;

- Definite, concrete, everyday language;

- Active voice;

- Tabular presentation or bullet lists for complex material, when-ever possible;

- No legal jargon or highly technical business terms; and

- No multiple negatives.[53]

In addition to the specific portions of the prospectus discussed above, Rule 421(b) mandates that the entire prospectus be "clear, concise, and under-standable." Pertinent standards to be followed in prospectus preparation include:

- Present information in clear, concise sections, paragraphs, and sentences . . . ;

- Use descriptive headings and subheadings;

- Avoid frequent reliance on glossaries or defined terms as the primary means of explaining information in the prospectus . . . ; and

- Avoid legal and highly technical business terminology.[54]

---

[52] Securities Act Release No. 7497 (1998).

[53] *Id*; Rule 421(d)(2), 17 C.F.R. § 230.421(d)(2).

[54] Rule 421(b), 17 C.F.R. § 230.421(b). Further, Rule 421(b) and Securities Act Release No. 7497 (1998) list the following drafting styles that the SEC believes make the prospectus harder to understand:

- Legalistic or overly complex presentations that make the substance of the disclosure difficult to understand;

- Vague "boilerplate" explanations that are imprecise and readily subject to differing interpretations;

The SEC makes clear, however, that certain business terms are often necessary to describe companies in certain industries (e.g., high-tech corporations). Therefore, the Commission proposes that, if certain technical terms are necessary, prospectuses attempt to clearly define the meaning of those terms the first time that they are used. Further, the Commission recognizes that sophisticated investors may want to read certain documents relating to the company in their entirety. For example, investors may wish to read the specific language of a contract that is highly pertinent to the company's future. In these situations, the Commission sets forth that information relating to such documents must be presented and explained in a clear fashion.[55]

[C] Disclosure of "Forward-Looking" Information

Although continuing to support strongly the need for a mandatory disclosure system, the Commission has responded to Professor Kripke and other critics by taking certain actions. Perhaps the most important is the adoption of the integrated disclosure system. A second is the Commission's promulgation of Securities Act Rule 175 (and Exchange Act Rule 3b-6) providing a "safe harbor" for projections.[56] A third is the SEC's adoption of Item 303 of Regulation S-K focusing on Management Discussion and Analysis (MD&A).[57] In this regard, the area encompassing issuer affirmative disclosure obligations (including such subjects as disclosure of "soft" information, merger negotiations, and "bad" news) is addressed at length in Chapter 10. And a fourth major development is the enactment of the Private Securities Litigation Reform Act of 1995. A key aspect of this Act is the provision of a safe harbor from liability in private actions for certain forward-looking statements made by publicly-held companies (for further discussion, see § 10.05).

Whereas "hard" information emphasizes historical data, "soft" information often focuses on forward-looking statements, such as projections, forecasts, and predictions. Until the mid 1970s, the SEC and the courts discouraged and even prohibited the disclosure of soft information. The major concern had been that investors, particularly the unsophisticated, might attach too much significance to information that is of questionable reliability.[58]

With the adoption of Rule 175 under the Securities Act, the SEC recognized that the flow of "soft" information to the marketplace may enable more informed investment decisions to be made. Generally, Rule 175 (as well as Rule 3b-6 under the Exchange Act) encourages issuer use of

- Complex information copied directly from legal documents without any clear and concise explanation of the provision(s); and
- Disclosure repeated in different sections of the document that increases the size of the document but does not enhance the quality of the information.

[55] Securities Act Release No. 7497 (1998).

[56] See SEC Securities Act Release No. 6084 (1979).

[57] See SEC Financial Reporting Release No. 36 (1989).

[58] See, e.g., *Gerstle v. Gamble-Skogmo, Inc.*, 478 F.2d 1281, 1294 (2d Cir. 1973).

financial projections in 1933 Act registration statements, 1934 Act reports, annual reports to shareholders, and other documents filed with the SEC. The rule establishes a "safe harbor" from liability for parties who invoke the rule.

Under Rule 175, "a safe harbor [is created] from the applicable liability provisions of the federal securities laws for statements [made by or on behalf of an issuer or by an outside re iewer retained by such issuer] relating to or containing (1) projections of reserves, income (loss), earnings (loss) per share or other financial items, such as capital expenditures, dividends, or capital structure, (2) management plans and objectives for future company operations, and (3) future economic performance included in management's statements."[59] In providing this "safe harbor," Rule 175 precludes liability for the making of issuer forward-looking statements unless the plaintiff establishes that any such statement was made or reaffirmed without a reasonable basis or was disclosed other than in good faith.[60]

It may be argued that the SEC went too far in permitting first-time public issuers to include "safe harbor" projections in their registration statements. Indeed, pursuant to the Commission's 1992 Small Business Initiatives, non-reporting issuers in Regulation A offerings also are entitled to invoke Rule 175.[61] Unlike reporting companies, many such issuers are start-up companies with no previous substantial earnings history. Moreover, in any event, these issuers have not been followed in the market. Hence, the SEC may have thrown its normal caution to the wind for the sake of encouraging projections. It can be argued, however, that, if such first-time issuers make projections with no previous earnings history, such projections are not within Rule 175's "safe harbor" because they are not made in "good faith" and "with a reasonable basis."[62]

The above argument, however, is unlikely to succeed. Projections for issuers engaged in IPOs or Regulation A offerings clearly are permitted within the confines of the safe harbor rule. Moreover, pursuant to legislation enacted by Congress in 1995, the safe harbor provisions have been broadened to encompass certain oral and written statements, even if not filed with the SEC, by an Exchange Act reporting company and those acting on its behalf (see § 10.05 *infra*). Nonetheless, perhaps in recognition that abuses may be rampant under an expansive safe harbor rule, Congress excluded issuers of speculative securities, such as penny stocks, from being entitled to invoke such safe harbor provisions.[63]

---

[59] Securities Act Release No. 6084 (1979).

[60] *Id.*

[61] See Securities Act Release No. 6949 (1992). See also, § 3.09[B][4] *supra*.

[62] See generally Fiflis, *Soft Information: The SEC's Former Exogenous Zone*, 26 U.C.L.A. L. Rev. 95 (1978); Poole, *Improving the Reliability of Management Forecasts*, 14 J. Corp. L. 547 (1989); Comment, *The Safe Harbor for Forecasts — A Step in the Right Direction?* 1980 Duke L.J. 607; Note, *Disclosure of Future-Oriented Information Under the Securities Laws*, 88 Yale L.J. 338 (1978).

[63] See discussion § 10.05[D] *infra*.

[D] Management Discussion and Analysis ("MD&A")

Responding further to critics that the Commission slights the importance of forward-looking information, the SEC adopted Item 303 of Regulation S-K (and Item 303 of Regulation S-B). Item 303 pertains to "Management Discussion and Analysis of Financial Condition and Results of Operation" (MD&A). This provision plays a significant role in the mandatory disclosure of forward-looking information in certain situations. As stated by one source, "the MD&A has become a major, if not the major, item of narrative disclosure that is studied, together with the financial statements, for investment decision and analysis purposes."[64]

Pursuant to the MD&A, the SEC has asserted that a disclosure obligation exists "where a trend, demand, commitment, event or uncertainty is both presently known to management and reasonably likely to have material effects on the registrant's financial condition or results of operation."[65] In circumstances where a trend, demand, commitment, event or uncertainty is known, the subject company's management must consider the following:

1. Is the known trend, demand, commitment, event or uncertainty likely to come to fruition? If management determines that it is not reasonably likely to occur, no disclosure is required.

2. If management cannot make that determination, it must evaluate objectively the consequences of the known trend, demand, commitment, event or uncertainty, on the assumption that it will come to fruition.

Disclosure is then required unless management determines that a material effect on the registrant's financial condition or results of operations is not reasonably likely to occur.[66]

Clearly, the SEC will bring enforcement actions when it deems the MD&A deficient. In view of these significant liability concerns, preparation of the MD&A demands careful planning, adequate time for reflection, and communication among the participants of the disclosure "team."[67]

[E] Disclosure of "Qualitative" Information

Purely qualitative information, unlike quantitative information, does not impact significantly on the earnings, assets, or economic viability of the registrant. Rather, such information more directly relates to the integrity and competency of corporate management. Under the Commission's rules and judicial decisions, disclosure is required, for example, of certain self-dealing transactions engaged in by management as well as adjudicated

---

[64] Schneider, *MD&A Disclosure*, 22 Rev. Sec. & Comm. Reg. 149, 150 (1989). See SEC Financial Reporting Release No. 36 (1989).

[65] SEC Financial Reporting Release No. 36, 6 Fed. Sec. L. Rep. (CCH) ¶ 73,193, at 62,842 (1989).

[66] *Id.* at 62,843.

[67] See, e.g., *In the Matter of Caterpillar, Inc.*, Administrative Proceeding No. 3-7692 (SEC 1992); discussion § 10.02 *infra*. See generally Hiler & Freeman, *Management's Discussion and Analysis: Known Trends in SEC Enforcement*, 8 Insights No. 12, at 11 (Dec. 1994); Schneider, *supra* note 64, at 155-56.

illegalities and certain other events (such as the imposition of an SEC injunction).[68] Absent self-dealing, an adjudicated illegality, or mandated disclosure called for by a specific SEC rule, courts are reluctant to require an issuer to disclose qualitative information that is not economically material.[69]

In this context, as well as others, where liability is premised on the failure to disclose, the information omitted in order to be actionable must be material (or called for by an SEC rule) and there must exist a disclosure obligation.[70] For example, in the insider trading context, the Supreme Court has made it clear that silence when trading on material nonpublic information is not actionable under Section 10(b) of the Exchange Act unless there exists a duty to disclose such information.[71]

As a general matter, Regulation S-K and Regulation S-B (for small business issuers) are the central sources for determining a publicly-held company's disclosure obligations under the federal securities laws. They are not, however, the only sources. For example, in the securities offering setting, Rule 408 of Regulation C provides:

> In addition to the information expressly required to be included in a registration statement, there shall be added such further material information, if any, as may be necessary to make the required statements, in the light of the circumstances under which they are made, not misleading.

Rule 12b-20 promulgated under the 1934 Act contains a similar requirement with respect to reports filed with the SEC pursuant to the Exchange Act.

Moreover, it may be argued that because the issuer itself is selling securities in the offering context, a fiduciary duty triggering a disclosure obligation arises between the issuer and purchasers of the securities. Although this view is not held by all courts, it may be posited that in the Securities Act registration setting, if the information is material, it must be disclosed.[72]

§ 4.08   State "Blue Sky" Law

Generally, under state Blue Sky law, as under the federal securities laws, every security offered to be sold in the applicable state must be registered or exempt from registration. Note one important caveat: If the securities

---

[68] See, e.g., *Maldonado v. Flynn*, 597 F.2d 789 (2d Cir. 1979); Items 402, 404 of Regulations S-K.

[69] See, e.g., *Gaines v. Haughton*, 645 F.2d 761 (9th Cir. 1981), *cert. denied*, 454 U.S. 1145 (1982). See generally Symposium, *Corporate Disclosure and its Impact on Corporate Morality/ Efficiency*, 48 Cath. U. L. Rev. No. 1 (1998); Ferrara, Starr & Steinberg, *Disclosure of Information Bearing on Management Integrity and Competency*, 76 Nw. U.L. Rev. 555 (1981).

[70] See, e.g., *Roeder v. Alpha Industries*, 814 F.2d 22 (1st Cir. 1987).

[71] See *Dirks v. SEC*, 463 U.S. 646 (1983); *Chiarella v. United States*, 445 U.S. 222 (1980).

[72] See *Chiarella v. United States*, 445 U.S. 222, 230 (1980). For discussion on this issue, see § 10.01 *infra*.

offered are listed on the New York or American Stock Exchange or traded on the NASDAQ National Market System, offerings of such securities are exempt from state registration requirements. Hence, companies whose stock is or will be listed on a major stock exchange or traded on the NASDAQ National Market System are exempt from the states' registration requirements.[73]

Traditionally, there are three types of registration which states may require. The first type, registration by coordination, is available to the issuer when a registered offering is being made under the Securities Act of 1933. This method of registration only requires the filing of three copies of the current federal prospectus as well as any additional information required by the state securities administrator. A second type of registration, registration by notification, requires the filing of a short-form registration statement and is available generally only when an issuer and its predecessors have had a seasoned business history for at least five years (e.g., no default and average net earnings). The third type of registration, registration by qualification, goes further than mandating full disclosure and authorizes the state securities administrator to engage in merit regulation. Under merit regulation, the state securities administrator can prevent an offering from going forward because it is not "fair, just and equitable."[74]

Although many states reject merit regulation, a number of others adhere to this approach. In states adopting merit regulation, full and fair disclosure alone is not enough. Rather, the offering also must be deemed "fair, just, and equitable." The debate over merit regulation generally has focused on whether full disclosure of material information concerning an offering is sufficient to protect investors, the propriety of paternalistic government regulation, and the economic costs versus benefits of such a system of regulation.[75] Generally, merit regulation is used to describe the securities laws of those states which, "in addition to requiring full disclosure, have granted their administrators power to analyze the securities to be offered, the terms of the offering, and the business of the issuer for purposes of determining, according to certain formal and informal rules, whether the securities are too speculative for public sale."[76]

In general, "tough" merit regulation states may deny registration where insiders or promoters have invested relatively little in relation to the amount of capital sought by the offering or if the promoters or insiders have received "cheap stock" (namely, stock received at significantly lower prices

---

[73] See Section 18(b)(1)(c) of the Securities Act, enacted as part of the National Securities Markets Improvement Act of 1996. See generally Manning, *The Status of the Marketplace Exemption from State Securities Registration*, 41 Bus. Law. 1511 (1986).

[74] See T. Hazen, The Law of Securities Regulation § 8.2 (3d ed. 1996). See generally J. Long, *Blue Sky Law* § 1.04 (1999).

[75] See generally Campbell, *An Open Attack on the Nonsense of Blue Sky Regulation*, 10 J. Corp. L. 553 (1985); Sargent, *The Challenge to Merit Regulation*, 12 Sec. Reg. L.J. 276, 367 (1984); Tyler, *More About Blue Sky*, 39 Wash. & Lee L. Rev. 899 (1982); American Bar Association, *Report on State Regulation of Securities Offerings*, 41 Bus. Law. 785 (1986).

[76] J. Mofsky, *Blue Sky Restrictions on New Business Promotions* 7-8 (1971). See authorities cited note 75 *supra*.

than the proposed public offering price). Further, registration may be denied in such states if the proposed offering price is deemed too high (e.g., the issuer's earnings history is not reflected in the proposed offering price), if the voting rights sought to be issued to the public are inequitable, or if the underwriter's commissions are unreasonable for the proposed offering. As a final example, merit regulation states may require that the proceeds from an offering of securities be held in escrow until a specified amount has been received by the issuer.[77]

---

[77] See J. Long, *supra* note 74, at § 1.05.

Chapter 5

RESALES AND REORGANIZATIONS

§ 5.01   Introduction

As seen from the foregoing materials, the Securities Act of 1933 was enacted in large part to help promote the dissemination of adequate and reliable information to the investing public in the distribution process. To achieve this objective, Section 5 requires registration for any offer or sale of a security unless such offer or sale is exempt from the registration provisions. The party seeking to invoke an exemption from registration has the burden of proving that such exemption has been perfected.[1]

We have examined the exemptions for issuers in Chapter 3. Attention now turns to exemptions for resales by persons other than an issuer. We begin by addressing Section 4(1), which provides the most important exemption in this context. By its terms, Section 4(1) exempts from the registration requirements of Section 5 "transactions by any person other than an issuer, underwriter or dealer." Hence, as a general proposition, the Section 4(1) exemption permits individual investors to resell their securities without registration, provided such resales are viewed as "transactions" (rather than as part of a "distribution") and such persons are not deemed underwriters.

Because Section 4(3) and Section 4(4) exempt most transactions by broker-dealers, the problems that arise under Section 4(1) generally involve underwriters. Underwriter status necessarily renders the Section 4(1) exemption unavailable.

Importantly, the National Securities Markets Improvement Act of 1996 preempts state regulation of Section 4(1), 4(3), and 4(4) of the Securities Act. Note, however, that state regulation is federally preempted with respect to the Section 4(1) and 4(3) exemptions only if the issuer of the subject security is an Exchange Act reporting company (see § 18(b)(4) of the Securities Act).

§ 5.02   The Concept of "Underwriter"

The concept of underwriter is fundamental to the framework of the 1933 Act. Congress contemplated that underwriters would play an integral role in both the initial and secondary distribution process. Underwriter status subjects applicable parties to the provisions of Section 5 and results in liability exposure for material misrepresentations and nondisclosures contained in the registration statement.

---

[1] See, e.g., *Pennaluna & Co. v. SEC*, 410 F.2d 861, 865 (9th Cir. 1969); *SEC v. Culpepper*, 270 F.2d 241, 246 (2d Cir. 1959).

Section 2(a)(11) of the Securities Act defines an "underwriter" as "any person who has purchased from an issuer with a view to, or offers or sells for an issuer in connection with, the distribution of any security, or participates or has a direct or indirect participation in any such undertaking, or participates or has a participation in the direct or indirect underwriting of any such undertaking, but such term shall not include a person whose interest is limited to a commission from an underwriter or dealer not in excess of the usual and customary distributors' or sellers' commission."[2] In this regard, see SEC Rules 141 and 142 which, in effect, exclude from underwriter status: (1) distributors and dealers who receive a commission from an underwriter or dealer not in excess of the usual and customary distributors' or sellers' commissions (Rule 141); and (2) those persons who, under the circumstances delineated in the rule, purchase for investment purposes all or a specified portion of the securities remaining unsold after the lapse of a defined period of time (Rule 142).

For the purposes of Section 2(a)(11) only (i.e., who should be regarded as an "underwriter"), the term "issuer" is defined to include a person who controls the issuer. SEC Rule 405 defines "control" as "the possession, direct or indirect, of the power to direct or cause the direction of the management and policies of a person, whether through the ownership of voting securities, by contract, or otherwise." Significantly, the inclusion of control persons within the definition of "issuer" for Section 2(a)(11) purposes signifies that sales by directors and executive officers create the risk that some party involved in the transaction is an "underwriter."

An examination of Section 2(a)(11) reveals that a person can become an underwriter in the following ways:

(1) By purchasing from the issuer with a view towards distribution;

(2) By offering or selling for an issuer in connection with a distribution;

(3) By participating, directly or indirectly, in the distribution or underwriting effort;

(4) By selling securities of the issuer on behalf of a control person in connection with the distribution of any security; and

(5) By purchasing securities of the issuer from a control person with a view towards distribution.

If a person falls within one of these categories, he or she will be deemed to be an underwriter. Note the lack of guidance Section 2(a)(11) provides. For example: What evidence shows intent to distribute? What circumstances constitute participation? What power must a person possess to be in control? The answers to these questions are necessarily based on the individual circumstances of each case. Judicial decisions are relatively scarce, and not surprisingly, have not eliminated fears of inadvertent underwriter status. Moreover, beyond Rule 144 (which will be examined in § 5.04), the SEC has promulgated few rules or regulations in this area.

---

[2] 15 U.S.C. § 77b(11).

[A] The Presumptive Underwriter Doctrine

In a registered offering of securities, an individual, a few investors, or an institution may purchase a substantial portion of the offering and thereafter resell the securities to the public. At least two problems may arise: First, the purchasers may hold the securities until the information in the registration statement becomes outdated; or second, the purchasers, perhaps seeking to take advantage of the rapid price increase normally associated with a "hot issue" (that is, an issue that, shortly after the registration statement has gone effective is trading in the aftermarket at a substantially higher price than the registered offering price), may sell large quantities of the subject securities (for substantial profit) within a short time period. If the Section 4(1) exemption were to apply, these sales would be free of the registration requirements, including, of course, the prospectus delivery obligation. Concerned with the lack of disclosure in this context, the SEC formulated (and later abandoned) the presumptive underwriter doctrine.[3]

Under the presumptive underwriter doctrine, one who purchases more than 10% of the securities offered in a registered offering may be deemed an underwriter unless such person establishes sufficient investment intent. The doctrine was subject to criticism by pension and employee benefit plans managed by life insurance companies and similar institutional investors. In fear of the doctrine, a number of institutional investors significantly limited their purchases of securities in registered public offerings.

Comments made by the SEC staff indicate that the presumptive underwriter doctrine has been abandoned. As stated by the Commission's then Director of the Division of Corporation Finance:

> For many years, a concept known as the "presumptive underwriter" doctrine existed. That doctrine assumed that a purchaser of a relatively large amount of securities covered by a registration statement (at one point 10 percent) was buying with a view to distribution and, therefore, should be deemed a statutory underwriter. The theory was most subjective, most difficult of explanation, and presented considerable problems both in compliance, as well as administration. In 1983, in the American Council of Life Insurance letter, the "presumptive underwriter" doctrine was for all intents and purposes abandoned. . . . Nothing in the Securities Act compelled the view that a person acquiring a substantial part of an offering should be treated differently from any other investor with a large position in the issuer, unless the purchaser becomes an affiliate as a result of the purchases.[4]

---

[3] See Ahrenholz & Van Valkenberg, *The Presumptive Underwriter Doctrine: Statutory Underwriter Status for Investors Purchasing a Substantial Portion of a Registered Offering*, 1973 Utah L. Rev. 773 (1973).

[4] Address by Linda C. Quinn, Esq. Before the ABA's Federal Regulation of Securities Committee (Nov. 22, 1986), *discussed in*, Barron, *The SEC Staff Finally Abandons the "Presumptive Underwriter" Doctrine*, 15 Sec. Reg L.J. 296 (1987). Note that an *"affiliate"* of an issuer generally is one who controls, is controlled by, or is under common control with, either directly or indirectly, such issuer.

[B] Participating in the Underwriting Effort

Based on the Second Circuit's decision in *SEC v. Chinese Consolidated Benevolent Association*,[5] the making of continual solicitations resulting in a distribution of securities renders the Section 4(1) exemption unavailable, irrespective of a party's motive or relationship with the issuer. This is so even if the party is a volunteer and receives no compensation for its efforts.

The above principle is not always literally applied, creating uncertainty in this area. For example, in one case, the court found that the defendant bank purchased shares on behalf of its customers in a public offering, acted as an important link in the chain of distribution, and issued reports touting the shares to its customers at the time it was buying and selling securities for its customers' accounts. Nevertheless, the court found that, as a matter of law, the bank was not an underwriter. It reasoned that:

> in no manner did [the defendant bank] have a relationship with [the issuer], [the principal underwriter], or the underwriting itself. Plaintiff, therefore, must properly plead some greater nexus between the investment management department of [defendant] and this underwriting of securities before such liability can attach.[6]

§ 5.03 Distributions by Controlling Persons or Affiliates

The concept of "control" is crucial to the understanding of secondary distributions. For the purposes of determining who is an "underwriter," Section 2(a)(11) defines the term "issuer" to include a controlling person. Therefore, underwriter status may be accorded to any person who sells securities on behalf of a controlling person in connection with the distribution of any security.

The possibility of inadvertent underwriter status is ever present because of the ambiguities associated with the meaning of "control." Moreover, the inclusion of control persons within the definition of "issuer" for Section 2(a)(11) purposes signifies that sales of securities by directors and executive officers create the risk that some party involved in the transaction is an "underwriter," irrespective of whether the securities are restricted or unrestricted. Indeed, control person status has been found to exist based on such factors as percentage of stock ownership, director or officer position held, and relationships with insiders. Because directors and executive officers frequently are shareholders and have relatively close relationships with other key insiders, this problem of potential underwriter status is a very practical and widespread one.

The lack of a precise definition for control frustrates counselors and corporate planners.[7] The Commission, in an effort to alleviate some of the uncertainty, promulgated Rule 405, which defines "control."

---

[5] 120 F.2d 738 (2d Cir. 1941). See *In re State Bank of Pakistan*, [1991-1992 Transfer Binder] Fed. Sec. L. Rep. (CCH) ¶ 84,946 (SEC 1992).

[6] *Zicklin v. Breuer*, 534 F. Supp. 745, 747 (S.D.N.Y. 1982).

[7] See Sommer, *Who's "In Control"? — S.E.C.*, 21 Bus. Law. 559 (1966).

Rule 405 defines "control" as "the possession, direct or indirect, of the power to direct or cause the direction of the management and policies of a person, whether through the ownership of voting securities, by contract, or otherwise." Rule 405 focuses on a person's ability to direct the management and policies of the corporation. Use of Rule 405 to define "control" in the Section 2(a)(11) context, however, has been criticized by commentators. These commentators suggest that an appropriate definition of "control" should stress a person's ability to compel the issuer to register an offering. They assert that Congress never intended a person to be deemed an issuer for Section 2(a)(11) purposes when that person did not possess the power to effect registration. Moreover, they argue that the SEC's use of Rule 405 to define "control" fails to relieve uncertainty. [8]

[A] Effecting a "Distribution"

The Securities Act does not explicitly hold the conduct of controlling persons illegal when they effect a distribution of unregistered shares through an underwriter. Of course, what a statute fails expressly to do, a court can accomplish through construing the statute's pertinent language, legislative history, and policy rationales. In *United States v. Wolfson*,[9] the Second Circuit held that a group of controlling persons (Wolfson and his cohorts) violated Section 5 because they effected an unregistered distribution of securities through several unwitting brokerage houses. As the court observed, Section 4(1) "by its terms exempts only transactions." Hence, because Wolfson and his cronies were effecting a "distribution," they could not avail themselves of the Section 4(1) exemption. As the Seventh Circuit more recently stated:

> Section 4(1) provides an exemption for *transactions, not individuals*. It was created to exempt routine trading *transactions* with respect to securities already issued and *not to exempt* distributions by issuers or acts of others who engage in steps necessary to such distributions.[10]

As an additional point from the *Wolfson* case, the six brokerage houses, although unable to invoke the Section 4(1) exemption, were not subject to the Section 5 requirements due to the Section 4(4) exemption. The court supported this conclusion by finding that each of the unwitting brokerage houses effected only "transactions" (unaware of the "distribution"), the "transactions" were solicited by Wolfson, and the "transactions" were executed in the over-the-counter market.

An earlier case, *Ira Haupt & Co.*,[11] had the effect of making brokers wary

---

[8] See *Pennaluna & Company v. SEC*, 410 F.2d 861 (9th Cir. 1969); 7B J.W. Hicks, *Exempted Transactions Under the Securities Act of 1933*, § 9.03[2][a] (1999); Campbell, *Defining Control in Secondary Distributions*, 18 B.C. Ind. & Comm. L. Rev. 37 (1976).

[9] 405 F.2d 779 (2d Cir. 1968).

[10] *SEC v. Holschuh*, 694 F.2d 130, 137-138 (7th Cir. 1982) (emphasis added). Accord, *SEC v. Murphy*, 626 F.2d 633, 648 (9th Cir. 1980); *In re DG Bank (Schweiz) AG*, [1991-1992 Transfer Binder] Fed. Sec. L. Rep. (CCH) ¶ 84,945 (SEC 1992).

[11] 23 SEC 589 (1946). See *In re Paulson Investment Co.*, [1991-1992 Transfer Binder] Fed. Sec. L. Rep. (CCH) ¶ 84,917 (SEC 1991).

of selling a controlling person's shares. There, an individual Schulte controlled Park & Tilford, Inc. He gave a series of sell orders, involving around 200 shares per order, to his broker Haupt. During a six-month period, 93,000 shares were sold pursuant to these orders. Haupt was charged with violating Section 5 for its role in effecting the unregistered offering. Haupt offered two defenses. First, Haupt argued that its sales of Park & Tilford shares were not a "distribution" because there was no plan to sell a specified number of shares. The Commission rejected this defense, finding that the facts and circumstances clearly put Haupt on notice that a distribution was anticipated.

Second, the broker Haupt claimed the Section 4(4) exemption, which, *inter alia*, exempts "brokers' transactions executed upon customers' orders on any exchange . . . ." In rejecting this defense, the SEC reasoned that the Section 4(4) exemption does not exempt brokers from Section 5 when they act as underwriters in a "distribution." The SEC defined a "distribution" as "[t]he entire process by which in the course of a public offering the block of securities is dispersed and ultimately comes to rest in the hands of the investing public." Here, Haupt was effecting a "distribution" rather than engaging in a "transaction." As will be discussed later in the chapter, to alleviate some of the concern generated by the *Haupt* decision, the SEC promulgated Rule 154 and thereafter Rule 144.

[B]   Secondary Offerings

As the foregoing discussion suggests, in order to effect a "distribution," a registered offering must take place. Irrespective of whether the offering is on behalf of an issuer or for the benefit of a control person, only the issuer can register a public offering. This consequence is not unduly onerous, according to proponents, because a controlling person has the leverage to induce the issuer to file a registration statement and to elicit adequate disclosure on the part of such an issuer. Because of the ambiguities associated with the concept of control, a person who may be viewed as an affiliate may contract with the issuer when he/she acquires the stock for the right of demand registration, thereby granting the control person the contractual right to demand that the issuer file a 1933 Act registration statement when the person wishes to dispose of his/her stock. If the purported "control person" does not have such leverage, he/she may settle for the right of "piggy-back" registration. This right, looking to the terms of the covenant negotiated, authorizes the control person to sell ("piggy-back") his/her stock or a portion thereof at the time that the issuer elects to file a registration statement.[12]

In any event, such "control person" should insist that the issuer covenant to provide Rule 15c2-11 information. Generally, Rule 15c2-11 prohibits broker-dealers from publishing a quotation for any security unless specified information is available with respect to the issuer and the security. In effect,

---

[12] See generally O'Hare, *Institutional Investors, Registration Rights, and the Specter of Liability Under Section 11 of the Securities Act of 1933*, 1996 Wisc. L. Rev. 217 (1996).

the rule prevents the widespread distribution of securities without certain minimal information being publicly available. Hence, Rule 15c2-11(a)(5) calls for certain mandated information to be reasonably current and to be made reasonably available by the subject broker or dealer upon the request of a prospective purchaser.[13] Importantly, if the control person induces the issuer to disseminate Rule 15c2-11 information, the "current information" requirement of Rule 144, which provides a safe harbor in the resale context, will be satisfied (see § 5.05[B] *infra*).

Even where the control person in a secondary distribution induces the issuer to file a registration statement, there remain significant pitfalls. One particular concern is disclosure. For example, where all or a part of the proceeds of the offering will be paid to selling shareholders rather than to the issuer, the registration statement must carefully disclose this consequence.[14] Another problem is that shareholders effecting a secondary registered offering may be tempted to manipulate the price of the stock. The SEC, aware of the potential for abuse, has brought enforcement actions in this context and has promulgated a number of rules designed to curtail such manipulative activity.[15]

---

[13] Hence, Rule 15c2-11 calls for the following information to be made available upon request to a prospective purchaser:

(i)   the exact name of the issuer and its predecessor (if any);

(ii) the address of its principal executive offices;

(iii) the state of incorporation, if it is a corporation;

(iv) the exact title and class of the security;

(v)   the par or stated value of the security;

(vi) the number of shares or total amount of the securities outstanding as of the end of the issuer's most recent fiscal year;

(vii) the name and address of the transfer agent;

(viii) the nature of the issuer's business;

(ix) the nature of products or services offered;

(x)   the nature and extent of the issuer's facilities;

(xi) the name of the chief executive officer and members of the board of directors;

(xii) the issuer's most recent balance sheet and profit and loss and retained earnings statements;

(xiii) similar financial information for such part of the two preceding fiscal years as the issuer or its predecessor has been in existence;

(xiv) whether the broker or dealer or any associated person is affiliated, directly or indirectly with the issuer;

(xv) whether the quotation is being published or submitted on behalf of any other broker or dealer, and, if so, the name of such broker or dealer; and

(xvi) whether the quotation is being submitted or published directly or indirectly on behalf of the issuer, or any director, officer or any person, directly or indirectly the beneficial owner of more than 10 percent of the outstanding units or shares of any equity security of the issuer, and, if so, the name of such person, and the basis for any exemption under the federal securities laws for any sales of such securities on behalf of such person.

[14] See, e.g., Item 507 of SEC Regulation S-K; *In the Matter of Universal Camera Corp.*, 19 S.E.C. 648 (1945).

[15] See e.g., SEC Regulation M; *In the Matter of Hazel Bishop, Inc.*, 40 S.E.C. 718 (1961).

§ 5.04 Purchasing from an Issuer with a View Towards Distribution

A person who has acquired "restricted securities" from an issuer often has obtained the securities pursuant to Section 4(2) of the Securities Act or pursuant to Rule 505 or 506 of Regulation D. One problem is that when an issuer sells unregistered securities to one or more persons in a non-public transaction, it is possible that the transfer is in reality a public offering in disguise — a two-step, indirect distribution in which the transferees function as "underwriters" for the issuer.

An affiliate of the issuer selling either restricted or nonrestricted securities faces a similar problem — because of his or her close connection with the issuer, an affiliate (absent the exercise of utmost care) may be viewed as an "underwriter" or involved in a "distribution" and thus unable to invoke the Section 4(1) exemption in any resale transaction involving securities of the issuer.

As discussed earlier in this chapter, if a person is deemed to be an "underwriter," he or she cannot rely on the exemption from registration provided by Section 4(1) of the Act to protect the resale transaction. Generally, although Section 4(1) exempts ordinary transactions such as a private resale of securities, it does so only with respect to *"transactions by any person other* than an issuer, *underwriter*, or dealer." The dilemma for persons holding *restricted securities* of an issuer and for affiliates of an issuer (regardless whether such affiliates seek to sell restricted or nonrestricted securities) comes into focus upon examining the statutory definition of "underwriter." Section 2(a)(11) of the Act defines an "underwriter" to include any person who "has purchased" securities from the issuer "with a view to . . . the *distribution* of any security."

Section 2(a)(11) does not provide an objective standard for determining whether a person acquiring securities from an issuer is taking with a view toward investment or with a view toward resale. For a non-affiliate holding *restricted securities*, a resale in purported reliance upon Section 4(1) carries the risk that such seller will be deemed to be an "underwriter" within the meaning of Section 2(a)(11), and therefore, unable to claim the desired exemption. For an affiliate who intends to sell any securities of the issuer, *restricted or not*, the same risk is present. As will be discussed in § 5.05, provided that the requirements of Rule 144 are met, the Rule provides a safe harbor to persons holding restricted securities of an issuer and to affiliates of an issuer who seek to resell either restricted or nonrestricted securities.[16]

[A] Holding Period

In determining whether a person has purchased from the issuer with a view to distribution, the amount of time that the person held the security prior to resale is deemed a relevant factor. In this regard, a "rule of thumb"

---

[16] See J.W. Hicks, *supra* note 8, at § 10.01[1]; discussion § 5.05 *infra*.

for ascertaining investment intent under the Section 4(1) exemption provides that the SEC normally should not initiate an enforcement action against a party who is not a "control" person and who held the securities for at least two years prior to resale. As discussed in § 5.05, Rule 144 shortens this time period, if certain criteria are met, to one year.

On the other hand, compared to noncontrol persons, affiliates (or control persons) are more likely to be engaged in a distribution (rather than a transaction) when they resell their securities. If that indeed is the situation, such affiliates may not avail themselves of the Section 4(1) exemption, irrespective of their stock holding period.[17]

[B]   Restrictive Legends — Change in Circumstances

Restrictive legends normally are placed on securities acquired in an unregistered (e.g., Rule 505 or 506) offering of restricted securities. Subject parties may claim that these restrictive legends establish their investment intent at the time of purchase. Not surprisingly, the courts have rejected this contention, holding that the purchase of stock from an issuer under an investment restriction is by no means a conclusive defense to underwriter status.[18] In certain situations, however, "change in circumstances" may serve as a valid defense to underwriter status. When invoking the change in circumstances doctrine, the subject party asserts that it bought the stock with investment intent but that subsequent unforeseen changes compelled the earlier than planned sale of the stock.[19]

When the SEC adopted Rule 144 (discussed in § 5.05 *infra*), the Commission stated that "the 'change in circumstances' concept should no longer be considered as one of the factors in determining whether a person is an underwriter . . . since the circumstances of the seller are unrelated to the need of investors for the protections afforded by the registration [requirement] and other provisions of the Act."[20] Hence, at least according to the SEC, the change in circumstances doctrine no longer retains its validity. On the other hand, it may be asserted that, to the extent that the change in circumstances defense is a valid test in terms of statutorily defining one who purchases with an intent to redistribute, the Commission cannot by administrative fiat change the meaning of the statute.[21]

[C]   Sales by Pledgees

The inadvertent underwriter problem (with the prospect of rendering the Section 4(1) exemption unavailable) also arises in connection with sales by

---

[17] See *United States v. Sherwood*, 175 F. Supp. 480 (S.D.N.Y. 1959).

[18] See *G. Eugene England Foundation v. First Federal Corporation*, [1976-1977 Transfer Binder] Fed. Sec. L. Rep. (CCH) ¶ 95,837 (10th Cir. 1973); *Gilligan, Will & Co. v. SEC*, 267 F.2d 461 (2d Cir. 1959).

[19] See, e.g., *Lectmor v. VTR, Inc.*, [1969-1970 Transfer Binder] Fed. Sec. L. Rep. (CCH) ¶ 92,707 (S.D.N.Y. 1970).

[20] Securities Act Release No. 5223 (1972).

[21] See T. Hazen, *The Law of Securities Regulation* 252 (3d ed. 1996).

pledgees (e.g., banks) of securities pledged by control persons (as well as sales by such pledgees of restricted securities pledged by either control persons or nonaffiliates).[22] For example, if the pledgor control person defaults on a bank loan secured by the pledge, can the bank sell the securities pledged without being deemed an underwriter? In *SEC v. Guild Films Co.*,[23] the pledgor, a controlling shareholder, pledged as collateral for a bank loan a substantial block of securities that bore a restrictive legend on the face of the securities. After the shareholder defaulted on the loan, the bank, knowing of the restrictive legend, sold some of the securities without a registration statement being filed. The Second Circuit held that the bank was an underwriter. Even though the bank may have taken the securities as collateral and had not directly dealt with the issuer, "the bank knew that [it] had been given unregistered stock and that the issuer had specifically forbidden that the stock be sold." Hence, to avoid Section 5 liability, the bank had to retain the securities pledged, invoke an exemption (e.g., Section "4(1½)", Rule 144, Rule 144A), or induce the issuer to file a registration statement.

Language contained in the *Guild Films* case may be criticized as being unduly onerous upon good faith pledgees. By asserting that a good faith pledgee participates in a distribution or takes with the view to distribute whenever a pledgor defaults, it may be asserted that the Second Circuit's rationale unfairly hampers legitimate commercial activity. On the other hand, it may be argued that the key issue is not the pledgee's culpability in facilitating the sale of unregistered securities to the investing public but rather whether such sales by the pledgee should be permitted where the effect is to place into the hands of uninformed investors securities that have never been part of a registered offering. To purchasers of such securities who have not received adequate disclosure, the pledgee's good faith is of little solace.[24]

In this regard, the potentially harsh result of the *Guild Films* decision on legitimate commercial activity may be mitigated in practice by a pledgee bank's use of: (1) a covenant by the pledgor to effect registration of the securities ("a registration covenant") in the event of the pledgor's default (in all likelihood, such a covenant would not be worth the paper it was written on); (2) the invocation of an exemption from registration, such as the Section "4(1½)" exemption (see § 5.06 *infra*); and (3) a more circumspect approach to accepting pledgor securities as collateral.

The thrust of the *Guild Films* decision evidently remains good law. The continued vitality of the court's broad language as it relates to good faith pledgees, however, is open to question. As the First Circuit opined, "[t]here is considerable support for the . . . view that a good faith pledgee who sells

---

[22] Note that a "pledge" is itself a "sale" under the Securities Act. See *Rubin v. United States*, 449 U.S. 424 (1981).

[23] 279 F.2d 485 (2d Cir.), *cert. denied*, 364 U.S. 819 (1960).

[24] See generally Rice, *The Effects of Registration on the Disposition of Pledged Securities*, 21 Stan. L. Rev. 1607 (1969); Sargent, *Pledgees and Foreclosure Rights Under the Securities Act of 1933*, 45 Va. L. Rev. 885 (1959).

unregistered shares at a foreclosure sale is not an 'underwriter.' "[25] Nonetheless, the SEC continues to adhere to the view that, under certain circumstances, the pledgee's sale of the securities pledged creates underwriter status.[26]

§ 5.05   Rule 144

[A]   Background

Historically, that a non-affiliate acquired securities pursuant to a Section 4(2) private placement exemption did not thereafter preclude such person from reselling the securities. For example, as discussed earlier, a non-affiliate holding restricted securities (e.g., securities acquired pursuant to offerings made under Section 4(2), Rule 505 or Rule 506) normally could resell such securities after a substantial holding period, such as two or three years. Moreover, in certain situations, such non-affiliates, who acquired restricted securities allegedly for investment, could resell them pursuant to Section 4(1), notwithstanding a relatively recent acquisition date, if the seller could demonstrate a "change of circumstances." Nonetheless, given that the burden of proving the perfection of an exemption is upon the seller,[27] prudent parties exercised utmost caution when disposing of their securities without registration.

The situation for affiliates, and broker-dealers that executed orders to sell securities for the account of affiliates, was even more onerous. As a result of the SEC's 1946 administrative proceeding in *Ira Haupt*,[28] discussed in § 5.03[A], it was difficult for the broker to determine whether an affiliate, when disposing of stock, was engaging in a "distribution" of the issuer's securities. The confusion that broker-dealers faced in attempting to determine whether a distribution would occur led the SEC to adopt Rule 154 in 1951.[29] Unfortunately, Rule 154 was of limited value because it was designed for brokers, but offered no protection to those persons on behalf of whom the sale was executed.[30]

After extensive analysis, the "Wheat Report" was issued in 1969.[31] The Report recommended a series of rules that sought to clarify the circumstances under which an affiliate or a non-affiliate could rely upon Section

---

[25] *A.D.M. Corporation v. Thompson*, [1982-1983 Transfer Binder] Fed. Sec. L. Rep. (CCH) ¶ 99,206 (1st Cir. 1983) (and SEC "no-action" letters cited therein).

[26] See SEC Rule 144(d)(4)(D); *In re DG Bank (Schweiz) AG*, [1991-1992 Transfer Binder] Fed. Sec. L. Rep. (CCH) ¶ 84,945 (SEC 1992); T. Hazen, *supra* note 21, at 249; Hueter, *The Plight of the Pledgee Under Rule 144*, 3 Sec. Reg. L.J. 111 (1975).

[27] See, e.g., *SEC v. Ralston Purina Co.*, 346 U.S. 119 (1953).

[28] 23 S.E.C. 589 (1946).

[29] See Securities Act Release No. 3421 (1951), *as amended by* Securities Act Release No. 3525 (1954).

[30] See S. Goldberg, *Private Placements and Restricted Securities* § 7.1 (rev. ed. 1982); J.W. Hicks, *supra* note 8, at § 10.02[1].

[31] See *Disclosure to Investors — A Reappraisal of Federal Administrative Policies Under the '33 and '34 Acts* (1969) ("Wheat Report").

4(1) for resale transactions. In 1970, the SEC set forth a single proposed rule as an alternative to the series recommended by the Wheat Report.[32] It was called Proposed Rule 144 and was designed to continue the SEC's efforts towards providing objective standards with respect to the availability of the Section 4(1) exemption. Finally, after lively debate and extensive public comments and suggestions, the final version of Rule 144 was adopted in 1972.[33]

Generally, Rule 144 acts as a safe harbor from incurring liability under the registration provisions of the Securities Act. It permits the public sale in ordinary trading transactions of limited amounts of securities owned by persons controlling, controlled by, or under common control with the issuer (i.e., "affiliates"), and by other persons who have acquired "restricted securities" of the issuer. Hence, Rule 144 protects certain resale transactions from the Securities Act's registration mandates when such transactions are engaged in by: (1) "non-affiliated" persons who have acquired securities from either the issuer or an affiliate of the issuer in a transaction not involving a public offering ("restricted securities"), (2) persons who are deemed to be "affiliates" of the issuer at the time they propose to resell any securities of the issuer (irrespective whether such securities are restricted or unrestricted), and (3) brokers who effect transactions in compliance with the Rule.

The safe harbor derived from Rule 144 is important to the functioning of the securities markets. Absent the availability of an exemption, all offers or sales of securities must be registered under Section 5 of the Act. The exemptions normally available in the resale context are Section 4(1) for sellers and Section 4(4) for brokers. Their application under a given set of conditions, however, may be problematic. By creating a safe harbor for perfecting these exemptions, Rule 144 seeks to provide greater clarity in this area.[34]

[B] Provisions of the Rule — Overview

Since its adoption in 1972, Rule 144 has been amended several times and substantially liberalized. The basic purpose of Rule 144, however, has remained the same. Generally, with certain caveats, Rule 144 provides a safe harbor under the Section 4(1) exemption for investors (e.g., institutional as well as individual investors) who are selling their securities without registration, and for brokers under the Section 4(4) exemption who are effecting sales of such securities. Rule 144 provides this safe harbor through an objective set of provisions, premised on the rationale that some relaxation of Securities Act disclosure and registration requirements is appropriate with respect to relatively small secondary transactions. If the investor and the broker make the sales in compliance with the conditions

---

[32] See Securities Act Release No. 5087 (1970).

[33] Securities Act Release No. 5223 (1972). See J.W. Hicks, *supra* note 8, at § 10.02[2].

[34] See M. Pollock, *Resale of Restricted Securities*, Corporate Practice Series (BNA) No. 46 (1986); Fogelson, *Rule 144 — A Summary Overview*, 37 Bus. Law. 1519 (1981).

set forth in Rule 144, they will not be deemed to be "underwriters" or engaged in a "distribution."[35]

An understanding of certain terms is crucial to an understanding of Rule 144. Rule 144 defines an "affiliate" of an issuer as a "person that directly, or indirectly through one or more intermediaries, controls, or is controlled by, or is under common control with, such an issuer." In addition, Rule 144 defines "restricted" securities as those "securities that are acquired directly or indirectly from the issuer, or from an affiliate of the issuer, in a transaction or chain of transactions not involving any public offering, or securities acquired from the issuer that are subject to the resale limitations of Regulation D under the Act, or securities that are subject to the resale limitations of Regulation D and are acquired in a transaction or chain of transactions not involving any public offering." Hence, such restricted securities include those acquired in offerings pursuant to Section 4(2), Rule 505, Rule 506, and Rule 701.

The foregoing definitions are important. In certain situations, Rule 144 treats affiliates and non-affiliates differently. For example, only non-affiliates can resell restricted securities free of Rule 144 requirements after holding the securities for two years (see Rule 144(k)).[36] In addition, Rule 144's holding requirements pertain only to restricted securities.

To utilize Rule 144 a person must meet five general requirements, some of which have been eliminated or substantially modified by the SEC in certain circumstances.

First, there must be adequate current information concerning the issuer (see Rule 144(c)). This requirement is in accord with the underlying policy of the Securities Act which is to protect investors through adequate and fair disclosure. The information requirement can be satisfied in either of two ways: (1) the issuer can be subject to and be currently complying with the reporting requirements of the Exchange Act, or (2) if the issuer is not a 1934 Act reporting company, the issuer can publicly make information available pursuant to Exchange Act Rule 15c2-11. If the purchaser has sufficient leverage, he or she may contract with the issuer that it be required to furnish the Rule 15c2-11 information.

A *second requirement* is that the person seeking to sell the restricted securities (e.g., stock acquired in a private offering) must meet the one-year holding period established by Rule 144 (see Rule 144(d)). The holding period seeks to ensure that the person assumed an investment stake in the prior purchase(s) and has not acted merely as the issuer's conduit for a sale to the public of unregistered securities. Note that the one-year holding period

---

[35] See D. Goldwasser, *A Guide to Rule 144* (2d ed. 1978); L. Loss & J. Seligman, *Securities Regulation* 1474-1575 (3d ed. 1989); Ash in 11 H. Sowards, *Federal Securities Act* § 6B.01 (1987); Gilroy & Kaufman in 3 A.A. Sommer, *Securities Law Techniques* § 38.01 (1987).

[36] See Securities Act Release No. 7390 (1997); Securities Act Release No. 6862 (1990). Note that under Rule 144, if non-affiliates continuously have held the subject securities for at least two consecutive years, then the current non-affiliated holder may resell such securities under Rule 144(k) even if such holder has held such securities for a shorter time period (i.e., less than two years). See *infra* note 42 and accompanying text.

runs from the date of purchase from the issuer or an affiliate of the issuer. Hence, a subsequent purchaser's acquisition of stock from a control person will trigger the start of the one-year holding period as will an initial purchase from the issuer. [37]

Third, Rule 144 places restrictions on the amount of sales a person can make during a given time period in reliance on the Rule (see Rule 144(e)). This requirement is designed to ensure that a "distribution" does not take place and to lessen the impact of these sales on the trading markets. Generally, *with certain exceptions* (see Rule 144(k) discussed later in this section), sales of securities by a person under Rule 144 during any three-month period cannot exceed the greater of: (1) 1% of the shares of that class outstanding as shown by the most recent statement of the issuer, or (2) the average weekly trading volume reported on all exchanges (and/or through NASDAQ or the consolidated transaction reporting system) for the four weeks preceding the filing of notice as specified in Rule 144(h). In order to determine whether the volume limitation applies, one must consider whether the holder is affiliated or unaffiliated with the issuer.

The fourth requirement under Rule 144 is that the securities must be sold in ordinary brokerage transactions within the meaning of Section 4(4) or in transactions directly with a market maker, without solicitation. Hence, a person seeking to rely on Rule 144 must not "solicit or arrange for the solicitation of orders to buy securities in anticipation of or in connection with such transactions." [38] Moreover, the broker must receive no more than the usual and customary broker's commission. Finally, with respect to sales during a three-month period that exceed 500 shares or have a sales price greater than $10,000, notice of each such sale must be filed with the SEC.

The "brokers' transactions" requirement referred to above (see Rule 144(f)) must be distinguished from the requirements with the same name in Rule 144(g). Rule 144(f) is one of the conditions that must be met by a seller intending to rely on the Rule. The broker also must find an exemption for its role in the transaction. Rule 144(g), by defining the term "brokers' transactions" and by delineating aspects of "reasonable inquiry" to be conducted by the broker, greatly assists the broker in meeting Rule 144's safe harbor and thereby perfect the Section 4(4) exemption. [39]

---

[37] See Securities Act Release No. 7390 (1997). In reducing the Rule 144 holding periods, the SEC asserted that this reduction will decrease "compliance burdens and costs without significant impact on investor protection. . . . [A]lso the [amendments] will promote market efficiency, investment and capital formation by reducing the liquidity costs of holding restricted securities and reducing issuers' cost of raising capital through the sale of restricted securities."

[38] Rule 144(f), 17 C.F.R. § 230.144(f).

[39] See Securities Act Release Nos. 4445 (1962), 5168 (1972); *In re Transactions in Securities of Laser Arms Corporation by Certain Broker-Dealers,* [1990-1991 Transfer Binder] Fed. Sec. L. Rep. (CCH) ¶ 84,724 (SEC 1991). In the *Laser Arms* proceeding, the Commission reaffirmed its position with respect to the appropriate level of a broker's diligence in this setting:

[A] dealer who offers to sell, or is asked to sell a substantial amount of securities must take whatever steps are necessary, to be sure that this is a transaction not involving an issuer, person in a control relationship with an issuer, or an underwriter. For this purpose, it is not sufficient for him merely to accept self-serving statements of his sellers and their counsel without reasonably exploring the possibility of contrary facts.

As will be discussed later in this section, Rule 144(k) is the major exception to the foregoing requirements. Provided that the non-affiliate holder has held the restricted securities for two years, such holder may resell such securities free of Rule 144's many restrictions. The two-year period is measured from the date of acquisition from the issuer or from an affiliate of the issuer.

To invoke the exemption from Securities Act registration provided by Rule 144, all conditions of the rule must be satisfied. Rule 144 is a "safe harbor" and, hence, is nonexclusive. Accordingly, even though a person has not met the conditions of Rule 144, he or she still may seek to invoke another exemption, such as the statutory Section 4(1) exemption.[40]

[C] Certain Sales by Non-Affiliates

[1] Restricted Stock

Paragraph (k) of Rule 144 eliminates the current public information, volume limitation, manner of sale, and notice requirements for certain non-affiliates who have not been affiliated with the issuer for the preceding three months and where the restricted securities have been beneficially owned by non-affiliates for at least two years prior to the resale. Generally, in determining the two-year holding period, a non-affiliate may "tack" to his or her own holding period those of prior holders unaffiliated with the issuer. Thus, Rule 144(k) effectively removes all restrictions when non-affiliates have held restricted securities for at least two years and allows such non-affiliates to freely resell such securities. Rule 144(k) accordingly eases the burdens that were placed on the liquidity of restricted securities.

Phrasing the foregoing description in other terms, the SEC revised paragraph (k) of Rule 144 in 1983 to include current public information among its exceptions.[41] In 1990, the Commission again amended Rule 144(k) to permit non-affiliates to "tack" the holding periods of prior non-affiliated holders.[42] Hence, as Rule 144 now stands, a person, who is not an affiliate

---

[40] Securities Act Release No. 5223 (1972).

[41] See Securities Act Release No. 6488 (1983).

[42] See Securities Act Release No. 6862 (1990). In expanding the "tacking" periods for non-affiliates owning restricted securities, the Commission explained:

Under Rule 144, as previously in effect, restricted securities generally were required to be held for at least two years before the holder could sell the securities in reliance upon the safe-harbor provisions of Rule 144. Except in limited instances, the holding period of predecessor owners was not combined with, or "tacked" to, the holding period of the person wishing to sell in reliance on Rule 144.

As a result of its reexamination of the tacking concept embodied in Rule 144, the Commission today is amending the Rule to permit holders of restricted securities acquired in a transaction or series of transactions not involving any public offering to add to their own holding period those of prior holders unaffiliated with the issuer. No such tacking will be permitted, however, where the seller has purchased from an affiliate of the issuer whose presence in the chain of title will trigger the commencement of a new holding period. . . .

. . .

Rule 144(k) is amended to permit a non-affiliate, who has been a non-affiliate for at least and who has held the restricted securities for at least two years (or when "tacked" with the holding periods of previous non-affiliated holders has held such securities for at least two years), can sell such securities to the public in any manner without any information whatsoever being available concerning the issuer.[43]

Consider this result with the SEC's assertion when it adopted Rule 144 in 1972:

> [T]he purpose and underlying policy of the [Securities] Act to protect investors requires . . . that there be *adequate current information concerning the issuer*, whether the resales of securities by persons result in a distribution or are effected in trading transactions. Accordingly, the availability of [Rule 144] is conditioned on the existence of adequate current public information.[44]

The SEC, with its amendments to Rule 144, essentially has nullified the above rationale. One justification proffered is the deregulatory assertion that "[t]he purpose of the amendments is to relax restrictions on resales of securities that are more burdensome than necessary."[45] But nowhere does the Commission adequately explain why such restrictions are "more burdensome than necessary," particularly in view of the investor protection concerns that are highlighted throughout the 1972 Rule 144 adopting release. Hence, Rule 144, as revised, may be viewed as inconsistent with a major objective of the 1933 Act, which is to protect investors by ensuring that their decisions are informed, and also as incompatible with a fundamental premise underlying the rule's adoption.

There is, of course, another side to this issue. In order to promote capital formation and induce investors to take a stake in start-up and similar enterprises, a non-affiliate who holds restricted securities must have a way to resell those securities if he or she chooses. Rule 144(k) now provides such shareholders with an opportunity to resell their securities after holding them for two years. In this way, the revised Rule meets prospective sellers' expectations and facilitates the flow of venture capital into the economy. The prospective purchaser is adequately protected, it may be asserted, by the application of the antifraud provisions. And, if a trading market for the subject issuer's securities should develop, then Rule 15c2-11 information will be made available.[46] Moreover, a prospective buyer is not compelled to purchase the restricted securities. The determination whether to acquire the securities if adequate current issuer information is unavailable should

---

three months, to resell restricted securities free of the restrictions imposed by paragraphs (c), (e), (f), and (h) of Rule 144 if a period of at least three [subsequently amended to two] years, as computed in accordance with amended paragraph (d) of the Rule, has elapsed since the later of the date the securities originally were acquired from the issuer or the date they were acquired from an affiliate of the issuer.

[43] In 1997, the SEC reduced the Rule 144(k) holding period from three to two years. See Securities Act Release No. 7390 (1997).

[44] Securities Act Release No. 5223 (1972) (emphasis supplied).

[45] Securities Act Release No. 6286 (1981). See Securities Act Release No. 6488 (1983).

[46] See *supra* note 13 and accompanying text.

be left to the prospective purchaser, and not foreclosed by government intervention.

It can be further argued that the Rule 144 amendments are not a significant departure from prior SEC practice. For example, under certain conditions, a party in secondary transactions may invoke the Section 3(a)(11) intrastate exemption which does not require the delivery of information to prospective purchasers (see § 3.13[A] *supra*). In such circumstances, as is arguably true under the Rule 144 amendments, the applicable state "blue sky" laws are the appropriate regulatory sources.

Nonetheless, it may be asserted that the SEC revisions to Rule 144 unduly liberalize certain restrictions, while other overly burdensome limitations of the Rule have been virtually ignored by the SEC. If adequate information is not available concerning the issuer, a prospective non-affiliated seller should not be permitted to unload unlimited quantities of restricted securities into the market. The prospective seller should only be allowed to resell the restricted securities in limited volumes over a period of time. In this way, the prospective seller will not have to rely on the unwilling, nonreporting issuer for public information and will not be locked into the investment, while at the same time, he or she will not be able to dump unlimited amounts of restricted securities into the market. In other words, paragraph (k) should permit a prospective non-affiliated seller to avoid the information requirements of Rule 144(c) only if that seller is willing to conform to the volume limitation restrictions of paragraph (e) of the Rule.

By promulgating paragraph (k), the SEC appears to take the position that the unloading of all of a non-affiliate's stock after a two-year holding period will never constitute a "distribution." Such a position in questionable. Given the substantial amount of restricted stock that a non-affiliate can unload in the marketplace under certain conditions, the SEC's blanket exemption spreads too far. A more sensible approach that would accommodate the competing interests would be to require a nonaffiliate to adhere to the volume limitations of Rule 144(e).

Moreover, the SEC's amendments to Rule 144 are inconsistent with the disclosure approach of Rules 505 and 506 of Regulation D. If the Commission's objective is to ensure the provision of adequate information to "unsophisticated" investors of restricted securities, it should be irrelevant whether the investor purchased the securities from the issuer (pursuant to Regulation D) or from a shareholder who is not affiliated with the issuer (by means of Rule 144). In either case, the prospective purchaser's need for sufficient information to make an intelligent investment decision remains the same. Only in the Rule 505 or 506 Regulation D offering context, however, is the investor entitled to such information.[47] In the Rule 144 setting, by contrast, there is no mandated disclosure when the investor purchases restricted securities from a non-affiliated party (who has met the two-year holding requirement) of an issuer that fails to provide current public information.

---

[47] See discussion in §§ 3.06, 3.08[B][2] *supra*.

[2] Nonrestricted Stock

Rule 144 does not expressly cover a non-affiliate's disposition of nonrestricted stock. Nonetheless, the SEC, by its promulgation of Rule 144(k), appears to take the position that the sale of a non-affiliate's stock is not a separate distribution. Moreover, the assumption of underwriter status may no longer be a pitfall for non-affiliates selling nonrestricted stock due to the SEC staff's apparent abandonment of the presumptive underwriter doctrine (see § 5.02[A] *supra*). These developments may lead to the conclusion that a non-affiliate can freely resell nonrestricted stock without limitation pursuant to the Section 4(1) exemption. The Commission, however, has declined to expressly address this issue.

If the above represents the SEC's position, it is misplaced. In certain circumstances, a non-affiliate can hold a substantial percentage of nonrestricted stock. Permitting such nonaffiliates to freely liquidate their positions conflicts with both the definition of underwriter under Section 2(a)(11) and the rationale underlying the Section 4(1) transactional exemption. In short, persons who dispose of large percentages of securities are, in actuality, engaging in a distribution rather than a transaction and, when they do so after a short holding period, are purchasing from an issuer with a view towards distribution. Support for this assertion may be premised on the fact that, if a substantial security holder were an affiliate, he/she would be subject to the volume limitation requirements of Rule 144(e). Yet, status as an affiliate in this context should not be determinative. At times, an affiliate may have more leverage to induce the issuer to file a registration statement for the securities such affiliate wishes to sell. Nevertheless, the detrimental effect on the capital trading markets and the investing public are identical, irrespective of whether one has affiliate status when reselling large quantities of stock.

The foregoing assertions are reinforced by the following scenario: Company X, for investment purposes, purchases 12% of Company Y's "unrestricted" stock over a six-month period on the New York Stock Exchange. Insiders of Company Y, who still retain 51% ownership of the public company's stock and are able to elect the entire board of directors, have no desire to share control. Company X, pleased with its investment, increases its ownership interest in Company Y's "unrestricted" stock during a three-year period to 19%. One year later, after the insiders reject Company X's request to have a seat on Company Y's board of directors, Company X elects to sell all of its stock in Company Y on the New York Stock Exchange during a ninety-day period.

Under the above scenario, Company X is not an "affiliate" of Company Y. It is neither in a "control" relationship nor can it compel Company Y to file a registration statement. Being a non-affiliate, its sales, by analogy to Rule 144(k), do not constitute a "distribution." Moreover, again in reference to Rule 144(d) and (k), a four-year holding period, as reflected in the illustration, indicates that Company X, not being a control person, acquired and held the securities with investment intent, hence mitigating against the assumption of underwriter status. The policies of the Securities

Act, however, demand that Company X, absent registration, should not be able within a fairly short time period to unload its securities on the investing public.

With the promulgation of Rule 144(k) and the apparent abandonment of the presumptive underwriter doctrine, the SEC appears to have given the impression that non-affiliates can resell nonrestricted stock without limitation. Non-affiliates and their counsel, however, should not act with the same certainty as other parties and transactions that clearly come within Rule 144's scope. Because unlimited sales by non-affiliates should not be permitted for the reasons provided, the SEC should prescribe a safe harbor volume limitation under the Section 4(1) exemption for non-affiliates selling nonrestricted stock. This pronouncement may be effected either by amending Rule 144 or by promulgating a separate rule.[48]

[D] Chart

The following chart seeks to clarify the various requirements that a seller must comply with in order to come within the Rule 144 safe harbor. Remember, however, that the chart may simplify some of the pertinent requirements. Attention therefore should be directed to the relevant SEC releases, the discussion contained herein, and the text of the Rule itself.

---

[48] For further discussion, see Steinberg & Kempler, *The Application and Effectiveness of SEC Rule 144*, 49 Ohio State L.J. 473 (1988). See also, Campbell, *Resales of Securities Under the Securities Act of 1933*, 52 Wash. & Lee L. Rev. 1333 (1995); Hicks, *The Concept of Transaction as a Restraint on Resale Limitations*, 49 Ohio St. L.J. 417 (1988).

RULE 144

REQUIREMENTS FOR AFFILIATES AND NON-AFFILIATES OF THE ISSUER

Requirement	Affiliate Selling Non-Restricted Securities	Affiliate Selling Restricted Securities	Non-Affiliate (Securities are Restricted)	Non-Affiliate Selling Restricted Securities Who Complies with Two Year Holding Requirement of Rule 144(k)
Rule 144(c) - Current Public Information	Must Comply	Must Comply	Must Comply	No Compliance Necessary
Rule 144(d) - Holding Period for Restricted Securities	No Compliance Necessary	Must Comply	Must Comply	Restricted Securities Must Be Held for Two Years by Holder or Prior Non-Affiliates
Rule 144(e) - Limitation on Amount of Securities Sold	Must Comply	Must Comply	Must Comply	No Compliance Necessary
Rule 144(f) - Manner of Sale	Must Comply	Must Comply	Must Comply	No Compliance Necessary
Rule 144(h) and (i) - Notice of Proposed Sale and Intention to Sell	Must Comply	Must Comply	Must Comply	No Compliance Necessary
Rule 144(j) - Non-Exclusion of the Rule	Applicable	Applicable	Applicable	Applicable

§ 5.06 The Section "4(1-1/2)" Exemption

One exemption thus far not discussed is the so-called Section "4(1-1/2)" exemption. This exemption, based largely on SEC no-action letters and other SEC pronouncements, seeks to fill a gap in the statutory exemptive scheme. Upon examining this framework, it appears that none of the statutory or regulatory exemptions expressly cover unlimited sales of securities by affiliates (as well as sales of restricted securities by non-affiliates) who desire to sell such securities in a routine private transaction after a short holding period. By way of example, Rule 144 neither helps a "control" person who wishes to sell all of his or her stock in a private transaction nor a non-affiliate who has not held restricted securities for a sufficient time period to invoke the Rule. Such sales frequently occur and the SEC, provided that certain conditions are met, appears not to be especially troubled by their presence. This should continue to be the case even in view of the Commission's adoption of Rule 144A. As will become evident (see § 5.07 *infra*), the Rule 144A exemption is unavailable in numerous situations.

Focusing on the Section "4(1-1/2)" exemption, the SEC has stated:

> In making such private sales, the affiliates presumably would rely on the so-called Section "4(1-1/2)" exemption. This is a hybrid exemption not specifically provided for in the 1933 Act but clearly within its intended purpose. The exemption basically would permit affiliates to make private sales of securities held by them so long as some of the established criteria for sales under both Section 4(1) and Section 4(2) of the Act are satisfied.[49]

Unfortunately, the Commission has declined to identify the pertinent "established criteria" of Section 4(1) and Section 4(2) that must be satisfied in order for a party successfully to invoke the Section "4(1-1/2)" exemption. However, certain criteria relevant for perfecting the exemption may be as follows:

- While the source of the Section "4(1-1/2)" exemption is Section 4(1), the determination of appropriate standards to govern the exemption is primarily derived from Section 4(2) authority.

- Advertising and general solicitation are not permitted.

- Although no finite number has been established, there is some limit on the number of offerees and purchasers.

- Whether the prospective seller must hold the securities for a certain length of time (such as two years) is uncertain. The holding period may be more relevant where there is no public information available concerning the issuer or where a large number of shares are sought to be sold to several unsophisticated investors.

- The purchasers' access to registration-type information (or the actual providing of such information) as well as purchaser sophistication are relevant, though not necessarily determinative, factors.[50]

---

[49] Securities Act Release No. 6188 (1980). See *Ackerberg v. Johnson*, 892 F.2d 1328 (8th Cir. 1989).

[50] See Olander & Jacks, *The Section 4(1-1/2) Exemption — Reading Between the Lines of the Securities Act of 1933*, 15 Sec. Reg. L.J. 339 (1988); Schneider, *Section 4(1-1/2) — Private Resales of Restricted or Control Securities*, 49 Ohio State L.J. 501 (1988); ABA Committee Report, *The Section "4(1-1/2)" Phenomenon: Private Resales of "Restricted" Securities*, 34 Bus. Law. 1961 (1979).

§ 5.07　Rule 144A

Rule 144A is a non-exclusive safe harbor from the Securities Act registration requirements with respect to the resale of restricted securities to qualified institutional buyers (QIBs) by persons other than the issuer of such restricted securities.[51]

Rule 144A is directed at providing resale markets in generally three different settings: (1) the sale of debt securities from underwriters to QIBs; (2) resales of restricted securities originally sold pursuant to private or limited offerings, such as pursuant to Rule 505 or 506 of Regulation D; and (3) resales of securities of foreign enterprises or of securities originally offered outside of the United States, such as pursuant to Regulation S (see § 3.17 *supra*). Rule 144A's objective generally has been achieved insofar as helping to attract foreign companies to the U.S. capital markets.

Rule 144A is being used by a number of issuers to avoid the federal registration requirements. For example, a company seeking to issue debt securities will place such securities with an underwriter pursuant to the Section 4(2) exemption who in turn will sell them to QIBs under Rule 144A. Rule 144A is deemed advantageous because such offerings can be effected almost instantaneously and without the rigorous disclosure requirements mandated in registered offerings.[52]

[A]　Requirements

The requirements of Rule 144A may strike the reader as being complicated. The following is a Summary that hopefully will make the conditions of the Rule more understandable.

[1]　Resales of Restricted Securities to Qualified Institutional Buyers (e.g., Eligible Insurance Companies, Investment Companies, Employee Benefit Plans, Venture Capital Firms)

Such qualified institutional buyer ("QIB") must have $100 million invested in securities (of issuers that are not affiliated with such buyer) at the conclusion of its most recent fiscal year (goes to amount invested in securities, *not* assets).

(a) In addition to $100 million invested in securities, banks and savings and loan associations must have a net worth of at least $25 million.

(b) Broker-dealers are not required to meet the $100 million invested in securities standard. Rather, an eligible broker-dealer must own and invest on a discretionary basis at least $10 million of securities of issuers that are not affiliated with such broker-dealer. In addition, a broker-dealer who acts solely in a riskless principal transaction on behalf of a

---

[51] See Securities Act Release No. 6862 (1990).

[52] See Raghaven, *Private Placement Market Is Proving Popular*, Wall St. J., April 1, 1997, at C14 (stating that in the first quarter of 1997, $17.8 billion of debt securities were sold pursuant to Rule 144A).

qualified institutional purchaser is itself treated as a QIB, regardless of whether it meets the $10 million invested in securities standard mentioned above.

[2] Qualifying the Prospective Purchaser

It is the seller's responsibility to qualify the prospective purchaser. In other words, the seller or its agent must "reasonably believe" that such purchaser is a QIB. The rule enumerates a number of non-exclusive means to satisfy this requirement, including such purchaser's most recent publicly available annual financial statements and the most recent information appearing in documents publicly filed by such prospective purchaser.

[3] Exclusion of Fungible Securities from Rule 144A

The "nonfungibility" condition arose due to concern that Rule 144A would result in the development of side-by-side public and private markets for the same class of securities, thereby resulting in loss of liquidity to the established trading markets. Hence, as adopted, Rule 144A is not available for securities that, at the time of their issuance, are of the same class (i.e., fungible) as securities trading on a U.S. exchange or quoted on the NASDAQ. Note that convertible securities, having an effective conversion premium at the time of issuance of less than ten percent, are treated as securities of both the convertible and the underlying securities.

[4] Provision of Information

Upon request to the issuer, such issuer must provide to the holder and to the prospective purchaser certain basic information concerning the issuer's business and its financial statements (if the issuer is not a 1934 Act reporting company and is not exempt from such reporting pursuant to Exchange Act Rule 12g3-2(b)). Information ordinarily would be obtained by the holder from the issuer pursuant to contractual rights negotiated at the time of issuance.

[5] Notice Requirement

The rule requires that the seller take reasonable steps to notify the QIB that the seller is relying on Rule 144A as an exemption from registration.

[B] Criticism

The "provision of information" condition of Rule 144A raised the ire of former SEC Commissioner Edward Fleischman. He contended that the delivery of information requirement will adversely affect "that class of business enterprises most needy of the benefits promised by the rule and most capable of magnifying those benefits to the advantage of the entire American economy, namely smaller domestic privately-owned issuers also known as'emerging growth companies.'"[53]

---

[53] Securities Act Release No. 6862 (1990) (Fleischman, Comm'r, dissenting in part).

On the other hand, Rule 144A has raised concerns that it will adversely impact individual investors. To such critics, the SEC's promulgation of Rule 144A represents yet another example of the Commission's solicitousness toward capital formation and institutional investors to the detriment of ordinary investors. In a letter to then SEC Chairman David Breeden, two influential Congressmen, John D. Dingell and Edward J. Markey, asserted that Rule 144A may be invalid as exceeding the scope of the Commission's authority in this area (namely, that the exemption, Rule 144A, exceeds the scope of the statutes, Section 4(1) and Section 4(4), upon which the Rule 144A exemption is based). The Congressmen also expressed their concern on a policy level:

> We strongly endorse what we understand to be policy goals underlying the Commission's adoption of Rule 144A. The Commission staff is to be commended for its creativity, hard work, and the high quality of its efforts in seeking to enhance the competitiveness of the U.S. in today's global markets. Nonetheless, we are concerned about the specific mechanism established to achieve these goals. In particular, we are concerned about the possible development of a two-tiered securities market for U.S. investors, one public and one private, and the serious negative implications of such a development; the diminished availability of many quality investments to smaller investors and, conversely, the greater likelihood that poor investments will be passed on to unwitting investors through mutual and pension funds or other avenues of leakage, and the rule's diminution of the amount and type of disclosure, particularly with regard to foreign companies about which U.S. investors have historically had little information.[54]

Rule 144A thus far has been most successful in attracting foreign companies to the U.S. capital markets. According to a report authored by the SEC staff, 69 of the first 95 issuers whose securities were sold by means of Rule 144A were foreign entities. The rule, however, has failed to stimulate a resale market in Regulation D and similar types of offerings. On the other hand, as discussed earlier in this Section, Rule 144A is being used extensively by companies marketing their debt securities to QIBs[55]

---

[54] Excerpts of the letter are contained and discussed in Barron, *Some Comments on SEC Rule 144A*, 18 Sec. Reg. L.J. 400 (1991).

[55] See 23 Sec. Reg. & L. Rep. (BNA) 1589 (1991); *supra* note 52 and accompanying text. For discussion on Regulation S, see § 3.17 *supra*. See generally Bradford, *Rule 144A and Integration*, 20 Sec. Reg. L.J. 37 (1992); Rumsey, *Rule 144A and Other Developments in the Resale of Restricted Securities*, 19 Sec. Reg. L.J. 157 (1991); Steinberg & Lansdale, *Regulation S and Rule 144A: Creating a Workable Fiction in an Expanding Global Securities Market*, 29 Int'l Law. 43 (1995).

§ 5.08   Corporate Reorganizations

[A]   In General

Corporations as well as other entities frequently engage in reorganizations. State corporation statutes, corporate charters, and similar controlling instruments normally require shareholder approval or consent of mergers, consolidations, transfer of assets and reclassifications of stock. These reorganizations normally result in the exchange of shares or the issuance of new stock. Rule 145(a) makes it clear that when such plans of reorganization are submitted to shareholders for approval, the corporation makes an "offer to sell" within the meaning of Section 2(a)(3) of the Securities Act. Rule 145, therefore, has several ramifications.

[B]   Rule 145 — Ramifications

Absent an exemption from registration, an offer to sell securities pursuant to Rule 145 triggers the registration requirements of Section 5 as well as due diligence obligations (including the rigorous culpability standards of Section 11). Rule 145 transactions may be registered pursuant to the Securities Act on Form S-4. The Form S-4 framework improves the effectiveness of the business reorganization prospectus by requiring that information be presented in a more accessible and meaningful format.[56]

By triggering the registration requirements, Rule 145 also triggers Section 5's "gun-jumping" prohibition.[57] Thus, communications designed to influence shareholders' votes may be viewed as constituting offers to sell in the pre-filing period and, hence, violations of Section 5(c). Rule 145(b) provides certain exceptions in this respect, authorizing the corporation to communicate basic information, including the issuer's name, a brief description of the business of the parties, and a brief description of the transaction. Compliance with the provisions of Rule 145(b) has the effect of protecting the communication from constituting an "offer to sell" under Section 2(a)(3) or from being deemed a "prospectus" under Section 2(a)(10). In this regard, the pre-filing publicity notice permitted under Rule 135 is also available for such transactions.[58]

---

[56] See Securities Act Release No. 6578 (1985). See generally Campbell, *Rule 145: Mergers, Acquisitions and Recapitalizations Under the Securities Act of 1933*, 56 Fordham L. Rev. 277 (1987).

[57] For discussion on conditioning the market ("gun-jumping"), see § 4.02[A][2] *supra*.

[58] Rule 135 is addressed in § 4.02[A][3] *supra*. In 1999, the SEC adopted new rules and amended existing rules to allow parties to communicate with fewer restrictions about planned business combination transactions during the pre-filing, waiting, and post-effective periods of registration. Under revised Rule 145, offerors are still allowed to use Rule 135 notices prior to the filing of a registration statement to solicit security holders; however, new Rule 425 imposes a filing requirement for such notices. Two newly promulgated rules, Rules 165 and 166, also exempt certain communications regarding business combination transactions from Section 5 of the Securities Act. Rule 165 is not limited to offerors and may be used by "any other participant that may need to rely on and complies with [Rule 165] in communicating about the transaction." Rule 166 permits communications by participants in a registered

[C] "Downstream Sales"

The ramifications of Rule 145 do not end after the shareholders approve a plan of reorganization. Rule 145(c) addresses the problem of "downstream sales." Depending on the circumstances, parties to a Rule 145 transaction who publicly sell or publicly offer to sell their securities may be deemed to be engaged in a distribution as well as being deemed underwriters within the meaning of Section 2(a)(11). These parties can avoid underwriter status, however, by meeting the criteria contained in Rule 145(d).

As an initial point, for parties who neither are affiliates of the acquired company nor affiliates of the acquiring company, the securities received in a Rule 145 transaction are nonrestricted securities, thereby having no restrictions on resale.

In regard to parties who are affiliates of an entity *acquired* pursuant to a Rule 145 transaction, the SEC, consistent with its Rule 144 modifications, has substantially relaxed the "resale" provisions of Rule 145. As a result, such parties (who are affiliates of the acquired, but not of the acquiring, entity) today have much greater leeway in reselling their securities without fear of assuming underwriter status. Accordingly, persons who are affiliates of the acquired entity that receive securities in registered business combinations and who subsequently transfer such securities will not be deemed underwriters if:

i. The securities are sold in compliance with the provisions of paragraphs (c), (e), (f), and (g) of Rule 144; or

ii. The person is a non-affiliate of the issuer (i.e., a non-affiliate of the acquiring company), has held the securities for at least a one-year period, and the issuer has complied with the current public reporting requirements of Rule 144(c) (by either being an Exchange Act reporting company or by making adequate information available); or

iii. The party is a non-affiliate of the issuer and has held the securities for at least two years. [59]

Consider the effect of the SEC's amendments to Rule 145 (with respect to persons who were affiliates of an entity acquired in a Rule 145 transaction and who are non-affiliates of the acquiring entity). First, such non-affiliates of the issuer (i.e., non-affiliates of the acquiring company) can dispose of all of their securities after one year if the issuer has maintained adequate current public information. Second, such non-affiliates, after a two-year holding period, can sell all of their shares even if the issuer is not making adequate current information available. Note that the holding period is measured from the date of acquisition from the issuer or from an

---

offering involving a business combination transaction before the first public announcement of the offering upon a showing that "all reasonable steps within their control [were taken] to prevent further distribution or publication of the communication until either the first public announcement is made or the registration statement related to the transaction is filed [with the Commission.]" See Securities Act Release No. 42055, [1999-2000 Transfer Binder] Fed. Sec. L. Rep. (CCH) ¶ 86,215 (SEC 1999).

[59] See Securities Act Release 7390 (1997); Securities Act Release No. 6508 (1984).

affiliate of the issuer. "Tacking" of the applicable holding period is permitted when transactions take place between non-affiliates.[60]

The public policy assessments made by the Commission in adopting these revisions can be questioned on much the same basis as was made with respect to the amendments to Rule 144 (see § 5.05[C]). Undoubtedly, the Commission's amendments to Rule 145 are a victory for deregulation and capital formation. Some may claim, however, that the costs are too great: By permitting non-affiliates of the issuer to "dump" their securities on the investing public with little or no information being available about the issuer deals a blow to two fundamental purposes underlying the federal securities laws, namely, to ensure the integrity of the financial marketplace and to enable investors to have adequate information before them so that they can make informed investment decisions.

[D] "Spin-Offs"

Spin-offs have many variations. The "classical" spin-off occurs when a parent corporation distributes shares of a privately-held subsidiary as a stock dividend to its current shareholders. In such event, it is only a matter of time before these shares become publicly traded. Absent the availability of an exemption, "spin-offs" thereby may have the effect of evading the registration requirements. Due to this concern, the SEC and the courts have held that this technique, depending on the circumstances, calls for Securities Act registration. Moreover, parent corporations that cause their subsidiaries to engage in such practices may be deemed to be "underwriters."[61]

Defendants, charged with failing to register a "spin-off" offering, have asserted that the stock dividend distributed to shareholders was not an "offer to sell" or "sale" within the meaning of Section 2(a)(3) of the Securities Act because it was not "for value," and hence, was not in violation of Section 5. The SEC and the courts frequently have rejected this argument, reasoning that the creation of a public market for the spun-off securities constitutes value to the parent corporation when the stockholders dispose of these securities.[62]

In 1997, the SEC's Division of Corporation Finance opined that a spin-off does not require Securities Act registration if the following five conditions are met: (1) shareholders of the parent corporation do not provide any consideration for the spun-off shares; (2) the shares spun-off are distributed pro rata to the parent corporation's shareholders; (3) adequate information about the subsidiary and the spin-off must be provided by the parent corporation to both the stockholders and the securities trading markets;

---

[60] See Securities Act Release No. 7390 (1997); Securities Act Release No. 6862 (1990); *supra* note 42 and accompanying text.

[61] *See SEC v. Datronics Engineers, Inc.*, 490 F.2d 250 (4th Cir. 1973), *cert. denied*, 416 U.S. 937 (1974); *SEC v. Harwyn Industries Corp.*, 326 F. Supp. 943 (S.D.N.Y. 1971). But see Isquith v. Caremark International, Inc., [1998 Transfer Binder] Fed. Sec. L. Rep. (CCH) ¶ 90,141 (7th Cir. 1998).

[62] See cases cited note 61 *supra*.

(4) the parent corporation has a valid business purpose justifying the spin-off; and (5) if the parent corporation elects to spin-off restricted securities, it must have held such securities for a least two years.[63] Note, moreover, that SEC Rule 15c2-11 effectively thwarts public trading of securities acquired in unregistered spin-offs by prohibiting broker-dealers from either initiating or continuing to provide price quotations for a security unless adequate public information is available with respect to both the issuer and the security.[64]

---

[63] See SEC Legal Bulletin No. 4 (Sept. 16, 1997).

[64] See T. Hazen, *supra* note 21, at 303; Bloomenthal, *Market-Makers, Manipulators and Shell Games*, 45 St. John's L. Rev. 597 (1971); Long, *Control of the Spin-Off Device Under the Securities Act of 1933*, 25 Okla. L. Rev. 317 (1972); Lorne, *The Portfolio Spin-Off and Securities Registration*, 52 Texas L. Rev. 918 (1974); Note, *Registration of Stock Spin-Offs Under the Securities Act of 1933*, 1980 Duke L.J. 965 (1980); cases cited note 61 *supra*; description of Rule 15c2-11, *supra* note 13 and accompanying text.

Chapter 6

DUE DILIGENCE AND SECURITIES ACT LIABILITY

§ 6.01 Introduction

This chapter addresses due diligence, liability consequences, and other ramifications in both registered and unregistered offerings. The chapter begins with a discussion of Section 11's statutory framework. A number of key concepts under the statute are reviewed, including persons subject to liability under Section 11, requirements for invoking the right of action, defenses (particularly the due diligence defenses), damages, contribution, and indemnification.

Concerning due diligence in the registered offering context, the *BarChris*[1] case still serves as the most appropriate vehicle for focusing on this concept. As *BarChris* illustrates, although technically a defense, due diligence is a necessary function to be performed. The discussion thereafter addresses the various parties who may assert the due diligence defense and the degree of investigation required for each such party, including: directors ("inside" as well as "outside"), signatories of the registration statement, underwriters, accountants (who serve as "experts"), and attorneys (who are not liable under Section 11 unless they "expertise" a portion of the registration statement, serve as a director, or act in some other capacity that brings them within the provision's reach).

After analyzing *BarChris* and its ramifications, the chapter discusses the controversial issue, particularly for underwriters, of due diligence in the integrated disclosure framework. These concerns, as the materials in § 6.07 point out, are accentuated in the shelf registration context. Many critics claim that the SEC's response, principally the adoption of Rule 176, is inadequate. The ultimate resolution reached should accommodate the legitimate concerns of underwriters yet be consistent with investor protection.

The last portion of the chapter focuses on Section 12(a)(2) of the Securities Act which contains a "reasonable care" defense that, depending on the circumstances, may be similar to Section 11's "due diligence" defense. Importantly, Section 12(a)(2) may be Section 11's remedial counterpart where an *unregistered* offering takes on the characteristics of a public offering. Also, Section 12(a)(2) may be invoked in the context of registered offerings.[2] Moreover, in either the registered or unregistered offering

---

[1] *Escott v. BarChris Construction Corporation*, 283 F. Supp. 643 (S.D.N.Y. 1968).

[2] See *Gustafson v. Alloyd Company*, 513 U.S. 561 (1995), discussed in, § 6.09[D] *infra*.

setting, plaintiffs always can seek to invoke Section 10(b) of the Securities Exchange Act.[3]

§ 6.02   The Registered Offering — Framework of Section 11

As discussed in the foregoing materials (you may wish to review the discussion in §§ 3.01 and 4.01 at this time), a registered offering under the Securities Act requires that a registration statement be utilized. A key policy underlying this requirement is to enable prospective purchasers to make informed investment decisions based upon the disclosure of adequate and truthful information regarding the issuer, its associated persons, and the offering. This policy is frustrated when a registration statement (including the prospectus that comprises part of the registration statement) contains materially false or misleading statements.

In view of the above, investors under certain conditions may recover their losses if they purchase securities pursuant to a registration statement that contains a material misrepresentation or nondisclosure. The federal law provision most likely to be invoked in this context is Section 11 of the Securities Act.

[A]   Parties Subject to Section 11 Liability

Section 11(a) of the Securities Act specifies the classes of persons who may be subject to liability for material misstatements or omissions contained in the registration statement (including the prospectus which is part of the registration statement). Parties subject to Section 11 liability include: (1) all persons who sign the registration statement (including, pursuant to Section 6(a) of the Securities Act, the "issuer, its principal executive officer or officers, its principal financial officer, its controller or principal accounting officer, and the majority of its board of directors or persons performing similar functions"); (2) every director (or person performing similar functions) or general partner of the issuer; (3) every person named with his/her consent in the registration statement as being or about to become a person stated in (2) above; (4) every expert "who has with his consent been named as having prepared or certified any part of the registration statement, or as having prepared or certified any report or valuation which is used in connection with the registration statement, with respect to the statement in such registration statement, report, or valuation which purports to have been prepared or certified by him"; (5) every underwriter of the offering; and (6) pursuant to Section 15, every control person of a party liable under Section 11.

Due to the statutory language and the exhaustive enumeration of those parties subject to suit under Section 11, courts refuse to impose "aiding and abetting" liability pursuant to that provision. For example, in *In re Equity Funding Corp. of America Securities Litigation*,[4] the court observed:

---

[3] See *Herman & MacLean v. Huddleston*, 459 U.S. 375 (1983), discussed in, § 7.07 *infra*.

[4] 416 F. Supp. 161 (D.C. Cal. 1976).

"[W]here a statute specifically limits those who may be held liable for the conduct described by the statute, the courts cannot extend liability, under a theory of aiding and abetting, to those who do not fall within the categories of potential defendants described by the statute."[5] The Supreme Court's decision in *Central Bank of Denver*, holding that aiding and abetting liability may not be imposed under Section 10(b) of the Exchange Act, further evidences that such liability is improper under Section 11.[6]

[B] Elements of the Section 11 Right of Action

Generally, provided that the interstate commerce requirement has been met and upon proof of a material misstatement or nondisclosure, a private action for damages under Section 11(a) may be brought by "any person acquiring such security" unless it can be shown that, at the time of purchase, the purchaser knew of the misstatement or omission. Privity between the purchaser and the defendant is not required for recovery. Moreover, as held by most courts, the Section 11 right of action is available in the initial offering setting as well as when those shares are subsequently traded in the aftermarket.[7] In practical effect, however, with respect to shares traded in the aftermarket, the "tracing" requirement often may have the effect of nullifying the Section 11 right of action. For example, in one such case, stockholders purchasing in the aftermarket were held to lack standing under Section 11 with respect to those shares that they were unable affirmatively to establish were purchased in the public offering.[8] Hence, pursuant to the tracing requirement, plaintiffs must show not that they "might" have purchased shares by means of a deficient registration statement in a particular offering, but that they in fact did purchase such shares pursuant to that specific offering (and registration statement). Given the practical difficulties of "tracing," this requirement frequently is a burdensome one for "aftermarket" Section 11 plaintiffs.[9]

---

[5] *Id.* at 181.

[6] *Central Bank of Denver v. First Interstate Bank of Denver*, 511 U.S. 164 (1994), discussed, §§ 9.01–9.02, 14.05[B] *infra*.

[7] The majority of courts allow Section 11 to be invoked in the aftermarket by allegedly aggrieved purchasers. However, based on the U.S. Supreme Court's decision in *Gustafson v. Alloyd Co.*, 513 U.S. 561 (1995) (discussed in § 6.09[D]), which limited Section 12(a)(2)'s scope to public offerings, some courts have confined Section 11's coverage to those securities purchased in the public offering itself. Compare *Hertzberg v. Dignity Partners, Inc.*, 191 F.3d 1076 (9th Cir. 1999) (holding purchasers who traced shares acquired in the aftermarket to the allegedly false registration statement had standing under § 11) and *Schwartz v. Celestial Seasonings, Inc.*, 178 F.R.D. 545 (D. Colo. 1998) (same), with *Brosious v. Children's Place Retail Stores*, [1999-2000 Transfer Binder] Fed. Sec. L. Rep. (CCH) ¶ 90,651 (D.N.J. 1999) (tracing not recognized to confer § 11 standing) and *Gould v. Harris*, 929 F. Supp. 353 (C.D. Cal. 1996) (same).

[8] See *Kirkwood v. Taylor*, 590 F. Supp. 1375 (D. Minn. 1984). For other cases raising the "tracing" issue, see, e.g., *Barnes v. Osofsky*, 373 F.2d 269 (2d Cir. 1967); *In re Newbridge Networks Securities Litigation*, 767 F. Supp. 275 (D.D.C. 1991); *Guenther v. Cooper Life Sciences, Inc.*, 759 F. Supp. 1437 (N.D. Cal. 1990); *McFarland v. Memorex Corp.*, 493 F. Supp. 631 (N.D. Cal. 1980); cases cited note 7 *supra*. See generally McMillin, *Recent Developments in Litigation Under the Securities Act of 1933*, 33 Rev. Sec. & Comm. Reg. 1 (2000).

[9] See cases cited notes 7–8 *supra*.

In addition, a plaintiff bringing suit under Section 11 normally need not show reliance upon the misstatement or omission. In fact, he/she need not even have read the prospectus. Pursuant to Section 11(a), however, where the plaintiff acquired the securities more than twelve months after the effective date of the registration statement and if the issuer has made generally available an "earnings statement" covering this twelve-month period, such plaintiff must prove reliance on the misstatement or omission. This showing of reliance may be made by means other than the actual reading of the prospectus.[10]

Another important point is that a plaintiff seeking to recover under Section 11 need not prove that the material misrepresentation or nondisclosure "caused" the loss. In this regard, however, Section 11(e), supported by case law, permits the defendant to reduce (either in part or totally) the plaintiff's monetary recovery by showing that the loss (or portion thereof) was attributable to factors other than the material misrepresentation(s) or nondisclosure(s) contained in the registration statement.[11]

Section 11's seemingly broad express right of action also is limited by a relatively short statute of limitations. Section 13 of the Securities Act provides that an action pursuant to Section 11 must be brought "within one year after the discovery of the untrue statement or the omission, or after such discovery should have been made by the exercise of reasonable diligence . . . [but] in no event shall any such action be brought . . . more than three years after the security was offered to the public."

To recap, under Section 11, *a plaintiff*:

- must have purchased the security where a means or instrumentality of interstate commerce was used in connection with the offer or sale;

- at the time of purchase, must not have known of the misrepresentation or nondisclosure;

- must show that the misrepresentation or nondisclosure was "material," meaning that reasonable investors would have considered the pertinent information important in making their investment decisions;

- need not establish privity;

- as held by most courts, can recover for aftermarket purchases but subject to the often difficult "tracing" requirement;

- normally need not show reliance upon the misrepresentation or nondisclosure;

- need not prove that the misrepresentation or nondisclosure "caused" the loss (in other words, causation is presumed once a material misstatement or nondisclosure has been shown to exist);

---

[10] See SEC Rule 158 (defining the terms: "earning statement," "made generally available to its security holders," and "effective date of the registration statement" for the purposes of the reliance requirement as set forth in the final paragraph of § 11(a)).

[11] See, e.g., *Akerman v. Orxy Communications, Inc.*, [1984 Transfer Binder] Fed. Sec. L. Rep. (CCH) ¶ 91,680 (S.D.N.Y. 1984), *aff'd*, 810 F.2d 344 (2d Cir. 1987).

- must bring the action within the time period set forth by Section 13's statute of limitations.

[C] Defenses

[1] General

Section 11(b) provides a number of due diligence defenses for persons other than the issuer. Generally, the only defenses available to the issuer, who otherwise is strictly liable, are the purchaser's knowledge of the misstatement or omission, lack of materiality, lack of causation, equitable defenses (such as in pari delicto), and expiration of the statute of limitations. These defenses, of course, are available to any defendant.

In addition to the above defenses and the "due diligence" defense (which will be addressed shortly), a non-issuer defendant, who discovers a material misstatement or omission in the registration statement, may avoid liability by taking the action specified in Section 11(b)(1) or (2), namely:

(1) *Before* the effective date of the registration statement or part thereof in question, he or she (1) resigns from or takes such steps as are permitted by law to resign from, or ceases or refuses to act in, every office, capacity or relationship ascribed to him or her in the registration statement, and (2) advises the SEC and the issuer in writing of the action taken and disavowing responsibility for such part of the registration statement.

(2) *After* such part of the registration statement has become effective, (1) if he or she was unaware that it had become effective, and (2) upon becoming aware of such fact, acts forthwith, (3) advises the SEC in writing as set forth above, and (4) gives reasonable public notice that such part of the registration statement had become effective without his or her knowledge.

[2] Due Diligence — Overview

The "due diligence" defenses are contained in Section 11(b)(3). As regards the *unexpertised portion* of the registration statement, a subject defendant must show that, *after* reasonable investigation he/she had reason to believe and did believe at the time such part of the registration statement became effective, there was no material misstatement or omission. As regards the *expertised part*, a defendant (other than the responsible expert) need show only that he/she had no reasonable ground to believe and did not believe that the expertised portion of the registration statement was defective. While a non-expert is not required to make an investigation of expertised information, he/she must "have no reasonable ground to believe" such information is inaccurate.[12]

An expert, on the other hand, is required to show that after reasonable investigation, he/she had reasonable ground to believe and did believe

---

[12] The same standard applies under Section 11(b)(3)(D) to statements in the registration statement purporting to have been made by a public official or purporting to be a copy or extract from a public official document.

his/her "expertised" statement to be accurate. In other words, an expert is required to exercise the same standard of care regarding the part expertised by him or her as a non-expert is required to exercise regarding the non-expertised portion of the registration statement. Experts are not subject to liability under Section 11 for misstatements or omissions in the unexpertised part of the registration statement merely by reason of their involvement as experts.

[3] Due Diligence Standard

Section 11(c) provides that the standard of reasonableness by which the concept of "reasonable investigation" is to be measured is that required of "a prudent man in the management of his own property." In this regard, the "prudent man" standard applies not only to the reasonableness of one's investigation but also to the reasonableness of one's belief.

While opinions may differ as to whether the standard is unitary or elastic, the *BarChris* decision, which is discussed in § 6.04, unequivocally indicates that the degree of responsibility, and a fortiori the extensiveness of the investigation required to establish due diligence, largely will depend upon the type of person and the nature of his/her relationship with the issuer. While *BarChris* let it be known that the statutory due diligence obligations are not to be treated lightly, the decision did not resolve many of the problems inherent in the vague "reasonable investigation" standard. Subsequently, the SEC adopted Rule 176 which lists a number of factors to be taken into account as "circumstances affecting the determination of what constitutes reasonable investigation." These factors are:

(a) The type of issuer;

(b) The type of security;

(c) The type of person;

(d) The office held when the person is an officer;

(e) The presence or absence of another relationship to the issuer when the person is a director or proposed director;

(f) Reasonable reliance on officers, employees, and others whose duties should have given them knowledge of the particular facts (in light of the functions and responsibilities of the particular person with respect to the issuer and the filing);

(g) When the person is an underwriter, the type of underwriting arrangement, the role of the particular person as an underwriter and the availability of information with respect to the registrant; and

(h) Whether, with respect to a fact or document incorporated by reference, the particular person had any responsibility for the fact or document at the time of the filing from which it was incorporated. [13]

---

[13] 17 C.F.R. § 230.176.

Critics contend that these guidelines do little to provide meaningful content to the "reasonable investigation" standard. Rule 176 and the ramifications of due diligence in the integrated disclosure framework will be addressed in §§ 6.05-6.07.

§ 6.03 Contribution and Indemnification

Under Section 11, violators generally are subject to joint and several liability. Accordingly, a plaintiff is entitled to recover the entire judgment against any violator. An exception to this framework exists with respect to outside directors who are liable only in proportion to their fault unless they had actual knowledge of the falsity.

In order to distribute judgment and settlement costs among joint violators, the two common techniques used are contribution and indemnification. While indemnification involves a shifting of the entire loss from one defendant to another person, contribution involves a sharing of the damages among the tortfeasors.

Section 11(f) of the Securities Act clearly provides for a right to *contribution*.[14] The provision, however, leaves unsettled the extent to which losses are to be shared among the parties. The traditional view is that the parties share the entire loss on a pro rata basis (i.e., equally among the joint tortfeasors irrespective of individual fault). The emerging view is that apportionment of damages should be premised upon a proportionate fault or pro tanto basis. The subjects of contribution and methods of allocating contribution in securities litigation are addressed in § 7.11.[15]

The right to *indemnification* is far less certain. Neither Section 11 nor any other provision of the securities laws provides for such a right. The SEC's position, as contained in Items 510 and 512(h) of Regulation S-K, is that indemnification of officers, directors, and controlling persons of the registrant for liability arising under the Securities Act is against public policy, and, hence, unenforceable. Interestingly, however, the SEC has no such hostility to the procurement of insurance. Rule 461(c) of Regulation C provides that normally "[i]nsurance against liabilities arising under the [Securities] Act, whether the cost of insurance is borne by the registrant, the insured or some other person, will not be considered a bar to acceleration [of the effective date of the registration statement]."

Another question concerns whether an underwriter, pursuant to an indemnity contract with the issuer or its controlling persons, may thereby avoid liability. With respect to intentional securities law violations by an

---

[14] See also, *Musick, Peller & Garrett v. Employers Insurance of Wausau*, 508 U.S. 286 (1993) (implied right to contribution recognized under § 10(b) of Exchange Act).

[15] See Steinberg & Olive, *Contribution and Proportionate Liability Under the Federal Securities Laws in Multidefendant Securities Litigation After the Private Securities Litigation Reform Act of 1995*, 50 SMU L. Rev. 337 (1996); Comment, *Apportioning Contribution Shares Under the Federal Securities Act: A Suggested Approach for an Unsettled Area*, 50 Fordham L. Rev. 450 (1981). See generally Ruder, *Multiple Defendants in Securities Law Fraud Cases: Aiding and Abetting, Conspiracy, In Pari Delicto, Indemnification and Contribution*, 120 U. Pa. L. Rev. 597 (1972).

underwriter, the courts have denied indemnification. Generally, the courts reason that, permitting a party to avoid monetary liability for its own reckless or willful misconduct, is contrary to the securities acts' objective of inducing parties to be scrupulous about their disclosure obligations. Moreover, the issuer's indemnification of the underwriter is suspect in that the funds ultimately come out of the shareholders' pockets, the very individuals who were damaged by the misconduct.[16] The foregoing reasons also are applicable for prohibiting indemnification where the underwriter has been negligent. Some courts, however, may enforce an indemnity contract where the underwriter's culpability does not surpass that of negligence.[17]

§ 6.04 Due Diligence in the Registered Offering Context

As an initial matter, it should be pointed out (see § 3.01) that, strictly speaking, due diligence is a defense that may be asserted by the subject party rather than an affirmative obligation. If the statements made in the registration statement are true or, alternatively, if no lawsuit is brought, no liability will be incurred for an individual's failure to exercise due diligence. On the other hand, if an action is instituted and a material misstatement or omission is shown, liability often may be avoided under Section 11 only by proving the performance of due diligence. For this reason, as a practical matter, due diligence is a necessity.

Although not a recent decision, the seminal case on due diligence in the Section 11 context is *Escott v. BarChris Construction Corporation*.[18] In *BarChris*, convertible debentures of BarChris Construction Corporation, the issuer, were sold to the public by means of a registration statement filed with the SEC. Plaintiffs, who were purchasers of these debentures, alleged that the registration statement contained material misstatements and omissions. Relief was sought against various defendants, including the directors, the persons who signed the registration statement, the underwriters, and the auditors. In imposing liability against the various parties, the *BarChris* court set forth several key principles.

[A] Directors

In analyzing the due diligence defense raised by the defendant directors, *BarChris* draws a distinction between inside and outside directors, and

---

[16] See, e.g., *Globus v. Law Research Serv., Inc.*, 418 F.2d 1276 (2d Cir. 1969), *cert. denied*, 397 U.S. 913 (1970).

[17] See *Eichenholtz v. Brennan*, 52 F.3d 478 (3d Cir. 1995) (not permitting right to indemnification when underwriter was negligent); *Globus*, 418 F.2d at 1288; L. Loss & J. Seligman, Securities Regulation 4632 (3d ed. 1988); Comment, *Allocation of Damages Under the Federal Securities Laws*, 60 Wash. U. L.Q. 211 (1982) (and cases cited therein). For discussion of contribution and indemnification under Section 10(b) of the Securities Exchange Act, see § 7.11 *infra*.

[18] 283 F. Supp. 643 (S.D.N.Y. 1968). See also, *Feit v. Leasco Data Processing Equip. Corp.*, 332 F. Supp. 544 (E.D.N.Y. 1971), for an extensive discussion of liability under Section 11 of the Securities Act.

between directors based upon the extent of their knowledge of or access to the pertinent facts. Certainly one would expect a director who also serves as the principal executive officer to be required to perform more diligently than an outside director who otherwise has no relationship with the issuer. As another example, many corporations have established executive committees, comprised of two or three directors who, in many cases, make decisions that otherwise would be within the province of the entire board of directors. Depending upon the circumstances, an inordinate hardship would be imposed upon directors not serving on those committees if they were held to the same degree of responsibility.

BarChris indicates that, while less may be required of certain outside directors in order to meet their due diligence obligations, reasonable investigation still requires affirmative action. Hence, even outside directors must endeavor to make some type of an independent verification of the information contained in the registration statement. Clearly, a director who makes no effort to investigate will not be able to sustain his/her burden of establishing that he/she acted with due diligence.

In one relatively recent case, an outside director met his due diligence defense under Section 11. In *Weinberger v. Jackson*, the district court stated:

> Since Valentine was an outside director, he was not obliged to conduct an independent investigation into the accuracy of all the statements contained in the registration statement. He could rely upon the reasonable representations of management, if his own conduct and level of inquiry were reasonable under the circumstances. He was reasonably familiar with the company's business and operations. He regularly attended board meetings at which the board discussed every aspect of the company's business. And he reviewed the company's financial statements. He was familiar with the company's development of its new product lines. He was involved with various company decisions. He reviewed six drafts of the registration statement and saw nothing suspicious or inconsistent with the knowledge that he had acquired as a director. And he discussed certain aspects of the registration statement with management. . . .
>
> Plaintiffs argue that Valentine did not make specific inquiries of the company's management with respect to the representations contained in the prospectus. But he had no duty to do so as long as the prospectus statements were consistent with the knowledge of the company which he had reasonably acquired in his position as director. He was also given comfort by the fact that the prospectus and the information in it were reviewed by underwriters, counsel and accountants. This met the standards of due diligence and reasonable inquiry. . . .[19]

---

[19] [1990–1991 Transfer Binder] Fed. Sec. L. Rep. (CCH) ¶ 95,693, at 98,256 (N.D. Cal. 1990). See generally Hamilton, *Reliance and Liability Standards for Outside Directors*, 24 Wake Forest L. Rev. 5 (1989).

It may be argued that an outside director should: seek to attend board of director meetings regarding the offering; review the registration statement with care (probing relevant corporate personnel and counsel on the factual contents and representations made therein); review the Exchange Act filed documents that are incorporated by reference into the registration statement; with the aid of competent advisers, assess the abilities of management as well as the company's reputation; ask questions and follow up if necessary. Although the performance of the foregoing actions may not guarantee absolution from liability, it should provide persuasive evidence that the outside director met his or her due diligence obligations.

[B] Signatories

Persons who sign the registration statement (normally inside directors and officers of the issuer) may be held to stringent due diligence obligations. This is despite the fact that, had they not signed, their respective duties of investigation, particularly in the case of officers not holding directorships, may have differed. The rationale for holding signatories, particularly those who are inside directors or who otherwise hold principal corporate offices (even if not directors), to a strict standard of due diligence is that prospective investors reasonably may assume that, by signing the registration statement, such signatories represent that it is an accurate statement of the information contained therein.

To a large extent, *BarChris* may be viewed as treating "inside" signatories in effect as guarantors of the accuracy of the registration statement (indeed the court may have said as much). Interestingly, however, Congress specifically rejected a proposal that would have made directors guarantors in this context. On the other hand, it may be said that *BarChris* "does not deny the [due diligence] defense [to such inside signatories], but recognizes the obvious difficulty of establishing it."[20]

[C] Attorneys

Due diligence is a concern for lawyers who are involved in a registered offering. For example, counsel may: (1) serve as a director of the issuer, (2) act as an expert within the meaning of Section 11(a)(4) (e.g., by rendering a tax opinion that is contained in the registration statement), and (3) perform due diligence investigations on behalf of a client (e.g., an underwriter) in its stead.

An SEC Advisory Committee has proposed that an issuer establish a disclosure committee comprised of outside directors to oversee the integrity of the company's disclosures. See Report of the Advisory Committee on the Capital Formation and Regulatory Processes, [1996–1997 Transfer Binder] Fed. Sec. L. Rep. (CCH) ¶ 85,834 (1996). Implementation of such disclosure committees raises a host of due diligence concerns.

[20] Folk, *Civil Liabilities Under the Federal Securities Acts: The BarChris Case*, 55 Va. L. Rev. 1, 22 (1969). See H.R. Rep. No. 85, 73d Cong., 1st Sess. 5 (1933); H.R. Rep. No. 152, 73d Cong., 1st Sess. 26 (1933); Landis, *The Legislative History of the Securities Act of 1933*, 28 Geo. Wash. L. Rev. 29, 48 (1959).

With respect to assuming "expert" status, it is clear that an attorney who renders legal advice or assists in the preparation of the registration statement does not thereby become an expert within the meaning of Section 11. Further, because Section 11 limits the class of potential defendants, attorneys cannot be held liable under Section 11 on an aiding and abetting theory.[21] Depending on the circumstances, they can be held liable as primary violators under Section 10(b) of the Securities Exchange Act, as "sellers" under Section 12 of the Securities Act, as "control persons" under both the 1933 and 1934 Acts, and under state law.[22]

In *BarChris* the young attorney, Birnbaum, while not a director at the time the registration statement originally was filed, was a director when he signed the later amendments. He thereby subjected himself to Section 11 liability as a director and as a signatory. Unfortunately, Birnbaum made no investigation whatsoever and relied on the statements of others. The court noted that, while Birnbaum was not an executive officer in any real sense, he was named as such in the prospectus. Further, by virtue of his duties as in-house counsel and keeper of the corporate minutes, he had considerable information about the corporation's affairs. While not aware of many of the inaccuracies in the prospectus, as a lawyer he must have appreciated some of them. He should have known his statutory obligations and made a reasonable investigation.

The court's opinion indicates that, even if he were not a signatory to the registration statement, Birnbaum nevertheless would have been subject to Section 11 liability. In this regard, note that his liability would have been based upon his status as a director and not as an attorney. However, the fact that Birnbaum was an attorney was taken into consideration in determining whether he conducted a reasonable investigation.

Grant, the issuer's outside counsel, was liable both as a director and as a signatory. The court in *BarChris* took into account his role of being primarily responsible for drafting the registration statement, reasoning that "more was required of him in the way of reasonable investigation than could fairly be expected of a director who had no connection with this work." The court indicated that, by its holding, it was not seeking to establish an unduly onerous standard for outside counsel who also serves as a director. Rather, each case must turn on its own facts. Here, even taking into account that BarChris' officers had misled Grant, "there . . . [were] too many instances in which Grant failed to make an inquiry which, if pursued, would have put him on his guard."[23]

As noted above, counsel who renders a formal legal opinion which is included in the registration statement with his/her consent is considered

---

[21] See *Central Bank of Denver v. First Interstate Bank of Denver*, 511 U.S. 164 (1994); *Herman & McLean v. Huddleston*, 459 U.S. 375, 386 n.22 (1983).

[22] See, e.g., *Molecular Technology Corp. v. Valentine*, 925 F.2d 910 (6th Cir. 1991); *In re Rospatch Securities Litigation*, [1992 Transfer Binder] Fed. Sec. L. Rep. (CCH) ¶ 96,939 (W.D. Mich. 1992); *Zendell v. Newport Oil Corp.*, 544 A.2d 878 (N.J. 1988); M. Steinberg, Corporate and Securities Malpractice (1992).

[23] 283 F. Supp. at 690–92.

an "expert" within the ambit of Section 11. For example, counsel may proffer an opinion that (1) the company and its subsidiaries are duly incorporated, (2) licenses are in order, (3) the company's securities are validly issued under state law and are non-assessable, and (4) there has been no default under material contracts. Such opinions rarely are problematic. More difficult issues arise when counsel proffers an opinion that is critical to the "deal" such as an opinion by counsel concerning the pertinent federal tax implications.[24]

A different question is presented where an attorney, acting as counsel for either the issuer or the underwriter, furnishes a "comfort opinion." A comfort opinion essentially is a statement that, based on counsel's participation in the preparation of the registration statement and conferences with representatives of the issuer, underwriters and public accountants, he/she has no reason to believe that the registration statement violates Section 11. In order not to be subject to Section 11 liability, counsel should ensure that neither the opinion nor its contents appear in the registration statement.

[D]   Delegation of Due Diligence

In practice, the issuer, directors and underwriters frequently delegate their due diligence investigations to counsel. Such delegation, as *BarChris* makes clear, is appropriate. In effect, while counsel seeks to perform an adequate investigation on behalf of his or her client, it is the client, and not counsel, who will be held liable under Section 11 if counsel fails to meet the requisite standard of care. In such instances, however, counsel may be faced with a legal malpractice suit under state law.[25]

When counsel performs due diligence on behalf of a client, counsel should stand in the client's "shoes." The scope of the due diligence obligation depends on such factors as the client's position, its relationship with the issuer, and its involvement in the preparation of the registration statement. The extensiveness of the appropriate investigation may range from that required of an outside director who has no other affiliation with the issuer to the extensive verification required of underwriters in the traditional public offering setting.[26]

[E]   Underwriters

The court in *BarChris* imposed a rigorous due diligence degree of investigation upon the underwriters. The court reasoned that the underwriters to a public offering are uniquely situated to verify the accuracy of the registration statement's contents. Underwriters not only have access

---

[24] See S. FitzGibbon & D. Glazer, Legal Opinions (1992); Rice & Steinberg, Legal Opinions in Securities Transactions, 16 J. Corp. L. 375 (1991).

[25] See sources cited note 22 *supra*.

[26] See L. Loss & J. Seligman, Securities Regulation 4246–78 (3d ed. 1992); Spanner, A Litigation Perspective on the Prospectus Preparation Process for an Initial Public Offering, 16 Sec. Reg. L.J. 115 (1988).

to the necessary information; they have the leverage in the traditional registration context to compel the issuer to fulfill its disclosure duties. Moreover, the investing public relies upon the underwriters' reputations and upon their participation in the offering as an endorsement of the registration statement's accuracy. As more recently stated by the SEC:

> An underwriter . . . occupies a vital position in an offering. The underwriter stands between the issuer and the public purchasers, assisting the issuer in pricing and, at times, in structuring the financing and preparing disclosure documents. Most importantly, its role is to place the offered securities with public investors. By participating in an offering, an underwriter makes an implied representation about the securities. Because the underwriter holds itself out as a securities professional, and especially in light of its position vis--vis the issuer, this recommendation itself implies that the underwriter has a reasonable basis for belief in the truthfulness and completeness of the key representations made in any disclosure documents used in the offerings. [27]

Nonetheless, an underwriter is not expected to have the intimate knowledge of corporate affairs that insider directors would possess, and consequently its duty to investigate should be considered in view of its more limited access. The *BarChris* court emphasized, nonetheless, that an underwriter is expected to exercise a high degree of care in the course of its investigation. Not only must underwriters make an independent verification of management's representations, they must play the devil's advocate. [28] As discussed in depth later in this chapter, in recognition of possible limitations on the underwriter's ability to investigate in certain circumstances, the SEC adopted Rule 176. [29]

Moreover, although not without exception, underwriters in a number of recent cases met the due diligence defense. In one such case, the underwriter conducted the following investigation:

> After reviewing the record, this court concludes that there is no genuine issue of material fact that the underwriters did meet the standards required of them by Section 11. . . . Their investigation of [the issuer] was conducted primarily by the managing underwriters. It was conducted by experienced people, who were assisted by attorneys and accountants. The underwriters reviewed the industry, the company, the company's management, and the company's

---

[27] Securities Exchange Act Release No. 26100 (1988).

[28] See *BarChris*, 283 F. Supp. at 697. See also, *In re Software Toolworks Inc. Securities Litigation*, 38 F.3d 1078, 1086 (9th Cir. 1994); *Feit v. Leasco Data Processing Equipment Corp.*, 332 F. Supp. 544, 581–82 (E.D.N.Y. 1971).

[29] See §§ 6.05–6.07 *infra*. See generally Fortenbaugh, *Underwriters' Due Diligence*, 14 Rev. Sec. Reg. 799 (1981); Freilich & Janvey, *Understanding "Best Efforts" Underwritings*, 17 Sec. Reg. L.J. 151 (1989); Greene, *Determining the Responsibilities of Underwriters Distributing Securities Within an Integrated Disclosure System*, 56 Notre Dame Lawyer 755 (1981); O'Hare, *Institutional Investors, Registration Rights and the Specter of Liability Under Section 11 of the Securities Act of 1933*, 1996 Wisc. L. Rev. 217 (1996).

past and projected manufacturing, sales and financial performance. The underwriters had over twenty meetings with various management personnel, covering all aspects of the company's business. Company personnel were specifically questioned about the development and scheduled availability of products, related operating systems and applications software. The underwriters also contacted many of [the issuer's] suppliers, customers, and distributors, who were asked extensive questions about the company's operations. The underwriters reviewed company documents including operating plans, product literature, corporate records, financial statements, contracts, and lists of distributors and customers. They examined trade journals and other industry-related publications to ascertain industry trends, market trends and competitive information. They also made physical inspections of the company's facilities. When any negative or questionable information was developed as a result of their investigation, the underwriters discussed it with the appropriate persons and arrived at informed decisions and opinions. The underwriters also obtained written representations from the selling stockholders and the company that as of the closing date of the public offering, there were no misstatements or omissions.

As a result of that investigation and due diligence, the underwriters reasonably believed the accuracy of the information contained in the prospectus, including the information alleged to be misrepresented or omitted here. The underwriters had no knowledge of any misrepresentations or omissions, and their work met the standards of the diligence and reasonable investigation required by Section 11. . . .[30]

One interpretation of this more recent case law is that, with certain exceptions, there may be a general trend toward construing the due diligence defense in a more flexible manner. Although the conducting of an investigation is clearly called for, the extent of such investigation required may be linked to the party's position and relationship to the issuer. In ascertaining the adequacy of the investigation conducted, a number of courts are declining to impose onerous standards upon underwriters and outside directors — parties who are not executive officers. This is due to the concept that, unlike those having such inside status, underwriters and outside directors neither have the same degree of knowledge nor access to corporate information and are all too often targeted as "deep pockets."

---

[30] *Weinberger v. Jackson*, [1990–1991 Transfer Binder] Fed. Sec. L. Rep. (CCH) ¶ 95,693. at 98,255 (N.D. Cal. 1990). See *In re International Rectifier Securities Litigation*, [1997 Transfer Binder] Fed. Sec. L. Rep. (CCH) ¶ 99,469 (C.D. Cal. 1997) (holding underwriters met due diligence defense). But see *In re Software Toolworks Inc. Securities Litigation*, 38 F.3d 1078 (9th Cir. 1994) (reversing grant of summary judgment that underwriters met their due diligence defense and concluding that whether such defense met presented jury question). See also, *In re Donaldson, Lufkin & Jenrette Securities Corp.*, [1992 Transfer Binder] Fed. Sec. L. Rep. (CCH) ¶ 85,035 (SEC 1992) (SEC enforcement action against underwriter for allegedly failing to investigate adequately where registration statement contained disclosure deficiencies).

[F] Accountants

When the court in *BarChris* turned to consider the liability of the accountants, it did so with respect to that "part of the registration statement purporting to be made upon the authority of [the accountant] as an expert."[31] The only part of the registration statement made on the authority of the accountants in *BarChris* was, as is usually the case, the certified financial statements. In considering the defense that the accountants acted with due diligence, the court stated that this defense must be assessed at the time that the part of the registration statement containing the allegedly false and misleading financial statements became effective. To accomplish this task, the court scrutinized the audit as well as the accountants' review of events that occurred after the date of the certified balance sheet contained in the registration statement but before the effective date of the registration statement.

The most blatant error found by the court was the accountants' failure to discover that a bowling alley constructed by the registrant, which had been recorded on the books as having been sold, had not been sold. In determining whether the accountants should be held liable for the resulting misstatements in the financial statements, the court carefully considered the various internal documentary evidence examined by the accountants during the course of their audit. In addition, the court considered certain accounting records that had not been examined but which, if examined, would have put the accountants on notice of the impropriety. After reviewing the audit procedures in this context, the court concluded that the accountants failed to prove that they had conducted a reasonable investigation and consequently, their ignorance of the true facts was unjustified.[32]

In scrutinizing the accountants' review of events subsequent to the date of the certified financial statements but prior to the effective date of the registration statement, the court concluded that the written work program utilized for the review conformed to generally accepted auditing standards (GAAS) and would have provided the accountants with the due diligence defense had it been properly executed. The program, with limited exceptions, only required a cursory review of the financial statements and certain specific accounts. Significantly, however, the court criticized the accountants for obtaining answers which they considered satisfactory without attempting to verify them. Thus, while limited review procedures may suffice as to "subsequent events," the court added the gloss that information obtained and examined in the course of such a review must be independently verified. As such, although accountants need not perform a complete audit when conducting a subsequent events review, any danger signals must be pursued and answers must be verified.[33]

---

[31] 283 F. Supp. at 698.

[32] *Id.* at 703. See also, *United States v. Benjamin*, 328 F.2d 854 (2d Cir.), *cert. denied*, 377 U.S. 953 (1964).

[33] See 283 F. Supp. at 700–03. See also, *In re Software Toolworks Inc. Securities Litigation*, 38 F.3d 1078 (9th Cir. 1994).

From an overall perspective, the court in *BarChris* believed that accountants "should not be held to a standard higher than that recognized in their profession."[34] Similarly, the Seventh Circuit's decision in *Hochfelder v. Ernst & Ernst*[35] is instructive on the standards by which an accountant's audit must be judged. The court, essentially agreeing with *BarChris*, held that accountants generally "are required to meet only the standard of care expected of persons holding themselves out as skilled accountants."[36] The Seventh Circuit, however, relying on Judge Learned Hand's opinion in *The T.J. Hooper*,[37] went on to assert that compliance with GAAS (Generally Accepting Auditing Standards) does not provide automatic insulation from liability. As the court pointed out, a determination must be made whether the prevailing professional practice constitutes reasonable prudence. Hence, while compliance with GAAS may strongly suggest that the requisite standard of care has been met, "[c]ourts must in the end say what is required; there are precautions so imperative that even their universal disregard will not excuse their omission."[38]

Generally, with respect to accountants' liability under Section 11 (as well as under other provisions of the federal securities law), the lead of *BarChris* concerning the proper standard of care has been followed. Accordingly, it appears that compliance with GAAS normally will provide a shield to charges of carelessness. Note, however, that:

> It is vitally important to point out that this shield only relates to an accountant's care in obtaining essential underlying facts. Compliance with GAAS will not be a shield to liability where an unreasonable judgment is made on the basis of adequate information properly obtained. The decisions scrutinizing accountants' audit procedures have at the same time considered the reasonableness of the judgments made on the basis of the information unearthed during the audit.
>
> In addition, compliance with GAAS will not act as a shield from liability for misleading presentation of information obtained during the course of a properly conducted audit. In other words, the "investigative" portion of the audit, in which the accountant obtains evidential matter to support the information ultimately presented in financial statements is only the first step in the evaluation of liability. The next step is to scrutinize the judgments made by the accountant on the basis of the information obtained, and the final step is to scrutinize the fairness of the financial statements taken as a whole. When financial statements are alleged to be false or

---

[34] 283 F. Supp. at 703.

[35] 503 F.2d 1100 (7th Cir. 1974), *rev'd on other grounds*, 425 U.S. 185 (1976).

[36] *Id.* at 1108. Accord, *SEC v. Arthur Young & Co.*, 590 F.2d 785 (9th Cir. 1979).

[37] 60 F.2d 737 (2d Cir. 1932).

[38] 503 F.2d at 1114, n.16 (quoting, *The T.J. Hooper*, 60 F.2d at 740).

misleading, carelessness at any of the three levels can lead to liability. [39]

§ 6.05   Impact of the Integrated Disclosure System

At this point, you may wish to review the discussion on the SEC's integrated disclosure system in § 4.06. Perhaps the most significant liability concern raised by the integrated disclosure system is that certain issuers can incorporate by reference Exchange Act periodic reports into their Securities Act registration statements. Such incorporation of 1934 Act reports may make it substantially more onerous for subject parties to satisfy Section 11's "due diligence" obligation (as well as Section 12(a)(2)'s "reasonable care" standard), thus resulting in greater liability exposure for, among others, directors, underwriters, and accountants.

The issue of *underwriter due diligence* in the integrated disclosure process has raised the most serious liability concerns. It has been argued that, given the practical realities, incorporation by reference severely hampers an underwriter's ability to perform the type of due diligence that *BarChris* sets forth. The reasons underlying this assertion include: (1) underwriters will not generally participate in the drafting of the disclosures incorporated by reference from the 1934 Act periodic reports into the 1933 Act registration statement; (2) underwriters, due to management's reluctance to modify previously filed SEC documents that it had approved (irrespective of SEC Rule 412), [40] will be unable to persuade management to improve the disclosures previously made; (3) by its nature, incorporation by reference drastically limits the time period during which such due diligence can be performed; and (4) adoption of the integrated disclosure system comes at a time of intense competition among underwriters.

Taking the above considerations into account, one may argue that it is inevitable that the underwriter's role as a key participant in the registration process significantly recedes in importance. In short, according to many in the securities industry, the SEC's integrated disclosure system has "rendered untenable the underwriter's traditional role and responsibilities in securities distributions." [41]

Due to these concerns, the Corporation Finance Committee of the Securities Industry Association (SIA) proposed that an underwriter should be deemed to satisfy its due diligence obligations if it "(1) had read the

---

[39] Gruenbaum & Steinberg, *Accountants' Liability and Responsibility: Securities, Criminal and Common Law*, 13 Loyola U.L.A. L. Rev. 247, 260–61 (1980). See also, *In re Software Toolworks Inc. Securities Litigation*, 38 F.3d 1078 (9th Cir. 1994); Ebke, *In Search of Alternatives: Comparative Reflections on Corporate Governance and the Independent Auditor's Responsibilities*, 79 Nw. U. L. Rev. 663 (1984); Fiflis, *Current Problems of Accountant's Responsibilities to Third Parties*, 28 Vand. L. Rev. 31 (1975).

[40] Rule 412 is designed to alleviate concerns regarding the modification of disclosures made in previously filed SEC documents. Among other things, the rule sets forth that a modifying or superseding statement made in an SEC filed document is not deemed an admission that the statement that undergoes such change violates the federal securities laws. See Fortenbaugh, *Underwriters' Due Diligence*, 14 Rev. Sec. Reg. 799, 805 (1983).

[41] Greene, *supra* note 29, at 797. See Hovdesven & Wolfram, *Underwriter Liability in the Integrated Disclosure System*, Nat. L.J., July 5, 1982, at 14.

registration statement and all exhibits and incorporated documents; (2) had discussed the registration statement with the registrant's representatives; and (3) after such review and discussion, did not know of any material misstatement or omission."

The SIA proposal has not been adopted because it neglects established case law and SEC policy that the element of independent verification by the underwriter is essential for establishing due diligence. Instead, the Commission has opted for Rule 176, which basically codifies Section 1704(g) of the American Law Institute's Federal Securities Code. According to the SEC, the rule's basic focus is to permit each person who has potential Section 11 liability to "evaluate the surrounding facts, including the extent of his prior relationship with the issuer, and utilize techniques of investigation appropriate to the circumstances of the offering."[42] Rule 176 provides:

In determining whether or not the conduct of a person constitutes a reasonable investigation or a reasonable ground for belief meeting the standard set forth in Section 11(c), relevant circumstances include, with respect to a person other than the issuer,

(a) The type of issuer;

(b) The type of security;

(c) The type of person;

(d) The office held when the person is an officer;

(e) The presence or absence of another relationship to the issuer when the person is a director or proposed director;

(f) Reasonable reliance on officers, employees, and others whose duties should have given them knowledge of the particular facts (in light of the functions and responsibilities of the particular person with respect to the issuer and the filing);

(g) When the person is an underwriter, the type of underwriter, the type of underwriting arrangement, the role of the particular person as an underwriter and the availability of information with respect to the registrant; and

(h) Whether, with respect to a fact or document incorporated by reference, the particular person had any responsibility for the fact or document at the time of the filing from which it was incorporated.[43]

As a general proposition, Rule 176 correctly recognizes the concepts of delegation and specialization for all potentially liable persons (except the issuer) under Section 11. Moreover, subsections (g) and (h) recognize, at least somewhat, the concerns of underwriters in the integrated disclosure system. Nonetheless, the SEC has been criticized for failing to recognize, in view of market realities, the difficult task that underwriters have to

---

[42] Securities Act Release No. 6383 (1982).

[43] 17 C.F.R. § 230.176.

independently verify the information contained in the registration statement. This criticism becomes accentuated when applied to the shelf registration process (discussed in § 6.07, *infra*).

In 1998, the SEC proposed amendments to Rule 176 that, if adopted, will
provide further guidance for underwriters in the integrated disclosure
framework with respect to their performance of due diligence.[44] One
practice set forth in the SEC proposals that is today a key part of underwriter due diligence in the shelf registration context is the issuer's designation of counsel for the (prospective) underwriter. Pursuant to this designation, counsel selected by the issuer acts on behalf of the prospective
underwriter in fulfilling such underwriter's continuous due diligence
functions.

It may be argued that the traditional role and responsibilities of the
underwriter in the distribution process remain necessary for investor
protection, at least until an adequate alternative approach has been
adopted. Although underwriters, for good reason, fear increased liability,
investor protection should not be lessened. As stated by the Second Circuit:

> No greater reliance in our self-regulatory system is placed on any
> single participant in the issuance of securities than upon the

---

[44] In 1998, the SEC proposed to amend Rule 176 to provide further guidance for underwriters in the integrated disclosure system. In the proposal, the Commission set forth six practices
that evidence the performance of underwriter due diligence under Section 11. The SEC stated
that these six factors are not exclusive and that an underwriter's failure to satisfy all six factors
should not be deemed determinative of such underwriter's lack of due diligence. These six
factors are:

- Whether the underwriter reviewed the registration statement and conducted a
  reasonable inquiry into any fact or circumstance that would cause a reasonable person
  to question whether the registration statement contains an untrue statement or
  material omission;

- Whether the underwriter discussed the information contained in the registration
  statement with the relevant executive officer(s) of the registrant (including, at
  minimum, the chief financial officer (CFO) or the chief accounting officer (CAO) (or
  designee)) and the CFO or CAO (or designee) certified that he or she has examined
  the registration statement and that to the best of his or her knowledge, it does not
  contain an untrue statement or material omission;

- Whether the underwriter received a Statement on Auditing Standards No. 72 comfort
  letter from the issuer's auditors;

- Whether the underwriter received a favorable opinion from issuer's counsel opining
  that nothing has come to its attention that has caused it to believe that the registration
  statement contains an untrue statement or omits to state a material fact;

- Whether the underwriter employed counsel that, after reviewing the issuer's
  registration statement, Exchange Act filings and other information, opined that
  nothing came to its attention that would lead it to believe that the registration
  statement contains an untrue statement or omits to state a material fact; and

- Whether the underwriter employed and consulted a research analyst that:
  - has followed the issuer or the issuer's industry on an ongoing basis for at least
    the six months immediately before the commencement of the offering; and
  - has issued a report on the issuer or its industry within the 12 months immediately
    before commencement of the offering.

Securities Act Release No. 7606A (1998), discussed in Jones & Baez, *New SEC Proposals for
the Regulation of Securities Offerings*, 27 Sec. Reg. L.J. 25, 42–43 (1999).

underwriter . . . . Prospective investors look to the underwriter —
a fact well known to all concerned and especially to the underwriter
— to pass on the soundness of the security and the correctness of
the registration statement and prospectus.[45]

While the above statement certainly remains valid in the IPO and related
offering context, it may be argued that its dogmatic application in the
integrated disclosure setting makes the underwriter, in essence, an insurer
for others' defalcations.

§ 6.06   Director Signing of Form 10-K

As part of its integrated disclosure framework, the SEC has mandated
that a majority of a registrant's directors sign the Form 10-K. In adopting
this requirement, the Commission reasoned:

> [A] requirement for the signatures [on the Form 10-K] of a majority
> of a registrant's directors — in addition to those of its principal
> executive officer, its principal financial officer, and its controller or
> principal accounting officer — is an appropriate one under the
> circumstances. The Commission believes that just as its rules and
> the administrative focus of the Division of Corporation Finance are
> being realigned to reflect the shift in emphasis toward relying on
> periodic disclosure under the Exchange Act, so too the attention of
> the private sector, including management, directors, accountants,
> and attorneys, must also be refocused towards Exchange Act filings
> if a sufficient degree of discipline is to be instilled in the system
> to make it work. With an expanded signature requirement, the
> Commission anticipates that directors will be encouraged to devote
> the needed attention to reviewing the Form 10-K and to seek the
> involvement of other professionals to the degree necessary to give
> themselves sufficient comfort. In the Commission's view, this added
> measure of discipline is vital to the disclosure objectives of the
> federal securities laws, and outweighs the potential impact, if any,
> of the signature on legal liability.[46]

Concerns have been expressed that the director signature requirement
for the Form 10-K may result in greater liability exposure. For example,
the signing of the Form 10-K by a subject director arguably may signify
that the director "caused" the filing, failed to act in "good faith," and/or acted
with "scienter," thereby giving rise to a host of both SEC and private liability concerns. Although it is still premature to assess whether the signature
requirement will alter existing legal liabilities, it appears that this requirement, at least to some extent, has induced directors to scrutinize the Form
10-K and to seek the advice of corporate counsel in this exercise to a much
greater degree than previously was the practice.[47]

---

[45] *Chris-Craft Industries, Inc. v. Piper Aircraft Corp.*, 480 F.2d 341, 380 (2d Cir.), *cert. denied*, 414 U.S. 910 (1973).

[46] Securities Act Release No. 6231 (1980).

[47] For a discussion of the director signature requirement on the Form 10-K and its potential
liability ramifications, see M. Steinberg, Securities Regulation: Liabilities and Remedies
§ 5.04[3] (2000).

§ 6.07　Shelf Registration

At this point, you may wish to review the discussion on shelf registration contained in § 4.06[B]. Generally, Rule 415 governs the registration of securities to be offered and sold on a continuous or delayed basis in the future. Significantly, the rule permits eligible issuers (namely, those offering securities that may be registered on Form S-3 or F-3) to engage in primary at-the-market offerings of equity securities which the issuer expects to offer within two years of the registration statement's effective date.

The Commission's decision to include equity offerings within Rule 415's scope drew a sharp dissent from then Commissioner Thomas who asserted that the rule should be limited to debt offerings. She argued that Rule 415, when applied to equity offerings,

> (1) jeopardizes the liquidity and stability of our primary and secondary markets by encouraging greater concentration of underwriters, market-makers, and other financial intermediaries and by discouraging individual investor participation in the capital markets thereby furthering the trend toward institutionalization of securities holders, and (2) reduces the quality and timeliness of disclosure available to investors when making their investment decisions. Incurring these risks is antithetical to the statutory duty of the Commission to protect investors and to maintain the integrity of our capital markets.[48]

There is little question that underwriter due diligence concerns are accentuated in the shelf registration setting. In this setting, underwriters assert that they will have little, if any, time to perform any meaningful due diligence.[49] The SEC has responded by promulgating Rule 176 and by advising potential underwriters to acquire "in advance a reservoir of knowledge" about the issuer. It is arguable, however, that the SEC's position overlooks the manner in which the shelf rule has impacted the role of underwriters. First, due to the competitive nature of the shelf registration process, the bargaining position of the underwriter to induce disclosure on the issuer's part has been greatly diminished. Second, potential underwriters have little incentive to develop "in advance a reservoir of knowledge," with its attendant costs, if there is only a possibility that they will be selected.[50]

Fortunately, it appears at this time that underwriters have determined how their due diligence functions will be performed in the shelf registration context in a seemingly adequate and cost effective manner. Today, the most

---

[48] See Securities Act Release No. 6499 (1983).

[49] See Ketels, *SEC Rule 415 — The New Experimental Procedures for Shelf Registration*, 10 Sec. Reg. L.J. 318, 335–36 (1982).

[50] See generally Banoff, *Regulatory Subsidies, Efficient Markets, and Shelf Registration: An Analysis of Rule 415*, 70 Va. L. Rev. 135 (1984); Fox, *Shelf Registration, Integrated Disclosure, and Underwriter Due Diligence: An Economic Analysis*, 70 Va. L. Rev. 1005 (1984); Maynard, *Blue Sky Regulation of Rule 415 Shelf-Registered Primary Offerings: The Need for a Limited Form of Federal Preemption*, 22 Ariz. St. L.J. 89 (1990).

prevalent way that such due diligence is conducted is by the issuer designating underwriter's counsel. Pursuant to this designation, counsel, acting on behalf of the prospective underwriters, conducts ongoing due diligence. Because counsel normally is selected by the issuer, conflicts of interest dilemmas arise. Nonetheless, at least this practice provides a means by which continuous due diligence can be conducted by the underwriter's designee. And, of course, it should be kept in mind that the due diligence responsibility remains with the underwriter(s).[51]

§ 6.08   Section 12(1) (as now amended Section 12(a)(1))

Section 12(1) (as now amended Section 12(a)(1)) of the Securities Act gives teeth to Section 5 by providing the purchaser of securities with an express private right of action against his/her seller if such seller offers or sells a security in violation of Section 5.[52] In an action brought under Section 12(a), the purchaser may seek rescission or, if he/she no longer owns the securities, damages. Section 12(a)(1) (as well as Section 12(a)(2) discussed in § 6.09) does not provide a plaintiff with a choice of remedies. As stated by the Second Circuit: "If [the] plaintiff owns the stock, he is entitled to rescission but not damages. If [the] plaintiff no longer owns the stock, he is entitled to damages but not rescission."[53]

If a violation of Section 5 has been committed by the seller, the purchaser ordinarily is entitled to recover. In other words, strict liability is imposed against the seller. The exercise of reasonable care or bona fide but unsuccessful efforts to perfect an exemption from registration are irrelevant. Hence, upon the purchaser establishing a prima facie case that the seller violated Section 5, a seller may avoid liability only, for example, by showing that the offering qualifies for an exemption from registration or that the plaintiff is in pari delicto (see § 7.10). The statute of limitations for Section 12(a)(1) claims is one year.[54]

A key issue under Section 12 is the meaning of the term "seller." Supreme Court and other case law focusing on this question are addressed in § 6.09[B].

---

[51] See Securities Act Release No. 6499 (1983) ("The trend toward appointment of a single law firm to act as underwriters' counsel is a particularly significant development. . . . Registrants appoint the law firm to act as underwriters' counsel either with or without consulting the prospective participating underwriters."); 22 Sec. Reg. & L. Rep. (BNA) 1634 (1990); Frerichs, *Underwriter Due Diligence Within the Integrated Disclosure System — If It Isn't Broken, Don't Fix It*, 16 Sec. Reg. L.J. 386 (1989); Nicholas, *The Integrated Disclosure System and Its Impact upon Underwriters' Due Diligence: Will Investors Be Protected?*, 11 Sec. Reg. L.J. 3 (1983); Note, *The Impact of the SEC's Shelf Registration Rule on Underwriter's Due Diligence Investigations*, 51 Geo. Wash. L. Rev. 767 (1983).

[52] The definition of "seller" for Section 12 purposes is addressed in § 6.09[B] *infra*.

[53] *Wigand v. Flo-Tek, Inc.*, 609 F.2d 1028, 1035 (2d Cir. 1979).

[54] See Section 13 of the Securities Act, 15 U.S.C. § 77m.

§ 6.09   Section 12(2) (as now amended Section 12(a)(2))

[A]   Overview

Aggrieved purchasers of securities acquired in a public offering by an issuer or its controlling shareholder(s) may seek to invoke Section 12(a)(2) of the Securities Act.[55] Generally, Section 12(2) (as now amended Section 12(a)(2)) affords an express right of action to a purchaser against his/her seller for rescission, or damages if the securities have been disposed of, when the purchaser acquired the securities by means of a prospectus or oral communication (that relates to a prospectus) which contained a material misstatement or omission. Proof of reliance is not required. Indeed, to recover under Section 12(a)(2), "a plaintiff need not prove that he ever received the misleading prospectus."[56] Accordingly, Section 12(a)(2)'s terms "do not require that the particular sale to an individual plaintiff directly be by means of the prospectus alleged to be misleading." Rather, it is sufficient that "the seller sold by means of a misleading prospectus securities of which those purchased by the plaintiff were a part." With respect to oral communications that relate to a prospectus, however, a different result might follow.[57]

Section 12(a)(2) provides the seller with a "quasi due diligence" defense. Once the purchaser has established a prima facie case, the onus is shifted to the seller to establish that he/she did not know, and in the exercise of reasonable care could not have known, of the untruth or omission.

In general terms, a comparison between the Section 12(a)(2) right of action with that provided under Section 11 reveals the following: First, whereas Section 11 only applies to registered offerings, due to the Supreme Court's restrictive decision in *Gustafson v. Alloyd Company*,[58] the Section 12(a)(2) remedy similarly is limited to purchasers of securities in a public offering by an issuer or its controlling shareholder(s). Clearly the remedy is available in registered offerings. Although unclear at the time, *Gustafson* suggests that Section 12(a)(2) also may apply in offerings that take on a public nature but are exempt from Securities Act registration pursuant to Section 3 of that Act. Such offerings may include those pursuant to Regulation A, Rule 504, and Section 3(a)(11)/Rule 147.[59] Prior to the *Gustafson* decision, lower courts uniformly held that Section 12(a)(2) was available in issuer private offerings exempt from registration (such as pursuant to Section 4(2) or Rule 506 of Regulation D);[60] and there existed

---

[55] See *Gustafson v. Alloyd Company*, 513 U.S. 561 (1995).

[56] *Sanders v. John Nuveen & Co., Inc.*, 619 F.2d 1222, 1226 (7th Cir. 1980), *cert. denied*, 450 U.S. 1005 (1981).

[57] *Id.* at 1226–27, n.8.

[58] 513 U.S. 561 (1995).

[59] See discussion of these exemptions in §§ 3.09[B], 3.10 *supra*.

[60] See, e.g., *Abell v. Potomac Insurance Co.*, 858 F.2d 1104 (5th Cir. 1988).

a split of authority whether the remedy was available in private secondary transactions.[61]

Second, Section 12(a)(2) extends liability only to those who "sold" the securities to the allegedly aggrieved purchasers. On the other hand, Section 11 specifically enumerates those parties who are subject to liability under that provision. In this regard, note that a dealer, although not subject to Section 11 liability, may be liable under Section 12 as a "seller" in a registered offering.[62]

Moreover, in contrast to the specific categories of possible defendants listed in Section 11, Section 12(a)(2) by its terms subjects only "sellers" to potential liability. In this respect, note that underwriters are not necessarily within the reach of Section 12(a)(2). As the Eleventh Circuit has observed: "Since § 12 does not provide for underwriter liability per se, an underwriter must also be a seller of the security in question to be liable under the section."[63]

Another distinction between Section 11 and Section 12(a)(2) lies in the standard of care defense. Whereas Section 11 establishes an affirmative defense of "reasonable investigation," Section 12(a)(2) provides that the seller exercise "reasonable care." This apparently lower standard of care is consistent with the general notion that sellers of securities may not be intimately involved with the offering and may not have the same access to information as do potential Section 11 defendants. However, as the Seventh Circuit's decision in *Sanders v. John Nuveen & Co., Inc.*[64] indicates, the degree of care to be exercised by sellers who are within the Section 12(a)(2) inner circle may converge with the reasonable investigation standard of Section 11.

[B] The Meaning of "Seller"

Prior to the Supreme Court's decision in *Pinter v. Dahl*,[65] the lower federal courts differed widely as to which parties were regarded as "sellers" under Section 12(a)(2) (as well as under Section 12(a)(1)). While some courts imposed a strict privity requirement,[66] most courts relaxed the privity

---

[61] Compare *Ballay v. Legg Mason Wood Walker, Inc.*, 925 F.2d 682 (3d Cir. 1991) (limiting § 12(2) to initial offerings), with *Pacific Dunlop Holdings, Inc. v. Allen & Co., Inc.*, 993 F.2d 578 (7th Cir. 1993) (holding that § 12(2) extends to secondary transactions). See generally Loss, *The Assault on Section 12(2)*, 105 Harv. L. Rev. 908 (1992); Maynard, *Liability Under Section 12(2) of the Securities Act of 1933 for Fraudulent Trading in Post-Distribution Markets*, 32 Wm. & Mary L. Rev. 847 (1991); Weiss, *The Courts Have It Right: Securities Act Section 12(2) Applies Only to Public Offerings*, 48 Bus. Law. 1 (1992).

[62] See discussion in §§ 6.02, 6.04 *supra*.

[63] *Foster v. Jessup and Lamont Securities Co., Inc.*, 759 F.2d 838, 845 (11th Cir. 1985).

[64] 619 F.2d 1222 (7th Cir. 1980), *cert. denied*, 450 U.S. 1005 (1981).

[65] 486 U.S. 622 (1988).

[66] See, e.g., *Collins v. Signetics Corp.*, 605 F.2d 110 (3d Cir. 1979); *McFarland v. Memorex Corp.*, 493 F. Supp. 631 (N.D. Cal. 1980). See generally Abrams, *The Scope of Liability Under Section 12 of the Securities Act of 1933: "Participation" and the Pertinent Legislative Materials*, 15 Fordham Urban L.J. 877 (1987).

requirement to some extent. Liability was imposed by a number of courts upon persons as "sellers" for being integrally connected with, or substantially involved in, the transaction.[67]

The Supreme Court in *Pinter* rejected both of the above approaches. While the decision expressly dealt with the definition of "seller" under Section 12(a)(1), lower federal courts overwhelmingly have applied the holding to cases arising under Section 12(a)(2).[68]

In *Pinter*, the Supreme Court construed the term "sell" to encompass those persons who engage in "solicitation" of the buyer. Upon examining the language and purpose of Section 12(a)(1), the Court thereupon defined "seller" under that provision as extending to one "who successfully solicits the purchase, motivated at least in part by a desire to serve his own financial interests or those of the securities owner."[69] Therefore, under Section 12, one may not recover against his/her seller's seller. As the Court stated, "liability under Section 12 is imposed "on only the buyer's immediate seller; remote purchasers are precluded from bringing actions against remote sellers. Thus, a buyer cannot recover against his seller's seller. . . ."[70] Accordingly, for purposes of Section 12, a "seller" includes: (1) one who owned the security sold to the purchaser, (2) an agent for a vendor (such as a broker) who successfully solicited the purchase, (3) one who solicited the purchase with the intent to personally benefit thereby, and (4) one who, without financial benefit to oneself, solicited the purchase with the motivation to serve the owner's financial interests.

The Court's construction of "seller" permits at least two groups of "participants" to avoid Section 12 liability. First, those persons who gratuitously provide advice on investment matters to friends, family members, and acquaintances are not "sellers" so long as they are not motivated by a desire to benefit the securities owner or themselves. Second, professionals, such as accountants and lawyers, whose involvement is solely the performance of their professional services (e.g., counsel drafting the offering document for the issuer-client), are not "sellers."[71]

[C] Secondary Liability

Prior to the Supreme Court's decision in *Central Bank of Denver v. First Interstate Bank of Denver*,[72] a few lower courts recognized secondary

---

[67] See, e.g., *Davis v. Avco Financial Services, Inc.*, 739 F.2d 1057 (6th Cir. 1984); *Croy v. Campbell*, 624 F.2d 709 (5th Cir. 1980). See generally O'Hara, *Erosion of the Privity Requirement in Section 12(2) of the Securities Act of 1933: The Expanded Meaning of Seller*, 31 U.C.L.A. L. Rev. 921 (1984).

[68] See, e.g., *Moore v. Kayport Package Express, Inc.*, 885 F.2d 531, 536 (9th Cir. 1989).

[69] 486 U.S. at 622.

[70] *Id.* at 644, n.21.

[71] *Id.* at 651. See *Wilson v. Saintine Exploration and Drilling Corporation*, 872 F.2d 1124 (2d Cir. 1989). See also, *Junker v. Crory*, 650 F.2d 1349 (5th Cir. 1981) (attorney, whose participation was a substantial factor in causing the transaction to take place, deemed a seller for § 12(2) purposes). See generally Klock, *Promoter Liability and In Pari Delicto Under Section 12(1): Pinter v. Dahl*, 17 Sec. Reg. L.J. 53 (1989); Prentice, *Section 12 of the 1933 Act: Establishing the Statutory Seller*, 40 Alabama L. Rev. 417 (1989).

[72] 511 U.S. 164 (1994).

liability under Section 12(a)(2) based upon an aiding and abetting ratio-nale.[73] The majority of courts, however, rejected such secondary liability as inappropriate.[74] As discussed in § 9.01, due to the Supreme Court's 1994 decision in *Central Bank of Denver*, it is clear today that liability under Section 12(2) is precluded when premised on such theories as aiding and abetting and conspiracy.[75]

[D] Limited to Public Offerings

As discussed in § 6.09[A], prior to the Supreme Court's decision in *Gustafson v. Alloyd Company*,[76] a split of authority existed in the lower courts as to whether Section 12(a)(2) could be used by purchasers in the secondary trading context.[77] Confining Section 12(a)(2)'s scope, the *Gustaf-son* Court limited the provision's application to public offerings by issuers or their controlling shareholders.[78] The consequence is that Section 12(a)(2) may be invoked only by purchasers in registered offerings under the 1933 Act and perhaps by purchasers in Section 3 exempt offerings provided that such exempt offerings take on a public nature (such as certain offerings conducted pursuant to Rule 504, Regulation A, or Section 3(a)(11)/Rule 147).[79]

In light of *Gustafson*, Section 12(a)(2) does not extend to secondary transactions (other than public offerings by controlling shareholders). Moreover, the decision makes clear that materially misleading offering doc-uments used in private placements (such as pursuant to the Section 4(2) or Rule 506 exemption) are not within the reach of Section 12(a)(2). Although this latter position may be viewed as dicta, the Court's language and analysis pointedly reflect this result.[80]

The key to the Court's decision was its interpretation of the term "prospectus" as contained in Section 12(a)(2). Although Section 12(a)(2) also provides a remedy based on an actionable "oral communication," such oral communication must relate to a prospectus.[81] Construing the term "pro-spectus," the Court examined three sections of the Securities Act — Sections 2(10), 10, and 12(a)(2) — in an effort to give the term a consistent meaning throughout the 1933 Act. Focusing on Section 10, which confines the defini-tion of "prospectus" to "public offerings by an issuer or its controlling shareholders," the Court concluded that this definition also applies to Section 12(a)(2). Turning to the definition of "prospectus" contained in

---

[73] See, e.g., *In re Caesars Palace Securities Litigation*, 360 F. Supp. 366 (S.D.N.Y. 1973).

[74] See, e.g., *Davis v. Avco Financial Services*, 739 F.2d 1067 (6th Cir. 1984).

[75] See discussion §§ 9.01–9.02 *infra*. See generally Steinberg, *The Ramifications of Recent U.S. Supreme Court Decisions on Federal and State Securities Regulation*, 70 Notre Dame L. Rev. 489 (1995).

[76] 513 U.S. 561 (1995).

[77] See *supra* note 60 and accompanying text.

[78] See 513 U.S. at 584.

[79] See *supra* notes 57–60 and accompanying text.

[80] See 513 U.S. at 579–88.

[81] *Id.* at 567–69.

Section 2(10), the Court likewise found that "the definitional part of [that] statute must be read in its entirety, a reading which yields the interpretation that the term prospectus refers to a document soliciting the public to acquire securities." Hence, by interpreting the term "prospectus" as "a term of art referring to a document that describes a public offering of securities by an issuer or controlling shareholder," the Court significantly limited the scope of Section 12(a)(2).[82]

To sum up this important decision, the *Gustafson* Court held that, in defining the term "prospectus," Section 12(a)(2) applies only to public offerings. The Court's language leaves some question whether Section 12(a)(2) is confined to registered offerings or whether its reach also extends to offerings that otherwise would require registration but for the presence of an exemption under Section 3 of the Securities Act. Under this second approach, an offering document conveyed to prospective purchasers pursuant to an exempt offering that takes on a public nature (such as under Rule 504, Regulation A, and Rule 147) would be defined as a "prospectus," thereby triggering Section 12(a)(2) availability. In any event, *Gustafson* evidently precludes application of the Section 12(a)(2) right of action for private initial (e.g., Rule 506) offerings as well as secondary (e.g., § 4(1)) transactions.[83]

[E] The Reasonable Care Defense

Under Section 12(a)(2), the defendant can avoid liability by showing that he/she did not know, and in the exercise of reasonable care could not have known, of the material misstatement or omission. Whether this standard imposes Section 11-type due diligence obligations has been met with mixed reaction.

In defining the meaning of "reasonable care" under Section 12(a)(2), it is important to distinguish the responsibilities of a so-called traditional underwriter from those of a "mere" seller. For example, to require a "seller" in a Rule 504 offering for $700,000 to comply with Section 11 due diligence would arguably impose too harsh a standard. Moreover, in many such offerings, the subject person neither may have the bargaining position to carry out a Section 11-type due diligence investigation nor be intimately involved in the preparation of the prospectus.

On the other hand, where an unregistered offering has many of the characteristics frequently associated with an offering that must be registered

---

[82] *Id.* at 581–86.

[83] See *Vannest v. Sage Rutty & Co., Inc.*, 960 F. Supp. 651 (W.D.N.Y. 1997) (holding that § 12(2) per Gustafson does not extend to Rule 506 private offering). For further analysis, see Bainbridge, *Securities Act Section 12(2) After the Gustafson Debacle*, 50 Bus. Law. 1231 (1995); Fiflis, *Gustafson v. Alloyd Co., Inc.: Judicial vs. Legislative Power*, 23 Sec. Reg. L.J. 423 (1996); Kerr, *Ralson Redux: Determining Which Section 3 Offerings Are Public Under Section 12(2) After Gustafson*, 50 SMU L. Rev. 175 (1996); Maynard, *The Impact of Gustafson and Its Methodology*, 24 Sec. Reg. L.J. 61 (1996); Thel, *Section 12(2) of the Securities Act: Does Old Legislation Matter?*, 63 Fordham L. Rev. 1183 (1995); Weiss, *Securities Act Section 12(2) After Gustafson v. Alloyd Co.: What Questions Remain?*, 50 Bus. Law. 1209 (1995); *supra* notes 75–81 and accompanying text.

(and hence triggers Section 12(a)(2) application even after *Gustafson*), "the standard of 'reasonable care' under Section 12(a)(2) may converge with the standàrd of 'reasonable investigation' prescribed under Section 11."[84] For example, in *Sanders v. John Nuveen & Co.*,[85] the Seventh Circuit held an underwriter liable under Section 12(a)(2) for failing to make a reasonable investigation. Although stating that it is far from clear that Congress intended to impose a more rigorous standard of care under Section 11 than under Section 12(a)(2), the court also opined: "Since what constitutes reasonable care under § 12(2) depends upon the circumstances, we, of course, do not intimate that the duty of a seller under § 12(2) is always the same as that of an underwriter in a registration offering under § 11."[86] In sum, under the circumstances at bar, the Seventh Circuit held that Section 12(a)(2)'s reasonable care standard required a reasonable investigation.

In a dissent from the denial of certiorari in *Sanders*, two Supreme Court Justices expressed concern that the Seventh Circuit's decision would "be read as recognizing no distinction between the standards of care applicable under §§ 11 and 12(2), and particularly as casting doubt upon the reasonableness of relying upon the expertise of certified public accountants."[87] Indeed, perhaps the most troubling aspect of the Seventh Circuit's analysis is that, by stating that the underwriter should have examined the company's audited financial statements, the lower court evidently required a higher investigative standard under Section 12(a)(2) than under Section 11. As stated in the dissent:

> Even under § 11 of the Act, an underwriter is explicitly absolved of the duty to investigate with respect to "any part of the registration statement purporting to be made on the authority of an expert" such as a certified accountant if "he had no reasonable ground to believe and did not believe" that the information therein was misleading. This provision is in the Act because, almost by definition, it is reasonable to rely on financial statements certified by public accountants. Yet, in this case, the Court of Appeals nevertheless seems to have imposed the higher duty prescribed by § 11 to investigate, but denied petitioner the right to rely on "the authority of an expert" that also is provided by § 11.[88]

Sanders, although an important case, should not be read, particularly in view of the Supreme Court's dissenters, as requiring underwriters to undertake independent financial investigations. Rather, as in Section 11, such persons should be entitled to rely, absent reason otherwise, on the accuracy of the issuer's audited financial statements. Nonetheless, the

---

[84] Brief of the Solicitor General at pages 7–8 in *Sanders v. John Nuveen & Co.*, 619 F.2d 1229 (7th Cir. 1980), *cert. denied*, 450 U.S. 1005 (1981), urging the Supreme Court to deny the petition for a writ of certiorari. See *In re Software Toolworks Inc. Securities Litigation*, 38 F.3d 1078 (9th Cir. 1994).

[85] 619 F.2d 1222 (7th Cir. 1980); *cert. denied*, 450 U.S. 1005 (1981).

[86] *Id.* at 1228.

[87] 450 U.S. 1005 (Powell, J., dissenting).

[88] *Id.* at 1009–10.

decision is significant because it conveys that underwriters of unregistered offerings (that are public in nature and thereby trigger Section 12(a)(2) application even after *Gustafson*) have substantial responsibilities in complying with the "reasonable care" obligation contained in Section 12(a)(2).[89]

In another case, the Sixth Circuit set forth the following factors in assessing the seller's "reasonable care" defense:

> We believe that the following considerations are pertinent to an analysis of whether a § 12(2) seller has established this affirmative defense [of reasonable care]: (1) the quantum of decisional (planning) and facilitative (promotional) participation, such as designing the deal and contacting and attempting to persuade potential purchasers, (2) access to source data against which the truth or falsity of representations can be tested, (3) relative skill in ferreting out the truth (for example, in this case [the seller's] manager had comparatively greater skill in evaluating judgments based on subsidiary facts, since he performed a similar function in the process of investigating the creditworthiness of borrowers), (4) pecuniary interest in the completion of the transaction, and (5) the existence of a relationship of trust and confidence between the plaintiff and the alleged "seller." These are the circumstances that determine whether a person has exercised due care in this context.[90]

[F]　Indemnification and Contribution

As a general statement, the vast majority of courts refuse to imply a right of action for either contribution or indemnification under Section 12(a)(2) of the Securities Act.[91] The Supreme Court thus far has not resolved this issue but its decision in *Musick, Peeler & Garrett v. Employers Insurance of Wausau*[92] (discussed in § 7.11) strongly points to the denial of this right of action as do other Supreme Court decisions to a lesser degree.[93]

---

[89] See generally Comment, *"Reasonable Care" in Section 12(a)(2) of the Securities Act of 1933*, 48 U. Chi. L. Rev. 372 (1981).

[90] *Davis v. Avco Financial Services, Inc.*, 739 F.2d 1057, 1068 (6th Cir. 1984). See *Ambrosino v. Rodman & Renshaw, Inc.*, [1992 Transfer Binder] Fed. Sec. L. Rep. (CCH) ¶ 96,969 (7th Cir. 1992) (although not conclusive, court found relevant that the defendant's "exercise of due diligence had been higher than the custom and practice of the industry at that time"); *Dennis v. General Imaging, Inc.*, 918 F.2d 496, 505 (5th Cir. 1990) (citations omitted): "While the exact requirements of this duty depend on the nature of the relationship of the seller at issue to his buyer, federal courts agree that a showing by the seller that he made reasonable inquiries into the possibility of fraud of the issuer and discovered nothing wrong or that no fraud could be discovered by the exercise of reasonable care, warrants a denial of liability." See generally, Maynard, *The Affirmative Defense of Reasonable Care Under Section 12(2) of the Securities Act of 1933*, 64 Notre Dame L. Rev. 57 (1993).

[91] These decisions, for example, include: *Baker, Watts & Company v. Miles & Stockbridge*, 876 F.2d 1101 (4th Cir. 1989); *In re Professional Financial Management*, 683 F. Supp. 1283 (D. Minn. 1988); *In re Olympia Brewing Company Securities Litigation*, 674 F. Supp. 597 (N.D. Ill. 1987).

[92] 508 U.S. 286 (1993).

[93] See, e.g., *Gustafson v. Alloyd Company*, 513 U.S. 561 (1995); *Central Bank of Denver v. First Interstate Bank of Denver*, 511 U.S. 164 (1994).

The leading federal appellate court decision is *Baker Watts & Co. v. Miles & Stockbridge*.[94] There, the court reasoned:

> First, [Section 12(2)] itself does not create such remedies [of contribution and indemnification]. Indeed, the statute's protection extends to investors who purchase securities based on misleading statements of material fact; it is not solicitous of unsuccessful defendants in a federal securities action. . . .

> Second, the 1933 Act's legislative history and the structure of the federal securities laws do not suggest the recognition of implied rights of contribution and indemnification. There is no indication in the 1933 Act's legislative history, for example, of any congressional intent to create these remedies in § 12(2). This fact, combined with the plain language of the statute, "reinforces our decision not to find such . . . right[s] of action implicit within the section." . . . Moreover, § 11(f) of the 1933 Act and §§ 9(e) and 18(b) of the Securities Exchange Act of 1934 expressly provide rights to contribution in specific circumstances. Congress knows how to define such a right of action in the federal securities laws, and we infer a lack of congressional intent to do so when the particular provision at issue is silent as to the existence of such a remedy. . . .

> Third, the underlying purpose of the 1933 Act is "regulatory rather than compensatory." . . . Negligence in the preparation of a securities prospectus was made actionable under § 12(2) of the 1933 Act in order to promote careful adherence to the requirements of the statute. . . . In particular, a right of action for indemnification would frustrate the statute's goal of encouraging diligence and discouraging negligence in securities transactions. An unsuccessful defendant in a federal securities action therefore cannot "escape loss by shifting his entire responsibility to another party." . . .

> In sum, we agree with the district court that Congress clearly did not provide private rights of action for contribution or indemnification in § 12(2). . . .[95]

[G] Affirmative Defense of Section 12(b)

The Private Securities Litigation Reform Act of 1995 amended Section 12 of the Securities Act by adding a new subsection (Section 12(b)). Section 12(b) provides that in actions brought under Section 12(a)(2) a defendant may avoid all or part of the damages that otherwise would be incurred by proving that all or part of the depreciation in the value of the securities in question resulted from factors unrelated to the material misstatement(s) or omission(s) that were contained in the prospectus or related oral communications.

---

[94] 876 F.2d 1101 (4th Cir. 1989).

[95] *Id.* at 1105–06.

APPENDIX 6

DUE DILIGENCE CHECKLIST

		NONE	NOT APPLICABLE (SET FORTH REASON)
1.	Articles of Incorporation for the Company and its subsidiaries, as amended.	_____ _____	_____
2.	Bylaws of the Company and its subsidiaries, as amended	_____ _____	_____
3.	Minutes of all Board of Directors Meetings from January 1996 forward for the Company and its subsidiaries.	_____ _____	_____
4.	Minutes of all Stockholders' Meetings from January 1996 forward for the Company and its subsidiaries.	_____ _____	_____
5.	Copies of reports, proxy statements, registration statements and similar documents filed with the Securities and Exchange Commission and state securities commissions, together with related correspondence.	_____ _____	_____
6.	Registration rights agreements with respect to any shares of capital stock or warrants to purchase such shares.	_____ _____	_____
7.	All other agreements relating to securities of the Company or any of its subsidiaries, including agreements and investment agreements, stock transfer restriction agreements, voting trusts, or any other such agreements	_____ _____	_____

		NONE	NOT APPLICABLE (SET FORTH REASON)
8.	Any agreements with regulatory authorities, including any state securities commissions or commissioners, regarding issuance of shares of capital stock of the Company	_____ _____	_____
9.	Any statements of the Board of Directors designating preferences, rights, etc., of any class or series of preferred stock	_____ _____	_____
10.	Schedule of all entities in which the Company owns any outstanding voting securities	_____ _____	_____
11.	List of all offices of the Company and its subsidiaries where the Company and its subsidiaries carry on a material amount of business	_____ _____	_____
12.	List of all offices of the Company and its subsidiaries and the states or other jurisdictions where the Company and its subsidiaries carry on a material amount of business	_____ _____	_____
13.	List and brief description of all material domestic and foreign governmental permits, licenses and approvals held by the Company and its subsidiaries, including those issued by customs authorities	_____ _____	_____

		NONE	NOT APPLICABLE (SET FORTH REASON)
14.	Any employee benefit plans or agreements, stock bonus, profit sharing, stock option, stock purchase, savings or retirement plans or agreements, and all collective bargaining, labor, employment or consulting contracts to which the Company or any of its subsidiaries is a party other than those otherwise called for herein	_____ _____	_____
15.	Employment Agreements between the company and key employees, together with amendments thereto	_____ _____	_____
16.	Any partnership or joint venture agreements to which the Company or any of its subsidiaries is a party	_____ _____	_____
17.	All debentures, notes, loans, lines of credit or revolving credit agreements, both secured and unsecured, mortgages, deeds of trust, security agreements, and other documents relating to indebtedness of the Company not otherwise called for herein	_____ _____	_____
18.	All guarantees by the Company or any of its subsidiaries of the indebtedness of others	_____ _____	_____

		NONE	NOT APPLICABLE (SET FORTH REASON)
19.	A brief description of the Company's insurance programs and policies (including keyman life insurance), together with any legal documents pertaining thereto and a list of claims against such insurance program currently pending	_____ _____	_____
20.	Form of any standard contracts used with the Company employees	_____ _____	_____
21.	Schedule of all loans and advances outstanding in the last three years (other than routine travel and business expense advances) by the Company or any subsidiary to any officer or director of the Company or any subsidiaries	_____ _____	_____
22.	All leases, options to lease or purchase or purchase contracts relating to real property	_____ _____	_____
23.	All material contracts, agreements, notes, or leases not otherwise called for herein to which the Company, its subsidiaries or any of their respective businesses, including any tax sharing agreements with any party	_____ _____	_____
24.	List of major vendors/suppliers	_____ _____	_____

	NONE	NOT APPLICABLE (SET FORTH REASON)

25. A schedule of all pending or threatened legal, administrative, arbitrative or other proceedings or governmental investigations pending or threatened against the Company or any other party which might result in (a) damages payable by the Company, (b) a permanent injunction against the Company or any of its subsidiaries, (c) a material deterioration of the business prospects of the Company and its subsidiaries, taken as a whole, or (d) a change in zoning or building ordinances materially affecting the property or leasehold interests of the Company:

(i) parties; _____ _____ _____
(ii) nature of the proceedings; _____ _____ _____
(iii) date commenced; and _____ _____ _____
(iv) amount of damages or other relief sought _____ _____ _____

26. Reports of independent certified public accountants relating to management and accounting procedures of the Company from January 1998 to this date ("management letters") _____ _____ _____

27. Attorneys' responses to auditor's letters of inquiry relating to the Company from January 1998 to this date _____ _____ _____

28. All news or press releases of the company for the past year. _____ _____ _____

		NONE	NOT APPLICABLE (SET FORTH REASON)
29.	A schedule describing any ongoing tax disputes, and copies of revenue agents' reports and correspondence respecting federal or state tax proceedings involving open years or items	_____ _____	_____
30.	Copies of any speeches delivered by any officer or director of the Company to securities or financial organizations	_____ _____	_____
31.	Copies of any articles published in any financial periodical or newsletter concerning the Company	_____ _____	_____
32.	List and brief description of all trademarks, trade names, copyrights, patents and other similar proprietary rights owned by, or used in the business of, the Company or any of its subsidiaries and all registrations relating thereto	_____ _____	_____
33.	Agreements, letters of intent and other documents relating to any pending sales or dispositions of any material portions of the Company's assets	_____ _____	_____

Chapter 7

SECTION 10(b) AND RELATED ISSUES

§ 7.01 Overview

This chapter explores developments under Section 10(b) of the Securities
Exchange Act and Rule 10b-5 promulgated thereunder by the SEC (as well
as certain related issues). Generally, the antifraud provisions of the
securities acts were designed to protect investors, to assure fair dealing in
the securities markets, and to promote ethical business practices. Consistent with these objectives, Section 10(b) makes it unlawful to employ
deceptive or manipulative devices "in connection with the purchase or sale
of any security." As enacted by Congress, Section 10(b) was designed to be
a "catch-all" provision and, as such, it encompasses a broad range of
practices.[1]

The language of Section 10(b) does not create an express private remedy
for its violation. Neither does the legislative history reveal that Congress
intended to create a private right of action under the statute at the time
of its passage. Nonetheless, the federal courts have routinely recognized
the existence of a private remedy under Section 10(b). As the Supreme
Court has recognized, "[t]he existence of this implied remedy is simply
beyond peradventure."[2]

In order to establish a successful claim under Section 10(b), a plaintiff
must prove certain elements. Many of these elements are explored in depth
in this chapter. These elements include that the plaintiff must (by proof
of the preponderance of the evidence):

(1) Establish the *requisite jurisdictional means*. This requirement is
normally met without difficulty. For example, as one appellate court has
pointed out, "proof of intrastate telephonic messages in connection with the
employment of deceptive devices or contrivances is sufficient to confer
jurisdiction in a Section 10(b) and Rule 10b-5 action."[3]

(2) Have the status as a *purchaser or seller* of the securities. Note that
the defendant need not be a purchaser or seller.[4]

(3) Prove *"manipulation" or "deception"* and not "merely" breach of
fiduciary duty.[5]

---

[1] See A. Bromberg & L. Lowenfels, Securities Fraud & Commodities Fraud (1999).

[2] *Herman & MacLean v. Huddleston*, 459 U.S. 375, 380 (1983).

[3] *Loveridge v. Dreagoux*, 678 F.2d 870, 874 (10th Cir. 1982).

[4] See *Blue Chip Stamps v. Manor Drug Stores*, 421 U.S. 462 (1977); *McGann v. Ernst &
Young*, 102 F.3d 390 (9th Cir. 1996); § 7.02 *infra*.

[5] See *Santa Fe Industries, Inc. v. Green*, 430 U.S. 462 (1977); § 7.05 *infra*.

(4) Show that a misstatement or nondisclosure of fact is *material*, signifying that a reasonable investor would consider such information important in making an investment decision. The investor need not show that the misstatement or nondisclosure, if accurately disclosed, would have changed the investment decision. Hence, to satisfy the materiality requirement, "there must be a substantial likelihood that the disclosure of the omitted fact would have been viewed by the reasonable investor as having significantly altered the 'total mix' of information made available."[6] Moreover, in the merger context as well as other situations involving uncertain events, the probability/magnitude standard has been applied. Under this standard, the existence of materiality depends "at any given time upon a balancing of both the indicated probability that the event will occur and the anticipated magnitude of the event in light of the totality of the company activity."[7]

(5) Establish that the defendant acted with "*scienter*," signifying knowing or intentional misconduct.[8]

(6) Where called for, show that the plaintiff *relied* on the alleged misrepresentation and exercised *due diligence*.[9]

(7) Establish *causation* between the defendant's wrongful conduct and the plaintiff's loss.[10]

(8) Related to the causation requirement, prove that the manipulative or deceptive practice was "*in connection with*" the purchase or sale of a security. Generally, in order to meet this requirement, the proscribed conduct must touch upon and be integral to the purchase or sale of the security.[11]

(9) Where liability is based upon *silence*, establish that the alleged primary violator had a *duty to disclose*.[12]

---

[6] *Basic, Inc. v. Levinson*, 485 U.S. 224, 232 (1988), quoting, *TSC Industries, Inc. v. Northway, Inc.*, 426 U.S. 438, 449 (1976).

[7] *SEC v. Texas Gulf Sulphur Co.*, 402 F.2d 833, 849 (2d Cir.) (en banc), *cert. denied*, 394 U.S. 976 (1969), quoted in, *Basic, Inc. v. Levinson*, 485 U.S. 224, 238 (1988). See also SEC Staff Accounting Bulletin No. 99, 64 Fed. Reg. 45150 (1999) (opining that "exclusive reliance on certain quantitative benchmarks to assess materiality in preparing financial statements and performing audits of those financial statements is inappropriate").

[8] See *Aaron v. SEC*, 446 U.S. 680 (1980); *Ernst & Ernst v. Hochfelder*, 425 U.S. 185 (1976); § 7.03 *infra*.

[9] See *Basic, Inc. v. Levinson*, 485 U.S. 224 (1988); *Affiliated Ute Citizens v. United States*, 406 U.S. 128 (1972); § 7.06 *infra*.

[10] Section 21D(b)(4) of the Exchange Act expressly provides that the plaintiff must prove loss causation in any private action arising under the Exchange Act. See *AUSA Life Insurance Co. v. Ernst & Young*, 206 F.3d 202 (2d Cir. 2000); 3 A. Bromberg & L. Lowenfels, *supra* note 1, at §§ 7.6, 8.7; Gabaldon, *Causation, Courts and Congress: A Study of Contradiction in the Federal Securities Laws*, 31 Boston Coll. L. Rev 1027 (1990).

[11] See *Superintendent of Life Insurance v. Bankers Life and Casualty Co.*, 404 U.S. 6 (1971); *In re Carter-Wallace, Inc. Securities Litigation*, 150 F.3d 153 (2d Cir. 1998); *Pross v. Katz*, 784 F.2d 455 (2d Cir. 1986); *Chemical Bank v. Arthur Andersen & Co.*, 726 F.2d 390 (2d Cir. 1984); Black, *The Second Circuit's Approach to the "In Connection With" Requirement of Rule 10b-5*, 53 Brooklyn L. Rev. 539 (1987); Fletcher, *The "In Connection With" Requirement of Rule 10b-5*, 16 Pepperdine L. Rev. 913 (1989).

[12] See *Chiarella v. United States*, 445 U.S. 222 (1980), discussed in Chapter 11.

(10) Prove the extent of *damages* suffered.[13]

In addition, the plaintiff must bring its action within Section 10(b)'s *statute of limitations* which is one year after the violation was or should have been discovered by the plaintiff and in no event more than three years after the violation.[14]

Note moreover that the plaintiff also *must plead fraud with particularity* in its Section 10(b) cause of action. Rule 9(b) of the Federal Rules of Civil Procedure provides: "In all averments of fraud or mistake, the circumstances constituting fraud or mistake shall be stated with particularity. Malice, intent, knowledge, and other condition of mind of a person may be averred generally."[15] As applied in the securities law context, Section 21D(b) of the Exchange Act generally requires that a plaintiff must specifically plead each alleged misrepresentation or nondisclosure and why such is misleading, and must allege specific facts as to each such disclosure deficiency supporting a "strong inference" that the subject defendant knew that the misstatement or omission was false.[16]

Also, as will be discussed in Chapter 9, only primary violators are liable in private actions under Section 10(b). In *Central Bank of Denver v. First Interstate Bank of Denver*, the Supreme Court held that in private actions Section 10(b) liability may not be imposed against aiders and abettors. Nonetheless, the SEC may institute enforcement actions against aiders and abettors for alleged violations of Section 10(b).[17]

The *defendant* may assert a number of *defenses*, including *in pari delicto*, *laches*, and *waiver*. The *in pari delicto* defense is addressed later in the chapter.[18]

With respect to *indemnification*, because the Supreme Court has ruled that scienter (e.g., deliberate or perhaps reckless misconduct) is required to state a successful Section 10(b) (and Rule 10b-5) claim under the Exchange Act,[19] it appears that indemnification would frustrate the public policy as well as the statutory underpinnings of the Act and therefore is prohibited in the Section 10(b) context.[20]

---

[13] See M. Kaufman, Securities Litigation: Damages (1989); Thompson, *The Measure of Recovery Under Rule 10b-5: A Restitution Alternative to Tort Damages*, 37 Vand. L. Rev. 349 (1984); discussion § 7.09 *infra*.

[14] See *Lampf, Pleva, Lipkind, Prupis & Petrigrow v. Gilbertson*, 501 U.S. 350 (1991); discussion § 7.08 *infra*.

[15] Rule 9(b) of the Federal Rules of Civil Procedure. See *Wexner v. First Manhattan Co.*, 902 F.2d 164 (3d Cir. 1996).

[16] For further discussion, see § 7.04 *infra*.

[17] See Section 20(f) of the Exchange Act (granting to the SEC authority to pursue aiders and abettors under the 1934 Act). *Central Bank of Denver v. First Interstate Bank of Denver*, 511 U.S. 164 (1994) (holding that aiders and abettors not subject to liability in § 10(b) private actions); §§ 9.02, 14.04 *infra*.

[18] See *Bateman Eichler, Hill Richards, Inc. v. Berner*, 472 U.S. 299 (1985); *Hecht v. Harris, Upham & Co.*, 430 F.2d 1202 (9th Cir. 1970); § 7.10 *infra*.

[19] See cases cited note 8 *supra*; § 7.03 *infra*.

[20] See, e.g., *Globus v. Law Research Serv., Inc.*, 418 F.2d 1276 (2d Cir. 1969); discussion § 6.09[F] *supra*.

The right to *contribution* under Section 10(b) likewise has been resolved. In the *Musick Peller* decision, the Supreme Court recognized such a right to contribution under Section 10(b). In the 1995 legislation, Congress codified this right to contribution.[21]

§ 7.02 Standing: The Purchaser-Seller Requirement

In *Blue Chip Stamps v. Manor Drug Stores*,[22] allegedly defrauded offerees asserted that had the defendant not deceived them, they would have purchased the securities offered. The Supreme Court ruled that the plaintiffs did not have standing to bring a Section 10(b) right of action because they were neither purchasers nor sellers. The Court premised its decision on a number of factors:

(1) The statutory language of Section 10(b) proscribes manipulation or deception "in connection with the purchase or sale" of securities. This language, along with the pertinent legislative history, indicated that Congress did not intend to grant standing to defrauded (but non-purchasing) offerees.

(2) Granting standing to offerees under the implied remedy of Section 10(b) would make the Section 10(b) remedy more expansive than the comparable express causes of action that Congress chose to delineate. Hence, granting offerees standing under Section 10(b) evidently would contravene Congress' intent.

(3) Looking to policy matters, the Court asserted that Section 10(b) litigation poses a greater danger of vexatiousness than litigation in general. According to the Court, this is due to the presence of "strike" suits, potential abuse of the liberal discovery provisions of the Federal Rules of Civil Procedure, and that "hazy issues of historical fact" will be adjudicated on the basis of "oral testimony."[23]

Hence, under the *Blue Chip* standing requirement, three principal types of potential plaintiffs are barred from instituting Section 10(b) litigation:

First are potential purchasers of shares, either in a new offering or on the Nation's post-distribution trading markets, who allege that they decided not to purchase because of an unduly gloomy representation or the omission of favorable material which made the issuer appear to be a less favorable investment vehicle than it actually was. Second are actual shareholders in the issuer who

---

[21] See *Musick, Peeler & Garrett v. Employers Insurance of Wausau*, 508 U.S. 286 (1993); § 7.11 *infra*. See generally Fallone, *Section 10(b) and the Vagaries of Federal Common Law: The Merits of Codifying the Private Cause of Action Under a Structuralist Approach*, 1997 U. Ill. L. Rev. 71 (1997); Prentice, *The Future of Corporate Disclosure: The Internet, Securities Fraud, and Rule 10b-5*, 47 Emory L.J. 1 (1998); Sachs, *Freedom of Contract: The Trojan Horse of Rule 10b-5*, 51 Wash. & Lee L. Rev. 879 (1994); Stern, *The Constitutionalization of Rule 10b-5*, 27 Rutgers L.J. 1 (1995).

[22] 421 U.S. 723 (1975), upholding the Birnbaum standing rule, *Birnbaum v. Newport Steel Corp.*, 193 F.2d 461 (2d Cir. 1952).

[23] 421 U.S. at 733-61.

allege that they decided not to sell their shares because of an unduly rosy representation or a failure to disclose unfavorable material. Third are shareholders, creditors, and perhaps others related to an issuer who suffered loss in the value of their investment due to corporate or insider activities in connection with the purchase or sale of securities which violate Rule 10b-5.[24]

In this regard, shareholders of the second and third categories above, although unable to bring a direct action, should be able to institute a derivative action on the issuer's behalf if such issuer is a purchaser or seller of its securities.

The *Blue Chip* standing requirement has been extended by some courts to plaintiffs seeking solely injunctive relief. Hence, when seeking injunctive relief under Section 10(b), the plaintiff must be a purchaser or seller of securities. The policy rationale is that *Blue Chip* applies to injunctive actions due to the need to deter strike suits and the rendering of hazy oral testimony.[25]

It is important to emphasize that, in order to bring a Section 10(b) cause of action, *only the plaintiff* (not the defendant) must be a "purchaser" or "seller." Moreover, applying the purchaser-seller requirement, the lower federal courts have recognized standing under Section 10(b) in a variety of circumstances, including: in a shareholder derivative action brought on behalf of an allegedly defrauded corporation where the corporation was a purchaser or seller of its securities; in a "forced" sale transaction, such as a "freeze-out" merger; where the plaintiff has "pledged" the securities; and where the plaintiff has entered into a contract to buy or sell the securities.[26]

§ 7.03   Requisite Culpability Level

[A]   Private Damages Actions

The Supreme Court in *Ernst & Ernst v. Hochfelder*[27] held that in private actions for damages pursuant to Section 10(b) *scienter* must be proven. The decision was largely predicated on a strict linguistic interpretation of Section 10(b). The construction of Rule 10b-5 was confined to that given the statutory source upon which the administrative rule (Rule 10b-5) is based, namely, Section 10(b). The *Hochfelder* Court, moreover, pointed out that: (1) the 1933 Act's statutory provisions granting private redress for negligent conduct are "subject to significant procedural restrictions not applicable under § 10(b)," and (2) except for the "short-swing" trading prohibition of Exchange Act Section 16(b),[28] "[e]ach of the provisions of the 1934

---

[24] *Id.* at 737-38.

[25] See, e.g., Cowin v Bresler, 741 F.2d 410 (D.C. Cir. 1984). For a decision contra, see *Granada Investments, Inc. v. DWG Corp.*, 717 F. Supp. 533 (N.D. Ohio 1989).

[26] For further discussion, see T. Hazen, The Law of Securities Regulation 774-87 (3d ed. 1996); L. Loss & J. Seligman, Securities Regulation 3703-17 (3d ed. 1991).

[27] 425 U.S. 185 (1976).

[28] 425 U.S. at 208-09. See Sections 11 and 12(a)(2) of the Securities Act, 15 U.S.C. §§ 77k, 1(a)(2). For discussion on Section 16(b), see § 11.08 *infra*.

Act that expressly create civil liability . . . contains a state of mind condition requiring something more than negligence."[29] Hence, extending Section 10(b) to include negligent conduct in private damages actions, the Court held, would "nullify the effectiveness of the carefully drawn procedural restrictions on these express actions."[30]

While the *Hochfelder* Court stated that the term "scienter" encompasses "a mental state embracing intent to deceive, manipulate, or defraud" and may be shown by "knowing or intentional misconduct,"[31] the Court declined to resolve whether "recklessness" constitutes scienter.[32] This issue is discussed later in this section. Moreover, as discussed in §§ 7.01 and 7.04, pursuant to Rule 9(b) of the Federal Rules of Civil Procedure and Section 21D(b) of the Exchange Act, a plaintiff must plead fraud with particularity when bringing a Section 10(b) right of action.

[B] SEC Actions for Injunctive Relief

After the Supreme Court's decision in *Hochfelder*, the question remained whether the SEC was required to establish scienter in an action for injunctive relief brought for violations of Section 10(b). Because the principal focus of an SEC injunctive proceeding ostensibly "is to protect the public against harm, not to punish the offender,"[33] it was argued by some authorities that an SEC action under Section 10(b) could be premised on negligent conduct. Others, relying upon a statutory linguistic analysis, asserted that scienter had to be proven under Section 10(b), irrespective of the plaintiff's identity.[34]

The Supreme Court resolved this issue in *Aaron v. SEC*.[35] Largely relying on the literal language of Section 10(b) and its legislative history, the Court concluded that "scienter is an element of § 10(b) and Rule 10b-5, regardless of the identity of the plaintiff or the nature of the relief sought."[36] From an SEC enforcement view, *Aaron* is an important case, further aspects of which are discussed in Chapters 8 and 14.

[C] "Recklessness"

A question left open by both *Hochfelder* and *Aaron* is whether reckless conduct constitutes scienter for Section 10(b) purposes. Overwhelmingly, the lower federal courts have concluded that recklessness satisfies the

---

[29] 425 U.S. at 209 n.28. See, e.g., Sections 9(e), 18 and 20 of the Exchange Act, 15 U.S.C. §§ 78i(e), (r), (t).

[30] 425 U.S. at 210.

[31] *Id.* at 193 n.12, 197.

[32] *Id.* at 193 n.12.

[33] *SEC v. Coven*, 581 F.2d 1020, 1027-28 (2d Cir. 1978).

[34] See generally M. Steinberg & R. Ferrara, Securities Practice: Federal and State Enforcement § 5.01 et. seq (1985 & 1999 Supp.).

[35] 446 U.S. 680 (1980). With respect to the portion of the decision addressing Section 17(a) of the Securities Act, that provision is discussed in Chapters 8 and 14.

[36] 446 U.S. at 691.

scienter requirement. This position is reinforced by the enactment of the Private Securities Litigation Reform Act of 1995 (PSLRA). That legislation strongly suggests that reckless conduct satisfies Section 10(b)'s scienter requirement except for forward-looking statements by publicly-held enterprises with respect to which the defendant's actual knowledge must be proven.

The vast majority of courts have construed reckless conduct within the Section 10(b) context to mean conduct that is "highly unreasonable" and which represents "an extreme departure from the standards of ordinary care" to the extent that the danger was "either known to the defendant or [was] so obvious that the [defendant] must have been aware of it."[37] A few courts have adopted a somewhat more relaxed standard. For example, one minority view holds that reckless conduct exists if the defendant had reasonable grounds to believe material facts existed that were misstated or omitted, but nonetheless failed to obtain and disclose such facts although he/she could have done so without extraordinary effort.[38] Another approach, termed the "barely reckless" standard, deems actionable an allegation that the defendant "should have known," with the proviso that such conduct surpasses that of negligence.[39]

[D] State Court Reaction

Due to the Supreme Court's decisions in the federal securities law area, which have had the effect of making a plaintiff's task in establishing a successful cause of action under Section 10(b) more difficult, counsel may deem it wise to consider bringing state common law and/or state securities law claims. In this regard, in construing their respective Blue Sky statutes, a number of state courts have elected not to follow the Supreme Court's lead in *Hochfelder* and *Aaron*, hence holding that scienter is not required to be shown. State court decisions holding that negligence is sufficient culpability to impose liability have distinguished Section 10(b)'s language from that contained in the respective state statute and have found no legislative history in the state statute comparable to that underlying Section 10(b).[40] The subject of state law remedies is discussed in greater detail in Chapter 8.

---

[37] See, e.g., *Hollinger v. Titan Capital Corporation*, 914 F.2d 1564, 1569 (9th Cir. 1990) (en banc); *Sanders v. John Nuveen & Co., Inc.*, 554 F.2d 790, 793 (7th Cir. 1977).

[38] See *Lanza v. Drexel & Co.*, 419 F.2d 1277, 1306 n.98 (2d Cir. 1973) (en banc).

[39] See *Stern v. American Bankshares Corp.*, 429 F. Supp. 818 (E.D. Wis. 1977). See generally Johnson, *Liability for Reckless Misrepresentations and Omissions Under Section 10(b) of the Securities Exchange Act of 1934*, 59 U. Cincinnati L. Rev. 667 (1991); Steinberg & Gruenbaum, *Variations of Recklessness After Hochfelder and Aaron*, 8 Sec. Reg. L.J. 179 (1980).

[40] See *Kittleson v. Ford*, 93 Wash. 2d 223, 608 P.2d 264 (1980). But see *Ohio v. American Equitel Corp.*, 60 Ohio Misc. 7, 395 N.E.2d 1355 (Ct. C.P. Ohio 1979) (requiring scienter to be shown). See generally J. Long, Blue Sky Law § 7.01 (1999); M. Steinberg & R. Ferrara, *supra* note 34, at § 12.18.

§ 7.04 Pleading Requirements

As discussed in § 7.01, in addition to pleading fraud with particularity pursuant to Rule 9(b) of the Federal Rules of Civil Procedure, a plaintiff bringing suit under Section 10(b) also must adhere to Section 21D(b) of the Exchange Act. Section 21D(b), enacted pursuant to the PSLRA, sets forth:

(1) A requirement that a plaintiff in the complaint in any private securities fraud action alleging material misstatements and/or omissions "specify each statement alleged to have been misleading; the reason or reasons why the statement is misleading; and if an allegation regarding the statement or omission is made on information and belief, the complaint shall state with particularity all facts on which that belief is formed."

(2) A requirement that in any private action under the 1934 Act in which the plaintiff "may recover money damages only on proof that the defendant acted with a particular state of mind, the complaint shall, with respect to each such act or omission alleged to violate [the 1934 Act], state with particularity facts giving rise to a strong inference that the defendant acted with the required state of mind."

As the Joint Explanatory Statement of the Conference Committee for this legislation recognized, the foregoing language derives "in part" from the Second Circuit's pleading requirement, which is "[r]egarded as the most stringent pleading standard." Nonetheless, the Conference Committee apparently believed that this "stringent pleading standard" was too lax, stating "[b]ecause the Conference Committee intends to strengthen existing pleading requirements, it does not intend to codify the Second Circuit's case law interpreting this pleading standard." In view of the new statute and its accompanying legislative history, the pleading requirement in private securities fraud actions undoubtedly poses a difficult barrier for plaintiffs to hurdle.

In cases decided after the PSLRA, the lower federal courts are divided with respect to the requisite pleading requirements in securities actions alleging fraud. Some courts continue to embrace the Second Circuit's standard while others have more strictly construed the PSLRA's pleading requirements. The following approaches, for example, have emerged: (1) The Second Circuit standard whereby a plaintiff must allege either (a) "motive" and "opportunity" by the defendant to commit fraud, or (b) "facts that constitute strong circumstantial evidence of conscious misbehavior or recklessness."[41] (2) A standard similar to that adhered to by the Second Circuit which "impose[s] strict procedural requirements," mandating the pleading of facts with particularity that show the defendant's motive and opportunity to perpetrate fraud or circumstantial evidence of either reckless or intentional misconduct.[42] (3) The Sixth Circuit standard holding that allegations of a defendant's motive and opportunity are not by themselves

---

[41] See, e.g., *Press v. Chemical Investment Serv. Corp.*, 166 F.3d 529, 537-38 (3d Cir. 1999). Accord, *Williams v. WMX Techs., Inc.*, 112 F.3d 175, 178 (5th Cir. 1997).

[42] See, e.g., *In re Advanta Corp. Securities Litigation*, 180 F.3d 525, 533-34 (3d Cir. 1999).

adequate for pleading scienter but that such allegations constitute a factor, among others, that a court may consider in ascertaining whether a plaintiff has set forth "a strong inference of fraudulent scienter."[43] (4) The most rigorous pleading requirement adhered to by the Ninth Circuit rejecting the motive and opportunity test and "requir[ing] plaintiffs to plead, at a minimum, particular facts demonstrating deliberate or conscious reckless-ness."[44] In view of the sharply differing approaches by the appellate courts, this issue awaits Supreme Court resolution.

§ 7.05   The "Manipulation" or "Deception" Requirement

[A]   Breach of Fiduciary Duty Not Sufficient

Santa Fe Industries, Inc. v. Green[45] involved the merger of the Kirby Lumber Corporation into its parent, Santa Fe Industries, Inc., which owned ninety-five percent of Kirby's stock. Santa Fe availed itself of a simplified Delaware procedure known as a "short-form" merger, under which a parent that owns at least ninety percent of a subsidiary's outstanding stock can absorb the subsidiary without being required to obtain approval by the shareholders of either corporation. The day after the merger became effective, Kirby's minority shareholders were informed that they would re-ceive $150 in cash for each of their shares, and that, if dissatisfied, they could seek appraisal in the Delaware courts.[46]

Santa Fe also provided the Kirby shareholders with an information statement containing facts and figures that convinced one of the recipients that Kirby stock was actually worth at least $772 a share. Rather than alleging that these materials contained misrepresentations and nondisclo-sures, the plaintiff claimed that the gross undervaluation of his shares was itself a "fraud" within the meaning of Section 10(b) and Rule 10b-5.[47]

The Supreme Court rejected this argument, holding that the transaction "was neither deceptive nor manipulative and therefore did not violate either § 10(b) of the [Exchange] Act or Rule 10b-5."[48] The Court largely premised

---

[43] See, e.g., *In re Comshare Inc. Securities Litigation*, 183 F.3d 542, 549 (6th Cir. 1999).

[44] See, e.g., *In re Silicon Graphics Inc. Securities Litigation*, 183 F.3d 970, 974 (9th Cir. 1999). After the PSLRA's enactment, an unresolved issue is whether the "group pleading" doctrine is still good law. As a general proposition, this doctrine recognizes "the presumption, for pleading purposes, that statements made in public documents, such as registration statements, prospectuses, and periodic SEC filings, constitute the collective actions of the officers and directors who signed the documents, and thus allow securities fraud to be pled without allegations of individualized conduct." Block & Hoff, *Liability for Persons Signing SEC Disclosure Documents*, N.Y.L.J., Aug. 26, 1999, at p. 5. Compare *In re Bank America Securities Litigation*, [1999-2000 Transfer Binder] Fed. Sec. L. Rep. (CCH) ¶ 90,733 (E.D. Mo. 1999) (recognizing validity of group pleading doctrine), with *Allison v. Brooktree Corp.*, 999 F. Supp. 1342 (C.D. Cal. 1998) (holding that group pleading doctrine no longer survives after the PSLRA).

[45] 430 U.S. 462 (1977).

[46] 430 U.S. at 466-67. See 8 Del. Code Ann. § 253 ("short-form" merger statute).

[47] 430 U.S. at 474.

[48] *Id.*

its decision on Section 10(b)'s language and the statute's legislative history, finding "no indication that Congress meant to prohibit any conduct not involving manipulation or deception."[49] Further support was found by examining the Exchange Act's fundamental purpose of implementing a philosophy of full and fair disclosure. Once adequate disclosure has taken place, the fairness of the transaction is at most a tangential concern of the federal Securities Acts. Therefore, claims challenging solely the fairness of transactions or internal corporate mismanagement are best relegated to state law.[50]

Santa Fe was scarcely a surprise after the Court's previous decisions in *Ernst & Ernst v. Hochfelder*[51] and *Cort v. Ash*.[52] *Hochfelder* held that there can be no implied private right of action for damages under Section 10(b) and Rule 10b-5, absent an allegation of scienter. The decision was largely predicated on a strict construction of Section 10(b). This approach to the language of the statute was expressly affirmed and adopted by the *Santa Fe* Court. In *Cort*, the Court demonstrated its reluctance to imply federal causes of action in areas traditionally left to state law. There, the Court observed that "corporations are creatures of state law, and investors commit their funds to corporate directors on the understanding that, except where federal law *expressly* requires certain responsibilities of directors with respect to stockholders, state law will govern the internal affairs of the corporation."[53] Both cases evidence the Court's contraction of the scope of

---

[49] *Id.* at 473. The term manipulation has been construed by the Supreme Court as a term of art encompassing market operations. Thus, the term encompasses such practices as matched orders, wash sales, and rigged prices that are designed to mislead investors by artificially affecting market activity (including the price of the subject company's securities). *Id.*

Note that manipulation is actionable under both Section 9(a)(2) of the Exchange Act and Section 10(b) of that Act. Generally, to prove manipulation under Section 9(a)(2) of the Exchange Act, the following must be shown: "(1) that the defendant effected a series of transactions in a security registered on a national securities exchange, (2) creating actual or apparent active trading in such security, or raising or depressing the price of such security, (3) for the purpose of inducing the purchase or sale of such security by others." McLucas & Angotti, *Market Manipulation*, 22 Rev. Sec. & Comm. Reg. 103, 105 (1989).

Manipulation under Section 10(b) is easier to prove than under Section 9(a)(2). Importantly, Section 10(b) covers stock manipulation that is perpetrated in the over-the-counter (OTC) market as well as on a stock exchange. Moreover, unlike Section 9(a)(2), market manipulation under Section 10(b) may be established without proof that the suspect transactions were engaged in for the purpose of inducing the purchase or sale of the security by others.

For commentary on manipulation, see A. Bromberg & L. Lowenfels, *supra* note 1, at §§ 7.3 et seq; Howard, *Frontrunning in the Marketplace: A Regulatory Dilemma*, 19 Sec. Reg. L.J. 263 (1989); Lowenfels & Bromberg, *Securities Market Manipulations: An Examination and Analysis of Domination and Control, Frontrunning and Parking*, 55 Albany L. Rev. 293 (1991); Poser, *Stock Market Manipulation and Corporate Control Transactions*, 40 U. Miami L. Rev. 671 (1986); Thel, *Regulation of Manipulation Under Section 10(b): Securities Prices and the Text of the Securities Exchange Act of 1934*, 1988 Colum. Bus. L. Rev. 359.

[50] 430 U.S. at 477-80. But see Thel, *The Original Conception of Section 10(b) of the Securities Exchange Act*, 42 Stan. L. Rev. 385 (1990).

[51] 425 U.S. 185 (1976). See § 7.03[A] *supra*.

[52] 422 U.S. 66 (1975) (declining to imply private right of action under federal statute, discussed in § 8.02[B] *infra*).

[53] *Id.* at 80 (emphasis in original).

the federal securities laws. *Santa Fe* combined the approaches of *Hochfelder* and *Cort*, employing a narrow approach to construction and stressing that the regulation of the internal management of corporations is within the ambit of state corporation law.

Santa Fe is one of the more important decisions that the Supreme Court has handed down in the federal securities law area. Had the decision gone the other way, garden variety suits for breach of fiduciary duty (irrespective of whether there had been adequate disclosure) would have been actionable under Section 10(b). *Santa Fe* thus signifies that a federal claim under Section 10(b) must allege manipulation or deception.

[B]   Federal Claims Premised on Breach of Fiduciary Duty

The *Santa Fe* decision had a second aspect, arising from the Court's comment in footnote 14 of the opinion. In that footnote, the Court stated that the failure to provide the minority with advance notice of the merger was not a material nondisclosure because, as the plaintiffs conceded, "under Delaware law [the plaintiffs] could not have enjoined the merger because an appraisal proceeding [was] their sole remedy in the Delaware courts for any alleged unfairness in the terms of the merger."[54] Today no plaintiff would make this concession in a *Santa Fe* situation.

[1]   Post-*Santa Fe* State Court Decisions

Subsequent to *Santa Fe*, Delaware[55] and a number of other state courts[56] held that appraisal is not a shareholder's sole remedy when a merger is unfair. Based on these decisions, under certain circumstances, aggrieved shareholders may bring suit in state court to enjoin a merger that has not been consummated. For example, in Delaware, a shareholder is not relegated to the appraisal remedy and may seek to enjoin a merger where "fraud, misrepresentation, self-dealing, deliberate waste of corporate assets, or gross and palpable overreaching are involved."[57]

[2]   Post-*Santa Fe* Federal Court Decisions

In view of these post-*Santa Fe* state court decisions, aggrieved shareholders not only may seek redress under state law, they also can institute a Section 10(b) right of action in certain circumstances. Where the material misrepresentation(s) or omission(s), if there had been adequate disclosure, would have enabled shareholders to take corrective steps to avoid financial

---

[54] 430 U.S. at 474 n.14.

[55] See *Weinberger v. UOP, Inc.*, 457 A.2d 701 (Del. 1983); *Singer v. Magnovox Co.*, 380 A.2d 969 (Del. 1977).

[56] See, e.g., *Alpert v. 28 Williams St. Corp.*, 63 N.Y. 2d 557, 483 N.Y.S. 2d 667, 473 N.E. 2d 19 (1984); *Perl v. IU International Corp.*, 607 P.2d 1036 (Hawaii 1980). But see *Steinberg v. Amplica, Inc.*, 42 Cal. 3d 1198, 233 Cal. Rptr. 249, 729 P.2d 683 (1986) (appraisal sole remedy).

[57] *Weinberger v. UOP, Inc.*, 457 A.2d 701, 714 (Del. 1983).

loss, such as procuring a state court injunction against the contemplated action, a federal Section 10(b) right of action may be invoked.[58] Hence, to a certain extent, federal claims under Section 10(b) based partially on breach of fiduciary duty under state law still survive. This rationale has been called the "*Goldberg* line of cases" or the "lost state remedy theory." The Supreme Court has raised but declined to resolve the validity of this theory.[59]

Stated differently, subject to certain caveats, minority shareholders are entitled to information needed to determine whether the board of directors has breached its fiduciary duty under state law. Failure to provide this information, according to a number of courts,[60] may be a material deception actionable under Section 10(b). This federal right to information extends well beyond the freeze-out merger situation. Indeed, subject to certain caveats, it encompasses every corporate transaction in securities that shareholders could have attacked under state law, had they known the facts.

[3] Caveats

There are a number of caveats to the foregoing. First, assuming that disclosure to shareholders is required, the board of directors need only disclose objective facts. There is no requirement for the board to engage in subjective revelation or characterize its actions with pejorative nouns or adjectives. As stated by one court, "[t]he unclean heart of a director is not actionable, whether or not it is 'disclosed' unless the impurities are translated into actionable deeds or omissions both objective and external."[61] Or, as more recently enunciated by the Supreme Court in *Virginia Bankshares, Inc. v. Sandberg*: "We hold disbelief or undisclosed motivation, standing alone, insufficient to satisfy [an actionable claim]."[62]

Moreover, the courts consistently have required Rule 10b-5 claims to allege more than the bare availability of state court injunctive relief. In derivative actions, when shareholder approval of a transaction is not required, the courts have reasoned that disclosure to a disinterested board of directors is equivalent to disclosure to the shareholders. Stated differently, the knowledge of the disinterested board is attributed to the corporation, thereby precluding a finding of deception.[63] Of course, in nonderivative actions, where an individual shareholder is the purchaser or seller of securities, a Section 10(b) claim need only allege that the shareholder was deceived. In such cases, the deception requirement is satisfied by alleging

---

[58] See, e.g., *Healey v. Catalyst Recovery, Inc.*, 616 F.2d 641 (3d Cir. 1980); *Alabama Farm Bureau Mutual Casualty Co. v. American Fidelity Life Insurance Co.*, 606 F.2d 602 (5th Cir. 1979); *Goldberg v. Meridor*, 567 F.2d 209 (2d Cir. 1977), *cert. denied*, 434 U.S. 1069 (1978). But see *Isquith v. Caremark International, Inc.*, 136 F.3d 531 (7th Cir. 1998) (rejecting Goldberg line of cases).

[59] *Virginia Bankshares, Inc. v. Sandberg*, 501 U.S. 1083, 1106-08 (1991).

[60] See cases cited in note 58 *supra*.

[61] *Stedman v. Storer*, 308 F. Supp. 881, 887 (S.D.N.Y. 1969), quoted in, *Biesenbach v. Guenther*, 588 F.2d 400, 402 (3d Cir. 1978). See *Goldberg v. Meridor*, 567 F.2d 209, 218 n.8 (2d Cir. 1977).

[62] 501 U.S. 1083, 1096 (1991).

[63] See, e.g., *Maldonado v. Flynn*, 597 F.2d 789 (2d Cir. 1979).

that there was a material misrepresentation or nondisclosure in the flow of information between the majority and the individual shareholder that deprived the plaintiff of an opportunity under state law to enjoin the transaction.[64]

A troublesome issue in determining whether a corporation has been deceived is the proper definition of a "disinterested" director. A director's "financial stake" in the subject transaction would clearly render such person "interested." What is not so clear is whether the presence of some other disability, such as a director's desire to maintain his/her position irrespective of the corporation's best interests, or the perpetuation of improper influence or deception upon a director by a controlling person (including the failure to apprise a director of material facts), would likewise render the director "interested." Relatively few courts hold that only the existence of a financial conflict disqualifies a director[65] — the better view is that other disabilities have the same effect.[66] The crucial criterion should be whether a director can exercise *independent judgment* on behalf of the corporation and its shareholders.

Based on the above, only if corporate action requires shareholder approval or if the directors are interested or not informed, will nondisclosure provide the basis for a claim of deception of a corporation in a derivative action under Section 10(b). Even in such cases, however, the bare allegation of nondisclosure will not suffice to state a federal claim. Another limitation imposed by *Santa Fe* is that the aggrieved shareholder must also allege that, had the corporate malfeasance been disclosed, state court remedies would have been available. In this vein, a question left unanswered after *Santa Fe* is whether the complainant must show not only that a suit in state court could been brought, but also that such a suit would have been won. The courts are split on this issue. While some courts appear to require that the complainant show that he/she would have been awarded relief in the state court action,[67] others require the plaintiff to show a reasonable basis or probability of success.[68] In *Virginia Bankshares*, the Supreme Court raised, yet declined to resolve, the validity of this rationale, coined the "lost state remedy theory."[69]

---

[64] See e.g., *Healey v. Catalyst Recovery Co.*, 626 F.2d 641 (3d Cir. 1980).

[65] See, e.g., *Tyco Labs., Inc. v. Kimball*, 444 F. Supp. 292 (E.D. Pa. 1977).

[66] See generally *Maldonado v. Flynn*, 597 F.2d 789 (2d Cir. 1979).

[67] See, e.g., *Madison Consultants v. Federal Deposit Insurance Corp.*, 710 F.2d 57 (2d Cir. 1983); *Kidwell ex rel. Penfold v. Meikle*, 597 F.2d 1273 (9th Cir. 1979).

[68] See e.g., *Healey v. Catalyst Recovery, Inc.*, 616 F.2d 641 (3d Cir. 1980); *Alabama Farm Bureau Mutual Casualty Co. v. American Fidelity Life Insurance Co.*, 606 F.2d 602 (5th Cir. 1979).

[69] 501 U.S. at 1106-08. Cases decided after *Virginia Bankshares* support the continued validity of the "lost state remedy" theory. See, e.g., *Wilson v. Great American Enterprises, Inc.*, 979 F.2d 924 (2d Cir. 1992); *Howing Company v. Nationwide Corporation*, 972 F.2d 700 (6th Cir. 1992); discussion in Steinberg & Reece, *The Supreme Court, Implied Rights of Action, and Proxy Regulation*, 54 Ohio St. L.J. 67, 101-13 (1993). But see *Isquith v. Caremark International, Inc.*, 136 F.3d 531 (7th Cir. 1998) (expressing disapproval of theory). For further discussion of *Virginia Bankshares*, see § 8.05[B] *infra*.

[4] Summation

Based on *Santa Fe* and its progeny, although unfairness alone is an insufficient basis for a federal claim, there are circumstances, subject to certain limitations, in which unfairness coupled with either a failure to disclose or an affirmative deception remains a firm foundation for a federal claim. Interestingly, the viability of any such Section 10(b) claim will present local law questions akin to those with which the federal judiciary grapples in diversity cases governed by the rule of *Erie Railroad Co. v. Tompkins*.[70] Significantly, however, unlike the *Erie* doctrine, under which federal courts apply state substantive law in order to recognize state created remedies and liabilities, *Santa Fe's* footnote fourteen, as construed by the lower federal courts, conditions the existence of a *federal* right upon the applicable *state* law.[71]

§ 7.06   The Reliance Requirement

[A]   Generally

Proof of reliance normally is required to help prove the causal connection between the defendant's wrongdoing and the complainant's loss. Positive proof of reliance has not been demanded of the plaintiff where unnecessary to show causation. In such instances, upon demonstrating materiality (e.g., of the nondisclosure), the complainant enjoys a presumption of reliance which the defendant can rebut (e.g., by showing that the plaintiff would not have acted differently had he/she known of the nondisclosure). As the Supreme Court stated in *Affiliated Ute Citizens v. United States*:[72]

> Under the circumstances of this case involving primarily a failure to disclose, positive proof of reliance is not a prerequisite to recovery. All that is necessary is that the facts withheld be material in the sense that a reasonable investor [would] have considered them important in the making of this decision. . . . This obligation to disclose and this withholding of a material fact establish the requisite element of causation in fact.[73]

Hence, in cases involving primarily a failure to disclose, the plaintiff's reliance is presumed. Although a number of courts have recognized this presumption in omission as well as "half-truth" cases,[74] others hold to the contrary. The Fifth Circuit, for example, has opined that the presumption of reliance extends only to situations involving "primarily a failure to

---

[70] 304 U.S. 64 (1938).

[71] The *Goldberg*-line of cases has been subject to criticism. See, e.g., *Healey v. Catalyst Recovery Co.*, 616 F.2d 641, 651 (Aldisert, J., dissenting). See generally Ferrara & Steinberg, *A Reappraisal of Santa Fe: Rule 10b-5 and the New Federalism*, 129 U. Pa. L. Rev. 263 (1980).

[72] 406 U.S. 128 (1972).

[73] *Id.* at 153-54.

[74] See, e.g., *Holmes v. Bateson*, 583 F.2d 545, 558 (1st Cir. 1978). See generally Langevoort, *Half-Truths: Protecting Mistaken Inferences by Investors and Others*, 52 Stan. L. Rev. 87 (1999).

disclose, implicating the first or third subparagraph of . . . Rule [10b-5] [and not to cases involving] primarily a misstatement or failure to state a fact necessary to make those statements not misleading [i.e., "half-truth" cases], classified under the second subparagraph of the Rule."[75]

[B] The "Fraud on the Market" Theory

Plaintiffs also may enjoy a presumption of reliance by invoking the "fraud on the market" theory. This theory postulates that investors assume that the market price of a security is determined by the available material information and that no unsuspected fraudulent conduct has affected the price. The use of this theory to apply a rebuttable presumption of reliance received Supreme Court approbation in *Basic, Inc. v. Levinson*.[76]

In *Basic*, the Court quoted from a lower court decision that explained the rationale of the fraud on the market theory in the following terms:

> In face-to-face transactions, the inquiry into an investor's reliance upon information is into the subjective pricing of that information by that investor. With the presence of a market, the market is interposed between seller and buyer and, ideally, transmits information to the investor in the processed form of a market price. Thus the market is performing a substantial part of the valuation process performed by the investor in a face-to-face transaction. The market is acting as the unpaid agent of the investor, informing him that given all the information available to it, the value of the stock is worth the market price.[77]

The Supreme Court's decision in *Basic* recognized the reality of the modern securities markets involving the trading of hundreds of millions of shares on a daily basis and that most ordinary investors do not read corporate reports or press releases. Acknowledging the presence of impersonal trading markets, the Court relied in part on economic theory and empirical studies to support its holding. In so ruling, the Court promoted the use of the class action to redress Section 10(b) violations. If the Court had required positive proof of individualized reliance from each plaintiff, individual issues may have predominated over the common ones, thereby precluding the pursuit of class actions in this context. Hence, the Court's decision looked to policy grounds as well to help ensure that ordinary investors have a viable recourse when they are defrauded in the impersonal trading markets.[78]

Accordingly, the Court concluded:

> An investor who buys or sells stock at the price set by the market does so in reliance on the integrity of that price. Because most

---

[75] *Huddleston v. Herman & MacLean*, 640 F.2d 534, 548 (5th Cir. 1981), *aff'd on other grounds*, 459 U.S. 375 (1983). Accord, *Binder v. Gillespie*, 172 F.3d 649 (9th Cir. 1999).

[76] 485 U.S. 224 (1988). Other aspects of the Basic decision are addressed in § 10.04 *infra*.

[77] 485 U.S. at 244, quoting, *In re LTV Securities Litigation*, 88 F.R.D. 134, 143 (N.D. Tex. 1980).

[78] 485 U.S. at 245-46.

publicly available information is reflected in market price, an investor's reliance on any public material misrepresentations, therefore, may be presumed for purposes of a Rule 10b-5 action.[79]

It should be observed that only six Justices took part in the *Basic* decision, with Chief Justice Rehnquist, Justice Scalia, and Justice Kennedy not participating. In a sharp dissent, Justice White, joined by Justice O'Connor, disagreed with the Court's embracement of the fraud on the market theory, asserting:

> [I]n adopting a "presumption of reliance," the Court *also* assumes that buyers and sellers rely — not just on the market price — but on the *"integrity"* of that price. It is this aspect of the fraud-on-the-market hypothesis which most mystifies me. . . .
>
> Even if securities had some "value" — knowable and distinct from the market price of a stock — investors do not always share the Court's presumption that a stock's price is a "reflection of [this] value." Indeed, "many investors purchase or sell stock because they believe the price *inaccurately* reflects the corporation's worth." If investors really believed that stock prices reflected a stock's "value," many sellers would never sell, and many buyers never buy. . . ."[80]

[1]   Characteristics of an "Efficient" Market

In order for the presumption of the efficient market theory to apply, the subject security must be traded in an *efficient* market. In making this determination, the principal focus is on the market for that particular security and not on the location (such as the New York Stock Exchange or the NASDAQ) where such security trades. Hence, for fraud on the market purposes, the market for each security is distinct, leading to the conclusion that a stock exchange (or over-the-counter market) can be efficient for some securities listed on such exchange (or traded on such OTC market) but not for others.[81]

Therefore, what factors generally comprise an efficient market to support the *Basic* presumption of reliance? In *Freeman v. Laventhol & Horwath*, the Sixth Circuit looked to the following five factors:

(1)   a large weekly trading volume,

(2)   the existence of a significant number of reports by securities analysts,

(3)   the existence of market makers and arbitrageurs in the security,

---

[79] *Id.* at 247.

[80] *Id.* at 256 (White, J., concurring in part and dissenting in part) (emphasis not supplied, citations omitted). See generally Langevoort, *Theories, Assumptions, and Securities Regulation: Market Efficiency Revisited*, 140 U. Pa. L. Rev. 851 (1992); Stout, *The Unimportance of Being Efficient: An Economic Analysis of Stock Market Pricing and Securities Regulation*, 87 Mich. L. Rev. 613 (1988); Wang, *Some Arguments That the Stock Market is Not Efficient*, 19 U.C. Davis L. Rev. 341 (1986).

[81] See *Harman v. Lyphomed, Inc.*, 122 F.R.D. 522, 525-26 (N.D. Ill. 1988); A. Bromberg & L. Lowenfels, *supra* note 1, at § 8.6.

(4)   the eligibility of the company to file an S-3 Registration Statement, and

(5)   a history of immediate movement of the stock price as the result of unexpected corporate events or financial releases.[82]

The foregoing five factors serve as indicia that a company's stock trades in an efficient market. While the satisfaction of all five factors normally should be conclusive, an efficient market nonetheless may be found to exist even if a particular factor may be absent (for example, where the subject stock barely missed or recently failed to satisfy the qualifications for Form S-3 registrants).[83]

[2]   Rebutting the Fraud on the Market Presumption of Reliance

In *Basic*, both the majority and the dissent observed that application of the fraud on the market theory creates a *rebuttable* presumption of reliance. In practice, this presumption generally has been rebutted when the disclosure deficiencies were corrected in the market by extensive media coverage. In such cases, because the press coverage credibly made available to the market accurate information, the otherwise actionable misstatement (or omission) was rendered immaterial. The defendants' task in making this showing is difficult. To rebut the *Basic* presumption of reliance in this context, therefore, it must be shown that "any material information which [the defendants] fail[ed] to disclose must [have been] transmitted to the public with a degree of intensity and credibility sufficient to effectively counterbalance any misleading impression created by the [defendants] . . . ."[84]

[C]   The "Fraud to Enter the Market" Theory

A more expansive version of the fraud-on-the-market theory, also called the "fraud to enter the market" theory, applies this doctrine to the offering context where no active trading market exists for the issuer's stock. The leading case is *Shores v. Sklar*[85] in which the Fifth Circuit sitting en banc adopted the theory, with ten judges dissenting. The Supreme Court has yet to rule on the theory's validity in this context.

In *Shores*, the plaintiff purchased bonds without reading the offering circular. He alleged in a Section 10(b) cause of action that the defendants had perpetrated a fraudulent scheme on the investment community by

---

[82] 915 F.2d 193, 199 (6th Cir. 1990).

[83] See *Cammer v. Bloom*, 711 F. Supp. 1264, 1287 (D.N.J. 1989); Bromberg & Lowenfels, *supra* note 1, at § 8.6. See generally Robinson, *Fraud-on-the-Market Theory and Thinly-Traded Securities Under Rule 10b-5: How Does a Court Decide if a Stock Market is Efficient?*, 25 Wake Forest L. Rev. 223 (1990).

[84] *In re Apple Computer Securities Litigation*, 886 F.2d 1109, 1116 (9th Cir. 1988). See *Raab v. General Physics Corporation*, 4 F.3d 286, 289 (4th Cir. 1993); *Wielgos v. Commonwealth Edison Co.*, 892 F.2d 509, 516 (7th Cir. 1989).

[85] 647 F.2d 462 (5th Cir. 1981) (en banc), *cert. denied*, 459 U.S. 1102 (1983).

bringing unmarketable securities into the open market. Invoking the fraud to enter the market theory, the court held that an investor is entitled to rely on the integrity of the market to the extent that the securities offered for sale are entitled to be in the marketplace. To recover under this theory, the plaintiff must establish that the bonds would never have been issued or marketed. Proof that the bonds would have been offered at a lower price is not sufficient. [86] Thus, "the fraudulent scheme [must be] so pervasive that without it the issuer would not have issued, the dealer could not have dealt in, and the buyer could not have bought [the securities], because they would not have been offered at any price." [87] As subsequently construed by the Fifth Circuit, securities are deemed not entitled to be marketed, "only where the promoters knew the enterprise itself was patently worthless." [88]

While the Fifth Circuit in *Shores* and its progeny examined how the market would have likely responded to the securities being offered absent the fraud, other courts have focused on the integrity of the regulatory process. For example, the Ninth Circuit held that reliance may be presumed if the investor "relie[d], at least indirectly, on the integrity of the regulatory process and the truth of any representations made to the appropriate agencies and the investors at the time of the original issue." [89]

The Seventh Circuit in *Eckstein v. Balcor Film Investors* [90] rejected the *Shores* "fraud to enter the market" theory. The court reasoned:

> *Shores* held that an investor may maintain an action under Section 10(b) by establishing that the fraud permitted the securities to exist in the market — that but for the fraud the securities would have been "unmarketable" — and that the investor relied on their existence. [We reject the *Shores* rationale.] . . . The existence of a security does not depend on, or warrant, the adequacy of disclosure. Many a security is on the market even though the issuer or some third party made incomplete disclosures. Federal securities law does not include "merit regulation." Full disclosure of adverse information may lower the price, but it does not exclude the security from the market. Securities of bankrupt corporations trade freely; some markets specialize in penny stocks. Thus the linchpin of *Shores* — that disclosing bad information keeps securities off the market, entitling investors to rely on the presence of the securities just as they would rely on statements in a prospectus — is simply false. [91]

---

[86] *Id.* at 469-71.

[87] *Id.* at 464 n.2. See A. Bromberg, & L. Lowenfels, *supra* note 1, at § 8.6.

[88] *Abell v. Potomac Insurance Company*, 858 F.2d 1104, 1121-22 (5th Cir. 1988), *vacated on other grounds*, 492 U.S. 914 (1988).

[89] *Arthur Young & Co. v. United States District Court*, 549 F.2d 686, 695 (9th Cir. 1977). The Tenth Circuit has adopted a similar approach. See *T.J. Raney & Sons, Inc., v. Fort Cobb, Okla. Irrigation Fuel Authority*, 717 F.2d 1330, 1332 (10th Cir. 1983).

[90] 8 F.3d 1121 (7th Cir. 1993).

[91] *Id.* at 1130-1131.

After rejecting the *Shores* rationale, the Seventh Circuit opted for a different approach. In *Eckstein*, the limited partnership offering was subject to a minimum sale requirement. To prevail on the issue of reliance, the Seventh Circuit required that plaintiffs prove that, absent the fraud, the limited partnership would not have met the minimum sale requirement.[92]

[D] Plaintiff Due Diligence

The plaintiff "due diligence" requirement has been equated by a number of courts with the requirement of justifiable reliance. The Tenth Circuit, upon reviewing pertinent case law, indicated that the following factors are relevant in determining whether the plaintiff's reliance was justifiable:

> (1) the sophistication and expertise of the plaintiff in financial and securities matters; (2) the existence of long standing business or personal relationships; (3) access to the relevant information; (4) the existence of a fiduciary relationship; (5) concealment of the fraud; (6) the opportunity to detect the fraud; (7) whether the plaintiff initiated the stock transaction or sought to expedite the transaction; and (8) the generality or specificity of the misrepresentations.[93]

Two policy rationales for the plaintiff due diligence requirement are: "First, general principles of equity suggest that only those who have pursued their own interests with care and good faith should qualify for the judicially created private [Rule] 10b-5 remedies. Second, by requiring plaintiffs to invest carefully, the court promotes the anti-fraud policies of the Acts and engenders stability in the markets."[94]

In light of the Supreme Court's decision in *Hochfelder* requiring a plaintiff to prove the defendant's scienter in order to recover under Section 10(b),[95] courts have altered the plaintiff's due diligence burden. Rather than mandating that the plaintiff establish due care, these courts now require that such plaintiff's burden simply is to negate that he/she acted recklessly when engaging in the securities transaction.[96]

Two interesting issues have surfaced in the plaintiff due diligence setting. The first issue, called the "bespeaks caution" doctrine (which has been

---

[92] *Id.* at 1131. See generally Black, *The Strange Case of Fraud on the Market: A Label in Search of a Theory*, 52 Albany L. Rev. 923 (1988); Carney, *The Limits of the Fraud on the Market Theory*, 44 Bus. Law. 1259 (1989); Herzog, *Fraud Created the Market: An Unwise and Unwarranted Extension of Section 10(b) and Rule 10b-5*, 63 Geo. Wash. L. Rev. 359 (1995); Newkirk, *Sufficient Efficiency: Fraud on the Market in the Initial Public Offering Context*, 58 U. Chi. L. Rev. 1393 (1991).

[93] *Zobrist v. Coal-X, Inc.*, 708 F.2d 1511, 1516 (10th Cir. 1983). This standard has been applied by many courts. See, e.g., *Myers v. Finkle*, 950 F.2d 165 (4th Cir. 1991).

[94] *Dupuy v. Dupuy*, 551 F.2d 1005, 1014 (5th Cir. 1977).

[95] See § 7.03[A] *supra*.

[96] *Mallis v. Bankers Trust Co.*, 615 F.2d 68, 79 (2d Cir. 1980). See *Landry v. All American Assurance Co.*, 688 F.2d 381, 392-93 (5th Cir. 1982); Gabaldon, *Unclean Hands and Self-Inflicted Wounds: The Significance of Plaintiff Conduct in Actions for Misrepresentation Under Rule 10b-5*, 71 Minn. L. Rev. 317 (1986); Sachs, *The Relevance of Tort Law Doctrines to Rule 10b-5: Should Careless Plaintiffs Be Denied Recovery?*, 71 Cornell L. Rev. 96 (1985).

codified by Congress), concerns whether disclosure of the pertinent risk factors (and other cautionary statements) in the written offering documents will render the plaintiff's reliance on certain forward-looking or "soft" statements contained in other portions of such offering materials unjustified. The second issue is whether a plaintiff justifiably relies on allegedly false oral statements when the written offering documents are accurate.

[1] The "Bespeaks Caution" Doctrine

The "bespeaks caution" doctrine may be viewed from both "materiality" and "reliance" perspectives. The doctrine provides that "where an offering statement, such as a prospectus, accompanies statements of future forecasts, projections and expectations with adequate cautionary language, those statements are not actionable as securities fraud."[97] Hence, under the "bespeaks caution" doctrine, cautionary statements make reliance on the projections or other soft information unreasonable and renders the statements, when read in conjunction with the cautionary language, immaterial.[98] The Private Securities Litigation Reform Act of 1995 codifies the "bespeaks caution" doctrine. This doctrine is addressed more fully in Chapter 10 (see § 10.05[D]).

[2] Reliance on Oral Statements Inconsistent with Written Offering Materials

Another interesting issue that surfaces in securities litigation is whether a plaintiff justifiably relies on allegedly false or misleading oral statements when the written offering documents (such as a prospectus or private placement memorandum) are accurate. In most jurisdictions, the fact that the written offering documents are accurate is not dispositive. When analyzing this issue, courts have focused on the reliance and materiality components.[99]

With respect to the issue of reliance (also referred to in this setting as plaintiff due diligence or justifiable reliance), many courts embrace the eight-factor test set forth above.[100] In adhering to this standard, "no single factor is determinative; all relevant factors must be considered and balanced to determine whether reliance was justified."[101] Nonetheless, as applied by a number of courts, a key determinant is whether there exists a fiduciary relationship between the defendant and plaintiff.[102] Some

---

[97] *In re Donald J. Trump Casinos Securities Litigation*, 793 F. Supp. 543, 544 (D.N.J. 1992), *aff'd*, 7 F.3d 357 (3d Cir. 1993).

[98] See, e.g., *Rubinstein v. Collins*, 20 F.3d 160, 167 (5th Cir. 1994). See generally O'Hare, *Good Faith and the Bespeaks Caution Doctrine: It's Not Just a State of Mind*, 58 U. Pitt. L. Rev. 619 (1997).

[99] See, e.g., *Myers v. Finkle*, 950 F.2d 165 (4th Cir. 1991).

[100] See *supra* note 93 and accompanying text.

[101] *Zobrist v. Coal-X, Inc.*, 709 F.2d 1511, 1516-17 (10th Cir. 1983).

[102] See, e.g., *Brown v. E.F. Hutton Group, Inc.*, 991 F.2d 1020, 1031-33 (2d Cir. 1993).

courts also give great weight to the level of the plaintiff's financial sophistication.[103]

That the plaintiff failed to read the offering document, allegedly because of the document's complexity, is irrelevant. In other words, provided that the offering document is timely transmitted and contains sufficient disclosure, the contents of such offering document are imputed to the investor even if not read by the investor.[104] Nonetheless, if key disclosures (such as risk factors) are buried in the offering document or indigestible, a different result may well follow.[105]

Some courts, particularly the Seventh Circuit, adhere to a more restrictive approach based on a "materiality" analysis. Stated generally, under this interpretation, (1) the written word trumps the oral; and (2) when statements in promotional sales materials and the formal written offering document conflict, the offering document "wins."[106] Hence, so long as the written words are clear and complete, "written words govern oral ones in order to reward truthful disclosures and facilitate accurate assessment of risk."[107] Under this analysis, an oral statement that contradicts disclosures in the written offering is deemed immaterial (because such oral statement does not significantly affect the mix of information on which the investor acts).[108]

§ 7.07 Cumulative Remedies

Under a cumulative interpretation of the securities laws, a party may invoke a remedy even though another statute may provide another remedy for the same conduct. In *Herman & MacLean v. Huddleston*,[109] the Supreme Court adopted a cumulative construction to Section 10(b), thereby recognizing an implied right of action for damages under Section 10(b) despite the apparent availability of an express cause of action under Section 11 of the 1933 Act. The Court reasoned that, unlike Section 11, Section 10(b) imposes a heavier burden on the plaintiff by mandating that the defendant's scienter be proven in order to recover. Moreover, while Section 11 applies solely in the registered offering context, Section 10(b) is a "catch-all" antifraud provision designed to reach manipulative or deceptive practices in connection with the purchase or sale of any security, whether traded in the primary or secondary markets.[110]

---

[103] See, e.g., *Myers v. Finkle*, 950 F.2d 165, 165-67 (4th Cir. 1991). See generally Fletcher, *Sophisticated Investors Under the Federal Securities Laws*, 1988 Duke L.J. 1081.

[104] 950 F.2d at 167 (stating that "[i]nvestors are charged with constructive knowledge of the risks and warnings contained in the private placement memoranda").

[105] See, e.g., *Kennedy v. Tallant*, 710 F.2d 711, 720 (11th Cir. 1983).

[106] See, e.g., *Eckstein v. Balcor Film Investors*, 8 F.3d 1121, 1131-32 (7th Cir. 1993); *Acme Propane, Inc. v. Tenexco, Inc.*, 844 F.2d 1317, 1325 (7th Cir. 1988).

[107] 844 F.2d at 1325.

[108] See, e.g., *Teamsters Local 282 Pension Trust Fund v. Angelos*, 762 F.2d 522, 530 (7th Cir. 1985). See *Flamm v. Eberstadt*, 814 F.2d 1169, 1173 (7th Cir. 1983); cases cited note 106 *supra*.

[109] 459 U.S. 375 (1983).

[110] *Id.* at 380-84.

Note that the Supreme Court's subsequent decision in *Lampf*, adopting a one year/three year statute of limitations for Section 10(b) claims, minimizes the importance of *Huddleston*. Prior to *Lampf*, federal courts generally "borrowed" the limitations period for the most analogous state statute to determine the applicable statute of limitations for the Section 10(b) claims. This "borrowing" often led to a longer statute of limitations under Section 10(b) than the one year/three year period provided by Section 13 of the Securities Act for Section 11 and 12(a)(2) claims. Due to *Lampf*, this no longer is the situation: the statute of limitations now basically is the same for all of the foregoing claims (namely, for claims under Sections 11 and 12(a)(2) of the 1933 Act and Section 10(b) of the 1934 Act).[111]

Also, although the Court in *Huddleston* did not directly hold, its language strongly suggests that a cumulative approach between Section 10(b) and other express rights of action, such as Section 12(a)(2) of the Securities Act and Section 18(a) of the Exchange Act is appropriate where the express remedy does not require the plaintiff to prove scienter. In other words, the various procedural restrictions that apply in actions invoking the express remedies (which restrictions are absent in suits brought under Section 10(b)) are counterbalanced by Section 10(b)'s scienter requirement. Based in large part on this rationale, the lower courts adhere to a cumulative approach where the express remedy invoked is Section 11 or 12(a)(2) of the Securities Act or Section 18(a) of the Exchange Act.[112]

After *Lampf*, *Huddleston's* significance in the Section 12(2)/Section 10(b) setting is lessened. Like Section 11, Section 12(a)(2) claims are easier to prove than Section 10(b) claims.[113] Generally, prior to *Lampf*, plaintiffs would seek to bring a Section 10(b) action in lieu of a Section 11 or 12(a)(2) claim only when the statute of limitations had run for the 1933 Act claims. After *Lampf*, however, Section 10(b) now has the same statute of limitations as Sections 11 and 12(a)(2). Hence, if the Section 11 or 12(a)(2) claim is time-barred, the same will hold true for the Section 10(b) claim.[114]

Huddleston retains far more vitality with respect to 1934 Act Section 18(a) claims. Section 18(a) provides an express right of action for damages (subject to a good faith defense) when an investor purchases or sells a security in reliance upon a materially false or misleading statement that is contained in a document filed with the SEC pursuant to the Exchange Act, where such statement affects the price of the security. Because of Section 18(a)'s strict reliance and causation requirements, a suit based solely on Section 18(a) evidently has never succeeded. Hence, although the limitations periods for Section 10(b) and Section 18(a) claims are virtually identical, the Section 10(b) action is the preferred route.[115]

---

[111] Lampf is discussed in § 7.08 *infra*.

[112] See, e.g., *Berger v. Bishop Investment Corp.*, 695 F.2d 302 (8th Cir. 1982); *Wachovia Bank & Trust Co. v. National Student Marketing Corp.*, 650 F.2d 342 (D.C. Cir. 1980); *Ross v. A.H. Robins, Co.*, 607 F.2d 545 (2d Cir. 1979).

[113] See §§ 6.02, 6.09 *supra*.

[114] For discussion on Lampf, see § 7.08 *infra*.

[115] See L. Loss & J. Seligman, Securities Regulation 4296-4300 (3d ed. 1992).

A more difficult issue is presented when a cumulative approach is sought to be invoked between Section 10(b) and Section 9 of the Exchange Act. Under Section 9 (which provides a private remedy for purchasers and sellers who have been victimized by stock manipulation), the plaintiff, in order to recover, must prove scienter, reliance, causation, and damages. Moreover, plaintiffs suing under Section 9 are subject to rigorous procedural limitations. As one court has observed: "Section 9(e) contains a relatively short statute of limitations, permits the court to require security for costs, limits damages to losses sustained by reason of the unlawful price manipulation, provides for contribution by persons not joined as defendants in the original action, and permits the court to assess attorneys' fees against either party."[116] Hence, due to the breadth of the Section 9 requirements, plaintiffs bringing suit under Section 10(b) are subject to no additional burdens. Indeed, when contrasted with the Section 9 express remedy, the Section 10(b) right of action is more attractive in many respects and is not less attractive in any respect.[117]

Nonetheless, cogent reasons exist for recognizing a cumulative remedy in this context. Perhaps the most persuasive is that an exclusive approach precluding a Section 10(b) right of action where a Section 9 express remedy is available would afford less protection to investors who trade on a national securities exchange than to those who trade in the over-the-counter market. It is beyond dispute that Section 9 applies by its terms only to transactions on a national securities exchange. To fill this vacuum, courts have uniformly held that such manipulative practices that occur in the over-the-counter market may be redressed by private claimants under Section 10(b).[118] Because these claimants are not saddled with the limitations of Section 9, they may successfully seek redress under Section 10(b) in situations in which injured investors who trade on a national securities exchange under an exclusive construction of remedies would be denied recovery.

Such a result is not only misplaced but is contrary to congressional intent. The Securities Acts Amendments of 1964 were the ultimate result of a congressionally-mandated special study conducted by the Securities and Exchange Commission.[119] The study recommended, inter alia, that Congress strengthen over-the-counter regulation. Congress followed this recommendation in order to provide, as much as practicable, equality of regulation between the national securities exchange and over-the-counter markets. At no time, however, did Congress intend to create greater rights on behalf of over-the-counter investors as compared to those given to investors who trade in stock exchange listed securities.

---

[116] *Wolgin v. Magic Marker Corp.*, 82 F.R.D. 168, 180 (E.D. Pa. 1979).

[117] See generally *Chemetron Corp. v. Business Funds, Inc.*, 718 F.2d 725 (5th Cir. 1983), 682 F.2d 1149 (5th Cir. 1982).

[118] See, e.g., *Wachovia Bank & Trust Co. v. National Student Marketing Co.*, 650 F.2d 342 (D.C. Cir. 1980).

[119] Report of Special Study of Securities Markets of the Securities and Exchange Commission, H.R. Doc. No. 95, 88th Cong., 1st Sess. (1963).

Thus, Congress' approach is sound and firmly rooted in the reality of the operations of the securities markets. In contrast, an exclusive construction of remedies fragmentizes the operational components of the securities markets and ignores that the markets operate as a unified whole where those desiring to buy or sell may do so with confidence. Denying private parties the use of Section 10(b) with respect to manipulative schemes in listed securities would insulate from monetary liability practices repugnant to the notions of honesty and fairness. Such a construction goes far toward undermining the very interests the securities laws were designed to promote.[120]

§ 7.08   Statute of Limitations

Being an implied right of action, Section 10(b) does not provide by its terms for a statute of limitations. In *Lampf, Pleva, Lipkind, Prupis & Petigrow v. Gilbertson*,[121] the Supreme Court set forth the applicable statute of limitations for private actions under Section 10(b) of the Exchange Act. Prior to *Lampf*, a majority of the appellate courts opted for the relevant state law statute that was most analogous to Section 10(b) and Rule 10b-5. Under this framework, the federal courts selected either the appropriate state's limitations period for common law fraud or the limitations period for securities fraud under the applicable blue sky statute.[122] Irrespective of which particular state statute was applied, the result was a lack of predictability, uniformity and certainty, even within individual federal circuits.[123]

In *Lampf*, the Supreme Court chose a one-year after discovery within a three-year period of repose scheme (one year/three year limitations period), selecting Section 9(e) of the Exchange Act as the language to govern Section 10(b) actions. Significantly, the Court held that the doctrine of equitable tolling was unavailable under Section 10(b).[124] Under this principle, the statute of limitations generally is tolled during the time in which the victim of a fraud remains in ignorance of it through no lack of diligence on his/her part. Prior to *Lampf*, this doctrine was applied with regularity by the federal courts to toll the running of the Section 10(b) statute of limitations.[125]

---

[120] See Steinberg, *The Propriety and Scope of Cumulative Remedies Under the Federal Securities Laws*, 67 Cornell L. Rev. 557 (1982). See also, Siegel, *Interplay Between the Implied Remedy Under Section 10(b) and the Express Causes of Action of the Federal Securities Laws*, 62 B.U. L. Rev. 385 (1982).

[121] 501 U.S. 350 (1991).

[122] Compare *Nesbit v. McNeil*, 896 F.2d 380 (9th Cir. 1990) (applying state fraud statute), with *O'Hara v. Krovens*, 625 F.2d 15 (4th Cir. 1980) (applying state securities law statute for fraud). See Committee on Federal Regulation of Securities, *Report of the Task Force on Statute of Limitations for Implied Actions*, 41 Bus. Law. 645 (1986).

[123] Compare *Nesbit v. McNeil*, 896 F.2d 380, 384 (9th Cir. 1990) (applying Oregon two-year statute) with *Reeves v. Teuscher*, 881 F.2d 1495, 1501 (9th Cir. 1989) (applying Washington three-year statute).

Prior to *Lampf*, a minority approach applied a uniform limitations period for Section 10(b) claims. See, e.g., *Cere Partners v. GEL Associates*, 918 F.2d 349 (2d Cir. 1990).

[124] 501 U.S. at 363.

[125] See, e.g., *Sumner v. Land & Leisure, Inc.*, 664 F.2d 965, 968 (5th Cir. 1981).

The Supreme Court in *Lampf* held that the one-year/three-year structure is fundamentally incompatible with the equitable tolling doctrine. The Court pointed out that the one year period begins after the plaintiff discovered the facts constituting the violation, thereby making tolling unnecessary. With respect to the three year limit, the Court reasoned that this period is one of repose and therefore is inconsistent with tolling. Hence, the Court concluded that Congress intended that the three year limitation serve as the final cutoff, thereby precluding equitable tolling during this period.[126]

In selecting a one year/three year limitations period, the *Lampf* Court observed that the Exchange Act provides for a number of express remedies, and with one exception, each employs some type of one year/three year framework. The Court also drew support from the Securities Act which likewise adopts the one year/three year structure.[127] Hence, the Court reasoned: "We can imagine no clearer indication of how Congress would have balanced the policy considerations implicit in any limitations provision than the balance struck by the same Congress in limiting similar and related protections."[128]

Applying its decision retroactively, the *Lampf* Court held that the plaintiffs' claims were time-barred, having been instituted more than three years after the alleged Section 10(b) violations.[129] In reaction to the perceived harshness of *Lampf*'s retroactive application, Congress enacted Section 27A of the Exchange Act to overrule such application.[130] This effort proved futile. In *Plaut v. Spendthrift Farm, Inc.*, the Supreme Court

---

[126] See 501 U.S. at 363-64.

[127] The one exception is Section 16(b) of the Exchange Act, which contains a two-year limitations period to remedy short-swing trading abuse (discussed in § 11.09 *infra*). Because Section 16(b) "differs in focus" from Section 10(b), the Court did "not find [it] to be an appropriate source to borrow a limitations period here." 501 U.S. at 360 n. 5. With respect to the Securities Act, the Court pointed out that "Congress . . . adopt[ed] the 1 and 3 year structure for each cause of action contained therein." *Id.*

[128] 501 U.S. at 359. The *Lampf* Court observed that, derived from the Rules of Decision Act (28 U.S.C. § 1652), it is customary to borrow an appropriate state statute of limitation whenever Congress has declined to enact such a statute for a federal cause of action. However, the Court concluded that, when a cause of action is implied rather than express and the statute (here the Exchange Act) from which the action is implied also contains an express cause of action having its own limitations period, a court should look to the statute of origin to determine the appropriate limitations period. The Court did not completely abrogate the tradition of borrowing analogous state limitations periods, but rather restricted its future application, thus: "When the statute of origin contains comparable express remedial provisions, the inquiry usually should be at an end. Only where no analogous counterpart is available should a court then proceed to apply state-borrowing principles." *Id.*

[129] *Id.* at 364, relying on, *James B. Bean Distilling Co. v. Georgia*, 502 U.S. 529, 544 (1991) (stating that "when the Court has applied a rule of law to the litigants in one case it must do so with respect to all others not barred by procedural requirements or res judicata").

[130] Generally, pursuant to Section 27A, actions filed before June 22, 1991, the date that *Lampf* was handed down, were governed by the limitations period and principles of retroactivity existing in the circuit of filing as the law existed on June 19, 1991.

declared Section 27A to be unconstitutional because the statute "effects a clear violation of the separation-of-powers principle."[131]

After *Lampf*, it was asserted that, in order for the one-year period to begin running under Section 10(b)'s limitations period, the plaintiff must have actual (rather than constructive) knowledge of the facts underlying the alleged violation. Although *Lampf* did not resolve this issue, the lower courts after *Lampf* overwhelmingly have rejected this approach. Accordingly, the subject plaintiff must initiate his/her Section 10(b) right of action within one year after the facts constituting the violation were known or should have been known to the plaintiff and in no event more than three years after the alleged violation.[132] This one year/three year statute of limitations also has been applied to other implied rights of action under the Exchange Act.[133]

§ 7.09 Measure of Damages

Much of the discussion that follows applies to damages under the securities laws in general. Because the proper measure of damages most often arises in Section 10(b) litigation, the subject will be treated here. For damages in insider trading cases, Chapter 11 should be consulted.

Section 28(a) of the Exchange Act has been construed by the courts to prohibit recovery of punitive, as opposed to compensatory damages, and to prevent double recovery by those who assert both state and federal claims

---

[131] 516 U.S. 211, 225 (1995). The Court stated:

> We think that [Section] 27A(b) offends a postulate of Article III . . . deeply rooted in our law . . . . Article III establishes a "judicial department" with the "province and duty . . . to say what the law is" in particular cases and controversies. *Marbury v. Madison*, 1 Cranch 137, 177 (1803). The record of history shows that the Framers crafted this charter of the judicial department with an expressed understanding that it gives the Federal Judiciary the power, not merely to rule on cases, but to decide them, subject to review only by superior courts in the Article III hierarchy — with an understanding, in short, that "a judgment conclusively resolves the case" because "a 'judicial Power' is one to render dispositive judgments." . . . By retroactively commanding the federal courts to reopen final judgments, Congress has violated this fundamental principle.

Id. at 218-19. See Johnson, *Bridging the Gap: Some Thoughts About Interstitial Lawmaking and the Federal Securities Laws*, 48 Wash. & Lee L. Rev. 879 (1991); Polden, *Drawing the Appropriate Statute of Limitations in Implied Causes of Action Under Rule 10b-5: A General Framework of Familiar Legal Principles*, 40 Drake L. Rev. 221 (1991).

[132] See, e.g., *Tregenza v. Great American Communications Co.*, 12 F.3d 717 (7th Cir. 1993); *Dodds v. Cigna Securities, Inc.*, 12 F.3d 346 (2d Cir. 1993). See also, *Berry v. Valence Technology, Inc.*, 175 F.3d 699 (9th Cir. 1999) (stating that regardless whether inquiry notice or actual discovery is the correct standard, "the Forbes article would not have led a reasonable investor to investigate the possibility of fraud").

But see Lowenfels & Bromberg, *SEC Rule 10b-5 and Its New Statute of Limitations: The Circuits Defy the Supreme Court*, 51 Bus. Law. 309 (1996) (asserting that constructive notice is the correct standard to commence the one-year period for § 10(b) limitations purposes).

[133] See, e.g., *Westinghouse Electric Corp. v. Franklin*, 993 F.2d 349 (3d Cir. 1993) (applying Lampf to § 14(a) claim).

that arise out of the same conduct.[134] The measures of compensatory damages adopted by the courts primarily include the out-of-pocket measure[135] and, in some circumstances, the rescissionary[136] and benefit-of-the-bargain measures.[137] In certain contexts, other measures of damages have been applied.[138] As a general proposition, however, "[t]he customary measure of damages in a Rule 10b-5 case is the out-of-pocket loss."[139]

Nonetheless, where the amount of damages can be determined with reasonable certainty, courts may apply the benefit-of-the-bargain measure, particularly if such application is necessary to prevent unjust enrichment.[140] A number of courts, however, have refused to apply this measure in cases involving defrauded purchasers due to the asserted speculative nature of the damages that would otherwise be awarded.[141]

The Private Securities Litigation Reform Act of 1995 added a new Section 21D(e) to the Exchange Act. In general, this provision places a limitation on damages in 1934 Act actions where the plaintiff attempts to establish such damages by reference to the market price of a security. In this context, the award of damages is the difference between the purchase or sale price paid or received by the plaintiff, as applicable, and the mean trading price of the security during the 90-day period beginning on the date on which the information correcting the misstatement or omission that is the basis for the action is disseminated to the market. For these purposes, the "mean trading price" of such security is the average of the daily trading price of such security, determined as of the close of the market each day during the 90-day period referred to above.

---

[134] See e.g., *Affiliated Ute Citizens v. United States*, 406 U.S. 128, 155 (1972); *Osofsky v. Zipf*, 645 F.2d 107, 111 (2d Cir. 1981); *Gould v. American-Hawaiian Steamship Co.*, 535 F.2d 761, 781 (3d Cir. 1976).

[135] See, e.g., *Estate Counseling Service, Inc. v. Merrill Lynch, Pierce, Fenner & Smith, Inc.*, 303 F.2d 527, 533 (10th Cir. 1962) (defining the out-of-pocket measure as "the difference between the contract price, or the price paid, and the real or actual value at the date of the sale, together with such outlays as are attributable to the defendant's conduct").

[136] See, e.g., *Blackie v. Barrack*, 524 F.2d 891, 909 (9th Cir. 1975). See also, *Randall v. Loftsgaarden*, 478 U.S. 647 (1986).

[137] See, e.g., *Osofsky v. Zipf*, 645 F.2d 107, 111-15 (3d Cir. 1981).

[138] See, e.g., *Chasins v. Smith Barney & Co.*, 428 F.2d 1167, 1173 (2d Cir. 1970) (awarding a defrauded buyer the value of the consideration paid for the security less the sale price of the security prior to plaintiff's awareness of the misconduct). For the disgorgement measure, see *infra* note 142 and accompanying text.

[139] *Hackbart v. Holmes*, 675 F.2d 1114, 1121 (10th Cir. 1982).

[140] *Id.* at 1122. See *Madigan, Inc. v. Goodman*, 498 F.2d 233, 239 (7th Cir. 1974).

[141] See e.g., *Barrows v. Forest Laboratories, Inc.*, 742 F.2d 54 (2d Cir. 1984). See generally Alexander, *Rethinking Damages in Securities Class Actions*, 48 Stan. L. Rev. 1487 (1996); Dickey & Mays, *Effect on Rule 10b-5 Damages of the 1995 Private Securities Litigation Reform Act: A Forward-Looking Assessment*, 51 Bus. Law. 1203 (1996); Easterbrook & Fischel, *Optimal Damages in Securities Cases*, 52 U. Chicago L. Rev. 611 (1985); Thompson, *Simplicity and Certainty in the Measure of Recovery Under Rule 10b-5*, 51 Bus. Law. 1177 (1996); Thompson, *The Measure of Recovery Under Rule 10b-5: A Restitution Alternative to Tort Damages*, 37 Vand. L. Rev. 349 (1984); Comment, *The Measure of Damages Under Section 10(b) and Rule 10b-5*, 46 Md. L. Rev. 1266 (1987).

In sum, the key measures of damages may be set forth as follows:

The benefit-of-the-bargain measure is generally understood as the difference between the represented value of the security purchased or sold and the fair value of the security on the date of the trade. Out-of-pocket relief . . . represents "the difference between the fair value of all that the [plaintiff] received and the fair value of what he would have received had there been no fraudulent conduct." . . . Disgorgement . . . returns to the plaintiff the amount of the defendant's unjust enrichment. Under the disgorgement theory, the plaintiff recovers the defendant's profit resulting from the fraud, rather than the plaintiff's losses. Finally, rescission, by contrast, is the judicial act of undoing a transaction, restor-[ing] each party to its pre-transaction condition.[142]

§ 7.10 *In Pari Delicto* Defense

In the past, considerable debate was generated regarding the propriety of the *in pari delicto* defense in securities litigation.[143] In the *Bateman Eichler* case,[144] the Supreme Court limited the availability of the defense in a Section 10(b) civil damages action where corporate insiders and a broker allegedly conveyed false "inside" information. In so doing, the Court applied a two-part test to ascertain whether the *in pari delicto* defense should be permitted. First, it looked to the relative culpability of the parties to the action. Second, the Court examined public policy considerations. Hence, a Section 10(b) action for damages may be barred on the grounds of the plaintiff's own culpability only where (1) as a direct result of his own actions, the plaintiff bears at least substantially equal responsibility for the violations he seeks to redress, and (2) preclusion of suit would not significantly interfere with the effective enforcement of the securities laws and protection of the investing public.[145]

Turning to the first prong, the *Bateman Eichler* Court found that the plaintiff "tippees" were less blameworthy than the defendant "tippers." As the Court stated, "[i]n the context of insider trading, we do not believe that a person whose liability is solely derivative can be said to be as culpable as one whose breach of duty gave rise to that liability in the first place."[146]

Regarding the second prong, the Court asserted that permitting private suits for damages in this context would enhance the enforcement of the securities laws and would serve as a deterrent to the perpetration of insider trading. Moreover, by bringing such an action and exposing oneself to civil and criminal penalties, a tippee would not enjoy a "heads-I-win,

---

[142] Kaufman, *No Foul, No Harm: The Real Measure of Damages Under Rule 10b-5*, 39 Cath. U. L. Rev. 29, 31 (1989). See M. Kaufman, Securities Litigation: Damages (1989); authorities cited note 141 *supra*.

[143] See e.g., Comment, *Rule 10b-5: The In Pari Delicto and Unclean Hands Defenses*, 58 Calif. L. Rev. 1149 (1970).

[144] *Bateman Eichler, Hill Richards, Inc. v. Berner*, 472 U.S. 299 (1985).

[145] *Id.* at 310-11.

[146] *Id.* at 313, citing, *Dirks v. SEC*, 463 U.S. 646 (1983).

tails-you-lose" scenario. Accordingly, public policy would be promoted by allowing such actions.[147]

After *Bateman Eichler*, it was uncertain whether the Court's analysis therein applied to the securities laws in general. The Court answered this question affirmatively in an action involving Section 12(1) [now 12(a)(1)] of the Securities Act, *Pinter v. Dahl*.[148] In *Pinter*, the Court held that the *Bateman Eichler* standard "provides the appropriate test for allowance of the *in pari delicto* defense in a private action under any of the federal securities laws."[149] The Court reasoned that, irrespective of whether the substantive statute imposes liability for willful or negligent misconduct or even is one of strict liability (such as Section 12(a)(1)), there may be occasions where the objective of deterring unlawful conduct is served better by precluding suit rather than by allowing recovery.[150]

Applying the *Bateman Eichler* standard to the Section 12(1) litigation at bar, the *Pinter* Court's analysis indicates that the *in pari delicto* defense will rarely be successful in this context. According to the Court, the defense can be used only when the plaintiff's role in the offer or sale of the securities is more that of a promoter than an investor. Whether a plaintiff primarily is an investor or a promoter depends on several factors, such as "the extent of the plaintiff's financial involvement compared to that of third parties solicited by the plaintiff, the incidental nature of the plaintiff's promotional activities, the benefits received by the plaintiff from his promotional activities, and the extent of the plaintiff's involvement in the planning stages of the offering."[151]

In the Section 12(a)(1) setting, where the plaintiff is deemed to be primarily an investor, the *in pari delicto* defense is unavailable. This is true even if the plaintiff-investor actively participates in the distribution of unregistered securities. The *Pinter* Court reasoned that a contrary holding would pose a significant obstacle to the effective enforcement of the Securities Act's registration provisions and to the goal of investor protection.[152]

§ 7.11 Contribution, Proportionate Liability, and Related Issues

In *Musick, Peeler & Garrett v. Employers Insurance of Wausau*,[153] the Supreme Court recognized an implied right of action for contribution under Section 10(b). The Court focused its inquiry on "how the 1934 Congress would have addressed the issue had the [Section 10(b)] action been included

---

[147] 472 U.S. at 315-16.

[148] 486 U.S. 622 (1988). For discussion on Section 12(a)(1), see § 6.08 *supra*.

[149] 486 U.S. at 622.

[150] *Id.* at 634.

[151] *Id.* at 639 (citations omitted).

[152] *Id.* at 638. See generally Klock, *Promoter Liability and In Pari Delicto Under Section 12(1): Pinter v. Dahl*, 17 Sec. Reg. L.J. 53 (1989).

[153] 508 U.S. 286.

as an express provision in the 1934 Act."[154] Of the eight liability provisions contained in the 1933 and 1934 Acts, the Court found that 1934 Act Sections 9 and 18 impose liability upon defendants who occupy a position most similar to Section 10(b) defendants for ascertaining entitlement to contribution. Since both Sections 9 and 18 expressly provide for contribution, the Court reasoned that "consistency requires us to adopt a like contribution rule for the right of action existing under Rule 10b-5."[155]

The Court rejected the argument that two of its relatively recent decisions outside of the securities law arena that declined to recognize an action for contribution[156] signified that contribution likewise was inappropriate under Section 10(b). The Court reasoned that these cases construed statutory provisions that allowed for express rights of action. While the ramifications of these cases may foreclose recognizing a right to contribution under express securities law remedial provisions that do not by their terms provide for this right of action (such as with respect to Securities Act Section 12(a)(2)),[157] a different analysis applies to implied rights. Here, because the judiciary has implied the Section 10(b) private right of action, it is the Court's role to elaborate, define, and shape the contours of this remedy.[158] Applying this analysis, the Court concluded that "[t]hose charged with liability in a [Section 10(b)] action have a right to contribution against other parties who have joint responsibility for the violation."[159]

The Supreme Court in *Musick* declined to focus on how contribution should be apportioned among the (alleged) tortfeasors. Historically, three methods emerged: pro rata, proportionate fault, and pro tanto.

The first measure, *the pro rata method*, was the least favored and has been rejected by Congress in its enactment of the Private Securities Litigation Reform Act of 1995. Under this approach, "the judgment amount is simply divided by the number of defendants, settling and non-settling, that are found liable."[160] Although this method of allocating contribution lends itself to ease of administration, its major disadvantage is that the parties' relative culpability is not a consideration.[161] Due to this drawback, the pro rata method is "rarely invoked."[162]

Under *the proportionate fault method*, the "jury assesses the relative culpability of both settling and non-settling defendants, and the non-settling

---

[154] *Id.* at 294.

[155] *Id.* at 297.

[156] See *Texas Industries, Inc. v. Radcliff Materials, Inc.*, 481 U.S. 630 (1981) (no right to contribution based on violation of § 1 of the Sherman Act); *Northwest Airlines, Inc. v. Transport Workers*, 451 U.S. 77 (1981) (no right to contribution pursuant to Equal Pay Act and Title VII of the Civil Rights Act of 1964).

[157] The issue of contribution under Section 12(a)(2) is addressed in § 6.09[F] *supra*.

[158] 508 U.S. at 291.

[159] *Id.* at 298.

[160] *In re Jiffy Lube Securities Litigation*, 927 F.2d 151, 161 (4th Cir. 1991).

[161] See *Smith v. Mulvaney*, 827 F.2d 558, 561 (9th Cir. 1987).

[162] *Cortec Industries, Inc. v. Sun Holding L.P.*, 839 F. Supp. 1021, 1026 (S.D.N.Y. 1993).

defendant pays a commensurate percentage of the judgment."[163] The Supreme Court has adopted this approach in the maritime context, holding that under the proportionate fault method "no suits for contribution from settling defendants are permitted, nor are they necessary, because the non-settling defendants pay no more than their share of the judgment."[164] Several courts have applied the proportionate fault method.[165] Under this method, the plaintiff assumes the risk of a "bad" settlement, and therefore has an incentive to procure from each settling defendant a share of damages that is proportionate to each such defendant's culpability. A key disadvantage to this method is that the factfinder must ascertain not only the degree of culpability of each nonsettling defendant but also of each of the settling parties who no longer are parties to the action.[166]

Turning to the third approach, *the pro tanto method* "reduces a nonsettling defendant's liability for a judgment against him/her in the amount paid by a settling defendant."[167] Or, phrased differently, under this approach, "when a plaintiff receives a settlement from one defendant, a nonsettling defendant is entitled to a credit of the settlement amount against any judgment obtained by the plaintiff against the nonsettling defendant so long as both the settlement and judgment represented common damages."[168] The pro tanto method is favorable for plaintiffs as the risk of a "bad" settlement is borne by the nonsettling defendants who must pay the balance of the plaintiff's damages. This prospect gives rise to concerns of collusion between the plaintiff and a "favored" defendant as well as the imposition of damages against a non-settling defendant out of proportion to such party's relative fault. Nonetheless, this method encourages settlement and eliminates the need for any further consideration of the culpability of settling defendants even if the remaining defendants proceed to trial. Moreover, a "fairness" hearing to approve a pretrial settlement may be conducted by the court, thereby helping to ensure that the settlement amounts resemble each settling party's relative culpability.[169]

Issues relating to contribution and proportionate fault were addressed by Congress' enactment of the Private Securities Litigation Reform Act of 1995 (PSLRA). Pursuant to that legislation, Congress amended the Exchange Act to add new Section 21D(g). This new section (1) circumscribes the scope of the current joint and several liability scheme; (2) creates a

---

[163] *In re Jiffy Lube*, 927 F.2d at 160 n.3.

[164] *McDermott, Inc. v. Amclyde*, 511 U.S. 202, 209 (1994).

[165] See, e.g., *Bragger v. Trinity Enterprise Corp.*, 30 F.3d 14, 17 (2d Cir. 1994) (dicta); *Franklin v. Kaypro Corporation*, 884 F.2d 1222 (9th Cir. 1989); *In re Del-Val Corporation Securities Litigation*, 868 F. Supp. 547 (S.D.N.Y. 1994).

[166] See *Alvarado Partners L.P. v. Mehta*, 723 F. Supp. 540, 552-53 (D. Colo. 1989).

[167] *In re Masters Mates & Pilots Pension Plan*, 957 F.2d 1020, 1029 (2d Cir. 1992).

[168] *Singer v. Olympia Brewing Co.*, 878 F.2d 596, 600 (2d Cir. 1989).

[169] See *In re Masters Mates & Pilots Pension Plan*, 957 F.2d at 1029; *Cortec Industries*, 839 F. Supp. at 1027; *MFS Municipal Income Trust v. American Medical Int'l, Inc.*, 751 F. Supp. 279, 287 (D. Mass. 1990). See generally Friedman, *Contribution and Partial Settlements in Securities Fraud Actions in Light of McDermott, Inc. v. AmClyde*, 23 Sec. Reg. L.J. 143 (1995); Moses & Sutton, *Contribution Under Rule 10b-5*, 26 Rev. Sec. & Comm. Reg. 159 (1993).

proportionate liability framework for actions brought against multiple defendants under the Exchange Act or against "outside directors" of the issuer whose securities are the subject of an action under Section 11 of the Securities Act; and (3) clarifies several issues relating to partial settlements in federal securities actions.

First, the statute limits the application of joint and several liability for damages to apply only if the trier of fact specifically determines that the defendant in question "knowingly committed" a violation of the federal securities laws. The section provides that the term "knowingly committed" requires actual knowledge as the scienter standard and specifically provides that recklessness cannot constitute a knowing violation. Further, the PSLRA codifies the right to contribution among such joint tortfeasors recognized by the Supreme Court in *Musick, Peeler*. Under this framework, the legislation provides that the liability of such defendants is to be premised upon findings of percentage of responsibility as to each jointly and severally liable defendant.

Second, by implication, in all actions wherein the "knowingly committed" scienter standard cannot be proven by the plaintiff but the lesser standard of recklessness may be shown, the PSLRA creates a proportionate liability scheme and (with certain exceptions) restricts liability for damages solely to that portion of the judgment that corresponds to the percentage of each individual defendant's responsibility for plaintiffs' losses. In addition, if certain individually liable defendants' shares of liability are uncollectible due to insolvency or some other reason, the statute requires additional proportionate contributions either from the jointly and severally liable defendants or, if still uncollectible, from other proportionately liable defendants for those uncollectible shares in certain specified circumstances.

The PSLRA further provides specific guidelines for determining the percentage of each individual defendant's responsibility for damages in the form of directing the court (1) to instruct the trier of fact to answer special interrogatories; or (2) to itself make special findings with respect to multiple defendants on specific issues. Such issues are to include, among other things, the percentage of responsibility of each defendant and whether the defendant "knowingly committed" violations so as to properly place that defendant within the joint and several liability scheme.

Third, the PSLRA evidently brings an end to the controversy generated by several recent decisions addressing issues of partial settlements in federal securities actions by providing for the discharge of all claims for contribution brought by any other persons, whether or not such persons have themselves settled with the plaintiff, against any defendant that has settled any private action at any time prior to judgment. Moreover, the section requires the implementation of a settlement bar order by the court constituting the discharge of all obligations to the plaintiff of the settling defendant "arising out of the action." The legislation makes clear that such bar orders apply to contribution actions brought by and against the settling defendant.

In addition, the PSLRA provides for a new judgment reduction method applicable in multidefendant partial settlement cases. This method serves to reduce the plaintiff's subsequent judgment against any nonsettling defendant by the greater amount of either (1) the proportionate responsibility of the settling defendant as determined by the court or jury, or (2) the amount that the settling defendant has already paid to the plaintiff pursuant to the respective settlement agreement.[170]

§ 7.12   The Private Securities Litigation Reform Act (PSLRA): Class Action Reform and Related Issues

[A]   Class Action Reform

The PSLRA amends both the Securities Act and the Exchange Act to add new Sections 27(a) and 21D(a), respectively. These sections are intended to address the problem of "professional plaintiffs" and other abusive practices in private securities class actions. The content of these sections includes the following:

(1) A requirement that each plaintiff seeking to serve as a representative party on behalf of a class file with the complaint a sworn certification that: (i) the plaintiff reviewed the complaint and authorized its filing; (ii) the plaintiff did not purchase the securities in question at the direction of counsel or in order to participate in a private action; (iii) the plaintiff is willing to both serve as a representative party on behalf of the class and provide both deposition and trial testimony; (iv) sets forth all of such plaintiff's particular securities transactions that are the subject of the class action; (v) identifies any other action filed during the preceding three-year period in which the plaintiff sought to serve as a representative party on behalf of a class; and (vi) the plaintiff will not accept payment for serving as a representative party on behalf of a class beyond the plaintiff's pro rata share of any recovery, except as approved by the court. The plaintiff's filed certification will not be deemed a waiver of the attorney-client privilege.

(2) Guidelines for early notice (not later than twenty days after the filing of the complaint) to class members pertaining to the appointment of the lead plaintiff. Such notice must appear "in a widely circulated national business-oriented publication or wire service." Within sixty days of such publication, any member of the purported class may seek to serve as lead plaintiff.

(3) Provisions requiring the court to consider any motion by a purported class member in response to the class notice to be appointed as the lead plaintiff. These provisions require the court to adopt a rebuttable presumption that the "most adequate plaintiff" is the person with the largest financial interest in the relief sought by the class, but allows for discovery

---

170 See Langevoort, *The Reform of Joint and Several Liability Under the Private Securities Litigation Reform Act of 1995: Proportionate Liability, Contribution Rights and Settlement Effects*, 51 Bus. Law. 1157 (1996); Steinberg & Olive, *Contribution and Proportionate Liability Under the Federal Securities Laws*, 50 SMU L. Rev. 337 (1996).

on such motions in limited circumstances. However, these provisions also mandate restrictions on "professional plaintiffs" in declaring that, except as the court may otherwise permit (such as with respect to institutional investors), a person may be a lead plaintiff (or an officer, director, or fiduciary of a lead plaintiff) in no more than five securities class actions brought as plaintiff class actions during any three-year period.

(4) Provisions limiting the lead plaintiff's recovery to its proportionate share of any judgment or settlement, as well as reasonable costs and expenses, including lost wages.

(5) The prohibition of settlements under seal except in limited circumstances.

(6) Provisions limiting the award of attorneys' fees and expenses to a "reasonable percentage" of the amount of any damages and prejudgment interest "actually paid" to the class. These provisions do not address how attorneys' fees should be calculated in cases where the relief awarded or settlement does not include monetary damages.

(7) Specific and mandatory procedures for the disclosure of settlement terms to class members (including disclosure of the amount of plaintiff recovery, statement of attorneys' fees and costs sought, identification of lawyers' representatives for the plaintiff class to answer questions, and statement of the reasons for settlement).

(8) Provisions requiring the court to determine whether an interest on the part of plaintiff's counsel in the securities in question constitutes a conflict of interest insufficient to disqualify the attorney from representing the party.

In addition, the 1934 Act is amended to authorize the court to require security for payment of class action fees and expenses.

These sections taken together should reduce the abusive practices of plaintiffs' counsel in securities class actions. However, it is evident that the efficacy of these sections will depend on the extent to which institutional investors choose to "come forward" and utilize the new framework.[171]

[B] Sanctions for Abusive Litigation

The PSLRA amends the 1933 and 1934 Acts to mandate court review, upon final adjudication of private securities actions thereunder, of the parties' or their attorneys' compliance with Rule 11(b) of the Federal Rules of Civil Procedure requirements for a good faith factual and legal basis as to any pleading or dispositive motion. If the court finds that there is a "substantial failure" of the parties or attorneys to comply with its provisions, the court is directed to impose mandatory sanctions in accordance with Rule 11.

The provisions set forth a rebuttable presumption that sanctions for violation of Rule 11(b) are the reasonable attorneys' fees and costs incurred

---

[171] See, e.g., Symposium, 51 Bus. Law. No. 4 (1996); Symposium, 33 San Diego L. Rev. No. 3 (1996); Symposium, 24 Sec. Reg. L.J. No 2 (1996); Symposium, 76 Wash. U. L.Q. No. 2 (1998).

as a direct result of such violation. This presumption may be rebutted by the sanctioned party or attorney only upon proof that (i) the award will present an unreasonable burden or (ii) the violation was "de minimis."[172]

[C] Stay of Discovery and Preservation of Evidence

The PSLRA amends the 1933 and 1934 Acts to provide for (i) a stay of discovery during the pendency of any motion to dismiss unless the court finds that particularized discovery is necessary to preserve evidence or to prevent undue prejudice to a party; and (ii) the preservation of evidence relevant to the allegations of the complaint during the pendency of any stay of discovery. A party aggrieved by the willful failure of an opposing party to comply with the provisions requiring preservation of evidence may seek appropriate sanctions. These provisions therefore enable defendants who succeed in their motions to dismiss to avoid the discovery and related expenses associated with securities litigation.[173]

[D] Auditor Disclosure of Corporate Fraud

The PSLRA amends the 1934 Act by adding a new Section 10A thereto. New Section 10A sets forth requirements for audits conducted by an independent public accountant of an issuer's financial statements to include certain procedures to (1) detect illegal acts that would have a direct and material effect on the determination of financial statement amounts; (2) identify related party transactions materials to financial statements; and (3) evaluate an issuer's ability to continue as a going concern. The statutory language makes clear that the above procedures are to be carried out in accordance with current generally accepted accounting principles (GAAP) "as may be modified from time to time by the [SEC]." The existing auditing standards provide for all three types of procedures prescribed in new Section 10A.

Section 10A further specifies notification and reporting guidelines for a public accountant who becomes aware of information indicating possible illegal activities during the course of an audit. The provisions also appear to codify current generally accepted accounting principles. If, in the course of an audit the public accountant detects or otherwise becomes aware of information indicating that an illegal act has or may have occurred, the accountant must (1) determine the likelihood that an illegal act has occurred; (2) determine the possible effect of the illegal act on the issuer's financial statements, including contingent effects such as fines, penalties, or damages; and (3) inform appropriate management and assure that the issuer's audit committee (or, if none, its board of directors) is adequately informed (unless such illegal act clearly is inconsequential).

The lone new requirement imposed on such accountants exists if such an accountant concludes that (1) the illegal act has a material effect on the

---

[172] See sources cited note 171 *supra.*

[173] See sources cited note 171 *supra.*

issuer's financial statements; (2) senior management has not taken "timely and appropriate remedial actions" in regard to the illegal act; and (3) the failure to take "remedial action" is likely to cause the accountant to depart from a standard report or to resign from its capacity as auditor. Under these conditions the accountant must, "as soon as is practicable," report such conclusions to the board of directors. A board of directors receiving a report from such an accountant must inform the SEC within one business day of receipt of the report and must give the accountant a copy of the notice sent to the SEC. If, however, the accountant does not receive a copy of the notice within this time, such accountant must resign from the engagement or provide the SEC with a copy of its report (or documentation of its oral report) to the board of directors within one business day after the issuer fails to provide to the accountant the notice copy. Even if the accountant resigns, it must still furnish the SEC with a copy of its report within the same time period.

As a last point, Section 10A stipulates that an accountant who furnishes a report to the SEC under this statute will not be held liable in any private action for any findings, conclusions, or statements in the report. However, the willful failure to file a required report will subject the accountant "and any other person that the [SEC] finds was a cause of such violation" to cease-and-desist proceedings as well as the imposition of civil penalties. [174]

§ 7.13 Extraterritorial Jurisdiction

Extraterritorial jurisdiction implicating the federal securities laws comes into play in a number of different contexts, including in civil litigation involving Section 10(b). For purposes of organization, this subject will be treated here.

[A] Transnational Fraud

The principal extraterritorial application of the federal securities laws has involved the area of transnational fraud. In an effort to protect American investors and to prevent this country from being employed as a base for deceptive conduct in transactions abroad affecting American or foreign investors, the U.S. courts have given broad extraterritorial application to the antifraud provisions of the federal securities laws. Under formulations to determine whether subject matter jurisdiction exists, two tests have developed: (1) the "conduct" test and (2) the "effects" test.

Under the *conduct* test, courts generally have applied Section 10(b) of the Exchange Act to foreign transactions occurring abroad when fraudulent conduct of material importance (e.g., a misstatement causing an investor's acquisition of a security) or conduct integrally associated with a fraud (e.g., the drafting of an inaccurate offering document used to sell stock) that directly caused the plaintiff's alleged damages took place within the United States. [175] Hence, in situations in which conduct transpiring in the United

---

[174] See sources cited note 171 *supra*.

[175] See, e.g., *Kautbar SDN BHD v. Steinberg*, 149 F.3d 659 (7th Cir. 1998); *Robinson v.*

States was merely preparatory to the fraud, courts frequently have declined to find subject matter jurisdiction where the complainant was a foreign, rather than a United States, citizen.[176] Nonetheless, subject matter jurisdiction would be appropriate in the case of a foreign plaintiff where key preparatory conduct in the United States, such as the drafting of a prospectus, directly caused the foreign investor's loss.[177]

Applying the *effects* test, courts have found subject matter jurisdiction when securities transactions outside of the United States had substantial and foreseeable injurious effects in this country. For example, fraudulent conduct undertaken abroad, which caused a decrease in the value of stock listed on a U.S. exchange, was viewed as coming within the ambit of the federal securities laws, irrespective that no conduct, preparatory or otherwise, took place in the United States in regard to the transaction abroad.[178] The number of defrauded U.S. residents compared to foreign residents also has been considered by U.S. courts under the effects test.[179]

[B]   Securities Act Registration

In 1990, the SEC adopted Regulation S in an attempt to clarify the extraterritorial application of Section 5 of the Securities Act. The ramifications of Regulation S and its impact on extraterritorial application are addressed in § 3.14. As a general matter, note that in this context antifraud issues are not implicated.

[C]   Tender Offers

Another area involving the extraterritorial application of the securities laws is tender offer regulation. Foreign issuers seeking to purchase the securities of other foreign issuers that have U.S. shareholders have been careful to restrict their public communications concerning the bid in order to avoid triggering the Williams Act as well as the SEC's tender offer rules. This approach may be successful in certain situations. In one such instance, for example, General Electric Company PLC made an offer to acquire a number of shares of the Plessey Company PLC. Both companies were doing business pursuant to Great Britain law. Plessey, however, had American

---

TCI/US West Cable Communications, 117 F.3d 900 (5th Cir. 1997); *Butte Mining PLC v. Smith*, 76 F.3d 287 (9th Cir. 1996) (setting forth a somewhat more relaxed standard); *Leasco v. Data Processing Equipment Corp.*, 468 F.2d 1326 (2d Cir. 1972). See also, *Zoelsch v. Arthur Andersen & Co.*, 824 F.2d 27 (D.C. Cir. 1987) (requiring the domestic conduct at issue to itself constitute a securities law violation).

[176] See, e.g., *Zoelsch v. Arthur Andersen & Co.*, 824 F.2d 27 (D.C. Cir. 1987); *Bersch v. Drexel Firestore, Inc.*, 519 F.2d 974 (2d Cir. 1978).

[177] See *ITT v. Cornfeld*, 619 F.2d 909 (2d Cir. 1980). See also, *Europe & Overseas Commodity Traders, S.A. v. Banque Paribas London*, 147 F.3d 118 (2d Cir. 1998) (declining to exercise jurisdiction even though key misstatements were made in the United States where none of the parties or companies were U.S. citizens or entities); cases cited note 175 *supra*.

[178] See, e.g., *Schoenbaum v. Firstbrook*, 405 F.2d 200, *modified en banc*, 405 F.2d 215 (2d Cir. 1969). See also, *Itoba Ltd. v. Lep Group PLC*, 54 F.3d 118 (2d Cir. 1995).

[179] See, e.g., *IIT v. Vencap, Ltd.*, 519 F.2d 1001 (2d Cir. 1975).

Depository Receipts (ADRs) trading in the U.S. securities markets and had certain other Dollar Shares registered in this country. To avoid implicating the United States tender offer regimen, General Electric refrained from issuing any press releases to the American press concerning the bid, made it clear in its communications to the press that the bid was neither being made in the United States nor was such bid for the Plessey ADRs or Dollar Shares, and took additional precautions to help guarantee that shares would not be accepted from stockholders in the United States.[180]

A United States district court ruled that the federal tender offer regimen did not extend to the General Electric offer. The court opined that, as contrasted with the antifraud provisions, it was more appropriate under the tender offer provisions to assess considerations of comity and policy in this area. As such, the court, after evaluating relevant factors, declined to invoke extraterritorial jurisdiction.[181] However, as the Second Circuit more recently held, if allegations of fraud are present in the tender offer setting, then the "conduct" and "effects" tests discussed above[182] are the proper standards.[183]

---

[180] *The Plessey Company PLC v. The General Electric Company PLC*, 628 F. Supp. 477, 479-86 (D. Del. 1986).

[181] *Id.* at 494-97.

[182] See *supra* notes 175-79 and accompanying text.

[183] See *Consolidated Gold Fields PLC v. Minorco, S.A.*, 871 F.2d 252 (2d Cir. 1989). See generally Choi & Guzman, *Portable Reciprocity: Rethinking the International Reach of Securities Regulation*, 71 S. Cal. L. Rev. 903 (1998); Lowenfels & Bromberg, *U.S. Securities Fraud Across the Border: Unpredictable Jurisdiction*, 55 Bus. Law. 975 (2000); Sachs, *The International Reach of Rule 10b-5: The Myth of Congressional Silence*, 28 Colum. J. Tran. L. 677 (1990); Thomas, *Extraterritorial Application of the United States Securities Laws: The Need for a Balanced Policy*, 7 J. Corp. L. 189 (1982).

Chapter 8

ALTERNATIVE REMEDIES

§ 8.01 Introduction

As Chapters 6 and 7 have discussed, Sections 11 and 12(a)(2) of the Securities Act and Section 10(b) of the Exchange Act play important roles in securities litigation. These provisions, however, may be unavailable to a complainant for a number of reasons. For example, the securities may have been purchased in the aftermarket, hence making the Section 11 right of action unavailable (unless the plaintiff meets the onerous "tracing" requirement). Or, alternatively, the complainant may be unable to invoke the Section 10(b) remedy because he/she is not a "purchaser" or "seller" or cannot establish that the defendant acted with scienter. Or, as a last example, the alleged violation may have occurred in connection with a proxy solicitation or tender offer. Under such circumstances, counsel should focus on the availability of alternative remedies, including the invocation of implied remedies.

Moreover, even where a right of action may be successfully established (such as under Section 10(b)), counsel, where appropriate, still should assess the viability of remedies afforded by other provisions. For example, recovery may be afforded under Section 14(a) based on the defendant's negligence whereas Section 10(b) mandates proof of scienter. As another example, Section 29(b) of the Exchange Act may provide an aggrieved party with the right to rescind the subject transaction.

As an additional point, counsel always should assess the advisability of seeking relief under the applicable state common and statutory (including "Blue Sky") laws.

§ 8.02 Implied Rights of Action — In General

[A] Pre-1975 Approach

Prior to 1975, the federal courts liberally recognized implied private rights of action, generally looking to whether the granting of an implied remedy would benefit the class sought to be protected by the statute. For example, in *J.I. Case Co. v. Borak*,[1] the Supreme Court recognized an implied right of action under Section 14(a) of the Exchange Act (the "proxy" provision), reasoning that such an implied right would promote investor protection and serve as a necessary supplement to SEC enforcement action.

---

[1] 377 U.S. 426 (1964).

[B] The *Cort* Formulation and Its Apparent Demise

The liberal construction to implied rights of action halted with the Supreme Court's decision in *Cort v. Ash*.[2] There, the Court formulated a four-prong standard:

> First, is the plaintiff "one of the class for whose especial benefit the statute was enacted," — that is, does the statute create a federal right in favor of the plaintiff? Second, is there any indication of legislative intent, explicit or implicit, either to create such a remedy or to deny one? Third, is it consistent with the underlying purpose of the legislative scheme to imply such a remedy for the plaintiff? And finally, is the cause of action one traditionally relegated to state law, in an area basically the concern of the States, so that it would be inappropriate to infer a cause of action based solely on federal law?[3]

In subsequent decisions, the Supreme Court embraced the *Cort* formulation with varying levels of enthusiasm.[4] Perhaps somewhat ironically (given the pre-1975 broad construction to implied rights), certain members of the Court criticized the *Cort* standard as being "an open invitation to federal courts to legislate causes of action not authorized by Congress."[5]

The evident demise of the *Cort* formulation was evidenced by *Transamerica Mortgage Advisors, Inc. v. Lewis*,[6] where the Supreme Court refused to imply a private right of action under the antifraud provision of the Investment Advisers Act, Section 206. There, the Court, relying on its prior decision in *Redington*,[7] stated that the central inquiry is to examine Congress' intent. Hence, the Court reasoned:

> The question whether a statute creates a cause of action, either expressly or by implication, is basically a matter of statutory construction. While some opinions of the Court have placed considerable emphasis upon the desirability of implying private rights of action in order to provide remedies thought to effectuate the purposes of a given statute, what must ultimately be determined is whether Congress intended to create the private remedy asserted . . . . We accept this as the appropriate inquiry to be made in resolving the issue presented by the case before us.[8]

Thus, in *Lewis* the Court adhered to what has been viewed as a restrictive approach. Some other cases, however, indicated that the *Cort* formulation

---

[2] 422 U.S. 66 (1975).

[3] *Id.* at 78.

[4] Compare *Cannon v. University of Chicago*, 441 U.S. 677 (1979), with *Touche Ross & Co. v. Redington*, 422 U.S. 560 (1979), *discussed* in Steinberg, *Implied Rights of Action Under Federal Law*, 55 Notre Dame Law. 33 (1979).

[5] See *Cannon v. University of Chicago*, 441 U.S. 677, 731 (1979) (Powell, J., dissenting).

[6] 444 U.S. 11 (1979).

[7] *Touche Ross & Co. v. Redington*, 442 U.S. 560 (1979) (holding that no implied private right of action exists under § 17(a) of the Exchange Act).

[8] 444 U.S. at 15-16.

possibly survived. *California v. Sierra Club*,[9] a non-securities law case, highlighted the disagreement on the Court concerning the continued viability of *Cort*. There, in declining to imply a right of action under the pertinent statute, the five-member majority adhered to the *Cort* formulation and asserted:

> Combined, these four factors present the relevant inquiries to pursue in answering the recurring question of implied causes of action. Cases subsequent to *Cort* have explained that the ultimate issue is whether Congress intended to create a private right of action, but the four factors specified in *Cort* remain the "criteria through which this intent could be discerned."[10]

Concurring in the judgment, Justice Rehnquist (joined by three other Justices) in a separate opinion believed that "the Court's opinion places somewhat more emphasis on *Cort v. Ash* than is warranted in light of several more recent 'implied right of action' decisions which limit it."[11]

Nonetheless, more recent U.S. Supreme Court decisions in *Virginia Bankshares*[12] and *Central Bank of Denver*[13] reflect a return to a more restrictive approach. In *Virginia Bankshares*, for example, the Court approvingly quoted from *Touche Ross v. Redington* that the "central inquiry remains whether Congress intended to create, either expressly or by implication, a private cause of action." Hence, the Court in *Virginia Bankshares* made clear that congressional intent is "accorded primacy among the considerations that might be thought to bear on any decision to recognize a private remedy."[14] Moreover, in *Central Bank of Denver*, the Court focused on the language of the statute as the controlling factor.[15]

§ 8.03   Availability of Implied Rights of Action Under Select Statutes

The lower federal courts have determined whether a private right of action should be implied under certain provisions of the federal securities laws. A number of these provisions are discussed later in this chapter.

The federal courts, for example, have:

- Generally refused to recognize an implied right of action under Section 6 of the Exchange Act (i) against a national securities

---

[9] 451 U.S. 287 (1981).

[10] *Id.* at 293.

[11] *Id.* at 302 (Rehnquist, J., concurring in the judgment).

[12] *Virginia Bankshares, Inc. v. Sandberg*, 501 U.S. 1083 (1991).

[13] *Central Bank of Denver v. First Interstate Bank of Denver*, 511 U.S. 164 (1994).

[14] 501 U.S. at 1103. Reflecting on the viability of the four-prong *Cort* test, the Seventh Circuit has opined that the test survives "only nominally." Hence, "courts may not recognize an implied remedy absent persuasive evidence that Congress intended to create one." *Spicer v. Chicago Board of Options Exchange, Inc.*, 977 F.2d 255, 258 (7th Cir. 1992).

[15] 511 U.S. at 173. See generally Grundfest, *Disimplying Private Rights of Action Under the Federal Securities Laws: The Commission's Authority*, 107 Harv. L. Rev. 961 (1994).

exchange based on the exchange's failure to enforce its own rules;[16] or (ii) against a broker-dealer, listed corporation, or other subject party based on a violation of exchange rules.[17]

- Declined to imply a private damages action under Section 7 of the Exchange Act on behalf of investors against financial institutions and brokers for violation of the margin requirements. In this regard, Section 7 authorizes the Federal Reserve Board to regulate margin transactions and prohibits violation of the Board's regulations. Generally, the regulations promulgated by the Board under the authority of Section 7 set the margin rate for securities purchased at 50 percent, meaning that the purchaser must advance the other 50 percent of the purchase price of the securities bought "on margin."[18] Declining to imply a Section 7 right of action, the Second Circuit reasoned:

  We . . . hold that no private right of action exists under Section 7. First, . . . there is simply no evidence that in passing Section 7 Congress intended to create a private action. . . . Second, Section 7 was clearly not passed for the "especial benefit" of individual investors. The major reason for enacting Section 7 was to control the excessive use of credit in securities transactions. . . . Finally, it is doubtful that allowing a private cause of action would be consistent with the underlying purposes of the legislative scheme. As stated above, the underlying purpose of Section 7 is to regulate the use of credit in securities transactions. As the addition of Section 7(f) makes clear, this regulation is aimed at both lenders and investors. While allowing a private cause of action could conceivably deter violations by lenders, it seems just as conceivable that it could encourage violations by investors seeking to shift the risk of loss.[19]

- In the tender offer setting, implied a private right of action for damages under the tender offer antifraud statute, Section 14(e) of the Exchange Act, on behalf of target corporation shareholders but not a damages remedy on behalf of the offeror.[20] With respect to the availability of *injunctive* (rather than monetary) relief

---

[16] See, e.g., *Walck v. American Stock Exchange, Inc.*, 687 F.2d 778 (3d Cir. 1982).

[17] See, e.g., *Jablon v. Dean Witter & Co.*, 613 F.2d 677 (9th Cir. 1980). But see for a more liberal construction, *Buttrey v. Merrill Lynch, Pierce, Fenner & Smith, Inc.*, 410 F.2d 135 (7th Cir. 1979).

[18] See *Walck v. American Stock Exchange, Inc.*, 687 F.2d 778 (3d Cir. 1982).

[19] *Bennett v. United States Trust Company of New York*, 770 F.2d 308, 312 (2d Cir. 1985).

[20] See *Piper v. Chris-Craft Industries, Inc.*, 430 U.S. 1 (1977) (applying *Cort*, defeated tender offeror does not have standing to bring an implied action for damages under § 14(e)); *Panter v. Marshall Field & Co.*, 646 F.2d 271 (7th Cir. 1981) (target shareholders sought relief under § 14(e)).

under Sections 13(d), 14(d), and 14(e) of the 1934 Act,[21] most courts recognize that an offeror has an implied right of action.[22]

• Implied private rights of action under certain provisions of the Investment Company Act[23] and the Trust Indenture Act.[24]

§ 8.04   Section 17(a) of the Securities Act

[A]   Generally

Section 17(a) of the Securities Act provides:

It shall be unlawful for any person in the offer or sale of any securities by the use of any means or instruments of transportation or communication in interstate commerce or by the use of the mails, directly or indirectly —

(1) to employ any device, scheme, or artifice to defraud, or

(2) to obtain money or property by means of any untrue statement of a material fact or any omission to state a material fact necessary in order to make the statements made, in the light of the circumstances under which they were made, not misleading, or

(3) to engage in any transaction, practice, or course of business which operates or would operate as a fraud or deceit upon the purchaser.

Section 17(a), the 1933 Act's antifraud provision, applies only to the offer or sale of securities. Hence, the prohibitions of Section 17(a) do not reach fraud in the purchase of securities. Based upon the Supreme Court's decisions in *United States v. Naftalin*[25] and *Aaron v. SEC*,[26] Section 17(a) has emerged as an attractive enforcement weapon for the SEC.

[B]   Supreme Court Decisions

The Supreme Court in *Naftalin* handed down three significant principles regarding Section 17(a). First, the protection afforded by Section 17(a)(1) extends beyond investors to encompass financial intermediaries such as broker-dealers. Second, the language of Section 17(a) relating to the

---

[21] These provisions were passed by Congress in 1968 as part of the Williams Act which, in effect, amended the Exchange Act. They are discussed in Chapter 13.

[22] See, e.g., *Indiana National Corp. v. Rich*, 712 F.2d 1180 (7th Cir. 1983); *Mobil Corp. v. Marathon Oil Co.*, 669 F.2d 366 (6th Cir. 1981). But see *Polaroid Corp. v. Disney*, [1988-1989 Transfer Binder] Fed. Sec. L. Rep. (CCH) ¶ 94,095 (3d Cir. 1988). See also, discussion in § 13.07 *infra*.

[23] See, e.g., *Fogel v. Chestnut*, 668 F.2d 100 (2d Cir. 1981).

[24] See, e.g., *Ziffiro v. First Pennsylvania Banking and Trust Co.*, 623 F.2d 290 (3d Cir. 1980). See generally Johnson, *The 'Forgotten' Securities Statute: Problems in the Trust Indenture Act*, 13 Toledo L. Rev. 92 (1981).

[25] 441 U.S. 768 (1979).

[26] 446 U.S. 680 (1980).

prohibition of fraud "in" an offer or sale of securities (as contrasted with Section 10(b)'s "in connection with" language) was sufficiently inclusive to cover Naftalin's misconduct. And third, Section 17(a) not only applies in the initial offering context but also extends to the secondary trading markets.[27] This last holding is particularly important. Prior to *Naftalin*, some authorities believed that, as part of the Securities Act which is directed at the regulation of initial offerings, Section 17(a) was likewise limited to the initial offering context. Hence, with respect to misconduct occurring in the aftermarket context involving the offer or sale of securities, *Naftalin's* effect is to subject such misconduct to the prohibitions of both Section 17(a) and Section 10(b).[28]

The importance of *Naftalin* to the SEC became evident when the Supreme Court handed down its decision in *Aaron*. In *Aaron*, the Court, applying a linguistic analysis, held that in SEC actions seeking injunctive relief, scienter must be proven to establish a violation of Section 10(b) of the Exchange Act and Section 17(a)(1) of the Securities Act.[29] To show violations of Section 17(a)(2) and 17(a)(3), on the other hand, the SEC need only establish the defendant's negligence.[30]

Note the effect of *Aaron*, when considered in light of *Naftalin*. Upon the making of a proper showing (i.e., a reasonable likelihood that, absent the ordering of an injunction, future violations will occur), the SEC can invoke Section 17(a)(2) or 17(a)(3) to obtain injunctive relief based on a defendant's negligent misconduct that occurred in the offer or sale of securities in the secondary trading markets. In view of this consequence, Section 17(a) becomes a more appealing enforcement weapon to the SEC in the "offer or sale" context than the traditional antifraud provision, Section 10(b), which requires the Commission to prove scienter.

Moreover, based upon legislation enacted in 1990, the SEC now has cease and desist authority.[31] This remedy, coupled with the effects of *Naftalin* and *Aaron*, provides the Commission with the authority to issue a cease and desist order based upon a party's negligent conduct. Hence, Section 17(a) is a powerful weapon in the SEC's arsenal.

[C] Availability of Implied Right of Action

Based upon a linguistic analysis (as the Supreme Court applied in *Aaron*), the assertion has been made that, if a private damages action were implied under Section 17(a), the requisite culpability standard would be that of negligence.[32] On the other hand, the Supreme Court has stressed that it is inappropriate to imply a private right of action that is significantly more

[27] 441 U.S. at 773-78.

[28] For further discussion, see Steinberg, *Section 17(a) of the Securities Act After Naftalin and Redington*, 68 Georgetown L.J. 163 (1979).

[29] 446 U.S. at 696.

[30] *Id.* at 696-97. The *Aaron* decision also is discussed in § 7.03[B] *supra*, § 14.05[A] *infra*.

[31] The SEC's cease and desist authority is discussed in § 14.04[A] *infra*.

[32] See *Landry v. All American Assurance Co.*, 688 F.2d 381, 387 (5th Cir. 1982).

expansive than the provisions that Congress expressly chose to provide. Because Sections 11 and 12(a)(2) of the Securities Act subject plaintiffs to certain procedural limitations and have a culpability standard resembling that of negligence, an argument can be made that liability should be imposed pursuant to Section 17(a) only for actions that are more blameworthy, namely, for intentional or reckless misconduct. [33]

Hence, perhaps the most important issue that has not been resolved by the Supreme Court in regard to Section 17(a) is whether an implied private right of action exists. Although a number of older cases implied such a remedy, [34] the more recent decisions with near unanimity have declined to do so. [35] Applying the *Cort* and more restrictive formulations, these courts have concluded that Congress did not intend to create a Section 17(a) private right of action. As stated by the Fifth Circuit:

> [I]t would appear that the *Cort* test as applied to § 17(a) of the Securities Act of 1933 points away from the implication of a private cause of action. This, together with the Supreme Court's conservative interpretation of the test in recent years, leads us to the conclusion that the district court correctly dismissed this theory of relief [thereby denying the existence of a § 17(a) private right of action]. [36]

§ 8.05   Section 14(a) of the Exchange Act

Section 14(a) of the Exchange Act and the SEC rules and regulations promulgated thereunder regulate the solicitation of proxies with respect to securities registered under Section 12 of that Act. Section 14(a) "was intended to promote the free exercise of the voting rights of stockholders by ensuring that proxies would be solicited with explanation to the stockholder of the real nature of the questions for which authority to cast his vote is sought." [37]

[A]   Elements of Private Right of Action

Generally, Rule 14a-9 prohibits the solicitation of proxies that contain any materially false or misleading statement. Due to the Supreme Court's decision in *J.I. Case v. Borak*, [38] it is clear that an implied private right of action exists under Section 14(a) and Rule 14a-9. Also, although not

---

[33] See *Ernst & Ernst v. Hochfelder*, 425 U.S. 185 (1976), discussed in § 7.03[A] *supra*.

[34] See, e.g., *Newman v. Prior*, 518 F.2d 97 (4th Cir. 1975).

[35] See, e.g., *Bath v. Bushkin, Gaims, Gaines & Jones*, 913 F.2d 817 (10th Cir. 1990); *Sears v. Likens*, 912 F.2d 889 (7th Cir. 1990); *Newcome v. Esrey*, 862 F.2d 1099 (4th Cir. 1988); *Currie v. Cayman Resources Corporation*, 835 F.2d 780 (11th Cir. 1988); *Krause v. Prettyman*, 827 F.2d 346 (8th Cir. 1987); *In re Washington Public Power Supply Securities Litigation*, 823 F.2d 1349 (9th Cir. 1987) (en banc).

[36] *Landry v. All American Assurance Co.*, 688 F.2d 381, 391 (5th Cir. 1982).

[37] *Mills v. Electric Auto-Lite Co.*, 396 U.S. 375, 381 (1970).

[38] 377 U.S. 426 (1964).

definitively resolved, it appears that an implied right of action exists under Rule 14a-8, the SEC shareholder proposal rule.[39]

The standard of materiality, as the Supreme Court held in *TSC Industries, Inc. v. Northway, Inc.*,[40] is that "there is a substantial likelihood that a reasonable shareholder would consider [such information] important in deciding how to vote."[41] Note that this standard does not require proof that accurate disclosure of the misrepresented or omitted fact would have caused a reasonable shareholder to change his/her vote but only that a substantial likelihood existed that accurate disclosure "would have been viewed by the reasonable investor as having altered the 'total mix' of information made available."[42]

The Supreme Court has addressed the issue of a plaintiff's task in establishing reliance and causation in a Section 14(a) action. In *Mills v. Electric Auto-Lite Co.*,[43] the Court held that, provided that the misstatement or omission is material and thus had "a significant propensity to affect the voting process," a plaintiff in a derivative or class action under Section 14(a) and Rule 14a-9 is ordinarily neither required to show reliance nor loss causation on the misleading proxy solicitation. Hence, according to the Supreme Court in *Mills*, upon a finding of materiality, "a shareholder has made a sufficient showing of causal relationship between the violation and the injury for which he seeks redress if . . . he proves that the proxy solicitation itself . . . was an essential link in the accomplishment of the transaction."[44] In the *Virginia Bankshares*[45] case, discussed in § 8.05[B], the Court elaborated upon Section 14(a)'s causation requirement.

Regarding the requisite state of mind for liability purposes, Section 14(a) and Rule 14a-9, unlike Section 10(b), do not by their terms require that deceptive or manipulative conduct be shown. As a consequence, where injunctive relief rather than damages is sought, some courts will order relief based upon the objective sufficiency of the disclosure (hence, ordering

---

[39] See *Roosevelt v. E.I. Du Pont De Nemours & Co.*, 958 F.2d 416 (D.C. Cir. 1992) (private right of action recognized under Rule 14a-8); *Rauchman v. Mobil Corporation*, 739 F.2d 205 (6th Cir. 1984) (leaving issue unresolved). For material on Rule 14a-8 as well as the SEC's rules relating to communications among shareholders, see Securities Exchange Act Release No. 40018 (1998); Brown, *The Shareholder Communication Rules and the Securities and Exchange Commission: An Exercise in Regulatory Utility or Futility?*, 13 J. Corp. L. 683 (1988); Cane, *The Revised SEC Shareholder Proxy Proposal System: Attitudes, Results and Perspectives*, 11 J. Corp. L. 57 (1985); Dent, *Toward Unifying Ownership and Control in the Public Corporation*, 1989 Wisc. L. Rev. 881; Fisch, *From Legitimacy to Logic: Reconsidering Proxy Regulation*, 46 Vand. L. Rev. 1129 (1993); Ryan, *Rule 14a-8, Institutional Shareholder Proposals, and Corporate Democracy*, 23 Ga. L. Rev. 97 (1988); Symposium on Proxy Reform, 17 J. Corp. L. No. 1 (1991); Thomas & Martin, *The Effect of Shareholder Proposals on Executive Compensation*, 67 U. Cin. L. Rev. 1021 (1999).

[40] 426 U.S. 438 (1976).

[41] *Id.* at 449.

[42] *Id.*

[43] 396 U.S. 375 (1970).

[44] *Id.* at 384-85.

[45] 501 U.S. 1083 (1991).

corrective disclosure without inquiry as to mental culpability).[46] Where damages are sought, most courts apply a negligence standard. For example, according to the Third Circuit:

> The language of Section 14(a) and Rule 14a-9(a) contains no suggestion of a scienter requirement, merely establishing a quality standard for proxy material. The importance of the proxy provision to informed voting by shareholders has been stressed by the Supreme Court, which has emphasized the broad remedial purpose of the section, implying a need to impose a high standard of care on the individuals involved. And, unlike Sections 10(b) and 18 of the Act, which encompass activity in numerous and diverse areas of securities markets and corporate management, Section 14(a) is specially limited to materials used in soliciting proxies. Given all of these factors the imposition of a standard of due diligence as opposed to actual knowledge or gross negligence is quite appropriate.[47]

On the other hand, in *Adams v. Standard Knitting Mills*[48] the Sixth Circuit took the position that scienter is required in private damage actions against accountants for false and misleading audited financial statements contained in proxy materials. In taking this position, the Sixth Circuit noted, however, that other circuits had prescribed a negligence standard under Section 14(a) when the defendant was a corporation issuing the proxy statement. The Sixth Circuit distinguished these cases, stating that scienter was required in the case at bar because accountants, among other things, are removed from the issuing corporation and do not stand to benefit from a misleading proxy statement.[49] A number of courts have disagreed with the Sixth Circuit's rationale, imposing liability against such parties as accountants and investment bankers based on negligence.[50]

[B] A Look at *Virginia Bankshares*

In a 1991 decision having significant ramifications, the Supreme Court examined Section 14(a) and Rule 14a-9. In *Virginia Bankshares, Inc. v. Sandberg*,[51] the Court addressed two outstanding issues in this area:

> [W]hether a statement couched in conclusory or qualitative terms purporting to explain directors' reasons for recommending certain corporate action can be materially misleading within the meaning of Rule 14a-9, and whether causation of damages compensable under § 14(a) can be shown by . . . member[s] of a class of minority shareholders whose votes are not required by law or corporate bylaw to authorize the corporate action subject to the proxy solicitation.[52]

---

[46] See, e.g., *Ash v. LFE Corp.*, 525 F.2d 215 (3d Cir. 1975). But see *Plant Industries, Inc. v. Bregman*, 490 F. Supp. 265 (S.D.N.Y. 1980).

[47] *Gould v. American Hawaiian S.S. Co.*, 535 F.2d 761, 797-98 (3d Cir. 1976).

[48] 623 F.2d 422 (6th Cir. 1980).

[49] *Id.* at 428.

[50] See, e.g., *Herskowitz v. Nutri/System, Inc.*, 857 F.2d 179 (3d Cir. 1988).

[51] 501 U.S. 1083 (1991).

[52] *Id.* at 1087.

As to the first issue, Justice Souter, writing for the Court, opined that statements of reason, opinion, or belief are not actionable without some misstatement of the facts underpinning the reason, opinion, or belief. Specifically, he noted that such statements contain two components: the opinion itself and the factual basis for the opinion. Assuming that the undergirding facts are neither false nor misleading, a statement of belief might be objectionable in one regard — "solely as a misstatement of the psychological fact of the speaker's belief in what he says."[53] However, to base Section 14(a) and Rule 14a-9 liability on mere disbelief or undisclosed belief would be to authorize litigation founded solely on the " 'impurities' of a director's 'unclean heart.' " This the Court refused to do. Rather, to impose liability, a plaintiff carries the burden of demonstrating "something false or misleading in what the statement expressly or impliedly declare[s] about its subject."[54]

Hence, nondisclosure of "true purpose"[55] is not actionable. However, when there is a material misstatement of reason, opinion or belief as well as the factual basis therefor, a Section 14(a) right of action exists under the reasoning of *Virginia Bankshares*. Note, moreover, that the rendering of such opinion or belief and the factual basis therefor by an eligible registrant may be phrased as "forward-looking" information, thereby invoking the safe harbor provisions of the Private Securities Litigation Reform Act (discussed in § 7.06[D] *supra*, § 10.05[D] *infra*).

Regarding the second issue, causation, the Court refused to extend the "essential link" test which it enunciated in *Mills v. Electric Auto-Lite Co.* The *Mills* Court held that once "there has been a finding of materiality, a shareholder has made a sufficient showing of causal relationship between the violation and the injury for which he seeks redress if . . . he proves that the proxy solicitation itself, rather than the particular defect in the solicitation materials, was an essential link in the accomplishment of the transaction."[56]

The Court in *Mills* left open the question of whether it was possible for minority shareholders to satisfy the causation requirement when their votes were not necessary to approve the transaction.[57] The Second Circuit in *Schlick v. Penn-Dixie Cement Corp.* addressed this issue, adverting to *Borak* and embracing the "broad remedial purposes" of the Securities Acts.[58] There, the court considered the defendant's argument that the "minority stockholders' votes [were] meaningless since the insiders . . . had enough votes to approve the transaction in any event."[59] Asserting that minority shareholder approval is not meaningless, but rather has value

---

[53] *Id.* at 1095.

[54] *Id.* at 1095-96.

[55] See discussion § 7.06[B] *supra*.

[56] 396 U.S. 375, 385 (1970).

[57] *Id.* at 385 n.7.

[58] 507 F.2d 374, 383 (2d Cir. 1974).

[59] *Id.* at 382.

"whether or not it is strictly essential to the power to act," the court answered the question left open in *Mills* in the affirmative.[60]

The Supreme Court rejected this purportedly expansive construction of *Mills* in *Virginia Bankshares*, holding that under the facts presented, shareholders whose votes were not necessary to consummate the transaction did not show the requisite causation for Section 14(a) purposes.[61] Structuring its inquiry around the policies of its seminal decision in *Blue Chip Stamps v. Manor Drug Stores*,[62] the Court reasoned that to recognize causation under the plaintiff minority shareholder's theory would produce hazy issues. Such a recognition would give rise to protracted litigation, the resolution of which would be unreliable: "Given a choice, we would reject any theory of causation that raised such prospects, and we reject this one."[63]

Even though rejecting the plaintiffs' arguments relating to causation in the case at hand, the Court nonetheless left a crucial issue unresolved: Whether the requisite showing of causation may be made if, due to a materially false or misleading statement or other deceptive conduct, the shareholder is lulled into bypassing a state remedy that otherwise would have been available to protect such shareholder from financial loss (called the "lost state remedy" theory).[64] Since *Virginia Bankshares*, a number of lower federal courts have given their approval to the "lost state remedy" theory in this context. In one such case, the Second Circuit ruled for the plaintiffs, reasoning that the defendants' deficient proxy statement may have induced the plaintiffs to forfeit their appraisal rights.[65] Similarly, the Third Circuit has stated that causation may be shown when "the [defendant's] misstatement or omission has caused the minority shareholders to forego an opportunity under state law to enjoin a merger."[66]

In conclusion, although *Virginia Bankshares* on its face is a proxy case, its implications reach far beyond the Section 14(a) region of securities law. Instead, the decision's ramifications flow into other areas of securities jurisprudence as well as into the unevenly treated context of actions implied under federal law.

[C]　Contexts Where Proxy Provisions Apply

Finally, it is important to point out that, while the areas covered by the proxy provisions are limited, the Section 14(a) right of action may be available in a variety of factual contexts. For example, the alleged failure

---

[60] *Id.* at 382-84.

[61] 501 U.S. at 1106-07.

[62] 421 U.S. 723 (1975), *discussed in*, § 7.02 *supra*.

[63] 501 U.S. at 1106.

[64] *Id.* at 1107-08. The subject of lost state remedies also is discussed in § 7.05[B] *supra*.

[65] *Wilson v. Great American Industries, Inc.*, 979 F.2d 924 (2d Cir. 1992).

[66] *Scattergood v. Perelman*, 945 F.2d 618, 626 n.4 (3d Cir. 1991). See *Howing Co. v. Nationwide Corp.*, 927 F.2d 700 (6th Cir. 1992); Steinberg & Reece, *The Supreme Court, Implied Rights of Action, and Proxy Regulation*, 54 Ohio St. L.J 67 (1993). But see *Isquith v. Caremark International, Inc.*, 136 F.3d 531 (7th Cir. 1998).

to disclose in a proxy statement information material to the shareholders' assessment of management's integrity or competence implicates Section 14(a). [67] Moreover, certain breach of fiduciary duty claims, patterned after the *Goldberg* Section 10(b) line of cases (see § 7.05[B]), are actionable under Section 14(a), provided that there is a proxy solicitation coupled with inadequacy of disclosure. [68] The Section 14(a) remedy also comes into play in proxy fights for corporate control. [69] And, as a final example, Section 14(a) may be invoked in connection with merger transactions. [70] Interestingly, because Section 14(a) does not have a purchaser-seller standing requirement and because the requisite culpability standard may be that of negligence, plaintiffs may be successful in a Section 14(a) right of action where such relief would be denied under Section 10(b). [71]

§ 8.06 Section 29(b) of the Exchange Act

Although rarely invoked since the Exchange Act's passage in 1934, Section 29(b) may serve as a powerful weapon for aggrieved litigants. Under the provision's language, every contract formed or performed in contravention of the 1934 Act or any rule or regulation prescribed thereunder "shall be void" as regards the rights of the violating party or his/her successor who takes with knowledge. This is the case even though the provision violated itself provides no private right of action. As the Supreme Court has stated, Section 29(b) impliedly "confers a 'right to rescind' a contract void under the criteria of the statute." [72]

Taken literally, Section 29(b)'s language, to quote Judge Friendly, is "[d]raconian." [73] Due to the "devastating meaning" of the provision's language, a number of courts have held that Section 29(b) merely codifies common law principles of illegal bargain in the application of the Exchange Act. [74]

---

[67] See, e.g., *Gaines v. Haughton*, 645 F.2d 761 (9th Cir. 1981).

[68] See, e.g., *Weisberg v. Coastal States Gas Corp.*, 609 F.2d 650 (2d Cir. 1979).

[69] See, e.g., *GAF Corporation v. Heyman*, 724 F.2d 727 (2d Cir. 1983); discussion in § 13.03 *infra*.

[70] See, e.g., *Pavlidis v. New England Patriots Football Club, Inc.*, 737 F.2d 1227 (1st Cir. 1984).

[71] See generally R. Thomas & C. Dixon, *Aranow & Einhorn on Proxy Contests for Corporate Control* (3d ed. 1998); Bainbridge, *Redirecting State Takeover Laws at Proxy Contests*, 1992 Wisc. L. Rev. 1071; Bradford, *The Possible Future of Private Rights of Action for Proxy Fraud: The Parallel Between Borak and Wilko*, 70 Neb. L. Rev. 306 (1991); Gelb, *Implied Private Actions Under SEC Rules 14a-9 and 10b-5: The Impact of Virginia Bankshares, Inc. v. Sandberg*, 76 Marquette L. Rev. 363 (1993); Hazen, *Corporate Mismanagement and the Federal Securities Act's Antifraud Provisions: A Familiar Path with Some New Detours*, 20 B.C. L. Rev. 819 (1979); Painter, *Civil Liability Under the Federal Proxy Rules*, 64 Wash. U. L.Q. 425 (1986); Steinberg, *Fiduciary Duties and Disclosure Obligations in Proxy and Tender Contests for Corporate Control*, 30 Emory L.J. 169 (1981); Symposium on Proxy Reform, 17 J. Corp. L. No. 1 (1991).

[72] *Transamerica Mortgage Advisors, Inc. v. Lewis*, 444 U.S. 11, 17 (1979). See *Mills v. Electric Auto-Lite Co.*, 396 U.S. 375, 387-388 (1970).

[73] *Pearlstein v. Scudder & German*, 429 F.2d 1136, 1149 (2d Cir. 1970) (Friendly, J., dissenting).

[74] See, e.g., *Occidental Life Insurance Co. v. Pat Ryan & Associates*, 496 F.2d 1255 (4th Cir. 1974).

Some courts, however, have construed Section 29(b) according to its language. In these decisions, the provision has been interpreted to provide plaintiffs with the relief sought, namely, the rescission of the subject transaction. For example, the Fifth Circuit has held that, pursuant to Section 29(b), a plaintiff can avoid a contract if it can be shown that: (1) the contract involved a "prohibited transaction," namely, that in the making or performance of the contract, there was perpetrated a violation of an Exchange Act provision or any rule or regulation prescribed thereunder; (2) there exists contractual privity between the plaintiff and the defendant; and (3) the plaintiff is in the class of persons the Exchange Act was designed to protect.[75] Once the plaintiff proves the above, the defendant may raise available equitable defenses, such as laches, estoppel, and "unclean hands."[76]

If the elements of the Section 29(b) right of action are satisfied, a plaintiff may rescind a contract, even after performance has been rendered. Given a remedial construction, Section 29(b) may subject every transaction, from an ordinary purchase of securities, to a complex merger, reorganization, proxy contest, or tender offer to which the Exchange Act applies, to its voidability provisions. However, in view of the Supreme Court's current approach, such an expansive interpretation of Section 29(b) is unlikely.[77]

§ 8.07 The Racketeer Influenced and Corrupt Organizations Act (RICO)

In 1995, Congress severely limited civil RICO actions in securities-related litigation.[78] Even prior to that legislation, the courts already had constricted civil RICO by setting forth various requirements.[79] Generally, prior to the 1995 legislation, civil RICO provided an express right of action to redress fraud in the sale of securities (as well as for mail and wire fraud).[80]

---

[75] *Regional Properties, Inc. v. Financial and Real Estate Consulting Company*, 678 F.2d 552, 559 (5th Cir. 1982).

[76] *Id.* at 562-63.

[77] See Gruenbaum & Steinberg, *Section 29(b) of the Securities Exchange Act of 1934: A Viable Remedy Awakened*, 48 Geo. Wash. L. Rev. 1 (1979). See also, Scott, *A Broker-Dealer's Civil Liability to Investors for Fraud: An Implied Private Right of Action Under Section 15(c)(1) of the Securities Exchange Act of 1934*, 63 Indiana L.J 687 (1988) (discussing the availability of an implied right of action under § 15(c)(1) as well as the application of the § 29(b) remedy).

[78] In enacting the Private Securities Litigation Reform Act of 1995, Congress amended Section 1964(c) of RICO.

[79] See, e.g., *International Data Bank v. Zepkin*, 812 F.2d 149 (4th Cir. 1987) (applying purchaser-seller standing requirement to civil RICO actions premised on securities fraud).

[80] 18 U.S.C. § 1964(c). See generally D. Abrams, *The Law of Civil RICO* (1991); Blakey & Gettings, *Racketeer Influenced and Corrupt Organizations (RICO): Basic Concepts — Criminal and Civil Remedies*, 53 Temple L.Q. 1009 (1980); Bridges, *Private RICO Litigation Based Upon "Fraud in the Sale of Securities,"* 18 Ga. L. Rev. 43 (1983); MacIntosh, *Racketeer Influenced and Corrupt Organizations Act: Powerful New Tool of the Defrauded Securities Plaintiff*, 31 Kansas L. Rev. 7 (1982); Mathews, *Shifting the Burden of Losses in the Securities Markets: The Role of Civil RICO in Securities Litigation*, 65 Notre Dame L. Rev. 896 (1990); Tyson & August, *The Williams Act After RICO: Has the Balance Tipped in Favor of Incumbent Management?*, 35 Hastings L.J. 53 (1983); Comment, *RICO and Securities Fraud: A Workable Limitation*, 83 Colum. L. Rev. 1513 (1983).

To state a claim for damages under RICO, the complainant first must allege a violation of the substantive RICO statute,[81] commonly referred to as "criminal RICO." The constituent elements of criminal RICO, as set forth by the Second Circuit, are "(1) that the defendant (2) through the commission of two or more acts (3) constituting a 'pattern' (4) of 'racketeering activity' (5) directly or indirectly invests in, or maintains an interest in, or participates in (6) an 'enterprise' (7) the activities of which affect interstate or foreign commerce."[82] After adequately alleging the foregoing, a private plaintiff, in order to invoke RICO's civil provisions for treble damages, attorneys' fees and costs, must satisfy a second burden, namely that he was "injured in his business or property *by reason* of a violation of Section 1962 [criminal RICO]."[83]

Pursuant to the Private Securities Litigation Reform Act of 1995, Congress amended Section 1964(c) of RICO to eliminate securities fraud as a predicate act in a civil RICO action. According to the Joint Explanatory Statement of the Conference Committee for the legislation, the Committee also "intend[ed] that a plaintiff may not plead other specified offenses, such as mail or wire fraud, as predicate acts under civil RICO if such offenses are based on conduct that would have been actionable as securities fraud." An exception is made, thereby permitting a civil RICO action to be initiated in this context, when any person has been criminally convicted in connection with the fraud, in which case the statute of limitations commences to run on the date the conviction becomes final.

§ 8.08 State Securities and Common Law Remedies

In the last two decades, the U.S. Supreme Court has handed down a number of restrictive decisions under the federal securities laws. Due to this development, the question arises whether investors should consider pursuing their state law actions with greater vigor.

[A] Obstacles to State Law Relief

[1] Overview

In some situations, plaintiffs should pursue their grievances under the federal securities acts. For example, a state such as New York declines to

---

[81] 18 U.S.C. § 1962.

[82] *Moss v. Morgan Stanley, Inc.*, 719 F.2d 5, 17 (2d Cir. 1983). Criminal RICO, therefore, makes unlawful:

(1) using income derived from a pattern of racketeering activity to acquire an interest in an enterprise;

(2) acquiring or maintaining an interest in an enterprise through a pattern of racketeering activity or collection of an unlawful debt;

(3) conducting the affairs of an enterprise through a pattern of racketeering activity; and

(4) conspiring to commit any of these offenses.

18 U.S.C. § 1962(a)-(d).

[83] 18 U.S.C. § 1964(c) (emphasis added).

recognize a private right of action for violation of its securities laws.[84] In addition, certain other states in their respective securities statutes provide private redress for purchasers only,[85] and afford a shorter statute of limitations than that prescribed by federal law.[86] Moreover, by premising liability upon the status of the primary violator as a seller, many of these statutes evidently cannot be invoked against a corporate defendant and its fiduciaries in secondary market frauds, such as when a company allegedly issues a deliberately false press release or earnings statement.[87] Adoption of a sufficiently broad definition of "seller" in this context would expand the statute's scope to encompass such situations.[88]

Another significant downside to state law is with respect to class action litigation. Unlike federal law which recognizes the fraud on the market theory to create a presumption of reliance,[89] thereby facilitating use of the class action mechanism, a number of state courts have declined to adopt this doctrine with respect to actions alleging common law fraud.[90] The consequence is that individualized proof of reliance is required, hence militating against class certification. For example, in rejecting the fraud on the market theory in cases alleging common law fraud, the California Supreme Court opined that recognition of the theory would eliminate the reliance requirement.[91] Similarly, the Delaware Supreme Court has held that "[a] class action may not be maintained in a purely common law or equitable fraud case since individual questions of law or fact, particularly

---

[84] See *CPC Int'l v. McKesson Corp.*, 70 N.Y.2d 268, 519 N.Y.S. 2d 804, 514 N.E.2d 116 (1987).

[85] See, e.g., North Dakota Comm. Code § 10-04-17, *construed in, Weidner v. Engelhart*, 176 N.W.2d 509, 513 (N.D. 1970); Ohio Rev. Code § 1707.43. See also, Section 410(a) of the Uniform Securities Act, *reprinted in*, 1 Blue Sky L. Rep. (CCH) ¶ 5500, at 1566 (Adopted 1956).

[86] See, e.g.; Ga. Code § 97-114(d); Mo. Code § 409.411(e); N.C. Securities Act § 78A-56(f); Va. Code § 13.1-522(D); *Clouser v. Temporaries, Inc.*, [1990-1991 Transfer Binder] Fed. Sec. L. Rep. (CCH) ¶ 95,846 (D.D.C. 1989) (holding claim was barred by the two-year District of Columbia blue sky statute of limitations, D.C. Code § 2-2613(e)).

[87] Hence, many states have adopted the Section 12(a)(2) counterpart but have declined to provide a private remedy for the Rule 10b-5 counterpart. Compare Texas Securities Act Art. 581-33A(2) (Section 12(a)(2) counterpart), with Washington Securities Act, RCW 21.20.010 (Rule 10b-5 counterpart).

[88] For example, holding that a company issuing a materially misleading press release aided the sale, played an integral role in the sale, or solicited the transaction for its financial benefit would, depending upon the standard adopted, confer "seller" status upon the entity, thereby subjecting it to liability exposure in secondary open market transactions.

[89] *Basic, Inc. v. Levinson*, 485 U.S. 224 (1988), *discussed in*, § 7.06[B] *supra*.

[90] Because many blue sky remedial statutes do not have a reliance requirement, this issue most frequently arises with respect to common law fraud claims. See, e.g., *Peil v. Speiser*, 806 F.2d 1154, 1163 n.17 (3d Cir. 1986) ("While the fraud on the market theory is good law with respect to the Securities Acts, no state courts have adopted the theory, and thus direct reliance remains a requirement of a common law securities fraud claim."); *Mirkin v. Wasserman*, 5 Cal. 4th 1082, 858 P.2d 568, 23 Cal. Rptr. 2d 101 (1993); *Gaffin v. Teledyne, Inc.*, 611 A.2d 467, 474 (Del. 1991); *Antonson v. Robertson*, 141 F.R.D. 501, 508 (E.D. Kan. 1991). But see *Hurley v. Federal Deposit Insurance Corp.*, 719 F. Supp. 27, 34 n.4 (D. Mass. 1989); Ohio Rev. Code § 1707.43 (no reliance requirement); *Arnold v. Dirrim*, 398 N.E.2d 426 (Ind. App. 1979).

[91] *Mirkin v. Wasserman*, 5 Cal. 4th 1082, 858 P.2d 568, 23 Cal. Rptr. 2d 101 (1993). Importantly, the court recognized that the state securities law provisions discussed at bar contained no reliance requirement.

as to the element of justifiable reliance, will inevitably predominate over common questions of law or fact."[92]

The availability of classwide treatment for plaintiff-investors in state securities and common law fraud cases has taken on greater significance in view of the U.S. Supreme Court's determination that Section 10(b) actions have a relatively short statute of limitations.[93] The practical consequence of these state court cases mandating individualized proof of reliance is that investors whose federal and state securities law claims are time-barred will also be prevented from obtaining class certification to bring their state common law action. In cases where prospective complainants sit on their rights perhaps this result is the correct one. But such a result arguably is unjust in cases of fraudulent concealment. In such situations, aggrieved investors may not learn of the fraud until several years (and even decades) after the event.[94] Given this reality, state courts and legislatures should recognize that application of the fraud on the market theory in common law fraud actions is a useful presumption in order to help ensure that unsophisticated investors in such situations have a forum to redress their grievances.[95]

[2] The Securities Litigation Uniform Standards Act

Enactment of the Securities Litigation Uniform Standards Act of 1998 (Uniform Standards Act) severely limits the availability of state law redress. Indeed, regarding securities class actions[96] involving nationally

---

[92] *Gaffin v. Teledyne, Inc.*, 611 A.2d 467, 474 (Del. 1992).

[93] See *Lampf, Pleva, Lipkind, Prupis & Pettigrow v. Gilbertson*, 501 U.S. 350 (1991) (construing statute of limitations for § 10(b) (1934 Act) claims to be within one year after discovery and in no event more than three years after the violation), *discussed in*, § 7.08 *supra*. See Section 13 of the Securities Act, 15 U.S.C. § 77m (providing statute of limitations for §§ 11 and 12(a)(2) claims of one year after plaintiffs knew or should have known of the violation and in no event more than three years after such violation).

[94] See, e.g., *Ernst & Ernst v. Hochfelder*, 425 U.S. 185 (1976) (fraud discovered decades later).

[95] A number of cases provide plaintiffs with some hope of receiving class certification of their common law claims. See, e.g., *In re College Bound Consolidated Litigation*, [1994-1995 Transfer Binder] Fed. Sec. L. Rep. (CCH) ¶ 98,328 (S.D.N.Y. 1994).

[96] Pursuant to the Securities Litigation Uniform Standards Act of 1998, a "covered class action" means:

(i) any single lawsuit in which —

(I) damages are sought on behalf of more than 50 persons or prospective class members, and questions of law or fact common to those persons or members of the prospective class, without reference to issues of individualized reliance on an alleged misstatement or omission, predominate over any questions affecting only individual persons or members; or

(II) one or more named parties seek to recover damages on a representative basis on behalf of themselves and other unnamed parties similarly situated, and questions of law or fact common to those persons or members of the prospective class predominate over any questions affecting only individual persons or members; or

(ii) any group of lawsuits filed in or pending in the same court and involving common questions of law or fact, in which —

(I) damages are sought on behalf of more than 50 persons; and

(II) the lawsuits are joined, consolidated, or otherwise proceed as a single action for any purpose.

traded securities,[97] the Uniform Standards Act[98] generally preempts state law.[99] Certain important exceptions exist, however, thereby preserving state securities and common law in those situations. For example, derivative actions may be pursued under state law.[100] State law also may be invoked in suits challenging the conduct of a subject issuer, any of its affiliates, or affected corporate fiduciaries with respect to specified actions—namely, going-private transactions, tender offers, mergers, and the exercise of appraisal rights.[101] Importantly, the Uniform Standards Act declines to preempt in any way the authority of the state securities commissions, thereby empowering the states to continue their investigatory and enforcement functions.[102]

The impact of the Uniform Standards Act is significant. Prior to its enactment, proponents asserted that publicly-held companies were reluctant to disclose forward-looking information,[103] irrespective of the safe harbor provided by the Private Securities Litigation Reform Act of 1995. The concern remained that such disclosure of forward-looking information

---

Section 101 of the Uniform Standards Act, *amending* § 16(f)(2)(A) of the Securities Act (15 U.S.C. § 77p(f)(2)(A)), and § 28(f)(5)(B) of the Exchange Act (15 U.S.C. § 78bb(f)(5)(B)).

[97] The term nationally traded security or "covered security" means a security that meets the standards set forth in Section 18(b) of the Securities Act, 15 U.S.C. § 77r(b). These securities include those that are listed for trading on the New York Stock Exchange, American Stock Exchange, and the NASDAQ National Market System (NMS). Securities issued by registered investment companies also are defined as nationally traded securities.

[98] Pub. L. No. 105-353, 112 Stat. 3227 (1998). See H. R. Rep. No. 105-803, 105th Cong., 2d Sess. (1998).

[99] See Section 101 of the Uniform Standards Act, *amending* Section 16 of the Securities Act (15 U.S.C. § 77p) and Section 28 of the Exchange Act (15 U.S.C. § 78bb).

[100] See Section 101 of the Uniform Standards Act, *amending* Section 16(f)(2)(B) of the Securities Act (15 U.S.C. § 77p(f)(2)(B)), and Section 28(f)(5)(C) (15 U.S.C. § 78bb(f)(5)(C)) (stating that "the term 'covered class action' does not include an exclusively derivative action brought by one or more shareholders on behalf of a corporation"). For the definition of "covered class action," see note 96 *supra*.

[101] See Section 101 of the Uniform Standards Act, *amending* Section 16(d)(1) of the Securities Act (15 U.S.C. § 77p(d)(1)), and Section 28(f)(3)(A)) of the Exchange Act (15 U.S.C. § 78bb(f)(3)(A)). In addition, the Uniform Standards Act excludes from federal preemption suits instituted by a state, a political subdivision thereof, or a state pension plan provided that such state, political submission thereof, or state pension plan is named as a plaintiff in such action and has authorized its participation in such action. See Section 101 of the Uniform Standards Act, *amending* Section 16(d)(2) of the Securities Act (15 U.S.C. § 77p(d)(2)), and Section 28(f)(3)(B) of the Exchange Act (15 U.S.C. § 78bb(f)(3)(B)). As another exception, "a covered class action that seeks to enforce a contractual agreement between an issuer and an indenture trustee may be maintained in a State or Federal court by a party to the agreement or a successor to such party." Section 101 of the Uniform Standards Act, *amending* Section 16(d)(3) of the Securities Act (15 U.S.C. § 77p(d)(3)), and Section 28(f)(3)(C) of the Exchange Act (15 U.S.C. § 78bb(f)(3)(C)).

[102] See Section 101 of the Uniform Standards Act, *amending* § 16(e) of the Securities Act (15 U.S.C. § 77p(e)), and Section 28(f)(4) of the Exchange Act (15 U.S.C. § 78bb(f)(4)) (stating that "[t]he securities commission (or any agency or office performing like functions) of any State shall retain jurisdiction under the laws of such State to investigate and bring enforcement actions").

[103] See sources cited in Levine & Pritchard, *The Securities Litigation Uniform Standards Act of 1998: The Sun Sets on California's Blue Sky Laws*, 54 Bus. Law. 1, 12 (1998).

would subject the applicable company to state court litigation.[104] The enactment of the Uniform Standards Act, generally preempting state law in securities class actions involving nationally traded securities,[105] should provide sufficient comfort to induce such companies to disclose forward-looking information.[106]

[B] Advantages of State Claims

On the other hand, there may be several distinct advantages for plaintiffs to bring state blue sky and common law claims.[107] Importantly, many state securities acts provide that, if appropriate, successful plaintiffs may recover reasonable attorneys' fees and punitive damages.[108] Another significant advantage relates to the statute of limitations issue. In *Lampf, Pleva, Lipkind, Prupis & Pettigrow v. Gilbertson*,[109] the Supreme Court held that the statute of limitations under Section 10(b) is one year from the date that the plaintiff discovered (or should have discovered) the facts constituting the violation and in no event more than three years after the violation.[110] Equitable tolling, the Court held, is not permitted.[111] A similar statute of limitations applies to claims brought under the Securities Act, including those brought pursuant to Section 12(a)(2).[112]

---

[104] See Grundfest, et al., *Securities Class Action Litigation in 1998: A Report to NASDAQ From the Stanford Law School Securities Class Action Clearinghouse*, 1070 PLI/Corp 69 (1998) ("Since passage of the Reform Act, a substantial portion of class action litigation has shifted from federal to state court in an apparent attempt to evade the Act's provisions."); Grundfest & Perino, *Securities Litigation Reform: The First Year's Experience — A Statistical Analysis of Class Action Securities Fraud Litigation Under the Private Securities Litigation Reform Act of 1995*, Stanford Law School (Feb. 27, 1997); *Securities Class Actions Seem to be Moving to State Courts, According to New Study*, 29 Sec. Reg. & L. Rep. (BNA) 311 (1997).

[105] Note, however, that the preservation of state derivative actions along with the Delaware Supreme Court's interpretations relating to a corporate fiduciary's duty of candor may not foreclose state litigation in the general disclosure context. See, e.g., *Malone v. Brincat*, 722 A.2d 5 (Del. 1998).

[106] See generally J. Hamilton & T. Trautmann, *Securities Litigation Uniform Standards Act of 1998: Law and Explanation* (CCH 1998); Casey, *Shutting the Doors to State Court: The Securities Litigation Uniform Standards Act of 1998*, 27 Sec. Reg. L.J. 141 (1999); Levine & Pritchard, note 103 *supra*; Painter, *Responding to a False Alarm: Federal Preemption of State Securities Fraud Causes of Action*, 84 Cornell L. Rev. 1 (1998).

[107] See Branson, *Collateral Participant Liability Under State Securities Laws*, 19 Pepp. L. Rev. 1027 (1992); Steinberg, *The Emergence of State Securities Laws: Partly Sunny Skies for Investors*, 62 U. Cin. L. Rev. 395 (1993).

[108] See, e.g., Uniform Securities Act § 410(a), *supra* note 85, at 1566; Ariz. Rev. Stat. § 44-2001; Wash. Rev. Code § 21.20.430(1), (2). Punitive damages also may be awarded in appropriate situations, such as where malice or egregious fraud is shown. See Ohio Rev. Code § 2315.21(B); *Price v. Griffin*, 359 A.2d 582, 589-590 (D.C. Ct. App. 1976).

[109] 501 U.S. 350 (1991), *discussed in*, § 7.08 *supra*.

[110] *Id.* at 364. (selecting § 9(e) of the Exchange Act as the language to govern the limitations period for § 10(b) actions).

[111] *Id.* at 363. The Court reasoned that the three-year outside limit was incompatible with equitable tolling principles.

[112] See Section 13 of the Securities Act, 15 U.S.C. § 77m (providing statute of limitations for §§ 11 and 12(a)(2) claims of one year after plaintiffs knew or should have known of the violation and in no event more than three years after such violation).

By contrast, many of the state blue sky statutes contain a longer statute of limitations under "Section 12(a)(2)/Section 10(b) types" of statutes. For example, Texas has a three year/five year limitations period. In other words, the Texas statute provides a statute of limitations barring such an action "more than three years after discovery of the untruth or omission, or after discovery should have been made by the exercise of reasonable diligence; or more than five years after the sale [or purchase]."[113] Other more flexible statutes of limitations include those of Florida (two year/five year),[114] Michigan (two year/four year),[115] Ohio (two year/four year),[116] California (one year/four year),[117] and Pennsylvania (one year/four year).[118] As to the outside limit, there appears to be no equitable tolling allowed.[119] Nonetheless, for those statutes that contain a flat period (for example, that suit must be brought within two years after the transaction), there is some authority that the statute may be tolled due to the defendant's fraudulent concealment.[120] Moreover, in cases of common law fraud, it is well established that the statute of limitations may be equitably tolled.[121]

Another example is that many state securities statutes provide for monetary damages based on negligent material misrepresentations or omissions made in the initial offering context as well as in the secondary trading markets.[122] Under federal law, if Section 10(b) is invoked, scienter must

---

[113] Tex. Civ. Stat. Ann. Art. 581-33H(2), (3). In addition, the Texas statute provides a limitations period of three years for registration violations. *Id.* Art. 581-33H(1). By contrast, the Securities Act generally provides a one-year statute of limitations for actions brought under Section 12(a)(1) for registration violations. See Section 13, 15 U.S.C. § 77m.

[114] Fla. Stat. Ann. § 95.11(4)(e). Accord, New Mexico Securities Act, N.M. Art. 58-13B-41 (two year/five year).

[115] Mich. Comp. Laws Ann. § 451.810(e).

[116] Ohio Rev. Code Ann. § 1707.43. For the two-year period in the statute, at least under some circumstances, that period "begins to run upon the actual discovery of the defect." *Eastman v. Benchmark Minerals, Inc.,* 34 Ohio App. 3d 255, 258, 518 N.E.2d 23, 25 (1986).

[117] Cal. Corp. Code § 25506.

[118] Pa. Stat. Ann. tit. 70, § 1-504(a).

[119] See, e.g.; *SEC v. Seaboard Corp.,* 677 F.2d 1301, 1308 (9th Cir. 1982) (interpreting California statute); *Gilbert Family Partnership v. NIDO Corporation,* 679 F. Supp. 679, 685 (E.D. Mich. 1988) (interpreting Michigan statute); *Bull v. American Bank & Trust Co.,* 641 F. Supp. 62, 67 (E.D. Pa. 1986) (interpreting Pennsylvania statute).

[120] See, e.g.; *Barton v. Peterson,* 733 F. Supp. 1482, 1492-93 (N.D. Ga. 1990) (interpreting Georgia law); *Platsis v. E.F. Hutton & Company, Inc.,* 642 F. Supp. 1277, 1304-05 (W.D. Mich. 1986), *aff'd,* 829 F.2d 13 (6th Cir. 1987) (construing § 410(e) of the Michigan Uniform Securities Act).

[121] See *Willis v. Maverick,* 760 S.W.2d 642, 644-45 (Tex. 1988); *Lampf,* 501 U.S. at 377-78 (Kennedy, J., dissenting) ("Only a small number of States constrain fraud actions with absolute periods of repose . . . .").

[122] For example, the Washington Supreme Court in *Kittilson v. Ford,* 93 Wash. 2d 223, 608 P.2d 264 (1980) (a civil action for damages), rejected the *Hochfelder* scienter standard. In distinguishing *Hochfelder* and holding that negligence is sufficient to impose liability, the *Kittilson* court reasoned:

We believe the holding in *Ernst & Ernst v. Hochfelder* [425 U.S. 185 (1976)] [is] inapplicable to our Securities Act. First, the "manipulative or deceptive" language of Section 10(b) of the 1934 Act is not included in the Washington Act. Secondly, in contrast to the federal scheme, the language of Rule 10b-5 is not derivative but is the statute in Washington. Finally, no legislative history similar or analogous to Congressional legislative history exists in Washington.

be shown.[123] In addition, these state securities statutory counterparts are more expansive than Section 12(a)(2). Accordingly, under a number of these statutes, plaintiffs may have a four or five-year limitations period to bring an action based on negligently made statements in the secondary markets.

Moreover, although some state courts have followed the Supreme Court's decision in *Pinter v. Dahl*[124] for defining who is a "seller" under the applicable state securities statute,[125] a number of states adhere to the more expansive "substantial factor" test.[126] This standard was used by several lower federal courts prior to *Pinter* for defining the term "seller" under Section 12 of the Securities Act.[127] Under this test, one is deemed a "seller" if his or her actions played an integral role or were a substantial contributing factor in the transaction.[128] Certainly, the liability net extends farther under this definition of "seller."

Also, a number of the state statutes extend liability exposure to those who materially aid in consummating the transaction.[129] This concept of secondary liability is particularly important in view of the U.S. Supreme Court's decision in *Central Bank of Denver* foreclosing aiding and abetting liability in private actions under Section 10(b).[130] Indeed, one who materially aids a sale under such a state statute is subject to liability unless he/she meets the reasonable care defense.[131] In effect, this standard may enable a plaintiff successfully to reach certain parties who would avoid liability under the federal securities laws, either because they were not "sellers"

---

[123] *Aaron v. SEC*, 446 U.S. 680 (1980); *Ernst & Ernst v. Hochfelder*, 425 U.S. 185 (1976).

[124] 486 U.S. 622 (1988) (defining seller under § 12(1) of the Securities Act as extending to one "who successfully solicits the purchase, motivated at least in part by a desire to serve his own financial interests or those of the securities owner"), *discussed in*, § 6.09[B] *supra*. Lower federal courts overwhelmingly have applied *Pinter* to Section 12(2) (now 12(a)(2)) actions. *Id.*

[125] See, e.g., *Baker, Watts & Co., v. Miles & Stockbridge*, 95 Md. App. 145, 620 A.2d 356 (1993); *State v. Williams*, 98 N.C. App. 274, 279, 390 S.E.2d 746, 749 (1990); *Brales v. Young*, 432 S.E.2d 482 (S.C. 1993).

[126] See, e.g., *Anders v. Dakota Land & Development Co.*, 380 N.W.2d 862, 867-68 (Minn. App. 1980); *Price v. Brydon*, 307 Or. 146, 764 P.2d 1370 (1988); *Hines v. Data Line Systems, Inc.*, 114 Wash. 2d 127, 787 P.2d 8, 20 (1990). An even more expansive definition of "seller" may have been recognized in *Lutheran Brotherhood v. Kidder Peabody & Co.*, 829 S.W.2d 300, 306 (Tex. App.), *set aside on other grounds*, 840 S.W.2d 384 (Tex. 1992) (stating that Texas' § 12(a)(2) counterpart, Art. 581-33(A)(2) "applies if the defendant was any link in the chain of the selling process").

[127] See, e.g., *Davis v. Avco Financial Services, Inc.*, 739 F.2d 1057, 1067-68 (6th Cir. 1984) (defining a seller as one who is integrally connected with or substantially involved in the transaction).

[128] *Id.*

[129] See, e.g., Ariz. Rev. Stat. Ann. § 44-2003; Or. Rev. Stat. § 59.115(3); Ohio Rev. Code § 1707.43. See generally J. Long, *Blue Sky Law* § 7.08 (1999).

[130] *Central Bank of Denver v. First Interstate Bank of Denver,* 511 U.S. 164 (1994), *discussed in*, §§ 9.01-9.03 *infra*.

[131] For application of the reasonable care standard as an affirmative defense, see, e.g., *Arnold v. Dirrim*, 398 N.E.2d 426, 434-35 (Ind. App. 1979); *McGarrity v. Craighill*, 83 N.C. App. 106, 111-12, 349 S.E.2d 311, 314-15 (1986).

under the *Pinter* test or were aiders and abettors rather than primary violators.[132]

There are other key advantages for plaintiffs under certain of the state securities provisions. For example, many states hold that reliance is not required to be shown under the applicable blue sky statute,[133] hence facilitating class action certification. Proving loss causation also may be dispensed with by plaintiffs in a number of states.[134] This more relaxed liability framework prompted Professor Cane to poignantly observe:

> It would seem that a plaintiff bringing a suit under [the Florida statute] could rescind [the transaction] without a showing of proximate cause, or any damage, or any scienter on the part of the defendant. . . . Was the intent of the Florida legislature to create a system of investor insurance?[135]

In addition to their state blue sky claims, investors also may emerge victorious when seeking relief on common law fraud, negligent misrepresentation, and breach of fiduciary duty grounds. In the *Virginia Bankshares* case, for example, although defeated on their federal and state securities law claims, the plaintiffs were awarded hefty damages on their breach of fiduciary duty claims.[136] In another case, even though not a purchaser or seller of stock, a shareholder under the circumstances at bar was entitled to bring a common law action for fraud.[137] And, as another example, the Eleventh Circuit held that, although unsuccessful on their federal and state securities law claims, the plaintiffs established a meritorious breach of fiduciary duty claim against their broker.[138] In so holding, the court asserted that "the [federal and state] securities fraud statutes do not co-opt the existence of separate claims under state fiduciary principles."[139]

In conclusion, the state securities laws are likely to be invoked by plaintiffs with greater frequency. Due to their more flexible construction,

---

[132] See, e.g., *Price v. Brydon*, 307 Or. 146, 764 P.2d 1370 (1988) (holding that attorney's actions in an offering could be viewed as materially aiding the sale). But see *Riedel v. Acutate of Colorado*, 773 F. Supp. 1055, 1066 (S.D. Ohio), *aff'd*, 947 F.2d 955 (6th Cir. 1991) (interpreting Ohio law, court stated that "an attorney providing professional services is not liable under Section 1707.43"). See generally Long, *Developments and Issues in Civil Liability Under Blue Sky Law*, 62 U. Cin. L. Rev. 439 (1993).

[133] See. e.g., Cal. Corp. Code §§ 25400, 25500; *Mirkin v. Wasserman*, 5 Cal. 4th 1082, 858 P.2d 568, 23 Cal. Rptr. 2d 101 (1993); Ohio Rev. Code § 1707.43; *Roger v. Lehman Bros. Kuhn Loeb, Inc.*, 621 F. Supp. 114, 118 (S.D. Ohio 1985) (interpreting Ohio Rev. Code Ann. § 1707.43); Texas Securities Act, Art. 581-33A(2); *Anderson v. Vinson Exploration, Inc.*, 832 S.W.2d 657 (Tex. App. 1992).

[134] See *E.F. Hutton & Company, Inc. v. Rousseff*, 537 So.2d 978, 981 (Fla. 1989).

[135] Cane, *Proximate Causation in Securities Fraud Actions for Rescission*, Fla. Bar Bus. Quart. Rep., Vol. 2, No. 2, at p. 14 (Spring 1989).

[136] See *Sandberg v. Virginia Bankshares, Inc.*, 979 F.2d 332, 342-48 (4th Cir. 1992).

[137] See *Gutman v. Howard Savings Bank*, 748 F. Supp. 254, 266 (D.N.J. 1990) (interpreting New Jersey law, standing to bring common law fraud claim granted and reliance may be shown in regard thereto where alleged misstatements were made directly to the complainant).

[138] *Gochnauer v. A.G. Edwards & Sons, Inc.*, 810 F.2d 1042 (11th Cir. 1987).

[139] *Id.* at 1050 (interpreting Florida law).

many of the state statutes provide the plaintiff with a right of action where such right may be lacking under federal law. Hence, the effect of the federal courts' restrictive approach to the remedial provisions of the Securities Acts may well be to induce plaintiffs more frequently to file their actions in the state courts. Given the broad relief awarded in some of these state court proceedings, this result in the end may be more detrimental to defendants. Hence, it indeed is ironic that many plaintiffs, by electing to bring suit in state court, may well be better off than they were prior to the time that the federal courts embarked on their restrictive approach.

Although plaintiffs may elect to bring their state claims along with their federal securities law claims in federal district court,[140] an increasing number of complainants are declining this option.[141] Perhaps this result is due to perceptions that state judges may be more inclined to permit issues to reach the jury and the relatively large number of significant damage verdicts awarded in the state courts.[142] Moreover, as evidenced by a number of decisions, there may be the concern that federal courts may construe the state securities laws at bar consistently with and no broader than federal law.[143] Such holdings, of course, provide an additional incentive for plaintiffs to institute their actions in state court and seek more remedial interpretations.

Nonetheless, as discussed earlier,[144] it must be emphasized that pursuant to the Securities Litigation Uniform Standards Act, state law (with certain exceptions) is preempted in class actions involving nationally traded securities. In such circumstances, federal law serves as the sole source for plaintiff redress.

---

[140] Of course, there are situations where only state law claims are available, hence mandating that suit be brought in state court (unless the requirements of diversity of citizenship jurisdiction are met). See 28 U.S.C. § 1332. One such example is where the applicable statute of limitations has expired for the federal securities law claims but not for the state law claims.

[141] By bringing the action in state court, a plaintiff therefore bypasses remedies afforded by the Exchange Act, such as Section 10(b), due to that Act's provision for exclusive federal jurisdiction. See Section 27 of the Exchange Act, 15 U.S.C. § 78aa. Electing to forego Exchange Act remedies and opt for the state court forum calls for counsel and client to address significant substantive and tactical questions.

[142] See, e.g., Moffett & Petzinger, *Pennzoil Wins $10.53 Billion in Suit Against Texaco; Verdict Is Called Highest Civil Judgment in History*, Wall St. J., Nov. 20, 1985, at 3.

[143] See, e.g., *Abell v. Potomac Insurance Company*, 858 F.2d 1104, 1130-31 (5th Cir. 1988), *vacated on other grounds, Fryer v. Abell*, 492 U.S. 914 (1989) (interpreting Louisiana law); *Capri v. Murphy*, 856 F.2d 473, 479 (2d Cir. 1988) (interpreting Connecticut law). See generally Branson, *Securities Litigation in State Courts — Something Old, Something New, Something Borrowed*, 76 Wash. U. L.Q. 509 (1998); Steinberg, *The Ramifications of Recent U.S. Supreme Court Decisions on Federal and State Securities Regulation*, 70 Notre Dame L. Rev. 489 (1995).

[144] See discussion *supra* notes 96-106 and accompanying text.

Chapter 9

SECONDARY LIABILITY

This chapter considers secondary liability under the federal securities laws. Three different theories of liability are highlighted: aiding and abetting, controlling person, and *respondeat superior*. Importantly, these theories also are applicable under many of the state securities statutes.[1] In addition, the ensuing discussion addresses distinctions between primary and secondary conduct.

§ 9.01 Aiding and Abetting Liability

Prior to the Supreme Court's decision in *Central Bank of Denver*,[2] virtually every lower federal court considering the issue recognized the propriety of aiding and abetting liability under Section 10(b) of the Exchange Act as well as certain other provisions.[3] However, in *Central Bank of Denver*, the Supreme Court held that Section 10(b) of the Exchange Act does not provide for the imposition of aiding and abetting liability in private litigation. The Court made crystal clear that its construction was based on "a strict statutory construction" and that the issue before it was one involving "the scope of conduct prohibited by § 10(b)."[4] Importantly, the Court's rationale extends to preclude aiding and abetting liability from being imposed by private plaintiffs for alleged violations of other federal securities law provisions.[5] Likewise, liability premised on the doctrine of "conspiracy" seems unavailable.[6] Moreover, prior to the enactment of the Private

---

[1] See J. Long, *Blue Sky Law* § 7.08 (1999); Branson, *Collateral Participant Liability Under State Securities Law*, 19 Pepp. L. Rev. 1027 (1992); Steinberg, *The Ramifications of Recent U.S. Supreme Court Decisions on Federal and State Securities Regulation*, 70 Notre Dame L. Rev. 489 (1995); discussion § 8.08 *supra*.

[2] 511 U.S. 164 (1994).

[3] See, e.g., *IIT v. Cornfeld*, 619 F.2d 909 (2d Cir. 1980); Olson, *The End of the Section 10(b) Aiding and Abetting Liability Fiction*, 8 Insights No. 6, at 3 (1994) ("The Court's decision overruled decisions from 11 federal courts of appeals which had recognized Section 10(b) aiding and abetting liability.").

[4] 511 U.S. at 173-75.

[5] After examining Sections 11 and 12 of the Securities Act and Sections 9, 16, 18, and 20A of the Exchange Act, the Court concluded that none of these express causes of action provided for aider and abettor liability. *Id.* at 178-80. Hence, the Court's analysis in *Central Bank of Denver* certainly should extend to other implied causes of action, such as Section 14(a) of the Exchange Act. Indeed, the statutory language of Section 14(a), like that of Section 10(b), "controls" and "bodes ill" for litigants who seek to hold collateral parties liable as aiders and abettors. *Id.* at 175.

[6] See 511 U.S. at 200 n.12 (Stevens, J., dissenting). Applying the analysis contained in *Central Bank of Denver*, lower courts overwhelmingly have rejected application of conspiracy doctrine under the federal securities laws. See, e.g., *Dinsmore v. Squadron, Ellenoff, Plesant, Sheinfield & Sorkin*, 135 F.3d 837 (2d Cir. 1998).

Securities Litigation Reform Act of 1995, the Court's restrictive approach was interpreted by many authorities to extend to the SEC, thereby precluding the Commission from bringing enforcement actions premised on aider and abettor liability (except where a statute provides for such liability).[7]

Nonetheless, discussion of aider and abettor liability principles should be undertaken for a number of reasons. For example, in view of Section 20(f) of the Exchange Act enacted as part of the Private Securities Litigation Reform Act, the SEC may pursue aiders and abettors for violations of the Exchange Act and rules prescribed thereunder.[8] Injunctions also may be procured by the Commission against those who aid and abet violations of the Investment Advisers Act.[9] Moreover, although the Commission's cease and desist power against those who are a "cause" of an alleged violation evidently is more expansive than aider and abettor liability principles,[10] the Commission still may draw on some of these principles to ascertain the parameters of the liability net. And, as a last example, a number of state securities statutes provide for aiding and abetting liability.[11] Prior to the Supreme Court's decision in *Central Bank of Denver*, the lower federal courts overwhelmingly held that aiding and abetting liability was appropriate under Section 10(b) of the Exchange Act as well as certain other provisions.[12] Although courts differed on the precise content of the various elements giving rise to aiding and abetting liability,[13] three basic prerequisites emerged: (1) a primary securities law violation by another, (2) substantial assistance by the alleged aider and abettor in the commission of the primary violation, and (3) requisite "knowledge" on the part of such alleged aider and abettor that his/her conduct was improper.[14]

In determining whether the requisite knowledge had been shown,[15] reckless conduct[16] sufficed if a fiduciary relationship existed between the

---

[7] See Gorman, *Who's Afraid of 10b-5? The Scope of a Section 10(b) Cause of Action After Central Bank of Denver*, 22 Sec. Reg. L.J. 247 (1994).

[8] See Sections 15(b)(4)(E), 15(b)(6)(A)(i), 20(f), 15 U.S.C. §§ 78o(b)(4)(E), 78o(b)(6)(A)(i), 78t(f).

[9] See Section 209(d), 15 U.S.C., § 80b-9(d).

[10] See Martin, Mirvis & Herlihy, *SEC Enforcement Powers and Remedies Are Greatly Expanded*, 19 Sec. Reg. L.J. 19, 23 (1991) (stating that the concept of a "cause" of a violation in relation to the SEC's cease and desist authority "would appear to go far beyond traditional concepts of aiding and abetting violations"). See Chapter 14 *infra*.

[11] See, e.g., Texas Securities Act Art. 581-33(F)(2); J. Long, *supra* note 1, at § 7.08. A number of state statutes are more expansive, imposing liabilities on those who "materially aid" the sale. See § 8.08 *supra*.

[12] See note 3 *supra*.

[13] Compare *Rolf v. Blyth, Eastman Dillon & Co., Inc.*, 570 F.2d 38 (2d Cir. 1978), with *Schatz v. Rosenberg*, 943 F.2d 485 (4th Cir. 1991).

[14] See, e.g., cases cited 511 U.S. at 192 n.1 (Stevens, J., dissenting); note 3 *supra*.

[15] Questions also arose as to whether the defendant's conduct constituted "substantial assistance." For a narrow view, see *Schatz v. Rosenberg*, 943 F.2d 485 (4th Cir. 1991) (lawyer drafting of key documents not substantial assistance). This view largely was rejected, even by those courts that otherwise adhered to a restrictive approach. See, e.g., *Abell v. Potomac Insurance Co.*, 858 F.2d 1104 (5th Cir. 1988), *vacated on other grounds*, 492 U.S. 914 (1989).

[16] Courts generally have adopted the "highly" reckless standard, defined as conduct that

complainant and the alleged aider and abettor.[17] Absent a fiduciary relationship, a number of courts required conscious intent,[18] particularly if the alleged violator was performing ordinary tasks constituting "the daily grist of the mill."[19] Disagreeing, other courts found recklessness to suffice where the alleged aider and abettor had reason to foresee that third parties would be relying on his/her conduct[20] or where he/she derived financial benefit from the wrongdoing.[21] Still other courts as a general principle deemed reckless conduct to satisfy the "knowledge" requirement.[22]

In view of the Supreme Court's decision in *Central Bank of Denver*, private parties increasingly will assert theories of liability based on primary violations. This subject is addressed in § 9.03.

§ 9.02   Application of *Central Bank of Denver* to the SEC

As a general proposition, prior to Section 20(f) of the Exchange Act enacted as part of the Private Securities Litigation Reform Act of 1995, a persuasive argument existed that the SEC could not bring an enforcement action premised on aider and abettor liability under Section 10(b). Although the Court's holding in *Central Bank of Denver* was confined to private parties, its rationale arguably extended to SEC actions. The Court made crystal clear that its interpretation was based on "a strict statutory construction" and that the issue before it was one involving "the scope of conduct prohibited by § 10(b)."[23] The situation present in *Central Bank of Denver* thus is akin to that of *Ernst & Ernst v. Hochfelder*.[24] There, the Court, applying a strict statutory construction to ascertain the scope of conduct proscribed by Section 10(b), held that scienter must be shown in private actions for damages under that statute.[25] Thereafter, applying *Hochfelder's* rationale, the Court in *Aaron v. SEC*[26] held that scienter must be proven in SEC enforcement actions for violation of Section 10(b).[27] Following this logic, it appeared as a general proposition that the SEC no

---

represents "an extreme departure from the standards of ordinary care . . . to the extent that the danger was either known to the defendant or so obvious that the defendant must have been aware of it." *Hollinger v. Titan Capital Corp.*, 914 F.2d 1564, 1569-70 (9th Cir. 1990) (en banc) (and cases cited therein). See § 7.03 *supra*.

[17] See, e.g., *Abell v. Potomac Insurance Co.*, 858 F.2d 1104 (5th Cir. 1988), *vacated on other grounds*, 492 U.S. 914 (1989).

[18] See, e.g., *Schatz v. Rosenberg*, 943 F.2d 485 (4th Cir. 1991).

[19] See, e.g., *Farlow v. Peat, Marwick, Mitchell & Co.*, 956 F.2d 982 (10th Cir. 1992).

[20] See, e.g., *Breard v. Sachnoff*, 941 F.2d 142 (2d Cir. 1991); *SEC v. Electronics Warehouse, Inc.*, 689 F. Supp. 53 (D. Conn.), *aff'd*, 891 F.2d 457 (2d Cir. 1989).

[21] See, e.g., *Walck v. American Stock Exchange, Inc.*, 687 F.2d 778, 791 n.18 (3d Cir. 1992); *Gould v. American-Hawaiian S.S. Co.*, 535 F.2d 761, 780 (3d Cir. 1976).

[22] See, e.g., *Stern v. American Bankshares, Inc.*, 429 F. Supp. 818 (E.D. Wis. 1977).

[23] 511 U.S. at 173-75. See discussion § 7.03 *supra*.

[24] 425 U.S. 185 (1976).

[25] *Id*. at 201.

[26] 446 U.S. 680 (1980).

[27] *Id*. at 689-95. See discussion § 7.03[B] *supra*, § 14.05[B] *infra*.

longer could institute an enforcement action under Section 10(b) based on aider and abettor liability. Note that this argument still may be asserted with respect to the viability of aider and abettor principles under the Securities Act.

Nonetheless, unlike the *Hochfelder-Aaron* scienter scenario, aiding and abetting a federal securities law violation gives rise by statute to criminal liability exposure. Accordingly, under this rationale, the criminal aid-abet statute provides ample authority for the SEC to pursue aiders and abettors.[28]

With respect to the Exchange Act, Congress resolved this issue in favor of the SEC by adding pursuant to the 1995 legislation a new subsection (f) to Section 20, thereby authorizing the SEC to seek injunctive relief and/or certain money penalties against aiders and abettors for violations of the 1934 Act (or any rule or regulation thereunder). Specifically, the section provides that any person who "knowingly provides substantial assistance" to another person in violation of the Exchange Act (or any rule or regulation thereunder) shall be liable "to the same extent as the person to whom such assistance is provided." Hence, this section preserves aiding and abetting liability in SEC enforcement actions brought for violations of the 1934 Act. Nonetheless, the mental culpability standard (although seemingly requiring actual knowledge) awaits clarification by the federal courts. Moreover, perhaps surprisingly, Congress has declined to provide the SEC with express authority to pursue aiders and abettors for 1933 Act violations. Accordingly, whether the Commission has aiding and abetting authority for Securities Act registration (Section 5) and antifraud (Section 17(a)) violations is uncertain. Hence, the applicability of *Central Bank of Denver* to SEC enforcement actions under the Securities Act remains unresolved.

§ 9.03 Distinguishing Primary from Secondary Conduct

In *Central Bank of Denver,* the Supreme Court invalidated one of the principal methods of recovery for private litigants under Section 10(b) of the Securities Exchange Act of 1934. The Court held that private litigants could no longer bring Section 10(b) claims against those who aid and abet a primary Section 10(b) violation.[29] On first impression, this holding seemingly released from liability so-called "secondary" actors (such as accountants, lawyers and underwriters) whose assistance was a substantial factor in the issuance of a materially misleading disclosure document or

---

[28] See 18 U.S.C. § 2(a) ("Whoever commits an offense against the United States or aids, abets, counsels, commands, induces or procures its commission, is punishable as a principal."); Bromberg, *Aiding and Abetting: Sudden Death and Possible Resurrection,* 24 Rev. Sec. & Comm. Reg. 133, 138 (1994) (pointing to criminal aid-abet statute as grounds for recognizing SEC authority to pursue aiders and abettors).

[29] 511 U.S. at 177 (focusing primarily on a textual analysis of § 10(b), the Court stated that "the statute prohibits only the making of a material misstatement (or omission) or the commission of a manipulative act. . . . The proscription does not include giving aid to a person who commits a manipulative or deceptive act").

other statement that was used in the securities marketplace. However, the Court held further that:

> The absence of §10(b) aiding and abetting liability does not mean that secondary actors in the securities market are always free from liability under the Securities Acts. Any person or entity, including a lawyer, accountant, or bank, who employs a manipulative device or makes a material misstatement (or omission) on which a purchaser or seller of securities relies may be liable as a primary violator under 10b-5, assuming all of the requirements for primary liability under Rule 10b-5 are met.[30]

This language opens the door to pursue liability against secondary actors for primary violations of Section 10(b). Yet, while the Supreme Court evidently approves the imposition of primary liability against secondary actors in certain situations under Section 10(b), the Court's language leaves numerous questions unresolved. This uncertainty plagues the lower courts to such a degree that there is little agreement between the circuits as to when such liability is appropriate.

The decisions of lower federal courts issued both before and after *Central Bank* have focused on activities engaged in by secondary actors to determine when primary liability under Section 10(b) is appropriate. Types of conduct that merit scrutiny include where the secondary actor speaks, where the secondary actor drafts or "authors" a statement for another, where the secondary actor's participation in the creation of the subject statement is deemed a substantial factor, and inquiry whether secondary actors have a duty to "blow the whistle" on their clients. The following discussion analyzes the judicial treatment of these various types of secondary actor activity associated with disclosure deficiencies.[31]

[A]   Primary Liability Where the Secondary Actor Speaks

There is much disagreement among the judiciary as to what constitutes primary activity sufficient to impose Section 10(b) liability upon secondary actors. However, one type of misconduct with respect to which courts nearly

---

[30] *Id.* at 191.

[31] Additionally, there are several recent law review articles discussing the issue of primary Section 10(b) liability for secondary actors. *See e.g.*, Branson, *Chasing the Rogue Professional After the Private Securities Litigation Reform Act of 1995*, 50 SMU L. Rev. 91 (1996); Evans & Floyd, *Secondary Liability Under Rule 10b-5; Still Alive and Well After Central Bank?* 52 Bus. Law. 13 (1996); Fisch, *The Scope of Private Securities Litigation: In Search of Liability Standards for Secondary Defendants*, 99 Colum. L. Rev. 1293 (1999); Harrison, *The Assault on the Liability of Outside Professionals: Are Lawyers and Accountants Off the Hook?*, 65 U. Cin. L. Rev. 473 (1997); Lowenfels & Bromberg, *Liabilities of Lawyers and Accountants Under Rule 10b-5*, 53 Bus. Law. 1157 (1998); Maxey, *Competing Duties? Securities Lawyers' Liability After Central Bank*, 64 Fordham L. Rev. 2185 (1996); Prentice, *Locating that Indistinct and Virtually Nondistinct Line Between Primary and Secondary Liability Under Section 10(b)*, 75 No. Car. L. Rev. 691 (1997); Rice, *Potential Liabilities for Legal Opinions in Securities Transactions*, 31 Rev. Sec. & Comm. Reg. 239 (1998); Warren, *The Primary Liability of Securities Lawyers*, 50 SMU L. Rev. 383 (1996).

universally agree is when a secondary actor makes a material misstatement in the form of a signed document or a direct oral misrepresentation to a third party. Where a secondary actor makes such a materially misleading statement, primary liability principles under Section 10(b) apply. [32]

Courts have little trouble agreeing that primary liability exposure is appropriate when a secondary actor makes direct *oral* misrepresentations to investors. [33] As stated by the Sixth Circuit, "while an attorney representing the seller in a securities transaction may not always be under an independent duty to volunteer information about the financial condition of his client, he assumes a duty to provide complete and non-misleading information with respect to subjects on which he undertakes to speak." [34]

Courts also have imposed primary liability on secondary actors with respect to direct *written* misrepresentations. For accountants, primary liability has been imposed on outside auditors when they have issued formal audit opinions or certifications of an issuer's financial statements that contain materially false representations. [35] Similarly, where a lawyer issues an opinion letter containing material misrepresentations, courts will apply primary liability principles. In fact, an attorney's use of cautionary language in the opinion seeking to dissuade third party reliance on the conclusions reached therein may not preclude the imposition of primary liability. [36] Further, even where counsel's opinion letter containing material disclosure deficiencies is intended only for the client, the lawyer nonetheless can be held primarily liable under Section 10(b) to the extent that the lawyer subsequently acquiesces in the circulation of the letter to potential investors. [37]

---

[32] See, e.g., *Anixter v. Home Stake Production Co.*, 77 F.3d 1215, 1225 (10th Cir. 1996) (concluding that "in order for accountants to 'use or employ' a 'deception' actionable under the antifraud law, they must themselves make a false or misleading statement (or omission) that they know or should know will reach potential investors").

[33] See *Rubin v. Schottenstein, Zox & Dunn*, 143 F.3d 263, 266-68 (6th Cir. 1998) (holding that primary liability under §10(b) appropriate where attorney for issuer falsely represented to third party investor about the financial condition of his client and when attorney knew that the investor would reasonably rely on his statements).

[34] *Rubin*, 143 F.3d at 268. *See also, Kline v. First Western Government Securities, Inc.*, 24 F.3d 480, 491 (3rd Cir. 1994) (stating that "when a professional 'undertakes the affirmative act of communicating or disseminating information,' there is a general obligation or 'duty' to speak truthfully").

[35] *See, e.g., Cooper v. Pickett*, 137 F.3d 616, 621 (9th Cir. 1997) (holding that plaintiff's §10(b) claim against accountant erroneously dismissed where complaint alleged that accountant knowingly certified false and misleading financial statements and also deliberately or recklessly did not comply with Generally Accepted Auditing Standards).

[36] See, e.g., *Kline v. First Western Government Securities, Inc.*, 24 F.3d at 483-90 (where law firm was put on notice that investors were relying on firm's tax opinion letters, law firm could be held primarily liable under §10(b) for misstatements and omissions contained in those letters even though firm stated in the letters that the opinions were based on assumed facts represented to the firm by the client and that the firm conducted no independent investigation into whether those represented facts accurately reflected reality).

[37] See, e.g., *Ackerman v. Schwartz*, 947 F.2d 841, 848 (7th Cir. 1991) (Although the attorney had no duty to the investors to blow the whistle on his client and he had no duty to correct a letter he had not authorized to be circulated in the first place, the attorney cannot evade primary §10(b) liability to the extent he permitted the promoters to release his opinion letter to the investors when he knew such letter contained material misrepresentations.).

Although frequently sued, accountants and lawyers are not the only professionals who risk primary liability for making affirmative statements. For example, investment bankers and underwriters may incur primary liability for rendering materially misleading valuations or forecasts regarding subject companies.[38]

[B] Primary Liability Where the Secondary Actor Drafts a Misstatement

One area in which the *Central Bank* decision has had a profound effect relates to situations in which the secondary actor has drafted a materially misleading document for her client. In order for primary liability exposure to arise, lower courts after *Central Bank* have assessed whether the secondary actor must actually sign, certify, or be named in a document containing material disclosure deficiencies.

[1] Pre-*Central Bank* Case Law

Prior to the Supreme Court's rejection of aiding and abetting liability in *Central Bank*, Section 10(b) claimants frequently sought recovery through the imposition of *primary* liability upon secondary actors.[39] A number of courts held that a claim alleging this type of misconduct was insufficient to sustain primary liability. Indeed, courts adhering to this approach concluded that by drafting documents to its client's specifications, counsel's services merely constituted "the daily grist of the mill."[40] The Fourth Circuit, rejecting primary liability principles in this context, perceived the defendant law firm as merely a "scrivener" of its client's disclosure materials.[41]

Courts often disagreed as to what conduct would suffice for the imposition of Section 10(b) liability. In *Abell v. Potomac Insurance Co.*,[42] for example, the underwriter's counsel included several misstatements in the bond offering documents at its client's request.[43] Although the law firm allowed

---

[38] See, e.g., *Cooper v. Pickett*, 137 F.3d at 629 (primary liability appropriate where underwriters' analysts allegedly were aware of undisclosed facts showing that there was no reasonable basis for their optimistic forecasts, and therefore, that they did not genuinely believe such forecasts).

[39] See e.g., *Abell v. Potomac Insurance Co.*, 858 F.2d 1104 (5th Cir. 1988); *vacated on other grounds*, 492 U.S. 914 (1989).

[40] *Id.* at 1128.

[41] *Schatz v. Rosenberg*, 943 F.2d 485, 497 (4th Cir. 1991) (stating that the law firm "did no more than 'paper the deal' or act as scrivener for [its client]").

[42] 858 F.2d 1104 (5th 1988), *vacated on other grounds,* 492 U.S. 914 (1989).

[43] See *id.* at 1111-12. As underwriter's counsel, defendant undertook the responsibilities of preparing and revising the bond offering documents and performing due diligence to ensure the accuracy and completeness of those documents. However, the documents did not disclose that the issuer had received a negative viability report with regard to the project. Also undisclosed was the fact that the issuer had obtained the land for the project through a less than arm's length transaction. And finally, the offering documents misrepresented the nature of the principal's pledge of collateral towards the success of the project.

its firm name to be included in the document as underwriter's counsel, the law firm did not sign the document or opine as to the completeness or accuracy of the statements contained therein.[44] Reversing the district court's findings of primary liability against underwriter's counsel, the Fifth Circuit found that counsel had not made any affirmative misstatements upon which plaintiffs had relied.[45]

In *Schatz v. Rosenberg*,[46] the Fourth Circuit reviewed the allegations presented in plaintiffs' pleadings to determine whether the allegations could sustain a finding of primary or secondary liability under Section 10(b). Plaintiffs alleged that the defendant law firm supplied a misstated letter to such plaintiffs regarding its client's financial position[47] and drafted closing documents containing misrepresentations made by its client.[48] The court held that by simply forwarding a letter from the law firm's client to plaintiffs, the law firm had not made any affirmative misstatement.[49] Further, by drafting closing documents containing representations by the law firm's client, the law firm did not warrant its client's probity.[50] The court concluded that the law firm could not be held liable under Section 10(b) for the misrepresentations made by the client, even though the lawyers incorporated the client's misrepresentations into legal documents necessary for closing the transaction.[51]

In *Molecular Technology v. Valentine*,[52] on the other hand, the Sixth Circuit took a broader approach to pre-*Central Bank* Section 10(b) liability. The defendant in *Molecular Technology* was a lawyer who drafted and edited various documents in connection with a merger between his client and a third party.[53] The attorney also played a similar role in several of the new company's subsequent securities offerings.[54] The court applied the "direct contacts" test for determining whether the defendant was liable as a primary violator.[55]

---

[44] *Id.* at 1126.

[45] *Id.* at 1123. The court noted that the defendant limited its role in the bond offering to the legal work it did for the bond underwriters. See note 43 *supra*. "Consequently, [defendant] *never made any statements* on its own behalf directly to the bondholders, but only checked and revised statements *made* in the offering statement." *Id.* (emphasis added).

[46] 943 F.2d 485 (4th Cir. 1991).

[47] *Id.* at 494.

[48] *Id.* Despite the fact that the client was actually insolvent at the time, the closing documents drafted by the defendant law firm represented that the client's net worth exceeded $7 million. *Id.* at 488.

[49] *Id.* at 494. Note that the plaintiffs did not allege that the law firm had made any representations other than those made by the law firm's client.

[50] *Id.* (asserting that the lawyers did not make any affirmative representations about their client to plaintiffs; rather they only put their client's representations to paper).

[51] *Id.* at 495.

[52] 925 F.2d 910 (6th Cir. 1991).

[53] *Id.* at 913-18.

[54] *Id.* at 913-14.

[55] *Id.* at 917. The court stated the test as follows:

[O]nly those individuals who had an affirmative obligation to reveal what was

Under the Sixth Circuit's application of the direct contacts test, attorneys who draft disclosure materials with the expectation that such materials will be furnished to investors are deemed primary participants.[56] The court held there was sufficient evidence to support a finding that the lawyer knew the information in the document was materially false and that such information was to be furnished to, and relied upon by, the third party. Further, the court found that there was adequate evidence that the attorney took a sufficiently active role in editing the information such that the subject misrepresentations could be deemed his own. Applying the "direct contacts" test, the court found that counsel had a duty to provide materially correct information to the third party. For breaching that duty, the attorney was subject to primary liability under Section 10(b).[57]

[2] Post-*Central Bank* Case Law

In the post-*Central Bank* era, plaintiffs in private actions no longer may seek to impose aiding and abetting liability upon secondary actors. Perhaps as a consequence, a number of courts may be expanding the theories of recovery under which secondary actors may be primarily liable.

In *In re Software Toolworks Incorporated Securities Litigation*,[58] for example, the Ninth Circuit addressed Section 10(b) claims brought against accountants and underwriters for drafting alleged misstatements that appeared in documents transmitted to the SEC. The Section 10(b) claims in *Software Toolworks* focused on a letter that was sent to the SEC by the company regarding its quarterly financial results.[59] Allegedly, the letter falsely stated that Software Toolworks did not have preliminary financial data available for the quarter and misleadingly described the nature of Software Toolworks' original equipment manufacturing contracts in its quarterly financial statements.[60]

In reversing the district court's grant of summary judgment for the underwriters and the accountants, the Ninth Circuit found that a jury could properly hold these secondary actors primarily liable under Section 10(b). According to the court, such liability would appropriately be based on findings that (1) the secondary actors were members of the drafting group; (2) that they had access to all information that was available; and (3) that those actors deliberately chose to conceal the truth about the figures in the SEC letter.[61]

---

allegedly omitted can be held as a primary participant in the alleged deception. A person undertaking to furnish information, which is misleading because of a failure to disclose a material fact, is a primary participant. Conversely, a person who does not undertake to furnish any information, and who is not aware of what information has been furnished, is under no duty to disclose material information in his possession.

[56] 925 F.2d at 917-18.

[57] *Id*. at 918.

[58] 50 F.3d 615 (9th Cir. 1994).

[59] *Id*. at 625-29.

[60] *Id*. at 628.

[61] *Id*. at 627, 629.

In *Klein v. Boyd*,[62] the Third Circuit addressed primary securities fraud charges against attorneys who allegedly compiled and drafted their client's private offering disclosure package. Specifically, in *Klein*, the defendant law firm drafted a disclosure package regarding its client, a limited partnership, to prospective investors. Plaintiffs alleged that the disclosure package omitted that the majority owner of the general partner had a record of securities fraud, regulatory sanctions, and claims of fraudulent conduct. The investors brought a Section 10(b) claim against the law firm for failing to disclose this information.[63]

The Third Circuit endorsed the Ninth Circuit's reasoning in *Software Toolworks* that primary liability is appropriate where the "secondary actor's participation in the creation of the fraudulent statement is so significant that the secondary actor can fairly be said to have made the statement."[64] Accordingly, the Third Circuit promulgated a four-factor test to determine when a lawyer in similar circumstances may be held primarily liable. Under the court's test, such an attorney may be held primarily liable under Section 10(b) when: (1) the lawyer knows (or is reckless in not knowing) that the statement will be relied upon by investors; (2) the lawyer is aware (or is reckless in not being aware) of the material misstatement or omission; (3) the lawyer played such a substantial role in the creation of the statement that the lawyer can fairly be said to be the "author" or "co-author" of the statement; and (4) the other requirements of primary liability are satisfied.[65] According to the court, such a lawyer may be a primary violator regardless of whether investors knew of the lawyer's involvement at the time the document was distributed.[66]

Subsequently, the Third Circuit granted a motion for reconsideration in which it vacated the judgment in *Klein*. The court then set the case for rehearing *en banc*.[67] After the judgment was vacated, however, the parties settled the matter before the rehearing took place. As a result, the court's decision in *Klein* may be of questionable value for ascertaining primary liability for secondary actors.

In an attempt to clarify the appropriate standard of primary liability for this type of misconduct, the SEC submitted a brief as *amicus curiae* in *Klein*. In its analysis, the Commission interpreted the Supreme Court's language in *Central Bank*. Specifically, the SEC reviewed the language from *Central Bank* establishing primary liability for secondary actors who "make a misstatement."[68]

The Commission argued that primary liability for a secondary actor who makes a false statement is not contingent upon public attribution of the

---

[62] [1998 Transfer Binder] Fed. Sec. L. Rep. (CCH) ¶ 90,136 (3d Cir. 1998).

[63] *Id.* at 90,318-90,320.

[64] *Id.* at 90,326 n.7.

[65] *Id.* at 90,318 n.1.

[66] *Id.* at 90,324.

[67] See [1998 Transfer Binder] Fed. Sec. L. Rep. (CCH) ¶ 90,165 (3d Cir. 1998).

[68] Brief of the SEC, *Amicus Curiae* in *Klein v. Boyd*, at 12, Nos. 97-1143, 97-1261 (3rd Cir. 1998).

statement to the secondary actor. To so limit *Central Bank* would be inconsistent with the language of Section 10(b). Section 10(b) makes it unlawful "for any person, directly or indirectly . . . [t]o use or employ . . . any manipulative or deceptive device or contrivance." To that end, a person who creates a misrepresentation, but takes care not to be identified publicly with it, "indirectly" uses or employs a deceptive device or contrivance and should be liable. The Commission argued further that it is the misrepresentation — not the person who made such misrepresentation — upon which a plaintiff must rely. By stating that liability exposure exists "where any person . . . makes a material misstatement on which a purchaser or seller relies," the focus is on the misrepresentation, not on the particular actor. Therefore, the Commission proposed the following standard:

> "[A] person who has the requisite *scienter* can be liable as a primary violator of Section 10(b) of the Securities Exchange Act of 1934 and Rule 10b-5 thereunder when he or she, acting alone or with others, *creates a misrepresentation*, whether or not the person is identified with the misrepresentation by name."[69]

[C]   Primary Liability Where the Secondary Actor Participates in the Misrepresentation

Distinguishing this category of misconduct from the preceding category at times may be problematic. The preceding discussion addressed primary liability for secondary actors who draft their clients' misleading documents. This subsection, on the other hand, focuses on primary liability for those secondary actors who participate in (but do not draft) the alleged misrepresentations. The inquiry's focus thus is as follows: "When a secondary actor is deemed a factor in the creation of her client's misstatements, what level of input by the secondary actor will give rise to primary liability exposure under Section 10(b)?"

Due to the fine points of distinction between actually drafting a client's misstatement and "merely" participating in the creation thereof, courts addressing secondary actors who engage in the latter type of misconduct often employ reasoning similar to the "drafting" lines of cases. For example, in *Carley Capital Group v. Deloitte & Touche, L.L.P.*,[70] the district court applied the SEC's standard from the *Klein amicus* brief to the actions of an accounting firm. In *Carley*, the plaintiff alleged that the defendant accounting firm specifically directed the premature inclusion of revenue and income from a contract in a report to be issued as part of a press release. Noting that the views of the SEC are entitled to consideration and some

---

[69] *Id.* at 15-20. Surprisingly, the SEC gratuitously conceded that "[u]nder the Commission's test, however, a person who prepares a truthful and complete portion of a document would not be liable as a primary violator for misrepresentations in other portions of the document. Even assuming such a person knew of misrepresentations elsewhere in the document and thus had the requisite scienter, he or she would not have created those misrepresentations." *Id.* at 18.

[70] 27 F. Supp. 2d 1324 (N.D. Ga. 1998).

deference, the judge specifically adopted the standard of primary liability for secondary actors suggested by the SEC in its *Klein amicus* brief. The judge found that, under the SEC's standard, plaintiffs had sufficiently alleged that the accounting firm had "created the misrepresentation by directing [its client] to include that revenue and income in the report."[71]

Similar reasoning has been accepted elsewhere where courts have found that accountants played "significant" or "central" roles in creating or drafting documents — financial or otherwise — that contained misstatements, even though such misstatements were not publicly attributed to the accountants at the time they were made.[72] However, this argument has met with disagreement in other circuits. In *Wright v. Ernst & Young, L.L.P.*,[73] for example, the Second Circuit reviewed allegations that an accounting firm had substantially participated in the creation of its client's false and misleading financial statements, thereby committing a primary violation of Section 10(b). Specifically, plaintiff alleged that the accounting firm substantially participated by orally approving its client's materially misleading financial statements, which the client had disseminated to the public in a press release. Affirming the trial court's dismissal of the complaint, the court held that "a secondary actor cannot incur primary liability under the [1934] Act for a statement not attributed to that actor at the time of its dissemination."[74]

[D] Duty to "Blow the Whistle"

The focus of the preceding discussion has been on primary liability under Section 10(b) for secondary actors' own conduct. Topics addressed included a secondary actor's exposure to primary liability for direct misrepresentations, a secondary actor's exposure to primary liability for drafting her client's misstatements, and a secondary actor's exposure to primary liability for conduct that constituted a "substantial factor" in creating her client's misstatements.

The following analysis focuses on the secondary actor's duty under the federal securities laws to disclose her client's misstatements to third parties when the secondary actor has not participated in the creation of those misstatements. In other words, when a secondary actor does not draft, review, revise, or advise with respect to her client's inclusion of misstatements in disclosure documents, must the secondary actor "blow the whistle" on her client to third parties who might rely on those misstatements?

---

[71] *Id.* at 1334-36.

[72] See, e.g., *In re ZZZZ Best Securities Litigation*, 864 F. Supp. 960, 970 (C.D. Cal. 1994) (accounting firm that was "intricately involved" in creating false documents published by client is a primary violator even though the investing public may not be able to reasonably attribute the misstatements and omissions to the accounting firm).

[73] 152 F.3d 169 (2d Cir. 1998).

[74] *Id.* at 175. See also, *Shapiro v. Cantor*, 123 F.3d 717, 720 (2d Cir. 1997) (stating that "[a]llegations of 'assisting,' 'participating in,' 'complicity in,' and similar synonyms used throughout the complaint fall within the prohibitive bar of *Central Bank*").

To establish Section 10(b) liability exposure on this basis, it is initially incumbent upon plaintiffs to prove that the secondary actor has a duty to disclose.[75] Several circuits have concluded that the federal securities laws are not the source of such a duty.[76] Further, absent a fiduciary duty that the plaintiff owes to the defendant, there is generally no liability for failing to blow the whistle at common law.[77] Rather, the secondary actor's duty to disclose may arise where a fiduciary or other confidential relationship is found to exist.[78] Where such a relationship can be established, courts have held that primary section 10(b) liability may be imposed for a breach of the duty to disclose that arises from that relationship.[79]

For lawyers, the duty to disclose or "blow the whistle" on their clients does not seem likely to arise. Rather, as stated by the Seventh Circuit in *Barker*, "[t]o the contrary, attorneys have privileges not to disclose."[80] Further, the Model Rules of Professional Conduct confine the acceptable actions of a lawyer such that only rarely should circumstances occur in which the lawyer's relationship with a third party would give rise to a duty higher than that owed to her clients.[81] As a result, courts overwhelmingly hold that a lawyer does not have a duty to disclose her client's fraudulent activities to third parties.[82]

---

[75] See, e.g., *Fortson v. Winstead, McGuire, Sechrest & Minick*, 961 F.2d 469, 472 (4th Cir. 1992), *citing, Chiarella v. United States*, 445 U.S. 222, 228 (1980) (*quoting* Restatement (Second) of Torts § 551(2)(a) (1976)).

[76] See, e.g., *Fortson v. Winstead, McGuire, Sechrest & Minick*, 961 F.2d at 472; *Schatz v. Rosenberg*, 943 F.2d at 490-92; *Abell v. Potomac Ins. Co.*, 858 F.2d at 1124; *Barker v. Henderson, Franklin, Starnes & Holt*, 797 F.2d 490, 496 (7th Cir. 1986).

[77] See 37 C.J.S. *Fraud* § 61(b)(3) (1943) ("Mere silence in the face of a third person's fraud will not render defendant liable unless there is a duty to speak."); Prentice, *supra* note 31, at 760.

[78] *Fortson*, 961 F.2d at 272 (*citing Windon Third Oil & Gas Drilling Partnership v. FDIC*, 805 F.2d 342, 347 (10th Cir. 1986)). See *Chiarella v. United States*, 445 U.S. 222, 228 (1980) (holding in § 10(b) insider trading context duty to disclose arises from a fiduciary or similar relationship of trust and confidence); *Barker*, 797 F.2d at 496 (finding that because neither §10(b) nor Rule 10b-5 imposes such a duty to disclose, any such duty "must come from a fiduciary relation outside the securities law").

[79] Before *Central Bank* the overwhelming majority of courts held that the duty to blow the whistle did not exist. *See e.g., Schatz v. Rosenberg*, 943 F.2d at 490-94; *Robin v. Arthur Young & Co.*, 915 F.2d 1120, 1125-26 (7th Cir. 1990).

[80] 797 F.2d at 497.

[81] *See* Model Rules of Professional Conduct Rule 1.6(b)(1) (stating that in this context an attorney may disclose only when necessary "to prevent the client from committing a criminal act that the lawyer believes is likely to result in imminent death or substantial bodily harm"); Model Rules of Professional Conduct Rule 1.7(b) (proscribing a lawyer's representation of a client if that representation "may be materially limited by the lawyer's responsibilities to another client or to a third person.").

[82] See, e.g., *Fortson*, 961 F.2d at 474-75 (holding that duty to investigate and disclose client's misstatements did not arise under state common law, ABA Ethics Opinions or Federal Treasury Regulations,); *Schatz*, 943 F.2d at 490-95 (concluding that duty to disclose client's misrepresentations did not arise under state ethics rules or state common law, and reasoning that "[t]he better rule — that attorneys have no duty to 'blow the whistle' on their clients — allows clients to repose complete trust in their lawyers." *Id.* at 493.).

For accountants, the question of whether a duty to disclose exists becomes more difficult. Accountants' duties differ from those of attorneys. Addressing this distinction in *United States v. Arthur Young & Co.*,[83] the Supreme Court stated:

> An independent certified public accountant performs a different role [than counsel whose role is to serve the client]. By certifying the public reports that collectively depict a corporation's financial status, the independent auditor assumes a public responsibility transcending any employment relationship with the client. The independent public accountant performing this special function owes ultimate allegiance to the corporation's creditors and stockholders, as well as to the investing public. This "public watchdog" function demands that the accountant maintain total independence from the client at all times and requires complete fidelity to the public trust.[84]

Notwithstanding the Supreme Court's language, lower courts have been reluctant to conclude that the requisite duty exists for Section 10(b) primary liability exposure.[85]

Nonetheless, enactment of Section 10A of the 1934 Act pursuant to the Private Securities Litigation Reform Act of 1995 may alter this duty analysis for purposes of accountant primary liability under Section 10(b). Arguably, an accountant's duty to blow the whistle may arise statutorily under recently enacted Section 10A. This provision requires accountants in certain situations to report their clients' illegal acts directly to the SEC.

Section 10A sets forth requirements for audits conducted by an independent public accountant of an issuer's financial statements to include certain procedures to (i) detect illegal acts that would have a direct and material effect on the determination of financial statement amounts; (ii) identify related party transactions material to financial statements; and (iii) evaluate an issuer's ability to continue as a going concern. The statutory language makes clear that the above procedures are to be carried out in accordance with current generally accepted accounting principles, "as may be modified from time to time by the [SEC]." The existing auditing standards provide for all three types of procedures prescribed in the new Section 10A.

Section 10A further specifies notification and reporting guidelines for a public accountant who becomes aware of information indicating possible illegal activities during the course of an audit. The provisions also appear to codify current generally accepted accounting principles. If, in the course of an audit the public accountant detects or otherwise becomes aware of

---

[83] 465 U.S. 805 (1984).

[84] *Id.* at 817.

[85] Prentice, *supra* note 31, at 767 (citing cases). *See Shapiro v. Cantor*, 123 F.3d 717 (2d Cir. 1997) (where an issuer's fraudulent omission from the offering statement relates to an area wholly distinct from the expertised portion of the offering statement certified by the accountants, the accountants have no duty to disclose the fraudulent misrepresentation to the third party purchaser).

information indicating that an illegal act has or may have occurred, notwithstanding such act's perceived materiality to the issuer's financial statements, the accountant must (i) determine the likelihood that an illegal act has occurred; (ii) determine the possible effect of the illegal act on the issuer's financial statements, including contingent effects such as fines, penalties, or damages; and (iii) inform appropriate management and assure that the issuer's audit committee or, if none, its board of directors, is adequately informed (unless such illegal act clearly is inconsequential).

The lone new requirement imposed by Section 10A arises if such an accountant concludes that (i) the illegal act has a material effect on the issuer's financial statements; (ii) senior management has not taken "timely and appropriate remedial action" with respect to the illegal act; and (iii) the failure to take "remedial action" is likely to cause the accountant to depart from a standard report or to resign from its capacity as auditor. Under these conditions, the accountant must, "as soon as is practicable," report its conclusions to the board of directors. A board of directors receiving a report from such an accountant must inform the SEC within one business day of receipt of the report and must give the accountant a copy of the notice sent to the SEC. If, however, the accountant does not receive a copy of the notice within this time, the accountant may resign from the engagement and must furnish the SEC with a copy of its report (or documentation of its oral report) to the board of directors within one business day after the issuer fails to provide to the accountant the notice copy.

Section 10A further stipulates that an accountant that furnishes a report to the SEC under that provision will not be held liable in any private action for any findings, conclusions, or statements in the report. However, the willful failure to file a required report will subject the accountant "and any other person that the [SEC] finds was a cause of such violation" to cease-and-desist proceedings as well as the imposition of civil penalties. Hence, pursuant to the mandates of Section 10A, a duty owed by auditors to the investing public may be held to exist.

Underwriters, like accountants, have been characterized as owing some type of duty to the investing public and therefore serving a role at times viewed as "adverse" to their issuer clients.[86] And, unlike attorneys, they owe no fiduciary duty to their clients.[87] The critical question as to underwriter liability, therefore, is whether an expansive duty to the public will find acceptance among the circuits. The adoption of such a duty would substantially increase the potential liability for underwriters who fail to disclose their clients' misstatements.

---

[86] See Prentice, *supra* note 31, at 768 n.354. See *Escott v. BarChris Constr. Corp.*, 283 F. Supp. 643, 696-97 (S.D.N.Y. 1968) ("In a sense, the positions of the underwriter and the company's officers are adverse. It is not unlikely that statements made by company officers to an underwriter to induce him to underwrite may be self-serving . . . unduly enthusiastic . . . [or], on occasion, be deliberately false.").

[87] See Prentice, *supra* note 31, at 768 n.354.

§ 9.04 Controlling Person Liability

Section 15 of the Securities Act imposes joint and several liability on any person who controls a person liable under Section 11 or 12 "unless the controlling person had no knowledge of or reasonable grounds to believe in the existence of the facts by reason of which the liability of the controlled person is alleged to exist." Section 20(a) of the Exchange Act provides that "every person who . . . controls any person liable under any provision of this title . . . shall also be liable jointly and severally with and to the same extent as such controlled person to any person to whom such controlled person is liable, unless the controlling person acted in good faith and did not directly or indirectly induce the act or acts constituting the violation or cause of action." As has been pointed out, "[t]he reason for this difference in language is hard to fathom, especially since Section 15 of the 1933 Act was amended in the bill which enacted the 1934 Act, and harder still to interpret."[88]

The term "control" is not defined in the Securities Acts. Pursuant to Rule 405, however, the Commission has defined the term to encompass "the possession, direct or indirect, of the power to direct or cause the direction of the management and policies of a person."[89] The courts generally are in accord with this standard. For example, as stated by one appellate court, control was established when the defendant "had the requisite power to directly or indirectly control or influence corporate policy."[90] Or, as stated by the Seventh Circuit: "We have looked to whether the alleged control-person actually participated in, that is, exercised control over, the operations of the person in general and, then, to whether the alleged control-person possessed the power or ability to control the specific transaction or activity upon which the primary violation was predicated, whether or not that power was exercised."[91]

As set forth above, Section 20(a) absolves the controlling person of liability if he/she acted in good faith and did not directly or indirectly induce the violation. The statutory language appears clear in placing the burden of proof on the controlling person to establish the good faith defense. This view has been overwhelmingly adopted.[92] With respect to the state of mind required to establish liability, the Supreme Court in *Hochfelder* stated that the controlling person provision "contains a state-of-mind condition requiring something more than negligence."[93]

Applying the above standards, a few courts have adopted the "culpable participant" test, signifying that the defendant's inaction, such as lack of supervision, "was deliberate and done intentionally to further the fraud."[94]

---

[88] See R. Jennings, H. Marsh, & J. Coffee, *Securities Regulation* 1131 (7th ed. 1992).

[89] 17 C.F.R. § 230.405.

[90] *G.A. Thompson & Co., Inc. Partridge*, 636 F.2d 945, 958 (5th Cir. 1981).

[91] *Harrison v. Dean Witter Reynolds, Inc.*, 974 F.2d 873, 881 (7th Cir. 1992).

[92] See, e.g., *Marbury Management, Inc. v. Kohn*, 629 F.2d 705, 716 (2d Cir. 1980).

[93] 425 U.S. 185, 209 (1976).

[94] *Sharp v. Coopers & Lybrand*, 649 F.2d 175, 185 (3d Cir. 1981). In a more recent case,

On the other hand, the overwhelming majority of courts have adopted a more remedial interpretation.[95] For example, the Second Circuit has opined that, in the brokerage house setting, the controlling person must show that "it has maintained and enforced a reasonable and proper system of supervision and internal control over sales personnel."[96] In *Hollinger v. Titan Capital Corp.*,[97] the Ninth Circuit, sitting en banc, stated:

> Section 20(a) provides that the "controlling person" can avoid liability if she acted in good faith and did not directly or indirectly induce the violations. By making the good faith defense available to controlling persons, Congress was able to avoid what it deemed to be an undesirable result, namely that of insurer's liability, and instead it made vicarious liability under § 20(a) dependent upon the broker-dealer's good faith.
>
> Contrary to the district court's ruling, the broker-dealer cannot satisfy its burden of proving good faith merely by saying that it has supervisory procedures in place, and therefore, it has fulfilled its duty to supervise. A broker-dealer can establish the good faith defense only by proving that it "maintained and enforced a reasonable and proper system of supervision and internal control."[98]

What constitutes "good faith" and "noninducement" under Section 20(a) should depend on the particular facts and circumstances. Although negligence theoretically is not sufficient to impose liability, a more relaxed form of reckless conduct should suffice. In determining whether the controlling person acted "recklessly," one should look to customary industry practice and the realistic practicalities of the trade. For example, the failure of a broker-dealer to institute adequate (not necessarily sure-proof) supervisory and internal control procedures should be viewed as reckless conduct. Under such circumstances, by ignoring an obvious danger, the controlling person's failure to institute such mechanisms constitutes a significant departure from the standards of ordinary care.[99]

§ **9.05** *Respondeat Superior* **Liability**

A controversial issue involves whether the common law principle of respondeat superior is compatible with the federal securities laws. Under

---

the Third Circuit may have relaxed this test, opining that "[t]he complaint contains no factual support for the conclusion that the [brokerage] firms knew *or should have known* of the [the broker's] misconduct or that any failure to adequately supervise him was to further the fraud." *Ash v. Ameritreat, Inc.*, [1999-2000 Transfer Binder] Fed. Sec. L. Rep. (CCH) ¶ 90,616, at 92,801 (3d Cir. 1999) (emphasis supplied).

[95] See cases cited *infra* notes 96-99 and accompanying text.

[96] *Marbury Management, Inc. v. Kohn*, 629 F.2d 705, 716 (2d Cir. 1980).

[97] 914 F.2d 1564 (9th Cir. 1990) (en banc).

[98] *Id.* at 1575-76. See *Harrison v. Dean Witter Reynolds, Inc.*, 974 F.2d 873 (7th Cir. 1992).

[99] See generally Carson, *The Liability of Controlling Persons Under the Federal Securities Acts*, 72 Notre Dame L. Rev. 263 (1997); Lowenfels & Bromberg, *Controlling Person Liability Under Section 20(a) of the Securities Exchange Act and Section 15 of the Securities Act*, 53 Bus. Law. 1 (1998).

this theory, a principal (e.g., a broker-dealer firm) is held liable for the securities law violations committed by its agent (e.g., a broker) when such agent acts within the scope of his/her employment having actual or apparent authority.[100]

A number of courts have rejected in all cases the application of respondeat superior liability under the federal securities laws. To hold otherwise, these courts reason, in effect would negate the controlling person provisions. For example, one court has reasoned:

> Noteworthy in each [controlling person] provision is the inclusion of a defense from liability based on "good faith" or lack of knowledge or reasonable belief. When originally passed by Congress, § 15 of the 1933 Act held controlling persons absolutely liable for § 11 and § 12 violations by controlled persons. Congress, in passing the 1934 Act, amended § 15 of the earlier Act, adding the language beginning at "unless the controlling person had no knowledge of or reasonable ground to believe in the existence of facts by reason of which the liability of the controlled person is alleged to exist." Likewise, the controlling person provision in the 1934 Act, § 20(a), contained the "good faith" defense to liability. Clearly Congress had rejected an insurer's liability standard for controlling persons in favor of a fiduciary standard — a duty to take due care.[101]

On the other hand, prior to the Supreme Court's decision in *Central Bank of Denver*, a majority of courts held that respondeat superior liability may be imposed under the federal securities laws. Those courts favoring imposition of respondeat superior liability reasoned that the controlling person provisions were enacted by Congress to supplement common law agency principles in order to reach individuals (such as intermediate and upper-level supervisors) who have no agency or employment relationship with the primary violator. As to the entity, the imposition of respondeat superior liability is appropriate.[102]

Thus, as a general principle, the common law doctrine of respondeat superior has been accepted in the federal securities law context by the overwhelming majority of federal appellate courts.[103] Nonetheless, in view of the Supreme Court's *Central Bank of Denver* decision, the continued vitality of respondeat superior liability is open to debate. There, the Court, applying a strict statutory construction, held that private actions based on aiding and abetting are not permitted under Section 10(b). The Court's language and tenor arguably signify that other common law theories of liability, unless provided for by statute, likewise will be rejected.[104]

---

[100] See, e.g., *Paul F. Newton & Co. v. Texas Commerce Bank*, 630 F.2d 1111 (5th Cir. 1980).

[101] *Carpenter v. Harris, Upham & Co., Inc.*, 594 F.2d 388, 393 (4th Cir. 1979).

[102] See, e.g., *Henricksen v. Henricksen*, 640 F.2d 880 (7th Cir. 1981). There are certain exceptions to this general proposition. See, e.g., Section 20A of the Exchange Act (Congress manifesting its intent that the doctrine of respondeat superior liability not apply in private rights of action brought by contemporaneous traders for alleged insider trading violations).

[103] See, e.g., *Hollinger v. Titan Capital Corp.*, 914 F.2d 1564 (9th Cir. 1990) (en banc) (and cases cited therein).

[104] See Booth, *Vicarious Liability and Securities Fraud*, 22 Sec. Reg. L.J. 347 (1995); Mathews, *The Supreme Court's Central Bank Decision*, Nat. L.J., May 23, 1994, at B4, B6.

This assertion is evidenced further by the Supreme Court's focus on the statutorily provided controlling person provision of the Exchange Act. In this regard, the Court stated:

> Congress did not overlook secondary liability when it created the private rights of action in the 1934 Act. Section 20 of the 1934 Act imposes liability on "controlling persons" . . . . This suggests that "when Congress wished to create such [secondary] liability, it had little trouble doing so."[105]

As Justice Stevens observed in his dissent, the majority's rationale suggests that lower court decisions recognizing respondeat superior liability "appear unlikely to survive."[106]

Nonetheless, even after *Central Bank of Denver*, lower courts have held that the doctrine of respondeat superior survives under the federal securities laws. In a case not arising under the federal securities laws,[107] the Third Circuit in a post-*Central Bank* decision reasoned:

> The language of *Central Bank* is undeniably broad, and the dissent warned that other mechanisms of common law secondary liability — such as "respondeat superior and other common-law agency principles" — may not survive the majority's construction of Section 10(b) of the Exchange Act. . . . Nonetheless, we do not believe that the Court's restrictive reading of the Exchange Act impacts on the determination of the scope of liability [in this case].

> In *Central Bank*, the Supreme Court primarily was concerned with broadening the range of unlawful conduct beyond that specifically proscribed by the Act. As the Court framed this issue, aiding and abetting constituted a separate cause of action, and in order to find such liability, the Court would have to imply a private right of action under the statute beyond that which already had been implied. . . .

> By contrast, courts imposing liability on agency theories are not expanding the category of affirmative conduct proscribed by the relevant statute; rather, they are deciding on whose shoulders to place responsibility for conduct indisputably proscribed by the relevant statute. The principal is held liable not because it committed some wrongdoing outside the purview of the statute which

---

[105] 511 U.S. at 184.

[106] *Id*. at 200 n.12 (Stevens, J., dissenting). The same holds true for the common law theory of conspiracy. *Id*. See *supra* note 6 and accompanying text.

[107] See, e.g., *Seolas v. Bilzerian*, 951 F. Supp. 978 (D. Utah 1997) (holding that *Central Bank* "does not abolish respondeat superior as a theory of liability under § 10(b)"); *In re Stat-Tech Securities Litigation*, 905 F. Supp. 1416 (D. Colo. 1995) (same). But see *ESI Montgomery County, Inc. v. Montenay International Corporation*, [1996-1997 Transfer Binder] Fed. Sec. L. Rep. (CCH) ¶ 99,345 (S.D.N.Y. 1996) (holding theory of respondeat superior eliminated in light of *Central Bank*). See also, Langevoort, *Words from on High About Rule 10b-5: Chiarella's History, Central Bank's Future*, 20 Del. J. Corp. L. 865, 893-96 (1995) (observing "a substantial difference between the aiding and abetting and respondeat superior issues").

assisted the wrongdoing prohibited by the statute, but because its status merits responsibility for the tortious actions of its agent.[108]

Note, however, that unlike many other federal statutes, the 1933 and 1934 Acts expressly allow for the imposition of secondary liability against principals by means of the controlling person provisions. This distinction may "bode ill" for those seeking to invoke the doctrine of respondeat superior liability under the federal securities laws.[109]

Even if the doctrine of respondeat superior liability ultimately is rejected by the federal courts, it may be useful to examine this issue from the standpoint of state securities law.[110] Moreover, when executive officers of a corporation or persons of similar status of any like enterprise improperly act with actual or apparent authority within the course and scope of their employment, it may be asserted that such enterprise should be held primarily liable. As stated by the Third Circuit, because executive officers make policy and generally have the authority to bind the corporation, "[t]heir action in behalf of the corporation is therefore primary, and holding a corporation liable for their action does not require respondeat superior."[111]

---

[108] *American Telephone and Telegraph Company v. Winback and Conserve Program, Inc.*, 42 F.3d 1421, 1430-31 (3d Cir. 1994) (interpreting liability under the Lanham Act).

[109] See 511 U.S. at 175; *id.* at 200 n.12 (Stevens, J., dissenting).

[110] See, e.g., Texas Securities Act Art. 581-33M ("The rights and remedies provided by this Act are in addition to any other rights (including exemplary or punitive damages) or remedies that may exist at law or in equity.").

[111] *Sharp v. Coopers & Lybrand*, 649 F.2d 175, 182 n.8 (3d Cir. 1981), *citing, Holmes v. Bateson*, 583 F.2d 542, 561 (1st Cir. 1978). See also, *In re Atlantic Financial Management*, 784 F.2d 29, 32 (1st Cir. 1986) (stating that "[t]here are strong reasons for believing that the 'direct or indirect' language of the Securities Act encompasses . . . common law agency liability").

Chapter 10

ISSUER AFFIRMATIVE DISCLOSURE OBLIGATIONS

§ 10.01 Overview

With certain exceptions, there is no affirmative duty for an issuer to disclose material nonpublic information. Despite the unwillingness of the courts and the SEC to recognize such a general mandate, there exist issuer affirmative disclosure requirements in a number of specific circumstances. As discussed in this chapter, these circumstances include:

(1) when SEC rules and regulations require disclosure of specified information;

(2) when mandatory disclosure of forward-looking information is called for by Item 303 of Regulation S-K, which pertains to "Management's Discussion and Analysis of Financial Condition and Results of Operation" (MD&A) (see § 4.07[D] *supra);*

(3) when selective dissemination of material information has been inadvertently made to investors or analysts, disclosure to the investing marketplace must be promptly made (see Regulation FD, § 10.08 *infra).*

(4) when the information revealed by the issuer contains a material disclosure deficiency at the time that the statement was made; under such circumstances, there exists a "duty to correct";

(5) when the issuer previously has made a public statement that, although accurate when made, continues to be "alive" in the marketplace and has become materially false or misleading as a result of subsequent events; under such circumstances, a "duty to update" may exist; and

(6) when material information has been leaked by, or rumors in the marketplace are attributable to, the issuer.

In other situations, the law is less clear as to the existence and scope of an issuer's affirmative duty to disclose, such as in the case of "soft" information, merger negotiations, and bad financial news. Moreover, the impact of "safe harbor" provisions with respect to an issuer's disclosure of certain forward-looking information (such as those contained in the 1995 federal legislation as well as in SEC rules) should be addressed in this context (see § 4.07[D] *supra,* § 10.05[D] *infra).*

In analyzing an issuer's obligations in this setting, the Supreme Court's decision in *Chiarella v. United States*[1] should be kept in focus. There, the Court held that, absent a duty to disclose, silence by a subject party will not incur Section 10(b) liability.

---

[1] 445 U.S. 222 (1980). For discussion of *Chiarella,* see Chapter 11.

Consistent with *Chiarella*, it may be posited that an issuer of securities has a duty to disclose all material information when it is purchasing or selling its securities. In other words, because a fiduciary relationship exists between shareholders and corporate directors (as well as executive officers), there arises an affirmative obligation to disclose all material information in the purchase-sale context even if such information is not specifically called for by SEC regulation. Recently, however, the First Circuit, rejecting this rationale, opined:

> Although in the context of a public offering there is a strong affirmative duty of disclosure, it is clear that an issuer of securities owes no absolute duty to disclose all material information. The issue, rather, is whether the securities law imposes on defendants a 'specific obligation' to disclose information of the type that plaintiffs claim was omitted.[2]

According to a number of authorities, the theoretical underpinnings for recognizing such a duty may be premised on two sources. First, by circulating a regular flow of information to the securities markets, a publicly-held company implicitly represents that information previously disclosed remains accurate. By failing to disclose, thereby inducing marketplace reliance that the previously disclosed information represents present conditions, the company has engaged in "deception" under Section 10(b).[3] Second, the "shingle" theory, currently applied to broker-dealers, could be extended to encompass publicly-held companies. Such companies, the argument generally posits, have a duty to deal fairly with their shareholders and the securities markets, the breach thereof constituting "deception" under Section 10(b).[4]

Despite the above arguments, neither the courts nor the SEC are willing to recognize such a general mandate. Hence, although the foregoing rationales arguably make good policy, they have not been accepted. Nonetheless, remember that in certain situations SEC rules may require that the issuer (or registrant) affirmatively disclose material events or transactions that are reasonably certain to occur in the future. At this time, you may wish to review the ramifications of Regulation S-K Item 303, Management Discussion and Analysis (MD&A), in § 4.07[D] *supra*. In addition, provided that the company is acting in good faith and with a reasonable basis, forward-looking information that is not required to be disclosed in the MD&A may be voluntarily disclosed pursuant to Securities Act Rule 175 and Exchange Act Rule 3b-6. The parameters of this safe harbor have been expanded pursuant to legislation enacted by Congress in 1995 (see § 4.07[C] *supra*, § 10.05[D] *infra*).

---

[2] *Cooperman v. Individual, Inc.*, 171 F.3d 43, 49–50 (1st Cir. 1999).

[3] See, e.g., Bauman, *Rule 10b–5 and the Corporation's Affirmative Duty to Disclose*, 67 Geo. L.J. 935 (1979). But see Sheffey, *Securities Law Responsibilities of Issuers to Respond to Rumors and Other Publicity: Reexamination of a Continuing Problem*, 57 Notre Dame Law. 755 (1982); Note, *Disclosure of Material Inside Information: An Affirmative Corporate Duty?*, 1980 Ariz. St. L.J. 795, 801.

[4] See Bauman, *supra* note 3, at 944–45. With respect to the "shingle theory," see, e.g., *Hanly v. SEC*, 415 F.2d 589 (2d Cir. 1969); discussion in § 12.03 *infra*.

§ 10.02   Impact of the "MD&A" Requirements

With respect to the mandatory disclosure of forward-looking information, Item 303 of Regulation S-K is playing an increasingly important role in requiring such disclosure in certain situations. Indeed, as stated by one source, "the MD&A has become a major, if not the major, item of narrative disclosure that is studied, together with the financial statements, for investment decision and analysis purposes."[5] On a number of occasions, the Commission has addressed a registrant's disclosure obligations under the "MD&A" — namely, under Item 303 pertaining to "Management's Discussion and Analysis of Financial Condition and Results of Operation."[6] The SEC has stated:

> As to prospective information, the MD&A Release sets forth the following test for determining when disclosure is required:
>
> > Where a trend, demand, commitment, event or uncertainty is known, management must make two assessments:
> >
> > (1) Is the known trend, demand, commitment, event or uncertainty likely to come to fruition? If management determines that it is not reasonably likely to occur, no disclosure is required.
> >
> > (2) If management cannot make that determination, it must evaluate objectively the consequences of the known trend, demand, commitment, event or uncertainty, on the assumption that it will come to fruition. Disclosure is then required unless management determines that a material effect on the registrant's financial condition or results of operations is not reasonably likely to occur.
> >
> > Where the test for disclosure is met, MD&A disclosure of the effects [of such uncertainty,] quantified to the extent reasonably practicable, [is] required.[7]

In view of SEC enforcement activity and the likelihood that private litigation in this area will ensue with some frequency, it has been contended that rigorous interpretations of the MD&A requirements will present a "gold mine" for the plaintiffs' bar. However, in view of the 1995 federal legislation providing for an expansive "safe harbor" for MD&A disclosures relating to forward-looking information and the imposition of rigorous pleading requirements, this consequence is unlikely to eventuate.[8]

---

[5] Schneider, *MD&A Disclosure*, 22 Rev. Sec. & Comm. Reg. 149, 150 (1989).

[6] See, e.g., SEC Financial Reporting Release No. 36, 6 Fed. Sec. L. Rep. (CCH) ¶¶ 73,192–73,193 (1989) (MD&A Release).

[7] *In the Matter of Caterpillar, Inc.*, SEC Administrative No. 3–7692 (1992), *quoting*, MD&A Release, note 6 *supra*.

[8] See *In re Sofamor Danek Group, Inc.*, 123 F.3d 394 (6th Cir. 1997) (rejecting that MD&A Item 303 creates a private right of action, stating that a § 10(b) action based on deficient MD&A disclosure is not precluded, and holding that under circumstances presented no § 10(b) recovery allowed).

Nonetheless, SEC enforcement developments may suggest that, even if the likelihood of a contingent event's actual occurrence is relatively remote, it would be prudent for the registrant to disclose in the MD&A any such contingency of substantial magnitude.[9]

§ 10.03 Rumors and Third Party Statements

The circulation of rumors in the marketplace concerning a material development affecting a particular issuer (e.g., being awarded a major contract or being the subject of a tender offer) is common. Also commonplace are forecasts by financial analysts regarding a company's forthcoming earnings. The question arises whether an issuer has a duty to respond to rumors or to third party misstatements under Section 10(b) when such communications are not attributable to the corporation. In the *Fluor* case, the Second Circuit construed this disclosure duty narrowly, asserting that "[a] company has no duty to correct or verify rumors in the marketplace unless those rumors can be attributed to the company."[10] Or, as more recently phrased by the Fourth Circuit, "[t]he securities laws require [the company] to speak truthfully to investors; they do not require the company to police statements made by third parties for inaccuracies . . . ."[11] Nonetheless, if the company adopts or becomes entangled with rumors or third party statements (such as analysts' forecasts), so as to render such statements attributable to the company, Section 10(b) liability may ensue. In the context of analysts' forecasts, a company may be deemed to be sufficiently entangled when, after reviewing such forecasts, it makes an express (or implied) representation that the information contained therein is accurate or is consistent with the company's own views. On the other hand, no entanglement exists if the company merely provides to analysts historical data or corrects solely factual inaccuracies contained in draft analyst documents.[12]

Applying a different rationale, note that both the district court and the Second Circuit in *Fluor* stated that the corporation had a justifiable business reason for delaying disclosure of the information. In this regard, *Fluor* represents the accepted view that practical justifications for delaying

---

[9] See Herlihy & Katz, *Recent Developments Concerning Disclosure,* 1991 M & A and Corp. Gov. L. Rep. 395, 411; Seamons, *Requirements and Pitfalls of MD&A Disclosure,* 25 Sec. Reg. L.J. 239 (1997); Note, *Environmental Disclosures and SEC Reporting Requirements,* 17 Del. J. Corp. L. 483 (1992); discussion § 4.07[D] *supra,* § 10.05[D] *infra.*

[10] *State Teachers Retirement Board v. Fluor Corp.,* 654 F.2d 843, 850 (2d Cir. 1981). See *State Teachers Retirement Board v. Fluor Corp.,* 500 F. Supp. 278, 292–93 (S.D.N.Y. 1980), *aff'd in part, rev'd in part,* 654 F.2d 843 (2d Cir. 1981), where the district court stated that a company may have a duty to respond under Section 10(b) where there are present widespread rumors, a substantial and rapid movement in the price of the subject corporation's stock, and the possession of a high degree of scienter.

[11] *Raab v. General Physics Corp.,* 4 F.3d 286, 288 (4th Cir. 1993).

[12] See, e.g., *Elkind v. Liggett & Myers, Inc.,* 635 F.2d 156, 163 (2d Cir. 1980); *In re Caere Corporate Securities Litigation,* 837 F. Supp. 1054, 1059 (N.D. Cal. 1999). See generally *Note, Securities Issuer Liability for Third Party Misstatements: Refining the Entanglement Standard,* 53 Vand. L. Rev. 947 (2000).

disclosure by an issuer of material nonpublic information generally fall into three categories: "delay while corporate officials ascertain and verify information [until] it is 'ripe for disclosure'; delay while a corporation pursues a business opportunity that would be jeopardized by immediate disclosure; and delay because disclosure would expose the corporation to undue and avoidable risk of loss."[13]

In certain circumstances, it is possible that an issuer may have a duty to seek a halt in the trading of its stock.[14] Moreover, the rules and other pronouncements of the self-regulatory organizations (SROs), including the New York and American Stock Exchanges, impose affirmative and timely disclosure requirements that are more rigorous than current Section 10(b) case law.[15] Violation of these rules, however, although perhaps resulting in SRO disciplinary action, do not provide investors with an implied right of action for damages under the federal securities laws (see § 8.03 *supra*). This position may stem from the belief that, where there are no prior inadequate disclosures, no particular SEC disclosure requirements, nor the presence of "insider" trading, disclosure determinations and the timing of such disclosure generally are left best to the discretion of management. Moreover, if regulation is to have a role in this setting, such regulation should be conducted and enforced by the self-regulatory organizations without the threat of monetary liability.

§ 10.04 Disclosure of Merger Negotiations

With respect to disclosure of merger negotiations, the Supreme Court's decision in *Basic, Inc. v. Levinson*[16] provides guidance. There, the issuer on three separate occasions falsely denied that it was engaged in merger negotiations. In assessing whether these misstatements were "material," the Supreme Court adopted the fact-specific inquiry of *Texas Gulf Sulphur*.[17] Under this standard, the materiality of merger negotiations "depend[s] at any given time upon a balancing of both the indicated probability that the event will occur and the anticipated magnitude of the event in light of the totality of the company activity."[18]

In applying this fact-specific inquiry in a given situation, the Court opined:

> Whether merger discussions in any particular case are material therefore depends on the facts. Generally, in order to assess the

---

[13] Vaughn, *Timing of Disclosure*, 13 Rev. Sec. Reg. 911, 913 (1980).

[14] See *Fluor*, 654 F.2d at 851 n.7.

[15] See, e.g., New York Stock Exchange Company Manual § A2, 2 Fed. Sec. L. Rep. (CCH) ¶ 23,121.

[16] 485 U.S. 224, 227–28 (1988). See generally Bagby & Ruhnka, *The Predictability of Materiality in Merger Negotiations Following Basic*, 16 Sec. Reg. L.J. 245 (1988); Brown, *Corporate Secrecy, the Federal Securities Laws, and the Disclosure of Ongoing Negotiations*, 36 Cath. U. L. Rev. 93 (1986); Gabaldon, *The Disclosure of Preliminary Merger Negotiations as an Imperfect Paradigm of Rule 10b-5 Analysis*, 62 N.Y.U. L. Rev. 1218 (1987).

[17] *SEC v. Texas Gulf Sulphur Co.*, 401 F.2d 833 (2d Cir. 1968) (en banc).

[18] 485 U.S. at 238, *quoting*, 401 F.2d at 849.

probability that the event will occur, a factfinder will need to look to indicia of interest in the transaction at the highest corporate levels. Without attempting to catalog all such possible factors, we note by way of example that board resolutions, instructions to investment bankers, and actual negotiations between principals or their intermediaries may serve as indicia of interest. To assess the magnitude of the transaction to the issuer of the securities allegedly manipulated, a factfinder will need to consider such facts as the size of the two corporate entities and of the potential premiums over market value. No particular event or factor short of closing the transaction need be either necessary or sufficient by itself to render merger discussions material. [19]

It should be emphasized that the Supreme Court's decision in *Basic* interpreted the issue of "materiality" for Section 10(b) purposes in the merger/acquisition setting. As the Court stated, the case did not address when, if ever, a company must affirmatively disclose the existence of such negotiations: "[T]his case does not concern the *timing* of a disclosure; it concerns only its accuracy and completeness." [20]

Hence, it is important to emphasize that the issuer in *Basic* elected to speak. Thus, the case neither involved the timing of disclosure nor an issuer's obligation to speak. [21] As a result, the decision may seem more expansive than, in actuality, it is. In this regard, absent the existence of certain triggering events, such as the presence of a competing tender offer where SEC Schedule 14D-9 requires disclosure of merger negotiations, [22] present law may not require the issuer affirmatively to disclose the existence of such negotiations, even if they are material. The SEC has taken this position:

> In urging that merger negotiations may become material before there is certainty of an agreement, we are not suggesting that material merger negotiations therefore have to be disclosed to the public as a matter of course. We agree with the court below that

---

[19] 485 U.S. at 239. For a recent decision interpreting *Basic* restrictively, see *Phillips v. LCI International, Inc.*, 190 F.3d 609 (4th Cir. 1999). But see *In re MCI Worldcom., Inc. Securities Litigation,* [2000 Transfer Binder] Fed. Sec. L. Rep. (CCH) ¶ 90,950 (E.D.N.Y. 2000) (alleged statements falsely denying existence of merger discussions held actionable under § 10(b)). With respect to the concept of materiality in audited financial statements, the SEC staff in SAB 99 rejected quantitative "rules of thumb" (such as 5%) as sole evaluators of materiality, stating that "exclusive reliance on certain quantitative benchmarks to assess materiality in preparing financial statements and performing audits of those financial statements is inappropriate." Staff Accounting Bulletin No. 99, 64 Fed. Reg. 45150 (1999).

[20] 485 U.S. at 235.

[21] *Id.*

[22] 17 C.F.R. § 240.14d–101, item 7 (calling for a subject company's management to disclose merger negotiations even though the terms of the prospective transaction and the potential offeror's identity need not be revealed if such disclosure would jeopardize the ongoing negotiations). See generally Branson, *SEC Nonacquiescence in Judicial Decisionmaking: Target Company Disclosure of Acquisition Negotiations*, 46 Md. L. Rev. 1001 (1987).

corporations ordinarily have no duty to disclose even material merger negotiations.[23]

One may inquire whether Item 303 MD&A disclosure impacts upon this analysis. As set forth by the SEC:

> While Item 303 could be read to impose a duty to disclose otherwise nondisclosed preliminary merger negotiations, as known events or uncertainties reasonably likely to have material effects on future financial condition or results of operations, the Commission did not intend to apply and has not applied, Item 303 in this manner. . . .
>
> [W]here disclosure is not otherwise required, and has not otherwise been made, the MD&A need not contain a discussion of the impact of such negotiations where, in the registrant's view, inclusion of such information would jeopardize completion of the transaction. Where disclosure is otherwise required or has otherwise been made by or on behalf of the registrant, the interests in avoiding premature disclosure no longer exist. In such case, the negotiations would be subject to the same disclosure standards under Item 303 as any other known trend, demand, commitment, event or uncertainty.[24]

In view of the *Basic* decision, issuers may well be inclined to remain silent until an agreement relating to price and structure of the transaction are reached. Moreover, a "no comment" statement, according to language in *Basic*, is "generally the functional equivalent of silence."[25] Unfortunately, issuer silence, absent justifiable business reasons for maintaining secrecy, conflicts with the disclosure policies of the federal securities acts. Nonetheless, given the enormous liability potential, issuer silence (or "no comment") may be a practical policy to implement.

§ 10.05   Disclosure of "Soft" Information

[A]   Generally

Traditionally, the securities laws have required disclosure of "hard" information, that is, factual, objectively verifiable data.[26] "Soft" information, on the other hand, predominantly focuses on forward-looking statements, such as projections, forecasts, and predictions.[27] Moreover, soft information need not necessarily relate to expectations regarding the future, but may include any statement that cannot be factually supported, whether due to a lack of substantiating data or because the information consists primarily of subjective evaluations or opinions. Accordingly, soft

---

[23] See Brief for the SEC as *Amicus Curiae* in *Levinson v. Basic, Inc.*, 786 F.2d 741 (6th Cir. 1986), *vacated and remanded*, 485 U.S. 224 (1988).

[24] SEC Financial Reporting Release No. 36, 6 Fed. Sec. L. Rep. (CCH) ¶ 73,197 (1989).

[25] 485 U.S. at 239 n.17.

[26] See generally Securities Act Release No. 6084 (1979).

[27] *Id.*

information may be defined as "statements of subjective analysis or extrapolation, such as opinions, motives, and intentions, or forward-looking statements, such as projections, estimates and forecasts."[28] Note, however, that under certain circumstances, such information is required to be disclosed today pursuant to the Item 303 MD&A disclosure mandates.[29]

Until the mid-1970s the SEC and the courts discouraged and even prohibited the disclosure of soft information.[30] The major concern was that investors, particularly the unsophisticated, might attach too much significance to information that is of questionable reliability.[31] On the other hand, the flow of soft information to the marketplace may enable sophisticated investors more intelligently to evaluate the total mix of information influencing their decisionmaking.[32]

Merger mania in the late 1970s and the 1980s brought the issue of disclosing soft information into sharper focus. For example, in a departure from its traditional view that forward-looking information is untrustworthy and, hence, discouraged, the SEC adopted Securities Act Rule 175 (as well as Exchange Act Rule 3b-6),[33] which encourages issuer use of financial projections and establishes a "safe harbor" for parties who invoke the rule (see § 4.07[B]).[34] Embracing the utility of soft information to a greater degree, legislation enacted by Congress in 1995 generally broadens the safe harbor provisions to encompass oral and written statements, even if not filed with the SEC, by publicly-held companies and those acting on their behalf.[35]

As a general proposition, even if not coming within the safe harbor provisions of Rule 175 and Rule 3b-6, "[f]orward-looking statements need

---

[28] *In re Craftmatic Securities Litigation*, 890 F.2d 628, 642 (3d Cir. 1989). See *Garcia v. Cordova*, 930 F.2d 826, 830 (10th Cir. 1990); Hiler, *The SEC and the Courts' Approach to Disclosure of Earnings Projections, Asset Appraisals, and Other Soft Information*, 46 Md. L. Rev. 1114 (1987); Karjala, *A Coherent Approach to Misleading Corporate Announcements, Fraud, and Rule 10b-5*, 52 Albany L. Rev. 957 (1988); Kerr, *A Walk Through the Circuits: The Duty to Disclose Soft Information*, 46 Md. L. Rev. 1071 (1987); Poole, *Improving the Reliability of Management Forecasts*, 14 J. Corp. L. 547 (1989); Rowe, *Projections, Appraisals, and Other Soft Information*, 23 Rev. Sec. & Comm. Reg. 37 (1990); Schneider, *Nits, Grits and Soft Information in SEC Filings*, 121 U. Pa. L. Rev. 254, 255 (1972).

[29] See §§ 4.07[D], 10.02, 10.04 *supra*.

[30] See, e.g., *Gerstle v. Gamble-Skogmo*, Inc., 478 F.2d 1281, 1294 (2d Cir. 1973); Securities Act Release No. 5180 (1971).

[31] See, e.g., *South Coast Services Corp. v. Santa Ana Valley Irrigation Co.*, 699 F.2d 1265, 1271 (9th Cir. 1982).

[32] See generally, Hiler, *The SEC and the Courts' Approach to Disclosure of Earnings Projections, Asset Appraisals, and Other Soft Information: Old Problems, Changing Views*, 46 Md. L. Rev. 1114 (1987); Kerr, *A Walk Through the Circuits: The Duty to Disclose Soft Information*, 46 Md. L. Rev. 1071 (1987).

[33] 17 C.F.R. § 230.175. See Securities Act Release No. 6084 (1979). The safe harbor rule under the Exchange Act in this setting is Rule 3b-6, 17 C.F.R. § 240.3b-6.

[34] Rule 175 is discussed in greater detail in § 4.07[C] *supra*. See generally Dennis, *Mandatory Disclosure Theory and Management Projections: A Law and Economics Perspective* 46 Md. L. Rev. 1197 (1987); authorities cited note 28 *supra*.

[35] See 10.05[D] *infra*.

not be correct; it is enough that they have a reasonable basis."[36] Isolated and general remarks about future results, not worded as guarantees, normally are not actionable as they are viewed as soft, "puffing" statements.[37] Recognizing that the securities laws do not serve as investment insurance,[38] courts have rejected conclusory allegations of fraud based on hindsight.[39] This "fraud-by-hindsight" defense has been applied by a number of courts, frequently by such courts granting motions to dismiss due to the plaintiff's failure to plead fraud with particularity as required by Rule 9(b) of the Federal Rules of Civil Procedure.[40] From a general prospective, the Private Securities Litigation Reform Act, enacted in 1995, codifies this judicial reluctance to impose monetary liability with respect to forward-looking statements.[41]

[B] Application to "Merger" Context

In the context of "mergers" and related transactions, a small number of courts have required companies to disclose forward-looking information in certain circumstances.[42] However, most courts continue to adhere to the traditional philosophical concerns as a basis for not imposing liability upon issuers who decline to disclose soft information.[43]

Hence, while soft information in the "merger" context historically has been treated as immaterial as a matter of law, an emerging, yet minority, view suggests that this is no longer so. The leading case for the proposition that there is an affirmative duty to disclose soft information when certain indicia of reliability are present is *Flynn v. Bass Brothers Enterprises.*[44] In that case the Third Circuit canvassed the events marking what it considered to be the emergence of a new public policy favoring the disclosure of soft information, spawned "in response to developing corporate trends, such as the increase in mergers,"[45] and held:

> In order to give full effect to the evolution of the law of disclosure, . . . today we set forth the law for disclosure of soft information as it is to be applied from this date on. Henceforth, the law is not that asset appraisals are, as a matter of law, immaterial. Rather, in appropriate cases, such information must be disclosed. Courts should ascertain the duty to disclose asset valuations and other soft

---

[36] *Wielgos v. Commonwealth Edison Co.*, 892 F.2d 509, 513 (7th Cir. 1989).

[37] See, e.g., *Raab v. General Physics Corp.*, 4 F.3d 286, 290 (4th Cir. 1993).

[38] See, e.g., *DiLeo v. Ernst & Young*, 901 F.2d 624, 627 (7th Cir. 1990).

[39] See, e.g., *Krim v. BancTexas Group, Inc.*, 989 F.2d 1435, 1448–50 (5th Cir. 1993).

[40] See, e.g., *Melder v. Morris*, 27 F.3d 1097 (5th Cir. 1994). For further discussion of Rule 9(b) see §§ 7.01, 7.03[A] *supra.*

[41] See § 10.05[D] *infra.*

[42] See, e.g., *Flynn v. Bass Brothers Enterprises, Inc.*, 744 F.2d 978 (3d Cir. 1984).

[43] See, e.g., *Starkman v. Marathon Oil Co.*, 772 F.2d 231 (6th Cir. 1985). Note, however, that disclosure may be required in certain circumstances pursuant to the Item 303 MD&A disclosure mandates. See §§ 4.07[D], 10.02 *supra.*

[44] 744 F.2d 978 (3d Cir. 1984).

[45] *Id.* at 986.

information on a case by case basis, by weighing the potential aid such information will give a shareholder against the potential harm, such as undue reliance, if the information is released with a proper cautionary note.

The factors a court must consider in making such a determination are: the facts upon which the information is based; the qualifications of those who prepared or compiled it; the purpose for which the information was originally intended; its relevance to the stockholders' impending decision; the degree of subjectivity or bias reflected in its preparation; the degree to which the information is unique; and the availability to the investor of other more reliable sources of information.[46]

Sharply contrasting *Flynn* is the Sixth Circuit's approach in *Starkman v. Marathon Oil Co.*,[47] in which the court declined to recognize a mandatory obligation to disclose asset appraisals or financial projections, unless "the predictions underlying the appraisal or projection are substantially certain to hold."[48] Criticizing the Third Circuit's approach in *Flynn*, the Sixth Circuit reasoned:

By its very nature . . . this sort of judicial cost-benefit analysis [referring to *Flynn*] is uncertain and unpredictable, and it moreover neglects the role of the market in providing shareholders with information regarding the target's value through competing tender offers. Our approach, which focuses on the certainty of the data underlying the appraisal or projection, ensures that the target company's shareholders will receive all essentially factual information, while preserving the target's discretion to disclose more uncertain information without the threat of liability, provided appropriate qualifications and explanations are made.[49]

Flynn represents an approach aimed at addressing investor concerns, whereas *Starkman* illustrates the disclosure concerns from an issuer's perspective. Both views have merit, but each is too one-sided. The cost-benefit analysis advocated by the Third Circuit does not promote certainty,

---

[46] *Id.* at 988.

[47] 772 F.2d 231 (6th Cir. 1985).

[48] *Id.* at 241.

[49] *Id.* at 242. The Sixth Circuit in *Starkman* observed that in a going private transaction implicating SEC Rule 13e-3 asset appraisals rendered by outside sources, such as an investment banker, must be disclosed in the Schedule 13E-3. The Sixth Circuit subsequently construed the disclosure parameters of outside appraisals rendered in going private transactions in *Howing Company v. Nationwide Corp.*, 972 F.2d 700 (6th Cir. 1992); 927 F.2d 263 (6th Cir. 1991), 826 F.2d 1470 (6th Cir. 1987). The Sixth Circuit opined:

The issuer in this case . . . choose to rely on the expertise of the [investment bank] First Boston. The problem with defendants adopting the First Boston opinion letter as their disclosure to shareholders is that this one-page letter is itself woefully inadequate when measured against the specific disclosure requirements of the Rule. An issuer cannot insulate itself from 13e-3 liability by relying on an investment banker's opinion letter which itself does not comply with the specific disclosure requirements of the Rule.

826 F.2d at 1479. See Kofele-Kale, *The SEC's Going-Private Rules — Analysis and Developments*, 19 Sec. Reg. L.J. 139 (1991).

because the approach calls for a court to determine the qualitative value of the enumerated factors with the benefit of hindsight and on an ad hoc basis. Under this approach, judicial guidelines may well have little stability, because the subjective nature of the inquiry is likely to result in the factors being applied differently under an ad hoc analysis. In addition, the Third Circuit's desire "to give full effect to the evolution in the law of disclosure"[50] overlooks the fact that, while the securities laws are designed to protect investors, they are not intended to impose undue hardship upon issuers. The issuer's duty to disclose should be based on what is fair and reasonable from both an investor's and an issuer's perspective.

On the other hand, the Sixth Circuit's approach in *Starkman* is too rigid. Disclosure, a key concept underlying the securities laws, is subordinated to the perceived need to avoid imposing liability in circumstances in which certainty cannot be assured. The *Starkman* court's concern is misplaced, because an important policy underlying the disclosure doctrine is issuer fair dealing through the sharing of information that is material to investor decisionmaking. Congress, the SEC, and the courts generally require issuers to make accurate and complete disclosure of specified information in order to enhance the level of investor decisionmaking and to ensure that the information disclosed is not materially misleading. All that should be required in the context of soft information is that the available material data be accurately disclosed; it need not be certain.

Clearly, there is a need for an approach that embraces both investor and issuer concerns. While an affirmative duty to disclose has been held to exist only in certain situations,[51] consistent application of the disclosure principle underlying the securities laws should require that, to ensure investor decisionmaking based on a flow of accurate information between the issuer and the financial markets, soft information must be affirmatively disclosed in certain circumstances.[52]

[C]　The "Bespeaks Caution" Doctrine

The "bespeaks caution" doctrine serves as an inducement for issuers to include cautionary warnings, qualifications, and disclaimers in regard to projections and other forward-looking information disseminated to the marketplace.[53] The bespeaks caution doctrine states that "where an offering statement [or other disclosure document], such as a prospectus, accompanies statements of future forecasts, projections and expectations with adequate cautionary language, those statements are not actionable

---

[50] 744 F.2d at 988.

[51] See §§ 4.07[D], 10.01–10.02 *supra*.

[52] For further discussion, see, e.g., Steinberg & Goldman, *Issuer Affirmative Disclosure Obligations — An Analytical Framework for Merger Negotiations, Soft Information and Bad News*, 46 Md. L. Rev. 923, 934–46 (1987).

[53] See Langevoort, *Disclosures That "Bespeak Caution,"* 49 Bus. Law. 481 (1994). O'Hare, *Good Faith and The Bespeaks Caution Doctrine: It's Not Just a State of Mind*, 58 U. Pitt. L. Rev. 619 (1997).

as securities fraud."[54] According to the doctrine, cautionary statements make reliance on the projections or other soft information unreasonable and that the statements, when read in conjunction with the cautionary language, are immaterial.[55] Moreover, the Private Securities Litigation Reform Act of 1995 codifies the "bespeaks caution" doctrine (see § 10.05[D] *infra*).

The Third Circuit's decision in *In re Donald J. Trump Casinos Securities Litigation*[56] provides an illustrative application of the bespeaks caution doctrine. There, a partnership offered $675 million in bonds to finance the completion of the Taj Mahal hotel/casino. Although the prospectus for the bonds stated the partnership believed that the operation of the business would generate funds sufficient to cover its debt service, the prospectus identified several risk factors and indicated that there could be no assurance that actual operating results would meet the disclosed expectations. When the partnership defaulted on the interest payments, the bondholders filed suit alleging securities fraud.[57]

In *Trump* the Third Circuit held that the prospectus included "warnings and cautionary language . . . tailored to the specific future projections, estimates or opinions in the prospectus."[58] The court held that the risk disclosures defeated the materiality of the forward-looking statements:

> [W]hen an offering document's forecasts, opinions or projections are accompanied by meaningful cautionary statements, the forward-looking statements will not form the basis for a securities fraud claim if those statements did not affect the "total mix" of information the document provided investors. In other words, cautionary language, if sufficient, renders the alleged omissions or misrepresentations immaterial as a matter of law.[59]

Importantly, the bespeaks caution doctrine is subject to limitations.[60] For example, not just any cautionary language will render accompanying forward-looking statements immaterial; the language must be "tailored to the specific future projections, estimates or opinions" at issue.[61] A blanket warning that an investment is risky is likely to be insufficient to ward off a securities fraud claim.[62] Another limitation stands for the proposition

---

[54] *In re Donald J. Trump Casinos Securities Litigation*, 793 F. Supp. 543, 544 (D.N.J. 1992), *aff'd*, 7 F.3d 357 (3d Cir. 1993).

[55] See, e.g., *In re Worlds of Wonder Securities Litigation*, 35 F.3d 1407, 1414 (9th Cir. 1994); *I. Meyer Pincus & Assoc., P.C. v. Oppenheimer & Co.*, 936 F.2d 759, 761 (2d Cir. 1992).

[56] 7 F.3d 357 (3d Cir. 1993).

[57] *Id*. at 365–71.

[58] *Id*. at 371–72.

[59] *Id*. at 371.

[60] As a general proposition, the "bespeaks caution doctrine applies only to cases where the disclosure of information was made in good faith and on a reasonable basis, unless . . . the forward-looking statement in controversy is so generalized and so significantly qualified by cautionary language that [it] is immaterial as a matter of law." Rosen, *Liability for 'Soft Information': New Developments and Emerging Trends*, 23 Sec. Reg. L.J. 3, 36 (1995).

[61] *Id*. See *Kline v. First Western Gov't Sec., Inc.*, 24 F.3d 480, 489 (3d Cir. 1994).

[62] See, e.g., *Rubinstein v. Collins*, 20 F.3d 160, 168 (5th Cir. 1994).

that the bespeaks caution doctrine does not apply to facts. As one court has stated, "[f]raud is still fraud, and all the cautionary language in the world will not replace a true material omission or misstatement of a fact which would matter to a reasonable investor."[63] Additionally, the bespeaks caution doctrine only applies to situations in which there was an affirmative disclosure of soft information, and therefore does not extend to allegations that there was a failure to disclose such information.[64] Moreover, there exists a concern among some courts that the doctrine may be applied too broadly.[65]

In sum, when reviewing disclosure documents, issuers and their counsel should assess whether the soft information conveyed is adequately counterbalanced by specific cautionary language. The nature of the cautionary language will depend on the circumstances and context in which the underlying soft information is being conveyed. For example, soft information relating to internal rates of return ordinarily will require more specific risk disclosures than will vague statements of optimism. Additionally, a more detailed disclosure of risks generally should be contained in a prospectus as compared to a press release.[66]

Thus, carefully crafted risk disclosure statements that bespeak caution can deter the bringing of securities fraud claims and can enhance the likelihood of successfully fending off such claims if litigation is initiated.

[D] The Private Securities Litigation Reform Act — Safe Harbor for Certain Forward-Looking Statements

The Private Securities Litigation Reform Act of 1995 amended the Securities Act by adding a new Section 27A and further amended the Securities Exchange Act by adding a new Section 21E. The new sections generally provide 1934 Act reporting companies (as well as those acting on their behalf and underwriters with respect to information furnished by or derived from information provided by such companies) with a safe harbor from liability in private actions for certain forward-looking statements (e.g., projections). The safe harbor is applicable to both forward-looking written and oral statements, so long as (1) the statement is identified as a forward-looking statement and is accompanied by meaningful cautionary statements, thus codifying the "bespeaks caution" doctrine; (2) the statement lacks materiality; or (3) the plaintiff fails to prove that the statement was made with actual knowledge of its falsity (irrespective of whether cautionary language is included).

The safe harbor also contains specific provisions for oral forward-looking statements made by an issuer or those acting on its behalf under (1) above.

---

[63] *In re Integrated Resources Real Estate Ltd. Partnership Securities Litigation*, 815 F. Supp. 620, 674 (S.D.N.Y. 1993).

[64] See *In re Worlds of Wonder Securities Litigation*, 814 F. Supp. 850, 858 (N.D. Cal. 1993), *aff'd in part, rev'd in part*, 35 F.3d 1407 (9th Cir. 1994).

[65] See, e.g., *Rubinstein v. Collins*, 20 F.3d 160 (5th Cir. 1994); *Mayer v. Mylod*, 988 F.2d 635 (6th Cir. 1993); *In re Synergen Securities Litigation*, 863 F. Supp. 1409 (D. Colo. 1994).

[66] See Rosen, *supra* note 60, at 34. See also, Langevoort, note 53 *supra*.

Such oral forward-looking statements are protected if such statements are accompanied by cautionary language and identify "readily available" documentation from which an investor can obtain additional information regarding the substance of such oral statements. The legislation provides that such documentation is to be deemed "readily available" if it is either filed with the SEC or otherwise generally disseminated (e.g., press release carried on the Dow Jones Broad Tape). The applicability of the safe harbor provisions are subject to enumerated exclusions in the form of certain excluded issuers (e.g., penny stock issuers) and certain statements in specific instances (e.g., tender offers).

In addition, the safe harbor section specifies that its provisions do not impose a duty to update a forward-looking statement. It is unclear whether this language is meant to eliminate the "duty to update" any forward-looking statement or merely to clarify that no implied "duty to update" may be gleaned from this section. Hence, the breadth of this language will be developed by the courts.

In regard to this legislatively enacted safe harbor for forward-looking information, the Joint Explanatory Statement of the Conference Committee is useful:

> The Conference Committee has adopted a statutory "safe harbor" to enhance market efficiency by encouraging companies to disclose forward-looking information. This provision adds a new Section 27A to the 1933 Act and a new Section 21E of the 1934 Act which protects from liability in private lawsuits certain "forward-looking" statements made by persons specified in the legislation.
>
> The first prong of the safe harbor protects a written or oral forward-looking statement that is: (i) identified as forward-looking, and (ii) accompanied by meaningful cautionary statements identifying important factors that could cause actual results to differ materially from those projected in the statement.
>
> Under this first prong of the safe harbor, boilerplate warnings will not suffice as meaningful cautionary statements identifying important factors that could cause actual results to differ materially from those projected in the statement. The cautionary statements must convey substantive information about factors that realistically could cause results to differ materially from those projected in the forward-looking statement, such as, for example, information about the issuer's business.
>
> Courts may continue to find a forward-looking statement immaterial — and thus not actionable under the 1933 Act and the 1934 Act — on other grounds. To clarify this point, the Conference Committee includes language in the safe harbor provision that no liability attaches to forward-looking statements that are "immaterial."
>
> The second prong of the safe harbor provides an alternative analysis. This safe harbor also applies to both written and oral

forward-looking statements. Instead of examining the forward-looking and cautionary statements, this prong of the safe harbor focuses on the state of mind of the person making the forward-looking statement. A person or business entity will not be liable in a private lawsuit for a forward-looking statement unless a plaintiff proves that person or business entity made a false or misleading forward-looking statement with actual knowledge that it was false or misleading. The Conference Committee intends for this alternative prong of the safe harbor to apply if the plaintiff fails to prove the forward-looking statement (1) if made by a natural person, was made with the actual knowledge by that person that the statement was false or misleading; or (2) if made by a business entity, was made by or with the approval of an executive officer of the entity with actual knowledge by that officer that the statement was false or misleading.

The Conference Committee recognizes that, under certain circumstances, it may be unwieldy to make oral forward-looking statements relying on the first prong of the safe harbor. Companies who want to make a brief announcement of earnings or a new product would first have to identify the statement as forward-looking and then provide cautionary statements identifying important factors that could cause results to differ materially from those projected in the statement. As a result, the Conference Committee has provided for an optional, more flexible rule for oral forward-looking statements that will facilitate these types of oral communications by an issuer while still providing to the public information it would have received if the forward-looking statement was written. The Conference Committee intends to limit this oral safe harbor to issuers or the officers, directors, or employees of the issuer acting on the issuer's behalf.

This legislation permits covered issuers, or persons acting on the issuer's behalf, to make oral forward-looking statements within the safe harbor. The person making the forward-looking statement must identify the statement as a forward-looking statement and state that results may differ materially from those projected in the statement. The person must also identify a "readily available" written document that contains factors that could cause results to differ materially. The written information identified by the person making the forward-looking statement must qualify as a "cautionary statement" under the first prong of the safe harbor (i.e., it must be a meaningful cautionary statement or statements that identify important factors that could cause actual results to differ materially from those projected in the forward-looking statement.) For purposes of this provision, "readily available" information refers to SEC filed documents, annual reports and other widely disseminated materials, such as press releases.

The safe harbor provision protects written and oral forward-looking statements made by issuers and certain persons retained or acting on behalf of the issuer. The Conference Committee intends the statutory safe harbor protection to make more information about a company's future plans available to investors and the public. The safe harbor covers underwriters, but only insofar as the underwriters provide forward-looking information that is based on or "derived from" information provided by the issuer. Because underwriters have what is effectively an adversarial relationship with issuers in performing due diligence, the use of the term "derived from" affords underwriters some latitude so that they may disclose adverse information that the issuer did not necessarily "provide." The Conference Committee does not intend the safe harbor to cover forward-looking information made in connection with a broker's sales practices.

The Conference Committee has determined that the statutory safe harbor should not apply to certain forward-looking statements. Thus, the statutory safe harbor does not protect forward-looking statements: (1) included in financial statements prepared in accordance with generally accepted accounting principles; (2) contained in an initial public offering registration statement; (3) made in connection with a tender offer; (4) made in connection with a partnership, limited liability company or direct participation program offering; or (5) made in beneficial ownership disclosure statements filed with the SEC under Section 13(d) of the 1934 Act.

This legislation also makes clear that nothing in the safe harbor provision imposes any duty to update forward-looking statements.

The Conference Committee does not intend for the safe harbor provisions to replace the judicial "bespeaks caution" doctrine or to foreclose further development of that doctrine by the courts.

An appellate court's application of the safe harbor provided by the 1995 legislation is illustrated by *Harris v. Ivax Corporation.*[67] There, the Eleventh Circuit, consistent with the 1995 Act's legislative history, reasoned that adequate cautionary language may be held to accompany the forward-looking statements even if the registrant fails to identify the particular factor that causes such forward-looking statements not to come to fruition. Moreover, the court opined that, at least in certain circumstances, the safe harbor encompasses a statement that is of a "mixed" nature — namely, of both known facts and forward-looking information: "[W]e hold that when the factors underlying a projection or economic forecast include both assumptions [i.e. "soft" information] and statements of known fact, and a plaintiff alleges that a material factor is missing, the entire list of factors is treated as a forward-looking statement."[68]

---

[67] 182 F.3d 799 (11th Cir. 1999).

[68] 182 F.3d 799, 805–06 (11th Cir. 1999). See generally Bloomenthal, *The Private Securities Litigation Reform Act — How Safe Is The Safe Harbor?*, 18 Sec. & Fed. Corp. L. Rep. 97 (1996); O'Hare, *Good Faith and The Bespeaks Caution Doctrine: It's Not Just a State of Mind*, 58 U. Pitt. L. Rev. 619 (1997); Symposium, 51 Bus. Law. No. 4 (1996); Symposium, 33 San Diego L. Rev. No. 3 (1996); Symposium, 24 Sec. Reg. L.J. No. 2 (1996).

Undoubtedly, judicial interpretation of the Private Securities Litigation Reform Act's safe harbor is at an early stage. The parameters of this safe harbor, hopefully, will be further refined by the courts during the next decade.

§ 10.06   Duty to Update

The duty to update may arise in a number of different circumstances. Generally, such a duty may be present when the issuer previously has made a statement that, although accurate when made, continues to be "alive" in the marketplace and has become materially false or misleading as a result of subsequent events. This duty may be implicated, for example, in the context of merger negotiations, disclosure of "soft" information, and responding to rumors.

Perhaps significantly the 1995 federal legislation specifies that its safe harbor provisions do not impose a duty to update forward-looking statements. It is unclear whether this language is intended to eliminate the "duty to update" in this context or merely to clarify that no implied duty to update may be derived from the 1995 legislation. Accordingly, the significance of this language will be construed by the courts.[69]

In certain settings, SEC rules specifically mandate a duty to update. In the tender offer context, for instance, SEC Rule 14e-2 calls for the subject company to disclose to its security holders its position toward the takeover bid and inform such security holders of any material change relating to the position previously taken.

Judicial decisions addressing the duty to update from a general perspective are relatively sparse. For example, the First Circuit in *Backman v. Polaroid Corp.* opined that, "in special circumstances, a statement, correct at the time, may have a forward intent and connotation upon which parties may be expected to rely." If that is the situation and if "there is a change, correction, more exactly, further disclosure, may be called for."[70]

Construing the First Circuit's decision in the foregoing case, one securities practitioner opined:

> For the first time, a court's careful analysis in a specific factual context makes completely clear that the duty to update is not nearly as broad as some of the authorities seem to suggest. The duty is not triggered simply because a prior statement would no longer be true if repeated at a later date in the light of intervening facts. [The court] did not articulate in detail precisely when an updating duty

---

[69] See *Phillips v. LCI International, Inc.*, 190 F.3d 609 (4th Cir. 1999) (suggesting no duty to update).

[70] 910 F.2d 10, 17 (1st Cir. 1990) (en banc). See *Weiner v. The Quaker Oats Company*, 129 F.3d 310 (3d Cir. 1997) (holding duty to update existed).

would exist, but the brief discussion suggests that the duty would arise primarily in special circumstances.[71]

§ 10.07   Duty to Disclose "Bad" News

"Bad news" usually refers to circumstances having an adverse financial impact upon the corporation, such as the loss of one or more major customers or valuable contracts, the initiation of a significant lawsuit or SEC enforcement action, or events giving rise to troubling liquidity problems, to mention but a few examples. Bad news also may refer to impending changes in corporate management, or the loss of access to or dismissal of special advisers upon whom corporate management has come to rely.

The reasons for issuer reluctance to disclose bad news concerning the company are axiomatic. Equally obvious is the significance of such information to investors. The periodic reports that issuers are required to file under the Exchange Act are comprehensive, and one generally cannot omit (material) bad news without violating the securities laws. However, certain disclosure loopholes exist, because there is no specific SEC rule mandating disclosure of material adverse financial information between periodic reports.

Hence, the affirmative disclosure issue relating to adverse financial information normally arises during an interval in which the issuer is not required to file a periodic report with the SEC. Under the Exchange Act an issuer is required, inter alia, to file annual reports on Form 10-K, quarterly reports on Form 10-Q and current reports on Form 8-K.[72] The regulations that mandate the filing of these reports are fairly specific as to what is required to be disclosed in the various line items. For example, the Form 10-K requires, among other things, an extensive discussion of the issuer's business, audited financial statements, disclosures regarding certain legal proceedings, and a management discussion and analysis ("MD&A").[73] With respect to the MD&A, mandated disclosures include identifying "any known trends or any known demands, commitments, events, or uncertainties that will result in, or that are reasonably likely to result in, the registrant's liquidity increasing or decreasing in any material way" and a description of "any known trends or uncertainties that have had or that the registrant reasonably expects will have a material favorable or unfavorable impact on net sales or revenues or income from continuing operations."[74]

Quarterly reports (on Form 10-Q) also must contain an MD&A and other extensive disclosures, including unaudited interim financial information

---

[71] Schneider, *The Uncertain Duty to Update — Polaroid II Brings a Welcome Limitation*, 4 Insights No. 10, at 2, 10 (1992). See Block, Radin & Carlinsky, *A Post-Polaroid Snapshot of the Duty to Correct Disclosure*, 1991 Colum. Bus. L. Rev. 139, 140 (1991); Rosenblum, *An Issuer's Duty Under Rule 10b-5 to Correct and Update Materially Misleading Statements*, 40 Cath. U. L. Rev. 289, 291 (1991); Note, *Rule 10b-5 and Voluntary Corporate Disclosures to Security Analysts*, 92 Colum. L. Rev. 1517, 1543–44 (1992).

[72] Small business issuers may utilize SEC forms promulgated for the use by such issuers. The same general requirements apply. See § 4.06[A] *supra*.

[73] See Form 10-K, Items 1–3, 6–9, 14, 17 C.F.R. § 249.310.

[74] Form 10-K, Item 7 (calling for information required by Item 303 of Regulation S-K).

prepared in accordance with generally accepted accounting principles ("GAAP").[75] Moreover, periodic disclosure, on Form 8-K, is required to facilitate current disclosure of certain significant events. A key ingredient of the Form 8-K disclosure obligation is that it is mandatory only with respect to certain specified events.[76] Disclosure of other events is permissive.[77] Although the Commission has issued a number of releases urging corporate managements to review their disclosure policies "and endeavor to set up procedures which will insure that prompt disclosure be made of material corporate developments, both favorable and unfavorable, so that investor confidence can be maintained in an orderly and effective securities market,"[78] the Commission has refrained from promulgating rules which mandate affirmative disclosure of bad news arising between quarterly reports. In addition, there is a dearth of judicial authority on the issue. Hence, because there currently is no general affirmative duty to disclose even material information regarding the issuer except in certain specific circumstances,[79] the disinclination by issuers to make such disclosure is not surprising.

Accordingly, the central issue in this context is one of timing. Issuers understandably wish to delay disclosure of adverse news as long as possible. For example, during the interim when the next Form 10-Q must be filed, perhaps new major contracts can be procured to replace the ones that were terminated. Immediate disclosure, according to management, could have a "snowball" effect, depressing the company's business and the price of its stock in the securities markets.

Generally, there is little judicial authority to support an affirmative duty to disclose adverse news during the period between SEC required reports (unless one of the disclosure mandates enumerated in § 10.01 is deemed to apply). Courts have held that the timing of disclosure is a matter of business judgment.[80] Under this concept, disclosure may be deferred until the information is ripe, or withheld if a valid business reason exists, such as where premature disclosure would jeopardize a contract. On the other hand, where the material information clearly is ripe and the business justifications proffered are not compelling, a plausible case exists for imposing liability for nondisclosure. A court should balance the potential impact of disclosing the bad news against the duty owed to shareholders.[81]

It is not surprising that questions concerning issuer affirmative disclosure obligations raise difficult public policy issues. In seeking to set forth

[75] Form 10-Q, Part I, Items 1-2, 17 C.F.R. § 249.308a.

[76] 17 C.F.R. § 249.308. The following items, for example, are mandatory under Form 8-K: Changes in Control of Registrant (Item 1), Acquisition or Disposition of Assets (Item 2), Bankruptcy or Receivership (Item 3), Changes in Registrant's Certifying Accountant (Item 4), and Resignations of Registrants Directors (Item 6).

[77] See Form 8-K, Item 5.

[78] See Securities Exchange Act Release No. 18271 (1981).

[79] See §§ 4.07[C], 10.01–10.02 *supra*.

[80] See, e.g., *Billard v. Rockwell International Corp.*, 683 F.2d 51 (2d Cir. 1982).

[81] Cf. *Flynn v. Bass Brothers Enterprises, Inc.*, 744 F.2d 978 (3d Cir. 1984).

a proper balance, legitimate concerns of both issuers and investors should be addressed. On the one hand, issuers should be required to affirmatively disclose only if there are sufficiently clear guidelines in effect and only if legitimate business interests will not be impeded by such disclosure. On the other hand, investors and the marketplace should be entitled to all material financial information that is ripe for disclosure, in a manner which is not misleading to investors, and that does not impose an unduly rigorous burden upon issuers.[82]

§ 10.08 Regulation FD

The SEC adopted Regulation FD (Fair Disclosure) in response to the perceived unfairness when companies selectively disclose material nonpublic information to analysts, institutional investors, and other securities market insiders. The Regulation's basic premise provides that "when an issuer, or person acting on its behalf, discloses material nonpublic information to [selective] persons . . . , it must make public disclosure of that information."[83] The timing of when the issuer must make such a public disclosure depends on whether the selective disclosure was intentional or non-intentional.

As summarized by the SEC:

> *Regulation FD (Fair Disclosure)* is a new issuer disclosure rule that addresses selective disclosure. The regulation provides that when an issuer, or person acting on its behalf, discloses material nonpublic information to certain enumerated persons (in general, securities market professionals and holders of the issuer's securities who may well trade on the basis of the information), it must make public disclosure of that information. The timing of the required public disclosure depends on whether the selective disclosure was intentional or non-intentional; for an intentional selective disclosure, the issuer must make public disclosure simultaneously; for a non-intentional disclosure, the issuer must make public disclosure promptly. Under the regulation, the required public disclosure may be made by filing or furnishing a Form 8-K, or by another method or combination of methods that is reasonably designed to effect broad, non-exclusionary distribution of the information to the public.[84]

---

[82] For further discussion, see Gulati, *When Corporate Managers Fear a Good Thing Is Coming to an End: The Case of Interim Nondisclosure,* 46 UCLA L. Rev. 675 (1999); Steinberg & Goldman, *supra* note 52, at 946–51.

[83] Selective Disclosure and Insider Trading, Securities Exchange Act Release No. 43154 (2000), 2000 SEC LEXIS 1672 (hereinafter the "Regulation FD Release"). The discussion in this Section is derived from the SEC Release.

[84] *Id.* As set forth in the Glossary to this text:

Regulation FD prohibits issuers or individuals acting on their behalf from selectively disclosing material nonpublic information to certain enumerated persons (generally securities market professionals and holders of the issuer's securities who may well trade on the basis of the information) without disclosing the information publicly. If the selective

[A] Purposes of Regulation FD

The SEC sought to address several concerns by promulgating Regulation FD. First, it believed that issuers often disclose important nonpublic information, such as advance warnings of earnings results, to securities analysts and/or institutional investors before making such information available to the general investing public. The Commission warned that as a result of this practice, the investing public might not believe that they are on an equal playing field with market insiders and may thereby lose confidence in the integrity of the securities markets. Second, the SEC stated that selective disclosure closely resembles the "tipping" of inside information, but noted that the current state of insider trading law may not create liability for an issuer's selective disclosure.[85] Third, the Commission perceived that the integrity of the securities markets was threatened by issuers selectively disclosing information as a means to secure favorable reviews by analysts. Specifically, analysts may feel pressured to report about a company in a positive light or risk losing their access to company personnel. Finally, the SEC opined that recent technological advances, particularly in the communications area, no longer pose undue impediments to timely public disclosure.

[B] Scope of Regulation FD

Regulation FD's scope focuses on those who are prohibited from selectively disclosing material nonpublic information and those to whom such selective disclosure is directed. The Regulation prohibits a company, or persons acting on such company's behalf, from selectively disclosing material inside information regarding such company or its securities.[86] For the purpose of the Regulation, an issuer includes a company that has a class of securities registered under Section 12 of the Exchange Act or is required to file reports under Section 15 of that Act.[87]

Regulation FD defines a "person acting on behalf of the issuer" as "any senior official of the issuer . . . or any other officer, employee, or agent of

---

disclosure is intentional, then the issuer must publicly disclose the information simultaneously by filing or furnishing a Form 8-K to the SEC or in a manner reasonably designed to provide broad distribution of the information. If the selective disclosure is unintentional, then the issuer must disclose the information to the public promptly, but in no event after the later of 24 hours or the opening of the next day's trading on the New York Stock Exchange. Violating Regulation FD exposes the issuer to SEC administrative and civil enforcement action, but does not by itself impose any Rule 10b-5 antifraud liability on the issuer or establish a private right of action.

[85] "[I]n light of the 'personal benefit' test set forth in the Supreme Court's decision in *Dirks v. SEC*, 463 U.S. 646 (1983), many have viewed issuer selective disclosures to analysts as protected from insider trading liability." Regulation FD Release, *supra* note 82, at n.7. Nevertheless, the Commission reiterated that it would institute enforcement actions based on violations of Section 10(b) where selective disclosures violated the insider trading prohibitions. See § 11.02 *infra*.

[86] 17 C.F.R. § 243.100(a).

[87] 17 C.F.R. § 243.101(b). Among other entities, the Regulation expressly excludes from the definition of "issuer" any foreign government or foreign private issuer.

an issuer who regularly communicates with any [enumerated recipient of information discussed below] . . . , or with holders of the issuer's securities."[88] This definition focuses on those whose job function regularly entails the disclosure of company-related information to the enumerated recipients. Selective disclosure by personnel who may occasionally interact with analysts or investors, for example, would not give rise to liability under Regulation FD. Thus, material nonpublic information disclosed in the due course of business to customers and suppliers would be outside the scope of the Regulation. The Commission, however, has noted that a senior official cannot escape liability by directing non-covered personnel to make a selective disclosure of information to someone within the classes of enumerated recipients. In such a case, the senior official would be held responsible for making the selective disclosure under Section 20(b) of the Exchange Act. Finally, the definition of a "person acting on behalf of the issuer" specifically excludes an "officer, director, employee, or agent of an issuer who discloses material nonpublic information in breach of a duty of trust or confidence to the issuer."[89] Such conduct would violate the insider trading prohibitions.[90]

Regulation FD applies when material nonpublic information is selectively disclosed to one of four enumerated classes of recipients outside the issuer:

- a broker or a dealer, or a person associated with a broker or dealer;

- an investment adviser, an institutional investment manager, or a person associated with either;

- an investment company or affiliated person thereof; or

- a holder of the issuer's securities, where it is reasonably foreseeable that the holder will purchase or sell the issuer's securities based on the information.[91]

The Regulation expressly excludes, and thus does not apply to, the following: a "person who owes a duty of trust or confidence to the issuer" (e.g., temporary insiders); a "person who expressly agrees to maintain the disclosed information in confidence"; a credit rating agency, "provided the information is disclosed solely for the purpose of developing a credit rating and the entity's ratings are publicly available"; and, with certain exceptions, in connection with "a securities offering registered under the Securities Act."[92] Furthermore, although not specifically referenced, disclosures to the media or communications to government agencies are outside the Regulation's scope.

---

[88] 17 C.F.R. § 243.101(c). The Regulation defines "senior official" as "any director, executive officer, investor relations or public relations officer, or other person with similar functions." 17 C.F.R. § 243.101(f).

[89] 17 C.F.R. § 243.101(c).

[90] See discussion §§ 11.02-11.03 *infra*.

[91] See 17 C.F.R. § 243.100(b)(1)(i)–(iv).

[92] 17 C.F.R. § 243.100(b)(2)–(3). The Regulation lists attorneys, investment bankers, and accountants as examples of those who may owe a duty of trust or confidence to the issuer.

[C]   Meaning of "Material" and "Nonpublic"

Although the Regulation refers to "material" and "nonpublic" information, it does not define those terms. Instead, the SEC relies on case law to define these terms. Thus, information is material if "there is a substantial likelihood that a reasonable shareholder would consider it important in making an investment decision . . . [and it is] a fact [that] would have been viewed by the reasonable investor as having significantly altered the total mix of information made available."[93] Information is nonpublic "if it has not been disseminated in a manner making [such information] available to investors generally."[94]

Although the Commission declined to establish a bright-line test for materiality, it offered several examples of information that likely would require issuers to make a materiality determination: (1) earnings information; (2) mergers, acquisitions, tender offers, joint ventures, or changes in assets; (3) new products or discoveries, or developments regarding customers or suppliers; (4) changes in control or in management; (5) change in auditors; (6) events regarding the issuer's securities; and (7) bankruptcies or receiverships. With this or any other information, the key for any materiality determination is on what significance a reasonable investor would place on the information.[95]

[D]   Intentional or Non-Intentional Selective Disclosure

Another important issue under Regulation FD involves whether the issuer selectively disclosed the information intentionally or non-intentionally. This assessment determines when the issuer must make the information publicly available. If the issuer intentionally and selectively discloses material nonpublic information, then it must disclose the same information simultaneously to the public. But if the selective disclosure is non-intentional, the issuer must disclose the information promptly, which is defined "as soon as reasonably practicable (but in no event after the later of 24 hours or the commencement of the next day's trading on the New York Stock Exchange) after a senior official of the issuer . . . learns that there has been a non-intentional disclosure by the issuer or person acting on behalf of the issuer of information that the senior official knows, or is reckless in not knowing, is both material and non-public."[96]

The standard for determining whether a selective disclosure was "intentional" meshes with the Regulation's definitions of materiality and nonpublic. The Regulation defines "intentional" to be that "the person making the

---

[93] Regulation FD Release, *supra* note 82, *quoting, TSC Industries, Inc. v. Northway, Inc.,* 426 U.S. 438, 449 (1976). The Regulation FD Release also cites SEC Staff Accounting Bulletin 99 (Aug. 12, 1999) (64 FR 45150) as authority supporting its definition of "materiality."

[94] Regulation FD Release, *supra* note 82, *citing, SEC v. Texas Gulf Sulphur,* 401 F.2d 833, 854 (2d Cir. 1968).

[95] See Regulation FD Release, note 82 *supra*. The Commission acknowledges that this information is not material per se.

[96] 17 C.R.F. § 243.101(d).

disclosure either knows, or is reckless in not knowing, that the information he or she is communicating is *both* material and nonpublic."[97] Thus, if an issuer were merely negligent in erroneously judging whether a certain piece of selectively disclosed information is either material or nonpublic, Regulation FD would not impose liability. By using this standard, the Commission seeks to provide "additional protection that issuers need not fear being second-guessed by the Commission in enforcement actions for mistaken judgments regarding materiality in close cases."[98] Nonetheless, the SEC warned that the determination of materiality should take into account all facts and circumstances. Thus, for example, a materiality judgment that might not be reckless in the context of an impromptu answer to an unexpected question at a press conference may be reckless in the context of a prepared written statement where the issuer has more time to evaluate the information it is about to disclose. Furthermore, if an issuer displays a pattern of "mistaken" judgments regarding materiality, that company's credibility would be harmed when it comes to future claims that any particular disclosure was not intentional.

[E] Methods for Making Public Disclosure

Regulation FD provides issuers with flexibility in determining how to publicly disclose material nonpublic information when they have engaged in selective disclosure of such information. Whatever method the issuer chooses must be "reasonably designed to provide broad, non-exclusionary distribution of the information to the public."[99] One clear method that an issuer can use is either to file or furnish a Form 8-K with the SEC.[100] The Regulation also provides that other methods of public disclosure may be acceptable, such as press releases, press conferences, or conferences that the public can attend or listen to by telephone or teleconference. In using these alternatives, however, the issuer must select a method or combination of methods that are reasonably calculated to provide a broad and effective

---

[97] 17 C.F.R. § 243.101(a) (emphasis added).

[98] See Regulation FD Release, note 82 *supra* (stating that "in the case of a selective disclosure attributable to a mistaken determination of materiality, liability will arise only if no reasonable person under the circumstances would have made the same determination").

[99] 17 C.F.R. § 243.101(e)(2).

[100] 17 C.F.R. § 243.101(e)(1). With respect to "filing" versus "furnishing" the information on Form 8-K, the SEC stated:

> [I]ssuers may choose either to "file" a report under Item 5 of Form 8-K or to "furnish" a report under Item 9 of Form 8-K that will not be deemed "filed." If an issuer chooses to file the information on Form 8-K, the information will be subject to liability under Section 18 of the Exchange Act. The information also will be subject to automatic incorporation by reference into the issuer's Securities Act registration statements, which are subject to liability under Sections 11 and 12(a)(2) of the Securities Act. If an issuer chooses instead to furnish the information, it will not be subject to liability under Section 11 of the Securities Act or Section 18 of the Exchange Act for the disclosure, unless it takes steps to include that disclosure in a filed report, proxy statement, or registration statement. All disclosures on Form 8-K, whether filed or furnished, will remain subject to the antifraud provisions of the federal securities laws.

public disclosure given that issuer's particular circumstances. Thus, for example, an issuer cannot rely solely on issuing a press release if it knows that its press releases are not routinely reported by the wire services. Furthermore, even though the Internet can be an effective method of disclosing information in conjunction with other methods, issuers cannot simply post information on their own Internet website as a sole means to satisfy Regulation FD's public disclosure requirements. In addition, the Commission will take into account whether a company deviated from its usual practices for making a public disclosure in determining whether the method of disclosure in any particular case complies with the Regulation.

The SEC, recognizing that a single method of disclosure may not be possible or desirable, offered a model for making a planned disclosure of material information. First, the issuer should issue a press release distributed through regular channels. Second, it should provide adequate notice through a press release and/or website posting of a scheduled conference call to discuss the particular information, giving investors information on the time and date of the call as well as how to access it. Third, the issuer should hold the conference call in an open manner, such that investors can listen to (but not necessarily ask questions during) the conference call either over the telephone or the Internet. The Commission also suggested that companies make taped replays of the conference call available for some time after they take place so as to allow other investors to listen to it.

[F] Exclusions

Because Regulation FD's disclosure requirements potentially could have conflicted with concerns relating to an issuer's "conditioning the market" during a registered offering, the Regulation generally "does not apply to disclosures made in connection with a securities offering registered under the Securities Act."[101] Registered shelf offerings, however, fall within Regulation FD's scope. Similarly, a reporting company's unregistered offerings are subject to Regulation FD. The Commission noted that in the context of such offerings, the company should either make selectively disclosed information public or secure a confidentiality agreement from the recipient. It also warned public companies undertaking unregistered offerings that if they fail to adhere to Regulation FD, they may risk losing their exemption from registration. A company's failure to adhere to Regulation FD, however, will not cause it to lose the availability of using short-form Securities Act registration forms S-2 or S-3 or cause its shareholders to lose their ability to sell their securities under Securities Act Rule 144(c).[102]

---

[101] Regulation FD Release, note 82 *supra*. As this book went to press, the SEC's Division of Corporate Finance was undertaking a review of the disclosure requirements during the offering process. The Commission noted that to the extent that selective disclosure may be a problem in the offering process, this review would be the more appropriate forum in which to consider establishing new regulations.

[102] See 17 C.F.R. § 243.103.

[G] SEC Enforcement, No Private Remedy

If an issuer violates Regulation FD, it will be subject to SEC enforcement action. The Commission, for example, could institute an administrative action seeking a cease-and-desist order or a civil action requesting an injunction and/or money penalties. The SEC also could bring administrative or civil actions against individuals affiliated with issuers who are responsible for violating the Regulation. The Regulation, however, does not create any private right of action. Furthermore, it expressly does not establish any Rule 10b-5 antifraud liability for cases based "solely" on an issuer's failure to comply with Regulation FD.[103] Nevertheless, Rule 10b-5 liability may still arise if, for example, the company's public disclosure, designed to satisfy Regulation FD, contains a material misstatement or omits material information.

[H] Impact of Regulation FD

Critics of Regulation FD contend that it will have a "chilling effect" on issuers' dissemination of information.[104] They believe that the Regulation will deter companies from disclosing certain information out of a concern for violating the Regulation. As a result, investors will end up receiving less, not more, information. The SEC, however, contends that the Regulation admirably serves investor interests, levels the "playing field," and has no "chilling effect." According to the SEC, the Regulation has been sufficiently tailored to provide meaningful safeguards against inappropriate liability. Moreover, the discipline and culture of the securities markets will continue to induce issuers to disclose information necessary for investors to make informed decisions.[105]

§ 10.09 Responding to Auditor Requests

A customary practice of auditors is to transmit audit inquiry letters to client corporations, which thereupon forward such requests to their counsel for assessment and response. Such a letter normally asks counsel to provide the auditor with certain information regarding the client's affairs. The information provided is employed by the auditor in opining on the corporation's annual financial reports. Among other items, the audit inquiry letter will seek information relating to contingent liabilities.

Such "loss contingency" requests may cause tension. On the one hand, there is counsel's desire to preserve the client's confidences and secrets, as

---

[103] See 17 C.F.R. § 243.102 ("No failure to make a public disclosure required solely by [Regulation FD] shall be deemed to be a violation of Rule 10b-5 . . . under the Securities Exchange Act."). Furthermore, because Regulation FD does not impose antifraud liability, issuers still maintain the safe harbor for forward-looking statements provided by the Private Securities Litigation Reform Act. See § 10.05(D) *supra*.

[104] See, e.g., August 10, 2000 Press Release by the Securities Industry Association "SEC Attempt to Cast More Light on Corporate Finances May Trigger 'Information Blackout,' Leaving Investors in the Dark."

[105] See Regulation FD Release, note 82 *supra*.

well as the client's desire to avoid disclosure of unfavorable information. For example, disclosure of a contingent unasserted liability may amount to advertising a client's possibly illegal conduct — a particularly undesirable event for the corporation where a potential plaintiff is ignorant of the possible claim. In addition, disclosure of a client's confidences incurs risk of waiving both the attorney-client and work product privileges. On the other hand, the auditor has a legitimate need to obtain adequate information in order to fulfill its duties consistent with the policy supporting public confidence in published financial statements.

Competing against these considerations is the ever-present threat that an attorney's failure to disclose material facts may subject the attorney and client to liability exposure under federal and state securities laws as well as under common law. In addition to potential liability under the securities acts' antifraud provisions, SEC Rule 13b2-2's "lying to the auditor" rule may impose Section 13(b)(2) liability on an officer or director of a registrant who, with the requisite intent, makes a materially false or misleading statement to an auditor.

In an effort to resolve these competing interests, the Financial Accounting Standards Board promulgated its Statement of Financial Accounting Standards No. 5 ("SFAS 5") and the ABA adopted its Statement of Policy Regarding Lawyers' Responses To Auditors' Requests for Information. Pursuant to the truce arrived at through these pronouncements, the following applies with respect to "loss contingencies":

> When properly requested by the client, it is appropriate for the lawyer to furnish to the auditor information concerning the following matters if the lawyer has been engaged by the client to represent or advise the client professionally with respect thereto and he has devoted substantive attention to them in the form of legal representation or consultation:
>
> > (a) overly threatened or pending litigation, whether or not specified by the client;
> >
> > (b) a contractually assumed obligation which the client has specifically identified and upon which the client has specifically requested, in the inquiry letter or a supplement thereto, [for] comment to the auditor;
> >
> > (c) an unasserted possible claim or assessment which the client has specifically identified and upon which the client has specifically requested, in the inquiry letter or a supplement thereto, [for] comment to the auditor.[106]

According to the ABA Policy Statement, counsel normally should not express judgment as to the outcome of claims delineated unless it appears to counsel that an unfavorable outcome is either "probable" or "remote." With respect to *unasserted possible claims or assessments*, where a potential claimant has not manifested an awareness of the potential claim, disclosure

---

[106] See American Bar Association, *Statement of Policy Regarding Lawyers' Responses to Auditors' Requests for Information*, 31 Bus. Law. 1709 (1976); Subcommittee on Audit Inquiry Responses, *Inquiry of a Client's Lawyer Concerning Litigation, Claims, and Assessments*, 45 Bus. Law. 2245 (1990).

is required only if the *client* concludes that "(i) it is probable that a claim will be asserted, (ii) there is a reasonable possibility, if the claim is in fact asserted, that the outcome will be unfavorable, and (iii) the liability resulting from such unfavorable outcome would be material to its financial condition."[107] Hence, by leaving the decision to reveal contingent liability for unasserted claims to the client, nondisclosure will be the likely consequence. Unless directed by the client, counsel has no duty under this framework to comment on such unasserted claims.[108]

---

[107] ABA Policy Statement, *supra* note 105, at 1713–14.

[108] Steinberg, *Attorney Liability for Client Fraud*, 1991 Colum. Bus. L. Rev. 1, 22–25 (1991). See Fuld, *Lawyers' Responses to Auditors — Some Practical Aspects*, 44 Bus. Law. 159 (1988); Hinsey, *Communications Among Attorneys, Management and Auditors,* 36 Bus. Law. 727 (1981); Hooker, *Lawyers' Responses to Audit Inquiries and the Attorney-Client Privilege*, 35 Bus. Law. 1021 (1980); Lorne, *The Corporate and Securities Adviser: The Public Interest, and Professional Ethics*, 76 Mich. L. Rev. 425, 448 (1978).

Chapter 11

INSIDER TRADING

§ 11.01 Overview

The subject of "insider" trading has been the focus of increased judicial scrutiny, vigorous SEC enforcement, and congressional attention. The Supreme Court has decided three major cases in this area. In *Chiarella v. United States*, the Court asserted that the imposition of liability under Section 10(b) and Rule 10b-5 for trading on material nonpublic information must be premised upon a duty to disclose.[1] In *Dirks v. SEC*, the Court held that the duty of tippers-tippees to disclose or abstain from trading under Section 10(b) and Rule 10b-5 depends on "whether the insider [tipper] personally will benefit [e.g., by receipt of pecuniary gain or reputational enhancement that will translate into future earnings], directly, or indirectly, from his disclosure. Absent some personal gain, there has been no breach of duty to stockholders. And absent a breach by the insider, there is no derivative breach [by the tippee]."[2] And, in *United States v. O'Hagan*, the Court upheld the validity of the misappropriation theory as well as SEC Rule 14e-3.[3]

Decided in the early 1980s, *Chiarella* and *Dirks*, although embracing certain traditional principles that had been adopted by the lower courts and the SEC,[4] posed difficulties for the SEC and private claimants. Generally, the SEC has met this challenge. In both *Chiarella* and *Dirks*, for example, the Court left unresolved the viability of the misappropriation theory. After *Chiarella*, the SEC and the Department of Justice successfully invoked this rationale. For example, in *United States v. Newman*,[5] the Second Circuit upheld an indictment on the grounds that the defendants had allegedly misappropriated valuable nonpublic information entrusted to them in the utmost secrecy. The court found that the defendants had "sullied the reputations" of their employers, investment banks, "as safe repositories of client confidences," and had deceived the clients of these investment banks "whose takeover plans were keyed to target company stock prices fixed by market forces, not artificially inflated through purchases by purloiners of

---

[1] 445 U.S. 222 (1980).

[2] 463 U.S. 646, 663 (1983).

[3] 117 S. Ct. 2199 (1997). Although it did not address the "misappropriation" theory in depth, another Supreme Court case in the insider trading area is *Carpenter v. United States*, 484 U.S. 19 (1987).

[4] See, e.g., *SEC v. Texas Gulf Sulphur Co.*, 401 F.2d 833 (2d Cir. 1968) (en banc), *cert. denied*, 394 U.S. 976 (1969) (imposing a duty on corporate officers and directors premised on the equal access theory to disclose or refrain from trading on material nonpublic information); *In re Cady, Roberts & Co.*, 40 S.E.C. 907 (1961) (same).

[5] 664 F.2d 12 (2d Cir. 1981).

confidential information."[6] Ultimately, as discussed in § 11.03, the Supreme Court upheld the misappropriation theory's validity in *United States v. O'Hagan*.[7]

After *Chiarella*, investors trading contemporaneously in the securities markets in misappropriation cases initially were left without a remedy. In *Moss v. Morgan Stanley*,[8] for example, the Second Circuit, in affirming the dismissal of an action seeking monetary damages for violations of Section 10(b), held that the plaintiffs failed to prove that the defendants breached a duty owed to them. In legislation passed in 1988, however, Congress enacted Section 20A of the Exchange Act to provide contemporaneous traders with an express right of action against those on the opposite side of the transaction who allegedly engaged in illegal insider trading of the same class of securities.[9]

Another example of the SEC's response to *Chiarella* was its promulgation, pursuant to Section 14(e) of the Williams Act, of Rule 14e-3, which seeks to deter insider and tippee trading in the tender offer setting. Generally, the rule, with certain exceptions, contains broad "disclose or abstain from trading" as well as "anti-tipping" provisions. With certain exemptions, Rule 14e-3 applies the disclose-or-abstain provision when an individual is in possession of material information relating to a tender offer and knows or has reason to know that such information is nonpublic and was obtained

---

[6] *Id.* at 17–18.

[7] 117 S. Ct. 2199 (1997).

[8] 719 F.2d 5 (2d Cir. 1983).

[9] 15 U.S.C. § 78t-1(a). For more discussion on *Chiarella*, *Dirks*, and their implications, see S. Bainbridge, *Insider Trading* (2000); A. Bromberg & L. Lowenfels, *Securities Fraud & Commodities Fraud* §§ 7.4–7.5 (1999); D. Langevoort, *Insider Trading: Regulation, Enforcement & Prevention* (1999); M. Steinberg & W. Wang, *Insider Trading* (1996 & 2000 supp.); Aldave, *Misappropriation: A General Theory of Liability for Trading on Nonpublic Information*, 13 Hofstra L. Rev. 101 (1985); Anderson, *Fraud, Fiduciaries, and Insider Trading*, 10 Hofstra L. Rev. 341 (1982); Branson, *Discourse on the Supreme Court Approach to SEC Rule 10b-5 and Insider Trading*, 30 Emory L.J. 263 (1981); Hiler, *Dirks v. SEC — A Study in Cause and Effect*, 43 Md. L. Rev. 292 (1984); Karjala, *Statutory Regulation of Insider Trading in Impersonal Markets*, 1982 Duke L.J. 627; Langevoort, *Insider Trading and the Fiduciary Principle: A Post-Chiarella Restatement*, 70 Calif. L. Rev. 1 (1982); Levmore, *Securities and Secrets: Insider Trading and the Law of Contracts*, 68 Va. L. Rev. 117 (1982); Mitchell, *The Jurisprudence of the Misappropriation Theory and the New Insider Trading Legislation: From Fairness to Efficiency and Back*, 52 Albany L. Rev. 775 (1988); Morgan, *The Insider Trading Rules After Chiarella: Are They Consistent with Statutory Policy?*, 33 Hastings L.J. 1407 (1982). See generally Bainbridge, *Insider Trading Regulation: The Path Dependent Choice Between Property Rights and Securities Fraud*, 52 SMU L. Rev. 1589 (1999); Bainbridge, *Incorporating State Law Fiduciary Duties into the Federal Insider Trading Prohibition*, 52 Wash. & Lee L. Rev. 1189 (1995); Carney, *Signalling and Causation In Insider Trading*, 36 Cath. U.L. Rev. 863 (1997); Dooley, *Enforcement of Insider Trading Restrictions*, 66 Va. L. Rev. 1 (1980); Easterbrook, *Insider Trading, Secret Agents, Evidentiary Privileges, and the Production of Information*, 1981 Sup. Ct. Rev. 309; Fried, *Reducing the Profitability of Corporate Insider Trading Through Pretrading Disclosure*, 71 So. Cal. L. Rev. 303 (1998); Haft, *The Effect of Insider Trading Rules on the Internal Efficiency of the Large Corporation*, 80 Mich. L. Rev. 1051 (1982); Macey, *From Fairness to Contract: The New Direction of the Rules Against Insider Trading*, 13 Hofstra L. Rev. 9 (1984); Prakash, *Our Dysfunctional Insider Trading Regime*, 99 Colum. L. Rev. 1491 (1999); Seligman, *The Reformulation of Federal Securities Law Concerning Nonpublic Information*, 73 Geo. L.J. 1083 (1985).

directly or indirectly from the offeror, the subject corporation, any of their affiliated persons, or any person acting on behalf of either company.[10]

In the release adopting Rule 14e-3, the Commission asserted that *Chiarella* did not limit its authority under Section 14(e) to prescribe such a mandate regulating insider trading in the tender offer context.[11] In *O'Hagan*, the Supreme Court upheld Rule 14e-3's validity at least as applied to the facts at bar.[12]

Congress also has been active in this area by enacting legislation in 1984 and 1988. Due to the difficulty in comprehensively defining "insider trading," Congress elected to leave the further development of this concept to judicial interpretation. Among other provisions, the legislation amended the Exchange Act to authorize the SEC to seek the imposition of a civil monetary penalty amounting to three times the profit received or loss avoided due to the violative transaction(s). As provided by the 1988 legislation, under certain conditions, broker-dealers, investment advisers, and others are subject to the treble monetary penalty for illegal inside trades effected by those persons who are under their control.[13]

§ 11.02   Supreme Court Decisions of the Early 1980s — *Chiarella & Dirks*

A fundamental tenet underlying the federal securities laws, at least since the SEC's decision in *Cady Roberts*,[14] is that "insiders" and, in certain circumstances, their tippees must either disclose material nonpublic information in their possession prior to trading or refrain from such trading. Unfortunately, although seemingly straightforward, the theoretical underpinnings for a duty to "disclose or abstain" from trading as well as its application to concrete factual situations and the persons to whom the duty should run have not always been clear.

In *Chiarella v. United States*,[15] the Supreme Court held that under Section 10(b) of the Exchange Act and Rule 10b-5 promulgated thereunder a

---

[10] See 17 C.F.R. § 240.14e-3.

[11] See Securities Exchange Act Release No. 17120 (1980).

[12] 117 S. Ct. 2189 (1997). For commentary on Rule 14e-3, see Gruenbaum, *The New Disclose or Abstain from Trading Rule: Has the SEC Gone Too Far?*, 5 Corp. L. Rev. 350 (1981); Heller, *Chiarella, SEC Rule 14e-3 and Dirks: "Fairness" Versus Economic Theory*, 37 Bus. Law. 517 (1982); Koprucki, *Market Insiders' Duty Under Section 10(b), Rule 10b-5, and Rule 14e-3 to Disclose Material Nonpublic Market Information*, 50 U. Cin. L. Rev. 558 (1981); Loewenstein, *Section 14(e) of the Williams Act and the Rule 10b-5 Comparisons*, 71 Geo. L.J. 1311 (1983). For further discussion, see § 11.07 *infra*.

[13] For further discussion, see §§ 11.06[B], 11.07 *infra*. For commentary on the 1984 and 1988 legislation, see Aldave, *The Insider Trading and Securities Fraud Enforcement Act of 1988: An Analysis and Appraisal*, 52 Albany L. Rev. 893 (1988); Friedman, *The Insider Trading and Securities Fraud Enforcement Act of 1988*, 68 N. Car. L. Rev. 465 (1990); Kaswell, *An Insider's View of the Insider Trading and Securities Fraud Enforcement Act of 1988*, 45 Bus. Law. 145 (1989); Langevoort, *The Insider Trading Sanctions Act of 1984 and Its Effect on Existing Law*, 37 Vand. L. Rev. 1273 (1984); Silver, *Penalizing Insider Trading: A Critical Assessment of the Insider Trading Sanctions Act of 1984*, 1985 Duke L.J. 960.

[14] *In re Cady, Roberts & Co.*, 40 S.E.C. 907 (1961).

[15] 445 U.S. 222 (1980).

financial printer — who purchased stock after deciphering information gleaned from confidential documents entrusted to his employer that certain companies were to be the targets of mergers or tender offers — did not breach a duty to the investing public.[16] In so doing, the Court rejected the parity of information[17] and parity of access to information[18] principles that a number of lower courts had embraced. Hence, the Court held that silence, absent a duty to disclose, will not give rise to Section 10(b) liability. Such liability based on silence, the Court asserted, "is premised upon a duty to disclose arising from a relationship of trust and confidence between parties to a transaction."[19]

With respect to insiders, the *Chiarella* Court reinforced the principle, expanded upon in *Dirks v. SEC*,[20] that a duty to disclose or abstain from trading arises where such persons possess material nonpublic information.[21] Quoting from the SEC's decision in *Cady Roberts*, the *Chiarella* Court stated that the obligation to disclose or abstain from trading derives from:

> an affirmative duty to disclose material information [which] has been traditionally imposed on corporate "insiders," particularly officers, directors, or controlling stockholders. We . . . have consistently held that insiders disclose material facts which are known to them by virtue of their position but which are not known to persons with whom they deal and which, if known, would affect investment judgment.[22]

Significantly, the *Chiarella* Court did not address the issue of whether the financial printer could have been held liable pursuant to the misappropriation theory under Section 10(b) and Rule 10b-5. Had this theory been applied, as it ultimately was embraced by the Court nearly two decades later in *O'Hagan*,[23] *Chiarella* would have breached a duty to the acquiring corporation and to his employer when he traded on the basis of information he procured by virtue of his strategic position.

Turning to the Supreme Court's decision in *Dirks*, the Court held that the duty of tippees to disclose or abstain from trading depends on whether

---

[16] *Id.* at 226–35.

[17] See, e.g., *SEC v. Texas Gulf Sulphur Co.*, 401 F.2d 833 (2d Cir. 1968) (en banc), *cert. denied*, 394 U.S. 976 (1969).

[18] See, e.g., *United State v. Chiarella*, 588 F.2d 1358 (2d Cir. 1978), *rev'd*, 455 U.S. 222 (1980).

[19] 445 U.S. at 230.

[20] 463 U.S. 646 (1983).

[21] 445 U.S. at 226–27.

[22] *Id., quoting, In re Cady Roberts & Co.*, 40 S.E.C. 907, 911 (1961). See generally Branson, *Discourse on the Supreme Court Approach to SEC Rule 10b-5 and Insider Trading*, 30 Emory L.J. 263 (1981); Langevoort, *Insider Trading and the Fiduciary Principle: A Post-Chiarella Restatement*, 70 Calif. L. Rev. 1 (1982); Wang, *Trading on Material Nonpublic Information on Impersonal Stock Markets: Who Is Harmed and Who Can Sue Whom Under SEC Rule 10b-5?*, 54 So. Cal. L. Rev. 1217 (1981).

[23] 117 S. Ct. 2199 (1997). See § 11.03 *infra*.

the tipper has him/herself breached a fiduciary duty to the corporation's shareholders by divulging the information to the tippee. "Thus, the test is whether the insider personally will benefit, directly or indirectly, from his disclosure. Absent some personal gain, there has been no breach of duty to stockholders. And absent a breach by the insider, there is no derivative breach [by the tippee]."[24] Such personal benefit may be shown by the insider's receipt of pecuniary gain or reputational enhancement that will translate into future earnings.[25] Also, the requisite showing of benefit may be made by the insider making a gift of confidential information to the tippee. In such circumstances, "[t]he tip and trade resemble trading by the insider himself followed by a gift of the profits to the recipient."[26] In order to hold the tippee liable under Section 10(b) for trading on the information conveyed by the insider, the tippee must or should have known that the insider breached his/her fiduciary duty by disclosing such confidential information to the tippee.[27]

By holding that (1) there must be a breach of the insider's fiduciary duty to the corporation's shareholders before the tippee inherits the duty to disclose or abstain and (2) by premising the existence of a breach on whether the insider will personally benefit from disclosing the information to the tippee, the Court in *Dirks* made it more difficult for the SEC and private claimants to prove liability. In imposing a motivational requirement, the Court arguably "excuses a knowing and intentional violation of an insider's duty to shareholders if the insider does not act from a motive of personal gain."[28] The task of proving such a motive in many cases must rest on circumstantial evidence and may be troublesome.[29] Moreover, the benefit apparently must be a personal one which, at least in most instances, must enrich the insider monetarily. Other types of benefits, such as an enhanced reputation that does not translate into future earnings, may be insufficient to find a breach. Liability also may not be imposed against the "loose-lipped" director or officer who divulges confidential corporate information to such persons as financial analysts, broker-dealers and golfing cronies without any intention to make a gift or personally benefit therefrom. This result constitutes a departure from prior lower court case law.[30]

In contrast to the generally restrictive nature of the holding, the *Dirks* Court recognized the "quasi-insider" principle, stating:

---

[24] 463 U.S. at 662.

[25] *Id.* at 664.

[26] *Id.*

[27] *Id.* at 660.

[28] *Id.* at 671–74 (Blackmun, J., dissenting).

[29] See, e.g., *SEC v. Switzer*, 590 F. Supp. 756 (W.D. Okla. 1984).

[30] See, e.g., *Elkind v. Liggett & Myers, Inc.*, 635 F.2d 156, 165 (2d Cir. 1980). Note that the SEC's Regulation Fair Disclosure (FD) regulates issuer selective disclosure practices. Interestingly, the Commission opted to adopt the rule pursuant to its asserted authority under Section 13(a) of the Exchange Act. See Securities Exchange Act Release No. 43154 (2000); § 10.08 *supra.* See generally Hiler, *Dirks v. SEC — A Study in Cause and Effect*, 43 Md. L. Rev. 292 (1984); Phillips, *Insider Trading Liability After Dirks*, 16 Rev. Sec. Reg. 848 (1983).

Under certain circumstances, such as where corporate information is revealed legitimately to an underwriter, accountant, lawyer, or consultant working for the corporation, these outsiders may become fiduciaries of the shareholders. The basis for recognizing this fiduciary duty is not simply that such persons acquired nonpublic corporate information, but rather that they have entered into a special confidential relationship in the conduct of the business of the enterprise and are given access to information solely for corporate purposes. . . . [W]hen such a person breaches his fiduciary relationship, he may be treated more properly as a tipper than as a tippee. . . . For such a duty to be imposed, however, the corporation must expect the outsider to keep the disclosed nonpublic information confidential, and the relationship at least must imply such a duty. [31]

Hence, under this rationale, individuals enjoying a special relationship with the corporation, such as accountants, attorneys, consultants, and underwriters, may be viewed as insiders when they trade on material nonpublic information that they legitimately received during the course of that relationship.

§ 11.03   The Misappropriation Theory

[A]   *United States v. O'Hagan*

The misappropriation theory posits that a person perpetrates fraud "in connection with" a securities transaction, and hence violates Section 10(b) of the Exchange Act and Rule 10b-5 promulgated thereunder, when he/she misappropriates material nonpublic information for securities trading purposes, breaching a fiduciary-like duty owed to the source of such information. This theory targets "outsiders" of an enterprise who become privy to confidential information but who owe no fiduciary duty to that enterprise's shareholders. Accordingly, the theory fills the gap left open by traditional insider trading liability in that the breach of a duty owed is not to a trader on the other side of the transaction but rather is owed to the source of the information. [32]

In *United States v. O'Hagan,* [33] the Supreme Court held that to establish liability under the misappropriation theory a fiduciary-like duty must exist between the misappropriator of the information and the source of such

---

[31] 463 U.S. at 677 n.14.

[32] See *United States v. O'Hagan*, 117 S. Ct. 2199, 2207 (1997). An example of a breach to the source of the information is an attorney who, in the course of her employment, learns of a client's contemplated merger for a target corporation and then purchases stock in the target corporation before the merger is publicly announced. See, e.g., *United States v. Grossman*, 843 F.2d 78, 86 (2d Cir. 1988). Another example is where an employee of an investment advisor learns of a prospective recommendation of a particular stock by his employer and purchases that stock in advance of the recommendation. *Cf. United States v. Carpenter*, 484 U.S. 19 (1987).

[33] 117 S. Ct. 2199 (1997).

information. Under this theory, the misappropriator is using his position to deceive those who entrusted him with the confidential information.[34] In other words, an enterprise's confidential information constitutes property with respect to which such enterprise has a right of exclusive use. And because the disclosure obligation is owed to the source of the information, the undisclosed misappropriation of such confidential information is viewed as fraud akin to embezzlement.[35]

Hence, deception by means of nondisclosure is fundamental to liability under the misappropriation theory.[36] Accordingly, "full disclosure [to the source of the information] forecloses liability under the misappropriation theory."[37] The deception underlying the misappropriation theory thus focuses on feigning fidelity to the information's source to whom a fiduciary-like duty is owed. Consequently, if the fiduciary reveals to such source that she plans to trade (or tip), there is no deception perpetrated and accordingly no Section 10(b) violation.[38] Nonetheless, even if the fiduciary makes such disclosure, she still may remain liable under state law, such as for breach of the duty of loyalty and under certain federal statutes, including mail and wire fraud.[39]

Section 10(b) mandates that "the misappropriator's deceptive use of information be 'in connection with the purchase or sale of [a] security.' "[40] Such deception occurs "in connection with" the purchase or sale of a security when the fiduciary's fraud is consummated. And the fraud under Section 10(b) is consummated, not when the fiduciary procures the confidential information, but when without revelation to his source(s), he utilizes the information to engage in securities trading (or to engage in "tipping").[41] Thus, the "in connection with" requirement limits liability under the misappropriation theory to using material confidential information in order to profit (or avoid loss) when engaging in securities transactions.[42]

---

[34] *Id.* at 2207.

[35] *Id.* at 2208.

[36] Misappropriation is a "deceptive device or contrivance" within the meaning of Section 10(b). *United States v. O'Hagan*, 117 S.Ct. 2199, 2208 (1997) (holding that a misappropriator engages in deception and stating "[a] fiduciary who pretends loyalty to the principal while secretly converting the principal's information for personal gain dupes or defrauds the principal").

[37] *Id.* at 2209.

[38] *Id.*

[39] *Id.* See *United States v. Carpenter*, 484 U.S. 19 (1987); *Diamond v. Oreamuno*, 24 N.Y.2d 494, 248 N.E.2d 910 (1969); *Brophy v. Cities Service Co.*, 31 Del. Ch. 241, 70 A.2d 5 (1949); W. Wang & M. Steinberg, *Insider Trading* § 16.2 (1996 & 2000 Supp.); Hazen, *Corporate Insider Trading: Reawakening the Common Law*, 39 Wash. & Lee L. Rev. 845 (1982).

[40] *United States v. O'Hagan*, 117 S. Ct. at 2209. See generally Black, *The Second Circuit's Approach to the "In Connection With" Requirement of Rule 10b-5*, 53 Brooklyn L. Rev. 539 (1987); Fletcher, *The "In Connection With" Requirement of Rule 10b-5*, 16 Pepp. L. Rev. 913 (1989).

[41] 117 S. Ct. at 2209.

[42] *Id.* See generally Symposium, 20 Cardozo L. Rev. No. 1 (1998); Nagy, *Reframing the Misappropriation Theory of Insider Trading: A Post-O'Hagan Suggestion*, 59 Ohio St. L.J. 1223 (1998); Painter, Krawiec & Williams, *Don't Ask, Just Tell: Insider Trading After United States*

[B] Family and Other Personal Relationships

After *O'Hagan*, the applicability of the misappropriation theory in the business setting — such as where an employee purloins material nonpublic information from his/her employer — is well established. In the context of family and other personal relationships, however, the misappropriation theory's impact is less certain.

For example, in *United States v. Chestman*,[43] the Second Circuit rejected the government's reliance on the misappropriation rationale under the facts presented when the wife entrusted inside information to her husband. The court asserted that "a fiduciary duty cannot be imposed unilaterally by entrusting a person with confidential information" and that "marriage does not, without more, create a fiduciary relationship."[44] No such duty arose in the case at bar because the inside information was gratuitously communicated to the husband by the wife with no promise by the husband to keep the information confidential. Further, the court concluded that the husband was not part of the family's "inner circle" (that included the wife's parents), signifying that a fiduciary or comparable duty was not present.[45]

So much for "family values." One can understandably be upset by the law giving greater sanctity to a shareholder's relationship with a director of a publicly-held company (with whom such shareholder has never spoken or met) than to one's spouse, parent, child, or sibling. Evidently by adopting Rule 10b5-2, the SEC agrees with the asserted absurdity of this approach. The Rule provides a non-exclusive list of three situations in which a person is deemed to have a relationship of trust and confidence for purposes of invoking the misappropriation theory. Rule 10b5-2 thus triggers application of the misappropriation theory when the person receiving the material nonpublic information trades or tips in the following situations: (1) when such recipient explicitly agreed to maintain the confidentiality of the information; (2) when a reasonable expectation of confidentiality existed due to the fact that the persons who had the communication(s) (including the misappropriator) enjoyed a history, practice, or pattern of sharing confidences; and (3) when the source of the information (i.e., the person providing such information) was a spouse, child, parent, or sibling of the person receiving the information, unless it can be established as an affirmative defense that on the facts and circumstances of the particular family relationship that no reasonable expectation of confidentiality existed.[46]

---

v. O'Hagan, 84 Va. L. Rev. 153 (1998); Ramirez & Christopher, *The Misappropriation Theory of Insider Trading Under United States v. O'Hagan*, 26 Sec. Reg. L.J. 162 (1998); Weiss, *United States v. O'Hagan: Pragmatism Returns to the Law of Insider Trading*, 23 J. Corp. L. 1 (1998).

[43] 947 F.2d 551 (2d Cir. 1991).

[44] *Id.* at 567–68.

[45] *Id.* at 570–71. Accord, *SEC v. Reed*, 601 F. Supp. 685 (S.D.N.Y.), *rev'd on other grounds*, 773 F.2d 447 (2d Cir. 1985). But see *SEC v. Falbo*, 14 F. Supp. 2d 508 (S.D.N.Y. 1998) (under facts at bar, invoking the misappropriation theory and finding breach of spouse's duty of confidentiality).

[46] Securities Exchange Act Release No. 43154, 2000 SEC LEXIS 1672 (2000).

§ 11.04   "Possession" vs. "Use"

When charged with insider trading, a defendant may contend that he/she had planned to purchase or sell the subject securities prior to coming into possession of the inside information. In response, the SEC's position generally has been that mere possession, rather than use, of the material nonpublic information is sufficient to trigger liability under Section 10(b).[47] Likewise, the Second Circuit, endorsing the "possession" standard, opined that "material information cannot lie idle in the human brain."[48]

Disagreeing, the Ninth and Eleventh Circuits,[49] held that proof of use rather than mere possession is consistent with Section 10(b)'s scienter requirement.[50] Language in the Supreme Court's decision in *O'Hagan* also supports the "use" approach.[51] In *SEC v. Adler*, the Eleventh Circuit held that Section 10(b)'s scienter requirement mandates that the Commission must establish that the defendant when he/she traded actually "used" the material nonpublic information. Phrased somewhat differently, the SEC must show that the defendant's knowledge of such information constituted a substantial factor in his/her decision to purchase or sell the subject securities at the particular price or at the particular time.[52] Importantly, however, the court held that a defendant's knowing possession of material nonpublic information when trading raises a strong inference of use. Such inference may be rebutted by the defendant establishing that he/she had independent, justifiable reasons for engaging in the particular transactions at that time and in the amount traded.[53] Similarly, the Ninth Circuit in *United States v. Smith* adopted the "use" rather than "possession" standard.[54] The court, however, declined to adhere to the Eleventh Circuit's inference of use (upon a showing of knowing possession) due to constitutional reasons arising from a criminal prosecution.[55]

Reacting to the Ninth and Eleventh Circuit decisions, the SEC adopted Rule 10b5-1.[56] The Rule triggers liability exposure when a person purchases or sells securities while "aware" of material nonpublic information. Hence, a trade is deemed to be "on the basis" of material nonpublic

---

[47] See, e.g., *Report of the Investigation in the Matter of Sterling Drug, Inc.*, Securities Exchange Act Release No. 14675 (1978) (asserting that "[i]f an insider sells his securities while in possession of material nonpublic information, such an insider is taking advantage of his position to the detriment of the public").

[48] *United States v. Teicher*, 987 F.2d 112, 120 (2d Cir. 1993).

[49] See *United States v. Smith*, 155 F.3d 1051 (9th Cir. 1998); *SEC v. Adler*, 137 F.3d 1325 (11th Cir. 1998).

[50] See § 7.03 *supra*.

[51] See *United States v. O'Hagan*, 117 S. Ct. at 2208 (stating that, under the misappropriation theory, "the fiduciary's fraud is consummated . . . when without disclosure to his principal, he *uses* the information to purchase or sell securities") (emphasis added).

[52] 137 F.3d at 1337.

[53] *Id.*

[54] 155 F.3d at 1066.

[55] *Id.* at 1067–69 (stating that "a knowing possession standard would . . . go a long way toward making insider trading a strict liability crime").

[56] Securities Exchange Act Release No. 43154, 2000 SEC LEXIS 1672 (2000).

information under Rule 10b5-1 if the trader was "aware" of such information at the time of the purchase or sale. The Rule reflects the position that one who is aware of inside information at the time of trading will have inevitably made use of such information. While the awareness standard expands the scope of insider trading liability (as compared to the Ninth and Eleventh Circuits' approaches), the SEC posits that Rule 10b5-1 enhances investor confidence and the integrity of the securities markets.

Under Rule 10b5-1, an affirmative defense generally is available if the trader engages in the specified transaction(s) pursuant to a pre-existing plan, contract, or instruction that is binding and specific. Under such circumstances, the inside information was not a factor in the trading decision. More specifically, to establish the affirmative defense, a person must satisfy the following criteria. First a person must demonstrate that prior to becoming aware of the inside information, he/she had entered into a binding contract to purchase or sell the security, had provided instructions to another person to execute the trade for the instructing person's account, or had adopted a written plan for trading securities. Second, the person must demonstrate that, with respect to the purchase or sale, the contract, instructions, or plan: expressly specified the amount(s), price(s), and date(s); provided a written formula, algorithm, or computer program for determining the amount(s), price(s), and date(s); or did not permit the person to exercise any influence over how, when, or whether to execute the trade(s) (and in the event that any other person exercised such influence, that person was not aware of the material, nonpublic information). Third, the person must demonstrate that the trade(s) that occurred were pursuant to the previously established contract, instructions, or plan. This means that the person neither may alter or deviate from the contract, instruction, or plan, nor enter into a corresponding or opposite hedging transaction with respect to those securities. Furthermore, the defense is governed by a good-faith requirement that the person did not enter into the contract, instruction, or plan as part of a scheme to avoid liability under Rule 10b5-1.[57]

Rule 10b5-1 provides another affirmative defense for trading parties that are entities. This defense is available as an alternative to the defense discussed above. Under the provisions of this defense, an entity will not be liable if it demonstrates that the individual responsible for the investment decision on behalf of the entity was not aware of the material inside information, and that the entity had implemented reasonable policies and procedures to prevent insider trading.[58]

---

[57] Rule 10b5-1(c); SEC Release, note 56 *supra.*

[58] Rule 10b5-1(c); SEC Release, note 56 *supra.* See generally, Horwich, *Possession Versus Use: Is There a Causation Element in the Prohibition on Insider Trading?,* 52 Bus. Law. 1235 (1997); Karmel, *The Controversy of Possession Versus Use,* N.Y.L.J., Dec. 17, 1998, at 3; McLucas & Walker, *Insider Trading Developments: Do the Adler and Smith Cases Portend Tougher Times for SEC Enforcement?,* 32 Rev. Sec. & Comm. Reg. 93 (1999); Nagy, *The "Possession" vs. "Use" Debate in the Context of Securities Trading by Traditional Insiders: Why Silence Can Never Be Golden,* 67 U. Cin. L. Rev. 1129 (1999).

§ 11.05   Right of Action for Contemporaneous Traders

After the Second Circuit's decision adopting the misappropriation theory in *United States v. Newman*,[59] the question remained whether purchasers and sellers of securities had a cause of action for monetary damages under Section 10(b) even though the defrauding parties who misappropriated the inside information owed them no fiduciary duty. In *Moss v. Morgan Stanley, Inc.*,[60] the Second Circuit held that in order to recover under Section 10(b) for monetary damages it must be shown that the defendant breached a duty owed to the plaintiff. Relying on *Chiarella*, the court asserted that the relationship giving rise to a duty to disclose must be between the parties to the transaction. Hence, because the misappropriators in *Moss* owed no fiduciary duty to the plaintiff, no Section 10(b) right of action was available.[61]

In subsequently enacted legislation, Congress nullified the *Moss* decision in this respect. In the Insider Trading and Securities Fraud Enforcement Act of 1988, Congress enacted Section 20A of the Exchange Act to provide an express right of action on behalf of "contemporaneous traders" who were trading the same class of securities on the opposite side of the transaction during the time that the allegedly illegal inside trade(s) occurred. Thus, to recover under this express right of action, the plaintiff must be trading contemporaneously with and on the opposite side of the transaction from the inside trader. Moreover, the damages available in an action instituted under Section 20A on behalf of contemporaneous traders are limited to the profit gained or loss avoided by the defendant's illegal trades.[62]

Importantly, Section 20A does not limit a complainant's entitlement to private rights of action under other provisions of the Exchange Act, such as Section 10(b). In this regard, a private right of action under Section 10(b) may be available against inside traders (as well as their tippers) on behalf of certain noncontemporaneous traders. Such a situation may arise when, due to insider trading that has increased the price of the target company's stock, a bidder must pay more to acquire such stock. In the House Report accompanying the 1988 legislation, the Committee took the position that a Section 10(b) right of action exists in the above situation and that a plaintiff should be able to recover the full extent of any actual damages incurred.[63]

Moreover, as part of the Insider Trading Sanctions Act of 1984, Congress added Section 20(d) to the Exchange Act. That provision states:

---

[59] 664 F.2d 12 (2d Cir. 1981), *discussed in,* § 11.01 *supra.*

[60] 719 F.2d 5 (2d Cir. 1983).

[61] *Id.* at 15–16. But see *O'Connor & Associates v. Dean Witter Reynolds, Inc.*, 529 F. Supp. 1179 (S.D.N.Y. 1981) (right of action extended to options trader even though insiders owed such person no fiduciary duty).

[62] See H.R. Rep. No. 100-910 to accompany H.R. 5133, 100 Cong., 2d Sess. (1988); Fed. Sec. L. Rep. (CCH) No. 1309 (Oct. 26, 1988); 20 Sec. Reg. & L. Rep. (BNA) 1623 (1988); authorities cited note 13 *supra.*

[63] H.R. Rep. No. 100-910, *supra* note 62, at 28. See *Litton Industries, Inc. v. Lehman Brothers Kuhn Loeb, Inc.*, 967 F.2d 742 (2d Cir. 1992).

> Wherever communicating, or purchasing or selling a security while in possession of, material nonpublic information would violate, or result in liability to any purchaser or seller of the security under any provision of this [Act], or any rule or regulation thereunder, such conduct in connection with a purchase or sale of a put, call, straddle, option, or privilege with respect to such security or with respect to a group or index of securities including such security, shall also violate and result in comparable liability *to any purchaser or seller of that security* under such provision, rule, or regulation. [64]

Section 20(d)'s effect is to provide, within the confines of *Chiarella* and *Dirks*, an option-trading plaintiff with a private right of action against an inside trader of options. [65] Note, however, that a distinct issue is presented as to whether an *option* trader has a private cause of action against an inside *stock* trader. Section 20(d) does not resolve this issue. The lower federal courts are divided. [66]

§ 11.06 Damages and Penalties

[A] Damages — Section 10(b) Actions

The measure of damages for insider trading in open market transactions under Section 10(b) has received diverse treatment from the relatively few courts that have considered the issue. *Shapiro v. Merrill Lynch, Pierce, Fenner & Smith, Inc.* [67] represents an expansive approach. There, the Second Circuit, relying on *Affiliated Ute Citizens v. United States,* [68] stated that "[t]he proper test to determine whether causation in fact has been established in a nondisclosure case is 'whether the plaintiff would have been influenced to act differently than he did if the defendant had disclosed to him the undisclosed fact.' "[69] After finding that causation in fact had been established (notwithstanding that all transactions occurred on a national securities exchange), the court formulated a potentially broad measure of damages:

> [W]e hold that defendants are liable in this private action for damages to plaintiffs who, during the same period that defendants traded in or recommended trading in Douglas common stock, purchased Douglas stock in the open market without knowledge of

---

[64] 15 U.S.C. § 78t(d) (emphasis supplied).

[65] See Thel, *Section 20(d) of the Securities Exchange Act: Congress, The Supreme Court, the SEC and the Process of Defining Insider Trading*, 69 N.C. L. Rev. 1261 (1991); Wang, *A Cause of Action for Option Traders Against Insider Option Traders*, 101 Harv. L. Rev. 1056 (1988).

[66] Compare *Deutschman v. Beneficial Corp.*, 841 F.2d 502 (3d Cir. 1988) (providing a right of action), with *Laventhall v. General Dynamics Corp.*, 704 F.2d 407 (8th Cir. 1983) (not permitting suit).

[67] 495 F.2d 228 (2d Cir. 1974).

[68] 406 U.S. 128 (1972).

[69] 495 F.2d at 239.

the material inside information which was in the possession of defendants.[70]

Having so held, the Second Circuit, however, left to the district court's discretion the proper measure of damages, noting its concern with the potential for draconian liability.[71]

In *Fridrich v. Bradford*,[72] the Sixth Circuit rejected the *Shapiro* analysis. Disagreeing with the Second Circuit, the *Fridrich* court found that the plaintiffs had failed to show that their loss was caused by the defendants' inside trading. The Sixth Circuit supported its holding by pointing out that an award of damages to contemporaneous traders in the open market would create a windfall for fortuitous investors while being essentially punitive. Although the court recognized that it could limit the amount of recovery to the defendants' profits, it declined to do so.[73]

Subsequently, in *Elkind v. Liggett & Myers, Inc.*[74] the Second Circuit, although not expressly rejecting the *Shapiro* rationale, greatly limited the potential damages recovery. There, the court considered three alternative measures of damages: (1) out-of-pocket, (2) market-repercussion, and (3) disgorgement. Rejecting the out-of-pocket measure, the court pointed out that this measure is normally directed toward compensating a trader for damages that are directly traceable to the defendant's perpetration of a fraud upon the trader. In an impersonal open market, however, "uninformed traders . . . are not induced by representations on the part of the tipper or tippee to buy or sell."[75] Secondly, the Second Circuit observed that the out-of-pocket measure posed serious proof problems as the "value" of the stock traded during the period of nondisclosure can often be hypothetical. Lastly, the court concluded that the out-of-pocket measure had the potential for the imposition of "draconian, exorbitant damages, out of all proportion to the wrong committed."[76]

The *Elkind* court also rejected the market-repercussion theory of damages. This measure would allow recovery of damages caused by erosion of the stock's market price that is traceable to the defendant's wrongful trading. The rationale underlying the theory is that "if the market price is not affected by the [defendant's] trading, the uninformed investor is in the same position as he would have been had the insider abstained from trading." Upon analysis, the Second Circuit rejected this theory due to the difficult problems of proof it would impose on plaintiffs and that adoption of the theory would frequently preclude recovery for an insider's breach of his/her duty to disclose the confidential information prior to trading.[77]

---

[70] *Id.* at 241.

[71] *Id.*

[72] 542 F.2d 307 (6th Cir. 1976).

[73] *Id.* at 318–22.

[74] 635 F.2d 156 (2d Cir. 1980).

[75] *Id.* at 169.

[76] *Id.* at 170.

[77] *Id.* at 171.

The *Elkind* court thereupon adopted a third alternative, the disgorgement measure of damages. This measure also is the proper measure of damages under Section 20A for contemporaneous traders who trade on the opposite side of the transaction from the defendant.[78] Under the *Elkind* formulation, the measure of damages is as follows:

> (1) [T]o allow any uninformed investor, where a reasonable investor would either have delayed his purchase or not purchased at all if he had the benefit of the tipped information, to recover any post-purchase decline in market value of his shares up to a reasonable time after he learns of the tipped information or after there is a public disclosure of it but (2) limit his recovery to the amount gained by the [subject violator] as a result of his selling at the earlier date rather than delaying his sale until the parties could trade on an equal informational basis. . . . Should the intervening buyers, because of the volume and price of their purchases, claim more than the [subject violator's] gain, their recovery (limited to that gain) would be shared *pro rata*.[79]

[B] Penalties

A number of different parties may be subject to a variety of monetary penalties under the federal securities laws for engaging in illegal insider trading. These parties may include actual traders, their tippers, as well as broker-dealers and investment advisers (when they fail to take appropriate steps to prevent the insider trading violation(s) or fail to maintain and enforce policies and procedures reasonably designed to prevent the occurrence of such trading). Penalties that may be levied in this context are (1) requiring the subject party to "disgorge" the ill-gotten profits (or loss avoided) in an SEC enforcement action,[80] (2) subjecting individuals to a maximum criminal fine of $1 million and ten years imprisonment,[81] and (3) in an SEC enforcement action, within a court's discretion, ordering the subject party to pay into the United States Treasury a treble damages penalty amounting to three times the profit gained or loss avoided.[82] These penalties, together with the imposition of jail terms and the availability of civil damages, are intended to strongly deter insider trading. As an additional measure to combat insider trading, the SEC may award "bounties" (up to ten percent of the amount disgorged or monetary penalty imposed) to persons who provide information concerning insider trading violations.[83]

---

[78] See H.R. Rep. No. 100-910, note 63 *supra*; see discussion § 11.05 *supra*.

[79] 635 F.2d at 172. See generally Dougherty, *A [Dis]semblance of Privity: Criticizing the Contemporaneous Trader Requirement in Insider Trading*, 24 Del. J. Corp. L. 83 (1999).

[80] See, e.g., *SEC v. Commonwealth Chemical Securities, Inc.*, 574 F.2d 90, 102–03 (2d Cir. 1978). See § 14.05[D] *infra*.

[81] See Section 32(a) of the Exchange Act, 15 U.S.C. § 78ff(a) (as amended by the Insider Trading and Securities Fraud Enforcement Act of 1988).

[82] See Section 21A of the Exchange Act, 15 U.S.C. § 78u-1.

[83] See Section 21A(e) of the Exchange Act, 15 U.S.C. § 78u-1(e); authorities cited note 13 *supra*. For discussion on liability of controlling persons in this context, see Steinberg & Fletcher, *Compliance Programs for Insider Trading*, 47 SMU L. Rev. 1783, 1788–89 (1994):

§ 11.07   Rule 14e-3

Subsequent to the Supreme Court's decision in *Chiarella*, the SEC, in an effort to regulate insider and tippee trading in the tender offer context, adopted Rule 14e-3 which establishes a "disclose or abstain from trading" rule under Section 14(e) of the Exchange Act. As adopted, with certain exceptions, Rule 14e-3 applies this disclose-or-abstain provision to the possession of material information relating to a tender offer where the person knows or has reason to know that the information is nonpublic and was received directly or indirectly from the offeror, the subject corporation, any of their affiliated persons, or any person acting on behalf of either company. Moreover, the rule contains a broad anti-tipping provision and provides for certain exceptions pertaining to sales to the offeror and to certain activities by multiservice financial institutions.[84]

In this regard, the rule exempts purchases and sales by multiservice financial institutions, such as broker-dealers, if it can be shown that "the individuals making the investment decision did not know the nonpublic information and that the [broker-dealer] had established policies and procedures, reasonable under the circumstances, to ensure that its [employees] would not violate [the] rule." Such procedures may "include Chinese Walls and restricted-list procedures designed to prevent individual decisionmakers from learning or using such information."[85]

In the release adopting Rule 14e-3, the Commission asserted that *Chiarella* did not limit its authority under Section 14(e) to prescribe such a mandate regulating insider trading in the tender offer context.[86] As

---

To recover these penalties [under the 1988 legislation], the Commission must prove that the controlling person "knew or recklessly disregarded the fact that such controlled person was likely to engage in the act or acts constituting the violation and failed to take appropriate steps to prevent such act or acts before they occurred."

. . .

    If the controlling person is a broker-dealer or investment advisor, [the 1988 legislation] provides the Commission with more potent ammunition for imposing the new monetary penalties. [It] sets forth an affirmative duty on broker-dealers and investment advisors to maintain adequate procedures to protect against insider trading and it defines a separate standard for controlling person liability in reference to that duty. First, [the legislation] added Section 15(f) of the Exchange Act and Section 204A of the Investment Advisors Act of 1940 which impose an affirmative duty on broker-dealers and investment advisors to maintain "written policies and procedures reasonably designed" to prevent insider trading violations. Second, Section 21A(b)(1)(B) subjects broker-dealers and investment advisors to controlling person liability if they "knowingly or recklessly failed to establish, maintain, or enforce" those procedures and "such failure substantially contributed to or permitted the occurrence" of the insider trading violation.

For further discussion, see *infra* note 85 and accompanying text.

[84] Securities Exchange Act Release No. 17120 (1980).

[85] M. Steinberg & W. Wang, *Insider Trading* § 9.2.3 (1996 & 2000 supp.). See *Koppers Co., Inc. v. American Express Co.*, 689 F. Supp. 1371, 1413 (W.D. Pa. 1988); SEC Division of Market Regulation, *Broker-Dealer Policies and Procedures Designed to Segment the Flow and Prevent the Misuse of Material Nonpublic Information*, [1989–1990 Transfer Binder] Fed. Sec. L. Rep. (CCH) ¶ 84,520 (1990); Poser, *Conflicts of Interest Within Securities Firms*, 16 Brook. J. Int'l L. 111 (1990).

[86] See Securities Exchange Act Release No. 17120 (1980).

applied to the facts presented in the cases thus far decided, Rule 14e-3 has been upheld, including by the Supreme Court in *O'Hagan*.[87] Limiting its holding to the charges brought against O'Hagan, the Supreme Court upheld Rule 14e-3's validity without requiring proof that a fiduciary duty was breached. The Court stated:

> [I]t is a fair assumption that trading on the basis of material, nonpublic information will often involve a breach of a duty of confidentiality to the bidder or target company or their representatives. The SEC, cognizant of the proof problem that could enable sophisticated traders to escape responsibility, placed in Rule 14e-3(a) a "disclose or abstain from trading" command that does not require specific proof of a breach of fiduciary duty. That prescription, we are satisfied, applied to this case, is a "means reasonably designed to prevent" fraudulent trading on material, nonpublic information in the tender offer context.[88]

§ 11.08 The Mail and Wire Fraud Statutes

Although not available to the SEC, the mail and wire fraud statutes,[89] as seen from the Supreme Court's decision in *Carpenter v. United States*,[90] are potent weapons in the U.S. Attorney's arsenal to combat alleged criminal offenses involving insider trading. Moreover, these statutes constitute predicate offenses under RICO,[91] thereby providing the U.S. Attorney with enhanced prosecutorial powers in this setting.[92]

§ 11.09 Section 16 — "Short-Swing" Trading

[A] Overview

Section 16 of the Exchange Act applies to directors, officers, and beneficial owners of more than ten percent of any class of equity security of an issuer (other than an exempted security),[93] with such class of equity security having been registered pursuant to Section 12(b) or 12(g) of the Exchange

---

[87] See *United States v.* O'Hagan, 117 S. Ct. 2199, 2217–19 (1997); *United States v. Chestman*, 947 F.2d 551, 559, 563 (2d Cir. 1991) (en banc).

[88] 117 S. Ct. at 2218–19.

[89] 18 U.S.C. §§ 1341, 1343.

[90] 484 U.S. 19 (1987). See *United States v. Bryan*, 58 F.3d 933 (4th Cir. 1995) (rejecting application of misappropriation theory under § 10(b) but affirming convictions based on mail and wire fraud).

[91] See 18 U.S.C. § 1961. RICO is discussed in § 8.07 *supra*.

[92] See D. Langevoort, *supra* note 9, at § 8.04[2]; W. Wang & M. Steinberg, *supra* note 9, at § 11.1 et seq.

[93] Exempt securities for purposes of Section 16 include, for example, municipal bonds, obligations of the United States, and securities issued in connection with certain employee benefit plans. See Securities Exchange Act Release No. 18114 (1981).

Act.[94] The statute seeks to deter insider trading based on the use of material nonpublic information by such persons. Section 16 contains three key provisions in attempting to meet this objective.

1. Section 16(a) of the Exchange Act requires that, upon becoming an officer, director, or ten percent equity shareholder of a Section 12(b) or 12(g) issuer, such individual must file with the SEC (and with the self-regulatory organization (SRO) with which the stock is listed or traded) a report disclosing the number of the corporation's shares beneficially owned. Subsequent reports must be filed on a timely basis to reflect changes in the number of shares beneficially owned.

2. Section 16(c) prohibits such insiders to transact short sales in their issuers' equity securities.

3. Generally, "Section 16(b) is designed to permit the corporation or a security holder bringing an action upon behalf of the corporation to recover for the benefit of the corporation short-swing profits arising from the purchase [and sale or sale and purchase] by insiders within any six-month period of equity securities of the company."[95]

Under Section 16(b), an irrebuttable presumption is created when "insiders" engage in such short-swing transactions. The profits that the insider gained from the transaction(s) are recoverable by the issuer in a suit initiated by it, or if it declines to do so, in a properly instituted shareholder's suit expressly authorized by the statute. In view of the broad remedial nature of the statute, a strict formula for computing "profit realized" has been established. Such a formula is designed "to squeeze all possible profits out of stock transactions, and thus to establish a standard so high as to prevent any conflict between the selfish interest of a fiduciary officer, director, or stockholder and the faithful performance of his duty."[96] The formula established matches the lowest price "in" with the highest price "out," thus ensuring recovery of all possible profits. In fact, this formula can yield a profit when in actuality a loss has been suffered.[97]

Moreover, an insider's intent to profit under a transaction that falls within Section 16(b)'s scope need not be shown in order for there to be recovery. As the Seventh Circuit (as well as other courts) pointed out, an insider is "deemed capable of structuring his dealings to avoid any possibility of taint and therefore must bear the risks of any inadvertent miscalculation."[98] In some situations, however, the courts, by finding that certain unorthodox

---

[94] Hence, these equity securities are either listed on a national securities exchange (§ 12(b)) or are securities of an issuer having at least 500 shareholders of record and $10 million in assets (§ 12(g) and Rule 12g-1).

[95] H. Bloomenthal, *Securities Law* 365 (1966).

[96] *Smolowe v. Delendo Corp.*, 136 F.2d 231 (2d Cir. 1943).

[97] See *Morales v. Consolidated Oil & Gas, Inc.*, [1982 Transfer Binder] Fed. Sec. L. Rep. (CCH) ¶ 98,796 (S.D.N.Y. 1982).

[98] *Bershad v. McDonough*, 428 F.2d 693, 696 (7th Cir. 1970). See *Whiting v. Dow Chemical Co.*, 523 F.2d 680, 687 (2d Cir. 1975) ("[T]he unwary who fall within [§ 16(b's)] terms have no one but themselves to blame.").

transactions do not constitute the predicate purchase or sale, have displayed a judicial reluctance to impose liability under Section 16(b) where no congressional purpose would be served.[99]

[B] Relevant Issues

The issues dealing with the construction of Section 16(b), at times, are complex. The following discussion seeks to highlight the key concepts. For more extensive treatment, other sources should be consulted.[100]

[1] Beneficial Ownership and the Concept of Attribution

A significant problem that arises with respect to the concepts of attribution and beneficial ownership in the context of Section 16(b) is in attempting to determine whether, and the extent to which, a corporate insider will be liable for short-swing trading profits when the securities are held by another person, group, or organization. This issue may arise, for example, within the context of family-related transactions, of a related trust, of a partnership in which the insider is a partner, or of a corporation in which the insider is an officer, director or shareholder. The question becomes one of the responsibility of the corporate insider for the acts of such parties and his/her relationship with these other parties.

The definition of "beneficial owner" for purposes of Section 16(b) focuses on whether the insider has a pecuniary interest. Subject to certain exceptions, Rule 16a-1(a)(2) defines "beneficial owner" as "any person who, directly or indirectly, through any contract, arrangement, understanding, relationship or otherwise, has or shares direct or indirect pecuniary interest in the equity securities." Under the SEC rules, a person has such a pecuniary interest when he/she has an opportunity to share in any profit generated from the subject securities transactions. On a non-exclusive basis, the rules provide a number of situations where an individual is deemed to have such an indirect interest. As one example, securities held by a member of an insider's "immediate family," who shares the same household as such insider, creates a presumption (that is rebuttable) that the insider beneficially owns the securities.[101]

Although the SEC's rules define the term "beneficial ownership" for purposes of Section 16, they leave a number of issues unresolved. Moreover, the Commission's approach is not binding on the courts. Therefore, case law remains important.

The cases involving beneficial ownership and the concept of attribution have failed to provide clear standards. Nonetheless, two important factors are (1) whether the insider exercised control over the securities and (2) the

---

[99] See, e.g., *Kern County Land Co. v. Occidental Petroleum Corp.*, 411 U.S. 582 (1973).

[100] See, e.g., P. Romeo & A. Dye, *Section 16 Treatise and Reporting Guide* (1999).

[101] See Securities Exchange Act Release No. 28869, [1990–1991 Transfer Binder] Fed. Sec. L. Rep. (CCH) ¶ 84,709 (1991).

insider's ability to benefit, directly or indirectly, from the profits generated from the short-swing transactions.[102] On the other hand, the Seventh Circuit has applied a more restrictive analysis. Rather than focusing on control over the securities, the court looked to whether the insider stood to receive a direct monetary benefit from the subject transactions. The court held that:

> profit realized by a corporate insider [for purposes of Section 16(b)] means direct pecuniary benefit to the insider. . . . [I]t is not enough that ties of affinity and consanguinity between the . . . recipient and the insider make it likely that the insider will experience an enhanced sense of well-being as a result of the receipt, or will be led to reduce his gift-giving to the recipient.[103]

[2] Directors

Directors and any person performing similar functions (irrespective of whether the business organization is incorporated) are subject to Section 16(b). A key issue in this setting is whether a business organization can be viewed as a director of another entity by virtue of that organization having a representative on the latter entity's board of directors.

Generally, the courts have answered the above question affirmatively, holding that a corporation may "deputize" one of its directors or other person to serve on a second corporation's board. For example, the Second Circuit in *Feder v. Martin Marietta Corp.*[104] imposed liability based on the deputization theory. There, the court found that the president and chief executive officer of Martin Marietta had been "deputized by or represented" Martin Marietta during the time he served as a director of Sperry Rand. Therefore, the court concluded that Martin Marietta was in effect a director of Sperry Rand and was forced to disgorge the profits it acquired in the short-swing trading of Sperry Rand stock.

[3] Officers

In determining whether an individual is an officer for Section 16 purposes, Rule 16a-1(f) focuses on whether such person performs significant policy-making functions. Consistent with this perspective, the rule specifically includes those individuals who clearly hold policy-making duties, such as the company's president, principal financial officer, and any vice-president in charge of a key business division.[105]

The SEC's position on this issue basically follows case law. The focus of the inquiry in ascertaining who is an officer for purposes of Section 16 is

---

[102] See, e.g., *Whittaker v. Whittaker Corp.*, 639 F.2d 516 (9th Cir. 1981); *Whiting v. Dow Chemical Co.*, 523 F.2d 680, 688 (2d Cir. 1975); *Atamil Corp. v. Pryor*, 405 F. Supp. 1222 (S.D. Ind. 1975).

[103] *CBI Industries, Inc. v. Horton*, 682 F.2d 643, 646 (7th Cir. 1982).

[104] 406 F.2d 260 (2d Cir. 1969).

[105] 17 C.F.R. § 240.16a1(f).

upon an individual's functions and responsibilities within the organizational structure. This matter can arise in several different settings. Primarily, however, the issue is whether one, lacking in a title representing him/her as an officer, nevertheless in fact had that status, or, conversely, whether one having the title of officer, for example as vice president, had a role so devoid of decision-making functions that he/she could not in reality be called an officer within the meaning of Section 16. For example, the Ninth Circuit has opined:

> [T]he title "Vice President" does no more than raise an inference that the person who holds the title has the executive duties and the opportunities for confidential information that the title implies. The inference can be overcome by proof that the title was merely honorary and did not carry with it any of the executive responsibilities that otherwise might be assumed. [106]

[4] Ten Percent Beneficial Owners

Unlike the situation for directors and officers, Section 16(b) imposes liability on a ten percent beneficial owner if that person had that status both when the securities were acquired and when they were sold. Hence, in *Foremost-McKesson, Inc. v. Provident Securities Co.,*[107] the Supreme Court held that "in a purchase-sale sequence, a beneficial owner must account for profits only if he was a beneficial owner before the purchase."[108] And, in *Reliance Electric Co. v. Emerson Electric Co.,*[109] the high Court ruled that liability pursuant to Section 16(b) normally cannot be based on a beneficial owner's sale of securities which takes place after his/her ownership was reduced to less than ten percent. This is so, even if at the time when the seller owned more than ten percent of the stock, he/she deliberately structured two separate transactions so as to reduce the extent of liability. For example, the first such sale transaction could be arranged so as to result in the beneficial owner holding 9.9% of the company's stock. In the second transaction, the beneficial owner could sell the remaining shares. Provided that in such a two-stage transaction the sales are not "legally tied" to one another,[110] the beneficial owner under *Reliance* is liable under Section 16(b) only as to the first transaction.[111]

[5] Objective Approach vs. Pragmatic Approach

Persons are subject to Section 16(b) liability only if they engage in a "purchase" and "sale" or "sale" and "purchase" of a subject security within

---

[106] *Merrill Lynch, Pierce Fenner and Smith v. Livingston,* 566 F.2d 1119, 1122 (9th Cir. 1978).

[107] 423 U.S. 232 (1976).

[108] *Id.* at 250.

[109] 404 U.S. 418 (1972).

[110] *Id.* at 421. See *Reece Corp. v. Walco National Corp.,* [1981–1982 Transfer Binder] Fed. Sec. L. Rep. (CCH) ¶ 98,289 (S.D.N.Y. 1981).

[111] 404 U.S. at 422–25.

a six-month period. As such, an insider's liability may turn upon whether there indeed has been a "purchase" and "sale" within Section 16(b)'s scope.

The traditional and still commonly used approach is objective. The "objective" approach works in a mechanical fashion. Courts applying it neither will inquire into an insider's reasons for engaging in the transaction nor will they ascertain his/her access to or use of inside information. Consequently, any transaction that can be viewed as a "purchase" or "sale" and brought within the ambit of the statute will result in liability.[112]

Due to its unfair consequences in certain situations, the objective approach is subject to criticism. As a result, the "pragmatic" approach has been employed in certain "unorthodox" transactions, such as stock reclassifications, dealings in options, warrants, and rights, stock conversions, and exchanges pursuant to mergers. As stated by one commentator:

> The pragmatic approach involves a number of elements. First, and most important, it applies only in certain unusual circumstances. If these circumstances exist, then the transaction is characterized as "unorthodox." Unorthodox transactions are ill-defined, but they usually have peculiar features that either make it unfair to apply Section 16(b) or make it difficult to determine whether or when a purchase or sale has taken place.[113]

The pragmatic approach received Supreme Court approbation in *Kern County Land Co. v. Occidental Petroleum Corp.*[114] The Court reasoned:

> In deciding whether borderline transactions are within the reach of the statute, the courts have come to inquire whether the transaction may serve as a vehicle for the veil which Congress sought to prevent — the realization of short-swing profits based upon access to inside information — thereby endeavoring to implement Congressional objectives without extending the reach of the statute beyond its intended limits. . . . [T]he prevailing view is to apply the statute only when its application would serve its goals. . . . [I]n interpreting the terms "purchase" and "sale," courts have properly asked whether the particular type of transaction is one that gives rise to speculative abuse.[115]

Several courts have employed the pragmatic approach in a variety of contexts. Using this approach, Section 16(b) liability has been imposed in some cases[116] but not in others.[117] From these cases as well as from the scholarly commentary, the key inquiries in applying the pragmatic approach include:

---

[112] See, e.g., *Park and Tilford, Inc. v. Shulte*, 160 F.2d 984 (2d Cir. 1947).

[113] Tomlinson, *Section 16(b): A Single Analysis of Purchases and Sales — Merging the Objective and Pragmatic Analyses*, 1981 Duke L.J. 941, 947 (1981).

[114] 411 U.S. 582 (1973).

[115] *Id.* at 594–95 (citations omitted).

[116] See, e.g., *Texas International Airlines v. National Airlines, Inc.*, 714 F.2d 533 (5th Cir. 1983).

[117] See, e.g., *Heublein, Inc. v. General Cinema Corp.*, 722 F.2d 29 (2d Cir. 1983).

(1) Is the transaction in question of a type that may be characterized as unorthodox?

(2) Did the insider have control over the timing of the decision involved in the transaction?

(3) Did the insider have access to inside information, irrespective of whether that information was in fact used?[118]

---

[118] M. Steinberg & W. Wang, *supra* note 9, at § 15.1 et seq. (and authorities cited therein); Tomlinson, *supra* note 113, at 949. See generally A. Jacobs, *Section 16 of the Securities Exchange Act* (1994); P. Romeo & A. Dye, *Section 16 Treatise and Reporting Guide* (1999); Ferber, *Short-Swing Transactions Under the Securities Exchange Act*, 16 Rev. Sec. Reg. 801 (1983); Hazen, *The New Pragmatism of Section 16(b) of the Securities Exchange Act of 1934*, 54 N.C. L. Rev. 1 (1975); O'Conner, *Toward a More Efficient Deterrence of Insider Trading: The Repeal of Section 16(b)*, 58 Fordham L. Rev. 309 (1989); Steinberg & Lansdale, *The Judicial and Regulatory Constriction of Section 16(b) of the Securities Exchange Act of 1934*, 68 Notre Dame L. Rev. 33 (1992); Taylor, *Teaching an Old Law New Tricks: Rethinking Section 16*, 39 Ariz. L. Rev. 1315 (1997); Thel, *The Genius of Section 16: Regulating the Management of Publicly Held Companies*, 42 Hastings L.J. 391 (1991); Tomlinson, *Section 16(b): A Single Analysis of Purchases and Sales — Merging the Objective and Pragmatic Analyses*, 1981 Duke L.J. 941; Wentz, *Refining a Crude Thumb: The Pragmatic Approach to Section 16(b) of the Securities Exchange Act of 1934*, 70 Nw. U. L. Rev. 221 (1975).

Chapter 12

BROKER-DEALER REGULATION

§ 12.01 Overview

Preceding chapters have discussed the availability of private rights of action under various provisions of the securities acts. Broker-dealers, of course, may be liable for a primary violation of these sections if their conduct falls within the established requirements already discussed. Under Section 11(a)(5) of the Securities Act, for example, if a broker-dealer acts as an underwriter with respect to the registered offering, such broker-dealer would be subject to liability for material misstatements or omissions contained in the registration statement.[1] In response, the broker-dealer may assert the Section 11(b)(3) due diligence defense. As an underwriter, however, the broker-dealer would be subject to the strengthened due diligence requirement outlined in *Escott v. BarChris Construction Corporation*.[2]

Under Section 12 of the Securities Act, a broker-dealer would be liable for an offer or sale of securities either in violation of the Section 5 registration requirements or the making of a material misrepresentation or omission contained in a prospectus (or oral communication). Earlier material discussed the construction that the Supreme Court has given the terms "seller" and "prospectus" under Section 12.[3] A dealer, by definition, would fall within Section 12's definition of "seller" if it acts as principal. A broker becomes a "seller" under Section 12 when, acting as an agent, it successfully solicits the transaction. As with Section 11, the broker-dealer has a diligence-based defense against Section 12(a)(2) liability. The broker-dealer may defend by showing that it exercised "reasonable care," a standard that, as applied by some courts, may require a stringent showing.[4] Note, moreover, the issue whether Section 12(a)(2) may be invoked in the secondary trading markets against such parties as broker-dealers has been resolved by the Supreme Court in *Gustafson* (where the Court held that Section 12(a)(2) applies only to public offerings by an issuer or its controlling shareholders).[5]

Broker-dealers are subject to a number of other provisions. For example, Section 17(a) of the Securities Act and Section 15(c) of the Exchange Act

---

[1] See, e.g., *Feit v. Leasco Data Processing Equipment Corp.*, 332 F. Supp. 544 (E.D.N.Y. 1971).

[2] 283 F. Supp. 643 (S.D.N.Y. 1968). See discussion §§ 6.02, 6.04 *supra*.

[3] *Gustafson v. Alloyd Company*, 513 U.S. 561 (1995), *discussed in*, § 6.09[A], [D] *supra*; *Pinter v. Dahl*, 486 U.S. 622 (1988), *discussed in*, § 6.09[B] *supra*.

[4] See *Sanders v. John Nuveen & Co.*, 619 F.2d 1222 (7th Cir. 1982); discussion § 6.09[E] *supra*.

[5] *Gustafson v. Alloyd Company*, 513 U.S. 561 (1995), *discussed in*, § 6.09[A], [D] *supra*.

are potent enforcement weapons against broker-dealers who engage in fraud in the offer or sale of securities.[6] Additionally, the insider trading provisions similarly affect the activities of broker-dealers.[7]

Moreover, a broker-dealer may be subject to liability under the Section 10(b) antifraud provision[8] as well as secondary liability principles.[9] The material in this chapter addresses special concepts and theories of liability with regard to broker-dealers.

Also, it should be pointed out that brokers and dealers must register under both federal and state law.[10] In addition, depending on the amount of assets under management, investment advisers must register under federal law or state law.[11] The failure to register may result in government enforcement action, including criminal prosecution. Also, plaintiffs may seek relief in private litigation based on a broker-dealer's failure to register. The Fifth Circuit's decision in *Regional Properties* (see § 8.06) serves as an example of relief being afforded to the plaintiffs even where the broker-dealer's failure to register caused the plaintiffs no harm.

Note also that self-regulatory organizations (SROs) play an important role in broker-dealer regulation. These SROs include the major stock exchanges, such as the New York Stock Exchange and the National Association of Securities Dealers (NASD).

Sections 5, 6, 15A, 17A, and 19 of the Exchange Act contain the general federal regulatory framework for SROs. For example, Sections 6 and 15A require adoption of rules governing the admission and conduct of an SRO's members; and Section 19(b) and (g) addresses the SEC oversight and the SRO enforcement of these rules. If a broker-dealer runs afoul of an SRO rule, such broker-dealer is subject to sanctions. However, private litigants may not sue for damages under the federal securities laws for broker-dealer violations of SRO rules.[12]

---

[6] See *United States v. Naftalin*, 441 U.S. 768 (1979), *discussed in*, § 8.04 *supra*.

[7] See §§ 11.01–11.08 *supra*.

[8] See Chapter 7 *supra*.

[9] See Chapter 9 *supra*.

[10] See R. Janvey, *Regulation of the Securities and Commodities Markets*, ¶¶ 4.01–4.02 (1992); D. Lipton, *Broker-Dealer Regulation (1990)*; Lipton, *A Primer on Broker-Dealer Regulation*, 36 Cath. U. L. Rev. 899 (1987).

[11] See Bagnall & Cannon, *The National Securities Markets Improvement Act of 1996: Summary and Analysis*, 25 Sec. Reg. L.J. 3, 13–15 (1997) (pointing out that under the 1996 federal legislation "investment advisers with assets under management of $25 million or more and advisers to [SEC] registered investment companies will fall exclusively under [SEC] jurisdiction" but that states still retain their enforcement powers against such advisers or associated persons where fraud has been committed); Friedman, *The Impact of NSMIA on State Regulation of Broker-Dealers and Investment Advisers*, 53 Bus. Law. 511 (1998).

[12] Early authority on the issue was mixed. Compare *Buttrey v. Merrill Lynch, Pierce, Fenner & Smith, Inc.*, 410 F.2d 135 (7th Cir. 1969) (allowing implied right), with *Plunkett v. Dominick & Dominick, Inc.*, 414 F. Supp. 885 (D. Conn. 1976) (rejecting implied right). Over the last two decades, as the Supreme Court has restricted the recognition of implied private rights of action, courts have uniformly rejected an implied private right of action for violations of SRO rules. See, e.g., *Carrott v. Shearson Hayden Stone, Inc.*, 724 F.2d 821 (9th Cir. 1984); *Thompson v. Smith Barney, Harris Upham & Co.*, 709 F.2d 1413 (11th Cir. 1983); *Jablon v. Dean Witter & Co.*, 614 F.2d 677 (9th Cir. 1980). For further discussion, see §§ 8.02–8.03, *supra*.

Also, many aspects of broker-dealer regulation and liability have been discussed in previous chapters. In examining the issues contained in this chapter, the materials in earlier parts of the text should be consulted. As further illustrations:

(1) With respect to the duty of a broker-dealer to register with the SEC and with the states and private liability ramifications for the failure to do so, see the *Regional Properties* case in § 8.06 *supra*.

(2) Broker-dealer liability for insider trading is addressed throughout Chapter 11 as well as the imposition upon a broker-dealer or investment adviser of a treble monetary penalty based upon the illegal inside trading of a controlled person.

(3) Defenses that a broker-dealer may raise, such as *in pari delicto*, are discussed in §§ 7.10, 8.06 *supra*.

(4) Secondary liability of broker-dealers for aiding and abetting, as control persons, and under *respondeat superior* is addressed in Chapter 9. Note that the SEC has express statutory authority to proceed in the broker-dealer and investment adviser contexts on the basis of aider and abettor liability principles.

Broker-dealers thus are subject to vigorous SEC oversight, including the bringing of enforcement actions. This subject is addressed in Chapter 14.

§ 12.02   Arbitration

[A]   Key Supreme Court Decisions

In *Shearson/American Express, Inc. v. McMahon*,[13] the Supreme Court held that pre-dispute arbitration agreements between brokerage firms and their customers did not contravene the Securities Exchange Act and the Racketeer Influenced and Corrupt Organizations Act (RICO). Hence, such claims ordinarily are arbitrable consistent with the terms of the applicable arbitration agreement. The following discussion focuses on the validity of such pre-dispute arbitration agreements under the securities laws.

In *McMahon*, the Supreme Court relied in large part on the Federal Arbitration Act (FAA),[14] which establishes a "federal policy favoring arbitration."[15] This policy is prevalent even when a claim is based on a federal statutory right. As a consequence, the burden is on the party opposing the validity of the arbitration agreement to show that Congress intended to preserve the availability of a judicial forum, irrespective of the terms of an arbitration agreement.[16] Accordingly, in order to preclude

---

[13] 482 U.S. 220 (1987).

[14] 9 U.S.C. § 1 et seq.

[15] *Moses H. Cone Memorial Hospital v. Mercury Construction Corp.*, 460 U.S. 1, 24 (1983).

[16] 482 U.S. at 227, *relying on, Mitsubishi Motors Corp. v. Soler Chrysler-Plymouth, Inc.*, 473 U.S. 614 (1985); *Dean Witter Reynolds, Inc. v. Byrd*, 470 U.S. 213 (1985); *Scherk v. Alberto-Culber Co.*, 417 U.S. 506 (1974).

application of the FAA, according to the Court, the party seeking to avoid arbitration "must demonstrate that Congress intended to make an exception to the Arbitration Act for claims arising under . . . the Exchange Act, an intention discernible from the text, history, or purposes of the statute."[17]

Upon examining Section 29(a) of the Exchange Act, which renders void any stipulation whereby a person waives compliance with any 1934 Act provision, the Court opined that Section 29(a) only proscribes waiver of the Exchange Act's *substantive* obligations. By contrast, Section 29(a) does not preclude parties from waiving a judicial forum in favor of an arbitral tribunal.[18]

The Court's holding in *McMahon* takes a far different view of arbitration than its 1953 decision in *Wilko v. Swan*.[19] In holding that pre-dispute arbitration agreements were not enforceable in actions brought pursuant to Section 12(2) [now 12(a)(2)] of the Securities Act, the *Wilko* Court invoked the anti-waiver provision of the Securities Act, Section 14, which is Section 29(a)'s counterpart. Underlying the *Wilko* Court's holding was its hostility to the arbitration process. Succinctly put, the Court believed that arbitration would fail to protect the investor's substantive rights. As a consequence, a judicial forum was necessary to ensure that the statutory rights created by Section 12(2) would be adequately protected.[20]

Although declining to overrule *Wilko* at that time,[21] the Supreme Court in *McMahon* asserted that, in view of the increased regulatory oversight of arbitration since *Wilko* was handed down, a party's 1934 Act substantive rights are not waived by enforcing a predispute arbitration agreement. Pursuant to the 1975 Amendments to the 1934 Act, the SEC now "has broad authority to oversee and to regulate the rules adopted by the [self-regulatory organizations] relating to customer disputes, including the power to mandate the adoption of any rules it deems necessary to ensure that arbitration procedures adequately protect statutory rights."[22] Accordingly, the *McMahon* Court held:

> We conclude, therefore, that Congress did not intend for § 29(a) to bar enforcement of all predispute arbitration agreements. In this case, where the SEC has sufficient statutory authority to ensure that arbitration is adequate to vindicate Exchange Act rights, enforcement does not effect a waiver of "compliance with any provision" of the Exchange Act under § 29(a).[23]

---

[17] 482 U.S. at 227.

[18] *Id.* at 228–38.

[19] 346 U.S. 427 (1953).

[20] *Id.* at 432–37. See generally Brown, Shell & Tyson, *Arbitration of Customer-Broker Disputes Arising Under the Federal Securities Laws and RICO*, 15 Sec. Reg. L.J. 3 (1987); Comment, *Predispute Arbitration Agreements Between Brokers and Investors: The Extension of Wilko to Section 10(b) Claims*, 46 Md. L. Rev. 339 (1987).

[21] 482 U.S. at 234 ("[S]tare decisis concerns may counsel against upsetting *Wilko's* contrary conclusion under the Securities Act").

[22] *Id.* at 233–34.

[23] *Id.* at 238. But see *id.* at 252–68 (Blackmun, J., concurring in part and dissenting in part).

Subsequently, in *Rodriguez De Quijas v. Shearson/American Express, Inc.*,[24] the Supreme Court overruled *Wilko*. Holding that predispute agreements to arbitrate claims under the Securities Act are enforceable, the Court stated:

> [I]n *McMahon* the Court declined to read § 29(a) of the Securities Exchange Act of 1934, the language of which is in every respect the same as that in § 14 of the 1933 Act, to prohibit enforcement of predispute agreements to arbitrate. The only conceivable distinction in this regard between the Securities Act and the Securities Exchange Act is that the former statute allows concurrent federal-state jurisdiction over causes of action and the latter statute provides for exclusive federal jurisdiction. But even if this distinction were thought to make any difference at all, it would suggest that arbitration agreements, which are "in effect, a specialized kind of forum-selection clause," . . . should not be prohibited under the Securities Act, since they, like the provision for concurrent jurisdiction, serve to advance the objective of allowing buyers of securities a broader right to select the forum for resolving disputes, whether it be judicial or otherwise. And in *McMahon* we explained at length why we rejected the *Wilko* Court's aversion to arbitration as a forum for resolving disputes over securities transactions, especially in light of the relatively recent expansion of the Securities and Exchange Commission's authority to oversee and to regulate those arbitration procedures. . . .[25]

[B] Aftermath of *McMahon* and *Rodriguez*

In the aftermath of *McMahon* and *Rodriguez*, many believe that securities arbitration favors the industry. As stated in a *New York Times* article: "The [brokerage] houses basically like the current system because they own the stacked deck."[26] A 1992 U.S. General Accounting Office Report on Securities Arbitration, however, does not agree: "GAO's analysis of statistical results of decisions in arbitration cases at both industry-sponsored and

---

[24] 490 U.S. 477 (1989).

[25] *Id.* at 482–83. Also, the Court in *Rodriguez* relied on the "strong language of the Arbitration Act" under which "the party opposing arbitration carries the burden of showing that Congress intended in a separate statute to preclude a waiver of judicial remedies, or that such a waiver of judicial remedies inherently conflicts with the underlying purposes of that other statute." *Id.* at 483.

For other Supreme Court decisions in the securities arbitration area, see, e.g., *First Options of Chicago, Inc. v. Kaplan*, 514 U.S. 938 (1995) (holding that (1) issue whether parties agreed to arbitrate a certain matter is question for the court to decide and (2) standard that court of appeals should apply when reviewing district court decision confirming an arbitration award "should proceed like review of any other district court decision . . . , i.e., accepting findings of fact that are not 'clearly erroneous' but deciding questions of law de novo"); *Mastrobuono v. Shearson Lehman Hutton, Inc.*, 515 U.S. 52 (1995) (holding that award of punitive damages in arbitration proceeding not precluded by terms of brokerage firm-client agreement where agreement did not expressly refer to punitive damages and was ambiguous in this regard, resulting in such ambiguity being construed against the drafter of the agreement — the brokerage firm).

[26] Galberson, *When the Investor Has a Gripe*, N.Y. Times, March 29, 1987, at 1, 8.

independent forums showed no indication of a pro-industry bias in decisions at industry-sponsored forums." Nonetheless, as Professor Wallace points out: "Given the prominence that securities arbitration enjoy[s], probing questions must be asked regarding the effectiveness [and] basic fairness of the procedures that effectuate it."[27]

Even though not finding a pro-industry bias, the GAO report nonetheless was critical, stating that "GAO's review of arbitration procedures showed that arbitration forums lacked internal controls to provide a reasonable level of assurance regarding either the independence of the arbitrators or their competence in arbitrating disputes." Needless to say, such lack of internal controls, as found by the GAO, bring into question the integrity of the arbitration process.

Fortunately, certain improvements have been made. For example, in cases involving public customers, an arbitration panel consists of a majority of public arbitrators. The new rules more rigorously define those who qualify as public arbitrators to exclude, for instance, securities industry retirees. Such individuals may serve only as industry arbitrators comprising a minority of the panel. The rules also call for: preservation of a record of the proceeding; disclosure to the parties of certain past or existing affiliations of the arbitrators that are likely to affect their impartiality; and providing in the statement of award the arbitrators' and parties' names, a summary of the relevant issues in controversy, the damages and/or other relief sought and awarded, a statement of any other issues resolved, and the signatures of the arbitrators who concurred in the award.[28]

[C] Arbitration Today

Arbitration today, although more complex than in yesteryear,[29] remains a relatively informal process. Rather than burdensome pleading requirements as frequently mandated by federal law, a complainant in arbitration need only specify the relevant facts and the remedies sought.[30] Although

---

[27] Wallace, *Securities Arbitration After McMahon, Rodriguez, and the New Rules: Can Investors' Rights Really Be Protected?*, 43 Vand. L. Rev. 1199, 1202 (1990).

[28] See Securities Exchange Act Release No. 26805 (1989). Two excellent books on securities arbitration are M. Cane & P. Shub, *Securities Arbitration: Law and Procedure* (1991) and C. Edward Fletcher, *Arbitrating Securities Disputes* (1990). For law review articles on arbitration, see e.g., Symposium, 40 Arizona L. Rev. 1039–1110 (1998); Symposium, 62 Brooklyn L. Rev. No. 4 (1996); Katsoris, *Securities Arbitration: A Clinical Experiment*, 25 Fordham Urban L.J. 193 (1998); Nichols, *Arbitrator Selection at the NASD: Investor Perception of a Pro-Securities Industry Bias*, 15 Ohio St. J. Disp. Res. 63 (1999); Poser, *Making Securities Arbitration Work*, 50 SMU L. Rev. 277 (1996); Ramirez, *Arbitration and Reform in Private Securities Litigation: Dealing with the Meritorious as Well as the Frivolous*, 40 Wm. & Mary L. Rev. 1055 (1999); Shell, *Arbitration and Corporate Governance*, 67 N.C. L. Rev. 517 (1989); Wallace, note 27 *supra*.

[29] See Report of the Arbitration Policy Task Force to the Board of Governors, National Association of Securities Dealers, Inc., [1995–1996 Transfer Binder] Fed. Sec. L. Rep. (CCH) ¶ 85,735, at 87,463–87,468 (1996) (hereinafter "Ruder Report").

[30] Securities Industry Conference of Arbitration (SICA), Uniform Code of Arbitration (UCA) § 13.

discovery is permitted to an increasing extent,[31] including written requests for information and document requests,[32] a number of the more costly and time-consuming aspects of discovery found in federal and state court litigation usually are not present.[33] Hence, depositions are rarely permitted and dispositive motions prior to the formal hearing are not encouraged.[34]

At the formal hearing, the panel is comprised of a majority of public arbitrators. Unlike a judicial proceeding, formal rules of evidence do not apply, thereby allowing the introduction of hearsay.[35] Relevance and materiality are key criteria in the arbitrators' determination relating to the weight given to evidence proffered.[36]

Arbitrators, not being bound by precise legal standards in their decisions, may render awards premised on the standards of applicable self-regulatory organizations' (SROs') standards, industry custom, or even concepts of equity and fairness. Indeed, damages may be awarded to claimants for violations of SRO rules where no monetary remedy is provided for such misconduct under federal or state securities law.[37] Moreover, many arbitrators are not attorneys and, even for those who are lawyers, they may not have expertise in securities law.[38]

No written decision generally is required by the arbitration rules;[39] only the names of the parties, a summary of the issues presented, the relief sought and awarded, a statement of other issues resolved (e.g., jurisdictional rulings), the names of the arbitrators, and the signatures of the arbitrators who concur in the award are necessary.[40] The rationale frequently provided for not requiring written opinions is that mandating such opinions would contravene the policies underlying arbitration which are to provide an expeditious, efficient, and informal forum of alternative dispute resolution.[41] Another argument advanced is that requiring written opinions would be time consuming and burdensome, thereby deterring many qualified individuals from agreeing to serve as arbitrators.[42]

---

[31] See Ruder Report, *supra* note 29, at 87,463.

[32] See *supra* note 30, UCA § 20(a)-(c).

[33] See Ruder Report, *supra* note 29, at 87,463.

[34] *Id*. See M. Cane & P. Shub, *Securities Arbitration: Law and Procedure* 114 (1991).

[35] M. Cane & P. Shub, *supra* note 34, at 37; S. Jaffee, *Broker-Dealers and Securities Markets: A Guide to the Regulatory Process* 19 (1977).

[36] See *supra* note 30, UCA § 21; A Bromberg & L. Lowenfels, *Securities Fraud and Commodities Fraud* §§ 16.01–16.05 (1999).

[37] See A. Bromberg & L. Lowenfels, *supra* note 36, at §§ 16.01–16.05; Sullivan, *The Scope of Modern Arbitral Awards*, 62 Tulane L. Rev. 1113 (1988).

[38] See Ruder Report, *supra* note 29, at 87,468-87,469.

[39] See, e.g., NASD Arbitration Code, Rule 41.

[40] *Id*.

[41] See, e.g., *Raiford v. Merrill Lynch, Pierce, Fenner & Smith Inc.* 903 F.2d 1410, 1413 (11th Cir. 1990); *Sargent v. Paine Webber Jackson & Curtis Inc.*, 882 F.2d 529, 532 (D.C. Cir. 1989); *Sobel v. Hertz, Warner & Co.*, 469 F.2d 1211, 1214 (2d Cir. 1972).

[42] See Katzler, *Should Mandatory Written Opinions Be Required in All Securities Arbitrations? The Practical and Legal Implications to the Securities Industry*, 45 Am. U. L. Rev. 151, 164 (1995).

There may well be another key reason why arbitrators avoid writing opinions: Because the panel's decision can be overturned by a federal court only on narrow grounds, such as bias, misconduct, or manifest disregard of the law,[43] the writing of an opinion draws a road map by which a disgruntled party will have greater likelihood of upsetting the arbitral award. Moreover, being pressed for time, inadequately paid, and not accomplished in authoring written opinions (particularly in a complex area like securities law), any written decision incurs the risk of being viewed with disfavor by a learned federal court. Because arbitrators perceive that they act in good faith, follow the spirit if not the letter of the applicable law, and seek to do justice, they thus are reluctant to explain their rationale in a written opinion. The end product is one that reaches a defined result with no reasoning provided to support such result and with the losing party having little likelihood of overturning such result.[44]

§ 12.03 Special Concepts of Fraud for Broker-Dealers

Under Section 10(b) as well as under certain other provisions (such as Section 17(a) of the Securities Act), a number of principles have been developed to hold broker-dealers to a fairly strict standard of conduct. One such theory is the shingle theory which posits that by hanging out its "shingle," a broker-dealer impliedly represents that its conduct and the behavior of its employees will be fair and will comport with professional norms. As the Second Circuit stated in *Hanly v. SEC*:[45] "A securities dealer occupies a special relationship to the buyer of securities in that by his position he impliedly represents he has an adequate basis for the opinions he renders."[46] One aspect of this duty, labeled the "suitability" theory, recognizes an implied representation by the broker that it will recommend only those securities suitable for each customer's investment objectives and economic status.[47]

A number of other implied representations have been recognized as coming within the shingle theory, including:

---

[43] Section 10 of the Federal Arbitration Act (FAA), 9 U.S.C. § 10. Although error of law is not provided as a basis for vacating an award pursuant to § 10, several courts have embraced a standard focusing on manifest disregard of the law by the arbitrators as a ground for vacating an award. See Cane and Shub, *supra* note 34, at 326–39 (citing cases). None the less, the burden to show 'manifest disregard' is a high one for aggrieved parties. See, e.g., *Merrill Lynch, Pierce, Fenner & Smith Inc. v. Jaros*, 70 F.3d 418, 421 (6th Cir. 1995); *Advest Inc. v. McCarthy*, 914 F.2d 6, 10 (1st Cir. 1990); *Merrill, Lynch, Pierce, Fenner & Smith Inc. v. Bobker*, 808 F.2d 930, 934 (2d Cir. 1986).

[44] See S. Jaffee, *supra* note 35, at 339; Steinberg, *Securities Arbitration: Better for Investors than the Courts?* 62 Brooklyn L. Rev. 1503 (1996).

[45] *Hanly v. SEC*, 415 F.2d 589 (2d Cir. 1969).

[46] *Id.* at 596–97. See generally, Karmel, *Is the Shingle Theory Dead?*, 52 Wash. & Lee L. Rev. 1271 (1995).

[47] See M. Cane & P. Shub, *supra* note 34, at 132–74; N. Poser, *Broker-Dealer Law and Regulation: Private Rights of Action* (1995); Booth, *The Suitability Rule, Investor Diversification, and Using Spread to Measure Risk*, 54 Bus. Law. 1599 (1999); Kerr, *Suitability Standards: A New Look at Economic Theory and Current SEC Disclosure Policy*, 16 Pac. L.J. 805 (1985); Lowenfels & Bromberg, *Suitability in Securities Transactions*, 54 Bus. Law. 1557 (1999).

(1) An implied representation of fair pricing, including any markup or markdown;

(2) An implied representation that the broker-dealer will execute only authorized transactions for its customers;

(3) An implied representation to disclose any special consideration that influences the broker-dealer's recommendation;

(4) An implied representation to execute promptly customers' orders; and

(5) An implied representation that any recommendation made by a broker-dealer to a customer has a reasonable basis.[48]

One may inquire, however, whether aspects of the shingle theory still provide the basis for a Section 10(b) right of action in light of the Supreme Court's holding in *Santa Fe* that deception or manipulation must be shown (see § 7.05). Although not definitively resolved, a number of courts have taken the position that certain components of the shingle theory no longer are viable. For example, in *Pross v. Baird, Patrick & Co., Inc.*,[49] a Section 10(b) claim based on unauthorized trading by a broker was dismissed. The court reasoned that the claim was in actuality one for breach of fiduciary duty not involving the element of deception necessary to invoke Section 10(b).[50]

Nonetheless, the shingle theory basically remains good law. Arguably, it should remain so in view of the investing public's reliance (which may be called a "relational reliance" interest) on broker-dealers, investment advisers, and other financial experts. The shingle theory is premised on the proposition that these experts make certain implied representations to their customers. Consequently, where a customer relies on a broker-dealer's fair dealing, the failure by such broker-dealer to disclose its noncompliance with the implied representation(s) made constitutes deception for Section 10(b) purposes.[51]

Another basis upon which brokers have been held liable is for churning. Generally, a claim for churning is established by the plaintiff showing "(1) that the trading in his account was excessive in light of his investment objectives; (2) that the broker in question exercised control over the trading in the account; and (3) that the broker acted with the intent to defraud or with the wilful and reckless disregard for the interests of his client."[52]

---

[48] M. Steinberg & R. Ferrara, *Securities Practice: Federal and State Enforcement* § 2:17 (1985 & 2000 supp.) (and authorities cited therein).

[49] 585 F. Supp. 1456 (S.D.N.Y. 1984).

[50] *Id.* at 1460–61. Accord, *Shamsi v. Dean Witter Reynolds, Inc.*, 743 F. Supp. 87, 91 (D. Mass. 1989). But see *Rivera v. Clark Melvin Securities Corp.*, [1999 Transfer Binder] Fed. Sec. L. Rep. (CCH) ¶ 90,524 (D.P.R. 1999); *Cruse v. Equitable Securities of New York, Inc.*, 678 F. Supp. 1023 (S.D.N.Y. 1987). See generally Weiss, *A Review of the Historic Foundations of Broker-Dealer Liability For Breach of Fiduciary Duty*, 23 J. Corp. L. 65 (1997).

[51] See Langevoort, *Fraud and Deception by Securities Professionals*, 61 Texas L. Rev. 1247, 1280–83 (1983).

[52] *Mihara v. Dean Witter & Co.*, 619 F.2d 814, 820–21 (9th Cir. 1980).

With respect to establishing "excessive trading" for churning purposes, courts often look to the "turnover ratio"[53] and the "commission ratio."[54] Nonetheless, as the Ninth Circuit opined, no single factor identifies excessive trading.[55]

As a final point, courts allow brokers to engage in certain nonactionable puffery. Such statements that "this deal will make you rich" and "I'm the best broker in Kansas City" are not actionable on such grounds as lack of materiality and lack of justifiable reliance (see § 7.06[D] *supra*). On the other hand, where specific and realistic percentages are communicated to the investor, such as "your return will be fifteen percent annually," many courts will find such a statement to constitute actionable misrepresentation.[56]

§ 12.04 Screening Procedures

Broker-dealers perform various functions including investment banking, brokerage activities, underwriting, research, investment advice, and investment management. Potential conflicts can arise when information gathering and investment decision functions affect the same issuer. The investment banking department could obtain material, nonpublic information on a publicly-held issuer while the brokerage section is recommending trades in the same issuer's securities or while the trading department is executing trades in the issuer's securities for the firm's own proprietary accounts or as a market maker.[57]

[A] In General

Screening (commonly called "Chinese Wall") procedures consist of policies and procedures designed to control the flow of material, nonpublic information within a multiservice financial firm.[58] In the broker-dealer context, a Chinese Wall isolates the investment banking department from the brokerage, research, and other departments and also limits the flow of

---

[53] The turnover ratio is "the ratio of the total cost of the purchases made for the account during a given period of time to the amount invested." A. Bromberg & L. Lowenfels, *supra* note 36, at § 5.7(322).

[54] The commission ratio is "the ratio of the broker's commissions generated by the account to the size of the customer's investment in that amount." *Id.*

[55] *Nesbit v. McNeil*, 896 F.2d 380, 383 (9th Cir. 1990).

[56] See, e.g., *Cohen v. Prudential-Bache Securities, Inc.*, 713 F. Supp. 653 (S.D.N.Y. 1989) (and cases discussed therein).

[57] See, e.g., Levine, et al, *Multiservice Securities Firms: Coping with Conflicts in a Tender Offer Context*, 23 Wake Forest L. Rev. 41 (1988); Lipton & Mazur, *The Chinese Wall Solution to the Conflict Problems of Securities Firms*, 50 N.Y.U. L. Rev. 459 (1975). The propriety of such procedures as Chinese Walls to limit a broker-dealer's liability has been criticized. For example, Professor Poser opines that "[t]he Chinese Wall . . . makes it difficult . . . for a multiservice firm to fulfill its duty of undivided loyalty to clients." *Poser, Conflicts of Interest Within Securities Firms*, 16 Brooklyn J. Int'l L. 111 (1990).

[58] See Securities Exchange Act Release No. 17120, [1980 Transfer Binder] Fed. Sec. L. Rep. (CCH) ¶ 82,646, at 83,461 (1980) (hereinafter "SEC Rule 14e-3 Release").

sensitive information on a need-to-know basis.[59] In the case of banks, the Chinese Wall segregates the trust department from the commercial lending as well as the securities underwriting departments.[60]

Although Chinese Wall policies and procedures differ among firms, institutions employ numerous such practices to control the flow of information between departments.[61] In addition to general written policies and educational programs, consideration should be given to the implementation of procedures such as the following: (i) physical separation of departments in different wings or floors of a building; (ii) maintenance of separate accounting systems, records, and support staff; (iii) clearly identifying sensitive documents, employing secure filing systems, and restricting access by persons in departments where a breach of confidentiality could occur, such as a bank's trust department or a broker-dealer's trading section; (iv) limiting attendance at meetings where sensitive topics will be discussed; (v) restricting the transfer of personnel from one department into another; (vi) restricting directors, officers and employees from serving dual roles in more than one market sensitive area, such as the arbitrage and underwriting sections of a broker-dealer; and (vii) using code names in documents to conceal the identity of issuers.[62]

Generally, these policies and procedures focus on the activities of the sections of a firm that will frequently come into possession of material, nonpublic information, such as the investment banking section of a broker-dealer. At times, persons in other departments must be consulted on sensitive matters, such as when an opinion must be obtained from an analyst in the research department. In these instances, the research analyst would be "brought over the wall": the analyst would be required to operate under the same procedures that limit the investment banking section.[63]

[B]　The Need for Reinforcement Measures

In addition to the information segregation measures outlined above, the SEC and commentators have focused on the need for financial intermediaries to maintain reinforcement mechanisms. These other procedures, primarily restricted and watch lists, frequently are employed by multiservice financial firms to cope with their conflicting duties and avert the imposition

---

[59] See In re Merrill, Lynch, Pierce, Fenner & Smith, 43 S.E.C. 933 [1967–1969 Transfer Binder] Fed. Sec. L. Rep. (CCH) ¶ 77,629 (1968) (Exhibit A) (providing example of Chinese Wall policy that Merrill Lynch agreed to employ in a settlement of charges of violating the anti-fraud provisions of the federal securities law).

[60] See Board of Governors of the Federal Reserve System, Policy Statement Concerning the Use of Inside Information, 43 Fed. Reg. 12,755, 12,756 (March 17, 1978) (hereinafter "Federal Reserve Policy").

[61] See SEC Division of Market Regulation, Broker-Dealer Policies and Procedures Designed to Segment the Flow and Prevent the Misuse of Material Nonpublic Information, [1989–1990 Transfer Binder] Fed. Sec. L. Rep. (CCH) ¶ 84,520, at 80,620–80,625 (1990) (hereinafter "SEC Division Report").

[62] See Federal Reserve Policy, supra note 60, at 12,756; Doty & Powers, Chinese Walls: The Transformation of a Good Business Practice, 26 Am. Crim. L. Rev. 155, 175–77 (1988).

[63] See Doty & Powers, supra note 62, at 175–77.

of liability. [64] Internal audits and other enforcement measures are also utilized to ensure compliance and to detect breaches of the wall. [65] When personnel are brought over the wall, they become subject to these reinforcement procedures as well. [66]

To prevent leaks of inside information, the implementation by multiservice financial firms of reinforcement measures are key components of an effective compliance program. [67] Thus, the Commission often describes adequate procedures for financial intermediaries to include Chinese Walls, [68] restricted lists, [69] watch lists, [70] and other procedures [71] designed to prevent violations of the securities laws.

---

[64] See SEC Rule 14e-3 Release, *supra* note 58, at 83,461; Levine, et al., *supra* note 57, at 58.

[65] See Doty & Powers, *supra* note 62, at 175–77.

[66] See *id.* at 177 (including restricted lists, limits on employee securities transactions, and internal audits).

[67] See SEC Division Report, *supra* note 61, at 80,623-80,625.

[68] See *supra* notes 57–67 and accompanying text.

[69] See Broker-Dealer Internal Control Procedures for High Yield Securities, Report by the SEC Division of Market Regulation, [1993 Transfer Binder] Fed. Sec. L. Rep. (CCH) ¶ 85,251, at 84,680 n. 15 (1993) (hereinafter "Commission Division Report"):

> When an investment banking transaction becomes "public" (through a filing with the Commission or otherwise), firms will add the issuer's securities to a "restricted" list accessible to personnel throughout the firm. Once this is done, most, if not all, trading by proprietary and employee accounts is prohibited for set time periods. In addition, other firm activities, such as the issuance of research recommendations concerning the issuer's securities, also are severely limited or prohibited for set periods. Because the effects of such restrictions are so wide-ranging, securities are not added to the list until deals are made public. Otherwise, adding a security to this list might send a signal both within and outside the firm that a nonpublic transaction is imminent.

[70] *Id.* at 84,680 n. 14.

> At most firms, the compliance or legal staff maintains a "watch" or "grey" list of securities. A security is added to this list whenever an investment banking engagement is entered into between the broker-dealer and the security's issuer — or in any other instance in which one part of the broker-dealer has received material, nonpublic information concerning the issuer. The compliance or legal staff uses this list to monitor the firm's activities. For example, if a firm employee buys or sells a security on this list, the compliance or legal staff needs to determine if this transaction is indicative of a "breach" of Chinese Wall procedures.

[71] *Id.* at 84,680 n. 16.

> Many firms have implemented a third type of list for use after a securities is added to the watch or grey list but before the security has been added to the restricted list. If compliance or legal personnel determines that the firm's or employees' activities should in some way be limited, the security is placed on this list. For example, just prior to the public announcement of an investment banking transaction, the compliance or legal staff may instruct the firm's market makers to trade the issuer's securities in a "passive" manner, (i.e., by executing only unsolicited customer trades).

[C] Regulatory Treatment of Chinese Walls

Although no definitive answer has emerged from case law regarding the propriety of screening (or Chinese Wall) procedures to limit a broker-dealer's liability to its investor-clients,[72] the SEC expressed its approval for such procedures in the tender offer setting when it adopted Rule 14e-3. Rule 14e-3 provides a safe harbor to that rule's "disclose or abstain" provision for entities that implement certain policies and procedures. With certain exceptions, Rule 14e-3 generally imposes liability on persons who are in possession of material, nonpublic information relating to a tender offer and who purchase or sell (or tip such information relating to) the subject securities, unless the information and its source are publicly disclosed in a timely manner.[73]

The rule provides a safe harbor for entities that would otherwise violate its provisions. This safe harbor covers purchases and sales by nonnatural persons, typically multiservice financial institutions, if the entity can show that the individuals making the investment decision did not know the nonpublic information and that the entity had established policies and procedures, reasonable under the circumstances, to ensure that its individuals would not violate Rule 14e-3. In determining the reasonableness of the policies and procedures, the rule takes into account the nature of the entity's business. Chinese Walls and restricted lists are specifically identified as examples of policies and procedures that may prevent individual decisionmakers from learning or using such inside information.[74]

§ 12.05 Secondary Liability

Principles relating to secondary liability, including liability based on aiding and abetting, control person, and respondeat superior, are discussed in Chapter 9. As discussed earlier, the SEC has express statutory authority to bring enforcement actions against broker-dealers and investment advisers as aiders and abettors.

Another basis for liability relating to SEC enforcement practice is premised on "failure to supervise." In this regard, Section 15(b)(4)(E) of the

---

[72] See, e.g., *Slade v. Shearson, Hammill & Co.*, [1973–1974 Transfer Binder] Fed. Sec. L. Rep. (CCH) ¶ 94,439 (S.D.N.Y.), *remanded*, 517 F.2d 398 (2d Cir. 1974); *Cotton v. Merrill Lynch, Pierce, Fenner & Smith, Inc.*, 699 F. Supp. 251 (N.D. Okla. 1988); discussion in Steinberg & Fletcher, *Compliance Programs for Insider Trading*, 47 SMU L. Rev. 1783, 1806–11 (1994).

[73] The person must know or have reason to know that the information has been acquired directly or indirectly from certain parties involved in the tender offer, including the offering person, the issuer of the target securities, and any persons acting on their behalf. See also SEC Rule 17j-l (requiring registered investment companies to adopt and enforce written codes of ethics, including conflict of interest situations where access persons obtain material nonpublic information).

[74] See SEC Rule 14e-3 Release, *supra* note 58, at 83,461. See generally Bromberg & Lowenfels, *supra* note 36, at § 7.2; D. Langevoort, *Insider Trading: Regulation, Enforcement & Prevention* § 12.02 (1999); W. Wang & M. Steinberg, *Insider Trading* § 13.5 (1996 & 2000 Supp.).

Exchange Act authorizes the SEC to sanction a broker-dealer if such broker-dealer or any of its associated persons fails reasonably to supervise another person who commits certain enumerated securities law violations, if such person is subject to his/her supervision. The statute contains a safe harbor provision, providing a defense if there have been established and implemented adequate procedures that would reasonably be expected to prevent and detect pertinent violations.[75]

---

[75] See 15 U.S.C. § 78o(b)(4)(E). For example, in a release entitled "Supervisory Responsibilities of Broker-Dealer Management," Securities Exchange Act Release No. 8404 (1968), the SEC asserted that the following supervisory functions should be fulfilled:

> (1) The review of the firm's methods of obtaining customers' accounts, including provisions for assuring that adequate information is obtained as to the customers' objectives, needs and finances. (2) The review of customer accounts, including a review for churning and switching of securities in customers' accounts as well as unsuitable recommendations and sales of unregistered securities. (3) The review of methods of recruiting and training of employees, including provisions for assuring that salesmen will not be hired unless the firm can adequately service the business created and maintain an appropriate ratio between sales personnel and back office personnel. . . . (4) The review of back office operations, i.e., all systems and procedures, including the currency and accuracy of books and records, the status and causes of "fails to receive" and "fails to deliver," net capital, credit extensions and financial reports. Attention also should be given to operations that can or should be automated. Prompt delivery of securities to customers and prompt disbursement of customers' funds should be emphasized. . . . (5) The review of sales techniques and methods of salesmen. Specifically, procedures should be used for the review of salesmen's telephone recommendations to customers, sales correspondence with customers, new issue sales, suitability of recommendations and discretionary accounts.

See *In re FSC Securities Corp.*, Securities Exchange Act Release No. 40765 (1998); *SEC v. Prudential Securities*, [1993 Transfer Binder] Fed. Sec. L. Rep. (CCH) ¶ 97,780 (D.D.C. 1993); *In re Gutfreund*, [1992 Transfer Binder] Fed. Sec. L. Rep. (CCH) ¶ 85,067 (SEC 1992); *In re Solomon Brothers, Inc.*, [1991–1992 Transfer Binder] Fed. Sec. L. Rep. (CCH) ¶ 84,948 (SEC 1992). See generally R. Ferrara, D. Rivkin & G. Crespi, *Stockbroker Supervision* (1989); ABA Task Force, *Broker-Dealer Supervision of Registered Representatives and Branch Office Operations*, 44 Bus. Law. 1361 (1989); Ferrara & Sanger, *Derivative Liability in Securities Laws: Controlling Person Liability, Respondeat Superior, and Aiding and Abetting*, 40 Wash. & Lee L. Rev. 1007 (1983); Janvey, *The Feuerstein Report of Investigation: Supervisory Responsibilities of Legal and Compliance Officers of Brokerage Firms*, 21 Sec. Reg. L.J. 166 (1993); Lowenfels & Bromberg, *Broker-Dealer Supervision: A Troublesome Area*, 25 Seton Hall L. Rev. 527 (1994).

Chapter 13

CORPORATE CONTROL ACQUISITIONS AND CONTESTS

§ 13.01 Introduction

This chapter addresses three types of corporate control acquisitions or contests: the proxy battle, the going-private transaction, and the hostile tender offer. Although state common law is very relevant in these contexts, emphasis is placed (due to the subject matter covered in the course) on securities regulation.

In focusing on this chapter, one should keep in mind that hostile proxy and tender offer fights, by their nature, are contests for corporate control. In this way, they are quite similar. As Judge Friendly stated in *Electronic Specialty Company v. International Controls Corp.*:[1]

> [T]ender offers [and] proxy contests . . . are alike in the fundamental feature that they generally are contests. This means that the participants on both sides act, not "in the peace of a quiet chamber," but under the stresses of the marketplace. They act quickly, sometimes impulsively, often in angry response to what they consider, whether rightly or wrongly, to be low blows by the other side. Probably there will no more be a perfect tender offer than a perfect trial. Congress intended to assure basic honesty and fair dealing, not to impose an unrealistic requirement of laboratory conditions that might make the new statute a potent tool for incompetent management to protect its own interests against the desires and welfare of the stockholders. These considerations bear on the kind of judgment to be applied in testing conduct — on both sides — and also on the issue of materiality.[2]

§ 13.02 Going-Private Transactions

Generally, "[a] going-private transaction is a transaction or series of transactions instituted by the controlling shareholders of a publicly-held corporation and designed to eliminate or substantially reduce the corporation's outstanding equity, thereby returning the corporation to private ownership."[3] Generally, these transactions often take the form of a cash-out (or more pejoratively "freeze-out" or "squeeze-out") merger and result in compelling the minority stockholders to exchange their shares for cash.[4]

---

[1] 409 F.2d 937 (2d Cir. 1969).

[2] *Id.* at 948.

[3] Comment, *Regulating Going-Private Transactions: SEC Rule 13e-3*, 80 Colum. L. Rev. 782 (1980).

[4] *Id.* See generally A. Borden, *Going Private* (1989).

[A] State Law

In *Singer v. Magnavox Co.*,[5] the Delaware Supreme Court held that, in order to adhere to a controlling shareholder's fiduciary duties to the subsidiary corporation and its minority shareholders, a cash-out merger must have a proper business purpose and must be entirely fair to the minority. A number of states adhere to the *Singer* standards.[6] The Delaware high court itself, however, in *Weinberger v. UOP, Inc.*,[7] abandoned the business purpose test and confined its inquiry to the "entire fairness" standard. In so doing, the court formulated a more liberal approach to valuation, permitting such elements as premiums over market price offered in similar transactions and future earnings potential (so long as not speculative) to be considered. The *Weinberger* court's approach facilitates mergers and normally relegates a minority shareholder to the appraisal remedy. However, as stated by that court, "[t]he appraisal remedy we approve may not be adequate in certain cases, particularly where fraud, misrepresentation, self-dealing, deliberate waste of corporate assets, or gross and palpable overreaching are involved."[8] In such cases, injunctive relief may be awarded prior to the merger's consummation and breach of fiduciary duty actions seeking monetary damages may be invoked after the transaction has been accomplished (and cannot be "undone").[9]

It should be pointed out that a number of states do not follow *Singer* or *Weinberger*. For example, in some states, absent fraud or illegality, appraisal is a minority shareholder's sole remedy in a cash-out merger.[10] A few states accomplish this result by statute. A Minnesota statute, for instance, provides that corporations may merge "with or without a business purpose" and that the remedy for lack of "entire fairness" is appraisal.[11]

In leveraged buy-outs where incumbent management takes a substantial equity position in the surviving entity, it appears that the *Revlon* principles[12] frequently will apply.[13] Unlike cash-out mergers, leveraged buy-outs enable incumbent managements to put up little cash of their own and, through the use of borrowed funds collateralized by corporate assets (the repayment of such funds to be made by means of future revenues or the sale of certain assets), eliminate the public shareholders and gain for themselves a substantial equity position. Critics view such transactions as implicating inherent conflicts of interest, calling for the application of

---

[5] 380 A.2d 969 (Del. 1977).

[6] See, e.g., *Alpert v. 28 Williams St. Corp.*, 63 N.Y. 2d 557, 473 N.E. 2d 19, 483 N.Y.S. 2d 667 (1984); *Perl v. IU Int'l Corp.*, 61 Hw. 622, 607 P.2d 1036 (1980).

[7] 457 A.2d 701 (Del. 1983).

[8] *Id.* at 714.

[9] *Id.* See Weiss, *Balancing Interests in Cash-Out Mergers: The Promise of Weinberger v. UOP, Inc.*, 8 Del. J. Corp. L. 1 (1983).

[10] See, e.g., *Steinberg v. Amplica, Inc.*, 42 Cal. 3d 1198, 233 Cal. Rptr. 249, 729 P.2d 683 (1986); *Yanow v. Teal Industries, Inc.*, 178 Conn. 262, 422 A.2d 311 (1979).

[11] Minn. Stat. Ann. § 302A.601.

[12] The *Revlon* principles are discussed in § 13.09[B] *infra*.

[13] See, e.g., *MacAndrews & Forbes Holdings v. Revlon, Inc.*, 506 A.2d 173 (Del. 1986).

heightened fiduciary duty standards. Given the conflicts of interest and potential for abuse present, leveraged buy-out proposals benefitting incumbent management should be left open for a substantial period of time in order to enable unaffiliated third parties to make competing bids, thereby effectuating the "auction" process.[14]

[B] Federal Law

In addition to Section 10(b) of the Exchange Act, Section 13e-3 and 13e-4 of the Exchange Act and the SEC rules promulgated thereunder (Rules 13e-3 and 13e-4) are the principal federal securities law provisions governing going-private transactions. Rule 13e-3 is a comprehensive rule that prohibits fraudulent, deceptive, or manipulative practices in connection with going private transactions and sets forth filing, disclosure, and dissemination requirements.[15] Rule 13e-4 is narrower in scope and applies to an issuer's tender offer for its own securities ("self tenders"). It, like Rule 13e-3, is an antifraud provision and mandates extensive disclosure.[16] Moreover, the same procedural requirements that apply in third-party tender offers pursuant to Section 14(d) generally are extended by Rule 13e-4 to issuer self tenders.[17] Note that an issuer self tender that comes under Rule 13e-4 also may be a going-private transaction within Rule 13e-3's reach. Under such circumstances, both Rule 13e-3 and Rule 13e-4 apply.[18]

Rule 13e-3 calls for subject parties to disclose extensive information with respect to a going-private transaction by filing a Schedule 13E-3 with the SEC. The disclosures include: (1) a description of both the benefits and detriments of the transaction to the issuer as well as to affiliated and unaffiliated shareholders; (2) disclosure of any report, opinion, or appraisal received from an outside party concerning the going-private transaction; (3) disclosure of any plans by the issuer to merge, reorganize, sell assets or make any other material change after the transaction; (4) disclosure of the source and total amount of funds for the transaction, an estimation of anticipated expenses, a summary of any loan agreements, and arrangements to finance and repay loans; and (5) disclosure of whether the subject parties reasonably believe that the transaction is fair to unaffiliated stockholders and the factors upon which they have that belief.[19]

As to the last disclosure listed above, some commentators assert that, by requiring that the subject parties disclose whether they "reasonably

---

[14] Id. See DeMott, *Directors' Duties in Management Buyouts and Leveraged Recapitalizations*, 49 Ohio St. L.J. 517 (1988); Lowenstein, *Management Buyouts*, 85 Colum. L. Rev. 730 (1985); Morrissey, *Law, Ethics and the Leveraged Buyout*, 65 U. Det. L. Rev. 403 (1988); Steinberg & Lindahl, *The New Law of Squeeze-Out Mergers*, 62 Wash. U. L.Q. 351 (1984).

[15] See Securities Exchange Act Release No. 16075 (1979).

[16] See Securities Exchange Act Release No. 16112 (1979). See also, Securities Exchange Act Release No. 42055 (1999).

[17] See [1985–1986 Transfer Binder] Fed. Sec. L. Rep. (CCH) ¶ 83,954 (SEC 1986).

[18] Securities Exchange Act Release No. 16112 (1979). See Manges, *SEC Regulation of Issuer and Third-Party Tender Offers*, 8 Sec. Reg. L.J. 275 (1981).

[19] Schedule 13E-3, 17 C.F.R. § 240.13e-100. *See Howing Co. v. Nationwide Corp.*, 826 F.2d 1470 (6th Cir. 1987), 927 F.2d 263 (6th Cir. 1991), 972 F.2d 700 (6th Cir. 1992).

believe" that the going-private transaction is fair, the SEC is engaging in impermissible substantive regulation.[20] In this respect, the Supreme Court's decision in *Schreiber* (discussed in § 13.09[A]) is relevant.[21] There, the Supreme Court held that Section 14(e) of the Exchange Act is premised on the truthful disclosure of adequate information rather than on the substantive fairness of the transaction. Because both Sections 13(e) and 14(e) were enacted as part of the Williams Act in 1968 (as an amendment to the Exchange Act) and contain in part similar language, the assertion that Rule 13e-3's "disclosure of fairness" provision is invalid may have an even stronger basis today. Nonetheless, an argument can be made that, in prescribing this requirement, the Commission has focused on its disclosure function rather than engaging principally in substantive regulation.[22] Note, moreover, that minority shareholders, provided they can show a material misrepresentation or nondisclosure along with the loss of an otherwise available state remedy in connection with the going private transaction, often can avail themselves of the Section 10(b) or Section 14(a) right of action.[23]

§ 13.03 Proxy Contests

Under federal law, proxy contests principally are governed by Section 14(a) of the Exchange Act and SEC rules prescribed thereunder. In this regard, the legal standards underlying a private right of action under Section 14(a) are addressed in § 8.05. That discussion should be reviewed at this point.

Until relatively recently, it generally was thought that the tender offer had replaced the proxy battle as the means for procuring corporate control or effecting a change in corporate policies. "This situation was attributed to the difficulty of ousting an incumbent management (unless it was demonstrably incompetent and the insurgents had a large stock position), the significant amount of money and time consumed by a proxy fight, and the impossibility of recouping proxy fight costs if the insurgents failed to take control."[24] To a degree, however, the proxy fight has seen a partial renaissance. While this renaissance arguably may be more in response to market conditions than to regulatory developments, it also reflects changes in the regulatory context. Indeed, with the proliferation of state takeover statutes, SEC tender offer regulations, and court battles, the costs of pursuing a hostile tender offer can be exorbitant (e.g., costs of acquiring

---

[20] See, e.g., Note, *Rule 13e-3 and the Going-Private Dilemma: The SEC's Quest for a Substantive Fairness Doctrine*, 58 Wash. U. L.Q. 883 (1980).

[21] 472 U.S. 1 (1985). *Schreiber* is discussed in § 13.09[A] *infra*.

[22] See generally Kofele-Kale, *The SEC's Going-Private Rules: Analysis and Developments*, 19 Sec. Reg. L.J. 139 (1991).

[23] See *Virginia Bankshares, Inc. v. Sandberg*, 501 U.S. 1083 (1991); *Wilson v. Great American Industries, Inc.*, 979 F.2d 924 (2d Cir. 1992); discussion §§ 7.05[B], 8.05[B] *supra*.

[24] Brown, *Changes in Offeror Strategy in Response to New Laws and Regulations*, 25 Case West. Res. L. Rev. 843, 865–66 (1978).

a controlling interest, attorney and investment banker fees, and, depending upon market conditions, high interest rates).[25]

Nonetheless, proxy contests normally are viable today when economic benefits accrue to the shareholders. A number of these battles have had as the insurgents' main objective the sale or liquidation of certain assets of the corporation, particularly where the company's stock was trading at what was viewed as an unreasonably low price. The proceeds from the sale of such assets then may be passed onto the shareholders as a cash distribution. More recently, insurgents have engaged in proxy contests to effectuate their takeover bids — the proxy contest being used as a means to successfully consummate an unsolicited tender offer.

Given the "hurly-burly" of proxy contests, courts generally apply a standard of fair accuracy.[26] "[N]it-picking should not become the name of the game."[27] Nonetheless, as discussed in Chapter 8, an implied private right of action exists to redress violations of Section 14(a), particularly where materially false or misleading statements have been made.[28]

Section 14(a) of the Exchange Act and SEC rules promulgated thereunder regulate the solicitation of proxies in regard to securities registered under Section 12 of the 1934 Act. These rules, contained in Regulation 14A, prescribe certain filing, dissemination, disclosure and substantive requirements with respect to proxy solicitations. Significantly, Rule 14a-12 authorizes the participants to make both oral and written communications to shareholders prior to the filing of a proxy statement, provided that: all such written communications are filed with the SEC on the date of their first use; no form of proxy is provided to shareholders; shareholders are advised of the identity of the participants in the solicitation and provided with a description of such participants' interests or are informed where to locate such information; and shareholders are advised to read the proxy statement prior to voting. Hence, although communications may be made prior to the filing of a proxy statement, no proxies may be sought before a proxy statement required by Rule 14a-3 is furnished. In addition, the antifraud provisions of Rule 14a-9 apply in this setting.[29]

---

[25] See generally Bainbridge, *Redirecting State Takeover Laws at Proxy Contests*, 1992 Wisc. L. Rev. 1071; Bebchuck & Kahan, *A Framework for Analyzing Legal Policy Towards Proxy Contests*, 78 Calif. L. Rev. 1071 (1990).

[26] See *General Time Corporation v. Talley Industries, Inc.*, 403 F.2d 159, 162 (2d Cir. 1968).

[27] *Kennecott Copper Corp. v. Curtiss-Wright Corp.*, 584 F.2d 1195, 1200 (2d Cir. 1978).

[28] See § 8.05[A] *supra*.

[29] See 17 C.F.R. § 240.14a-12; Securities Exchange Act Release No. 42055 (1999). See generally, R. Thomas & C. Dixon, *Aranow & Einhorn on Proxy Contests for Corporate Control* (3d ed. 1998); M. Waters, *Proxy Regulation* (1992); Fisch, *From Legitimacy to Logic: Reconstructing Proxy Regulation*, 46 Vand. L. Rev. 1129 (1993); Steinberg, *Fiduciary Duties and Disclosure Obligations in Proxy and Tender Contests for Corporate Control*, 30 Emory L.J. 169 (1981); sources cited note 25 *supra*.

§ 13.04   A Primer on the Williams Act

[A]   Introduction

By the mid-1960's the frequency of cash tender offers had risen to levels that made many people uncomfortable. This discomfort was felt from the corridors of the SEC, where secret corporate control transactions that had somehow slipped between the regulatory cracks were viewed with great suspicion, to the boardrooms of many of the nation's corporations, where fear of being swallowed up by corporate raiders was spreading. The rate of tender offers, although small when compared to today's world of merger mania, had increased from 8, involving $200 million in 1960, to 107, involving $1 billion by 1966.[30]

There were many reasons for this takeover boom, not the least of which was a thriving economy that had left many corporations cash-rich and looking for investments. The perfect vehicle for investment in many cases proved to be the cash tender offer; there was little regulation compared to other control transaction devices (such as public exchange offers and proxy contests); and, results could be achieved swiftly and often with little resistance from the surprised incumbent managements.

Some viewed these new developments as a natural consequence of a pent-up economy that was showing signs of growth. Indeed, many saw the movement as a healthy signal of a mature, capitalist economy that promoted competition between managements as well as between products. In this kind of economy, most inefficient managements would gradually give way to those best able to accumulate and distribute earned profits to shareholders. Others were not quite as optimistic and feared that once-proud companies were falling prey to larger corporate raiders that would all too frequently victimize the smaller companies. In the process, shareholders, who had little understanding of these corporate maneuvers, would suffer.

The Williams Act of 1968,[31] which amended the Securities Exchange Act of 1934, was the legislative attempt at accommodating both of these viewpoints. The Act required offerors to disclose information that was material to a shareholder's decision whether to tender his/her shares, while, at the same time, not imposing too stringent regulations that would impede the efficacy of the cash tender offer vehicle.

The Williams Act, as adopted, was the ultimate product of the dialogue engendered by congressional proposals. The first attempt at legislation in this area came in 1965 when Senator Harrison Williams of New Jersey introduced S. 2731. Stories of giant corporate raiders swallowing or gutting small proud companies upset many members of Congress, particularly since this situation was due, at least in part, to a loophole in the securities laws.

Before the Williams Act's passage, an offeror could avoid federal filing, dissemination, and disclosure obligations by procuring control through a

---

[30] 113 Cong. Rec. S. 24,664 (daily ed. Aug. 30, 1967) (statement of Senator Williams).
[31] S. 510, Pub. L. 90-439, 82 Stat. 454 (1968).

cash tender offer.[32] Corporations and individuals took advantage of another disclosure loophole by buying up shares of an acquisition prospect in the open market until they had gained control or had acquired a substantial percentage of the company's stock. This could be accomplished swiftly and secretly without the attendant regulation that accompanied other merger vehicles such as the public exchange offer or the proxy contest.[33]

Although the philosophy of the proposed 1965 legislation was attractive to some members, hearings were never held and the bill died. One reason for that bill's failure was the feeling that it was too favorable to the incumbents in a tender offer contest, and, hence, would stifle economically beneficial corporate combinations. For example, one provision of the bill would have required a bidder to give incumbent management twenty days notice of its intention to commence a tender offer. Many felt that this kind of notice would have effectively eliminated hostile cash tender offers by allowing incumbent managements more time to implement various defensive tactics, thereby causing the defeat of hostile takeover bids.[34]

By 1967 proponents had refined their proposals. The major advocates for the legislation were the SEC and a coalition of corporate leaders who feared that, without some regulation, a detrimental tender offer fever would sweep the country, causing great harm to the American economy. These strange bedfellows provided a rather broad base of support for S. 510.

[B] Legislation

The legislation, as enacted in 1968, added Sections 13(d), (e), and 14(d), (e), and (f) to the Exchange Act. Many of the tender offer provisions in the Act are set forth in Section 14(d). That section principally contains disclosure mandates and provisions designed to give shareholders sufficient time in a noncoercive setting to make informed investment decisions. A number of these provisions have been modified by the SEC pursuant to its rulemaking powers.[35] Section 14(e) is a broad antifraud provision that makes it unlawful for any person to make false or misleading statements of material fact, or to engage in fraudulent, deceptive or manipulative acts or practices in connection with a tender offer. In 1970, Congress amended Section 14(e) to give the SEC broad rulemaking authority under that statute.

Some of the procedural provisions evidently did not provoke much debate. For example, Section 14(d)(5) allows a shareholder to withdraw his/her tendered shares within seven days after the offer commences and after sixty days following the commencement of the offer. This provision now has been expanded by SEC Rule 14d-7 to permit a shareholder to withdraw the

---

[32] See *Piper v. Chris-Craft Industries, Inc.*, 430 U.S. 1, 22 (1977); R. Clark, *Corporate Law* § 13.3 (1986).

[33] See Cohen, *A Note on Takeover Bids and Corporate Purchases of Stock*, 22 Bus. Law. 149 (1966).

[34] See discussion in Brudney, *A Note on Chilling Tender Solicitations*, 21 Rutgers L. Rev. 609 (1967).

[35] See discussion in § 13.08 *infra*.

shares tendered during the entire period that the offer remains open.[36] This withdrawal right changes the pre-Williams Act irrevocability of tendered shares, thereby enabling the shareholder to withdraw his/her shares and not be indefinitely held to a decision to tender that is not in one's best interest. Moreover, Section 14(d)(6) softens the "stampede" effect of coercing shareholders to rapidly tender their stock in first-come first-serve offers by providing for a pro rata purchase of all shares tendered within ten days of the initial offer. As with the withdrawal right, the SEC pursuant to Rule 14d-8 has expanded this right to proration to encompass the entire offering period.[37]

The disclosure provisions of Sections 13(d)(1) and 14(d)(1) are what apparently caused the greatest stir in Congress and among the academics. Section 13(d)(1) requires disclosure within ten days from any person (or group) who becomes the direct, indirect, or beneficial owner of five percent of a company's outstanding stock. This post-transaction filing requirement is principally directed at providing notice to the marketplace where a potential shift in corporate control may take place.[38] Section 14(d)(1) governs the cash tender offer and mandates the filing by an offeror of essentially the same information as required by Section 13(d)(1). These disclosures include:

(1)   the background and identity of the offeror;

(2)   the source and amount of funds used;

(3)   the purpose of the contemplated purchases;

(4)   the number of shares owned;

(5)   information regarding any special arrangements involving the offer; and

(6)   such additional information as the SEC may prescribe.[39]

A fundamental purpose of these disclosures is to protect shareholders from having to make hasty and uninformed decisions on whether or not it would be in their best interests to tender their shares for the offered price. Critics, on the other hand, believe that the information required to be disclosed is largely irrelevant to the shareholder's decision and that by, forcing disclosure, the economic incentive to embark on a takeover bid is needlessly impaired.[40]

Nonetheless, Section 13(d) has a significant loophole. Because the disclosures required by Section 13(d) need not be made until ten days after attaining five percent ownership, additional purchases may be made during

---

[36] 17 C.F.R. § 240.14d-7. Note, however, that Rule 14d-11 allows a bidder to have a subsequent offering period without withdrawal rights immediately after the offer's termination. See discussion § 13.08 *infra*.

[37] 17 C.F.R. § 240.14d-8. See Bloomenthal, *The New Tender Offer Regimen, State Regulation and Preemption*, 30 Emory L.J. 35 (1981).

[38] See *Treadway Companies, Inc., v. Care Corp.*, 638 F.2d 357, 380 (2d Cir. 1980).

[39] 17 C.F.R. §§ 240.13(d)(1), 240.14(d)(1).

[40] See generally Brudney, *supra* note 34, at 617–20.

this period so long as they do not constitute a "tender offer." This ten-day "window" permits potential acquirors to enhance their ownership level well beyond that contemplated by Congress through means of open market purchases and privately negotiated transactions. In this regard, however, the mandates of the Hart-Scott-Rodino Antitrust Improvements Act of 1976 in many situations will limit such purchases. [41]

Another provision of the Williams Act, Section 14(e), is designed to protect shareholders from fraud, deception and manipulation in connection with tender offers. Prior to enactment of this legislation, shareholders had to rely on the reach of Section 10(b), which is directed at preventing such practices in connection with the purchase or sale of any security. The problem is that Section 10(b) does not reach far enough due to at least two reasons: (1) generally, in cases of nondisclosure (i.e., silence), the statute is deemed not to be applicable unless there is a duty to disclose, [42] and (2) there must be a purchase or sale to trigger the statute's application. [43] In the pre-Williams Act era, therefore, unless a tender offer actually commenced and shares were purchased or sold, there was presumably no effective federal remedy for the SEC and private parties to invoke. Moreover, disclosure was not generally required until the offeror became a controlling shareholder with all the fiduciary duties that came with that status or unless the insurgent was receiving material nonpublic information derived from a corporate source. [44] Thus, Section 14(e) filled the need for legislation in this area and gave further substance to the disclosure requirements under Section 14(d).

As enacted, the legislation was designed to protect the valid interests of the target corporation's stockholders and to enable both the bidder and target managements to present their positions to the stockholders. [45] The neutral position taken by the Act was emphasized by its primary sponsor, Senator Williams: "We have taken extreme care to avoid tipping the scales either in favor of management or in favor of the person making the takeover bid." [46] Hence, the even-handed disclosure approach of the Act was adopted in an attempt to ensure that target corporation shareholders had sufficient

---

[41] See discussion § 13.07 *infra*.

[42] See *Chiarella v. United States*, 445 U.S. 222 (1980). See also, Note, *The Regulation of Corporate Tender Offers Under Federal Securities Law: A New Challenge for Rule 10b-5*, 33 U. Chicago L. Rev. 359, 373 (1966).

[43] See *Blue Chip Stamps v. Manor Drug Stores*, 421 U.S. 723 (1975).

[44] See *SEC v. Texas Gulf Sulphur Co.*, 401 F.2d 833 (2d Cir. 1968) (en banc); *Diamond v. Oreamuno*, 24 N.Y. 2d 494, 248 N.E. 2d 910 (1969).

[45] See House Comm. on Interstate and Foreign Commerce, Disclosure of Corporate Equity Ownership, H.R. Rep. No. 1711, 90th Cong., 2d Sess. 4, *reprinted in*, 1968 U.S. Code Cong. & Ad. News 2811, 2813; Senate Comm. on Banking and Currency, Full Disclosure of Corporate Equity Ownership and in Corporate Takeover Bids, S. Rep. No. 550, 90th Cong., 1st Sess. 3 (1967).

[46] 113 Cong. Rec. 24664 (1967).

information, and the time necessary, to make informed uncoerced invest-ment decisions.[47]

[C] Debate

The advocates of the legislation insisted that the disclosure provisions of the Williams Act were absolutely essential for protection of sharehold-ers.[48] Critics, on the other hand, were convinced that the disclosure provisions were irrelevant to a shareholder's decision to tender his/her shares. They viewed with cynicism the motives of the proponents seeking legisla-tion, arguing that the primary beneficiaries of the disclosure provisions were the potential target managements, not the shareholders.[49] As for the SEC, its interests were shareholder protection and maintaining the integ-rity of the securities markets. Irrespective of such warranted SEC concerns, critics felt that the requirement of disclosure was unnecessary in light of the dampening effect it would have on the efficient combinations of busi-nesses.[50] The ultimate issue therefore is whether the disclosure provisions designed to protect shareholders and the securities markets justify the alleged discouragement of business combinations.

Generally, critics took exception to the disclosure provisions for three alleged reasons: First, as mentioned above, the disclosure required was asserted to be irrelevant to a shareholder's decision on whether to tender the shares. Second, the legislation, at least in part, confused a free market philosophy with that of a distribution of wealth philosophy. And third, the practical effects of the legislation would destroy the climate for efficient business combinations.[51]

To the proponents, the disadvantages of the legislation were overwhelm-ingly outweighed by the advantages that would be gained from it. As one Senator put it, "[d]espite the sneers of a few cynics back in 1934, full disclosure has provided a strong stimulus to the American investor. Now is the time to eliminate the few areas where full disclosure is not avail-able."[52] In other words, the protection of shareholders and the integrity of the market as a whole outweighed any dampening effect on the efficient combinations of businesses.

Despite the controversy stirred, there was in fact relatively little opposi-tion to the bill once it reached the floor of both Houses. In fact, it passed both the House and the Senate on a voice vote.[53] There may be a number

---

[47] See Statement by Senator Kuchel, Full Disclosure of Corporate Ownership and in Corpo-rate Takeover Bids: Hearings on S. 510 Before the Senate Subcomm. on Securities of the Comm. on Banking and Currency, 90th Cong., 1st Sess. 46 (1967); sources cited in notes 45–46 *supra*.

[48] See Cohen, *supra* note 33, at 156–57.

[49] See Manne, *Cash Tender Offers for Shares — A Reply to Chairman Cohen*, 1967 Duke L.J. 231 (1967).

[50] *Id*. at 245.

[51] *Id*. at 245–53. See also, Brudney, *supra* note 34, at 616–41.

[52] 111 Cong. Rec. S. 28,260 (daily ed. Oct. 22, 1965) (Statement of Senator Williams).

[53] S. 510, 90th Cong., 2d Sess., 114 Cong. Rec. H. 21,484 (daily ed. July 15, 1968) and 114 Cong. Rec. S. 21,954 (daily ed. July 18, 1968).

of explanations accounting for this development. First, there was a broad consensus between the SEC and the corporate sector, which gave great impetus to the legislation. Second, the legislation was politically feasible to support since it was ostensibly aimed at protecting the securities markets and innocent shareholders of large publicly-held corporations. Also, as contrasted with today's attitudes, tender offers were viewed by many somehow as a sneaky, "ungentlemanly" way to conduct corporate transactions. Hence, the Williams Act's approach based on full disclosure, with no side purportedly having an unfair advantage over the other and the shareholder being the ultimate beneficiary, merited support.

§ 13.05　Definition of Tender Offer

The conventional tender offer generally is easily identified. Its characteristics frequently are a publicized bid to purchase shares of stock at a premium over market price made directly to the target corporation's shareholders with certain conditions attached, frequently including a time limit for the duration of the offer, financing contingencies, and a quantity limit on the total number of shares that the bidder is willing to acquire.[54] Tender offers, however, also may be unconventional. One such unconventional tender offer, for example, involved a bid made to approximately thirty sophisticated investors who owned 34% of the outstanding stock. Solicitors acting on behalf of the bidder followed a prearranged script, offered a premium over market price with no room for negotiation, and left the offer open for a short time period. Applying an eight-factor analysis discussed below, the court held that the solicitations constituted a tender offer under the Williams Act.[55]

The significance of the above holding is that conventional as well as unconventional tender offers trigger application of the Williams Act's regulatory framework. Unconventional tender offers are unlikely to satisfy the requirements of Section 14(d) and SEC rules thereunder, such as the twenty-business-day time period within which an offer remains open and the right of shareholders during the offer to withdraw their shares tendered. Moreover, an offeror must file a Schedule TO providing detailed disclosures.[56]

The unconventional tender offer today is a rare occurrence. That is because courts hold that (1) open market purchases on a stock exchange or in the over-the-counter market,[57] as well as (2) privately negotiated transactions between an acquiror and sophisticated investors,[58] normally do not constitute a tender offer. In making this determination, a number of courts apply the following eight-factor test:

---

[54] See *Hanson Trust PLC v. SCM Corporation*, 774 F.2d 47, 54–55 (2d Cir. 1985).

[55] *Wellman v. Dickinson*, 475 F. Supp. 783 (S.D.N.Y. 1979), *aff'd on other grounds*, 682 F.2d 355 (2d Cir. 1982).

[56] See § 13.08 *infra* for further discussion on the SEC's tender offer rules.

[57] See, e.g., *SEC v. Carter Hawley Hale Stores, Inc.*, 760 F.2d 945 (9th Cir. 1985).

[58] See, e.g., *Brascan Ltd. v. Edper Equities, Ltd.*, 477 F. Supp. 773 (S.D.N.Y. 1979).

(1) active and widespread solicitation of public shareholders for the shares of an issuer;

(2) solicitation made for a substantial percentage of the issuer's stock;

(3) offer to purchase made at a premium over the prevailing market price;

(4) terms of the offer are firm rather than negotiable;

(5) offer contingent on the tender of a fixed number of shares, often subject to a fixed maximum number to be purchased;

(6) offer open only for a limited period of time;

(7) offeree subjected to pressure to sell the stock;

(8) public announcements of a purchasing program concerning the target company precede or accompany rapid accumulation of large amounts of the target company's securities.[59]

The eight-factor test, although flexible, is uncertain in its application. In any given situation, solicitations may constitute a tender offer even though some of the eight factors are not satisfied. Conversely, a tender offer may not exist even though many of the factors are present. Hence, the eight-factor test is akin to an ad hoc balancing test in which the various factors are weighed.[60]

Due to the uncertainty of the above standard, the Second Circuit has adopted a different formulation. In *Hanson Trust PLC v. SCM Corporation*,[61] a corporation withdrew its tender offer after being confronted with a competing offer and with tactics engaged in by target management favoring the "white knight." After terminating its offer, the corporation, engaging in what is called a "market sweep," purchased shares from five arbitrageurs constituting about 25% of the target's stock. In ascertaining whether these solicitations were a tender offer, the court reasoned:

> [S]ince the purpose of § 14(d) is to protect the ill-informed solicitee, the question of whether a solicitation constitutes a "tender offer" within the meaning of § 14(d) turns on whether, viewing the transaction in the light of the totality of circumstances, there appears to be a likelihood that unless the pre-acquisition filing strictures of that statute are followed, there will be a substantial risk that solicitees will lack information needed to make a carefully considered appraisal of the proposal put before them.[62]

Looking at such factors as the small number of solicitees and the solicitees' high level of financial acumen, the Second Circuit held that a tender offer had not been made.[63]

---

[59] See *SEC v. Carter Hawley Hale Stores, Inc.*, 760 F.2d 945, 950 (9th Cir. 1985).

[60] See *id.* at 950–52.

[61] 774 F.2d 47 (2d Cir. 1985).

[62] *Id.* at 57.

[63] *Id.* at 57–58.

Critics assert that the Second Circuit's decision in *Hanson Trust* provides a means by which an acquiror can "sidestep" the Williams Act and SEC regulations thereunder. The Wall Street Journal evidently believed this to be the case and reacted favorably to this perceived development. In an editorial entitled "A Happy Jig," the Journal applauded the *Hanson Trust* decision as signaling the emergence of a "new deregulated takeover market" in which acquirors would no longer "hav[e] to worry about the costs and delays of securities regulations," hence resulting in "more simplified takeovers — and more profits for shareholders."[64] On the other hand, although full disclosure certainly is the principal objective of the Williams Act, it may be asserted that another purpose is to ensure the evenhanded treatment of all shareholders, including the small unsophisticated shareholder. "Market sweeps" discriminate against the ordinary investor and, arguably, should not be permitted.

In 1983, the SEC established an Advisory Committee on Tender Offers. After conducting a series of meetings, the Advisory Committee issued its Report, consisting of fifty recommendations. Most pertinent for our purposes here, Recommendation 14 provided:

> No person may acquire voting securities of an issuer, if, immediately following such acquisitions, such person would own more than 20% of the voting power of the outstanding voting securities of that issuer unless such purchases were made (i) from the issuer or (ii) pursuant to a tender offer. The Commission should retain broad exemptive power with respect to this provision.[65]

Moreover, in an apparent but not vigorous effort to restrain the use of market sweeps, the Commission in 1987 proposed Rule 14d-11. That proposal, which was not adopted by the SEC, would have imposed a cooling-off period for the purchase of a target's stock upon a party who has withdrawn a tender offer.[66]

§ 13.06 Constitutionality of State Takeover Statutes

In *Edgar v. MITE*,[67] the Supreme Court, in an opinion written by Justice White, declared the Illinois Business Takeover Act unconstitutional on interstate commerce grounds, reasoning that the burdens imposed on interstate commerce by the Act were excessive in relation to the local interests served. Another portion of Justice White's opinion, not joined in by the

---

[64] Editorial, "A Happy Jig," *Wall St. J.*, Oct. 7, 1985.

[65] See Advisory Committee on Tender Offers, U.S. SEC, Report of Recommendations (1983). See generally Quinn & Martin, *The SEC Advisory Committee on Tender Offers and Its Aftermath — A New Chapter in Change-of-Control Regulation*, contained in, *Tender Offers: Developments and Commentaries* at 9 (M. Steinberg ed. 1985).

[66] See Securities Exchange Act Release No. 24976 (1987). See generally Tyson, *The Williams Act After Hanson Trust v. SCM Corporation: Post-Tender Offer Purchases by the Tender Offeror*, 61 Tulane L. Rev. 1 (1986).

[67] 457 U.S. 624 (1982).

majority of the Court, asserted that the Illinois Act was unconstitutional under the Supremacy Clause.[68]

In the aftermath of the Supreme Court's decision in *MITE*, several state statutes, having provisions similar to the Illinois Act, were declared unconstitutional by the lower federal courts. Cognizant of the constitutional infirmities of their takeover statutes, several states responded by enacting "second generation" statutes which sought to pass constitutional scrutiny.[69]

[A] The *CTS* Decision

In *CTS Corp. v. Dynamics Corp. of America*,[70] the Supreme Court upheld one version of the second-generation statutes. There, the Court held that the Control Share Acquisitions Chapter of the Indiana Business Corporation Law[71] does not violate the Constitution on either preemption or interstate commerce grounds. In brief, the Indiana statute, which applies to corporations chartered in Indiana and which have certain other connections with that state, focuses on the acquisition of "control shares" in such a corporation. Under the Act, a control share acquisition is one which, but for the operation of the Act, would raise the purchaser's voting power to or above any of three thresholds: (1) one-fifth and less than one-third, (2) one-third and less than a majority, or (3) above a majority. When a control share transaction occurs, the acquiring entity does not have voting rights with respect to those shares unless a majority of the disinterested shares[72] entitled to vote approves the transaction. Such vote must take place within fifty days if the acquiring entity so requests.[73]

Even though the fifty day period of the Indiana statute exceeds the minimum twenty business day period that a tender offer must remain open under the Williams Act, the Supreme Court stated that this extra delay was permissible. Only unreasonable delays, the Court asserted, are unconstitutional. Moreover, to preempt the Indiana Act, the Court felt, would bring into question the constitutionality of a wide variety of state corporate laws of hitherto unquestioned validity. Such statutes include permitting corporations to have cumulative voting and the staggering of director terms, which, like the Indiana statute, may delay or limit the exercise of control by a successful bidder. Hence, the Court concluded:

> In our view, the possibility that the Indiana Act will delay some
> tender offers is insufficient to require a conclusion that the Williams

---

[68] *Id.* at 630–40. See generally, Sargent, *On the Validity of State Takeover Regulation: State Responses to MITE and Kidwell*, 42 Ohio St. L.J. 689 (1981).

[69] See Romano, *The Political Economy of Takeover Statutes*, 73 Va. L. Rev. 111 (1987); discussion § 13.06[A] *infra*.

[70] 481 U.S. 69 (1987).

[71] Ind. Code § 23-1-42-1 to 23-1-42-11.

[72] "Interested shares" are those beneficially controlled by the entity acquiring the corporation, an officer or an inside director of the subject corporation. *Id.* § 23-1-42-3.

[73] *Id.* § 23-1-42-7. Such a request must be made when the acquiror files an "acquiring person statement" with the corporation. The expenses of the meeting are to be paid by the acquiring person. *Id.* For further details of the Indiana Act, see 481 U.S. at 72–75.

Act pre-empts the [Indiana] Act. The longstanding prevalence of state regulation in this area suggests that, if Congress had intended to preempt all State laws that delay the acquisition of voting control following a tender offer, it would have said so explicitly.[74]

Likewise, the *CTS* Court found that the Indiana statute does not offend the Commerce Clause. Upon examination, the Indiana Act neither discriminates against interstate commerce nor does it create an impermissible risk of inconsistent regulation by the various states. As a basis for its holding, the Court relied on the premise that a state's authority to regulate domestic corporations is a fundamental precept of corporate law. In its role as regulator of corporate governance, a state has an interest in facilitating stable relationships among the participants in its domestic corporations. Applying these principles, the Court stated:

> The primary purpose of the [Indiana] Act is to protect the shareholders of Indiana corporations. It does this by affording shareholders, when a takeover offer is made, an opportunity to decide collectively whether the resulting change in voting control of the corporation, as they perceive it, would be desirable. A change of management may have important effects on the shareholders' interest; it is well within the State's role as overseer of corporate governance to offer this opportunity.[75]

[B]   The "Third-Generation" Statutes

After *CTS*, a number of different types of state "anti-takeover" statutes exist. These statutes, many of which have been upheld as constitutional,[76] play an integral role in the takeover process. Significantly, unlike the Illinois statute declared unconstitutional in *MITE*, these third-generation statutes do not directly impact upon an offeror making a tender offer for all shares outstanding. Nonetheless, aspects of these statutes may deter prospective offerors from engaging in takeover bids.

In addition to the control share acquisition type of statute upheld as constitutional in *CTS*, other types of statutes include:

"Fair Price" Statute — This type of statute reaches fundamental "second step" transactions, such as mergers or sales of substantially all assets, which frequently follow a hostile tender offer for a bare majority of the target's shares. The statute basically provides that such a transaction can be undertaken only if: (1) a majority of the disinterested shares of the subject corporation approve or (2) the same price is paid in the second-step

---

[74] 481 U.S. at 86.

[75] *Id.* at 91. See *AMP, Inc. v. Allied Signal Corp.,* 168 F.3d 649 (3d Cir. 1999) (interpreting Pennsylvania control share acquisitions statute). See generally Langevoort, *The Supreme Court and the Politics of Corporate Takeovers: A Comment on CTS Corp. v. Dynamics Corp. of America,* 101 Harv. L. Rev. 96 (1987).

[76] The Delaware statute has been upheld as constitutional. See, e.g., *BNS Inc. v. Koppers Co.,* 683 F. Supp. 458 (D. Del. 1988). The Wisconsin Statute was constitutionally upheld in *Amanda Acquisition Corporation v. Universal Foods Corporation,* 877 F.2d 496 (7th Cir. 1989).

transaction as was paid in the first-step tender offer. There are a number of variations to this type of statute.[77]

"Right of Redemption" Statute — With certain exceptions, this type of statute (enacted in Pennsylvania) provides that once a person or group owns twenty percent of a class of voting shares registered under the Exchange Act, that person or group is deemed to be a controlling shareholder. Attainment of that status requires such shareholder "to offer to purchase the remaining shares of all of the other shareholders at a statutorily defined price reflecting the highest premium paid by [such shareholder] in accumulating target stock."[78]

"Classified Board" Statute — This statute, enacted in Massachusetts, requires all publicly-held companies to have classified boards of directors, divided into three classes (being equal or nearly as equal in number as possible). Generally, each class is to serve staggered three-year terms. Removal of directors may be only for cause.[79]

"Other Constituency" or "Stakeholder" Statute — This type of statute, enacted in a majority of the states, authorizes a corporation's board of directors to consider non-shareholder interests, such as those of employees, customers, communities and suppliers, when making business decisions. Whereas most states apply this type of statute to directors' conduct in general, some states limit its application to takeovers.[80]

"Disgorgement" Statute— Enacted in Pennsylvania, a target company or any of its shareholders suing derivatively may bring an action against a controlling person (or group) seeking disgorgement of any profits made upon the sale of such person's shares in the company if the sale is within eighteen months after such person attained control status. Under the statute, control status is achieved when, for example, the person or group has voting power over at least 20% of the corporation's voting stock.[81]

"Business Combination Restriction" Statute — This type of statute, codified in such states as Delaware, New Jersey, New York, and Pennsylvania, generally provides that, with certain exceptions, if a person acquires a certain percentage of stock (e.g., 15% or more under the Delaware statute) without the approval of the board of directors of the subject corporation, that person becomes an interested shareholder and may not consummate a business combination (e.g., a merger) with the subject corporation for a substantial period of time (three years under the Delaware statute and five

---

[77] See generally Scriggins & Clarke, *Takeovers and the 1983 Maryland Fair Price Legislation*, 43 Md. L. Rev. 266 (1984).

[78] Bainbridge, *supra* note 25, at 1099, *interpreting*, 15 Pa. Cons. Stat. Ann. §§ 2542–2546. See generally Newlin & Gilmer, *The Pennsylvania Shareholder Protection Act: A New State Approach to Deflecting Corporate Takeover Bids*, 40 Bus. Law. 111 (1984).

[79] H.B. 5556, 1990 Mass. Adv. Legis. Serv. 5–6 (Law. Co-op).

[80] Tyler, *Other Constituency Statutes*, 59 Mo. L. Rev. 373, 379–80 (1994) (citing state statutes). See Bainbridge, *Interpreting Nonshareholder Constituency Statutes*, 19 Pepp. L. Rev. 971 (1992); Committee on Corporate Laws, *Other Constituencies Statutes: Potential for Confusion*, 45 Bus. Law. 2253 (1990); Symposium, 21 Stetson L. Rev. No. 1 (1991).

[81] See Bainbridge, *supra* note 25, at 1090–96.

years under the New York statute). There are certain exceptions where the business combination restriction does not apply. One such exception under the Delaware statute is that the acquisition by a controlling shareholder of at least 85% of the voting stock[82] in a tender offer or other acquisition entitles the interested shareholder to engage in a merger without being subject to the three-year prohibition. Another exception occurs when the target's board of directors approves the contemplated business combination before the time that the prospective acquiror becomes an interested share-holder.[83]

[C]   Need for Federal Preemption

To proponents of takeover activity, the *CTS* decision and the enactment of the state anti-takeover statutes signal a defeat for the American economy, market efficiency, and shareholder protection for at least three reasons. First, because there will be fewer tender offers, shareholders will be denied the opportunity to realize the full value of their stock, hence losing the opportunity for substantial profits. Second, inefficient managements will become more entrenched, thereby making their removal more difficult. This consequence harms not only shareholders but also the proficiency of American industry and our nation's quest to maintain its status as a world economic leader. Third, the efficient deployment of corporate assets to their most productive capacity will be impeded, again resulting in harm to shareholders, market efficiency, and our nation's economic proficiency.[84]

Given the adverse effect that the state anti-takeover statutes have on our nation's as well as the international securities markets, it is incumbent upon the Congress to preempt this area. The consequences of takeover activity present dilemmas of national and worldwide concern. They are not adequately debated and resolved by the respective states enacting legislation to protect their parochial interests. The time is now for Congress to act.

As former SEC Chairman (and now Professor) David S. Ruder has remarked:

---

[82] Shares owned by the target's directors and officers are not counted when determining whether the interested shareholder attains 85% stock ownership. See 8 Del. Code Ann. § 203.

[83] See 8 Del. Code Ann. § 203; N.Y. Bus. Corp. Law § 912(b). See generally Bainbridge, *State Takeover and Tender Offer Regulations Post-MITE: The Maryland, Ohio and Pennsylvania Attempts*, 90 Dick. L. Rev. 731 (1986); Booth, *The Promise of State Takeover Statutes*, 86 Mich. L. Rev. 1635 (1988); Bradford, *Protecting Shareholders from Themselves? A Policy and Constitutional Review of a State Takeover Statute*, 67 Neb. L. Rev. 459 (1988); Brown, *Regulatory Intervention in the Market for Corporate Control*, 23 U.C. Davis L. Rev. 1 (1989); Butler & Ribstein, *State Anti-Takeover Statutes and the Commerce Clause*, 57 U. Cin. L. Rev. 611 (1988); Cox, *The Constitutional "Dynamics" of the Internal Affairs Rule — A Comment on CTS Corporation*, 13 J. Corp. L. 317 (1988); Hazen, *State Anti-Takeover Legislation: The Second and Third Generations*, 23 Wake Forest L. Rev. 77 (1988); Johnson & Millon, *Misreading the Williams Act*, 87 Mich. L. Rev. 1862 (1989); Palmiter, *The CTS Gambit: Stanching the Federalization of Corporate Law*, 69 Wash. U. L.Q. 445 (1991); Pinto, *The Constitution and the Market for Corporate Control: State Takeover Statutes After CTS Corp.*, 29 Wm. & Mary L. Rev. 699 (1988); sources cited notes 68–81 *supra*.

[84] See Judge Posner's opinion in *CTS*, 794 F.2d 250 (7th Cir. 1986), *rev'd*. 481 U.S. 69 (1987).

Limitations on the free transferability of securities of corporations which are owned by shareholders nationwide diminish the efficiency, depth, and liquidity of the nation's securities markets. Accordingly, I believe that federal law should control in that area by preempting state statutes that unduly interfere with the free transferability of securities. I believe that corporations whose activities and ownership are national in scope should not be given protection against takeovers by the states where their primary production facilities are located. Just as I believe it to be imprudent for Congress to regulate internal corporate affairs through tender offer regulation, I believe it is imprudent for states to use their authority over matters of internal governance as a means of regulating the interstate market for corporate control.[85]

§ 13.07   Disclosure of Beneficial Ownership Interest

As discussed in § 13.04[B], Section 13(d)(1) of the Exchange Act and Rule 13d-1 prescribed thereunder require any person or group of persons agreeing to act together who acquire beneficial ownership of more than five percent of a class of equity security registered under Section 12 of the Act to disclose, within ten days, specific information by filing a Schedule 13D with the SEC and by sending copies to the issuer and to each exchange on which the security is traded. In short, "Schedule 13D requires disclosure of the identity of the issuer and the security, the identity, background, and citizenship of the reporting persons, the source and amount of funds used to acquire the securities, the purpose of the transaction, the reporting person's interest in the securities including trading history for the last 60 days and any contracts, arrangements, understandings or relationships with respect to the securities to which the reporting person or group is a party."[86] Note that certain passive investors are allowed to file an abbreviated Schedule 13G rather than a Schedule 13D. See Securities Exchange Act Release No. 39538 (1998).

Importantly, the requirements of Section 13(d) apply irrespective of whether the person (or group) acquiring five percent beneficial ownership intends to make a tender offer. The objective of the statute is to alert the securities markets of potential shifts in corporate control.[87] Although courts have declined to recognize a damages remedy under Section 13(d),[88] a

---

[85] "Federal Preemption of State Anti-Takeover Legislation," Remarks of David S. Ruder, Chairman, Securities and Exchange Commission, Before the 26th Annual Corporate Counsel Institute, at 8–9 (Chicago Oct. 7, 1987), *reported in*, Fed. Sec. L. Rep. (CCH) No. 1256, at 8–9 (1987). See generally Coffee, *Regulating the Market for Corporate Control: A Critical Assessment of the Tender Offer's Role in Corporate Governance*, 84 Colum. L. Rev. 1145 (1984).

[86] Bialkin, Attora and D'Alimonte, "Why, When and How to Conduct a Proxy Battle for Corporate Control," in *Proxy Contests and Battles for Corporate Control* at 87, 117 (1981). See Block & Rudoff, *Schedule 13D Problems Associated with Large Accumulations of Stock*, 10 Sec. Reg. L.J. 3 (1982).

[87] See *GAF Corp. v. Milstein*, 453 F.2d 709, 719 (2d Cir. 1971).

[88] See, e.g., *Stromfeld v. Great Atlantic and Pacific Tea Co., Inc.*, 484 F. Supp. 1264 (S.D.N.Y. 1980).

majority of courts have implied a private right of action for injunctive relief under Sections 13(d) and 14(d)-(e) on behalf of an issuer corporation.[89] The rationale is that, despite the Supreme Court's holding in *Piper v. Chris-Craft Industries*[90] that a defeated tender offeror does not have standing under Section 14(e) to bring an action for damages, the target company frequently may be the only willing party with the resources to maintain an injunctive action against a prospective bidder. In situations where the bidder's potential conduct may harm the company and its shareholders, granting standing to the target corporation to seek injunctive relief is therefore a practical approach to protecting shareholders and the marketplace.[91]

With respect to the type of relief awarded for a Section 13(d) violation, the usual remedy has been to require the violating party to amend its previous disclosures and to prohibit additional purchases until such corrective disclosure has been made. Some courts, however, have deemed such relief insufficient and have ordered disgorgement, disenfranchisement, divestiture, or rescission of shares acquired during the period that the misleading Section 13(d) disclosures were disseminated in the marketplace.[92] While some may applaud these measures, it also should be kept in mind that such actions for equitable relief under Section 13(d) may serve as a delaying tactic, thereby providing target management with sufficient time to develop and implement a successful defensive strategy to fend off the hostile offeror.

A major problem with Section 13(d) that has drawn attention is that a beneficial owner of more than five percent of a subject security need not disclose such ownership status until ten days after attaining that status. As a result, such parties may acquire additional shares through privately negotiated transactions and open market purchases during that ten-day "window" period so long as the acquisitions do not constitute a "tender offer." This loophole makes possible the accumulation of securities, representing a potential shift in corporate control, without adequate notification and disclosure of pertinent information to the marketplace. It has been proposed that Congress should close this loophole by either: (1) prohibiting additional accumulations above the five percent level unless there has been prior disclosure of the requisite information[93] or (2) deeming acquisition of more than twenty (or some other) percent of an equity security, with certain exceptions, to constitute a tender offer, thereby triggering the disclosure and dissemination requirements of the Williams Act.[94]

---

[89] See, e.g., *Indiana National Corp. v. Rich*, 712 F.2d 1180 (7th Cir. 1983). But see *Polaroid Corp. v. Disney*, [1988 Transfer Binder] Fed. Sec. L. Rep. (CCH) ¶ 94,095 (3d Cir. 1988).

[90] 430 U.S. 1 (1977).

[91] See, e.g., *Mobil Corp. v. Marathon Oil Co.*, 669 F.2d 366, 371 (6th Cir. 1981).

[92] See, e.g., *SEC v. First City Financial Corporation, Ltd.*, 688 F. Supp. 705 (D.D.C. 1988), aff'd, [1989–1990 Transfer Binder] Fed. Sec. L. rep. (CCH) ¶ 94,801 (D. C. Cir. 1989).

[93] See, e.g., Advisory Comm. on Tender Offers, U.S. SEC, Report of Recommendations 21–22 (1983).

[94] *Id.* at 23–23. See Tender Offer Reform Act of 1987, H.R. 2172, 100th Cong., 1st Sess. (1987) (if enacted, would have prohibited, with certain exceptions, the acquisition of more than ten percent of a target's stock except by means of a tender offer). See generally Steinberg, *Tender Offer Regulation: The Need for Reform*, 23 Wake Forest L. Rev. 1 (1988).

Nonetheless, in practical effect, application of the Hart-Scott-Rodino Anti-trust Improvements Act will limit such purchases in many situations.

Generally, the Hart-Scott-Rodino Antitrust Improvements Act of 1976 (HSR Act) imposes upon certain tender offerors and their targets in specified transactions pre-acquisition notification and disclosure require-ments. Pursuant thereto, information relevant to the transaction must be furnished to the Antitrust Division of the Department of Justice and the Federal Trade Commission. [95]

Under the HSR Act, an acquiring entity that is of a certain size generally must file and follow that Act's preacquisition waiting period prior to purchasing more than $15 million of the target corporation's voting securi-ties. Hence, "notification under the [HSR] Act may be required at a time when the acquiring company owns a much lower percentage of the target's voting securities than it could purchase by the time a Schedule 13D is required to be filed."[96] Stated another way, "an accumulation of stock prior to making a hostile raid may trigger the obligation to file a Form [under the HSR Act], and thereby compel the raider to surface and disclose its intentions, even if it does not meet the five-percent reporting threshold for the filing of a Schedule 13D."[97]

§ 13.08   SEC Tender Offer Rules

As evidenced by its 1999 amendments,[98] the SEC has been active in the tender offer rulemaking setting. The rules are quite extensive, mandating, inter alia, that both the offeror and the subject (i.e., target) corporations file detailed disclosure schedules. For example, a Schedule TO must be filed with the SEC in issuer and third-party tender offers. Moreover, Rule 14d-9 requires the subject company to file with the Commission a Schedule 14D-9 which calls for the disclosure of specified information. [99] The SEC "believes that the disclosure elicited by the Schedule will assist security holders in making their investment decisions and in evaluating the merits of a solicitation/recommendation."[100] Such information includes, if material, a description of any arrangement or other understanding and conflicts of interest between, among others, the offeror, the subject corporation, and their affiliates. Disclosure is also required in the Schedule of certain negotiations and transactions (e.g., merger negotiations) undertaken by the target company in response to the tender offer. [101] Moreover, in order to

---

[95] See generally, S. Axinn, B. Fogg & N. Stoll, *Acquisitions Under the Hart-Scott-Rodino Antitrust Improvements Act* (1991); Easterbrook & Fischel, *Antitrust Suits by Targets of Tender Offers*, 80 Mich. L. Rev. 1155 (1982).

[96] Axinn, Fogg & Stoll, *Contests for Corporate Control Under the New Law of Preacquisition Notification*, 24 N.Y.L.S. L. Rev. 857, 866–67 (1979).

[97] M. Lipton & E. Steinberg, *Takeovers and Freezeouts* § 7.02[5] (1999).

[98] Securities Exchange Act Release No. 42055 (1999).

[99] 17 C.F.R. § 240.14d-9.

[100] See Securities Exchange Act Release No. 16384 (1979).

[101] Compare this disclosure requirement with the duty affirmatively to disclose merger and

adhere to the disclosure requirements of Rule 14e-2,[102] the subject company in the Schedule 14D-9 must advise shareholders of its position in regard to the tender offer and the reasons therefor.

The SEC's tender offer rules cover a number of other matters. Rule 14d-6(d), for instance, expressly requires an offeror to disclose promptly any material change in the information provided to shareholders.[103] Rule 14e-8 prohibits a bidder from engaging in fraudulent or manipulative conduct when announcing a tender offer. For example, violation of Rule 14e-8 would occur if the supposed bidder had no intention or financial means to commence and complete the tender offer within a reasonable time period.[104] Also, to reduce the previous regulatory imbalances between cash tender offers and stock exchange offers, the SEC in 1999 elected to allow exchange offers to commence upon the filing of a registration statement. Nonetheless, the bidder cannot purchase any securities tendered in the exchange offer until the effectiveness of the registration statement and the dissemination of a prospectus supplement to security holders containing all material changes that have occurred.[105]

Another SEC tender offer rule, Rule 14d-8, extends the proration period from the previous ten-calendar-day period to the entire period that the offer remains open (under Rule 14(e)(1) a tender offer must remain open for at least twenty business days).[106] Generally, Rule 14d-8 obligates a bidder in an oversubscribed partial tender offer "to take up and pay for" shares tendered on a pro rata basis "during the period such offer, request, or invitation remains open." The rule precipitated comment on the extent of the Commission's rulemaking authority and on the broader question of its effect on the balance between the bidder and target in two-tier offers, particularly where the pressure on shareholders to tender is accentuated by a price differential between the tender offer and the proposed subsequent merger.[107] Rule 14d-11 adopted in 1999, allows bidders in third-party tender offers to have a subsequent offering period, lasting from three to twenty business days, as selected by the bidder, during which no withdrawal rights are permitted. If the bidder elects to have a subsequent

---

similar negotiations in other contexts, discussed in § 10.04 *supra*. Rule 14d-9 allows target companies to solicit and make recommendations to their security holders to the same degree that offerors are permitted to do so, provided that any such communication is filed with the SEC on the date of first use and contains a legend advising security holders to read the Schedule 14D-9 disclosure document where it is provided. See Securities Exchange Act Release No. 42055 (1999).

[102] SEC Rule 14e-2, 17 C.F.R. § 240.14e-2 (Rule 14e-2 generally obligates the target company to transmit to its shareholders within ten business days of the commencement of the tender offer a statement of its position in regard thereto).

[103] 17 C.F.R. § 240.14d-6(d).

[104] 17 C.F.R. § 240.14e-8. See Securities Exchange Act Release No. 42055 (1999).

[105] Securities Exchange Act Release No. 42055 (1999).

[106] 17 C.F.R. § 240.14d-8.

[107] See Brennan, "SEC Rule 14d-8 and Two-Tier Offers," contained in, *Tender Offers: Developments and Commentaries* at 109 (M. Steinberg ed. 1985).

offering period, the same consideration must be paid as was paid in the initial period. [108]

Other significant SEC actions in the tender offer context include the adoption of the "all holders" mandate under Rules 13e-4 and 14d-10. [109] The practical effect of these rules is to nullify the Delaware Supreme Court's decision in *Unocal v. Mesa Petroleum Co.* [110] In *Unocal*, the Delaware high court, applying a modified version of the business judgment rule, upheld the target management's use of a discriminatory issuer tender offer that excluded the hostile shareholder from participation. Under the SEC's "all holders" rule, by contrast, both issuer and third-party tender offers must be open to all shareholders and the best price paid to any tendering security holder must be paid to any other tendering security holder. Thus, the SEC's rule signifies that exclusionary tender offers for publicly-held companies no longer remain a viable defensive strategy.

§ 13.09   Substantive Regulation of Defensive Tactics

[A]   Federal Law

With respect to the legitimacy of defensive tactics under federal law, the key issue is whether Section 14(e), the antifraud provision of the Williams Act, regulates substantive conduct. In other words, is Section 14(e)'s purpose solely that of ensuring adequate and fair disclosure or does the statute have a broader reach? In adhering to the former approach, the Supreme Court definitively resolved this issue in *Schreiber v. Burlington Northern, Inc.* [111] The statutory analysis and policy implications of that decision merit attention.

Prior to the Supreme Court's decision in *Schreiber*, the Williams Act could have been applied in either of two ways to ensure that target shareholders normally had an opportunity to accept or reject a tender offer. First, conduct by management that deprives shareholders of an opportunity to tender may be held to constitute "constructive fraud" within the meaning of Section 14(e) of the Williams Act. Although the Supreme Court held in *Santa Fe Industries, Inc. v. Green* [112] that "mere" breaches of fiduciary duty not amounting to "manipulation" or "deception" do not violate Section 10(b) of the Exchange Act and Rule 10b-5 promulgated thereunder, Section 14(e) ought to be interpreted differently. Unlike Section 10(b), Section 14(e) by its terms prohibits "fraudulent" acts or practices. This difference in statutory language and the legislative history of Section 14(e) support giving it a broader reach than Section 10(b). Second, defensive tactics, the practical effect of which prevent shareholders from tendering in response to a bid, could have been viewed as "manipulative" under Section 14(e). Under this

---

[108] 17 C.F.R. § 240.14d-11. See Securities Exchange Act Release No. 42055 (1999).

[109] 17 C.F.R. §§ 240.13e-4, 240.14d-10; Securities Exchange Act Release No. 23421 (1986).

[110] 493 A.2d 946 (Del. 1985).

[111] 472 U.S. 1 (1985).

[112] 430 U.S. 462 (1977), *discussed in*, § 7.04 *supra*.

rationale, target management could be found to have engaged in "manipulative" practices proscribed by Section 14(e) when it artificially impedes the operation of a fair market for the corporation's stock by such tactics as granting options on valuable corporate assets to friendly third parties.[113]

Prior to *Schreiber*, a few courts held that certain defensive tactics engaged in by target management, even though fully disclosed, constituted "manipulation" under Section 14(e).[114] The Supreme Court in *Schreiber* rejected this interpretation, holding that Section 14(e)'s reach is limited to that of disclosure. In assessing Section 14(e)'s scope, the Court stated: "All three species of misconduct listed in Section 14(e), i.e., fraudulent, deceptive or manipulative . . . are directed at failure to disclose."[115] Hence, the *Schreiber* decision clearly limits the availability of federal law remedies in a tender offer situation. In so doing, the Supreme Court echoed the rationale of *Santa Fe* and relegated the policing of the substantive fairness of tender offers to state corporation law. Consequently, after *Schreiber*, to support a Section 14(e) right of action, a plaintiff must allege either misrepresentation or nondisclosure.

The *Schreiber* Court's decision signifies that, with certain exceptions such as the "all holders rule,"[116] the legitimacy of takeover maneuvers employed in multibillion dollar tender offers having both national and international ramifications will be examined solely under state law. To proponents of corporate accountability and shareholder democracy, the states' continual "race for the bottom" signals that meritorious interests will be neglected.[117] The decision also means that the state of Delaware, being the predominant state of incorporation for publicly-held companies, may well have the principal voice in determining the validity of takeover tactics.[118]

[B] State Law

The following discussion succinctly treats the application of state law with respect to the legitimacy of takeover tactics engaged in by a target

---

[113] Steinberg, *supra* note 94, at 19–20. See Junewicz, *The Appropriate Limits of Section 14(e) of the Securities Exchange Act of 1934*, 62 Texas L. Rev. 1171 (1984); Loewenstein, *Section 14(e) of the Williams Act and the Rule 10b-5 Comparisons*, 71 Georgetown L.J. 1311 (1983); Weiss, *Defensive Responses to Tender Offers and the Williams Act's Prohibition Against Manipulation*, 35 Vand. L. Rev. 1087 (1982).

[114] See, e.g., *Mobil Corp. v. Marathon Oil Co.*, 669 F.2d 366 (6th Cir. 1981) (target oil company's grant to competing tender offeror of certain options considered "manipulative" within meaning of § 14(e)); *Data Probe Acquisition Corp. v. Datatab, Inc.*, 568 F. Supp. 1538 (S.D.N.Y.) (self-serving grant of option to purchase shares of target by target's management was "manipulative device"), *rev'd*, 722 F.2d 1 (2d Cir. 1983), *cert. denied*, 465 U.S. 1052 (1984).

[115] 472 U.S. at 8.

[116] See Rules 13e-4, 14d-10, discussed in, § 13.08 *supra*.

[117] See generally Cary, *Federalism and Corporate Law: Reflections Upon Delaware*, 83 Yale L.J. 663 (1974).

[118] See Fiflis, *Of Lollipops and Law — A Proposal for a National Policy Concerning Tender Offer Defenses*, 19 U.C. Davis L. Rev. 303, 306 (1986) ("One may properly ask whether it is appropriate for Delaware, which conceivably may not be the abode of a single Unocal shareholder, to fix national policy in an international securities market, while Congress and the federal courts, Nero-like, abdicate a policymaking role.").

corporation's board of directors. Generally, in a number of jurisdictions, so long as the target's board (relying upon outside directors and experts) adopts defensive tactics for the purpose of maintaining the company as an independent viable entity, the business judgment rule will apply to insulate those actions from successful challenge.[119] The business judgment rule basically provides that corporate officers and directors will be shielded from judicial inquiry into the propriety of their decisions and from liability for harm to the corporation resulting from their decisions, so long as (1) the decision was within management's authority to make, and (2) such corporate fiduciaries (a) made reasonable inquiry and were reasonably informed with respect to the determination, (b) acted in good faith and had no disabling conflict of interest, and (c) had a rational basis for believing that the business judgment was in the corporation's best interests.[120] As the Supreme Court of Delaware has pointed out, the doctrine is an acknowledgment of the managerial prerogatives of corporate directors under state law: "It is a [rebuttable] presumption that in making a business decision the directors of a corporation acted on an informed basis, in good faith and in the honest belief that the action taken was in the best interests of the company."[121]

In ascertaining whether the business judgment rule will be applied in a given situation involving defensive tactics undertaken by the target's board of directors, a distinction has been made between defensive maneuvers employed to maintain the corporation as an independent, viable entity and those measures implemented to favor one bidder over another in a "sale" or "auction" setting. In the "sale" context, courts have refused to apply the business judgment rule to target management's actions.[122] Where "lock-up" and "no-shop" clauses are extended to management's favored suitor in such an active bidding situation, thereby precluding the auction process from ultimately resulting, the directors must demonstrate "some rationally related benefit accruing to the stockholders."[123]

Significantly, however, the business judgment rule continues to be the prevalent standard when assessing target management's actions taken for the purpose of maintaining the company as an on-going independent

---

[119] *Unitrin, Inc. v. American General Corp.*, 651 A.2d 1361 (Del. 1995); *Paramount Communications, Inc. v. Time, Inc.*, 571 A.2d 1140 (Del. 1990); *Moran v. Household International, Inc.*, 500 A.2d 1346 (Del. 1985); *Unocal Corp. v. Mesa Petroleum Co.*, 493 A.2d 946 (Del. 1985); *GAF Corp. v. Union Carbide Corp.*, [1985–1986 Transfer Binder] Fed. Sec. L. Rep. (CCH) ¶ 92,408 (S.D.N.Y. 1985) (applying New York law).

[120] See Principles of Corporate Governance and Structure: Analysis and Recommendations § 4.01 (1994).

[121] *Aronson v. Lewis*, 473 A.2d 805, 812 (Del. 1984). Generally, to overcome the presumption of the business judgment rule, the plaintiff must show "gross negligence." *Id.*

[122] See, e.g., *Edelman v. Fruehauf Corp.*, [1986–1987 Transfer Binder] Fed. Sec. L. Rep. (CCH) ¶ 92,863 (6th Cir. 1986) (applying Michigan law); *Hanson Trust v. ML SCM Acquisition, Inc.*, 781 F.2d 264 (2d Cir. 1986) (applying New York law); *MacAndrews & Forbes Holdings v. Revlon, Inc.*, 506 A.2d 173 (Del. 1986).

[123] Revlon, 506 A.2d at 182. See *Paramount Communications, Inc. v. QVC Network, Inc.*, 637 A.2d 34 (Del. 1994).

entity.[124] This standard has been applied to show-stop tactics, such as the taking on of $10 billion of debt,[125] unilateral adoption by a board of directors of an anti-takeover "poison pill" amendment to the corporation's by-laws which, if triggered, would result in the entity's liquidation,[126] invocation of the "Just Say No" defense,[127] and to corporate recapitalizations and restructurings, such as issuer self-tenders, dividend pay-outs, and related techniques.[128] Moreover, a number of courts have held that the grant of a lock-up to a potential acquiring entity, when no other bidder is on the scene, is also protected by the business judgment rule.[129]

As commentators have pointed out,[130] the Delaware Supreme Court in the takeover setting has not applied the business judgment rule in its traditional form. In *Unocal Corp. v. Mesa Petroleum Co.*,[131] the Delaware high court acknowledged that "[b]ecause of the omnipresent specter that a board may be acting primarily in its own interests . . . there is an enhanced duty which calls for judicial examination at the threshold before the protections of the business judgment rule may be conferred."[132] Hence, before the business judgment rule may be invoked, target management must show that there were "reasonable grounds for believing that a danger to corporate policy and effectiveness existed" and that the action taken was "reasonable in relation to the threat posed."[133]

Thus far, opinions differ whether this modified application of the business judgment rule has had a major substantive impact.[134] An interesting point is that, at least under Delaware law, by retaining outside advisers (such as investment bankers and lawyers) and relying extensively on outside

---

[124] See, e.g., *Gearhart Indus. v. Smith Int'l*, 741 F.2d 707 (5th Cir. 1984) (applying Texas law); *Turner Broadcasting Sys. v. CBS*, 627 F. Supp. 901 (N.D. Ga. 1985) (applying New York law); *Moran v. Household Int'l*, 500 A.2d 1346 (Del. 1985). But see *Dynamics Corp. of Am. v. CTS Corp.*, 794 F.2d 250 (7th Cir. 1986) (applying Indiana law), rev'd on other grounds, 481 U.S. 69 (1987); *Norlin Corp. v. Rooney, Pace, Inc.*, 744 F.2d 255 (2d Cir. 1984) (applying New York law).

[125] See, e.g., *Paramount Communications, Inc. v. Time, Inc.*, 571 A.2d 1140 (Del. 1990).

[126] E.g., *Revlon*, 506 A.2d at 180.

[127] *Moore Corp. v. Wallace Computer Services, Inc.*, 907 F. Supp. 1545 (Del 1995) (interpreting Delaware law, upholding target board's refusal to redeem the subject corporation's poison pill when faced with an all-cash, all-share offer at a substantial premium).

[128] E.g., *Unocal*, 493 A.2d at 954.

[129] See, e.g., *Revlon*, 506 A.2d at 181.

[130] See, e.g., Bainbridge, *Exclusive Merger Agreements and Lock-Ups in Negotiated Corporate Acquisitions*, 75 Minn. L. Rev. 239 (1990); Bradford, *Stampeding Shareholders and Other Myths: Target Shareholders and Hostile Tender Offers*, 15 J. Corp. L. 417 (1990); Chiapinelli; *The Life and Adventures of Unocal — Part I: Moore the Marrier*, 23 Del. J. Corp. L. 85 (1998); Johnson, *Corporate Takeovers and Corporations: Who Are They For?*, 43 Wash. & Lee L. Rev. 781 (1986); Taylor, *New and Unjustified Restrictions on Delaware Directors' Authority*, 21 Del. J. Corp. 837 (1996).

[131] 493 A.2d 946 (Del. 1985).

[132] *Id.* at 954.

[133] *Id.* at 955.

[134] See Gilson & Kraakman, *Delaware's Intermediate Standard for Defensive Tactics: Is There Substance to Proportionality Review?*, 44 Bus. Law. 247 (1989); Steinberg, *Nightmare on Main Street: The Paramount Picture Horror Show*, 16 Del. J. Corp. L. 1, 18–26 (1990).

directors, the board, in all probability, will be able to rebut assertions that the defensive maneuvers implemented were primarily motivated by entrenchment purposes, i.e., a desire to retain control.[135] As a result, under Delaware law, if a breach were shown, it would be of the duty of care rather than of loyalty. Consequently, pursuant to the 1986 statutory amendments to Delaware law, the directors would be absolved from monetary liability unless their actions constituted bad faith or intentional misconduct.[136]

A minority of courts, on the other hand, have declined to invoke the business judgment rule to management's tactics that evidence an intention to retain control.[137] Instead, in these situations, the burden is placed upon the board to "prove that the transaction was fair and reasonable to the corporation."[138] This standard is more protective of shareholder interests but its strict implementation has certain deficiencies. From a practical standpoint, it is undeniable that incumbent corporate management in nearly all hostile takeover bid situations wishes to retain control.[139] This attitude may be based on financial self-interest, prestige, or a sincere (but perhaps misguided) belief that the incumbent's continued stewardship is in the corporation's best interests. Hence, attention should focus on both the motive and effect of the directors' actions upon shareholder decisionmaking.

Unfortunately, vigorous application of a fairness standard may subject directors to astronomical monetary damages, totaling hundreds of millions, if not billions, of dollars.[140] The present director and officer insurance crisis would be exacerbated and outside directors would become even less inclined to serve on corporate boards. The consequence may be that courts would respond by making overly lenient factual determinations to whatever legal standard is applied in assessing alleged director misconduct, except perhaps in cases seeking exclusively injunctive relief. A better approach may be to: (1) recognize that takeovers deeply affect corporate constituencies in addition to shareholders, (2) permit management to take these non-investor interests into account in certain circumstances, (3) scrutinize defensive tactics by their effect on shareholder decisionmaking, (4) apply a fairly strict standard when assessing the legitimacy of "show-stopper" and similar

---

[135] *Revlon*, 506 A.2d at 181.

[136] See Delaware S. Bill 533, L. 1986, *amending*, Del. Code Ann. tit. 8, § 102. This comment presumes that the limitation on liability provision has been added to the corporation's articles of incorporation. See generally Balotti & Gentile, *Elimination or Limitation of Director Liability for Delaware Corporations*, 12 Del. J. Corp. L. 5 (1987).

[137] E.g., *Dynamics Corp. of America v. CTS Corp.*, 794 F.2d 250 (7th Cir. 1986) (applying Indiana law), *rev'd on other grounds*, 481 U.S. 69 (1987); *Norlin Corp. v. Rooney, Pace, Inc.*, 744 F.2d 255 (2d Cir. 1984) (applying New York law); *Heckmann v. Ahmanson*, 168 Cal. App. 3d 119, 214 Cal. Rptr. 177 (1986).

[138] *Norlin*, 744 F.2d at 265.

[139] See *Johnson v. Trueblood*, 629 F.2d 287, 292–93 (3d Cir. 1980) (construing Delaware law).

[140] See *Panter v. Marshall Field & Co.*, 646 F.2d 271 (7th Cir. 1981) (applying Delaware law) (over $200 million in damages sought).

maneuvers, and (5) implement a functional ceiling on damages that promotes the competing policies at stake.[141]

§ 13.10 Views of Commentators

Several commentators have expressed their opinions regarding the need for tender offer reform. The following summarizes a number of these divergent views.

1. *Application of the Business Judgment Rule* — These commentators believe that the business judgment rule, if the requirements of the rule are met, should govern the legitimacy of defensive takeover tactics.[142]

2. *Reliance on Outside Directors* — This view posits that deference to defensive tactics undertaken by a target's board of directors should be given by courts only if the outside directors have a significant role in determining the target's response to the takeover bid.[143]

3. *"Fairness" Standard* — Under this standard, the business judgment rule would not apply in the takeover setting. Rather, target management would have the burden of establishing that the defensive actions taken were fair to the corporation and its shareholders.[144]

4. *"Freeze" Period* — This proposal would establish a "freeze" period during which a hostile tender offer would remain open for a substantial period of time, such as six months, in order to enable shareholders to make informed decisions. During this "freeze" period, any "structural" change in the company (for example, an option to sell the target's "crown jewel") would require shareholder approval.[145]

5. *"Modified Shareholder Choice"* — Pursuant to this proposal, target shareholders would have an unimpeded right to tender their shares to the hostile bidder, subject to the exception that target management may take appropriate steps to fend off a hostile bid if it affirmatively shows that the

---

[141] For further discussion, see Steinberg, note 94 *supra*. See generally Johnson & Millon, *Misreading the Williams Act*, 87 Mich. L. Rev. 1862 (1989); Johnson & Siegel, *Corporate Mergers: Redefining the Role of Target Directors*, 136 U. Pa. L. Rev. 315 (1987); Lipton, *Corporate Governance in the Age of Finance Corporatism*, 136 U. Pa. L. Rev. 1 (1987); Loewenstein, *Toward An Auction Market for Corporate Control and the Demise of the Business Judgment Rule*, 63 So. Cal. L. Rev. 65 (1989); McGinty, *Replacing Hostile Takeovers*, 144 U. Pa. L. Rev. 983 (1996).

[142] See, e.g., Lipton, *Takeover Bids in the Target's Boardroom*, 35 Bus. Law 101 (1979); Steinbrink, *Management's Response to the Takeover Attempt*, 28 Case W. Res. L. Rev. 882 (1978).

[143] See, e.g., Gelfond & Sebastian, *Reevaluating the Duties of Target Management in a Hostile Tender Offer*, 60 B.U.L. Rev. 403 (1980); Williams, *Role of Directors in Takeover Offers*, 13 Rev. Sec. Reg. 963 (1980).

[144] See generally Prentice, *Target Board Abuse of Defensive Tactics: Can Federal Law Be Mobilized to Overcome the Business Judgment Rule?*, 8 J. Corp. L. 337 (1983).

[145] See, e.g., Goldberg, *Regulation of Hostile Tender Offers: A Dissenting View and Recommended Reforms*, 43 Md. L. Rev. 225 (1984); Lowenstein, *Pruning Deadwood in Hostile Takeovers: A Proposal for Legislation*, 83 Colum. L. Rev. 249 (1983).

offeror constituted a clear threat to the target's business, including the equity interests of the shareholders.[146]

6. *"The Passivity Approach"* — Tender offers are viewed as beneficial to shareholders and the economy under this approach. They encourage managerial efficiency, competition, proficient use of corporate assets, and shareholder gain. As a result, when a tender offer is made, target management under this approach must remain totally passive. Under this approach, no defensive tactics are permitted.[147]

7. *"The Auction Model"* — This approach takes on a number of variations. Basically, this proposal entitles target management to communicate to shareholders regarding its position on the takeover bid but does not permit the use of significant defensive maneuvers. Moreover, target management may (or "should" or "must" depending on the particular approach) put the corporation up for "auction," seeking out more favorable bids from other prospective offerors.[148]

---

[146] See, e.g., Steinberg, note 94 *supra.*

[147] See, e.g., Easterbrook & Fischel, *The Proper Role of Target Management in Responding to a Tender Offer*, 94 Harv. L. Rev. 1161 (1981)

[148] See e.g., Bebchuck, *The Case for Facilitating Competing Tender Offers*, 95 Harv. L. Rev. 1028 (1982); Gilson, *A Structural Approach to Corporations: The Case Against Defensive Tactics in Tender Offers*, 33 Stan. L. Rev. 819 (1981); Oesterle, *Target Managers as Negotiating Agents for Shareholders in Tender Offers: A Reply to the Passivity Thesis*, 71 Cornell L. Rev. 53 (1985). See also, Bebchuck & Ferrell, *Federalism and Corporate Law: The Race to Protect Managers from Takeovers*, 99 Colum. L. Rev. 1168 (1999).

Chapter 14

SEC ENFORCEMENT

§ 14.01 Introduction

Congress enacted the federal securities laws in light of a perceived need to protect investors and the integrity of the marketplace. To help ensure that the purposes of the securities laws are fulfilled, Congress vested the SEC with broad investigatory and enforcement powers. As part of its investigatory authority, the Commission may subpoena witnesses and records. Once the Commission obtains sufficient information to believe that a violation of the federal securities laws has occurred, it may bring an enforcement action either administratively or in a federal district court.

The overwhelming percentage (about ninety percent) of SEC enforcement actions are settled pursuant to the consent negotiation process where the defendant neither admits nor denies the Commission's allegations. Parties generally consent rather than litigate due to a number of factors. These include that the SEC may have a strong case, the financial costs involved in litigating with the Commission, avoidance of adverse publicity that would be generated by prolonged litigation, disruption of normal operations that would otherwise result due to management's attention being diverted, and fear of offensive collateral estoppel should the SEC emerge victorious. With respect to this last factor, there is the concern that an adverse decision in an SEC contested matter may result in the initiation of private damages actions in which the claimants seek to estop the defendants from relitigating issues resolved against them in the prior SEC action.[1]

SEC enforcement (as well as state "blue sky" enforcement) raises a multitude of issues. A number of the key topics are discussed in this chapter. For more extensive treatment, other sources should be consulted.[2]

---

[1] See *Parklane Hosiery Co., Inc. v. Shore*, 439 U.S. 322 (1979); authorities cited note 2 *infra*.

[2] See, e.g., American Bar Association, *The Securities Enforcement Manual: Tactics and Strategies* (Kirkpatrick & Lockhart, LLP 1997); A. Bromberg & L. Lowenfels, *Securities Fraud & Commodities Fraud* (1999); H. Friedman, *Securities and Commodities Enforcement* (1981); J. Long, *Blue Sky Law* (1999); M. Steinberg & R. Ferrara, *Securities Practice: Federal and State Enforcement* (1999).

State securities law enforcement mechanisms are fairly similar to those employed under federal law and comprise an important part of securities law enforcement. As stated by Dean Sargent:

> Blue sky enforcement actions are not only large in number, but varied in purpose · and form. They may be used to combat both fraud and registration violations. They also may be used to discipline securities professionals carrying on business within the state. The action may take the shape of an informal investigation, a formal administrative proceeding, a civil suit by the administrator or a criminal prosecution. These actions frequently end in settlement, but they also may conclude with application of one or more of a variety of possible remedies, including denial,

§ 14.02 SEC Subpoena Power

[A] Overview

SEC investigations normally are nonpublic and may take the form of a preliminary inquiry or a formal investigation. Frequently, a substantial portion of the materials in the Commission's files is obtained in the informal stage through cooperation. However, if the SEC is unable to elicit the needed information informally, it must initiate a formal investigation and seek authorization from the courts to compel uncooperative sources to supply the desired information. An informal inquiry can be commenced by the SEC's enforcement division and does not involve the use of subpoenas. The formal investigation, on the other hand, requires Commission authorization and, when necessary, court enforcement as well.[3]

Pursuant to a formal order of investigation, which outlines the general scope of the Commission's inquiry, the SEC can issue subpoenas if it determines that the documents and witnesses ordered produced may be relevant. If the party to whom the subpoena is issued refuses to voluntarily produce the requested information, the Commission must petition a federal district court for an order that compels compliance with the subpoena.[4] Because the Commission's subpoena enforcement power is expansive and constitutes a necessary element of its investigations, the courts frequently order enforcement.[5]

An SEC investigation serves to uncover facts that may reveal whether a violation of the securities laws has occurred.[6] Because such an investigation by itself carries no formal sanctions, judicial intervention may be necessary to enforce compliance with an SEC subpoena. Accordingly, the courts possess the power to hold a party in contempt for noncompliance with subpoenas they have ordered enforced.[7] A party commits civil contempt by disobeying a court order after knowledge that the order has been issued.[8]

---

suspension, or revocation of a securities exemption or of a broker-dealer, agent, or investment adviser registration, an injunction, an appointment of a receiver, or a criminal conviction.

Sargent, *Blue Sky Enforcement Actions — Some Practical Considerations*, 14 Sec. Reg. L.J. 343, 344 (1987). See generally Karmel, *Creating Law at the Securities and Exchange Commission: The Lawyer as Prosecutor*, 61 Law & Contem. Prob. 33 (1998); Long, *A Guide to the Investigative and Enforcement Provisions of the Uniform Securities Act*, 37 Wash. & Lee L. Rev. 739 (1980); McLucas, Taylor & Matthews, *A Practitioners Guide to the SEC's Investigative and Enforcement Process*, 70 Temple L. Rev. 53 (1997); Williams, *The Securities and Exchange Commission and Corporate Social Transparency*, 112 Harv. L. Rev. 1197 (1999).

[3] See SEC Rules of Practice, 17 C.F.R. § 202.5; Securities Act Release No. 6345 (1981).

[4] See, e.g., § 21(b) of the Exchange Act, 15 U.S.C. § 78u(b).

[5] See, e.g., *SEC v. Brigadoon Scotch Distributing Co.*, 480 F.2d 1047 (2d Cir. 1973).

[6] See, e.g., *United States v. Morton Salt Co.*, 338 U.S. 632 (1950).

[7] See, e.g., § 21(c) of the Exchange Act, 15 U.S.C. § 78u(c).

[8] See *Penfield Co. v. SEC*, 330 U.S. 585 (1947).

[B] Supreme Court Standards

The Supreme Court has established standards that must be met by an administrative agency before a subpoena will be enforced by the lower courts. In *United States v. Powell*,[9] the Court determined that an agency seeking enforcement of a subpoena does not have the burden of establishing probable cause. Rather, the agency must show "that the investigation will be conducted pursuant to a legitimate purpose, that the inquiry may be relevant to the purpose, that the information sought is not already within the [agency's] possession, and that the administrative steps required by the [federal statutes] have been followed."[10] If the Commission can establish these four elements, it will be deemed to have affirmatively established agency good faith, and the burden thereupon will shift to the opposing party to challenge on an appropriate ground.[11]

To procure enforcement under the *Powell* standards, the SEC is not required to provide evidence of probability of coverage under the securities statutes or the likelihood of a violation of these statutes.[12] Rather, the agency must demonstrate that the investigation falls within the mandate Congress granted to the SEC and that the documents sought are reasonably relevant to the inquiry.[13] The subpoena cannot be issued in bad faith,[14] its scope cannot be too indefinite,[15] and compliance with the subpoena cannot be too burdensome.[16]

Although demonstrating agency bad faith is difficult for those opposing enforcement of an SEC subpoena, this sometimes can be shown.[17] However, the other appropriate grounds for fending off enforcement of such a subpoena, including the assertion of first,[18] fourth,[19] and fifth[20] amendment constitutional challenges, rarely succeed. Hence, although judicial enforcement of an SEC subpoena may not be automatic, such enforcement generally is likely if the purpose of the SEC's request is legitimate and if the information sought is relevant to that purpose.

---

[9] 379 U.S. 48 (1964).

[10] *Id*. at 57–58.

[11] *Id*. at 58.

[12] *Id*. at 51–58.

[13] See *Oklahoma Press Publishing v. Walling*, 327 U.S. 186 (1946).

[14] 379 U.S. at 58.

[15] See *SEC v. Blackfoot Bituminous, Inc.*, 622 F.2d 512 (10th Cir. 1980).

[16] See *SEC v. Savage*, 513 F.2d 188 (7th Cir. 1975) (per curiam).

[17] See *SEC v. Wheeling-Pittsburgh Steel Corp.*, 648 F.2d 118 (3d Cir. 1981) (en banc). See generally Comment, *SEC v. Wheeling-Pittsburgh Steel Corp. — Informant Bad Faith Defense to Enforcement of an Administrative Subpoena*, 7 J. Corp. L. 121 (1984).

[18] See, e.g., *SEC v. McGoff*, 647 F.2d 185 (D.C. Cir. 1981).

[19] See, e.g., *See v. City of Seattle*, 387 U.S. 541 (1967).

[20] See, e.g., *Couch v. United States*, 409 U.S. 322 (1973).

[C]   Notice to Third Parties

The formal order of investigation, to which the Commission's subpoena power attaches, ordinarily names the initial subject(s) of the SEC's inquiry. In practice, the Commission may not include the identification of all or even a substantial number of the parties who may be implicated in the investigation. Also, the formal order does not indicate the third parties to whom the Commission may issue subpoenas. A target of an investigation, unless informed by a third party who receives a subpoena, thus may remain ignorant of the parties from whom the Commission seeks information.

In *SEC v. Jerry T. O'Brien, Inc.*,[21] the Supreme Court refused to require the Commission to provide notice to the targets of subpoenas issued to third parties in nonpublic investigations. In reaching its decision, the Court explored three sources from which such a requirement had to be derived if it were to be imposed upon the Commission: "a constitutional provision; an understanding on the part of Congress, inferable from the structure of the securities laws, regarding how the SEC should conduct its inquiries; or the general standards governing judicial enforcement of administrative subpoenas enunciated in . . . *Powell*."[22]

The Court found that neither the fourth, fifth nor sixth amendment mandated that notice of third party subpoenas be given in order to protect the target's constitutional rights. The fourth amendment affords no support because a third party provides information to the Commission. Even though the target may have communicated the subpoenaed information to the third party in confidence, the target may not rely on the third party's fourth amendment protection to claim an unreasonable search or seizure when the third party relinquishes the information. Neither the due process clause nor the self-incrimination clause of the fifth amendment apply to the third party notice situation. The due process clause under such circumstances does not apply because no adjudication of legal rights occurs in an administrative investigation. The self-incrimination clause does not apply because a third party answers the subpoena; the target is not compelled to act as a witness against himself. Finally, the protection of the sixth amendment's confrontation clause arises only upon the initiation of criminal proceedings.[23]

The Court rejected the structural statutory argument for requiring notice because, rather than supporting the purpose of the securities laws, notice to targets of third party subpoenas undermines Congress' intent to provide the Commission with expansive power to issue and enforce subpoenas. The federal securities laws contain no specific provision relating to notice of third party subpoenas, and the Court found no evidence that Congress desired the Commission to adopt any procedures to implement the practice. Instead, the Court determined that "Congress intended to vest the SEC

---

[21] 467 U.S. 735 (1984).

[22] *Id.* at 741.

[23] *Id.* at 742–43.

with considerable discretion in determining when and how to investigate possible violations of the statutes administered by the Commission."[24]

Finally, the Court considered the argument that the right to notice of third party subpoenas issued in an SEC investigation stems from the standards governing judicial enforcement of administrative subpoenas embraced in *Powell*. The Court rejected the argument on two bases: "[f]irst, administration of the notice requirement . . . would be highly burdensome for both the Commission and the courts"; and, "[s]econd, the imposition of a notice requirement on the SEC would substantially increase the ability of persons who have something to hide to impede legitimate investigations by the Commission."[25] In its holding, the Court recognized that, when the Commission initiates an investigation, it frequently does not know which parties will be "targets" of the investigation. To police the SEC's process of identifying targets, the district court would have to intervene by conducting a hearing "to determine the scope and thrust of the ongoing investigation." Moreover, if a target had notice of third party subpoenas, the target could delay the investigation by discouraging third parties from complying with the subpoenas.[26]

Also, a target, following the progress of the Commission's inquiry by knowing to whom subpoenas were issued, could destroy crucial evidence before the SEC could gain possession. The Court concluded that the SEC was not prohibited from notifying a target of any subpoena it issues, but refused to impose a judicial mandate that would "curtail the Commission's discretion to determine when such notice would be appropriate and when it would not."[27]

§ 14.03 Parallel Proceedings

Parallel proceedings, that is, concurrent or successive civil proceedings by the SEC (or another administrative agency) and criminal investigation by the U.S. Attorney (or another prosecutorial entity) generally are constitutional. As stated by the Fifth Circuit: "There is no general federal constitutional, statutory, or common law rule barring the simultaneous prosecution of separate civil and criminal actions by different federal agencies against the same defendant involving the same transactions."[28]

Hence, parallel proceedings are restricted only in very limited circumstances.[29] A key issue that has arisen but is not yet resolved is whether SEC subpoenas issued pursuant to a Commission investigation may be enforced after a criminal indictment has been returned. One federal appellate court has framed this issue as follows:

---

[24] *Id.* at 745.

[25] *Id.* at 748.

[26] *Id.* at 749–50.

[27] *Id.* at 750–51. For further discussion, see Steinberg, *SEC Subpoena Enforcement Practice*, 11 J. Corp. L. 1 (1985).

[28] *SEC v. First Financial Group of Texas, Inc.*, 659 F.2d 660, 666 (5th Cir. 1980).

[29] See *United States v. Kordel*, 397 U.S. 1 (1970).

Other than where there is specific evidence of agency bad faith or malicious governmental tactics, the strongest case for deferring civil proceedings until after completion of criminal proceedings is where a party under indictment for a serious offense is required to defend a civil or administrative action involving the same matter. The noncriminal proceeding, if not deferred, might undermine the party's Fifth Amendment privilege against self-incrimination, expand rights of criminal discovery beyond the limits of Federal Rule of Criminal Procedure 16(b), expose the basis of the defense to the prosecution in advance of criminal trial, or otherwise prejudice the case. If delay of the noncriminal proceeding would not seriously injure the public interest, a court may be justified in deferring it. In some such cases, however, the courts may adequately protect the government and the private party by merely deferring civil discovery or entering an appropriate protective order. [30]

In many such instances, the most feasible alternative may well be to place protective conditions on the exercise of the SEC's power to transmit information after return of an indictment. This approach would permit the Commission to pursue its civil enforcement functions, yet prevent undue expansion of discovery by prohibiting disclosure (of the information uncovered) between the SEC and the pertinent prosecuting entity. [31]

Today, the potential adverse ramifications incurred from parallel proceedings no longer are confined to SEC-Department of Justice referrals. As a number of episodes illustrate, [32] there is the distinct possibility that information transmitted to the SEC will be referred to other federal and state regulatory agencies. Moreover, pursuant to requests under the Freedom of Information Act, [33] the Commission may release documents and other information to private litigants involving matters that previously were subject to SEC scrutiny. Hence, in today's expanding world of parallel proceedings, the adverse consequences that may flow from providing information to the SEC can be massive. [34]

§ 14.04 SEC Administrative Enforcement Remedies

The SEC has a number of administrative enforcement remedies it may invoke when alleged violations of the federal securities laws have been perpetrated by persons and entities subject to the Commission's administrative jurisdiction. The following discussion highlights key SEC administrative enforcement remedies.

---

[30] *SEC v. Dresser Industries, Inc.*, 628 F.2d 1368, 1375–76 (D.C. Cir. 1980) (en banc).

[31] *Id.* at 1376, 1391.

[32] See, e.g., *Permian Corp. v. United States*, 665 F.2d 1214 (D.C. Cir. 1981).

[33] 5 U.S.C. § 552.

[34] For more extensive treatment of parallel proceedings, see Pickholz, *The Expanding World of Parallel Proceedings*, 53 Temple L.Q. 1100 (1982); Steinberg & Brennan, *Parallel Proceedings*, 8 Corp. L. Rev. 335 (1985); Note, *Using Equitable Powers to Coordinate Parallel Civil and Criminal Actions*, 98 Harv. L. Rev. 1023 (1985).

[A] Cease and Desist Orders

In legislation enacted in 1990, Congress granted the SEC authority to seek an administrative cease and desist order against *any* person based on *any* violation of the federal securities laws. A cease and desist order also may be imposed against any person who is deemed a "cause" of the subject violation, signifying that such person knew or should have known that his/her conduct would contribute to the violation. Moreover, the order entered may require not only that the party cease and desist from the proscribed acts but that he/she effect compliance within prescribed time periods and pursuant to specified conditions.[35] Under this authority, the SEC has ordered subject parties to effect "undertakings" in a variety of factual settings.[36] Importantly, in regard to "regulated" persons (such as broker-dealers, investment advisers and their "associated" persons), the Commission in a cease and desist action can procure an order for an accounting as well as disgorgement.[37]

Note that in order to obtain the foregoing relief, the SEC still must establish a violation of the securities laws. Nonetheless, the cease and desist remedy may be more easily obtained than an injunction. Unlike the procuring of injunctive relief, which requires the Commission to show a reasonable likelihood of future violative conduct by the defendant,[38] the SEC apparently takes the position that for a cease and desist order it need establish only that the subject party engaged in the proscribed conduct. Whether the SEC's position is correct awaits judicial resolution.[39]

[B] Money Penalties

The SEC in administrative actions may levy money penalties against "regulated" persons, provided that the Commission concludes that the penalty imposed is in the "public interest" and that the defendant engaged

---

[35] See § 8A of the Securities Act, § 21C of the Exchange Act, § 9(f) of the Investment Company Act, § 203(k) of the Investment Advisors Act, codified at, 15 U.S.C. §§ 77h-1, 78uu-3, 80a-9(f), 80b-3(k).

[36] See Mathews, Citera & Greenfield, *1991–1992 Securities Enforcement Review*, 7 Insights Nos. 1, 2 (Jan., Feb. 1993) (discussing proceedings).

[37] See § 21B(e) of the Exchange Act, 15 U.S.C. § 78u-2(e). Regulated persons include brokers, dealers, investment advisers, investment companies, and their associated persons. The SEC also can seek a temporary cease and desist order against regulated persons on an emergency basis.

[38] See § 14.05[A] *infra*.

[39] Compare *In re BC Financial Corp.*, 1994 WL 317454 (ALJ 1994) (no showing or reasonable likelihood required by SEC to procure cease and desist order) with *In re Warren G. Trepp*, Admin. Proc. File No. 3-8833 (ALJ 1997) (showing of reasonable likelihood required). See discussion in M. Steinberg & R. Ferrara, *supra* note 2, at § 5A:15 (and authorities cited therein). But see Hansen, *The Securities and Exchange Commission's Use of Cease and Desist Powers*, 20 Sec. Reg. L.J. 339, 347–48 (1993) (asserting that SEC should be held to same showing in cease and desist proceeding as that required for an injunction). See also, *Precious Metals Assoc., Inc. v. CFTC*, 620 F.2d 900, 912 (1st Cir. 1980) (requiring Commodity Futures Trading Commission (CFTC) to show defendant's "proclivity to violate the law" to obtain cease and desist order).

in the prohibited conduct (such as willfully violating the federal securities law, aiding and abetting, or failing reasonably to supervise another person under such party's control). In determining whether a money penalty and the extent to which such penalty is in the "public interest," Congress enumerated several factors that the Commission may consider.[40] Moreover, generally, the more severe the violation committed, the greater the money penalty that may be levied. Since 1990 (when this provision was enacted), the SEC frequently has ordered money penalties in its administrative proceedings.[41]

[C] Refusal and Stop Orders

Section 8 of the Securities Act generally governs the time in which SEC filed registration statements of securities offerings and amendments thereto become effective. Section 8(b) and Section 8(d) respectively authorize the Commission to issue refusal orders and stop orders in connection with materially incomplete, inaccurate, or false and misleading registration statements. Furthermore, Section 8(e) empowers the SEC to make an examination in any case in order to determine whether a stop order should be issued under Section 8(d).[42]

[D] Summarily Suspending Trading in a Security

Summary suspensions of over-the-counter or exchange trading of a security are imposed by the SEC under Section 12(k) of the Exchange Act. This sanction is not to exceed ten days. The Supreme Court in *SEC v. Sloan*[43] held that the Commission was not authorized to summarily suspend trading in a security for successive ten-day periods, unless such successive suspension was based on new circumstances. The Court thus required the SEC to provide notice and right to a hearing with regard to suspensions for extended periods of time.

---

[40] Three tiers of money penalties exist with more severe penalties associated with each tier: tier (1) — technical violations; tier (2) — violations that encompass fraud, manipulation, or deliberate disregard of a regulatory mandate; tier (3) — violations that came within tier (2) above and that result (or pose the risk of resulting) in substantial losses. Moreover, in determining whether the penalty is in the "public interest," relevant factors include the severity of the defendant's conduct, the harm resulting from such conduct, the extent of unjust enrichment, whether the defendant is a repeat offender, the need to deter such conduct, and "such other matters as justice may require." See § 21B of the Exchange Act, §203(i) of the Investment Advisors Act, § 9(d) of the Investment Company Act, codified at, 15 U.S.C. §§ 78u-2, 80b-3(i), 80a-9(d).

[41] See, e.g., *In re Nasdaq Fraud Investigation,* [1999 Transfer Binder] Fed. Sec. L. Rep. (CCH) ¶ 86,105 (SEC 1999); *In re Invesco, MIM, PLC,* Securities Exchange Act Release No. 30878, 51 SEC Docket 1333 (1992). When the Commission seeks a money penalty, a five-year statute of limitations evidently applies. See *3M Corporation v. Browner,* 17 F.3d 1453 (D.C. Cir. 1994) (construing 28 U.S.C. § 2462); § 14.08 *infra.*

[42] See McLucas, *Stop Order Proceedings Under the Securities Act of 1933: A Current Assessment,* 40 Bus. Law. 515 (1985).

[43] 436 U.S. 103 (1978).

[E] Broker-Dealer Disciplinary Sanctions

Broker-dealer (and associated persons) disciplinary sanctions may be imposed pursuant to several provisions contained in the Exchange Act. Persons or entities registered as broker-dealers, as well as any person "associated" with a broker-dealer, are vulnerable to SEC discipline under these provisions. After providing notice and opportunity for a hearing, broker-dealer sanctions may include outright revocation of registration (or denial of registration), suspension of registration, censure, or barring an associated person from associating with a broker-dealer (see Section 15(b)(4) and 15(b)(6) of the 1934 Act). Moreover, pursuant to Section 15A, a broker-dealer or associated person, inter alia, can be barred from becoming a member (or becoming associated with a member) of a registered securities association (i.e., the NASD). Also, pursuant to Section 19(h) of the Exchange Act, the SEC can suspend or revoke the registration or take other disciplinary action against a registered securities association as well as suspend or expel a member or person associated with a member of such association.[44] As a final example, under the 1990 legislation, the Commission may levy money penalties against broker-dealers and their associated persons who engage in violative conduct.[45]

[F] Section 15(c)(4) Disciplinary Proceedings

Administrative proceedings involving certain defective Exchange Act reports filed with the SEC may be adjudicated pursuant to Section 15(c)(4) of the 1934 Act. Section 15(c)(4) authorizes the Commission to order compliance with the provisions of Section 12, 13, 14 or 15(d) of the Exchange Act and the rules or regulations thereunder. For example, if a Section 12 or 15(d) registrant fails to comply with, in any material way, the continuous reporting requirements of Section 13, such as the timely and accurate filing of annual and other periodic reports, the Commission may, after notice and opportunity for hearing, publish its findings and issue an order requiring compliance. The order may be directed not only to the registrant but also to any person who "caused" such registrant's failure to comply.[46]

In 1984 Congress enacted the Insider Trading Sanctions Act (ITSA). ITSA, inter alia, expanded Section 15(c)(4) so as to enable the SEC to bring administrative actions to remedy violations of the proxy and tender offer provisions contained in Section 14 of the Exchange Act. The Act also clarified that the Commission may proceed administratively against persons (such as officers, directors, and perhaps attorneys) who are a "cause" of a failure to comply with Section 12, 13, 14 or 15(d).[47] Nonetheless, in view of

---

[44] See Mathews, *Litigation and Settlement of SEC Administrative Enforcement Proceedings*, 29 Cath. U. L. Rev. 215, 222–23 (1980). For SEC disciplinary proceedings against investment advisers, see § 203(e), (f) of the Investment Advisers Act, 15 U.S.C. § 80b-3(e), (f).

[45] See discussion § 14.04[B] *supra*.

[46] See McLucas & Romanowich, *SEC Enforcement Proceedings Under Section 15(c)(4) of the Securities Exchange Act of 1934*, 41 Bus. Law. 145 (1985).

[47] *Id.*

legislation enacted in 1990 granting the SEC cease and desist power,[48] Section 15(c)(4) today is invoked on a far less frequent basis.[49]

[G] Section 21(a) Reports of Investigation

Section 21(a) of the Exchange Act allows the Commission, in its discretion, to "make such investigations as it deems necessary to determine whether any person has violated, is violating, or is about to violate any provision of this title," and "to publish information concerning any such violations." Moreover, pursuant to Section 21(a), the SEC "may require or permit any person to file with it a statement in writing . . . as to all the facts and circumstances concerning the matter . . . investigated."[50] Although a Section 21(a) report is not actually an adjudicatory type of proceeding, it is used by the SEC as a substitute for administrative disciplinary or civil injunctive suits in marginal, nonegregious cases, at times having the effect of inducing subject parties to settle.

These settlements frequently enable the Commission to present its position regarding the conduct in question, thereby providing notice of the SEC's future enforcement posture on the issue. Moreover, through the Section 21(a) report procedure, the Commission can avoid the usual requirement of having to find an actual violation while persuading subject parties to modify their conduct or take, what the SEC views as, corrective steps. Hence, in these Section 21(a) reports, the Commission criticizes policies and decisions made by subject parties, thus directing to all concerned the areas in which the Commission desires reform.[51]

§ 14.05   SEC Injunctions

[A] Standards for Injunctive Relief

As in any other type of case where permanent injunctive relief is sought, a defendant's violation of the federal securities laws is not by itself sufficient for the SEC to obtain an injunction. Rather, the test generally applied is whether there is a reasonable likelihood that the defendant, if not enjoined, will again engage in the violative conduct.[52] In identifying the relevant factors that demonstrate a reasonable likelihood of future violations, one appellate court pointed to "the degree of scienter involved, the sincerity of defendant's assurances against future violations, the isolated or recurrent nature of the infraction, defendant's recognition of the wrongful nature of

---

[48] See § 14.04[A] *supra.*

[49] See *In re Kern*, [1988–1989 Transfer Binder] Fed. Sec. L. Rep. (CCH) ¶ 84,342 (ALJ 1988), *aff'd solely as to discontinuation of proceedings*, [1991 Transfer Binder] Fed. Sec. L. Rep. (CCH) ¶ 84,815 (SEC 1991). See generally *Report of the ABA's Section of Business Law Task Force on SEC Section 15(c)(4) Proceedings,* 46 Bus. Law. 255 (1990).

[50] 15 U.S.C. § 78u(a).

[51] For further discussion, see M. Steinberg & R. Ferrara, *supra* note 2, at § 4:01 *et seq.*

[52] See, e.g., *SEC v. Advance Growth Capital Corp.*, 470 F.2d 40, 53 (7th Cir. 1972).

his conduct, and the likelihood, because of defendant's professional occupation, that future violations might occur."[53] Other factors deemed relevant include the gravity of the offense committed,[54] the time elapsed between the violation and the court's decision,[55] whether the defendant, in good faith, relied on advice of counsel,[56] and the adverse effect an injunction would have on the defendant.[57]

The Supreme Court's decision in *Aaron v. SEC*[58] casts light on this issue. There, the Court held that the SEC must prove scienter in civil enforcement actions to enjoin violations of Section 10(b) of the Exchange Act, Rule 10b-5 promulgated thereunder, and Section 17(a)(1) of the Securities Act,[59] but need not prove scienter under Section 17(a)(2) or 17(a)(3).[60] The Court noted that under Section 17(a)(2) and 17(a)(3), "the degree of intentional wrongdoing evident in a defendant's past conduct" is an important factor in determining whether the Commission has "establish[ed] a sufficient evidentiary predicate to show that such future violation may occur."[61] The presence or lack of scienter is "one of the aggravating or mitigating factors to be taken into account" in a court's exercise of its equitable jurisdiction.[62] In a concurring opinion, former Chief Justice Burger asserted that the SEC "will almost always" be required to show that the defendant's past conduct was more culpable than negligent. The Chief Justice concluded that "[a]n injunction is a drastic remedy, not a mild prophylactic, and should not be obtained against one acting in good faith."[63]

It has been contended that the *Aaron* Court's language, even apart from the former Chief Justice's concurring opinion, could require the SEC to prove scienter in order to make a "proper showing" for obtaining injunctive relief under *any* section of the securities acts.[64] Indeed, during the last decade, the SEC has experienced greater difficulty in procuring injunctions.[65] Nonetheless, the absence of scienter may not preclude the granting of such relief where the applicable statutory provision requires only negligent culpability. For example, where a defendant has committed prior

---

[53] See, e.g., *SEC v. Cavanagh*, 155 F.3d 129 (2d Cir. 1998); *SEC v. Universal Major Indus. Corp.*, 546 F.2d 1044, 1048 (2d Cir. 1976).

[54] See, e.g., *SEC v. Manor Nursing Centers, Inc.*, 458 F.2d 1082, 1102 (2d Cir. 1972).

[55] See, e.g., *SEC v. Monarch Fund*, 608 F.2d 938, 943 (2d Cir. 1979).

[56] See, e.g., *SEC v. Lum's, Inc.*, 365 F. Supp. 1046, 1066 (S.D.N.Y. 1973).

[57] See, e.g., *SEC v. Manor Nursing Centers, Inc.*, 458 F.2d 1082, 1102 (2d Cir. 1972).

[58] 446 U.S. 680 (1980).

[59] *Id.* at 687–96.

[60] *Id.* at 696–700.

[61] *Id.* at 701.

[62] *Id.*

[63] *Id.* at 703 (Burger, C.J., concurring).

[64] See Huffman, *Aaron Restricts SEC Enforcement*, Legal Times, June 9, 1980, at 2.

[65] See, e.g., *SEC v. Steadman*, 967 F.2d 1636 (D.C. Cir. 1992) (denying SEC's request for injunctive relief, court stated that "injunctive relief is reserved for willful lawbreakers or those whose operations are so persistently sloppy as to pose a continuing danger to the investing public"). See generally Eisenberg, *Litigating with the SEC — A Reasonable Alternative to Settlement*, 21 Sec. Reg. L.J. 421 (1994).

violations, where his/her carelessness has been egregious, where public investors have been severely injured, or where the defendant's occupation increases the probability of future violations, a court (considering the totality of the circumstances) may order injunctive relief.[66]

Importantly, under certain state securities law provisions, injunctions and even criminal convictions may be obtained without proof of scienter. As Dean Sargent comments: "The current trend among the intermediate state appellate courts . . . seem[s] to be moving away from proof of guilty knowledge, mens rea, evil purpose, or even recklessness in criminal cases for securities fraud."[67]

[B] Implications of *Central Bank of Denver* and the PSLRA

As discussed earlier,[68] the Supreme Court's decision in *Central Bank of Denver* was believed by many authorities to preclude the SEC in certain situations from bringing an enforcement action premised on aider and abettor liability. However, unlike the *Hochfelder / Aaron* analogy addressed earlier,[69] aiding and abetting a federal securities law violation statutorily gives rise to criminal liability exposure.[70] Under this rationale, the criminal aid-abet statute provided ample authority for the SEC to pursue aiders and abettors.[71]

With respect to violations of the Exchange Act, it is now clear that the SEC has such aiding and abetting authority. In 1995, the Private Securities Litigation Reform Act (PSLRA) was enacted, amending Section 20 of the Securities Exchange Act by adding a new subsection (f). Section 20(f) authorizes the SEC to seek injunctive relief and/or certain money penalties against aiders and abettors for violations of the 1934 Act (or any rule or regulation thereunder). Specifically, the section provides that any person who "knowingly provides substantial assistance" to another person in violation of the Exchange Act (or any rule or regulation thereunder) shall be liable "to the same extent as the person to whom such assistance is provided."[72] Hence, this section preserves aiding and abetting liability in certain SEC enforcement actions. Nonetheless, the mental culpability standard (although seemingly requiring actual knowledge) may require clarification. Moreover, the PSLRA declines to grant the SEC express aiding and abetting authority with respect to Securities Act violations.

---

[66] See *SEC v. Washington County Utility District*, 676 F.2d 218 (6th Cir. 1982); *SEC v. Murphy*, 626 F.2d 633 (9th Cir. 1980). For further discussion *on Aaron*, see §§ 7.03[B], 8.04[B] *supra*.

[67] Sargent, *A Blue Sky State of Mind: The Meaning of "Willfully" in Blue Sky Criminal Cases*, 20 Sec. Reg. L.J. 96, 98 (1992). See J. Long, *supra* note 2, at § 8.04[3].

[68] See §§ 7.03[B], 9.02 *supra*.

[69] See §§ 7.02[A]-[B], 9.01-9.02 *supra*.

[70] 18 U.S.C. § 2(a).

[71] See Bromberg, *Aiding and Abetting: Sudden Death and Possible Resurrection*, 24 Rev. Sec. & Comm. Reg. 133, 136 (1994).

[72] Section 20(f) of the Exchange Act, 15 U.S.C. § 78t(f).

Besides its aiding and abetting authority, the SEC has powerful enforcement weapons. For example, the Commission may bring an administrative cease and desist proceeding against persons who are a "cause" of the alleged violation, thus encompassing those persons who "should have known" that their conduct "would contribute" to such violation.[73] Hence, even though the SEC must proceed administratively, the Commission should be able to spread the liability net as far. After all, establishing one as a "cause" of a violation should prove easier than proving aiding and abettor liability.[74]

Moreover, in view of Section 15(b)(4)(E) and Section 15(b)(6)(A) of the Exchange Act,[75] the Commission has express statutory authority to proceed against brokers and dealers (and associated persons) who aid and abet securities law violations.[76] Similarly, those who aid and abet violations of the Investment Advisers Act are subject to SEC enforcement action.[77] Hence, *Central Bank of Denver* thus far has not been problematic for the SEC's enforcement program. With respect to financial intermediaries, this is especially true given the Commission's rigorous use of the "controlling person" and "failure to supervise" provisions to hold broker-dealer executives, supervisors, and branch managers accountable.[78] As a last point, whereas prior to *Central Bank of Denver* the Commission was content to allege aider and abettor liability, the SEC now seeks an expansion of conduct that constitutes primary liability (see § 9.03 *supra*).

[C] Collateral Consequences

The primary purpose of injunctive relief under the federal securities laws is to deter future violative conduct, not to punish the violator.[79] As Judge Friendly noted, however, an injunction can have severe collateral consequences.[80] For example, an injunction not only harms one's reputation but it also serves as the basis for contempt sanctions if the injunctive order subsequently is violated.[81] Issuance of an SEC injunction can cause the suspension or revocation of a broker-dealer's registration, or constitute grounds for prohibiting any person from associating with a broker-dealer.[82]

---

[73] See § 14.04[A] *supra*.

[74] See Martin, Mirvis & Herlihy, *SEC Enforcement Powers and Remedies Are Greatly Expanded*, 19 Sec. Reg. L.J. 19, 23 (1993).

[75] 15 U.S.C. § 78o(b)(4)(E), 78o(b)(6)(A)(i).

[76] *Id.*

[77] 15 U.S.C. § 80b-9(d).

[78] See, e.g., *In re Prudential Securities, Inc.*, [1993 Transfer Binder] Fed. Sec. L. Rep. (CCH) ¶ 85,238 (SEC 1993); discussion § 12.04 *supra*.

[79] See *Aaron v. SEC*, 446 U.S. 680 (1980); *Hecht Co. v. Bowles*, 321 U.S. 321 (1944). Note that when the SEC seeks injunctive and other equitable relief (such as disgorgement), no applicable statute of limitations evidently applies. See, e.g., *SEC v. Rind*, 991 F.2d 1486 (9th Cir. 1993); § 14.08 *infra*.

[80] See *SEC v. Commonwealth Chemical Securities, Inc.*, 574 F.2d 90, 99 (2d Cir. 1978).

[81] See, e.g., *United States v. Custer Channel Wing Corp.*, 327 F.2d 675 (4th Cir. 1967).

[82] See § 15(b)(4)(C) of the Exchange Act, 15 U.S.C. § 78o(b)(4)(C); *SEC v. Geon Indus., Inc.*, 531 F.2d 39, 55 (2d Cir. 1976).

Similarly, an injunction disqualifies the subject party from serving as a director, officer, or employee of a registered investment company.[83] It can constitute a basis for barring an attorney, accountant, or other professional from practicing before the SEC.[84] Additionally, a Regulation A exemption from Securities Act registration may be unavailable to an enjoined issuer of securities.[85] As a final example, the Commission frequently requires that an injunction be disclosed in certain filings, reports, statements, or other information sent to shareholders and investors.[86]

Largely because of these consequences, the courts have required the SEC "to go beyond the mere facts of past violations and demonstrate a realistic likelihood of recurrence."[87] Employing this standard, courts have concluded in a number of cases that the SEC has not made a sufficient showing and have denied the Commission's request for injunctive relief.[88]

[D]　Ancillary or Other Equitable Relief

Over the years, the SEC has sought, and successfully obtained, ancillary or other equitable relief against an enjoined party. Examples of such relief include disgorgement, appointment of a receiver, appointment of independent members to the board of directors, and appointment of a special counsel.[89] Proponents assert that the authority for ordering such relief derives from the general equitable powers of the federal courts.[90] Indeed, even if a court refuses to grant the SEC's request for an injunction, it may nevertheless grant other equitable relief.[91] Some authorities assert,

---

[83] See § 9(a)(2) of the Investment Company Act, 15 U.S.C. § 80a-9(a)(2). The SEC can lift or waive this disqualification pursuant to Section 9(c) of the Act.

[84] See SEC Rule 102(e)(3)(i), 17 C.F.R. § 201.2(e)(3)(i). Rule 102(e) is discussed in § 14.09[A] *infra*.

[85] See Rule 262 of Regulation A, 17 C.F.R. § 230.262.

[86] See Item 401(d) of Regulation S-K, 17 C.F.R. § 229.401(d). See generally Andre, *The Collateral Consequences of SEC Injunctive Relief: Mild Prophylactic or Perpetual Hazard?*, 1981 U. Ill. L. Rev. 625.

[87] *SEC v. Commonwealth Chemical Securities, Inc.*, 574 F.2d 90, 100 (2d Cir. 1978).

[88] See, e.g., *SEC v. Caterinicchia*, 613 F.2d 102 (5th Cir. 1980); discussion § 14.05[A] *supra*.

[89] See, e.g., *SEC v. Colello*, 139 F.3d 674 (9th Cir. 1998) (recouping proceeds from illegal conduct); *SEC v. Mayhew*, 121 F.3d 44 (2d Cir. 1997) (disgorgement); SEC v. Huffman, 996 F.2d 800 (5th Cir. 1993) (holding that a disgorgement order does not amount to a "debt" under the Debt Collection Act); *SEC v. Rind*, 991 F.2d 1486 (9th Cir. 1993) (holding no right to jury trial when SEC seeks disgorgement of alleged illicit profits); *CFTC v. American Metals Exchange Corp.*, 991 F.2d 71 (3d Cir. 1993) (stating that proper measure of disgorgement is amount of defendant's ill-gotten gains, not amount of investors' losses); *SEC v. Manor Nursing Centers, Inc.*, 458 F.2d 1082 (2d Cir. 1972) (disgorgement); *SEC v. Fifth Ave. Coach Lines, Inc.*, 280 F. Supp. 3 (S.D.N.Y. 1968), *aff'd*, 435 F.2d 510 (2d Cir. 1971) (receiver); *SEC v. Coastal States Gas Corp.*, SEC Lit. Rel. No. 6054 (S.D. Tex. Sept. 12, 1973) (independent members of board of directors). See generally Farrand, *Ancillary Remedies in SEC Civil Enforcement Suits*, 89 Harv. L. Rev. 1779 (1976).

[90] See *SEC v. Wencke*, 622 F.2d 1363, 1369 (9th Cir. 1980). See generally Hazen, *Administrative Enforcement: An Evaluation of the Securities and Exchange Commission's Use of Injunctions and Other Enforcement Methods*, 31 Hastings L.J. 444 (1979).

[91] See, e.g., *SEC v. Commonwealth Chemical Securities, Inc.*, 574 F.2d 90, 102–03 (2d Cir. 1978).

however, that a number of the more far-reaching forms of equitable relief, such as an appointment of directors, may exceed the scope of a court's equitable powers.[92]

[E] Modification or Dissolution of SEC Injunctions

In view of the collateral consequences imposed by SEC injunctions, subject parties may seek to have the particular injunction modified or dissolved. The traditional view, derived from the Supreme Court's decision in *United States v. Swift & Co.*,[93] places a heavy burden upon the party seeking modification or dissolution. Writing at the time he was a federal appellate judge, former Justice Blackmun construed *Swift* as follows:

> (1) [T]hat, where modification and amendment of an existing decree is under consideration, there are "limits of inquiry" for the decree court and for the reviewing court; (2) that the inquiry is "whether the changes are so important that dangers, once substantial have become attenuated to a shadow"; (3) that the movants must be "suffering hardship so extreme and unexpected" as to be regarded as "victims of oppression"; and (4) that there must be "[n]othing less than a clear showing of grievous wrong evoked by new and unforeseen conditions." Phrased in other words, this means for us that modification is only cautiously to be granted; that some change is not enough; that the dangers which the decree was meant to foreclose must almost have disappeared; that hardship and oppression, extreme and unexpected, are significant; and that the movants' task is to provide close to an unanswerable case. To repeat: caution, substantial change, unforeseenness, oppressive hardship, and a clear showing are the requirements.[94]

Swift's stringent guidelines have been applied by numerous courts in a variety of contexts, including where modification or dissolution of an SEC injunction is sought.[95] A number of courts, however, have declined to follow *Swift's* rigorous requirements. These courts reason that subsequent Supreme Court decisions have departed from *Swift's* restrictive standards.[96] Hence, the Second Circuit, while noting that changes in fact or law provide the strongest reasons for modifying an injunction, held that modification or dissolution also is appropriate "where a better appreciation of the facts in light of experience indicate that the decree is not properly adapted to accomplishing its purposes."[97] Moreover, in view of the Supreme Court's decision in *Central Bank of Denver*, it remains to be seen the extent to which

---

[92] See Dent, *Ancillary Relief in Federal Securities Law: A Study in Federal Remedies*, 67 Minn. L. Rev. 865 (1983).

[93] 286 U.S. 106 (1932).

[94] *Humble Oil & Refining Co. v. American Oil Co.*, 405 F.2d 803, 813 (8th Cir. 1969).

[95] See, e.g., *SEC v. Advance Growth Capital Corp.*, 539 F.2d 649 (7th Cir. 1976).

[96] See *Rufo v. Inmates of Suffolk County Jail*, 502 U.S. 367 (1992); *United States v. United Shoe Machinery Corp.*, 391 U.S. 244 (1968); *System Federation v. Wright*, 364 U.S. 642 (1961).

[97] *King-Seeley Thermos Co. v. Aladdin Industries, Inc.*, 418 F.2d 31, 35 (2d Cir. 1979).

parties subject to SEC injunctions move to dissolve such injunctions on the basis of a change in the governing law. Thus far, such motions to dissolve have not occurred with frequency.[98]

A significant decision departing from the *Swift* standards in the securities law area is *SEC v. Warren*.[99] Distinguishing *Swift*, the district court in *Warren* exercised its "inherent equitable power to weigh the severity of the alleged danger which the injunction was designed to eliminate against the continuing necessity for the injunction and the hardship brought by its prospective application."[100] Weighing these factors, the court granted the motion to dissolve the injunction.[101] On appeal, the Third Circuit affirmed on substantially the same reasoning.[102]

Another development in this area has been that, even where the SEC makes the necessary showing, some courts have hesitated to order an unconditional permanent injunction. The conditions that courts have attached to the imposition of an injunction include automatic dissolution after a fixed number of years, suspension after the defendant fulfills certain requirements, and permitting a petition for dissolution after a fixed period of time on a lesser showing than that required by *Swift*.[103] Although the SEC, at times, has agreed to certain of these limitations pursuant to the consent process, the Commission's position appears to be that upon making a proper showing, it is entitled as a matter of statutory right to the ordering of a permanent injunction.[104]

Hence, the continued viability of the stringent *Swift* standard is open to debate. Perhaps a better approach would be for courts faced with a motion to modify or dissolve an injunction to apply an ad hoc balancing test. This standard would consider such factors as (1) subsequent change of fact or law, (2) the extent of adverse, unforeseen collateral consequences, (3) whether the injunction has fulfilled its objectives, (4) whether the individual deterrent effect of the injunction has ceased, (5) the decree's effect on societal deterrence, (6) whether a government entity is a party to the litigation and the adverse effect that granting of the motion would have on the entity's resources, and (7) the extent and nature of the public or other countervailing interest involved.[105]

---

[98] See discussion in §§ 7.03, 9.02 *supra*.

[99] 76 F.R.D. 405 (W.D. Pa. 1977), *aff'd*, 583 F.2d 115 (3d Cir. 1978).

[100] 76 F.R.D. at 408.

[101] *Id.* at 407–08.

[102] 583 F.2d at 120–22.

[103] See, e.g., the district court's order as set forth in *SEC v. Blazon Corp.*, 608 F.2d 960 (9th Cir. 1979), the validity of which the Ninth Circuit did not resolve.

[104] See Brief of the SEC at 10, *SEC v. Associated Minerals, Inc.*, Nos. 79-1449, 79-1450 (6th Cir. 1980).

[105] For further discussion, see Steinberg, *SEC and Other Permanent Injunctions — Standards for Their Imposition, Modification, and Dissolution*, 66 Cornell L. Rev. 27, 71–73 (1980).

§ 14.06   Officer and Director Bars

The SEC may seek in federal court an order prohibiting a person from serving as an officer or director of a publicly-held enterprise. Such an order may be conditional or unconditional; it may be of permanent duration or for a specified time period as directed by the court. The conditions for an officer or director bar are that the individual violated the antifraud provisions of Section 17(a)(1) of the 1933 Act or Section 10(b) of the 1934 Act (or any rule thereunder) and that such conduct demonstrated substantial unfitness to serve in this fiduciary capacity.[106]

Even prior to Congress' enactment of an officer/director bar provision in 1990, the SEC occasionally procured such orders as a type of equitable relief.[107] In one such case, the Second Circuit focused on proscribed conduct that occurred prior to the 1990 legislation. Granting broad equitable relief, the court ordered disgorgement of illicit profits, an officer/director bar, and a voting trust to sterilize the violators' controlling interests in publicly-held entities.[108] Not surprisingly, the Commission may be inclined to invoke this remedy with greater vigor in view of the express statutory authority now provided by federal law.[109]

§ 14.07   Court-Ordered Money Penalties

The SEC also may seek court ordered money penalties against *any* person for *any* violation of the securities laws or of an SEC cease and desist order. The penalty amount levied by the court is determined in view of the facts and circumstances and increases in amount according to the severity of the violation committed. As set forth by one source:

> The penalties are subject to three-tier maximums for each "violation." First, [with respect to so-called technical violations,] the maximum is the greater of $5,000 for a natural person or $50,000 for corporation or other entity, or the "gross amount of pecuniary gain to such defendant" resulting from the violation. Second, if the violation included "fraud, deceit, manipulation, or deliberate disregard of a regulatory requirement," the maximums are $50,000 and $250,000, respectively, or the gross pecuniary gain. Third, if the violation in addition resulted in or created, directly or indirectly, "substantial losses" or "a significant risk of substantial losses to others," the maximums are $100,000 [for a natural person] and

---

[106] See § 20(e) of the Securities Act, 15 U.S.C. § 77t(e); § 21(d)(2) of the Exchange Act, 15 U.S.C. § 78u(d)(2).

[107] See, e.g., *SEC v. Florafax Int'l, Inc.*, SEC Litig. Release No. 10617, 31 SEC Docket 1038 (N.D. Okla. 1984).

[108] *SEC v. Posner*, 16 F.3d 520 (2d Cir. 1994).

[109] See, e.g., *SEC v. Softpoint, Inc.*, 958 F. Supp. 846 (S.D.N.Y. 1997); Callcott, *Patterns of SEC Enforcement Under the 1990 Remedies Act: Officer-And-Director Bars*, 21 Sec. Reg. L.J. 347, 360 (1994) (citing cases). See also, *SEC v. Patel*, 61 F.3d 137 (2d Cir. 1995) (order of permanent bar of corporate officer vacated and remanded for justifiable factual basis for such bar order).

$500,000 [for a corporation or other entity], or the gross pecuniary gain. [110]

§ 14.08 Statutes of Limitations

As a general principle, the courts have held that there exists no applicable statute of limitations when the SEC seeks equitable relief. [111] Although some sources disagree, [112] this principle extends not only to Commission requests seeking injunctive relief but also to other equitable remedies, such as disgorgement. [113] Nonetheless, the SEC's pursuit of stale claims certainly is relevant in a court's determination whether to grant the relief requested. [114] Moreover, when the SEC institutes an action for monetary penalties, a five-year statute of limitations applies. This five-year limitations period also extends to non-monetary disciplinary sanctions that are viewed as punitive rather than remedial. [115]

§ 14.09 Professional Responsibility

This section will address select issues with respect to a securities lawyer's professional responsibilities. In addition to discussing Rule 102(e) [formerly Rule 2(e)], the section will focus on counsel's obligations when his/her client engages in violations of law.

[A] Rule 102(e) [formerly Rule 2(e)]

SEC Rule of Practice 102(e) provides that the Commission may suspend, limit, or bar "any person" from practicing before it "in any way." Despite the broad language of Rule 102(e), its application to date has been limited to disciplining attorneys, accountants, engineers, and other similar professionals. Although the securities laws do not give the SEC explicit authority to discipline such professionals, the Commission and the courts have held

---

[110] Martin, Mirvis & Herlihy, *supra* note 74, at 21, *interpreting,* § 21(b)(3) of the Exchange Act, 15 U.S.C. § 78u(d)(3). See Laby & Callcott, *Patterns of SEC Enforcement Under the 1990 Remedies Act: Civil Money Penalties,* 58 Albany L. Rev. 5 (1994). See generally Ferrara, Ferrigno & Darland, *Hardball! The SEC's New Arsenal of Enforcement Weapons,* 47 Bus. Law. 33 (1991). See also, *Hudson v. United States,* 118 S. Ct. 488 (1997) (holding that double jeopardy constraints apply if the sanction at issue is so punitive in nature as to "transform what has been denominated a civil penalty into a criminal penalty").

[111] See, e.g., *SEC v. Rind,* 991 F.2d 1486 (9th Cir. 1993).

[112] See, e.g., Riesenberg, *Application of Statutes of Limitations to SEC Disgorgement Actions,* 8 Insights No. 2, at p. 17 (Feb. 1994).

[113] See, e.g., *SEC v. Williams,* 886 F. Supp. 28 (D. Mass. 1995).

[114] See, e.g., *SEC v. Rind,* 991 F.2d at 1492.

[115] See, e.g., 28 U.S.C. § 2462; *Johnson v. SEC,* 87 F.3d 484 (D.C. Cir. 1996) (under facts of case, SEC imposition of censure and six-month suspension deemed a "penalty," thereby invoking § 2462's five-year limitations period). See generally Brodsky & Eggers, *The Statute of Limitations in SEC Civil Enforcement Actions,* 23 Sec. Reg. L.J. 123 (1995); Gordon, *SEC Administrative Proceedings: Five-Year Statute of Limitations Period Held Applicable,* 24 Sec. Reg. L.J. 420 (1997).

that the Rule is a necessary adjunct "to the Commission's power to protect the integrity of its administrative procedures and the general public."[116]

It has been argued without success that the SEC is exceeding or abusing whatever Rule 102(e) authority it may have by administratively litigating matters involving conduct that arguably does not come within the ambit of "practicing before the Commission."[117] This assertion stems from the fact that the SEC defines "practicing before the Commission" in a broad manner. Thus, the disciplinary authority of Rule 102(e) may come into play in connection with the registration provisions, as well as the periodic and other reporting requirements, to the extent that any or all of these filings and registration applications can be defined as "practicing" before the SEC. For example, attorneys who, under Rule 102(e), engage in improper counseling of their clients with respect to required reports filed with the SEC, can be suspended from practicing before the Commission.[118]

[B]　Legal and Ethical Standards

Under the American Bar Association's Model Rules of Professional Conduct, a lawyer, with certain exceptions, is obligated to preserve his or her client's confidences and secrets.[119] This duty is more protective of client

---

[116] *Touche Ross & Co. v. SEC*, 608 F.2d 570, 582 (2d Cir. 1979). See *In re Carter & Johnson*, [1981 Transfer Binder] Fed. Sec. L. Rep. (CCH) ¶ 82,847 (SEC 1981). In 1998, Rule 102(e) was amended, defining "improper professional conduct" for accountants to include:

(A)　Intentional or knowing conduct, including reckless conduct, that results in a violation of applicable professional standards; or

(B)　Either of the following two types of negligent conduct:

   (1)　A single instance of highly unreasonable conduct that results in a violation of applicable professional standards in circumstances in which an accountant knows, or should know, that heightened scrutiny is warranted.

   (2)　Repeated instances of unreasonable conduct, each resulting in a violation of applicable professional standards, that indicate a lack of competence to practice before the Commission.

Amendments to Rule 102(e) of the Commission's Rules of Practice, [1998 Transfer Binder] Fed. Sec. L. Rep. (CCH) ¶ 86,052 (SEC 1998). One SEC Commissioner dissented, opining that the SEC lacked authority to impose a negligence standard. *Id.* at 80,852. In view of the controversy underlying the implementation of a negligence standard, the validity of the 1998 amendments will be subject to judicial scrutiny.

For more recent Rule 102(e) proceedings against accountants, see, e.g., *Potts v. SEC*, 151 F.3d 810 (8th Cir. 1998) (upholding Rule 102(e)(1) sanctions against concurring partner on an audit reasoning that accountant's conduct reasonably could be viewed as reckless); *Checkowsky v. SEC*, 139 F.3d 221 (D.C. Cir. 1998) (dismissing Rule 102(e) proceeding against two auditors due to SEC's failure to articulate applicable legal standard); *In the Matter of Price Waterhouse Coopers LLP*, [1999 Transfer Binder] Fed. Sec. L. Rep. (CCH) ¶ 86,106 (SEC 1999) (settlement in regard to auditor independence rules where firm partners and managers acquired securities of such firm's audit clients).

[117] See *In re Keating, Muething & Klekamp*, [1979 Transfer Binder] Fed. Sec. L. Rep. (CCH) ¶ 82,124 (SEC 1979) (Karmel, Comm'r, dissenting); Kelleher, *Scourging the Moneylenders from the Temple: The SEC, Rule 2(e), and the Lawyers*, 17 San Diego L. Rev. 501 (1980).

[118] See, e.g., *In re Fields*, [1972–1973 Transfer Binder] Fed. Sec. L. Rep. (CCH) ¶ 79,407 (SEC 1973), *aff'd without opinion*, 495 F.2d 1075 (D.C. Cir. 1974).

[119] See Rule 1.6 of the Model Rules of Professional Conduct (1983).

confidentiality than the attorney-client privilege, applying "not merely to matters communicated in confidence by the client but also to all information relating to the representation, whatever its source."[120] In this regard, however, counsel should be wary when the client is engaging in violations of law. Under such circumstances, counsel's rendering of substantial assistance with knowledge of the fraud (such as the drafting by counsel of an SEC disclosure document that the lawyer knows presents a materially false impression of the issuer's financial condition) may result in liability under the Model Rules, the federal securities laws, and state law.[121]

The Model Rules make clear that a lawyer has discretion to reveal to third parties information relating to the representation of a client only to the extent counsel reasonably believes such disclosure is necessary to prevent the client from engaging in a criminal act that "is likely to result in imminent death or substantial bodily harm."[122] Hence, counsel under the Model Rules may not disclose information in order to prevent the client from perpetrating a crime or fraudulent act which counsel believes is likely to result in serious economic harm. Under such circumstances, counsel if he/she stays in the representation, must be careful to become neither a "cause" of the client's violation nor an aider or abettor. An alternative is for counsel to withdraw from the representation.[123] In this regard, however, a number of states have adopted a modified version of the Model Rules which permits counsel to disclose to third parties otherwise confidential information relating to a crime in order to prevent the client from unlawfully causing serious financial injury.[124]

The disclosure obligations in the securities law area are magnified by the concept that commission of a past unlawful act may materially impact on the present financial condition of the issuer. Accordingly, nondisclosure of the unlawful act(s) (and their financial consequences) may violate the federal securities laws and thereby constitute an ongoing fraud. Hence, the securities lawyer's dilemma when counseling a client in this setting can be unsettling.[125]

---

[120] *Id.* (comment to Rule 1.6). See *Upjohn v. United States*, 449 U.S. 383 (1981).

[121] See, e.g., Rule 1.2(d) of the Model Rules; *SEC v. National Student Marketing Corp.*, 457 F. Supp. 682 (D.D.C. 1978).

[122] Model Rule 1.6(b).

[123] *Id.* Rule 1.16. See *In re Carter & Johnson*, [1981 Transfer Binder] Fed. Sec. L. Rep. (CCH) ¶ 82,847 (SEC 1981).

[124] See Hall, *States Modifying ABA's Ethics Rules*, Legal Times, Aug. 12, 1985, at 1. See also, Hacker & Rotunda, *Representing the Corporate Client and the Proposed Rules of Professional Conduct*, 4 Corp. L. Rev. 269 (1981).

[125] See generally M. Steinberg, *Corporate and Securities Malpractice* (1992); Gruenbaum, *Clients' Frauds and Their Lawyer's Obligations*, 68 Georgetown L.J. 191 (1979); Kramer, *Clients' Frauds and Their Lawyer's Obligations: A Study in Professional Irresponsibility*, 67 Georgetown L.J. 991 (1978); Lorne, *The Corporate and Securities Adviser, the Public Interest, and Professional Ethics*, 76 Mich. L. Rev. 425 (1978); Maxey, *SEC Enforcement Actions Against Securities Lawyers: New Remedies vs. Old Policies*, 22 Del. J. Corp. L. 539 (1997); Painter, *The Moral Interdependence of Corporate Lawyers and their Clients*, 67 So. Cal. L. Rev. 507 (1994); Painter & Duggan, *Lawyer Disclosure of Client Fraud: Establishing a Firm Foundation*, 50 SMU L. Rev. 225 (1996); Seamons, *Inside the Labyrinth of the Elusive Standard Under the SEC's Rule 2(e)*, 23 Sec. Reg. L.J. 57 (1995); Sonde, *The Responsibility of Professionals Under the Federal Securities Laws — Some Observations*, 68 Nw. U. L. Rev. 1 (1973).

In the securities law context, counsel may be retained by the corporate entity. Generally, directors, officers, shareholders, employees, and affected communities may be considered constituents of the corporation.[126] In determining to whom to look as embodying the various interest groups of the corporation, the incumbent board of directors (elected by the shareholders) and members of executive management (who in turn are appointed by the board) may be deemed as the appropriate decisionmakers of corporate policy.[127]

In this regard, decisions made by an executive officer, properly designated to make such determinations, generally should be accepted by the lawyer as one made by the corporation. However, when such determinations involve violations of law, different considerations apply. In such situations, counsel should take appropriate measures which may include (depending on the seriousness of the situation and the corrective steps, if any, taken): (1) asking the officer or other decisionmaker to reconsider the matter; (2) if the situation is not corrected, referring the matter to higher authority in the corporation, such as the chief executive officer or the board of directors; (3) advising that a separate legal opinion on the matter's legality be procured; (4) fully informing the independent directors of the matter and its consequences; (5) if all else fails and the client seeks to engage in the illegal action without taking corrective action, resigning from the representation; and (6) in some states, having discretion to inform shareholders, affected third parties, and government agencies of the fraud.[128]

The SEC in the *Carter and Johnson*[129] proceeding focused on this subject. Although the Commission held that the respondents did not violate Rule 2(e) (now Rule 102(e)), it set forth standards that apply today:

> The Commission is of the view that a lawyer engages in "unethical or improper professional conduct" under the following circumstances: When a lawyer with significant responsibilities in the effectuation of a company's compliance with the disclosure requirements of the federal securities laws becomes aware that his client is engaged in a substantial and continuing failure to satisfy those disclosure requirements, his continued participation violates professional standards unless he takes prompt steps to end the client's non-compliance. . . .
>
> We do not imply that a lawyer is obliged, at the risk of being held to have violated Rule 2(e), to seek to correct every isolated disclosure action or inaction which he believes to be at variance with applicable disclosure standards, although there may be isolated disclosure

---

[126] See Model Rule 1.13 (comment).

[127] *Id.* See Steinberg, *Corporate / Securities Counsel — Conflicts of Interest*, 8 J. Corp. L. 577 (1983); *Developments in the Law — Conflicts of Interest in the Legal Profession*, 94 Harv. L. Rev. 1244 (1981).

[128] See Model Rule 1.13(b), (c) (and comment thereto). See *supra* note 124 and accompanying text.

[129] *In re Carter and Johnson*, [1981 Transfer Binder] Fed. Sec. L. Rep. (CCH) ¶ 82,847 (SEC 1981).

failures that are so serious that their correction becomes a matter of primary professional concern. It is also clear, however, that a lawyer is not privileged to unthinkingly permit himself to be co-opted into an ongoing fraud and cast as a dupe or a shield for a wrongdoing client.

Initially, counselling accurate disclosure is sufficient, even if his advice is not accepted. But there comes a point at which a reasonable lawyer must conclude that his advice is not being followed, or even sought in good faith, and that his client is involved in a continuing course of violating the securities laws. At this critical juncture, the lawyer must take further, more affirmative steps in order to avoid the inference that he has been co-opted willingly or unwillingly, into the scheme of non-disclosure.

The lawyer is in the best position to choose his next step. Resignation is one option, although we recognize that other considerations, including the protection of the client against foreseeable prejudice, must be taken into account in the case of withdrawal. A direct approach to the board of directors or one or more individual directors or officers may be appropriate; or he may choose to try to enlist the aid of other members of the firm's management. What is required, in short, is some prompt action that leads to the conclusion that the lawyer is engaged in efforts to correct the underlying problem, rather than having capitulated to the desires of a strong-willed, but misguided client.

Some have argued that resignation is the only permissible course when a client chooses not to comply with disclosure advice. We do not agree. Premature resignation serves neither the end of an effective lawyer-client relationship nor, in most cases, the effective administration of the securities laws. The lawyer's continued interaction with his client will ordinarily hold the greatest promise of corrective action. So long as a lawyer is acting in good faith and exerting reasonable efforts to prevent violations of the law by his client, his professional obligations have been met. In general, the best result is that which promotes the continued, strong-minded and independent participation by the lawyer.

We recognize, however, that the "best result" is not always obtainable, and that there may occur situations where the lawyer must conclude that the misconduct is so extreme or irretrievable, or the involvement of his client's management and board of directors in the misconduct is so thorough-going and pervasive that any action short of resignation would be futile. We would anticipate that cases where a lawyer has no choice but to resign would be rare and of an egregious nature. [130]

It should be emphasized that the Commission in the *Carter and Johnson* proceeding focused on counsel's obligations to seek the undertaking of

---

[130] *Id.* at 84,172–84,173.

corrective action *within* the corporate structure when fraud is afoot. The SEC did not address counsel's duty to disclose to the public or to affected third parties.[131]

---

[131] *Id.* at 84,173 n.78. See authorities cited note 125 *supra*.

APPENDIX 14

SEC Order Directing a Private Investigation

UNITED STATES OF AMERICA
BEFORE THE
SECURITIES AND EXCHANGE COMMISSION

In the Matter of XYZ Corporation :	ORDER DIRECTING A PRIVATE INVESTIGATION AND DESIGNATING OFFICERS TO
File No. _____ :	TAKE TESTIMONY

I

The Commission's public files disclose that XYZ Corporation is a corporation with its principal executive offices in Sandusky, Ohio. Its common stock is registered with the Commission pursuant to Section 12(g) of the Securities Exchange Act of 1934 (the "Exchange Act") and is quoted on the National Association of Securities Dealers Automated Quotation System ("NASDAQ"). XYZ Corporation has filed with the Commission registration statements and annual, quarterly and other periodic reports pursuant to Section 13 of the Exchange Act.

II

Members of the staff have reported information to the Commission tending to show that, during the period from on or about April 15, 1999, through the present:

A. XYZ Corporation, its present and former officers, directors, employees, affiliates and other persons or entities, directly and indirectly, in connection with the purchase or sale of securities, may have employed, or may be employing, devices, schemes or artifices to defraud, may have made, or may be making, untrue statements of material facts and may have omitted, or may be omitting, to state material facts necessary in order to make the statements made, in the light of the circumstances under which they were made, not misleading, and may have engaged, or may be engaging in transactions, acts, practices or courses of business which operate or have operated as a fraud and deceit upon other persons, including purchasers and sellers of such securities, concerning, among other things, the inventory, sales, payroll taxes, cash flow and the financial condition and performance of XYZ Corporation.

B. XYZ Corporation, its present and former officers, directors, employees, affiliates and other persons or entities, directly or indirectly, may have filed or caused to be filed with the Commission certain annual, quarterly and other reports pursuant to the Exchange Act which may have contained untrue statements of material facts or may have omitted information or material facts necessary in order to make the statements made, not misleading, and which may have failed to contain information required to be set forth therein concerning, among other things, the matters referred to in Paragraph II.A. above.

C. XYZ Corporation, its present and former officers, directors, employees, affiliates and other persons or entities, directly and indirectly, may have failed to or caused the failure to:

    1.   make and keep books, records, and accounts which, in reasonable detail, accurately and fairly reflect transactions and dispositions of the corporate funds of XYZ Corporation, and

    2.   devise and maintain a system of internal accounting controls sufficient to provide reasonable assurances that:

        a.   transactions are executed in accordance with management's general or specific authorization;

        b.   transactions are recorded as necessary to permit preparation of financial statements in conformity with generally accepted accounting principles or any other criteria applicable to such statements and to maintain accountability for assets;

        c.   access to assets is permitted only in accordance with management's general or specific authorization; and

        d.   the recorded accountability for assets is compared with the existing assets at reasonable intervals and appropriate action is taken with respect to any differences.

D. XYZ Corporation, its present and former officers, directors, employees, affiliates and other persons or entities, directly or indirectly, may have falsified, or caused the falsification of, books, records and accounts referred to in Subparagraphs II.C.1 and 2 above.

III

The Commission, having considered the foregoing, and deeming such acts and practices, if true, to be in possible violation of Section 17(a) of the Securities Act of 1933 and Sections 10(b), 13(a) and 13(b)(2)(A) and (B) of the Exchange Act of 1934 ("Exchange Act") and Rules 10b-5, 12b-20, 13a-1, 13a-13, 13b2-1, and 13b2-2 thereunder, finds it necessary and appropriate and hereby:

ORDERS, pursuant to Section 20(a) of the Securities Act and Section 21(a) of the Securities Exchange Act that a private investigation be conducted to determine whether any person, persons or entities have engaged, are engaging, or are about to engage in any of the aforesaid acts or practices, or in acts or practices of similar purport or object; and

FURTHER ORDERS, pursuant to Section 19(b) of the Securities Act and Section 21(b) of the Securities Exchange Act, that, for the purpose of such investigation, Louise Bennett, Anthony Davis, Lewis Goldstein, Christopher Hanna, George Martinez, and Kathleen Vaughan, and each of them, are hereby designated as officers of this Commission and each of them are empowered to administer oaths and affirmations, subpoena witnesses, compel their attendance, take evidence, and require the production of any books, papers, correspondence, memoranda or other records and materials deemed relevant or material to the investigation, and to perform all other duties in connection therewith as prescribed by law.

By the Commission

_____

Secretary

SEC Subpoena Order

SUBPOENA DUCES TECUM
UNITED STATES OF AMERICA
SECURITIES AND EXCHANGE COMMISSION

To T.J. Maloney, P.O. Box 934,
 Los Angeles, CA 90024

At the instance of the Securities and Exchange Commission you are hereby required to appear before Kathleen Vaughan, George Martinez, Christopher Hanna, Madeline Bates, Officers of the Securities and Exchange Commission, at 801 Cherry Street, 19th Floor in the City of Fort Worth, TX 76102 on the 14th day of July, 2000, at 9:00 o'clock a.m. of that day, to testify in the matter of XYZ Enterprises, Inc. involving a private investigation by the Commission pursuant to Section 20(a) of the Securities Act of 1933 and Section 21(a) of the Securities Exchange Act of 1934.

And you are hereby required to bring with you and produce at said time and place the following books, papers, and documents:

All monthly and quarterly brokerage account statements for your own account and for any account under your direction or control from March 15, 1999 through December 31, 1999; all calendars, logs, day timers or other documents reflecting meetings held or to be held from March 15, 1999 through December 31, 1999; all business, personal, mobil, and cellular telephone records for the period March 15, 1999 through December 31, 1999; all expense reports and supporting documentation from March 15, 1999 through December 31, 1999; all bank records for all accounts under your control or in which you have a direct or indirect or beneficial interest from March 15, 1999 through December 31, 1999.

Fail not at your peril,

> In testimony whereof, the seal of the Securities and Exchange Commission is affixed hereto, and the undersigned, a member of said Securities and Exchange Commission, or an officer designated by it, has hereunto set his hand at Fort Worth, Texas, this 30th day of June, 2000.

Kathleen Vaughan

GLOSSARY

This Glossary is designed to familiarize the reader with key securities law terms, statutes, rules, and other regulations. Although not intended to be comprehensive or exhaustive, the Glossary should prove useful.

General Terms

Acceleration Process by which the SEC can expedite a registration statement's effective date, thereby avoiding § 8(a)'s twenty day waiting requirement. *See § 8(a) of the Securities Act; Rule 460.*

Accredited Investor Class of investor defined in such provisions as § 2(15) of the Securities Act and Rule 501(a), for purposes of the exempt offering provisions of Regulation D and § 4(6) of the Securities Act, to include certain institutional investors as well as financially sophisticated and/or wealthy investors. *See Uniform Limited Offering Exemption (ULOE); § 4(6) of the Securities Act; Rules 505 and 506; Regulation D.*

Affiliate Generally, an affiliate of an issuer is one who controls, is controlled by, or is under common control with, either directly or indirectly through one or more intermediaries, such issuer. *See Controlling Person; Rule 405.*

"All-or-None" Offering Type of offering whereby all the securities offered must be sold at a specified price within a specified time with the amount due to the seller at a specified date and where the purchase price will be refunded if the offering is not fully subscribed. Pursuant to Rule 10b-9, such offerings are prohibited unless such conditions are met.

American Stock Exchange (AMEX) Exchange where the securities of smaller and perhaps newer companies are traded, as compared to the New York Stock Exchange with its larger companies and more stringent listing requirements. *See Securities Exchanges.*

Annual Report to Security Holders Pursuant to Rule 14a-3 and Rule 14c-3, an annual report is to be furnished to an issuer's security holders. The annual report is not deemed a filed document for Exchange Act § 18(a) liability purposes. *See § 14(a) of the Exchange Act; Rule 14a-9.*

Auditor Disclosure of Corporate Fraud Section 10A of the Exchange Act sets forth requirements for audits conducted by an independent public accountant of an issuer's financial statements to include certain procedures to (i) detect illegal acts that would have a direct and material effect on the determination of financial statements; (ii) identify related party transactions material to financial statements; and (iii) evaluate an issuer's ability to continue as a going concern. The statutory language makes clear that the above procedures are to be carried out in accordance with current generally accepted accounting principles, "as may be modified from time to time by the [SEC]." *See § 10A of the Exchange Act.*

"Bad Boy" Disqualifications Refers to provisions contained in certain SEC rules (such as Rule 262) disqualifying an issuer from using certain exemptions from registration if the issuer or its affiliated persons, executive officers, directors, or other like persons have been subject to disciplinary action during the previous five years (or ten years for Rule 262(b)(1)), including a criminal conviction relating to the sale of securities and the imposition of an SEC injunction.

"Bespeaks Caution" Doctrine Provides that forward-looking statements included in a disclosure document (such as a registration statement) are not actionable as securities fraud provided that such statements are accompanied by specific and meaningful cautionary language. *See Forward-Looking Statement; Safe Harbor for Certain Forward-Looking Statements; "Soft" Information.*

"Best Efforts" Underwriting Type of underwriting arrangement where the underwriters agree to act as agents for the issuer and use their "best efforts" in finding purchasers for the securities being offered. To the extent that the underwriters are unsuccessful in finding purchasers, the securities are not sold. *See Underwriting; "Firm Commitment" Underwriting.*

"Blank Check" Company A developmental stage company issuing penny stock that has (1) no specific business plan or purpose, or (2) the business plan of which is to merge with an unidentified company or companies. *See "Blank Check" Offering; Penny Stock; § 7 of the Securities Act.*

"Blank Check" Offering The offering of securities of a "blank check" company. *See "Blank Check" Company; Penny Stock; § 7 of the Securities Act.*

"Blue Sky" Laws Term used to refer to the body of state securities laws. Some states have statutes that only require disclosure of material information, while other states have merit regulation which requires, in addition to full disclosure, that the securities offered meet a test of substantive fairness. *See Merit Regulation; Regulation by Qualification.*

Bond Type of security which evidences a debt on which the issuing governmental body or corporation promises to pay the holder of the bond a specified amount of interest for a predetermined length of time, with repayment of the principal amount at a specified expiration date. A bond (as distinguished from a debenture or other debt security) is secured by the corporation's assets. *See Debentures; Debt Securities.*

Broker Generally, a "person" engaged in the business of purchasing or selling securities for the account of others.

Cease and Desist Order Pursuant to the 1990 Enforcement Remedies Act, an order issued by the SEC prohibiting a subject "person" from carrying on its proscribed conduct. *See Enforcement Remedies Act; § 8A of the Securities Act; § 21C of the Exchange Act.*

"Change in Circumstances" Doctrine Doctrine which holds that the concept of underwriter status can be avoided if a party can establish that he/she purchased the subject securities with investment intent but that subsequent unforeseen changes compelled the earlier than planned sale of the securities. Although the SEC has evidently rejected this defense to underwriter status, courts nonetheless may accept its validity.

Churning Refers to the practice of a broker-dealer engaging in excessive trading in a customer account over which it has control for the purpose of generating commissions.

Comfort Opinion A statement furnished by an attorney, acting either as counsel for the issuer or for the underwriter, providing that, based on counsel's participation in the preparation of the registration statement and conferences with representatives of the issuer, underwriters and public accountants, he/she has no reason to believe that the registration statement violates § 11. In order to avoid § 11 liability, counsel should ensure that neither the opinion nor its contents appear in the registration statement.

Conditioning the Market See *"Gun-Jumping."*

Controlling Person Pursuant to Rule 405, a controlling person is any person who directly or indirectly possesses the power to direct the management or policies of an entity. *See Rule 405.*

Covered Security Pursuant to the National Securities Markets Improvement Act of 1996, the SEC is granted exclusive authority over the registration of specified "covered" securities, thereby preempting state regulation of such offerings. *See National Securities Markets Improvement Act of 1996; § 18 of the Securities Act.*

Crown Jewel Antitakeover device whereby the target company sells (or grants an option to purchase) its most valuable asset — its "crown jewel" — to a third party in order to make the company less attractive to an unfriendly bidder.

Dealer Generally, a "person" engaged in the business of purchasing or selling securities for its own account.

Debentures Type of debt security that is not secured by a mortgage on the issuing corporation's assets, but is only backed by the company's general credit. Issuances of debentures are subject to the Trust Indenture Act of 1939 as well as the Securities Act of 1933. The antifraud provisions of § 10(b) of the Exchange Act also apply. *See Bonds; Debt Securities.*

Debt Securities Refers to bonds, notes, debentures, and other evidences of indebtedness in which investors furnish capital to a corporation in return for a promise by the corporation to repay the principal in full at a future specified date and to pay the investor a fixed rate of interest thereon for the term of the loan. The issuance of debt securities is subject to the Trust Indenture Act of 1939 and to the Securities Act. The antifraud provisions of § 10(b) of the Exchange Act apply as well. *See Bonds; Debentures.*

Deficiency Letter Letter sent by the SEC's Division of Corporation Finance to an issuer notifying it of deficiencies in its registration statement. Amendments to the registration statement are subsequently filed in response thereto. This letter also is known as a "letter of comments."

Derivatives Instruments, the value of which are limited to, or derived from, the worth of an underlying asset (e.g., stock, currencies, or commodities), indices (e.g., a stock market index), or interest rates.

Director/Officer Bar A court order prohibiting a person from serving as an officer or director of a publicly-held entity who has violated certain securities acts' antifraud provisions and whose conduct demonstrates "substantial unfitness." *See § 20(e) of the Securities Act; § 21(d) of the Exchange Act.*

"Disclose or Abstain" Rule Doctrine promulgated by the courts in the insider trading context which provides that under certain circumstances (see *Chiarella*, 445 U.S. 222 (1980), *Dirks*, 463 U.S. 646 (1983) and *O'Hagan, 117 S. Ct. 2199 (1997)),* one with material nonpublic information concerning a company's securities, the affairs of a company, or the market for the company's stock must either refrain from trading (or tipping) based on such information or must disclose such information to the investing public before trading (or tipping) on it.

Due Diligence In the securities offering context, refers to the functions performed by various parties, including underwriters, to help ensure that the prospectus contains no material misstatement or omission. The standard of conduct required of parties to successfully invoke the due diligence defense varies depending on such factors as the statute implicated (*e.g.,* § 11 of the Securities Act as compared to § 10(b) of the Exchange Act), the party's relationship with the issuer, whether the defendant is an expert or non-expert, and whether the portion of the offering document in question is an expertised or non-expertised portion.

Due Diligence In the securities litigation context, particularly with respect to the issue of justifiable reliance under § 10(b) of the Exchange Act and the one-year period of constructive notice under applicable statutes of limitations, refers to the plaintiff's obligation to protect his/her investment interests. *See Justifiable Reliance; Statute of Limitations.*

"Economic Reality" Looking at the prefatory language, "unless the context otherwise requires," contained in § 2 of the Securities Act and § 3(a) of the Exchange Act, courts, in ascertaining whether a security exists, decipher the economic reality of a transaction rather than applying a literal construction.

"Economic Risk" Test Under Rule 146 (which has been superseded by Rule 506), test used to determine whether offerees or purchasers of securities are able to bear the economic risks of the investment and, hence, help qualify the offering for exemption from registration pursuant to § 4(2). Rule 506 has eliminated this test. The test, however, still may be applicable under certain states' Blue Sky laws.

Efficient Market Theory See "Fraud on the Market" theory.

Electronic Data Gathering, Analysis, and Retrieval System (ED-GAR) Registrants subject to EDGAR must file with the SEC virtually all documents by means of electronic submission.

Enforcement Remedies Act This Act, enacted in 1990, authorized the SEC, *inter alia*, to issue cease and desist orders, obtain monetary penalties, order disgorgement in specified situations, and procure director and officer bar orders from the federal courts.

Exempt Securities Specific securities or categories of securities which are never required to be registered under § 5 of the 1933 Act. The exemption is predominantly due to the intrinsic character or nature of the issuer itself. Examples of exempt securities include certain short-term promissory notes or bills of exchange, securities issued or guaranteed by municipalities, state or federal governments, and securities issued by nonprofit, religious, educational or charitable organizations. *See Transactional Exemptions.*

Express Causation Requirement Enacted as part of the PSLRA, Section 21D(b)(4) of the Exchange Act expressly requires that a plaintiff prove loss causation is any private action under the Exchange Act. *See Private Securities Litigation Reform Act (PSLRA).*

"Family Resemblance" Test Test adopted by the U.S. Supreme Court (see *Reves*, 494 U.S. 56 (1990)) to determine whether a note is a security. Beginning with the presumption that a note of greater than a nine-month duration is a security, the family resemblance test analyzes each note by examining four factors: (1) the motivations that would prompt a reasonable buyer and seller to enter into the transaction; (2) the plan of distribution; (3) the reasonable expectations of the investing public concerning the note in question; and (4) any relevant risk reducing factors, such as a regulatory scheme or collateralization.

"Firm Commitment" Underwriting Type of underwriting arrangement whereby the underwriters agree to purchase from the issuer the securities being offered for the purpose of reselling them to participating dealers and the public. To the extent that the underwriters are not successful in finding purchasers, they must pay for and hold the securities for their own account. *See Underwriting; "Best Efforts" Underwriting.*

Float The aggregate market value of an entity's voting securities held by nonaffiliates.

Foreign Corrupt Practices Act (FCPA) A 1977 amendment to the Exchange Act, this legislation requires a reporting company to maintain reasonably accurate and detailed books and records (in addition to its normal Exchange Act reporting requirements) and to devise and maintain an internal accounting system that will reasonably insure proper accountability of assets and internal control of accounting practices and procedures. Foreign bribery also is prohibited. *See §§ 13(b)(2) and 30A of the Exchange Act.*

Forward-Looking Statement Generally refers to "soft" future-oriented information rather than historical "hard" information, encompassing projections of future performance and appraisals of specified assets. *See "Bespeaks Caution" Doctrine; "Soft" Information; Private Securities Litigation Reform Act.*

"Fraud on the Market" Theory Theory used by courts (and acquiesced in by the Supreme Court) to apply the presumption of reliance in securities litigation (*e.g.,* § 10(b) litigation). This theory posits that the market price of an issuer's stock reflects all available public information regarding the issuer.

"Free Writing" Term used to refer to written sales literature (unless otherwise provided, such as a § 10 prospectus, tombstone ad, or identifying statement) that is prohibited during the pre-filing and waiting periods and only permitted in the post-effective period. However, if there is such "free writing" in the post-effective period, a statutory § 10(a) prospectus (or its equivalent) must precede or accompany it or such "free writing" will be deemed a separate prospectus under § 2(a)(10), thereby resulting in a violation of § 5(b)(1).

General Solicitation Lack of general solicitation is a necessary condition to perfect certain exemptions from Securities Act registration, such as Rules 505 and 506 of Regulation D and the Section 4(2) and 4(6) exemptions. According to the SEC, the presence of a preexisting relationship with the offeree is an important factor in determining the lack of general solicitation. The substantial compliance standard of Rule 508 provides no defense if there is general solicitation. *See Private Offering Exemption; § 4(2); § 4(6); Rule 505; Rule 506; Rule 508.*

Glass-Steagall Act Popular name for the Banking Act of 1933. In essence, this legislation required that investment banking be separated from commercial banking. It has been repealed. *See Gramm-Leach-Bliley Act; Investment Banking.*

Going-Private Refers to a transaction or series of transactions in a publicly-held company whereby the controlling (or other) group substantially reduces or eliminates entirely the number of shares held by the public by inducing shareholders to exchange their stock for cash, thereby causing the company to attain private status. Such transactions are regulated by Rules 13e-3 and 13e-4 and, of course, state law. *See Leveraged Buyout (LBO); § 13(e) of the Exchange Act; Rules 13e-3, 13e-4; Schedule 13E-3.*

Going-Public Process whereby an issuer embarks upon a plan of financing in which securities are sold to the investing public. The issuer thereby becomes subject to the reporting requirements of the Exchange Act. *See Initial Public Offering (IPO).*

Golden Parachute A generous severance package that compensates certain key executives if control of a target company changes in the event of a corporate takeover.

Gramm-Leach-Bliley Act Act repealing the Glass-Steagall Act of 1933, the 1999 legislation, among other things, creates a regulatory framework premised on "functional regulation," authorizes the formation of "financial holding companies" that can provide a full array of financial products, and permits subsidiaries of banks (rather than banks themselves) to take part in an expansive range of financial activities.

"Greenmail" The purchase of a substantial block of the subject company's securities by a (potentially) unfriendly suitor with the primary purpose of inducing the subject company to repurchase the block at a premium over the amount paid by the potential suitor.

"Gun-Jumping" The publication of information of an offering or other conduct in the pre-filing period resulting in a conditioning of the public market or a stimulation of interest in the securities to be registered, thereby resulting in a violation of the § 5(c) proscription against offers to sell in the pre-filing period.

Horizontal Commonality One of the two types of "common enterprise" for purposes of the *Howey* investment contract test. Generally, horizontal commonality looks to the relationships which exist between an individual investor and the pool of other investors. A pooling of the interests of the investors is essential to finding the presence of horizontal commonality; all courts have held that horizontal commonality is sufficient to meet the common enterprise requirement of the *Howey* test. *See Vertical Commonality; Howey Test.*

"Hot Issue" Occurs where the price of an offering of securities quickly rises to a substantial premium above the initial offering price. The demand for the securities offered may be accompanied by an investor stampede to purchase the coveted "hot" stock.

Howey **Test** Test promulgated by the Supreme Court in the *Howey* case, 328 U.S. 293 (1946), to determine when an investment contract exists for purposes of § 2(a)(1) of the Securities Act and § 3(a)(10) of the Exchange Act. "The test is whether the scheme involves an investment of money in a common enterprise with profits to come solely from the efforts of others." The test subsequently has been elaborated upon by the lower courts. *See Investment Contract.*

Identifying Statement Pursuant to Rule 134, a communication concerning an offering, not deemed to be a prospectus under § 2(a)(10), which may be published or transmitted during the waiting period (and post-effective period). The identifying statement is used to ascertain what parties are interested in the securities and the extent of such interest. Mention of the price of the securities is permitted. *See Rule 134.*

In Registration Refers to the entire registration process, generally from the pre-filing period until the prospectus delivery requirements have been satisfied.

Initial Public Offering (IPO) The first public offering of securities that an issuer makes. By so doing, the issuer "goes public" and becomes subject to the Exchange Act's reporting obligations. *See "Going-Public".*

Insider Trading Sanctions Act (ITSA) Enacted in 1984, and amended in 1988, this legislation authorizes the SEC, *inter alia*, to seek the imposition of a civil monetary penalty amounting to three times the profit received or loss avoided against any person unlawfully purchasing or selling securities while in possession of material nonpublic information, unlawfully tipping material nonpublic information, or substantially contributing to the violation's occurrence by a brokerage firm's (or investment adviser's) failure to maintain and enforce an adequate law compliance monitoring system. Under certain circumstances, other "entities" (such as corporations, accounting and law firms) also may be subject to a treble money penalty. *See Insider Trading and Securities Fraud Enforcement Act (ITSFEA).*

Insider Trading and Securities Fraud Enforcement Act (ITSFEA) Enacted in 1988, this Act increases the SEC's enforcement powers with respect to insider trading through, *inter alia*, enhanced money penalties, more rigorous provisions with respect to control person liability, and authorization for awarding bounties to informants. *See Insider Trading Sanctions Act (ITSA).*

Integrated Disclosure Refers to the Commission's integrated disclosure framework which simplifies registrant reporting by (1) making uniform the disclosure requirements under the Securities Act and the Exchange Act, (2) allowing periodic reporting under the Exchange Act to satisfy much of the Securities Act registration statement disclosure requirements, and (3) encouraging (but not requiring) the use of informal shareholder communications to satisfy certain of the Act's formal disclosure requirements.

Integration of Offerings Doctrine by which seemingly separate offerings are construed as one integrated offering, thereby vitiating otherwise exempt offerings and usually resulting in a violation of the Securities Act's registration requirements. The SEC has set forth criteria to determine when integration should apply as well as establishing certain safe harbor rules. *See Rules 147(b)(2) and 502(a).*

Investment Advisors Act of 1940 Requires registration of all non-exempt investment advisors and obligates such advisers to conform their conduct to statutory norms. The Act, *inter alia*, addresses fee arrangements between advisors and clients, prohibits fraudulent practices, precludes assignment of an investment advisory contract without the client's consent, requires advisors to maintain books and records consistent with rules that may be promulgated by the SEC, and authorizes the SEC to inspect such books and records.

Investment Company Act of 1940 Requires companies engaged primarily in the business of investing, reinvesting, and trading in securities and whose securities are offered to and held by the investing public to register with the SEC and to disclose their financial condition and investment policies. The Act contains anti-fraud provisions and private remedies. Investment companies also may be subject to the provisions of the 1933 and 1934 Acts.

"Investment Contract" Term used in § 2(a)(1) of the Securities Act and § 3(a)(10) of the Exchange Act as a type of instrument that constitutes a security. *See Howey Test.*

Justifiable Reliance An objective or reasonable person test in determining whether a plaintiff's reliance on an alleged misrepresentation was justifiable in cause of action under § 10(b) of the Exchange Act. Factors relevant to this determination include *(Myers v. Finkle,* 950 F.2d 165 (4th Cir. 1991)): "(1) the sophistication and expertise of the plaintiff in financial and securities matters; (2) the existence of long standing business or personal relationships; (3) access to the relevant information; (4) the existence of a fiduciary relationship (5) concealment of the fraud; (6) the opportunity to detect the fraud; (7) whether the plaintiff initiated the stock transaction or sought to expedite the transaction; and (8) the generality or specificity of the misrepresentations." *See Due Diligence; Statute of Limitations.*

Letter of Comments *See Deficiency Letter.*

Letter of Intent Signed letter between an issuer and its managing underwriter outlining the proposed terms of the offering as well as the underwriting compensation, but not binding either party, with the possible exception of a provision concerning payment of expenses upon abandonment by one of the parties. *See Firm Commitment Underwriting; Market Out Clause.*

Leveraged Buyout (LBO) Corporate control transaction frequently characterized by public shareholders of a corporation being cashed-out, with corporate insiders obtaining a substantial equity interest in the ongoing enterprise. The funds borrowed to finance the acquisition are collaterized by the corporation's assets, with repayment of the loans to be made out of the company's future revenue stream and the sale of certain divisions or subsidiaries. *See Going-Private.*

Lock-Up An arrangement, made in connection with the contemplated acquisition of a publicly-held entity, that gives the prospective acquiror an advantage in acquiring the subject company over other potential acquirors.

Management Discussion and Analysis (MD&A) Item 303 of Regulation S-K (as well as Item 303 of Regulation S-B) requires disclosure of Management's Discussion and Analysis of Financial Condition and Results of Operation (MD&A). In short, the MD&A disclosure requirements seek to provide investors with management's analysis of historical and prospective material events, trends, and uncertainties. Generally, disclosure is required where the subject event, trend or uncertainty is reasonably likely to occur and to have a material impact on the company's financial condition or results of operation. *See Regulations S-B and S-K.*

Market Information Information about the market for a particular entity's securities as contrasted with information about the corporation or its business.

Market Maker Refers to a broker-dealer in the over-the-counter market who buys and sells securities as a principal for its own account on a regular or continual basis. The market maker conducts "two-way" bids; *i.e.*, it stands willing to both buy and sell the securities for which it is making a market. Market makers are subject to regulation by the National Association of Securities Dealers (NASD) and the SEC. *See NASD.*

Market Out Clause Permits an underwriter to avoid its commitment to acquire securities from the issuer prior to the closing of the offering if certain specified event(s) transpire. *See Firm Commitment Underwriting; Letter of Intent.*

Merit Regulation Refers to state Blue Sky statutes that, in addition to requiring full and adequate disclosure, require that securities offerings be substantively fair, just, and equitable. *See "Blue Sky" Laws; Registration by Qualification.*

Misappropriation Theory Generally extends liability for insider trading to persons who trade or tip material nonpublic information in breach of a duty owed to the source of the information (namely, to a source other than the subject corporation and its shareholders). See Rule 10b5-2.

Model Accredited Investor Exemption A model transactional exemption drafted by the North American Securities Administrators Association (NASAA) and adopted in full or in part by a number of states. Provides that issuers may avoid state registration requirements if the securities are sold only to "accredited" investors. The model exemption allows the issuer to use a general advertisement to "test the waters" if such advertisement contains certain specified information. Similar to Rules 505 and 506 of SEC Regulation D, limitations on resale apply. There is no federal exemption that entirely coordinates with NASAA's model exemption. *See Testing the Waters; Rule 1001; Regulation A.*

Money Penalties Authorizes the SEC to impose administrative civil money penalties against regulated persons and to seek the levying of civil money penalties against all "persons" pursuant to order of a federal court. *See § 20(d) of the Securities Act; §§ 21(d), 21A, 21B of the Exchange Act.*

NASD (National Association of Securities Dealers, Inc.) Self-regulatory organization (SRO) of broker-dealers organized and governed under the supervision of the SEC pursuant to § 15 of the Exchange Act.

NASDAQ (National Association of Securities Dealers Automated Quotation System) Electronic means of publicizing buy and sell quotes to be used in the over-the-counter market. *See Market Maker; Over-The-Counter Market.*

NASAA (North American Securities Administrators Association) A voluntary organization composed of securities regulatory authorities of the 50 states, the Commonwealth of Puerto Rico, Guam, as well as Mexico and the provinces of Canada.

National Market System Exemption Preempts from state registration oversight, securities that are listed (or are authorized for listing) on the American Stock Exchange, the New York Stock Exchange, or the NASDAQ (National Market System). *See Covered Security; National Securities Markets Improvement Act (NSMIA); § 18 of the Securities Act.*

National Securities Markets Improvement Act of 1996 (NSMIA) 1996 federal legislation preempts state regulation of securities registration with respect to offerings of four classes of "covered" securities. The SEC has exclusive authority over the registration of these securities. Generally, these securities include: (1) securities offered by SEC registered investment companies; (2) securities offered to "qualified purchasers" as such term may be defined by SEC rule; (3) all securities listed (or authorized to be listed) on the American Stock Exchange, the New York Stock Exchange, or quoted in the NASDAQ National Market System (NMS); and (4) securities offered in specified transactions deemed exempt from Securities Act registration (e.g., Rule 506 offerings). *See Covered Security; National Market System Exemption; § 18 of the Securities Act.*

New-Issue Markets That part of the securities market which consists of initially issued securities. These securities are issued to the investing public through a network of underwriters and dealers. *See Trading Markets.*

New York Stock Exchange (NYSE) The dominant stock exchange in the United States. Most of this country's largest commercial and industrial companies have their securities listed and traded on the NYSE. *See Securities Exchanges.*

"No-Action" Letter Letter issued by the SEC's staff, sought by a party prior to engaging in the contemplated conduct, in order to help ensure that such conduct will not raise the Commission's ire. After a no-action letter has been issued, the SEC is not precluded from subsequently bringing an enforcement action; however, as a practical matter, the chances of such an action being initiated are slim. Prospective plaintiffs are not precluded from bringing suit by the issuance of an SEC no-action letter.

Over-The-Counter Market (OTC Market) Generally, securities transactions in the secondary trading markets which do not take place on exchanges are said to be conducted over-the-counter. *See Market Maker; NASDAQ; Pink Sheets.*

Pac-Man Defense A tender offer by the subject company for the securities of the bidder.

Penny Stock Generally, penny stocks are highly speculative, low priced securities that are traded in the over-the-counter market (OTC). *See NASDAQ; Over-the-Counter Market; Pink Sheets.*

"Piggy-Back" Registration Term used to refer to a manner in which a control person can register his/her stock in a public offering. If a control person has covenanted with the issuer for the right of "piggy-back" registration, he/she is authorized to "piggy-back" his/her stock or a portion thereof at the time that the issuer elects to file a registration statement.

Pink Sheets System used (now largely outdated) in the over-the-counter market to record quotes and reports of transactions of securities not traded on the NASDAQ System. *See Over-The-Counter Market.*

Plain English Disclosure Refers to SEC requirements that are designed to make disclosure documents (primarily offering documents) easier for individual investors to understand by mandating that the documents be free of highly technical and legalistic language. Other requirements include the use of clear and concise paragraphs and sentences, prominent risk factor disclosure, limited use of glossaries to explain information in the prospectus, and the use of descriptive headings.

Pleading Requirements Enacted as part of the PSLRA, Section 21D(b) of the Exchange Act requires that: a plaintiff in the complaint in any private securities fraud action alleging material misstatements and/or omissions "specify each statement alleged to have been misleading; the reason or reasons why the statement is misleading; and if an allegation regarding the statement or omission is made on information and belief, the complaint shall state with particularity all facts on which that belief is formed;" and (2) in any private action under the 1934 Act in which the plaintiff "may recover money damages only on proof that the defendant acted with a particular state of mind the complaint shall, with respect to each such act or omission alleged to violate the 1934 Act, state with particularity facts giving rise to a strong inference that the defendant acted with the required state of mind." *See Private Securities Litigation Reform Act (PSLRA)*.

Poison Pill Generally, an antitakeover provision (also called a "shareholder rights plan") whereby certain securities (such as rights or warrants) of the target company are triggered upon consummation of any enumerated transaction or event into the common stock or other security of the target or of the acquiror or cash.

PORTAL A securities market established to allow trading of securities pursuant to Rule 144A. Purchasers of such securities must be qualified institutional buyers ("QIBs") as defined by Rule 144A. *See Qualified Institutional Buyer; Rule 144A*.

Post-Effective Period Time period after the registration statement filed with the SEC becomes effective. Sales can be made only by means of a statutory § 10(a) prospectus; "free-writing" is permitted if accompanied or preceded by a statutory § 10(a) prospectus (or its equivalent); certain broker-dealer published information is permitted pursuant to Rules 137–139; the "tombstone ad" and "identifying statement" may be used; prospectus delivery requirement for dealers generally applies; unsolicited brokers' transactions without prospectus delivery requirements generally permitted if, *inter alia*, transactions executed on an exchange or in the over-the-counter market.

Pre-Filing Period Time period before a registration statement has been filed with the SEC. Subject to certain exceptions, offers to sell as well as offers to buy are prohibited; sales are prohibited; negotiations and agreements with underwriters who are or will be in privity with the issuer are permitted; Rule 135 announcements are permitted; certain broker-dealer published information is permitted pursuant to Rules 137–139. *See Gun-Jumping*.

Preliminary Prospectus Prospectus used pursuant to Rule 430 in the waiting period as a written offer in satisfaction of § 10's prospectus delivery requirement. The preliminary prospectus contains substantially the same information as the § 10(a) statutory prospectus. A legend in red ink must be included, stating among other things, that the registration statement has yet to become effective. This document also has been called a "red herring" prospectus. *See Rule 430*.

Presumptive Underwriter Doctrine Under this doctrine, one who purchases more than ten percent of the securities offered in a registered offering may be deemed an underwriter unless such person establishes sufficient investment intent. The SEC staff evidently has abandoned the presumptive underwriter doctrine.

Private Offering Exemption Transactions by an issuer which are exempt from the registration requirements of § 5 of the Securities Act because they do not involve any public offering, and hence, fall within the § 4(2) exemption of the Securities Act. *See § 4(2) of the Securities Act; Rule 506.*

Private Securities Litigation Reform Act (PSLRA) Enacted by Congress in 1995, this comprehensive legislation, for example, provides for: securities class action reform, sanctions for abusive litigation, stays of discovery, auditor disclosure of corporate fraud or illegality, proportionate liability (and related issues), enhanced pleading requirements, SEC aiding and abetting authority, RICO reform, and a safe harbor from liability for certain forward-looking statements.

Proportionate Liability (& Related Issues) Enacted as part of the PSLRA in 1995, Congress circumscribed the former joint and several liability scheme. Except where actual knowledge of the falsity is shown, there now exists a proportionate liability framework for actions brought against multiple defendants under the Exchange Act or against outside directors of the issuer whose securities are the subject of an action under Section 11 of the Securities Act. The legislation also clarified several issues relating to partial settlements in federal securities actions. *See Private Securities Litigation Reform Act (PSLRA).*

Prospectus Generally, as defined under § 2(a)(10) of the Securities Act, with certain exceptions, any written communication (or by radio or television) which offers any security for sale or confirms the sale of any security, including confirmations, letters, brochures, circulars, notices, and advertisements. Solely oral communications (if not by radio or television) do not constitute a prospectus.

As construed by the U.S. Supreme Court (*Gustafson*, 115 S. Ct. 1061 (1995)), the term "prospectus" as used in § 12(a)(2) of the Securities Act generally means the type of information that must be contained in a 1933 Act registration statement.

Public Utility Holding Company Act of 1935 Statute regulating interstate holding companies which are engaged through their subsidiaries in the retail distribution of manufactured or natural gas or in the electric utility business. This Act requires such holding companies, unless exempted by the Act, to register with the SEC and to file initial and periodic reports detailing the financial structure, organization, and operations of such companies and their subsidiaries.

Qualified Institutional Buyer (QIB) Only QIBs can purchase securities in the Rule 144A market. A QIB generally must have at least $100 million invested in securities of issuers who are not affiliated with such QIB. Banks and savings and loan associations also must have a net worth of at least $25 million. Broker-dealers are subject to less rigorous standards. *See Regulation S; Rule 144A; PORTAL.*

Racketeer Influenced and Corrupt Organizations Act (RICO) RICO establishes criminal offenses and penalties as well as a civil private right of action for treble damages and attorneys' fees.

Although enacted largely due to the concern of the extent to which organized crime had penetrated the national economy, controversy has arisen regarding the use of the private monetary right of action against accepted, legitimate businesses.

In reaction to this concern, legislation enacted in 1995 precludes private parties from bringing RICO civil actions based on alleged violations of securities-related provisions, unless a criminal conviction has been procured.

"Red Herring" *See Preliminary Prospectus; Rule 430.*

Refusal Order Proceeding initiated by the SEC pursuant to § 8(b) of the Securities Act empowering the Commission, after providing an opportunity for a hearing, to declare a registration statement deficient on its face, and thereby issue a refusal order. To issue a refusal order, the SEC must act within ten days after the filing of such registration statement. The effect of the Commission's order is to prevent the registration statement from becoming effective until amended in accordance with such order. *See § 8(b) of the Securities Act.*

Regional Exchanges The Boston (BSE), Philadelphia (Phix), Midwest (MSE), and Pacific (PSE) stock exchanges are examples of exchanges known as regional exchanges. The volume of trading conducted on such exchanges accounts for only a small percentage of all the trading done in the securities markets. *See Securities Exchanges; New York Stock Exchange; American Stock Exchange.*

Registration by Coordination Type of state Blue Sky registration available to an issuer when a registered offering is being made under the U.S. Securities Act. This type of state registration requires only the filing of three copies of the 1933 Act registration statement as well as any additional information required by the state securities administrator.

Registration by Notification Type of state Blue Sky registration requiring the filing of a short-form registration statement. Such form of registration generally is available only when an issuer and its predecessors have had a seasoned business for at least five years (*e.g.*, no default and average net earnings).

Registration by Qualification Type of state Blue Sky registration requiring, in addition to full and adequate disclosure, that the offering meet the strictures of merit regulation; *i.e.*, that the offering be substantively fair, just, and equitable. *See Merit Regulation.*

Registration Statement The basic disclosure document which must be filed with the SEC pursuant to the 1933 Act's registration requirements for public offerings. The registration statement consists of the § 10(a) statutory prospectus (or its equivalent), which must be delivered to prospective purchasers before or at the time that sales are consummated, and supplemental information which is placed on file and available for public inspection at the SEC's office.

Reporting Company Generally refers to issuers subject to the periodic reporting requirements of the Exchange Act. With certain exceptions, these registrants include: (1) those which have had a public offering under the Securities Act (*see § 15(d) of the Exchange Act*), (2) those which have securities traded on a national stock exchange (*see § 12(b) of the Exchange Act*), and (3) those which have more than $10 million in assets and a class of equity securities owned by at least 500 persons (*see § 12(g) of the Exchange Act, Rule 12g-1 of the Exchange Act*).

Repurchase Agreement Financing arrangement whereby a person owning securities agrees to transfer the securities to another party for cash at a certain price. The original owner also simultaneously agrees to "repurchase" these securities at a fixed, higher price from the other, "lending" party, on a fixed date, the price differential being the return to the lender on the investment. Whether a "repo" is construed as a purchase and sale of a security or as a loan will determine how it will be scrutinized under the securities laws.

Restricted Security Generally, securities acquired directly or indirectly from an issuer or its affiliate in a nonpublic offering, or securities subject to the Regulation D resale limitations. *See Rule 144.*

"Risk Capital" Test Under this test, an investment contract generally may be found if an investor invests money, property, or services in an enterprise or venture with the expectation of some pecuniary or non-pecuniary benefits to the investor to be derived essentially from the efforts of others; horizontal or vertical commonality need not be required. This important alternative to the *Howey* Test has been embraced by a number of states, although generally not by the federal courts. *See Howey Test.*

Safe Harbor for Certain Forward Looking Statements This safe harbor extends only to private securities actions. Section 27A of the 1933 Act and Section 21E of the 1934 Act each provides a safe harbor provision for certain forward looking statements. Both written and oral statements are covered as long as certain requirements are met. These requirements generally are: (1) the statement must be identified as forward looking and accompanied by meaningful cautionary statements; (2) the statement lacks materiality; or (3) the plaintiff fails to prove that the statement was made with actual knowledge of the falsity. *See "Bespeaks Caution" Doctrine; Forward-Looking Statement; Private Securities Litigation Reform Act (PSLRA); "Soft" Information; § 27A of the Securities Act; § 21E of the Exchange Act.*

Sale of Business Doctrine This doctrine, rejected by the Supreme Court in the companion cases of *Landreth Timber Co.*, 471 U.S. 681 (1985), and *Gould*, 471 U.S. 701 (1985), provides that the transfer of stock incidental to the sale of a business does not constitute a security.

Scorched Earth Defense Antitakeover device whereby the directors of the subject company take actions to sell off the subject company's assets, or failing this, to destroy the character of the company in an effort to defeat the bidder's tender offer.

Section "4(1-1/2)" Exemption A hybrid exemption from registration, not enumerated in the Securities Act, yet ostensibly within its intent. This exemption, based largely on SEC no-action letters and other SEC pronouncements, seeks to fill the gap in the statutory exemptive scheme concerning sales of securities by affiliates, and sales of restricted securities by non-affiliates, who desire to sell such securities in a routine private transaction. Certain "established criteria" of the § 4(1) and § 4(2) exemptions must be met in order for a person to successfully invoke this exemption.

Securities Act of 1933 The first federal securities statute enacted, this "Truth in Securities" Act focuses on the initial offering context. It requires all securities offered for sale, unless otherwise exempted, to be registered with the SEC. The Act sets forth the requirements for registration of securities that are offered for sale to the public. The Act also contains exemptions from registration, private remedies, and antifraud provisions. Full disclosure, and not merit regulation, is the guiding principle.

Securities Exchange Act of 1934 Federal statute establishing the Securities and Exchange Commission (SEC) and setting forth provisions governing the public trading of securities. The Act, for example, contains antifraud provisions, extensive reporting as well as other requirements for certain issuers of securities, oversight of broker-dealers and national securities exchanges, requirements focusing on proxy solicitation, and provisions covering tender offers and going-private transactions.

Securities Exchanges Forum with established rules and procedures where securities are traded by exchange members. The securities must be admitted to trading by the exchange and the members thereof trade for either their own accounts or for customers. By the provisions of the Exchange Act, the exchanges are subject to SEC oversight. *See American Stock Exchange; New York Stock Exchange; Regional Exchanges; § 6 of the Exchange Act.*

SEC Aiding and Abetting Authority The PSLRA added a new subsection (f) to Section 20 of the Exchange Act authorizing the SEC to seek injunctive relief and/or certain money penalties against aiders and abettors for violation of the Exchange Act or any rule or regulation thereunder. *See Private Securities Litigation Reform Act; § 20(f) of the Exchange Act.*

"Shark Repellents" Amendments to a company's certificate of incorporation or by-laws that have been devised to discourage unsolicited approaches from unwanted bidders.

"Shelf" Registration Refers to Rule 415 which concerns Securities Act registration of securities to be offered or sold on a delayed or continuous basis in the future. Rule 415 allows, *inter alia*, Form S-3 (or F-3) issuers to file primary-at-the-market offerings of equity securities which they plan to offer within two years of the effective date of the registration statement. *See Rule 415.*

Shell Corporation A thinly capitalized entity normally consisting of few if any assets, little or no cash flow, and basically no business functions or operations. Shell corporations frequently are employed to shield promoters from personal liability and as a marketing tool in the securities law context.

Shingle Theory Posits that broker-dealers are to be held to a fairly strict standard of conduct, because by hanging out its "shingle," a broker-dealer impliedly represents that its conduct and the behavior of its employees will be fair and will comport with professional norms. *See Suitability Theory.*

Short Sale Practice where an investor places an order to sell at the current market price a security which he/she does not then own. By so doing, he/she incurs an obligation to sell which is to be fulfilled by purchasing the securities at a later date, hopefully for a lower price, and thereafter delivering such securities to the purchaser. Rules promulgated by the SEC pursuant to its § 10(b) authority regulate short sales. Moreover, § 16(c) of the 1934 Act prohibits short sales by insiders.

Short-Swing Profits For purposes of § 16(b) of the 1934 Act, short-swing profits are profits realized by insiders (directors, officers, 10% shareholders) from the purchase and sale (or sale and purchase) of an equity security within a six-month period. Pursuant to § 16(b), such profits are subject to disgorgement to the corporation. Strict liability attaches in order to effectuate the remedial purpose of the statute. *See § 16(a), 16(b), 16(c) of the Exchange Act.*

Small Business Issuer Defined as a U.S. or Canadian entity having annual revenues of less than $25 million, provided that such entity's voting stock held by non-affiliates (*i.e.*, "public float") is less than $25 million. Investment companies are excluded. Moreover, if the entity is a majority owned subsidiary of another enterprise, its parent also must be a small business issuer. *See Float.*

Small Corporate Offering Registration Form (SCOR) Adopted by NASAA, SCOR provides a simplified state registration form for small offerings that are exempt from 1933 Act registration due to Rule 504 of Regulation D.

"Soft" Information Refers to appraised asset valuations, projections, future earnings, and other less than "hard" information about an issuer which traditionally have not been required to be disclosed to investors and shareholders, but which today are frequently disclosed. *See "Bespeaks Caution" Doctrine; Forward-Looking Information; MD&A; Safe Harbor for Certain Forward-Looking Statements; § 27A of the Securities Act; § 21E of the Exchange Act; Rule 175.*

Specialist A trader on a securities exchange who, pursuant to SEC and self-regulatory organization (SRO) regulations and for the purpose of maintaining "a fair and orderly market," purchases securities for his/her own account or executes orders for other broker-dealers, while specializing in the securities of particular issues or companies.

Statute of Limitations With respect to claims brought for alleged violations of §§ 11 and 12(a)(2) of the Securities Act and § 10(b) as well as certain other provisions of the Exchange Act, the statute of limitations is one year after the plaintiff knew or should have known of the facts constituting the violation and, in no event, more than three years after such violation. No equitable tolling applies. *See § 13 of the Securities Act.*

Statutory Prospectus The § 10(a) (of the 1933 Act) prospectus (or its equivalent) which is used only after the registration statement becomes effective and must be sent or given to the investor before or at the time that a sale is effectuated. The statutory prospectus constitutes the first portion of the registration statement and must conform with the requirements set forth in Schedule A of the 1933 Act. *See § 10(a) of the Securities Act; Rules 430A and 434.*

"Stickering" Refers to the practice of using a prospectus supplement, a "sticker," to update a registration statement to reflect "material" changes. Such "stickering" may be used in a "shelf" registration. *See "Shelf" Registration.*

Stock Type of corporate security, the purchase of which by an investor generally gives him/her the potential to share in the corporation's profits in the firm by way of dividends as well as (normally in regard to common stock) the right to elect the directors of the corporation and to vote on matters that will fundamentally change the structure or nature of the corporation. Stockholders, as equity owners of the corporations, can be said to own the corporation.

Stock Exchanges *See Securities Exchanges.*

"Stop Order" Proceeding initiated by the SEC pursuant to § 8(d) of the Securities Act in response to materially false, incomplete, inaccurate, or misleading information in a registration statement. Once such a proceeding is initiated, and violations are found, the effectiveness of the registration statement becomes suspended until amended in accordance with the stop order. The Commission must provide notice and an opportunity for a hearing. *See § 8(d), (e) of the Securities Act.*

Strike Suit A lawsuit of questionable merit initiated largely, if not solely, for its nuisance value and which seeks to induce the named defendants to settle the action. *See Private Securities Litigation Reform Act (PSLRA).*

Substantial Compliance Although not a defense in SEC or state enforcement proceedings, Rule 508 of Regulation D provides that minor and inadvertent errors in perfecting an exemption under

Regulation D will not result in the loss of the exemption. To meet this standard, the person relying on the exemption must show: (1) that the term, condition or requirement was not "directly intended to protect that particular individual;" (2) that the failure to comply was "insignificant with respect to the offering as a whole;" and (3) that a "good faith and reasonable attempt was made to comply" with all of the Regulation's terms, conditions and requirements. *See Rule 508.*

Suitability Theory As one aspect of the shingle theory, the suitability theory is premised on an implied representation by the broker that it will recommend only those securities suitable for each customer's investment objectives and economic status. *See Shingle Theory.*

Summary Prospectus Prospectus that may be used by reporting companies pursuant to Rule 431 and § 10(b) of the 1933 Act as a written offer in the waiting period and for solicitation purposes only in the post-effective period. *See Rule 431.*

Target Company Refers to a company that is the subject (target) of a takeover bid.

Tender Offer A means frequently used to acquire control of a corporation characterized by active solicitation to purchase a substantial percentage of the target's stock from the target's shareholders at a premium over the market price, offered for a limited period of time and often contingent upon the tender of a specific number of shares. Tender offers are governed by the Williams Act which was enacted by Congress as an amendment to the Exchange Act as well as state law. *See Williams Act; §§ 13(d), (e), 14(d), (e), and (f) of the 1934 Act.*

Testing the Waters The ability of companies under a Regulation A, Rule 1001, or the NASAA Model Accredited Investor Exemption to solicit potential investor interest in the company prior to the filing and delivery of the mandated offering statement. Testing the waters provisions are meant to provide developing companies with an opportunity to measure investor interest in the company before the company decides to undertake the substantial cost of compliance. In general, the written test the waters document is a free writing subject to the inclusion of certain information, including that no funds are being solicited or will be accepted and that a detailed offering document will follow.

"Tombstone Ad" Advertisement of an offering, not deemed to be a prospectus under § 2(a)(10) of the 1933 Act, which may be published during the waiting period (and post-effective period). It provides basic information about the offering and identifies the members of the underwriting syndicate. Such an ad is used to ascertain what parties are interested in the securities and the extent of such interest. Mention of the price of the securities is permitted.

Trading Markets Generally, consisting of securities that have been previously issued. These securities are bought and sold on stock exchanges and in the over-the-counter market.

Transactional Exemptions Refers to transactions which are exempt from the registration requirements of § 5 of the Securities Act due to perfection of one of the Securities Act's statutory exemptions (or pursuant to an exemption prescribed by the SEC under its rulemaking authority). Usually, state securities law exemptions also must be perfected.

Trust Indenture Act of 1939 Generally, federal legislation regulating the issuance of debentures, notes, bonds, and similar debt securities offered to the public pursuant to trust indentures. Often these securities also must be registered under the 1933 Act. The Trust Indenture Act regulates the conduct of the indenture trustee and the issuer and provides rights for security holders.

Two-Tier Offer A two-step acquisition technique in which the first-step (front-end) is a cash tender offer and the second-step (back-end) often is a merger in which remaining shareholders of the subject company may receive securities of the bidder valued below the cash consideration offered in the first-step tender offer.

Underwriter Any person who has purchased securities from an issuer (or from a controlling person) with a view to their distribution, offers or sells for an issuer (or for a controlling person) in connection with the distribution of securities, or directly or indirectly participates in any such undertaking, or the direct or indirect underwriting thereof. *See § 2(a)(11) of the 1933 Act; "Best Efforts" Underwriting; "Firm Commitment" Underwriting.*

Uniform Limited Offering Exemption (ULOE) Provides issuers with a uniform exemption from state registration and is intended to coordinate with SEC Regulation D. Most of the states have adopted some form of ULOE and it is the goal of the SEC and the North American Securities Administrators Association (NASAA) to achieve general uniformity in all the states. Note that state regulation of Rule 506 has been preempted by the National Securities Markets Improvement Act of 1996 (NSMIA).

Uniform Standards Act The Securities Litigation Uniform Standards Act of 1998, with certain exceptions, preempts state law with respect to securities class actions involving nationally traded securities. The authority of state securities commissioners is preserved. State actions also may be brought in the derivative suit context as well in going private actions, tender offers, and mergers.

Vertical Commonality One of the two types of "common enterprise" for purposes of the *Howey* test. Vertical commonality generally requires that the fortunes of the investor(s) and promoter (or third party) rise or fall together or that the success of the venture depends essentially on promoter expertise. The lower federal courts widely disagree on whether vertical commonality satisfies the *Howey* common enterprise element. *See Horizontal Commonality; Howey Test.*

Waiting Period Time period after a registration statement has been filed with the SEC but before it becomes effective. Oral offers and written offers by means of a § 10 prospectus are permitted; however, only in the post-effective period, may securities be sold and offers to buy be accepted; certain broker-dealer published information is permitted pursuant to Rules 137–139; the § 2(a)(10) "tombstone ad" and Rule 134 "identifying statement" may be used.

White Knight The name given to a party sought out by a subject company in an attempt to fend off an unwanted bidder. Action taken by a white knight may include purchasing a large block of the target company's stock or making a competing tender offer.

Williams Act Act adopted in 1968 as an amendment to the Exchange Act dealing generally with tender offers. Provisions of the Williams At include §§ 13(d), (e), 14(d), (e) and (f) of the Exchange Act. *See Tender Offer.*

Securities Act of 1933

Section 2 Provides the definitions of terms used throughout the Securities Act.

Section 3(a) Specifies and enumerates specific securities or categories of securities that are exempt from Securities Act (§ 5) registration, largely due to the intrinsic character or nature of the issuer itself. These exempt securities include, for example, certain short-term promissory notes or bills of exchange, securities issued or guaranteed by municipalities, state or federal governments, and securities issued by nonprofit, religious, educational or charitable organizations. Certain of the exempt securities, although not subject to 1933 Act registration, are regulated by other agencies (*e.g.*, securities issued by national banks are subject to regulation by the Comptroller of the Currency). Section 3(a)(2) through 3(a)(8) provides a listing of the exempt securities. Even an exempt security, however, is subject to the securities acts' antifraud provisions.

Section 3(a)(9) Provides that securities exchanged by an issuer exclusively with its existing security holders, except those exchanged in a Title 11 bankruptcy proceeding, are exempt from Securities Act registration, provided that no commission or other remuneration is paid for soliciting such an exchange.

Section 3(a)(10) Generally exempts from Securities Act registration securities which are issued in exchange for bona fide legal claims, securities, or property interests when a court or other specified tribunal, after conducting an adversary proceeding on the transaction's fairness, grants such approval.

Section 3(a)(11) The "intrastate" exemption provides an exemption from Securities Act registration for securities offered and sold only to persons resident within the same state as the issuer is resident and doing business (or incorporated and doing business). *See Rule 147.*

Section 3(b) Empowers the SEC, through the promulgation of rules and regulations, to define additional exemptions from registration where, in the Commission's view, the public interest and the protection of investors does not require such securities to be registered either because of the limited character of the offering or the small amount involved. However, no offering of over $5,000,000 may be exempted under this subsection. *See Rules 504, 505, 701, 1001; Regulation A.*

Section 4(1) Exempts from the registration requirements of § 5 "transactions by any person other than an issuer, underwriter, or dealer." Hence, this provision generally permits individual investors who are not affiliates to resell their securities without registration, provided such resales are viewed as "transactions" rather than as part of a "distribution." *See Underwriter; Rule 144.*

Section 4(2) The private offering exemption provides that "transactions by an issuer not involving any public offering" are exempt from the registration requirements of § 5 of the Securities Act. The requirements for perfecting the § 4(2) exemption are detailed. There is no monetary limit to the amount of funds that can be raised under this exemption. *See General Solicitation; Private Offering Exemption; Rule 506.*

Section 4(3) This exemption concerns the prospectus delivery requirements of dealers. The prospectus delivery time periods have been shortened by the SEC pursuant to Rule 174. Nonetheless, a participating dealer selling part of its allotment is subject to the prospectus delivery requirements, irrespective of the time period elapsed. *See Rule 174.*

Section 4(4) Exempts from the registration requirements of § 5 "brokers' transactions executed upon customers' orders on any exchange or in the over-the-counter market but not the solicitation of such orders." *See Rule 144.*

Section 4(6) Provides an exemption for offerings not exceeding $5,000,000. Available to an unlimited number of accredited investors only. No general solicitation or advertising is permitted, there are no issuer qualifications, restrictions on resale apply, and no specific information need be furnished to investors. *See General Solicitation.*

Section 5(a) Prohibits the use of the mails or any instrument or means of interstate commerce to sell or to deliver a security for purposes of sale before the effective date of the registration statement. *See Pre-Filing Period; Waiting Period.*

Section 5(b) Prohibits the use of the mails or any other means of interstate commerce to transmit any prospectus, unless such prospectus meets the requirements of § 10. Also, the provision prohibits securities to be carried through the mails or in interstate commerce for purposes of sale or for delivery after sale unless accompanied or preceded by a § 10(a) prospectus. *See Post-Effective Period; Prospectus; Rules 430 and 431.*

Section 5(c) Prohibits, subject to certain exceptions, the use of the mails or any means of interstate commerce to offer to sell or offer to buy the securities offered in the time period before a registration statement has been filed with the Commission or while the registration statement is the subject of a stop order, refusal order, or any public proceeding or examination under § 8. *See "Gun-Jumping"; Pre-Filing Period.*

Section 6 Sets forth the filing requirements for registration statements including who must sign the statement, the effect of a signature affixed thereto, and the fee to be paid upon filing. This section also states that a registration statement is deemed effective only as to the securities offered therein, that the registration statement or amendments thereto are considered to be filed as of the receipt thereof by the SEC (provided the proper fee accompanies the statement), and that the information contained in or filed with a registration statement shall be available for public inspection and copying.

Section 7 Generally provides that a registration statement shall contain the information and be accompanied by the documents specified in Schedule A. The statute also grants to the SEC rulemaking authority with respect to registration statements filed by blank check issuers. *See "Blank Check" Company; "Blank Check" Offering; Penny Stock; § 10(a) of the Securities Act; Schedule A.*

Section 8(a) Provides that the effective date of a registration statement is the twentieth day after it is filed or such earlier date as the SEC may determine (based upon factors stated therein). The statute also provides that the effective date of a registration statement begins to run anew if amendments are filed thereto (unless filed with the SEC's consent or pursuant to an SEC order). *See Rule 460.*

Section 8(b) Provides that if the Commission determines that a registration statement is deficient on its face, upon affording an opportunity to a hearing, the SEC can issue a refusal order, so long as it acts within ten days after the filing thereof, preventing the registration from becoming effective until amended in accordance thereto. *See "Refusal Order."*

Section 8(d) Provides that the SEC may initiate a stop order in response to materially false, incomplete, inaccurate, or misleading information in a registration statement, suspending the effectiveness of the registration statement until amended in accordance with the stop order. Notice and an opportunity for a hearing must be provided. *See Stop Order.*

Section 8(e) Empowers the SEC to make an investigation into whether a stop order under § 8(d) should issue. *See Stop Order.*

Section 8A Empowers the SEC to issue cease and desist orders. *See Cease and Desist Order; § 21C of the Exchange Act.*

Section 10(a) Provides that a statutory prospectus must contain the information contained in the registration statement (see § 7) except the documents referred to in paragraphs (28) through (32) of Schedule A (or paragraphs (13) and (14) of Schedule B for foreign governmental issuers); however the SEC may by rules or regulations omit this required information from any prospectus if it determines that such information is not necessary or appropriate for the protection of investors and the public interest. Also provides under certain circumstances for the updating of information in a prospectus that is used more than nine months after the effective date of the registration statement. *See Statutory Prospectus; Schedule A.*

Section 10(b) Empowers the SEC to promulgate rules and regulations permitting the use of prospectuses that will satisfy § 5(b)(1). *See Preliminary Prospectus; Summary Prospectus; § 5(b) of the Securities Act; Rules 430 and 431.*

Section 11(a) Establishes a private right of action for damages on behalf of purchasers against an enumerated list of persons and entities who may be subject to civil liability for material misstatements or omissions contained in the registration statement (including the prospectus which is part of the registration statement). The action may be brought by "any person acquiring such security" unless it can be shown that, at the time of the purchase, the purchaser knew of the misstatement or omission.

Section 11(b) Provides defenses for subject parties other than the issuer for claims arising under § 11(a) of the Securities Act, the most important of which is the "due diligence" defense of § 11(b)(3). *See Due Diligence; Rule 176.*

Section 11(c) States that the appropriate standard of reasonableness in determining what constitutes reasonable investigation and reasonable grounds for belief for purposes of the § 11(b)(3) "due diligence" defense is "that required of a prudent man in the management of his own property." *See Due Diligence; Rule 176.*

Section 11(e) Provides for the measure of damages in suits brought under § 11(a) of the 1933 Act, as well as the payment of costs and attorney's fees. The provision also permits a defendant in a § 11(a) action to prove that the plaintiff's loss was due to factors other than the material misrepresentation(s) or nondisclosure(s) contained in the registration statement. The statute limits the damages of an underwriter to the dollar amount of the securities offered to the public by such underwriter.

Section 11(f) With the exception of outside directors, provides for joint and several liability for the subject parties specified in § 11(a). Unless outside directors act with actual knowledge of the falsity, such directors are liable only in proportion to their fault. The statute also allows for contribution unless the parties who are liable were guilty of fraudulent misrepresentation and the others were not.

Section 11(g) Prohibits recovery under § 11 of an amount exceeding the public offering price of the security.

Section 12(a)(1) Provides the purchaser of securities with an express private right of action for rescission (or if he/she no longer owns the securities, for damages) against his/her seller if such seller offers or sells a security in violation of § 5. Generally, if a violation of § 5 has been committed by the seller, strict liability is imposed.

Section 12(a)(2) Affords an express private right of action to a purchaser against his/her seller for rescission (or damages if the securities have been disposed of) where the purchaser acquired the securities by means of a prospectus or oral communication which contained a material misstatement or omission. The seller under § 12(a)(2) has a "reasonable care" defense. *See Due Diligence.*

Section 12(b) Provides that in actions brought under Section 12(a)(2), a defendant may avoid all or part of the damages that otherwise would be incurred by proving that all or part of the depreciation in the value of the securities in question resulted from factors unrelated to the misstatement(s) or omission(s).

Section 13 Provides the statute of limitations for actions brought under §§ 11, 12(a)(1), and 12(a)(2) of the 1933 Act.

Section 14 Provides that any provision, condition, or stipulation that binds any person acquiring a security to waive compliance with any provision of the 1933 Act or the SEC's rules and regulations thereunder shall be void. *See § 29(a) of the Exchange Act.*

Section 15 Provides that a person who controls a person held liable under § 11 or § 12 of the 1933 Act shall be jointly and severally liable with such controlled person, unless such controlling person did not have knowledge of the facts or reasonable grounds to believe in the existence of such facts upon which the controlled person's liability is predicated. *See Control; § 20(a) of the Exchange Act.*

Section 16 Provides that the rights and remedies provided by the 1933 Act shall be in addition to whatever rights or remedies exist at law or in equity.

Section 17(a) Makes it unlawful to engage in fraudulent or deceptive practices in the offer or sale of securities.

Section 17(c) Provides that the exemptions from registration contained in § 3 of the 1933 Act shall not apply to the provisions of § 17.

Section 18 Defines the classes of "covered" securities subject to exclusive SEC authority in regard to the registration of such securities, thereby preempting state regulation of such offerings. *See Covered Security; National Securities Markets Improvement Act of 1996.*

Section 19(a) Empowers the SEC to promulgate rules and regulations deemed necessary to carry out the provisions of the 1933 Act. Also states that good faith reliance on SEC rules or regulations will preclude 1933 Act liability.

Section 19(b) Empowers the SEC to subpoena witnesses, administer oaths and affirmations, take evidence, and request the production of documents for the purpose of enforcing the Securities Act.

Section 19(c) Authorizes the SEC to cooperate with state securities regulators in order to achieve greater uniformity and effectiveness of federal and state regulations and minimum interference with capital formation, particularly for small businesses.

Section 20(b) Empowers the SEC, when it appears that a person is engaged in or is about to engage in a practice or act violative of the 1933 Act or the rules or regulations promulgated thereunder, to bring an action in United States District Court to enjoin such practice or act, and upon a proper showing, an injunction or restraining order shall be granted. The statute also authorizes the SEC to transmit evidence concerning such practices or acts to the Attorney General who may bring the appropriate criminal proceedings.

Section 20(e) Authorizes the SEC to seek a court order barring a person from serving as an officer or director of a publicly-held company if such person violated § 17(a)(1) of the Securities Act and his/her conduct "demonstrates substantial unfitness to serve as an officer or director of any such issuer." *See Director/Officer Bar; § 21 of the Exchange Act.*

Section 22(a) Provides that the United States District Courts shall have jurisdiction over offenses and violations under the 1933 Act and the rules and regulations promulgated thereunder, and concurrent jurisdiction (consistent with the Uniform Standards Act) with the states for suits at law or in equity brought to enforce any duty or liability created by the 1933 Act. The statute also provides for venue of suits; service of process, and judicial review. It prohibits the removal of properly instituted 1933 Act cases from state court to federal court. *See Uniform Standards Act.*

Section 22(b) Provides that, if a person refuses to obey a subpoena, a federal district court, upon application by the SEC, may issue an order to such person requiring him/her to appear before the SEC and produce evidence; failure to obey such order is punishable by contempt of court.

Section 23 States that just because a registration statement has been filed or is in effect or no stop order has been issued in no way implies that the SEC represents that the registration statement is true and accurate and devoid of material misrepresentations or omissions or that the SEC has passed upon the merits of the security, and any representation to the contrary to any prospective purchaser shall be unlawful.

Section 24 States that any person who willfully violates any provision of the 1933 Act or any rule or regulation promulgated thereunder, or who willfully makes a material misrepresentation or omission in a registration statement, shall upon conviction be subject to fines and/or imprisonment. *See § 32(a) of the Exchange Act.*

Section 27A Enacted pursuant to the PSLRA, provides a safe harbor from liability for certain oral and written forward-looking statements made by 1934 Act reporting companies as well as certain persons acting on behalf of such issuers. *See Private Securities Litigation Reform Act (PSLRA); Safe Harbor for Forward-Looking Statements; § 21E of the Exchange Act.*

Securities Exchange Act of 1934

Section 2 States the necessity for the Securities Exchange Act of 1934, and enumerates reasons in support thereof.

Section 3(a) Provides the definition of terms used throughout the Exchange Act.

Section 4(a) Establishes the SEC and sets forth the criteria and rules governing the appointment of its five commissioners and the terms of their office.

Section 6(a) Permits an exchange to be registered as a national securities exchange pursuant to the terms and conditions of § 6 of the 1934 Act and the provisions of § 19(a) of the Act upon filing a registration application with the SEC in such form as the SEC may, by rule, prescribe containing the rules of such exchange and any other information or document as the SEC, by rule, may prescribe as germane for the public interest or the protection of investors.

Section 6(b) Sets forth basic conditions that must, in the Commission's view, be satisfied in order for an exchange to be registered as a national securities exchange.

Section 7(a) Provides that the Federal Reserve Board shall prescribe rules and regulations regarding the amount of credit which may be initially extended and subsequently maintained on a non-exempt security, and sets forth a standard upon which such rules and regulations shall be based for the initial extension of credit.

Section 7(b) States that notwithstanding the provisions of § 7(a), the Federal Reserve Board may from time to time raise or lower margin requirements for the initial extension of credit or the maintenance thereof.

Section 9 Provides an express private remedy for purchasers and sellers injured by manipulation of securities which are traded on a national securities exchange.

Section 10(b) The basic antifraud provision of the securities laws makes it unlawful to employ deceptive or manipulative devices in connection with the purchase or sale of securities. *See Rule 10b-5.*

Section 10A Sets forth requirements with respect to auditor disclosure of corporate fraud or illegality. *See Auditor Disclosure of Corporate Fraud.*

Section 12(a) Makes it unlawful for any broker or dealer to conduct transactions in securities on a national securities exchange (other than for an exempted security) that has not been registered pursuant to the 1934 Act.

Section 12(b) Provides for 1934 Act registration of a security which is listed on a national securities exchange by filing an application with the exchange as well as with the SEC containing specified information.

Section 12(g) Requires registration of a security for 1934 Act purposes by the issuer filing specified information with the SEC. Pursuant to Rule 12g-1, this requirement occurs when the issuer has assets of greater than $10 million and has a class of equity security held of record by at least 500 persons.

Section 13(a) Requires any issuer of a security registered pursuant to § 12 of the Exchange Act to file annual and other periodic reports as the Commission shall prescribe containing specified information. This periodic reporting obligation also is incurred by publicly-held issuers under § 15(d). *See § 15(d); Forms 8-K, 10-K, 10-Q, 10-KSB, 10-QSB.*

Section 13(b)(2) Generally requires publicly-held issuers to maintain reasonably accurate books and records and internal accounting controls. This statute was passed as part of the Foreign Corrupt Practices Act. *See Foreign Corrupt Practices Act (FCPA).*

Section 13(d) Requires any person (or group) who acquires, either directly or indirectly, a greater than five percent beneficial ownership interest in any equity security of a class subject to the 1934 Act's reporting requirements to file a Schedule 13D statement of ownership with the SEC within ten business days after attaining such percentage of ownership. *See Schedule 13D.*

Section 13(e) Makes it unlawful for any 1934 Act § 12 reporting company to purchase its own shares in contravention of SEC rules. *See Going-Private; Rules 13e-3, 13e-4; Schedule 13E-3.*

Section 14(a) Gives the SEC broad authority to regulate the solicitation of proxies with respect to securities registered under § 12 of the Exchange Act. The statute makes it unlawful for any person to violate SEC rules and regulations prescribed pursuant to § 14(a). *See Annual Reports to Security Holders; Rule 14a-9.*

Section 14(d) Requires any person making a tender offer to equity securities subject to the Exchange Act's reporting requirements and registered pursuant to § 12 of the Exchange Act to file with the SEC certain materials. Also, the statute sets forth procedural mandates, such as the offering period, pro rata rights, and the time within which tendered shares may be withdrawn. *See Tender Offer; Regulation M-A; Schedules TO, 14D-9.*

Section 14(e) Prohibits deceptive, manipulative, and fraudulent practices in connection with any tender offer, invitations or requests for tenders, or any solicitation of security holders for or against any such offer, invitation, or request. *See Tender Offer.*

Section 14(f) Requires a tender offeror to file with the Commission disclosures of the names and descriptions of individuals who are to be elected directors and other agreements affecting directors that will occur in connection with a change of management control pursuant to a tender offer for Exchange Act reporting equity securities.

Section 15(c)(1) Prohibits fraudulent, deceptive, or manipulative conduct by broker-dealers in the over-the-counter market (or on exchanges of which they are not members) in connection with the purchase or sale of securities.

Section 15(c)(4) Authorizes the Commission in an administrative proceeding, after providing notice and an opportunity for hearing, to order compliance by subject parties with the provisions of §§ 12, 13, 14, and 15(d) of the Exchange Act and SEC rules and regulations promulgated thereunder. The SEC also may proceed administratively against persons who are deemed to be a "cause" of a failure to comply with § 12, 13, 14, or 15(d).

Section 15(d) Generally obligates issuers of public offerings of securities made pursuant to the Securities Act to file annual, periodic, and other specified reports with the SEC. *See Forms 8-K, 10-K, 10-Q, 10-KSB, 10-QSB.*

Section 16(a) Requires beneficial owners of over ten percent of any non-exempt security registered pursuant to § 12 of the 1934 Act and directors and officers of the issuer of such stock to file with the SEC (and with any national securities exchange that such stock is listed on) a statement specifying how much of the issuer's stock is owned by such person and monthly changes in such ownership interest.

Section 16(b) Provides that profits realized by insiders (as defined in § 16(a) from the purchase and sale (or sale and purchase) of stock within a six-month period are subject to disgorgement to the corporation; strict liability attaches. If the corporation does not institute the action, a shareholder may bring the suit on behalf of the corporation. *See Short-Swing Profits.*

Section 16(c) Generally prohibits short sales and sales against the box by insiders (as defined in § 16(a)). *See Short-Sale.*

Section 18(a) Provides an express right of action for damages when an investor purchases or sells a security in reliance upon a materially false or misleading statement that is contained in a document filed with the SEC pursuant to the Exchange Act. Section 18(a) has strict reliance and causation requirements.

Section 20(a) Imposes joint and several liability on persons directly or indirectly controlling one held liable under the Exchange Act (or rules or regulations promulgated thereunder), unless such controlling person acted in good faith and neither directly nor indirectly induced the violation. *See Control; § 15 of the Securities Act.*

Section 20(f) Grants to the SEC the authority to bring suit and obtain relief against aiders and abettors of Exchange Act violations. *See SEC Aiding and Abetting Authority.*

Section 20A Enacted as part of the Insider Trading and Securities Fraud Enforcement Act of 1988, this statute provides an express private right of action for those who traded securities contemporaneously with, and on the opposite side of, a transaction from the insider trader.

Section 21 Gives the SEC broad authority to investigate possible violations, subpoena witnesses, require the production of memoranda and other records, initiate contempt proceedings, transmit evidence to the Attorney General (who may institute criminal proceedings), and bring actions for injunctive relief. Also, the statute permits the Commission to seek a treble monetary penalty against those engaged in insider trading. In addition, pursuant to the statute, the SEC may request a federal court to order director and officer bars and to levy money penalties for violation of any provision of the Exchange Act or any rule or regulation prescribed thereunder. *See Director/Officer Bar; Money Penalties; § 20(e) of the Securities Act.*

Section 21A Enacted as part of the Insider Trading and Securities Fraud Enforcement Act of 1988, this statute imposes an affirmative duty upon broker-dealers and investment advisers to maintain and enforce reasonable supervisory mechanisms to prevent insider trading violations and imposes treble monetary penalties under specified conditions. The statute also addresses the amount of penalties that can be assessed against a controlling person, contains procedures for collection, and gives the SEC authority to award bounties to informants. *See Insider Trading and Securities Fraud Enforcement Act (ITSFEA).*

Section 21B Provides the SEC with the authority to levy civil money penalties in administrative proceedings against regulated persons. *See Money Penalties.*

Section 21C Empowers the SEC to issue cease and desist orders. *See Cease and Desist Order; § 8A of the Securities Act.*

Section 21D(b)(1)-(2) Sets forth strict pleading requirements for plaintiffs in private securities fraud suits. *See Pleading Requirements.*

Section 21D(b)(4) Requires that a plaintiff establish causation between the defendant's wrongful conduct and such plaintiff's loss. *See Express Causation Requirement.*

Section 21D(e) Places a limitation on damages in Exchange Act actions where a plaintiff attempts to establish damages by reference to the market price of a security. In this context, the award of damages is the difference between the purchase or sale price paid or received by the plaintiff, as applicable, and the mean trading price of the security during the 90-day period beginning on the date on which the information correcting the misstatement or omission that is the basis for the action is disseminated to the market.

Section 21E Enacted pursuant to the PSLRA, provides a safe harbor from liability for certain oral and written forward-looking statements made by 1934 Act reporting companies as well as certain persons acting on behalf of such issuers. *See Private Securities Litigation Reform Act (PSLRA); Safe Harbor for Forward-Looking Statements; § 27A of the Securities Act.*

Section 24(d) Provides a basis for withholding disclosure under the Freedom of Information Act of certain records obtained from a foreign securities authority. Section 24(d) was enacted as part of the International Securities Enforcement Cooperation Act of 1990 and essentially enables the SEC to cooperate confidentially with foreign securities regulators.

Section 28(a) Provides that the rights and remedies contained in the Exchange Act shall be in addition to any other rights and remedies that may exist at law or in equity. The statute limits recovery in 1934 Act private damages actions to actual damages. It also states that nothing in the Exchange Act shall affect the jurisdiction of state securities commissions to the extent that the latter do not conflict with the Act or the rules and regulations promulgated thereunder.

Section 29(a) Provides that any condition, stipulation or provision binding a person to waive compliance with any provision of the 1934 Act or any SEC rule or regulation thereunder (or any stock exchange rule) shall be void. *See § 14 of the Securities Act.*

Section 29(b) Provides that every contract formed or performed in contravention of the 1934 Act or any rule or regulation prescribed thereunder "shall be void" as regards the rights of the violating party or his/her successor who takes with knowledge.

Section 30A Enacted as part of the Foreign Corrupt Practices Act, the provision makes it unlawful for any publicly-held registrant or any person acting on behalf of such issuer to engage in bribery of any foreign official, foreign political party, or candidate for foreign political office. *See Foreign Corrupt Practices Act (FCPA).*

Section 32(a) Generally provides for fines and/or imprisonment for willful violation of any provision of the Exchange Act or any pertinent SEC rule or regulation thereunder. The provision states, however, that no person shall be subject to imprisonment for the violation of any rule or regulation if he/she proves that he/she had no knowledge of such rule or regulation. *See § 24 of the Securities Act.*

SEC Rules

Securities Act Rules

Rule 134 Rule specifying what may be included in an "identifying statement." An identifying statement meeting the terms of Rule 134 is a communication not deemed to be a § 2(a)(10) prospectus and may be published or transmitted during the waiting period (and post-effective period). It is used to ascertain what parties are interested in the securities and the extent of such interest. *See "Identifying Statement."*

Rule 135 Permits a pre-filing announcement by an issuer of a proposed registered offering that will not be deemed a violation of § 5. This rule provides that certain enumerated information may be publicly disseminated by the issuer as long as the notice contains only specified information and states that the offering will only be made by means of a prospectus. Statements identifying the underwriter and the offering price generally are not permitted. Communications under Rule 135 relating to business combination transactions must be filed with the SEC as required by Rule 425. *See Prospectus; § 5 of the Securities Act; Rule 425.*

Rule 137 Permits a dealer not participating in a distribution to publish and distribute in its regular course of business information, recommendations, and opinions regarding securities of a reporting company that has filed or proposes to file a registration statement, provided that the dealer receives no remuneration from the issuer for such activities or from the ensuing distribution. The rule applies to the pre-filing, waiting, and post-effective periods.

Rule 138 Permits dealers participating in an offering of non-convertible senior securities which are registered on Form S-2 or S-3 (as well as Form F-2 or F-3) to publish recommendations and opinions concerning the issuer's common stock, and vice-versa. The rule applies to the pre-filing, waiting and post-effective periods.

Rule 139 Generally permits participating dealers to publish recommendations or opinions concerning offerings of S-2 (or F-2) issuers as long as said publication is (1) disseminated at regular intervals, (2) includes similar information regarding a substantial number of companies in the registrant's industry or is part of a comprehensive list of securities currently recommended by such dealer, (3) does not give special prominence to the issuer, and (4) does not give a more favorable opinion or recommendation with respect to the issuer than the last previous opinion issued before the dealer became a participant. With respect to S-3 (or F-3) issuers, a participating dealer is given greater latitude under Rule 139. The rule mandates only that, with respect to such issuers, the recommendation must be contained in a publication which is distributed with reasonable regularity in the normal course of the dealer's business.

Rule 144 Provides a safe harbor under the § 4(1) exemption for non-affiliated shareholders who are selling their restricted securities and for affiliates who are selling their unrestricted and/or restricted securities without registration. The rule also provides a safe harbor for brokers under the § 4(4) exemption who execute such transactions. If shareholders or brokers make a sale in compliance with the full set of objective conditions of Rule 144, they will not be deemed to be underwriters or involved in a distribution. *See § 4(1) and 4(4) of the Securities Act.*

Rule 144A Provides a non-exclusive safe harbor exemption from the Securities Act's registration requirements for resales to eligible institutions (QIBs) of certain restricted securities. *See Qualified Institutional Buyer (QIB); PORTAL; Regulation S.*

Rule 145 Unless an exemption from registration is available, Rule 145 requires that securities issued in connection with mergers, consolidations and certain other recapitalizations must be registered under the Securities Act. The rule also addresses issuer communications in the pre-filing period, allowing communications that comply with Rules 135, 165 and 166 to be made prior to the filing of the registration statement. Applicable restrictions on resales by persons other than the issuer are also addressed. *See Form S-4.*

Rule 146 Former SEC safe harbor rule to the § 4(2) exemption from Securities Act registration. Rule 146 is no longer in effect and has been superseded by Rule 506 of Regulation D. *See § 4(2) of the Securities Act; Rule 506.*

Rule 147 Safe harbor to the § 3(a)(11) intrastate exemption. Generally, the rule includes an 80% "in state" business requirement upon the issuer, a nine-month out-of-state resale prohibition, a principal residence test for purchasers and offerees, and precautions against interstate offers and sales. The doctrine of integration applies. Unlike the § 3(a)(11) exemption, the rule is only available for offerings by issuers. *See § 3(a)(11) of the Securities Act.*

Rule 165 Permits offers in connection with a business combination transaction during the pre-filing, waiting, and post-effective periods. The rule defines a business combination transaction as any such transaction specified in Rule 145(a) or an exchange offer. To rely on Rule 165, a prospectus must be filed and applicable tender offer, proxy and information statement rules must be complied with. *See Rule 425.*

Rule 166 Provides that communications by participants in a registered offering involving a business combination transaction before the first public announcement of the offering are not in violation of § 5(c) of the Securities Act upon a showing that reasonable steps were taken to prevent further distribution of the communication until either the initial public announcement is made or the registration statement is filed with the Commission.

Rule 174 Provision, promulgated by the SEC pursuant to § 4(3) of the Securities Act, nullifying to a large degree, the prospectus delivery requirements of said statute. The rule generally provides that a dealer is not subject to the prospectus delivery requirements if the issuer is a reporting company under the Exchange Act. Moreover, the time period in which a prospectus must be delivered under § 4(3) for first-time issuers has been significantly shortened pursuant to Rule 174. Participating dealers selling part of their allotment, however, must comply with the prospectus delivery requirements irrespective of the time period elapsed. *See § 4(3) of the Securities Act.*

Rule 175 Provides a safe harbor for forward-looking statements made by an issuer in a 1933 Act registration statement and in an SEC filed document pursuant to the Exchange Act by a reporting company if made with a reasonable basis and in good faith. The 1934 Act's counterpart to Rule 175 is Rule 3b-6. *See Forward-Looking Statement; "Soft" Information.*

Rule 176 Lists a number of factors for an adjudicator to take into account as "circumstances affecting the determination of what constitutes reasonable investigation" for purposes of the due diligence defense of § 11(b)(3). *See Due Diligence; § 11(b) of the Securities Act.*

Rule 405 Sets forth the definition of terms used throughout Regulation C. *See Regulation C.*

Rule 412 Provides, *inter alia*, that modification of disclosures made in previously filed SEC documents are not an admission that the earlier statements are materially misleading.

Rule 415 Concerns the Securities Act registration of securities to be offered or sold on a delayed or continuous basis in the future. Allows, *inter alia*, Form S-3 (or F-3) issuers to file primary-at-the-market offerings of equity securities which they plan to offer within two years of the effective date of the registration statement. *See "Shelf" Registration.*

Rule 425 Identifies all written communications under Rule 165 as prospectuses and sets forth filing requirements for such prospectuses as well as communications made under Rule 135 in connection with business combination transactions. The rule also requires all Rule 165 prospectuses and Rule 135 notices to identify to the investor the filer and its filing number with the SEC. *See Rule 135, Rule 165.*

Rule 430 Authorizes the use of a preliminary prospectus or so-called "red herring" to be used in the waiting period as a written offer in satisfaction of the prospectus delivery requirements. *See Preliminary Prospectus; § 10(b) of the Securities Act.*

Rule 430A Under this rule, issuers engaging in offerings of securities for cash are not required to file a pre-effective "pricing" amendment (*i.e.*, information relating to price and the underwriting syndicate). The information omitted in reliance on Rule 430A must be contained either in the final prospectus which will be deemed a part of the registration statement if filed within five business days after the registration statement's effective date or in a post-effective amendment to the registration statement.

Rule 431 Provides for the use of a summary prospectus by reporting companies under § 10(b) of the 1933 Act for purposes of § 5(b)(1) of the Act. *See Summary Prospectus; § 10(b) of the Securities Act.*

Rule 434 As set forth by the SEC, Rule 434 permits participants in eligible offerings "to convey prospectus information in more than one document and allows such documents to be delivered to investors at separate intervals and in varying manners. Rule 434 does not require that a final, integrated prospectus be delivered to investors. In the aggregate, however, all required information will still be disclosed to investors prior to or at the same time as a confirmation is sent . . . ."

Rule 460 Declares the SEC's policy of not accelerating a registration statement's effective date unless the preliminary prospectus has been distributed to underwriters and participating dealers of the offering.

Rule 501 Sets forth the definitions of terms used throughout Regulation D.

Rule 502 Sets out four general conditions that are applicable to Regulation D offerings. The conditions concern the integration of offerings, with a safe harbor provided therefor; the information that must be disclosed by an issuer to purchasers under a Regulation D offering (except for offerings made pursuant to Rule 504 or solely to accredited investors); the prohibitions against advertising and general solicitation (with the exception of Rule 504(b)(1)); and the limitations on resale (except as provided in Rule 504(b)(1)).

Rule 503 Sets forth the requirements for filing a Form D with the SEC pursuant to a Regulation D offering.

Rule 504 Provides an exemption from Securities Act registration under § 3(b) for offerings not exceeding $1,000,000 in any twelve-month period. The number of investors is unlimited, there are no investor qualifications, and reporting companies and investment companies do not qualify for use of the exemption. Generally, if the securities are state registered or sold only to accredited investors in accordance with applicable state law, the prohibitions on general solicitation and advertising and the restrictions on resale do not apply. Otherwise, no advertising or general solicitation is allowed and restrictions on resale apply. Pursuant to federal law, no information need be specifically disclosed. Nonetheless, the federal antifraud provisions apply to Rule 504 offerings.

Rule 505 Provides an exemption under § 3(b) for offerings not exceeding $5 million in any twelve-month period. The exemption is limited to 35 non-accredited purchasers plus an unlimited number of accredited investors. Specified information must be delivered to all non-accredited purchasers. The prohibitions on general solicitation and advertising apply, as well as the restrictions on resale. Investment companies and issuers disqualified under Regulation A do not qualify for use of the exemption.

Rule 506 Safe harbor to the § 4(2) exemption. The exemption permits sales to 35 non-accredited purchasers plus an unlimited number of accredited investors. Information supplying requirements (to non-accredited purchasers), investor sophistication requirements (unless the purchaser is accredited), resale limitations, and prohibitions on advertising and general solicitation apply. No dollar limitation applies to Rule 506 offerings. State regulation of Rule 506 offerings has been federally preempted. *See § 4(2) of the Securities Act.*

Rule 507 Eliminates the timely filing requirement of Form D as a condition to the Regulation D exemptions. However, Rule 507 serves as a disqualification to the use of Regulation D for future transactions by any issuer, if it, or a predecessor or affiliate, has been enjoined by a court for violating the filing obligation of Rule 503.

Rule 508 Provides that a failure to comply with one or more of the conditions of a Regulation D exemption will not make that exemption unavailable, provided that, the condition is not designed to protect specifically the complaining person; the failure to comply is insignificant to the offering as a whole; and there has been a good faith and reasonable attempt to comply with all requirements of the regulation. Rule 508 specifies that the provisions of Regulation D relating to general solicitation, the dollar limits of the Rules 504 and 505 exemptions, and the limits on non-accredited investors in Rules 505 and 506 are significant to every offering and thus are not subject to the Rule 508 defense. Further, Rule 508 does not apply to the SEC or the state regulators. *See General Solicitation; Substantial Compliance.*

Rule 701 Adopted pursuant to § 3(b) of the Securities Act. The rule generally provides an exemption from registration according to a specified formula during any twelve-month period for offers and sales of securities for certain compensation benefit plans adopted for the participation of employees, officers, directors, consultants, and advisers of an eligible company. This amount may not exceed the greatest of (1) $1 million, (2) 15% of the outstanding securities of the applicable class; or (3) 15% of the issuer's total assets. If more than $5 million of securities are sold, specific disclosure is required. The exemption can only be used for compensatory purposes (rather than for capital raising purposes) and can be used only by nonreporting companies. Restrictions on resale apply to securities sold in Rule 701 offerings.

Rule 1001 Also called the California Exemption. The exemption provides a coordinating federal exemption under § 3(b) for offers not exceeding $5 million in any 12-month period that are exempt under paragraph (n) of Section 25102 of the California Corporations Code.

This exemption is limited to issuers that are substantially connected to California and to investors who are determined to be "qualified" purchasers, as defined by the applicable California statutes and regulations. Rule 1001 allows an eligible issuer to "test the waters" by distributing a written general announcement that contains certain specified information. As a general rule, all offers are limited to qualified purchasers and all securities issued pursuant to the exemption are "restricted." *See Model Accredited Investor Exemption; Testing the Waters.*

SEC Rules

Exchange Act Rules

Rule 10b-5 Promulgated pursuant to § 10(b) of the 1934 Act, this rule makes it unlawful to employ any deceptive or manipulative device in connection with the purchase or sale of a security. *See § 10(b).*

Rule 10b5-1 Subject to certain affirmative defenses, this Rule subjects a person to insider trading exposure if such person trades while "aware" of material nonpublic information concerning the company or the market for its securities. See "Disclose or Abstain" Rule; Misappropriation Theory.

Rule 10b5-2 Sets forth a non-exclusive list of three situations in which a person is deemed to have a relationship of trust and confidence for purposes of invoking the misappropriation theory under § 10(b). See "Disclose or Abstain" Rule; Misappropriation Theory.

Rule 13e-3 Generally, the rule prohibits fraudulent, deceptive, and manipulative acts or practices in connection with going-private transactions and prescribes filing, disclosure, and dissemination requirements as a means reasonably designed to prevent such acts or practices. *See Going-Private; § 13(e) of the Exchange Act.*

Rule 13e-4 Governs issuer tender offers for a company's own securities. The rule prohibits fraudulent, deceptive, and manipulative acts and practices and establishes filing, disclosure, and dissemination requirements. An issuer tender offer regulated by Rule 13e-4, that also constitutes a going-private transaction under Rule 13e-3, must comply with both rules. *See Going Private; Tender Offer; § 13(e) of the Exchange Act; Rule 13e-3; Schedule 13E-3.*

Rule 14a-9 Prohibits the solicitation of proxies which contain any materially false or misleading statement. *See Annual Report to Security Holders; § 14(a) of the Exchange Act.*

Rule 14a-12 Permits management to solicit security holders in proxy contests before furnishing a proxy statement. However, a company is not allowed to secure promises to vote before a proxy statement is furnished to security holders.

Rule 14d-1 Sets forth the scope of Regulations 14D and 14E and the definitions applicable thereto.

Rule 14d-2 Provides when a tender offer is deemed to "commence." The rule also requires all written communications relating to a tender offer to be filed either under cover of Schedule TO or Rule 425 if the Securities Act is applicable. The rule further provides that a legend is to be included on written communications advising security holders to read the tender offer statement when it is received.

Rule 14d-8 Extends the right of shareholders to receive proration of their shares in a tender offer that is oversubscribed from the previous ten-calendar-day period (as provided in § 14(d)(6)) to the entire period that the offer remains open.

Rule 14d-9 Allows target companies to communicate with security holders to the same degree bidders are permitted. The rule requires targets to file all written communications relating to the transaction on the date the communication is made and include a legend advising security holders to read the recommendation that is to be provided.

Rule 14d-10 Requires that a tender offer be open to all shareholders and that the best price paid to any security holder be paid to any other tendering security holder.

Rule 14d-11 Provides bidders the option to have a subsequent offering period in a third party cash or stock tender offer during which no withdrawal rights are available. The subsequent offering period may last from 3 to 20 business days at the bidder's discretion. The rule sets forth that the same consideration must be used for both offering periods but has no specific requirement that a minimum number of shares be tendered in the initial offering.

Rule 14e-3 Prohibits insider and tippee trading in the tender offer context by applying the disclose-or-abstain provision where an individual is in possession of material information relating to a tender offer when he/she knows or has reason to know that such information is nonpublic and was obtained directly or indirectly from the offeror, the subject corporation, any of their affiliated persons, or any person acting on behalf of either company.

Rule 14e-5 Provides that from the "public announcement" until the expiration of a cash tender offer or exchange offer, a person making the offer is prohibited from purchasing the security that is the subject of the offer other than as part of the offer.

Rule 14e-8 Antifraud rule intended to prevent fraudulent and misleading communications concerning proposed tender offers by prohibiting bidders from announcing an offer that the bidder does not have the intent and/or financing to complete or that is meant to manipulate the price of the bidder's or the target's securities.

Rule 15c2-8(b) Provides that, if the issuer is not a reporting company, the broker or dealer must "deliver a copy of the preliminary prospectus to any person who is expected to receive a confirmation of sale at least 48 hours prior to the mailing of such confirmation."

Rule 15c2-11 Generally prohibits broker-dealers from publishing a quotation for any security unless specified information is available with respect to the issuer and the security.

SEC Regulations

Regulation A Provides an exemption from Securities Act registration for offerings of securities not exceeding $5 million in any twelve-month period. Pursuant to this exemption, a Regulation A offering is available to an unlimited number of investors with no investor qualification requirements. No investment companies are permitted to use the exemption and issuers and underwriters subject to "bad boy" prohibitions are disqualified. The issuer is subject to certain disclosure and notification requirements that resemble a "mini registration." Restrictions on resale do not apply. Moreover, companies relying on the Regulation A exemption may "test the waters" for potential investor interest. *See Testing the Waters.*

Regulation C Sets forth the procedural rules (Rules 400 through 494) governing the registration of securities under the 1933 Act. *See Rule 405.*

Regulation FD Prohibits issuers or individuals acting on their behalf from selectively disclosing material nonpublic information to certain enumerated persons (generally securities market professionals and holders of the issuer's securities who may well trade on the basis of the information) without disclosing the information publicly. If the selective disclosure is intentional, then the issuer must publicly disclose the information simultaneously by filing or furnishing a Form 8-K to the SEC or in a manner reasonably designed to provide broad distribution of the information. If the selective disclosure is unintentional, then the issuer must disclose the information to the public promptly, but in no event after the later of 24 hours or the opening of the next day's trading on the New York Stock Exchange. Violating Regulation FD exposes the issuer to SEC administrative and civil enforcement action, but does not by itself impose any Rule 10b-5 antifraud liability on the issuer or establish a private right of action.

Regulation M Governs the activities of issuers, underwriters, and certain other participants in connection with securities offerings and is designed to prevent manipulative conduct by persons who have an interest in the subject offering. Regulation M consists of five rules as well as a definitional rule.

Regulation M-A Found in Regulation S-K, this regulation contains disclosure requirements for issuer tender offers, third-party tender offers, tender offer recommendation statements and going-private transactions, as well as certain requirements for cash merger proxy statements. The regulation also addresses the difficulty of under-standing disclosure documents in business combination transactions by requiring a plain English summary sheet for all cash tender offers and mergers.

Regulation S-B Sets forth the substantive disclosure requirements for small business issuers for filing forms under the 1933 and 1934 Acts.

Regulation S-K Sets forth the substantive disclosure requirements for filing forms under the 1933 and 1934 Acts.

Regulation S-X Delineates the accounting rules and procedures to be followed in the preparation of the audited financial statements and SEC filings required by the 1933 and 1934 Acts.

Regulation S Generally provides that § 5 of the 1933 Act does not apply to offers and sales outside of the United States and specifies the elements for determining whether an offer and sale is outside the United States. Regulation S is intended to clarify the extraterritorial reach of U.S. securities registration provisions and to enhance the U.S. position in international securities markets. Besides the general statement which is analyzed under all relevant facts and circumstances, Regulation S also provides several safe harbors for extraterritorial offers, sales, and resales of securities. *See Rule 144A.*

SEC Forms

Form S-1 Used primarily by first-time issuers, this is the basic, long-form registration statement and requires full registrant and transaction-related information to be contained in the prospectus. No incorporation by reference is permitted.

Form S-2 Generally available to companies which have reported for three or more years, this registration form allows incorporation by reference from the Form 10-K and other SEC periodic reports into the prospectus. Issuers using this registration form also must deliver a copy of the annual security holder report along with the prospectus describing the offering or present registrant-oriented information in the prospectus comparable to that contained in the annual security holder report along with a description of the offering.

Form S-3 Available to companies reporting under the 1934 Act for a 12-month period and, for issuer primary offerings of common stock that prior to any such offering, have a public float (representing the aggregate market value of the company's voting stock held by non-affiliates) of at least $75 million. Companies meeting these requirements are allowed the fullest incorporation by reference of 1934 Act documents into the registration statement. They need only include the transaction-specific description of the offering in the prospectus, as well as events that occurred after the filing of the most recent 1934 Act report incorporated by reference.

Form S-4 Form which may be used for the registration of securities issued in combinations, mergers, consolidations, recapitalizations, acquisitions of assets, and other transactions that require registration under Rule 145. *See Rule 145.*

Form S-8 Available to reporting companies offering securities to their employees or their subsidiaries' employees pursuant to a stock benefit plan.

Form SB-1 Used by small business issuers to register up to $10 million of securities to be sold for cash if no more than $10 million in securities, including the present offering, is registered in any twelve month period. *See Small Business Issuer.*

Form SB-2 Generally used by small business issuers to register securities sold for cash. Form SB-2 has no dollar limit for offerings and may be used for any offering by a small business issuer. *See Small Business Issuer.*

Form 8-K Form that requires disclosure of specified events that may arise in the period between 1934 Act periodic filings. Disclosure of events other than those called for by the form are permissive rather than mandatory. *See §§ 13(a), 15(d) of the Exchange Act.*

Form 10-K The form used by issuers which are Exchange Act reporting companies for filing their annual reports pursuant to § 13 or § 15(d) of the Exchange Act. Information required to be included in the Form 10-K includes, for example, audited financial statements, a meaningful description of the issuer's business and financial condition, and financial data summaries appropriate for trend analysis. *See §§ 13(a), 15(d) of the Exchange Act.*

Form 10-Q The form used by issuers which are Exchange Act reporting companies for the filing of quarterly reports pursuant to § 13 or § 15(d) of the 1934 Act. *See §§ 13(a), 15(d) of the Exchange Act.*

Form 10-KSB Used by small business issuers which are Exchange Act reporting companies for filing their annual reports pursuant to § 13 or § 15(d) of the Exchange Act. *See Small Business Issuer.*

Form 10-QSB Used by small business issuers which are Exchange Act reporting companies for the filing of quarterly reports pursuant to § 13 or § 15(d) of the 1934 Act. *See Small Business Issuer.*

SEC Schedules

Schedule A Sets forth the information required to be contained in a statutory § 10(a) prospectus, which is filed as part of the registration statement. *See §§ 7 and 10(a) of the 1933 Act.*

Schedule 13D Statement of ownership disclosure form which must be filed pursuant to § 13(d) of the 1934 Act when a person (or group) acquires over five percent beneficial ownership of a reporting class of equity security. The purpose is to alert investors, the marketplace, and the target company's management of a potential change in corporate control. *See § 13(d) of the Exchange Act.*

Schedule 13E-3 A comprehensive disclosure document which must be filed by an issuer (and its affiliates) pursuant to Rule 13e-3 in the event of a going private transaction. *See Going-Private; § 13(e) of the Exchange Act; Rules 13e-3 and 13e-4.*

Schedule 14D-9 Statement which must be filed with the SEC by a subject (target) company of a tender offer, pursuant to Rule 14d-9, and containing information including, if material, a description of any arrangement or other understanding and conflicts of interest between, among others, the offeror, the subject corporation, and their affiliates. Certain negotiations and transactions undertaken by the target company in response to the tender offer and its position in regard to the tender offer (and the reasons therefor) must be disclosed. *See Tender Offer; § 14(d) of the Exchange Act; Rule 14d-9.*

Schedule TO This schedule refers to Regulation M-A for all substantive disclosure requirements and incorporates such requirements for, *inter alia,* issuer and third-party tender offers as well as going-private transactions. The Schedule must contain information regarding the tender offeror, including its identity and background, as well as its purpose for the tender offer and its proposals or plans.

TABLE OF CASES

[References are to page numbers]

[References are to page numbers]

[References are to page numbers]

F

G

[References are to page numbers]

T

[References are to page numbers]

U

V

TABLE OF STATUTES, RULES AND REGULATIONS

[References are to pages and footnotes]

Securities Act of 1933

Rule

Securities Exchange Act of 1934

Section

Securities Exchange Act of 1934

Rule

Text Section

WXYZ

Williams Act of 1968

Section

STATE STATUTES

ARIZONA/ARKANSAS

Arizona Revised Statutes

Section

CALIFORNIA/CANAL ZONE

California Corporation Code

Section

DELAWARE/DISTRICT OF COLUMBIA

Delaware Code

Title:Section

District of Columbia Code

Section

FLORIDA/GEORGIA

Florida Statutes

Section

Georgia Code

Section

ILLINOIS/INDIANA

Indiana Code

Section

MICHIGAN/MINNESOTA

Michigan Compiled Laws

Article:Section

Michigan Uniform Securities Act

Section

	Text Section
410(e)	245n120

Minnesota Statutes

Section

	Text Section
302A.601	334n11

MISSISSIPPI/MISSOURI

Missouri Code of State Regulations

Section

	Text Section
409.411(e)	241n86

NEW MEXICO/NEW YORK

New Mexico Securities Act

Article

	Text Section
58-13B-41	245n114

New York Business Corporation Law

Section

	Text Section
912(b)	349n83

NORTH CAROLINA/NORTH DAKOTA

North Carolina Securities Act

Section

	Text Section
78A-56(f)	241n86

North Dakota Commerical Code

Section

	Text Section
10-04-17(e)	241n85

OHIO/OKLAHOMA

Ohio Revised Code

Section

	Text Section
1707.43	241n85, n90; 245n116; 246n129; 247n133

2315.21(B)	244n108

Oklahoma Statutes

Title:Section

	Text Section
71:2(20)(P)	22n77, n78

OREGON/PENNSYLVANIA

Oregon Revised Statutes

Section

	Text Section
59.115(3)	246n129

Pennsylvania Consolidated Statutes

Title:Section

	Text Section
15:2542–2546	348n78
70:1-203	53n79
70:1-205	53n79
70:1-504(a)	245n118

Pennsylvania Statutes

Title:Section

	Text Section
70:1-504(a)	245n118

TEXAS

Texas Civil Statute Annotated

Article

	Text Section
581-33H(1)	245n113
581-33H(2)	245n113
581-33H(3)	245n113

Texas Securities Act

Article

	Text Section
581-33A(2)	241n87; 247n133
581-33(F)(2)	250n9

VIRGIN ISLANDS/VIRGINIA

Virginia Code

Section

	Text Section
13.1-522(D)	241n86

INDEX

[References are to pages.]

[References are to pages.]

[References are to pages.]

E

[References are to pages.]

[References are to pages.]

[References are to pages.]

[References are to pages.]

[References are to pages.]

[References are to pages.]

R

RACKETEER INFLUENCED AND CORRUPT ORGANIZATIONS ACT (RICO)
Damages under, claim for . . . 239-240
Insider trading . . . 312

REASONABLE CARE DEFENSE
Generally . . . 153-154
Definition . . . 179-181
False registration statement; Section 12(a)(2) . . . 179-181
Integrated disclosure system . . . 169

RECAPITALIZATIONS
Exemptions; Section 3(a)(9) . . . 62

RECKLESSNESS
Deceptive or manipulative devices . . 174-175

RECLASSIFICATIONS OF STOCK (See REORGANIZATIONS)

REFUSAL ORDERS
Generally . . . 368

REGISTRATION
Generally . . . 31-34; 93-95
Acceleration, SEC's power of . . . 102-103
Blue sky laws . . . 122-124
Disclosure requirements (See DISCLOSURE)
Exemptions from (See EXEMPTIONS FROM REGISTRATION; EXEMPT TRANSACTIONS)
"In registration" defined . . . 95
Post-effective period (See POST-EFFECTIVE PERIOD)
Pre-filing period (See PRE-FILING PERIOD)
Prospectus (See PROSPECTUS)
Reorganizations (See REORGANIZATIONS)
Section 5 (See subhead: Time periods)
Shelf registration (See SHELF REGISTRATION)
Spin-offs . . . 151-152
Time periods
    Generally . . . 93-95
    Chart . . . 106-108
    Post-effective period (See POST-EFFECTIVE PERIOD)
    Pre-filing period (See PRE-FILING PERIOD)
    Waiting period . . . 101-103
Transactional exemptions (See EXEMPT TRANSACTIONS)
Types of . . . 123
Waiting period
    Generally . . . 101-103
    Acceleration, SEC's power of . . 101-103

REGISTRATION STATEMENTS
Generally . . . 32-33; 93
Acceleration, SEC's power of . . . 102-103
Attorneys; due diligence defense . . . 162-164
Directors; due diligence defense . . . 160-162
Disclosure system, integrated
    Generally . . . 113-116
    False registration statements . . . 169-172
Expertised portion; due diligence . . . 157-158
False statements (See FALSE REGISTRATION STATEMENTS)
Form S-1; complete disclosure requirements . . . 114
Form S-2
    Distribution of information about S-2 issuers . . . 99-100
    Incorporation by reference . . . 114
Form S-3
    Distribution of information about S-3 issuers . . . 99-101
    Incorporation by reference . . . 114
Form S-4; reorganizations . . . 149
Incorporation by reference . . . 114
Integrated disclosure system
    Generally . . . 113-116
    False registration statements . . . 169-172
Post-effective period (See POST-EFFECTIVE PERIOD)
Section 11 (See FALSE REGISTRATION STATEMENTS)
Signatories; due diligence defense . . . 162
Unexpertised portion; due diligence 157-158

REGULATION A EXEMPTION
Limited offerings . . . 52-53

REGULATION D EXEMPTION
Form D, filing of . . . 42-43
General solicitation; Rule 502(c) . . . 43-48
Private offering exemption; Rule 506 . . . . . . 40-42; 64-67
Rule 502(c); general solicitation . . . 43-48
Rule 506; private offering exemption 40-42; 64-67
Rule 507 . . . 42-43
Rule 508; substantial compliance standard . . . 42-43; 65-66
Substantial compliance standard; Rule 508 . . . 42-43; 65-66

REGULATION FD (See ISSUER AFFIRMATIVE DISCLOSURE REQUIREMENTS)

REGULATION S
Generally . . . 67-69

[References are to pages.]

[References are to pages.]

[References are to pages.]

[References are to pages.]